Handbook of Research on Global Institutional Roles for Inclusive Development

Neeta Baporikar
Namibia University of Science and Technology, Namibia & University of Pune, India

A volume in the Practice, Progress, and Proficiency in Sustainability (PPPS) Book Series

Published in the United States of America by
    IGI Global
    Information Science Reference (an imprint of IGI Global)
    701 E. Chocolate Avenue
    Hershey PA, USA 17033
    Tel: 717-533-8845
    Fax: 717-533-8661
    E-mail: cust@igi-global.com
    Web site: http://www.igi-global.com

Copyright © 2022 by IGI Global. All rights reserved. No part of this publication may be reproduced, stored or distributed in any form or by any means, electronic or mechanical, including photocopying, without written permission from the publisher. Product or company names used in this set are for identification purposes only. Inclusion of the names of the products or companies does not indicate a claim of ownership by IGI Global of the trademark or registered trademark.

Library of Congress Cataloging-in-Publication Data

Names: Baporikar, Neeta, editor.
Title: Handbook of research on global institutional roles for inclusive
  development / Neeta Baporikar, editor.
Description: Hershey, PA : Information Science Reference, [2022] | Includes
  bibliographical references and index. | Summary: "This book explores a
  very broad range of ideas and institutions and provides case studies and
  best practices in the context of broader theoretical analysis of the
  impact of global multilateral institutions such as the World Bank and
  IMF have on development and enhances the understanding of how the ideas
  travel within the systems and how they are translated into policy,
  modified, distorted, or resisted"-- Provided by publisher.
Identifiers: LCCN 2021050144 (print) | LCCN 2021050145 (ebook) | ISBN
  9781668424483 (hardcover) | ISBN 9781668424506 (ebook)
Subjects: LCSH: Financial institutions, International. | International
  agencies. | Sustainable development--Developing countries--Case studies.
  | International economic relations. | Globalization--21st century.
Classification: LCC HG3881 .G57553 2022 (print) | LCC HG3881 (ebook) |
  DDC 332/.042--dc23/eng/20211206
LC record available at https://lccn.loc.gov/2021050144
LC ebook record available at https://lccn.loc.gov/2021050145

This book is published in the IGI Global book series Practice, Progress, and Proficiency in Sustainability (PPPS) (ISSN: 2330-3271; eISSN: 2330-328X)

British Cataloguing in Publication Data
A Cataloguing in Publication record for this book is available from the British Library.

All work contributed to this book is new, previously-unpublished material. The views expressed in this book are those of the authors, but not necessarily of the publisher.

For electronic access to this publication, please contact: eresources@igi-global.com.

Practice, Progress, and Proficiency in Sustainability (PPPS) Book Series

Ayman Batisha
International Sustainability Institute, Egypt

ISSN:2330-3271
EISSN:2330-328X

Mission

In a world where traditional business practices are reconsidered and economic activity is performed in a global context, new areas of economic developments are recognized as the key enablers of wealth and income production. This knowledge of information technologies provides infrastructures, systems, and services towards sustainable development.

The **Practices, Progress, and Proficiency in Sustainability (PPPS) Book Series** focuses on the local and global challenges, business opportunities, and societal needs surrounding international collaboration and sustainable development of technology. This series brings together academics, researchers, entrepreneurs, policy makers and government officers aiming to contribute to the progress and proficiency in sustainability.

Coverage

- Green Technology
- Eco-Innovation
- Environmental informatics
- Innovation Networks
- Outsourcing
- Technological learning
- Global Business
- Socio-Economic
- Strategic Management of IT
- Sustainable Development

IGI Global is currently accepting manuscripts for publication within this series. To submit a proposal for a volume in this series, please contact our Acquisition Editors at Acquisitions@igi-global.com or visit: http://www.igi-global.com/publish/.

The Practice, Progress, and Proficiency in Sustainability (PPPS) Book Series (ISSN 2330-3271) is published by IGI Global, 701 E. Chocolate Avenue, Hershey, PA 17033-1240, USA, www.igi-global.com. This series is composed of titles available for purchase individually; each title is edited to be contextually exclusive from any other title within the series. For pricing and ordering information please visit http://www.igi-global.com/book-series/practice-progress-proficiency-sustainability/73810. Postmaster: Send all address changes to above address. © © 2022 IGI Global. All rights, including translation in other languages reserved by the publisher. No part of this series may be reproduced or used in any form or by any means – graphics, electronic, or mechanical, including photocopying, recording, taping, or information and retrieval systems – without written permission from the publisher, except for non commercial, educational use, including classroom teaching purposes. The views expressed in this series are those of the authors, but not necessarily of IGI Global.

Titles in this Series

For a list of additional titles in this series, please visit: http://www.igi-global.com/book-series/practice-progress-proficiency-sustainability/73810

Innovative Economic, Social, and Environmental Practices for Progressing Future Sustainability
Chai Lee Goi (Curtin University, Malaysia)
Engineering Science Reference • © 2022 • 369pp • H/C (ISBN: 9781799895909) • US $195.00

Impact of Artificial Reefs on the Environment and Communities
Jorge H. P. Ramos (CinTurs, University of Algarve, Portugal)
Engineering Science Reference • © 2022 • 304pp • H/C (ISBN: 9781668423448) • US $215.00

Wetland Biodiversity, Ecosystem Services, and the Impact of Climate Change
Abdelkrim Ben Salem (Mohammed V University, Morocco) Laila Rhazi (Mohammed V University, Morocco) and Ahmed Karmaoui (University of Moulay Ismail, Morocco & Southern Center of Culture and Science, Morocco)
Engineering Science Reference • © 2022 • 310pp • H/C (ISBN: 9781799892892) • US $225.00

Handbook of Research on Organizational Sustainability in Turbulent Economies
Rafael Ignacio Perez-Uribe (Santo Tomas University, Bogota, Colombia) Carlos Salcedo-Perez (Politecnico GranColombiano University Institución, Colombia) and Andres Carvajal-Contreras (EAN University, Colombia)
Business Science Reference • © 2022 • 428pp • H/C (ISBN: 9781799893011) • US $295.00

Examining Algae as a Sustainable Solution for Food, Energy, and the Environment
Mostafa M. El-Sheekh (Tanta University, Egypt) Norhayati Abdullah (Universiti Teknologi Malaysia, Malaysia) and Imran Ahmad (Universiti Teknologi Malaysia, Malaysia)
Engineering Science Reference • © 2022 • 330pp • H/C (ISBN: 9781668424384) • US $195.00

Implications for Entrepreneurship and Enterprise Development in the Blue Economy
Lukman Raimi (Universiti Brunei Darussalam, Brunei) and Jainaba M. L. Kah (Office of the President, Gambia)
Business Science Reference • © 2022 • 302pp • H/C (ISBN: 9781668433935) • US $245.00

Technological Development and Impact on Economic and Environmental Sustainability
Yilmaz Bayar (Bandirma Onyedi Eylul University, Turkey) Mahmut Unsal Sasmaz (Usak University, Turkey) and Omer Faruk Ozturk (Usak University, Turkey)
Engineering Science Reference • © 2022 • 352pp • H/C (ISBN: 9781799896487) • US $215.00

701 East Chocolate Avenue, Hershey, PA 17033, USA
Tel: 717-533-8845 x100 • Fax: 717-533-8661
E-Mail: cust@igi-global.com • www.igi-global.com

Editorial Advisory Board

Elena Burdenko, *Plekhanov Russian University of Economics, Russia*
Mukund Deshpande, *Independent Researcher, India*
Teresa Dieguez, *ICPA, Portugal*
Sheikh Mohammed Rafiul Huque, *Jahangirnagar University, Bangladesh*
Yanamandra Ramakrishna, *Skyline University College, United Arab Emirates*
José Manuel Saiz-Álvarez, *Catholic University of Santiago de Guayaquil, Ecuador*
José Vargas-Hernández, *University of Guadalajara, Mexico*

List of Reviewers

Dileep Baragde, *G. S. Moze College, Savitribai Phule Pune University, India*
Elena Burdenko, *Plekhanov Russian University of Economics, Russia*
Gordana Petar Djukic, *University of Belgrade, Serbia*
Mufaro Dzingirai, *Midlands State University, Zimbabwe*
Meng Kui Hu, *University of Science, Malaysia*
Biljana Ilic, *Megatrend University of Belgrade, Serbia*
Vaisahli Mahajan, *Symbiosis International University, India*
Kannan Rajagopal, *Symbiosis International University, India*
Yanamandra Ramakrishna, *Skyline University College, UAE*
Booysen Tubulingane, *Namibia University of Science and Technology, Namibia*

List of Contributors

Alcívar-Avilés, María Teresa / *Catholic University of Santiago de Guayaquil, Ecuador*.................... 1

Angombe, Simon T. / *University of Namibia, Namibia*.. 39

Baragde, Dileep B. / *G. S. Moze College, India* 303

Burdenko, Elena Viktorovna / *Plekhanov Russian University of Economics, Russia* 198

Castillo-Nazareno, Uriel Hitamar / *Catholic University of Santiago de Guayaquil, Ecuador* 1

Cvetkovski, Tatjana / *Megatrend University in Belgrade, Serbia*.. 118

Deshpande, Mukund Vasant / *Independent Researcher, India* 244

Dieguez, Teresa / *Polytechnic Institute of Cávado and Ave, Portugal* 60

Dixit, Ramnath / *Symbiosis International University, Pune, India*.. 285

Djukic, Gordana P. / *Faculty of Economics, University of Belgrade, Serbia* 19, 118

Dzingirai, Mufaro / *Midlands State University, Zimbabwe* 99

Hu, Meng Kui / *Universiti Sains Malaysia, Malaysia*... 139

Ilic, Biljana Stojan / *Megatrend University of Belgrade, Serbia*... 118, 261

Jadhav, Amit Uttam / *G. S. Moze College, India* 303

Kadyan, Jagbir Singh / *Swami Shraddhanand College, University of Delhi, India*.......................... 80

Kadyan, Sneha / *O. P. Jindal Global University, India*.. 80

Kee, Daisy Mui Hung / *Universiti Sains Malaysia, Malaysia* 139

Mahajan, Vaishali / *Symbiosis Centre for Management and Human Resource Development, Symbiosis International University, Pune, India*.. 220

Ndava, Rodgers / *Midlands State University, Zimbabwe* 99

Rajagopal, Kannan / *Symbiosis Centre for Management and Human Resource Development, Symbiosis International University, Pune, India*.. 220

Randa, Isaac Okoth / *Namibia University of Science and Technology, Namibia* 175

Saiz-Alvarez, Jose Manuel / *Catholic University of Avila, Spain & Catholic University of Santiago de Guayaquil, Ecuador* 1

Sinha, Vinita / *Symbiosis Centre for Management and Human Resource Development, Symbiosis International University, Pune, India*.. 285

Tubulingane, Booysen Sabeho / *Namibia University of Science and Technology, Namibia & University of Giessen, Germany & UNICAF, Cyprus* 39

Vargas-Hernández, José G. / *Instituto Tecnológico Mario Molina, Zapopan* 157, 318

Table of Contents

Preface xvii

Acknowledgment xxiii

Chapter 1
Asian Infrastructure Investment Bank and Development: A Chinese Soft Power Tool for Global
Leadership 1
*Jose Manuel Saiz-Alvarez, Catholic University of Avila, Spain & Catholic University of
Santiago de Guayaquil, Ecuador*
Uriel Hitamar Castillo-Nazareno, Catholic University of Santiago de Guayaquil, Ecuador
María Teresa Alcívar-Avilés, Catholic University of Santiago de Guayaquil, Ecuador

Chapter 2
Digital Inclusion for Vulnerable Groups and Transformation: A Comparative Case Study 19
Gordana P. Djukic, Faculty of Economics, University of Belgrade, Serbia

Chapter 3
Education Quality and Offerings Intersection Post Pandemic for Inclusive Development: A Case
Study 39
*Booysen Sabeho Tubulingane, Namibia University of Science and Technology, Namibia &
University of Giessen, Germany & UNICAF, Cyprus*
Simon T. Angombe, University of Namibia, Namibia

Chapter 4
Entrepreneurship: Higher Education and Gender – Equity and Access for Inclusive Development.... 60
Teresa Dieguez, Polytechnic Institute of Cávado and Ave, Portugal

Chapter 5
Exploring Ethical Consumption for Equity and Inclusiveness: Bridging Thoughts and Action of
Consumers 80
Sneha Kadyan, O. P. Jindal Global University, India
Jagbir Singh Kadyan, Swami Shraddhanand College, University of Delhi, India

Chapter 6
Global Institutional Role to Promote Achievement of the Sustainable Development Goals in
Zimbabwe... 99
Mufaro Dzingirai, Midlands State University, Zimbabwe
Rodgers Ndava, Midlands State University, Zimbabwe

Chapter 7
Global Institutional Roles in Access to Inclusive Education: Comparison of Serbia and Europe 118
Biljana Stojan Ilic, Megatrend University of Belgrade, Serbia
Gordana P. Djukic, Faculty of Economics, The University of Belgrade, Serbia
Tatjana Cvetkovski, Megatrend University in Belgrade, Serbia

Chapter 8
Global Institutions and ESG Integration to Accelerate SME Development and Sustainability 139
Meng Kui Hu, Universiti Sains Malaysia, Malaysia
Daisy Mui Hung Kee, Universiti Sains Malaysia, Malaysia

Chapter 9
Institutional Transformation of Participatory Governance 157
José G. Vargas-Hernández, Instituto Tecnológico Mario Molina, Zapopan

Chapter 10
Integrated Reporting for Inclusive and Sustainable Global Capitalism.. 175
Isaac Okoth Randa, Namibia University of Science and Technology, Namibia

Chapter 11
International Financial Organizations: Russian Experience of Cooperation for Three Decades........ 198
Elena Viktorovna Burdenko, Plekhanov Russian University of Economics, Russia

Chapter 12
International Organizations' Aid for Educational Transformation and Inclusive Development 220
Kannan Rajagopal, Symbiosis Centre for Management and Human Resource Development,
Symbiosis International University, Pune, India
Vaishali Mahajan, Symbiosis Centre for Management and Human Resource Development,
Symbiosis International University, Pune, India

Chapter 13
Policy Framework and Planning in Global Institutions 244
Mukund Vasant Deshpande, Independent Researcher, India

Chapter 14
Poverty and Poverty Indicators in the Republic of Serbia: The Impact of Uneven Regional
Development 261
Biljana Stojan Ilic, Megatrend University of Belgrade, Serbia

Chapter 15
Role of Global Institutions in Competency Development 285
    Ramnath Dixit, Symbiosis International University, Pune, India
    Vinita Sinha, Symbiosis Centre for Management and Human Resource Development,
        Symbiosis International University, Pune, India

Chapter 16
Role of Global Institutions in Economic Development of India... 303
    Amit Uttam Jadhav, G. S. Moze College, India
    Dileep B. Baragde, G. S. Moze College, India

Chapter 17
Socio-Intercultural Organizational Development 318
    José G. Vargas-Hernández, Instituto Tecnológico Mario Molina, Zapopan, Mexico

Compilation of References 337

About the Contributors 389

Index... 395

Detailed Table of Contents

Preface.. xvii

Acknowledgment... xxiii

Chapter 1
Asian Infrastructure Investment Bank and Development: A Chinese Soft Power Tool for Global
Leadership... 1
    Jose Manuel Saiz-Alvarez, Catholic University of Avila, Spain & Catholic University of
        Santiago de Guayaquil, Ecuador
    Uriel Hitamar Castillo-Nazareno, Catholic University of Santiago de Guayaquil, Ecuador
    María Teresa Alcívar-Avilés, Catholic University of Santiago de Guayaquil, Ecuador

In October 2013, at the Asia-Pacific Economic Cooperation Summit in Jakarta, Indonesia, China's President Xi Jinping proposed creating a new multilateral development bank: the Asian Infrastructure Investment Bank (AIIB). Headquartered in Beijing, launched in October 2014, and operational on January 16, 2016, the AIIB has a governance structure similar to other MDBs to achieve green, technology-enabled, sustainable, and high-quality infrastructure focused on promoting regional, national, and international connectivity. Although there is US opposition, the AIIB has grown up to 103 approved members worldwide to promote regional cooperation and partnerships to address development challenges by working closely with other multilateral and bilateral development institutions and the private sector. This chapter aims to show how China is using the AIIB as a tool to be the first economic power on the planet shortly.

Chapter 2
Digital Inclusion for Vulnerable Groups and Transformation: A Comparative Case Study................. 19
    Gordana P. Djukic, Faculty of Economics, University of Belgrade, Serbia

The aim of the chapter is to highlight different regional approaches to digital inclusion from the social and economic aspects by academic researchers. The chapter presents the concept of digital literacy and digital inclusion and social and economic benefits in some European countries. The research observes individual European countries in which digital literacy with incorporated digital inclusion is equally important. The subject of the research will be digital inclusion on a regional level with an emphasis on the social, economic component in Denmark, Greece, and Serbia. The use of digital technology creates an opportunity for better public service in various sectors, especially in education, health, e-government, etc., which would favor better inclusion of the poor and socially disadvantaged. Technological transformation has contributed to the introduction of the most developed information and communication technologies (ICT) in a large number of countries in Europe and other countries around the world.

Chapter 3
Education Quality and Offerings Intersection Post Pandemic for Inclusive Development: A Case
Study 39
    Booysen Sabeho Tubulingane, Namibia University of Science and Technology, Namibia &
        University of Giessen, Germany & UNICAF, Cyprus
    Simon T. Angombe, University of Namibia, Namibia

Contact learning and teaching was suspended in 2020 at many universities globally, including in Namibia, to counter the spread of COVID-19 transmission. The study assessed the impact of the COVID-19 outbreak on student academic performance per respective offering type (online and contact) using quantitative inferential statistical regression analysis. Data from a total of 20770 student population for 2019 and 2020 academic years was applied in the study. The study established that online rather than contact education offering is associated with improved student academic performance at the Namibian university. However, Namibian students do not benefit from online education equally due to socio-economic inequality. A correlation between internet access and online student academic performance was established. The study has also demonstrated the importance of equality in student offering modes in upholding the quality of higher education. An academic research directed at evaluating the level of plagiarism associated with online and contact offering at the Namibian university needs to be conducted.

Chapter 4
Entrepreneurship: Higher Education and Gender – Equity and Access for Inclusive Development.... 60
    Teresa Dieguez, Polytechnic Institute of Cávado and Ave, Portugal

Sustainable development has become a buzzword in all fields and domains. Since the Brundtland Report, several attempts to exactly define the meaning of it appeared, even if not always consensual, inclusive, or convergent. However, SD is a holistic notion, encompassing economic, social, cultural, political, and environmental dimensions. Inclusive development is one of the 17 central elements of the Sustainable Development Goals. It follows the United Nations Development Programme's human development approach and joins in the standards and values of human rights. The chapter aims to reflect on the gender inequality problematic and explore how higher education can have an important role on this ongoing process. After a literature review, a co-creation project in IPCA, Portugal is presented. Conclusion seems to point out that education for entrepreneurship, namely through active learning methodologies, can develop the needed 21st century skills, especially if learned in active entrepreneurial education systems and oriented to reach inclusive sustainable development.

Chapter 5
Exploring Ethical Consumption for Equity and Inclusiveness: Bridging Thoughts and Action of
Consumers... 80
    Sneha Kadyan, O. P. Jindal Global University, India
    Jagbir Singh Kadyan, Swami Shraddhanand College, University of Delhi, India

This chapter is directed at examining this gap in everyday practices and is a step towards bridging thoughts and action of consumers towards sustainable social change. Utilizing a qualitative approach, purchasing practices of consumers with strong beliefs about ethical consumption are critically assessed to examine how individuals think and act with respect to their purchasing decisions. The findings of this chapter suggest that transparency and communication of the ethical investment of consumers in purchasing and consuming ethical products needs to be more pronounced for thoughts to reflect in ethical conscious practices.

Chapter 6
Global Institutional Role to Promote Achievement of the Sustainable Development Goals in
Zimbabwe.. 99
    Mufaro Dzingirai, Midlands State University, Zimbabwe
    Rodgers Ndava, Midlands State University, Zimbabwe

The role of institutions in development discourse when it comes to inclusive development is hotly debated in recent years. Nonetheless, little is known about the role of global institutions in achieving the Sustainable Development Goals in the context of the global pandemic widely known as the COVID-19 pandemic. Given this information, this chapter will focus on the role of global institutions in promoting the achievement of sustainable development goals in Zimbabwe. This study establishes that global institutions play an enabling role when it comes to the achievement of SDGs in Zimbabwe through developmental policy advocacy and guidance, sensitization and dissemination of information, capacity building, and financing developmental programs. Based on these findings, a plethora of recommendations has been proposed that includes expansion of collaboration, improvement of governance systems and practices, improvement on international co-operation, and unlocking of international finance.

Chapter 7
Global Institutional Roles in Access to Inclusive Education: Comparison of Serbia and Europe 118
    Biljana Stojan Ilic, Megatrend University of Belgrade, Serbia
    Gordana P. Djukic, Faculty of Economics, The University of Belgrade, Serbia
    Tatjana Cvetkovski, Megatrend University in Belgrade, Serbia

The aim of the chapter is to point the importance of global institutions and their role in access to inclusive education. Globalization as a world phenomenon has brought great changes both in the way of doing business and in other social spheres. First of all, a positive attitude towards the acceptance of diversity among people is the key word concerning at the social component. The modern world is facing great changes and the most important issues can be solved by education for sustainable growth and development. The authors will emphasize the comparison of Serbia and one developed European country in terms of inclusive education to highlight good practice and to apply it in Serbia.

Chapter 8
Global Institutions and ESG Integration to Accelerate SME Development and Sustainability 139
    Meng Kui Hu, Universiti Sains Malaysia, Malaysia
    Daisy Mui Hung Kee, Universiti Sains Malaysia, Malaysia

Since the adoption of the Sustainable Development Goals (SDGs) by the United Nations in 2015, all its 193 member states committed themselves to implementation at the national, regional, and international levels. In particular, the private sector is called upon to play an active role in driving the integration of environmental, social, and governance (ESG) principles among businesses, including SMEs. Armed with adequate resources, global institutions can influence SMEs and lead the way in educating and providing them with sound guidance towards ESG adoption. In collaboration with the local government, global institutions can intensify their efforts in promoting ESG adoption among SMEs. This chapter looks at how SMEs can leverage global institutions for guidance, support, and good practices in charting ESG integration in their business operations, enabling them to achieve business sustainability in the long term. Moreover, this chapter will specifically draw on experiences of ESG integration by Malaysian SMEs.

Chapter 9

Institutional Transformation of Participatory Governance 157
  José G. Vargas-Hernández, Instituto Tecnológico Mario Molina, Zapopan

This chapter is aimed to analyze the institutional transformation of participatory governance from the socio-intercultural perspective and interethnic relationships. The analysis of the public culture is based on the assumption that socio-intercultural and interethnic relations are a broader social field considered in the context of the analysis of the institutions of governance to understand the social institutions and events. The method used is reflective analytical based on the literature review and empirical study. It is concluded that these institutional transformations of participatory governance have been sourced and evolved into governance structures to govern the behaviors of the communities, organizations, leadership, and members.

Chapter 10

Integrated Reporting for Inclusive and Sustainable Global Capitalism.. 175
  Isaac Okoth Randa, Namibia University of Science and Technology, Namibia

There is growing universal agreement that neoliberalism, a form of political economy governance, has under-delivered for a majority of people over many years. This is exhibited in the extent of job losses, reduced tax revenues, dwindling overall savings, and so on. Whereas several contributory factors are identifiable, fundamentally these policy ambiguities are issues of failing global governance. This chapter analytically describes the influence of integrated reporting as an instrument for embedding corporate transparency, accountability, and responsibility, hence inclusive corporate governance for the common good in emerging economies. This investigation identified three channels through which integrated reporting connects with sustainable and inclusive capitalism, transparency and adequate disclosures in capital markets, stakeholder engagement, and corporate legitimacy. Integrated reporting provides the required cultural shift in corporate management by emphasising multi-capital long-term value creation, which ultimately promotes long-term behaviour in capital markets.

Chapter 11

International Financial Organizations: Russian Experience of Cooperation for Three Decades........ 198
  Elena Viktorovna Burdenko, Plekhanov Russian University of Economics, Russia

The chapter examines Russia's cooperation with international financial organizations for the period from 1992 to 2021. Attention is paid to cooperation programs with the International Monetary Fund and projects implemented jointly with the International Bank for Reconstruction and Development, the Multilateral Investment Guarantee Agency, and the International Finance Corporation. The participation of Russia in the projects of the International Development Association is shown. The chapter analyzes the problems of Russia's cooperation with "old" international organizations.

Chapter 12
International Organizations' Aid for Educational Transformation and Inclusive Development 220
 Kannan Rajagopal, Symbiosis Centre for Management and Human Resource Development,
  Symbiosis International University, Pune, India
 Vaishali Mahajan, Symbiosis Centre for Management and Human Resource Development,
  Symbiosis International University, Pune, India

There has been several research studies and articles on foreign aid for education which predominantly deliberates on the aspects that really works effectively in favor of aid and on the points which indicate the main reasons for the failures of such education aid initiatives. In fact, studies have abundantly shown that these foreign aids for education have made positive contributions to the education aid-recipient nations specifically in terms of enhancing the enrolment percentages under the basic education levels. However, there is also strong evidence on the existence of a wide gap on what the aid does to the nation and what it is intended to possibly achieve specifically in terms of the quality of education anticipated to be achieved. Overall findings of the research studies suggest that interventions are more effective at improving student performance and learning when social norms and intertemporal choices are factored in the design of educational policies and when two or more drivers of change are combined.

Chapter 13
Policy Framework and Planning in Global Institutions 244
 Mukund Vasant Deshpande, Independent Researcher, India

Global institutions play a central role in developing nations. Each nation has its own identity, and therefore, single policy for one nation rarely matches with the other. As a result, a variety of dimensions is essentially searched while planning a policy especially in a global institution. Although policies on food, habitation, and clothing are considered as common need of people in the globe, peoples' living entirely depends upon variety of characteristics such as their philosophy, environment, and desire to make development creating heavy influence on policy making. Therefore, this chapter is planned to understand how ideas and concepts are developed amongst the policy designers and converted into policy making.

Chapter 14
Poverty and Poverty Indicators in the Republic of Serbia: The Impact of Uneven Regional
Development 261
 Biljana Stojan Ilic, Megatrend University of Belgrade, Serbia

Poverty has become one of the most important categories of the global social and economic order and thus part of sustainability. Poverty is a product of harmful and excessive inequalities in the world as well as in almost every individual society. The aim of the chapter is to point to the importance of poverty indicators in the Republic of Serbia, as well as the impact of uneven regional development on poverty. Therefore, for Serbia, as well as for other countries in transition, it is vital to ensure sustainable and dynamic growth of real per capita income. The chapter also provides an overview of developing strategic directions for poverty alleviation.

Chapter 15
Role of Global Institutions in Competency Development 285
    Ramnath Dixit, Symbiosis International University, Pune, India
    Vinita Sinha, Symbiosis Centre for Management and Human Resource Development,
        Symbiosis International University, Pune, India

This chapter aims to highlight the role of global institutions in facilitating competency development for people from different nationalities spread across diverse geographies. Training and development is an essential step towards accomplishing inclusive development and is closely connected with social and economic development on a universal scale. Although multilateral institutions are taking efforts towards providing timely and regular training to people worldwide, there is ample scope for ensuring the successful implementation of knowledge and skills disseminated through various training initiatives. It is in this context that transfer of training or learning transfer gains prominence as a game changer in shaping the development initiatives driven by global institutions. This chapter thus delves deeper on the need to ensure a robust training transfer ecosystem and the significance of global institutions in facilitating the same to achieve competency development. The chapter concludes with pragmatic recommendations to enhance competency development universally.

Chapter 16
Role of Global Institutions in Economic Development of India 303
    Amit Uttam Jadhav, G. S. Moze College, India
    Dileep B. Baragde, G. S. Moze College, India

The International Monetary Fund (IMF), the World Bank, and the International Trade Organisation were conceived at the Bretton Woods Conference in July, 1944 as institutions to strengthen international economic cooperation and to help create a more stable and prosperous global economy. Instead, the General Agreement on Tariffs and Trade, through successive rounds of negotiations, got transformed into what has come to be known as the World Trade Organisation. The various institutions have been set up to govern international economic relations. While all the institutions work in close coordination with each other, each of these institutions has its own specific area of responsibilities. The IMF promotes international monetary cooperation and provides member countries with policy advice, temporary loans, and technical assistance so they can establish and maintain financial stability and external viability and build and maintain strong economies. The World Bank promotes long-term economic development and poverty reduction by providing technical and financial support.

Chapter 17
Socio-Intercultural Organizational Development 318
    José G. Vargas-Hernández, Instituto Tecnológico Mario Molina, Zapopan, Mexico

This chapter analyzes socio-intercultural organizational development as a novel perspective in organizational sciences. The analysis departs from the assumption that an effective socio-intercultural management and organizational long-term development based on the collaboration among all the stakeholders must be based on the cultural basic assumptions, values, and beliefs of participants involved in intercultural communication and dialogue, committed, and acting on equal basis despite the cultural differences and the challenges derived. The method employed is the transdisciplinary reflective-analytical approach. The analysis concludes that the transdisciplinary and socio-intercultural perspective of organizational development and effective management competence is based on intercultural communication and dialogue.

Compilation of References 337

About the Contributors 389

Index 395

Preface

Various processes that have come to be known collectively as globalization pose a major threat to nations and identities created and supported by the concept of the nation. The argument is perfectly straightforward even though it is commonly expressed in far from accessible language. Put simply, economic, political, cultural, and ideological trends, supported by a pervasive and all-powerful global approach inevitably destroy the distinctiveness upon which nations, nationalism, and national identities depend for their very existence. What emerges is the struggle between the national and the global creating a 'territorial trap', since it, ignores the fact that global systems are by their very nature entropic and challenge the very notion of the bounded region. Here the necessity arises to understand the role that global institutions like World Bank, IMF, UNO, or ILO play to ensure that all nations do get a level playing field to contribute not only to global good and development but also at the same time drive their national agenda to ensure their growth and national development.

For more than a century and a half, the most powerful national governments have created institutions of multilateral governance that promise to make a more inclusive world, a world serving women, working people, the colonized, the "backward," the destitute, and the despised. That promise and the real impact need deliberation, discussion, and probe. This book intends to do that only. The subject matter will be to examine what exists, to what extent these systems of global institutions function appropriately, and what they have not done. With the history of multilateral governance and the impact of the global pandemic, there is no doubt that we are at a cusp, a transition, between the system that marked the decades after the Second World War and a more extensive system of international governance that will characterize the world for the next generation. That system may keep the long-standing promise to serve the world's least advantaged, or it may serve to marginalize them further.

Handbook of Research on Global Institutional Roles for Inclusive Development examines the concepts that have powerfully influenced development policy and, more broadly, examines the role of ideas in these institutions and how they have affected the current development discourse. It enhances the understanding of how these ideas travel within systems and how they are translated into policy, modified, distorted, or resisted. Covering topics such as ethical consumption, academic migration, and sustainable global capitalism, this book is an essential resource for government officials, activists, management, academicians, researchers, students and educators of higher education, and educational administration and faculty.

OBJECTIVE OF THE BOOK

The impact global multilateral institutions such as the World Bank, UNO, and IMF have on development is hotly debated, but few doubt their power and influence. Therefore the main aim of this book is to examine the concepts that have powerfully influenced development policy and, more broadly, look at the role of ideas in these institutions and how they have affected current development discourse. With this aim, the objectives, therefore, are to enhance the understanding of how the ideas travel within the systems and how they are translated into policy, modified, distorted, or resisted. It is not about creating something fundamentally new, nor is it about completely transcending the efforts of these global institutions. Rather, it is about creating effective global institutions at a global level, which can aid in social and economic development globally. Hence, this unique book intends to explore a broad range of these ideas and institutions, and provide case studies and best practices in the context of broader theoretical analysis.

TARGET AUDIENCE

The scholarly value of the proposed publication is self-evident because of the increase in the emphasis placed on global institutions and the role they play for corporate governance, innovation, and sustainability globally and it is going to be more crucial post-pandemic when the economies restart and more so in emerging economies. Moreover, there is a dire need for understanding comprehensively the complexity in the process of how these global institutions work and function multi-laterally. Further, providing a qualified reference book to its proposed target market/constituents will expand the fields of global policy, governance, economics, and international management and learning. The proposed topic for publication will not only facilitate in identifying the role of global institutions, governance mechanisms, frameworks, competencies, and skills, which is imperative for economic development but help in benchmarking global practices. It will also aid entrepreneurs, and organizations globally to develop effectively and efficiently. It will also aid the institutions of higher learning and educators to focus properly and help policymakers in designing and implementing policies that are more effective in the new global world order. In particular, it will be of immense interest and use to: Academics and Researcher Community; Postgraduate/Masters Students/Economics/MBA/Executive Education, and Practitioners and Policy Makers in this new world order.

TOPICS OF INTEREST

The book includes, among others, the following topics of interest for academics and practitioners:

- Access to Higher Education
- Competency Development
- Digital Inclusion
- Economic Development
- Educational Transformation
- Ethical Consumption
- Participatory Governance

Preface

- Small and Medium-Sized Enterprises (SMEs)
- Socio-Intercultural Organizational Development
- Sustainable Development Goals
- Sustainable Global Capitalism
- Uneven Regional Development
- Case Studies

This book presents a collection of 17 chapters contributed by academicians, researchers, practitioners, and managers, who are experts in the field, and each chapter addresses a key topic. A brief outline of these 17 chapters follows.

Chapter 1, *Asian Infrastructure Investment Bank and Development: A Chinese Soft Power Tool for Global Leadership,* explores the growth, and role of AAIB, and how China is using the AIIB as a tool to be the first economic power on the planet shortly.

Chapter 2, *Digital Inclusion for Vulnerable Groups and Transformation: A Comparative Case Study,* aims to highlight different regional approaches to digital inclusion from the social and economic aspects by academic researchers. The chapter presents the concept of digital literacy and digital inclusion and social and economic benefits in some European countries. The research observes individual European countries in which digital literacy with incorporated digital inclusion is equally important. The subject of the research will be digital inclusion on a regional level with an emphasis on the social, and economic components, in Denmark, Greece, and Serbia. The use of digital technology creates an opportunity for better public service in various sectors, especially in education, health, e-government, etc. which would favor better inclusion of the poor and socially disadvantaged.

Chapter 3, *Education Quality and Offerings Intersection Post Pandemic for Inclusive Development: A Case Study,* assesses the impact of COVID-19 outbreak on student academic performance per respective offering type (online and contact) using quantitative inferential statistical regression analysis. Data from a total of 20770 student populations for the 2019 and 2020 academic years was applied in the study. The study established that, online than contact education offering is associated with improved student academic performance at the Namibian university, although, Namibian students do not benefit from online education equally due to socioeconomic inequality. The study has also demonstrated the importance of equality in student offering modes in upholding the quality of higher education.

Chapter 4, *Entrepreneurship: Higher Education and Gender – Equity and Access for Inclusive Development,* aims to reflect on the gender inequality problem and explore how Higher Education can have an important role in this ongoing process. After a literature review, critical discussion follows on a co-creation project in IPCA, Portugal. The conclusion seems to point out that education for entrepreneurship, namely through active learning methodologies, can develop the needed 21st-century skills, especially if learned in the active entrepreneurial education system and oriented to reach inclusive sustainable development.

Chapter 5, *Exploring Ethical Consumption for Equity and Inclusiveness: Bridging Thoughts and Action of Consumers,* is directed at examining this gap in everyday practices and is a step towards bridging thoughts and actions of consumers towards sustainable social change. Utilizing a qualitative approach, purchasing practices of consumers with strong beliefs about ethical consumption are critically assessed to examine how individuals think and act in their purchasing decisions. The findings of this paper suggest that transparency and communication of the ethical investment of consumers in purchasing and consuming ethical products need to be more pronounced for thoughts to reflect in ethical conscious practices.

xix

Chapter 6, *Global Institutional Role to Promote Achievement of Sustainable Development Goals in Zimbabwe,* focuses on the role of global institutions in promoting the achievement of sustainable development goals in Zimbabwe. This study establishes that global institutions play an enabling role when it comes to the achievement of SDGs in Zimbabwe through developmental policy advocacy and guidance, sensitization and dissemination of information, capacity building, and financing of developmental programs. Based on these findings, a plethora of recommendations have been proposed which include expansion of the collaboration, improvement of governance systems and practices, improvement of international cooperation, and unlocking of international finance.

Chapter 7, *Global Institutional Roles in Access to Inclusive Education: Comparison of Serbia and Europe,* deals with the importance of global institutions and their role in access to inclusive education. Globalization as a world phenomenon has brought great changes both in the way of doing business and in other social spheres. First of all, a positive attitude towards the acceptance of diversity among people is the keyword concerning the social component. The modern world is facing great changes and the most important issues can be solved by education for sustainable growth and development. The authors will emphasize the comparison of Serbia and one developed European country in terms of inclusive education to highlight good practice and apply it in Serbia.

Chapter 8, *Global Institutions and ESG Integration to Accelerate SMEs Development and Sustainability,* looks at how SMEs can leverage global institutions for guidance, support, and good practices in charting ESG integration in their business operations, enabling them to achieve business sustainability in the long term. Moreover, this chapter will specifically draw on experiences of ESG integration by Malaysian SMEs.

Chapter 9, *Institutional Transformation of Participatory Governance,* analyzes the institutional transformation of participatory governance from the socio-intercultural perspective and interethnic relationships. The analysis of the public culture is based on the assumption that socio-intercultural and interethnic relations are a broader social field considered in the context of the analysis of the institutions of governance to understand the social institutions and events. The method used is reflective analytical based on the literature review and empirical study. It is concluded that these institutional transformations of participatory governance have been sourced and evolved into governance structures to govern the behaviors of the communities, organizations, leadership, and members.

Chapter 10, *Integrated Reporting for Inclusive and Sustainable Global Capitalism,* analytically describes the influence of integrated reporting as an instrument for embedding corporate transparency, accountability and responsibility, hence inclusive corporate governance for the common good in emerging economies. This investigation identified three channels through which integrated reporting connects with sustainable and inclusive capitalism; transparency and adequate disclosures in capital markets, stakeholder engagement, and corporate legitimacy. Integrated reporting provides the required cultural shift in corporate management by emphasizing multi-capital long-term value creation, which ultimately promotes long-term behavior in capital markets.

Chapter 11, *International Financial Organizations Russian Experience of Cooperation for Three Decades,* examines Russia's cooperation with international financial organizations for the period from 1992 to 2021. Attention is paid to cooperation programs with the International Monetary Fund; projects implemented jointly with the International Bank for Reconstruction and Development, the Multilateral Investment Guarantee Agency, and the International Finance Corporation. The participation of Russia in the projects of the International Development Association is shown. The chapter analyzes the problems of Russia's cooperation with "old" international organizations.

Preface

Chapter 12, *International Organizations' Aid for Educational Transformation and Inclusive Development,* critically looks at what the international organizational aid does to the nation and what it is intended to possibly achieve specifically in terms of the quality of education anticipated to be achieved. Overall findings of the research studies suggest that interventions are more effective at improving student performance and learning when social norms and inter-temporal choices are factored in the design of educational policies, and when two or more drivers of change are combined.

Chapter 13, *Policy Framework and Planning in Global Institutions,* focuses on the planning and policy framework of global institutions. It examines the fundamentals of policymaking, the discussion helps to understand how ideas and concepts develop amongst the policy designers, and they in turn convert into policies in practice.

Chapter 14, *Poverty and Poverty Indicators in the Republic of Serbia: The Impact of Uneven Regional Development,* discusses the importance of poverty indicators in the Republic of Serbia, as well as the impact of uneven regional development on poverty. Therefore, for Serbia, as well as for other countries in transition, it is vital to ensure sustainable and dynamic growth of real per capita income. The chapter also provides an overview of development strategic directions for poverty alleviation.

Chapter 15, *Role of Global Institutions in Competency Development,* highlights the role of global institutions in facilitating competency development for people from different nationalities spread across diverse geographies. Training and development are essential steps toward accomplishing inclusive development and are closely connected with social and economic development on a universal scale. Although multilateral institutions are taking efforts toward providing timely and regular training to people worldwide, there is ample scope for ensuring the successful implementation of knowledge and skills disseminated through various training initiatives. It is in this context, that transfer of training or learning transfer gains prominence as a game-changer in shaping the development initiatives driven by global institutions. This chapter thus delves deeper into the need to ensure a robust training transfer ecosystem and the significance of global institutions in facilitating the same to achieve competency development. The chapter concludes with pragmatic recommendations to enhance competency development universally.

Chapter 16, *Role of Global Institutions in Economic Development of India,* reviews and examines the role of the three global institutions namely; the International Monetary Fund (IMF), the World Bank, and the International Trade Organisation in the Indian context.

Chapter 17, *Socio-Intercultural Organizational Development,* analyzes socio-intercultural organizational development as a novel perspective in organizational sciences. The analysis departs from the assumption that effective socio-intercultural management and organizational long-term development based on the collaboration among all the stakeholders must be based on the cultural basic assumptions, values, and beliefs of participants involved in intercultural communication and dialogue, committed, and acting on equal basis despite the cultural differences and the challenges derived. The method employed is the Transdisciplinary reflective–analytical approach. The analysis concludes that the Transdisciplinary and socio-intercultural perspective of organizational development and effective management competence based on intercultural communication and dialogue,

In short, this book includes a wide variety of approaches, problems, and discussions in the area of global institutional roles in equity and access for inclusive development. It provides color and a fresh look at some difficult concepts and a field that is difficult to unify as it is dynamic and complex. The expertise provided herein comes from all over the world, and although there are common themes among the chapters, each provides a unique viewpoint that results from cultural and geographic differences. I believe that such diversity of thought is a necessary component in the advancement of the body of

xxi

knowledge, regardless of the discipline of inquiry. I hope that you agree and enjoy the contributions of our authors. I also trust that the book will provide an opportunity to learn about global institutional roles in equity and access for inclusive development based on a cross-cultural context.

The book also focuses on expanding and improving global institutional roles in equity and access for inclusive development, teaching, and knowledge-transfer activities, for policymakers to appropriate support initiatives and frameworks apart from enhanced understanding stimulating additional research in this area for this global crisis period and beyond. The need to ensure that all economies not only survive the pandemic but flourish in these trying times globally is ambitious. However, together, we can make minimize the impact of this global crisis and even treat it as an opportunity for all stakeholders to ensure that global institutions also do their bit to aid all nations and economies equitably so that they not only survive but also come out unharmed for a better world for all.

In sum, *Handbook of Research on Global Institutional Roles for Inclusive Development* is a step in that direction by presenting an inclusive analysis and blends of the research streams on global institutional roles, for sustaining education, innovation, SMEs, and entrepreneurship development in the post-pandemic era, and new world order. It provides an understanding of this complex and multi-faceted process. It is useful in guiding future research as it presents comprehensive knowledge relating to the role of global institutions, their contribution, and significance to enhance access and equity for inclusive development. It is the first book that gives systematic information about global institutional roles in equity and access for inclusive development so that all nations and economies continue to not only sustain but evolve better and grow stronger in times to come.

Neeta Baporikar
Namibia University of Science and Technology, Namibia & University of Pune, India

Acknowledgment

I thank the editorial staff at IGI Global for providing the opportunity to create this timely *Handbook of Research on Global Institutional Roles for Inclusive Development* reference book. It was indeed an interesting and enjoyable experience, due to their smooth and supportive process.

Handbook of Research on Global Institutional Roles for Inclusive Development examines the concepts that have powerfully influenced development policy and, more broadly, examines the role of ideas in these institutions and how they have affected the current development discourse. It enhances the understanding of how these ideas travel within systems and how they translate into policy, modified, distorted, or resisted. Further, in this crucial post-pandemic these global institutions will have a greater role to play to ensure inclusive development remains a priority and does not take the backseat. The contributors of the chapters undoubtedly provided the opportunity to create a resource that I think will benefit researchers, practitioners, and the global community. Hence, I would like to express my heartfelt thanks to all the authors for their high-quality contributions and reviewers for their effort in providing constructive comments and useful suggestions. The successful completion of this book has been the result of the cooperation of many people, including the editorial advisory board. I express my thanks and gratitude to all of them.

I am indebted to my husband Jayant and daughter Neha. Their continued support in my writing and research journey enables me to see the value of discovering and applying new-fangled knowledge with the hope, that fresh opportunities open up for one and all.

Chapter 1
Asian Infrastructure Investment Bank and Development:
A Chinese Soft Power Tool for Global Leadership

Jose Manuel Saiz-Alvarez
ⓘⅅ https://orcid.org/0000-0001-6435-9600
Catholic University of Avila, Spain & Catholic University of Santiago de Guayaquil, Ecuador

Uriel Hitamar Castillo-Nazareno
Catholic University of Santiago de Guayaquil, Ecuador

María Teresa Alcívar-Avilés
Catholic University of Santiago de Guayaquil, Ecuador

ABSTRACT

In October 2013, at the Asia-Pacific Economic Cooperation Summit in Jakarta, Indonesia, China's President Xi Jinping proposed creating a new multilateral development bank: the Asian Infrastructure Investment Bank (AIIB). Headquartered in Beijing, launched in October 2014, and operational on January 16, 2016, the AIIB has a governance structure similar to other MDBs to achieve green, technology-enabled, sustainable, and high-quality infrastructure focused on promoting regional, national, and international connectivity. Although there is US opposition, the AIIB has grown up to 103 approved members worldwide to promote regional cooperation and partnerships to address development challenges by working closely with other multilateral and bilateral development institutions and the private sector. This chapter aims to show how China is using the AIIB as a tool to be the first economic power on the planet shortly.

INTRODUCTION

In October 2013, at the Asia-Pacific Economic Cooperation Summit in Jakarta, Indonesia, China's President Xi Jinping proposed creating a new multilateral development bank (MDB): the Asian Infrastructure

DOI: 10.4018/978-1-6684-2448-3.ch001

Copyright © 2022, IGI Global. Copying or distributing in print or electronic forms without written permission of IGI Global is prohibited.

Investment Bank (AIIB). Headquartered in Beijing, launched in October 2014 with the signature of a Memorandum of Understanding by 21 Asian countries (including China), and operational on January 16, 2016, the AIIB has a governance structure similar to other MDBs (Weiss, 2018). It is an MDB devoted to achieving green, technology-enabled, by financing sustainable and high-quality infrastructure to promote regional, national and international connectivity. Although the US opposition by affirming the AIIB would not meet global transparency, environmental and labor standards, procurement requirements, and other safeguards (Bustillo & Maiza, 2018), it has grown up to 103 approved members worldwide (data 2021). Today, the AIIB capitalizes at USD100 billion and is Triple-A-rated by the major international credit rating agencies. As a new addition to the MDB family, the AIIB's mandate includes promoting regional cooperation and partnerships to address development challenges by working closely with other multilateral and bilateral development institutions.

Xiao (2016) summarizes four driving forces to explain the creation of the AIIB. First, the arrival in November 2012 of Xi Jinping, as the new China's president, changed the traditional economic policies developed by his predecessors Jiang Zemin and Hu Jintao, guided by a conservative strategy focused on transforming China. The brand-new president focused on his policies following the so-called "double circulation," defined by simultaneously developing domestic welfare and international competition. Second, setting the goal of achieving development based on building infrastructures as a priority to avoid severe bottlenecks in China and abroad, especially in the Asian region. Third, to compensate Beijing's frustration over the Western, especially the US dominance of the existing international multilateral bodies. And fourth, the arrival of a new 'Eurasian shift' to link Europe and Asia by land and sea.

Creating the AIIB as an MDB is a central component of President Xi's regional economic and foreign policy. It aims to boost economic connectivity from China to Central and South Asia, the Middle East, and Europe (through the Silk Road Economic Belt) and, along a maritime route, from Southeast Asia to the Middle East, Africa, and Europe (the 21st Century Maritime Silk Road) (Weiss, 2018). As a result, the creation and launch of the AIIB are much more than promoting business and social interconnectivity and economic integration in the Asian-Pacific region and cooperation with existing MDBs (Xiao, 2016).

Added to the Silk Economic Belts (Road and Maritime), China is most likely to conduct an inclusive institutional balancing strategy to provide extra benefits to followers. Among them, the AIIB's founders have benefited from pooling support and strengthening the AIIB's legitimacy (He & Feng, 2019). In short, a nation joining the AIIB bets on the winning horse.

The success of this AIIB's legitimacy and attraction is seen in its rapid growth and international recognition. In 2018, the AIIB was granted Permanent Observer status in the deliberations of both the United Nations General Assembly and the Economic and Social Council. The AIIB represented about 79 percent of the global population and 65 percent of global gross domestic product (GDP) in 2020. Headed by China, the AIIB is defined by self-governing, rules-and treaty-based, AAA-rated, with preferred creditor status focused on assuring structural change and economic growth. As a result, the AIIB is becoming an instrument of development for developing countries, especially in Africa and Asia, and to a lesser extent in Latin America and the Caribbean, as this bank is one of the main tools used by China to turn into the first world economic power during this decade. China has economic potential in terms of development and growth far superior to the economic potential of the United States. The American nation is declining in terms of less economic power, in general, for its citizens due to higher domestic poverty rates, especially in blacks (19.5%) and Hispanics (17%), according to data from the US poverty statistics (https://federalsafetynet.com/us-poverty-statistics.html), among other reasons.

China's structural transformation is unstoppable, especially after Xi Jinping's inaugural speech of the so-called National Rejuvenation (2021-2049). After this vital speech, China launched its entire industry with its brands and designs based on Industry 4.0 and the 6G technology, which will create new technology to eliminate its dependence on the United States (Table 1). The AIIB becomes a valuable instrument to achieve this structural transformation in this changing process.

Table 1. Chinese vs. US technologies

CHINA	USA
Hu Lian Wang	World Wide Web
Huawei's 6G	6G based in the USA
C-Sky Architecture	X-86/ARM Architecture
Ark OS	IOS/Android
Beidou	GPS
IoT China	IoT USA
Yuan Wire	Fed Wire

Source: Adapted from www.statista.com

The AIIB's mission is to finance all sorts of infrastructures for tomorrow, especially in Asian (China included) and African developing countries. By investing in sustainable infrastructures, the AIIB lends facilities and capital with low-interest rates, grace periods, and repayment of long-term loans, converting them into returns with negative interest rates in real terms in many cases. Besides, the AIIB facilitates the adoption of new technologies. Strategies also focused on addressing climate change and connecting the Asian continent with the principal commercial routes through the Silk Road Economic and the Maritime Belt to operate to the highest standards. Europe has a crucial role to play. As Ghiasy and Zhou (2017) affirm: "the Belt is a still-evolving, long-term Chinese vision for Eurasian infrastructural development, connectivity, and economic cooperation. There is a vast vacuum of critical infrastructure in large parts of Eurasia, which many relevant states cannot fill, even with the aid of existing multilateral development funds. The Belt intends to fill much of this vacuum" (p. IX). As a result, China's growing prominence in the international economic, political, social, and business environments is countering the traditional hard power exerted by the US in the rest of the world after the Second World War. The US influence is decreasing in specific regions and continents, now in Asia and Africa.

As a result, Europe, Asia, and Africa are significant beneficiaries of China's rise to its world economic supremacy. China is heavily investing in hydroelectric plants, highways, and railways because the implementation of good transport networks helps accelerate economic development. In this way, the African continent can become the future factory of the world in the medium-term once operating costs in Southeast Asia increase due to wealth creation.

China is the future, so the countries collaborating with this Asian giant will have a brighter future. Rooted in the *heping jueqi* (peaceful rise), China is playing an increasing role in its area of influence. This power situation strengthened with the signing of trade agreements with a global impact, such as the Regional Comprehensive Economic Partnership (RCEP) signed on November 15, 2020; the most significant trade agreement in the world will increase China's influence worldwide. These trade agreements benefit countries in the European Union (EU), Asia, Africa, and Latin America.

This chapter aims to analyze and describe the history and strategies conceived and put into practice after signing the Shanghai Cooperation Organization (SCO) on June 15, 2001. To cope with this goal, a descriptive-explanatory methodology will be used. The prospective impact of these strategies will be summarized in a SWOT analysis to analyze the internal and external factors affecting the Chinese political and economical design and organizations. Finally, the chapter will forecast the future impact the AIIB will have on its country beneficiaries.

BACKGROUND

Since 2016, China has become the world's top economic power in the gross domestic product (GDP) in terms of purchasing parity power. Based on a Constructivist process rooted in five core assumptions (ideas, identity, agency, natural and social facts, and institutional facts) inserted in the AIIB, Mendez and Turzi (2020) argue that the traditional Latin American customary modes of behavior can be reinforced with the AIIB's help to foster economic growth in the region. The AIIB represents an excellent opportunity for developing countries to overcome the socio-economic problems caused by COVID19. In fact, one of the Chinese vaccines used to contain the pandemic (Sinovac) has been the most widely distributed in these countries, especially in Africa, Asia, and Latin America.

China is fully aware of its growing economic, geopolitical, and social strength on the planet. In fact, Chinese assertiveness pertains to grand strategic change, not lying low anymore, and not renouncing leadership any longer (Åberg, 2016). In reality, from an economic point of view, a significant stake of the United States' public debt is in Asian hands, mainly Chinese and Japanese, which makes the United States an economic giant with feet of clay. The fiscal cliff is constantly threatening the balance of the US fiscal and budgetary policies. And China knows it.

For this reason, it is essential for the United States to avoid trade wars with China, as it is a growing economic giant. For this reason, the authors of this chapter believe that an excellent strategy to benefit the contenders and the entire planet is to join forces, leaving aside political and economic differences. As Sun Tzu said centuries ago in his famous book "The Art of War": "If you cannot defeat your enemy, ally with him."

The AIIB is a cornerstone in strengthening China globally. This organization takes a hybrid layered approach to sustainable infrastructure investment, similar to other MDBs, and uses safeguards to avoid and compensate for adverse social and environmental impacts. Also, it encourages investment and innovation on sustainable infrastructures to generate positive developmental spillovers (Costa & Chin, 2019). As a result of this investment process, China is displacing the United States in the Asia-Pacific countries (APAC), especially in the Philippines, Malaysia, and Thailand, with the strengthening of trade routes, city-building (e.g., New Clark City in the Philippines) and the introduction of the Chinese culture (soft power) in the region. In this way, from an economic point of view, China has been transformed from being a closed system based on socialism to an open one rooted in so-called state capitalism.

The emergence of this state capitalism in China, accelerated after the success of Special Economic Zones (SEZ) in China, links to the transformation of the Chinese party-state, as some authors claim it. In this respect, Hameiri and Jones (2018) argue that "the full extent of China's challenge to global governance cannot be understood without reference to the ongoing transformation of the Chinese party-state: the contested fragmentation, decentralization and internationalization of state apparatuses. These processes mean that the AIIB is just one institution among many in China's messy international development financing field - alongside policy and commercial banks, active ministries, provincial governments, and state-owned enterprises" (p. 1).

This strong connection between political and economic powers in a single country is unique to the AIIB. It differentiates it from the rest of the MDBs (Table 2), where one country member's political and economic preponderance is more diluted. Also, the AIIB is the only MDBs born in the 21st century, which shows China's geostrategic interest in establishing and peacefully enforcing its own rules in the world.

Table 2. The AIIB vs. other MDBs

	Creation	Members	
		Founders	Today
The European Investment Bank (EIB)	1957	6	28
The Inter-American Development Bank (IADB)	1959	21	48
The African Development Bank (AfDB)	1963	33	80
The Asian Development Bank (ADB)	1965	33	68
The European Bank for Reconstruction and Development (EBRD)	1990	40	68
The Asian Infrastructure Investment Bank (AIIB)	2016	57	103

Source: Adapted from Liechtenstein (2019) and http://www.aiib.org

It is important to note that, contrary to other MDBs, the AIIB focuses on infrastructure development, not poverty reduction; loans are extended at commercial rates, and recipients are required to demonstrate repayment capacity as part of the business case for projects funded (Hameiri & Jones, 2018). By not focusing on poverty reduction, the AIIB prevents countries from being dependent on the aid granted by the MDBs. All European countries, defined by implementing the welfare state after the Second World War, finally emerged from the economic poverty caused by the war. However, many developing countries continue with poverty and social inequality after independence, especially those located in Africa. The focus on the construction of infrastructures favors trade and the growing growth axes between cities, which leads to the creation of wealth for society.

In addition to the creation of growth axes between cities, a fact especially visible with the formation of the largest city in the world (more than 70 million inhabitants) doubling the size of Tokyo and equivalent to the economic power of the state of New York and Silicon Valley in the USA, State-centric approaches offer insights into China's decision to engage in new institution building via the AIIB. In this respect, Stephen and Skidmore (2019) find that, while conforming considerably to existing institutional models, the AIIB promotes social and economic development by constructing infrastructures and China's integration into global social networks. As a result, the AIIB strengthens state-led development pathways and is associated with the Chinese norm of non-interference.

Being an MDB, the AIIB is especially sensitive and responsive to the poorest countries. One of the particularities of the AIIB's voting powers (Table 3) is the voice increase of smaller shareholders, generally the poorest countries. Consequently, the weight of shareholding is limited by AIIB's combination of non-shareholding votes (primary votes, equaling 12 percent) and innovative Founding Member votes (600 votes for each of the potential 57 Founding Members, including many US allies).

Table 3. Voting powers in the MDBs

	Voting Powers
The European Investment Bank (EIB)	100%
The Inter-American Development Bank (IADB)	99%
The African Development Bank (AfDB)	99%
The Asian Development Bank (ADB)	80%
The European Bank for Reconstruction and Development (EBRD)	94.5%
The Asian Infrastructure Investment Bank (AIIB)	85%

Source: Adapted from Liechtenstein (2019) and http://www.aiib.org

The AIIB has established partnership arrangements with international organizations with the sole exception of the Caribbean Development Bank and joint and co-financed projects with other MDBs (Chin, 2019). This union of resources and work experiences allows the AIIB to impact its countries and strengthen cooperation significantly.

The AIIB is consistent with the Chinese political-economic system and the China model (Gransow & Price, 2018). It works as a multilateral financing alternative to bilateral flows for China's massive Maritime and Road Silk Belt Initiatives. As a result, the AIIB is a crucial factor for China to expand the Chinese culture, language, and history worldwide (soft power) and enlarge businesses and investments abroad.

All this process of change will lead to the structural transformation of China. This process will continue until the increase in wages generated by the development and a possible future technological obsolescence will lead to the loss of competitiveness and, therefore, to reducing exports. However, it is not foreseeable that these economic problems will be generated during the next two decades due to government plans to develop the entire economy harmoniously with the creation of growth axes in the country.

However, not everything is positive in China when facing risks and uncertainties, as shown in a SWOT analysis applied for the AIIB (Table 4). The Euro-Asian collaboration, with the placement of European managers in critical positions, strengthens the impact and recognition of the bank in the world and supports it internationally by having a double Eastern–Western vision. This double vision, different from the rest of MDBs whose thinking focuses on a specific regional area, makes it easier for the AIIB to attract more countries, which has made it the largest MDBs on the planet. Besides, the combination of the emulation and novelty effects makes the AIIB more attractive to join due to the potential opportunities that may arise along the way. As a result of these advantages, AIIB's financial strength and credibility are increasing, as shown internationally by the achievement of AAA ratings.

Asian Infrastructure Investment Bank and Development

Table 4. A SWOT analysis for the AIIB

Strengths	Weaknesses
• Financial strength • Emulation effect • Novelty effect • Euro-Asian collaboration	• High dependence on Chinese political-related issues • Dependence on the prices of building materials
Opportunities	Threats
• Strong investment in developing countries • Growing collaboration with international companies • Help to position China as the world's leading economic power • Fight to reduce poverty, especially in Africa	• Financial risk • Political corruption in recipient countries • Negative reaction from the US • The arrival of a new international financial crisis

Source: Author

As a result of these strengths, some opportunities emerge, mainly with structural economic reforms and fighting to reduce poverty, especially in Africa. The substantial investment made by AIIB in developing countries creates social wealth and economic development. Also, it tends to reduce regional imbalances with the construction of infrastructures, mainly seaports, land facilities, highways, railways, and dams, to generate electric power. In Latin America and the Caribbean, Africa, and parts of Asia, a lack of road infrastructure produces isolation that hurts exports and domestic trade. For this reason, the role played by the AIIB is essential to alleviate this problem in developing countries. Structural transformation results will be fully achieved in the long term, provided that these countries' political and economic corruption levels decrease.

The USA is the great loser in this entire process of structural change in economic and political terms. A possible US reaction may be to fight against China's growing supremacy, which is detrimental to both countries, or collaborate. However, the USA has not signed the agreement to join the AIIB, and there is no interest on the part of China that the US do so, especially after the start of the nonrational trade war launched by the Trump administration. For this reason, it is foreseeable that the United States will gradually lag. Once they are overcome, China will not give up its newly conquered position of world leadership. For the first time in history, the change in world leadership will occur without a bloody war but instead through an economic war.

The following section will include some thoughts concerning the impact and results generated by the AIIB in the EU, Russia, and Africa.

IMPACT AND RESULTS

Higher Economic Cooperation with the EU-27

The impact caused by the AIIB in the EU-27 is remarkable. Before Brexit, the United Kingdom (UK), as the biggest and most faithful US ally in Europe, announced on March 12, 2015, its desire to become a founding member state of the AIIB. This British wish provoked a dispute with the White House (Bustillo & Andoni, 2018; Dyer & Parke, 2015) and was soon followed by Germany, France, and Italy (Xiao, 2016). The European support and favor by the strongest EU-27 economies of the future AIIB, backing the China proposal defying Washington's unwise opposition to creating an MDB, was crucial and essential for the AIIB's success. This fact explains why EU-27 top managers in key positions in the AIIB vigorously work hand-by-hand with the Chinese authorities.

Respecting the AIIB, distant nations demand higher shares relative to their GDP at the AIIB due to their higher membership costs, as in the European case. However, given its excellent political and economic relations with the Great Dragon, China is inclined to accommodate these demands for institutional legitimacy and the potential benefit of attracting distant countries (Kaya & Woo, 2021). As a result, 24 non-regional European members, of which 18 belong to the EU-27. Therefore, the European presence in the bank is essential and not only at the managerial and organizational level of the bank (Table 5).

Table 5. European non-regional and prospective members in the AIIB

	Membership date	Subscription (in million USD)	In % of total	Number of votes	Voting power (in %)
NON-REGIONAL MEMBERS					
Austria	Dec 25, 2015	500.8	0.5175	7,165	0.6346
Belarus	Jan 17, 2019	64.1	0.0662	2,198	0.1947
Belgium	Jul 10, 2019	284.6	0.2941	4,403	0.3900
Denmark	Jan 15, 2016	369.5	0.3818	5,852	0.5183
Finland	Jan 7, 2016	310.3	0.3207	5,260	0.4659
France	Jun 16,2016	3,375.6	3.4883	35,913	3.1810
Germany	Dec 25, 2015	4,484.2	4.6339	46,999	4.1630
Greece	Aug 20, 2019	10	0.0103	1,657	0.1468
Hungary	Jun 16, 2017	100	0.1033	2,557	0.2265
Iceland	Mar 4, 2016	17.6	0.0182	2,333	0.2066
Ireland	Oct 23, 2017	131.3	0.1357	2,870	0.2542
Italy	Jul 13, 2016	2,571.8	2.6576	27,875	2.4691
Luxembourg	Dec 25, 2015	69.7	0.0720	2,854	0.2528
Malta	Jan 7, 2016	13.6	0.0141	2,293	0.2031
Netherlands	Dec 25, 2015	1,031.3	1.0657	12,470	1.1045
Norway	Dec 25, 2015	550.6	0.5690	7,663	0.6788
Poland	Jun 15, 2016	813.8	0.8596	10,475	0.9278
Portugal	Feb 8, 2017	65	0.0672	2,807	0.2486
Romania	Dec 28, 2018	153	0.1581	3,087	0.2734
Serbia	Aug 15, 2019	5	0.052	1,607	0.1423
Spain	Dec 15, 2017	1,761.5	1.8203	19,772	1.7513
Sweden	Jun 23, 2016	630	0.651	8,457	0.7491
Switzerland	Apr 25, 2016	706.4	0.73	9,221	0.8168
United Kingdom	Dec 25, 2015	3,054	3.1567	32,704	2.8968
PROSPECTIVE MEMBERS					
Armenia					

Source: Adapted from www.aiib.org (Last visit: October 22, 2021).

Many European countries have joined the AIIB to participate in bilateral dialogue to significantly influence and reshape global governance norms (for better or worse) related to international development (Prinsloo, 2019). In the case of Spain, its AIIB accession was due to support Latin America and the Caribbean countries to foster economic structural change and growth because they belong to the Ibero-American Community of Nations, in addition to Andorra, Equatorial Guinea, and Puerto Rico. Japan, South Korea, Timor-Leste, France, Italy, Morocco, Western Sahara, and the Philippines are observers in this organization.

The UK departure from the EU-27 has generated numerous economic and social problems within the island. In fact, the UK weakened its relations with China, both from an economic and political point of view. Being described as a psychodrama, Hughes (2019) assures that "Brexit attitudes are frequently projected as symptoms of pathological thought. People who voted Remain are labeled 'Remoaners,' implying the presence of chronically disordered mood. Those who voted Leave are dismissed as 'Brextremists,' which hints at sociopathy. The language of psychiatry is often used to decry Brexit as an act of national 'self-harm,' with little apparent regard for the sensitivities of people for whom actual self-harm is a lived reality" (p. 2). As Adam (2020) poses, "Brexit is unlikely to deliver what demagogues have promised, and disillusioned voters naively believed. Once the extent of this deceit becomes apparent, feelings could turn nasty. Accumulated frustration and discontent could explode in violence" (p. 299). These problems are compounded by possible Scottish independence, with the celebration of a future poll for the Scottish independence in 2022 or 2023 and, in practice, the Irish reunification in economic terms, as there is no physical border between Ireland and Northern Ireland. As a result, the UK is now more concerned with solving the initial consequences of Brexit, rather than looking exclusively towards Asia, except to attract immigrants from the Commonwealth, given the aging of the British population.

Russia

The post-Soviet economic and political cooperation with Russia began on June 15, 2001, creating the SCO, conceived as an international intergovernmental organization led by Russia and China and formed by six Asian countries (China, Russia, Kazakhstan, Kyrgyzstan, Tajikistan, and Uzbekistan). The SCO's origin is in the "4+1" Cooperation Treaty, signed between Russia, Kazakhstan, Kyrgyzstan, and Tajikistan plus China, in the late 1980s when these republics, four of them integrated into the Soviet Union, agreed to reduce border and military tensions in the region and to increase educational and economic exchanges among them (Saiz-Alvarez, 2009).

The AIIB contributes to accelerating the necessary reforms in economic policy focused on narrowing the productivity gap between Russian and Western industries, partly caused by an excessive governmental intervention in the private sector and the weakness of property rights. These factors disincentive work efforts and foreign direct investment, so judicial, administrative, social, and banking reforms are needed to assure future sustainable economic growth (Berglöf, Kunov, Shvets, & Yuaeva, 2003).

The AIIB fosters infrastructure projects linked to three thematic priorities: sustainable infrastructure, cross-border connectivity, and private capital mobilization (Mendez, 2019). In the Russian case, the construction of infrastructures with the most advanced technology is essential to avoid collapses in extreme weather conditions, as happens in Siberia, where temperatures vary almost 100 degrees Celsius between summer (+30 °C) and winter (-70 °C). In addition, such construction must be as respectful as possible with the environment. Given the climatic extremes and the long distances, there is a tendency to use more air transport than land transport to reach remote areas. In this way, the environmental impact is much lower.

The entry of AIIB funds into Russia after accession on December 28, 2015, complements the EU-27 funds traditionally submitted to this Slavic country to ease the construction of infrastructures for benefiting local industries and population. Despite this fact, significant social and economic differences persist in Russia. The Russian economy is a politicized economic system where political leaders established in Moscow make a three-fold solid economic intervention and control, as the economic system is roughly divided into the oil and gas industry (rent creating sector), a sector dependent on incomes from oil and gas (rent dependent sector) and the new private sector, mainly formed by small and middle-sized firms (SMEs)(Granberg & Sätre, 2017, p. 215; Gaddy & Ickes, 2015; Oxenstierna, 2015, p. 100).

With 67,519 votes in the bank, equivalent to 5.9806% of the total votes, Russia is the second country with the highest voting power in the AIIB after China (299,961 votes 26.5693% voting power). However, it is noteworthy that, unlike other MDBs, neither China nor the combination of China and Russia reaches the majority of the votes. Hence, decisions have to be made by consensus, taking into account the opinions and suggestions of the smaller countries. In this way, it is possible to achieve more harmonious development of the APAC region, which benefits all the countries in the area and moves the geographic center of international trade from the North Atlantic to the Pacific Ocean.

The EU-27 continued commitment to strengthening the political association and economic integration of Ukraine with the EU-27, based on the Association Agreement and its Deep and Comprehensive Free Trade Area, causes tensions with Russia, as this country has border problems with Ukraine. The Russian military incorporation of Crimea (February 23–March 18, 2014) against Ukraine is very recent, and war conflicts have continued in the Russian-speaking regions of Ukraine (Donbass) since 2014. The EU sanctions towards Russia lead to the AIIB becoming increasingly important given the good political relations between Russia and China. These good relations are expected to be strengthened in the future as China takes on a more significant international role.

Towards a New Africa

The creation of the AIIB has meant a change in world geopolitics, with an accelerated weakening of the hegemonic world influence of the US. Thanks to AIIB, China has entered the African continent, which in the future will be the continuation of the assembly plants that currently exist in Southeast Asia, especially in the Philippines, Vietnam, and Laos.

Africa's estimated infrastructure finance deficit is between $68 and $108 billion annually (Prinsloo, 2019). To solve this financial imbalance, ten African countries have joined the AIIB as non-regional members to benefit from loans at preferential interest rates (Table 6). In the coming years, the influence of the AIIB will be more intense in Africa, especially in the countries bordering the Mediterranean Sea. As a result, this influence would revive the failed Arab Common Market signed in 1964 between Mauritania, Morocco, Argelia, Tunisia, Libya, Sudan, Egypt, Somalia, Djibouti, Comoros, Palestine, Jordan, Lebanon, Syria, Iraq, Saudi Arabia, Kuwait, Bahrein, Qatar, United Arab Emirates, Oman, and Yemen. Besides, the influence of the AIIB can strengthen the different bilateral good-neighborly policies signed between Morocco, Algeria, Tunisia, and the EU.

Table 6. African non-regional and prospective members in the AIIB

	Membership date	Subscription (in million USD)	In % of total	Voting power (in %)	Number of votes
NON-REGIONAL MEMBERS					
Algeria	Dec 27, 2019	5	0.0052	0.1423	1,607
Benin	May 25, 2020	5	0.0052	0.1423	1,607
Côte d'Ivoire	Feb 26, 2020	5	0.0052	0.1423	1,607
Egypt	Aug 4, 2016	650.5	0.6722	0.7672	8,662
Ethiopia	May 13, 2017	45.8	0.0473	0.1703	1,923
Ghana	Feb 21, 2020	5	0.0052	0.1423	1,607
Guinea	Jul 12, 2019	5	0.0052	0.1423	1,607
Liberia	Jan 4, 2021	5	0.0052	0.1423	1,607
Madagascar	Jun 25, 2018	5	0.0052	0.1423	1,607
Rwanda	April 16, 2020	5	0.0052	0.1423	1,607
PROSPECTIVE MEMBERS					
Kenya, Libya, Morocco, Senegal, South Africa, Togo, and Tunisia					

Source: Adapted from www.aiib.org (Last visit: October 22, 2021).

One of the most promising projects for Africa is the construction of solar-related energy infrastructures. In fact, the AIIB finalized an Energy Sector Strategy that emphasizes proactive support to client countries to develop intermittent renewable energy, including solar, as set in a joint declaration dated March 10, 2018, between the International Solar Alliance, a treaty-based international inter-governmental organization launched on November 30, 2015, and the AIIB for the promotion of solar energy globally.

Added to the renewal energies, broader cross-regional benefits for industrial development and domestic production in African countries by facilitating market linkages with Asian countries to maximize economic growth, especially in the most impoverished rural areas, due to the strong synergies created between the infrastructure development agendas of the African Union and the AIIB (Prinsloo, 2019).

China's Greatest Dominance in the Pacific

The Chinese government has implemented the "going out" strategy to push Chinese firms to invest overseas through foreign direct investment (FDI)(Ly, 2020). FDI permits economic growth and wealth creation in the destination country, so positive externalities are created. Combining the Belt and Road Initiative and AIIB will help China find new impetus for growth and achieve economic and diplomatic strategic goals (Ly, 2020; Cai, 2018).

The AIIB has two mandates: to improve infrastructure connectivity in the Asia-Pacific region and reform the existing international financial and economic system to benefit developing countries (Zhu, 2019). the construction of infrastructures in different industries allows the generation of harmonious development in the territory. Structures that are sustainable from an environmental point of view if they incorporate new technologies to reduce the carbon footprint. Given the ecological deterioration of the planet, AIIB loans are preferentially directed to projects with low (or even zero) environmental impact, which benefits the world and future generations.

The projects supported by AIIB in South Asia cover sustainable infrastructure development, including rural roads, urban infrastructure renewal (water supply, telecommunications, and energy supply), and hydroelectric power plants (Kumar & Arora, 2019). As a result, there is a structural and radical transformation of the territory and the opening of new business opportunities for companies based in the region, which results in higher levels of social and economic well-being.

Together with the AIIB, the ADB is of fundamental importance in its area of influence. Compared with the ADB, the AIIB is probably more efficient and economically sustainable, improving traditional MDBs (Zhao, Gou, & Li, 2019) (Table 7). The diversification and openness achieved in the AIIB permit transform the bank into a global corporation defined by its project sensibility, efficiency, and quality of the project's implementation.

Table 7. ADB vs. AIIB projects

	ADB	AIIB
Management structure	**Integrated and specific**	**Diversified and open**
Procurement	Specific and open information of procurement; more stringent screening criteria on the procurement process	Significant in the procurement scale, a realization of the information platform operation in the entire process of project procurement
Economic analysis	Higher information transparency of the project's economic income, a stricter criterion of the project sensitivity evaluation, more robust financial stability of the project	Covers the main contents and comprehensively analyzes the project sensitivity
Risks	It covers more risk types	Relative simplification of the risk assessment
Safeguard and supervision	Focus on the use of project funds and safeguards in the social dimensions with a values preference	Focus on the efficiency and quality of the project's implementation

Source: Adapted from Zhao, Gou, and Li (2019).

Besides North Korea, Japan highlights as one of the missing regional members of the bank. In fact, Japan worries about the AIIB diluting the influence of post-WWII Bretton Woods institutions, such as the International Monetary Fund, the World Bank Group, and the Asian Development Bank. Indeed, Japan holds the second-largest voting share in the International Monetary Fund and the World Bank Group. Opting to join the AIIB would weaken its position and influence in both multilateral organizations (Katada, 2016). For this reason, and combined with bloody historical events that occurred between China and Japan, it is expected that Japan will not apply to join the AIIB. Or, if this nation applies, it is very plausible that China would not accept a possible future Japanese accession. The same situation happens in Colombia due to the military support of the Andean nation to the US during the Second World War.

Finally, Wang (2018) poses that less democratic countries, in terms of reduced polity score, political constraints, civil liberties, and lack of political rights, are more likely to join the AIIB as founding members. Also, nations closer to China and countries under-represented in the ADB are more likely to join the AIIB.

Asian Infrastructure Investment Bank and Development

A NEW Post-COVID19 World

The US-China relationships have been negatively impacted recently due to the immense (and unfortunately extreme deadly) health crisis caused by COVID-19 (Coronavirus, SARS-CoV-2), the US-China trade war, the US rejection of accessing the AIIB, the US sanctions on Russia and Iran, two of AIIB member countries, the US support for Hong Kong's demands, the US backing for Tibet, and the Chinese intention and active actions of exerting a territorial control of the South China Sea, among other international issues. The US faces high risks and bears geopolitical and economic costs by standing outside the AIIB. First, the influence of the World Bank and the ADB will be diminished, especially in the APAC region. Second, as the AIIB gains stature, it will be considered a potential alternative to US-preferred policies, norms, and standards set in the APAC and African regions (Freeman, 2019).

Some geopolitical problems continue today. Both Russia and Iran have substantial infrastructure needs. Still, they have been excluded from the European Bank for Reconstruction and Development (EBRD) and the World Bank Group's loans since Moscow's intervention in Ukraine in 2014 (Freeman, 2019; Buckley, 2017). As a result, China is now playing the role of the US. A US prominence that tended to be hegemonic until the end of the 20th century. In other words, The US is beginning to lose influence and economic, geostrategic, and cultural power in large regions of the planet.

In this changing process, technology has a fundamental role to play. In fact, technology will be of great importance in the post-COVID19 world by becoming a strategic value for competitiveness. The current economic world defined by industry 4.0 and the IoT, thanks to the 6G technology led by China, will change consumption and purchasing habits in millions of consumers worldwide and make the world much smaller and more competitive. In this change process, the solidarity born of the Chinese model will play a growing role. It will determine the economic development of the planet, especially in the areas of influence of China (APAC, Africa, and, to a lesser extent, Latin America and the Caribbean countries). It is essential to emerging a sustained public-private collaboration based on triple helix models (HEIs, Government, and business) throughout this process, as is the case in China.

In the post-COVID19 era, will have increasing importance aspects such as attention to business opportunities, passion at work, innovation in the product and service offered in the market, the implementation of training and professional promotion policies within organizations (private and public) so that people grow within them, the introduction and implementation of digitization processes (ERP and wearables) and continuous improvement of processes (*kaizen*), to increase efficiency in products and processes. It is also necessary to dispose of competitive collaboration, money value, scientific knowledge implementation and transfer to the industry, laboratories development, and ecosystems collaboration between industry, universities, and technological centers. This collaboration will transmit knowledge and implement production processes leading to greater competitiveness and quality of life for the population living in the countries.

Infrastructural development tends to increase the citizens' quality of life and firms using them, which is fixed to the population in a territory. Consumers' access to a more significant number and variety of products and services will avoid emigration to other cities, regions, and countries. For the new services created to be fully internalized by consumers, it is also necessary to set up educational programs. For this reason, education is usually part of the comprehensive packages of measures aimed at improving the quality of life of the citizens, especially those living in developing countries.

Design and construction of infrastructures linked to the transportation and energy sectors and financed by the AIIB will encourage the creation of intelligent citizens in developing countries and the development of Rural Innovation Hubs that will promote the use of new technologies and digitization of commerce. As a result, both the digital gap and the digital illiteracy will decrease.

Given the disastrous experience of the pandemic in the world, throughout this process of change, it is also essential to have a developed health system that leads to an effective and rapid response capacity in the face of any health contingency. Therefore, it would be necessary to build road and sanitary infrastructures of all kinds, especially in developing countries, to better combat the consequences of the pandemic with a greater degree of efficiency.

Recommendations and Managerial Implications

Combining a more substantial Chinese soft power globally, the signature of commercial agreements and more vital China-Russia collaboration opens new perspectives to China. Its global impact will accelerate after President Xi's historic speech on July 1, 2021, which began the National Rejuvenation's period expected to end in 2049, leading non-Chinese companies to adapt to the new circumstances peacefully imposed by China.

As a result, it is foreseeable that the expansion of Chinese companies in the Pacific will accelerate, along with greater collaboration between Chinese and European companies, thanks to the existing silk routes on the planet (Maritime, Land, and Polar, the latter in partnership with Russia). In my opinion, for the survival of non-Chinese organizations is good to launch more active cooperation strategies with Chinese firms rooted in a win-win collaboration process, primarily if the business activity is focused on satisfying the global market.

Also, this deeper collaboration among countries and firms is seen in the Pacific Ocean, where the RCEP (Regional Comprehensive Economic Partnership), led by China and signed on Nov. 15, 2020, integrates more than 2,000 million inhabitants of the planet. The signing of trade agreements between companies located in RCEP member countries will further strengthen China and shift the geographic center of world trade from the North Atlantic to the Pacific. For this reason, I think it is positive that Western companies are beginning to implement some of the management practices carried out in Chinese companies to facilitate the implementation of strategic alliances that are beneficial for all organizations.

As a result, the business and educational world will change from being monopolar after the fall of the Soviet Union more than three decades ago to a bipolar world between the USA and economically led by China. The economic shock of these two superpowers will be firmer in Latin America, as it is the natural area of influence of the United States. This influence will gradually decrease over time as the US political and cultural domination plans of Latin American countries have failed, contrary to what happened in the Philippines. Thus, a process of adaptation of Latin American entrepreneurs to the new Chinese model, based more on a spirit of participation in business, the supremacy of the collective over the individual, and the elimination of corrupt practices, becomes necessary.

CONCLUSION

The AIIB has signed a co-financing framework agreement with the World Bank and the Asian Development Bank, and Memorandums on joint cooperation with: the African Development Bank, the African Development Fund, the Asian Development Bank, the Eurasian Development Bank, the European Bank for Reconstruction and Development, the European Investment Bank, the European Stability Mechanism, the Inter-American Development Bank and Inter-American Investment Corporation, the International Fund for Agricultural Development, the Islamic Development Bank Group, the New Development Bank, and the World Bank Group. The signing of these agreements demonstrates the global nature of the AIIB by not limiting itself to developing the APAC region. The growing commercial rivalry between the US and China will notably impact poorer nations in favor of China. Developing countries are more vulnerable to the political leveraging of international financial institutions (Prinsloo, 2019), as many of them are partly controlled by the US, especially the World Bank and the International Monetary Fund.

The double health and economic crises caused by COVID19 are changing the global geopolitical balance and are shifting global leadership from the US to China. The changing process accelerated over time as the Asian giant began in 2021 the so-called "National Rejuvenation" stage that will end in 2049. China is the only country on the planet that competes simultaneously with first-order (R&D and innovation) and second-order (lower labor costs) competitive advantages. What is more, the use of dumping policies (economic, social, and ecological) leads to a reduction in prices that allows Chinese companies to compete successfully in international markets, including foreign companies established in special economic zones of China.

Contrary to other world leadership transitions made through warfare, the "leadership transition" between the US and China in global governance will be peaceful through institutional competition to transform the international system peacefully (He & Feng, 2019). This result is based on China's *heping hueqi* (peaceful ascent) policy that stands up to the traditional US warmongering policy.

In short, COVID19's arrival will lead to a reorganization of economic power and political influence globally, with the strengthening of China, the only country in the world (along with Guyana) to have achieved unstopped economic growth since the start of the pandemic. This fact will cut the distance in terms of GDP with the US, which China's GDP has already surpassed in purchasing power parity since 2016.

FUTURE RESEARCH DIRECTIONS

Given the growing importance of China and the AIIB in the world, a possible future line of research could be given to study the impact of the AIIB in developing countries, especially in Africa, Asia, and Latin America. Second, Ecuador is becoming an important gateway for China in South America and Mexico for the Latin American countries located in Central America and the Caribbean. A process of change for the benefit of China that was accelerated in response to the economic policies carried out during the Trump Administration and that the new T-MEC treaty has tried to alleviate but has not succeeded.

REFERENCES

Åberg, J. H. S. (2016). A Struggle for Leadership Recognition: The AIIB, Reactive Chinese Assertiveness, and Regional Order+. *Contemporary Chinese Political Economy and Strategic Relations*, 2(3), 1125–1171.

Adam, R. G. (2020). *Brexit. Causes and Consequences*. Springer. doi:10.1007/978-3-030-22225-3

Berglöf, E., Kunov, A., Shvets, J., & Yuaeva, K. (2003). *The New Political Economy of Russia*. The MIT Press. doi:10.7551/mitpress/5007.001.0001

Bustillo, R., & Andoni, M. (2018). China, the EU and multilateralism: The Asian Infrastructure Investment Bank. *Revista Brasileira de Política Internacional*, *61*(1), e008. doi:10.1590/0034-7329201800108

Cai, K. G. (2018). The one belt one road and the Asian infrastructure investment bank: Beijing's new strategy of geoeconomics and geopolitics. *Journal of Contemporary China*, *27*(114), 831–847. doi:10.1080/10670564.2018.1488101

Chin, G. T. (2019). The Asian Infrastructure Investment Bank – New Multilateralism: Early Development, Innovation, and Future Agendas. *Global Policy*, *10*(4), 569–581. doi:10.1111/1758-5899.12767

Costa, K., & Chin, G. T. (2019). The AIIB and Sustainable Infrastructure: A Hybrid Layered Approach. *Global Policy*, *10*(4), 593–603. doi:10.1111/1758-5899.12771

Dyer, G., & Parker, G. (2015). US attacks UK's constant accommodation with China. *Financial Times*. Accessed Oct 20, 2021. https://www.ft.com/content/31c4880a-c8d2-11e4-bc64-00144feab7de

Freeman, C. P. (2019). Constructive Engagement? The US and the AIIB. *Global Policy*, *10*(4), 667–676. doi:10.1111/1758-5899.12764

Gaddy, C. G., & Barry, W. I. (2015). Putin's rent management system and the future of addiction in Russia. In S. Oxenstierna (Ed.), *The Challenges for Russia's Politicized Economic System* (pp. 11–32). Routledge.

Ghiasy, R., & Zhou, J. (2017). The Silk Road Economic Belt: Considering security implications and EU–China cooperation prospects. SIPRI (Stockholm International Peace Research Institute) and Friedrich Ebert Stiftung (Germany).

Granberg, L., & Sätre, A.-M. (2017), *The Other Russia. Local experience and societal change*, Routledge.

Gransow, B., & Price, S. (2019). Social Risk Management at AIIB – Chinese or International Characteristics? *Journal of Chinese Political Science*, *24*(2), 289–311. doi:10.100711366-018-9553-8

Hameiri, S., & Jones, L. (2018). China challenges global governance? Chinese international development finance and the AIIB. *International Affairs*, *94*(3), 573–593. doi:10.1093/ia/iiy026

He, K., & Feng, H. (2019). Leadership Transition and Global Governance: Role Conception, Institutional Balancing, and the AIIB. *The Chinese Journal of International Politics*, *12*(2), 153–178. doi:10.1093/cjip/poz003

Hughes, B. M. (2019). *The Psychology of Brexit. From Psychodrama to Behavioural Science*. Springer. doi:10.1007/978-3-030-29364-2

Katada, S. N. (2016). At the Crossroads: The TPP, AIIB, and Japan's Foreign Economic Strategy. *Asia-Pacific Issues*, *125*, 1–8.

Kaya, A., & Woo, B. (2021). China and the Asian Infrastructure Investment Bank (AIIB): Chinese Influence Over Membership Shares? *The Review of International Organizations*. Advance online publication. doi:10.100711558-021-09441-1

Kumar, N., & Arora, O. (2019). Financing Sustainable Infrastructure Development in South Asia: The Case of AIIB. *Global Policy*, *10*(4), 619–624. doi:10.1111/1758-5899.12732

Ly, B. (2020). The rationale of European countries' engagement in AIIB. *Cogent Business & Management*, *7*(1), 1772619. Advance online publication. doi:10.1080/23311975.2020.1772619

Mendez, A. (2019). Latin America and the AIIB: Interests and Viewpoints. *Global Policy*, *10*(4), 639–644. doi:10.1111/1758-5899.12733

Mendez, A., & Turzi, M. (2020). *The Political Economy of China–Latin America Relations. The AIIB Membership*. Springer. doi:10.1007/978-3-030-33451-2

Oxenstierna, S. (Ed.). (2015). *The Challenges for Russia's Politicized Economic System*. Routledge. doi:10.4324/9781315757780

Prinsloo, C. (2019). AIIB Membership for African Countries: Drawcards and Drawbacks. *Global Policy*, *10*(4), 625–630. doi:10.1111/1758-5899.12734

Saiz Álvarez, J. M. (2009). La Organización de Cooperación de Shanghai. Claves para la creación de un futuro líder mundial. *Revista de Economía Mundial*, *23*, 307–326.

Stephen, M. D., & Skidmore, D. (2019). AIIB in the Liberal International Order. *The Chinese Journal of International Politics*, *12*(1), 61–91. doi:10.1093/cjip/poy021

Wang, Y. (2018). The Political Economy of Joining the AIIB. *The Chinese Journal of International Politics*, *11*(2), 105–130. doi:10.1093/cjip/poy006

Weiss, M. A. (2018). Asian Infrastructure Investment Bank (AIIB). *Current Politics and Economics of South, Southeastern, and Central Asia*, *27*(1/2), 1–29.

Xiao, R. (2016). China as an institution-builder: The case of the AIIB. *The Pacific Review*, *29*(3), 435–442. doi:10.1080/09512748.2016.1154678

Zhao, J., Gou, Y., & Li, W. (2019). A New Model of Multilateral Development Bank: A Comparative Study of Road Projects by the AIIB and ADB. *Journal of Chinese Political Science*, *24*(2), 267–288. doi:10.100711366-018-9580-5

Zhu, J. (2020). Is the AIIB a China-controlled Bank? China's Evolving Multilateralism in Three Dimensions (3D). *Global Policy*, *10*(4), 653–659. doi:10.1111/1758-5899.12763

ADDITIONAL READING

Bossuyt, F., & Bolgova, I. (2020). Connecting Eurasia: Is Cooperation Between Russia, China, and the EU in Central Asia Possible? In M. Lagutina (Ed.), *Regional Integration and Future Cooperation Initiatives in the Eurasian Economic Union* (pp. 234–250). IGI Global. doi:10.4018/978-1-7998-1950-9.ch013

Chung, M., & Mascitelli, B. (2019). The Case of Australian Reluctance with the Chinese Belt and Road Initiative. In I. Ordoñez de Pablos (Ed.), *Dynamic Perspectives on Globalization and Sustainable Business in Asia* (pp. 11–21). IGI Global. doi:10.4018/978-1-5225-7095-0.ch002

Kar, B. B., & Eğri, T. (2019). The China Model in the Global Economy. In W. Liu, Z. Zhang, J.-X. Chen, & S.-B. Tsai (Eds.), *The Belt and Road Strategy in International Business and Administration* (pp. 1–27). IGI Global. doi:10.4018/978-1-5225-8440-7.ch001

Rodrigues, C., & Steenhagen, P. (2022). SEZs and China's Development Promotion: Policy Exchanges Under the Belt and Road Initiative. In P. G. Figueiredo, F. J. Leandro, & Y. Li (Eds.), *Handbook of Research on Special Economic Zones as Regional Development Enablers* (pp. 21–38). IGI Global. doi:10.4018/978-1-7998-7619-9.ch002

Saiz-Alvarez, J. M. (2018). *Business Strategies and Advanced Techniques for Entrepreneurship 4.0*. IGI Global. doi:10.4018/978-1-5225-4978-9

Shahriar, S. (2019). Literature Survey on the "Belt and Road" Initiative: A Bibliometric Analysis. In A. Anna Visvizi, M. Lytras, X. Zhang, & J. Zhao (Eds.), *Foreign Business in China and Opportunities for Technological Innovation and Sustainable Economics* (pp. 79–115). IGI Global. doi:10.4018/978-1-5225-8980-8.ch005

Syed, H., & Genç, S. Y. (2020). United States-China Trade War 2019: Its Impacts on European Economies. In R. A. Castanho (Ed.), *Cross-Border Cooperation (CBC) Strategies for Sustainable Development* (pp. 132–151). IGI Global. doi:10.4018/978-1-7998-2513-5.ch008

KEY TERMS AND DEFINITIONS

21st Century Maritime Silk Road: It is the China-Europe maritime route, crossing Southeast Asia, the Middle East, and Africa, to end in the European seaports.

ERP: Acronym for Enterprise Resource Planning, it consists of a set of information systems to integrate operations related to production, logistics, inventory, shipping, and accounting to achieve fast response times.

Heping Juequi: Strategy related to politics and used in international relations to make China a world leader without provoking warfare

Industry 4.0: Type of industry defined by the intensive use of robotics and new technologies throughout the production process, which promotes productivity, efficiency and reduces the need for human resources.

IoT: Acronym of the Internet of Things, it consists of objects and devices ("things") connected with sensors, software, and other technologies to transmit and receive data from other objects and devices, thus increasing people's quality of life and productivity and interactivity between companies and people.

Kaizen: From Japanese "kai" (change) and "zen" (better), it is defined as continuous improvement of production and distribution processes in the firms.

National Rejuvenation: It is a concept that encompasses the economic and international policy followed by China until 2049 to make the country the leading global economic power and the most influential political actor on the planet.

Silk Road Economic Belt: With high-speed trains, it connects China with Central and South Asia, the Middle East, and Europe.

Chapter 2
Digital Inclusion for Vulnerable Groups and Transformation:
A Comparative Case Study

Gordana P. Djukic
https://orcid.org/0000-0001-5419-0725
Faculty of Economics, University of Belgrade, Serbia

ABSTRACT

The aim of the chapter is to highlight different regional approaches to digital inclusion from the social and economic aspects by academic researchers. The chapter presents the concept of digital literacy and digital inclusion and social and economic benefits in some European countries. The research observes individual European countries in which digital literacy with incorporated digital inclusion is equally important. The subject of the research will be digital inclusion on a regional level with an emphasis on the social, economic component in Denmark, Greece, and Serbia. The use of digital technology creates an opportunity for better public service in various sectors, especially in education, health, e-government, etc., which would favor better inclusion of the poor and socially disadvantaged. Technological transformation has contributed to the introduction of the most developed information and communication technologies (ICT) in a large number of countries in Europe and other countries around the world.

INTRODUCTION

The United Nations adopted Resolution 56/183 in 2001, which adopted the World Summit on the Information Society, in two phases. During the first Summit in Geneva in 2003, goals were set to take measures with political support to build an information society "for all". In the second phase, at the second meeting of the Summit in Tunis in 2005, the need to activate the Geneva Action Plan, as well as to reach an agreement on Internet governance, to achieve an inclusive and development-oriented information society, in which everyone has the right to create and exchange information (UN, 2020a). Digital portals create opportunities for online education, e-courses, as well as for people with disabilities to work from home and increase opportunities for the inclusion of non-digital populations (ITU, 2021). In March 2018, the

DOI: 10.4018/978-1-6684-2448-3.ch002

Copyright © 2022, IGI Global. Copying or distributing in print or electronic forms without written permission of IGI Global is prohibited.

European Parliament - Department for Civil Rights and Constitutional Affairs Policies published a study "Basic Causes of Digital Gender Difference and Possible Solutions for Improved Digital Inclusion of Women and Girls". The study highlights the need to address the exclusion of women in terms of access to information technology. The idea of the Digital Agenda for Europe (DAE) is that everyone in Europe has equal access to information and communication technologies (ICT) and digital skills, to halt the growing trend of inequalities and disparities in access to education, services, and information; to reduce the digital divide between the rich who have resources and the poor who have little or no resources. The extent to which some countries formulate and implement digital inclusion in their documents cannot be fully explained. In addition, it is debatable how countries report on the implementation of policies related to access, literacy, awareness, and engagement (Helsper, 2014).

Based on research by Dutta and Lanvin (2020), in 2019, about two-thirds of the world's population owned a mobile phone, and just over 55 percent of the world's population had access to the Internet. It is pointed out that with the prevailing technology and at current rates of increase, it will take another 50 years for the whole world to be digitized. According to Dijk (2017), barriers to digital inclusion are: (1) access; (2) skill and (3) attitude. Approaches are different: 1. motivational - use of digital technology, 2. material (physical) approach - possession of a computer device and Internet connection, 3. access to skills - possession of digital skills. Inclusion from the social aspect and digital infrastructure is not satisfactory in Serbia. A large number of students, especially in rural and impoverished areas, are at a disadvantage. They do not have computers or adequate digital infrastructure. The digital divide and inequality are also seen in other vulnerable groups such as the elderly population who do not have enough education or the digital literacy to access online public services. Limited services to the socially vulnerable population in the field of e-health, e-education, or online services of public companies continuously deepen the digital divide and inequality. This chapter will discuss opportunities to support the digital inclusion of vulnerable and poor people in Serbia.

The author of the paper will use the following methods: a descriptive method that will serve to define and more clearly understand the concept of digital inclusion and the effectiveness of digital inclusion. The concept of social inclusion, the digital divide, and inequality, will be explained. A valid metric model of the digital economy development index will be used. Based on a comparative method the observed selected countries in Europe will be analyzed in terms of individual parameters of digital literacy. The index of the digital economy and society in the paper will be included to identify the digital divide in some countries and Serbia. The results of the research will be obtained by the method of analysis and synthesis in the following paragraphs that would indicate how Serbia could approach better inclusion when it comes to digitization and transformation of ICT. Digital literacy of the observed countries is reflected in the results based on indicators for each country. Based on the results of the research, the initiative is given to the Government of Serbia to create innovative programs for inclusive and digital development, following the directives and documents of international organizations and the example of a successful country, such as Denmark.

The contribution of the paper is to point out to politicians, academics, and other decision-makers the importance of adopting an adequate digital strategy, following the example of successful countries such as Denmark, to make public internet service even more effective, efficient and accessible, and to ensure that all people have equal knowledge, skills, and competencies for digital communication and technology. A good example of some European countries could serve Serbia to pave the way for greater technological transformation and progress in terms of digitalization, ie the application of improved levels of digital literacy for socially vulnerable individuals, children, youth, and all citizens. In this way, it would contribute to improving social inclusion and combating social vulnerability and inequality.

BACKGROUND

Following Perez (2002), and Gomez-Mejia (2017), the impact of technology on the economy is manifested in its mass use, in education, production activities, business administration in companies, institutions, etc. For economic growth to be sustainable and for the industry to be globally competitive, there is a need for continuous technological innovation, because economic growth depends on the speed of innovation. Gomez-Mejia explained that the effects of technological innovation have been reflected in the need creation of intellectual capital and the need for a higher level of education for employees. Still in the domain of neoclassical liberal theory and from the time of Adam Smith human capital was involved, as a factor of the production function. Nowadays, the theoretical concept is based on the "Knowledge Economy" (through continuous learning and creating human capital), as a specific component of ICT. Gomez-Mejia (2017) argued that technological progress affects the global dynamics and sustainability of the golden age. In that sense, it is necessary to understand the technological process and its release "an understanding of the historical moment, and a willingness to clarify socio-political choice ", i.e. understanding the historical theoretical concept of technological development and the impact on the economy". Further it is pointed out that financial support from the International Community's is necessary to provide development assistance underdeveloped and poor countries, "just how the Marshall Plan helped reconstruction of Europe, with an increase in transatlantic trade." The identification of new and effective ways to support sustainable development is necessary for the international community and new ICT opportunities, (i.e. for digital inclusion), in the context of globalization.

Today, at the time of COVID-19, social isolation affected the greater need for digital inclusion. The use of the Internet, computers, and phones are not the same for everyone. Certain poor or marginalized groups don't have digital devices, any online access to business, health or financial services, and education. All over the world, information education is crucial for social (family, partnership, or friendship), as well as for business communications. In that sense, there are richer groups of people who have inclusive advantages, because they are materially better situated than those who are materially endangered and socially excluded, which has resulted in social marginalization and the digital divide. According to Sapic (2021), to alleviate the digital divide, social exclusion, and inequality, it is necessary to apply a systemic approach by the state, the decision-maker. A systematic approach based on which information technologies, knowledge, competencies, digital skills are improved through state policy, programs (and strategies), in the field of work, education, while respecting the needs of the population, their privacy, and security, is called digital inclusion (Sapic, 2021; Jaeger et al., 2012).

Concept of Digital Inclusion

Jeager et al., have defined digital inclusion as a growing technology in modern life that is of great importance for access to all in areas such as employment, government, education, civic participation, socialization, and include elements: 1. Digital division, which implies a gap in terms of socio-economic status, education, national or regional affiliation, age, Internet access, etc., 2. Digital literacy, which includes knowledge of software for successful internet navigation, and 3. Promotional policy for the development of digital education, i.e. literacy. According to National Digital Inclusion Alliance, (NDIA) (2021), digital inclusion is activities with five elements: 1. broadband service which is robust and affordable, 2. access to digital literacy, 3. access to digital devices, 4. adequacy technical support, and 5. applications and online designed content for self-sufficiency. On the national level, digital inclusion needs government strategies and investments to access and use technology (NDIA, 2021). According to Martin and Grudziecki (2006), digital literacy is defined as consciousness, attitude, and ability to adequately access digital tools and use large and diverse opportunities in individual identification: management, integration, evaluation, analysis, and synthesis of digital resources, building new knowledge, creating media expression and communication with others, for constructive social action. According to Martin (2005), initially, it should be based on having appropriate skills in research, building, and connecting to the web. It represents "the ability to succeed in encounters with the electronic infrastructures and tools that make possible the world of the twenty-first century" (Martin, 2005).

The initial phase is basic digital competence and includes basic levels of knowledge and skills, as higher levels of conceptual approaches, and also implies the attitudes and consciousness of individuals, i.e. competence is a combination of skills, knowledge, attitudes, and include know-how. DigEuLit Working Group regards the "key competences" as an "underpinning element" of digital literacy. Key features of Key Competencies are: portability, applicability to multifunctionality, when achieving goals and solving various problems, and are important for personal competencies. Digital Transformation is the third phase after the acquired Digital Usage in the second phase, creates opportunities for a higher level of knowledge, professional creativity, and encourages change and innovation (Martin and Grudziecki, 2006). A Model Digital Literacy (Murray and Perez, 2014) contains related components of knowledge, skills, and attitudes that are incorporated into the context of reflexive self-awareness and purposeful intentions. In this way, computer users are given opportunities to achieve general (generative) goals. The characteristic of the model is the generative ability to create new skills and knowledge. Nowadays, most students at the university are "exposed" to digital technology. It is pointed out that such a lower level of knowledge is not enough, but a higher academic level of technological knowledge is needed, which is acquired during continuous formal education, experience, and practice (Abah,2019; Murray and Perez, 2014). The development of digital technologies should accelerate economic development and created greater opportunities for service delivery, which had effects on the growing interconnectedness between people, businesses, and governments (Abah, 2019).

Effectiveness of Digital Inclusion

According to Bellini (2018), digital inclusion affects the relationship between people and information communication technology (ICT). The moment an individual digitally engages in a digital society a human-ICT relationship emerges. The author explained that when they get involved in the digital society, there is a tendency to advance and equalize digital abilities and digital possibilities. They increasingly prefer the digital world in society. The outcome of progression and equalization is a developed personal relativistic perception of efficiency when digital efficiency emerges. An individual's digital efficiency has three dimensions: access, cognition, and behavior. Dimensions are causally related, in a situation where they exist constraints of one dimension, it affects another. In a situation where there is insufficient invocation of digital skills in an individual, technophobia or fear of ICT develops, which has consequences for the congestive limitation and behavior of the individual.

Digital Inclusion for Vulnerable Groups and Transformation

Due to the causal relationship of constraints, the application of constraint measurements is necessary instead of measuring the digital efficiency of individuals. Further argued that digitized society, demands increasing digital inclusion, improved digital capabilities, and fewer restrictions, which is "the concern of individuals and groups." To that end, a public policy is needed that promotes digitalization and "purposeful" ICT, ie digital efficiency, which can be achieved through interaction with people and ICT. It is emphasized that the measurement of digital efficiency is possible by applying indicators of three dimensions, namely: 1. an indicator of the first dimension of individuals who have limited access to ICT because of material deprivation (vulnerability), i.e. social exclusion, is digital limitations - Access limitations (Alim). An Indicator of the second dimension refers to limitations: neurological (mental disorders) or educational, limitation in possibilities and practical experiences (disabilities) is - Cognitive limitations - (Clim).

The third dimension indicator refers to barriers to behavior (negative beliefs, attitudes, opinions) regarding ICTs, is Behavior limitations - (Blim). "The digital effectiveness value is the difference between the aggregated, normalized digital capabilities and limitations in all three dimensions of access, cognition, and behavior". Based on Bellini's research, it can be concluded that a high level of digital efficiency has positive implications on the entire (and global) community, in terms of education, health, culture, social and digital inclusion. The accelerated process of digitalization has influenced the expansion of the concept of social (and digital) inclusion by adopting new regulations: the strategy "Connectig for European Gigabit Society", 2016, by the European Commission, General data protection Regulation, 2018 (General EU regulations on data protection (GDPR), then ePrivacy legislation, 2018. In addition, the 2018 strategy was adopted, "Digital Age of Consent" by the Department of Justice and Equality in Ireland. Regulations have been enacted to increase the digital protection and security of citizens and to provide adequate infrastructure for safe access.

Social Exclusion (Vulnerability)

The concept of social exclusion is a "dynamic process in which individual is excluded from any economic, political, social and cultural social events: "feels partially or completely closed" in the social system that determines the status of the individual in society; unlike the concept of poverty, social exclusion implies systematic multiple deprivations over a longer time (Walker, 1997). In addition, social exclusion encompasses 1. Extreme effects of social deprivation on endangered social groups that are relatively concentrated on certain endangered geographical locations; 2. Desirability of social inclusion of the vulnerable in society. The broader term encompasses: 1. Vulnerability of a large part of the population to situations of exclusion in various spheres of social life (and digital inequality); 2. Equal rights of all citizens to protection from poverty; 3. "Cohesive" societies in which the rights to social inclusion are respected (Muddiman, 2000). The activities defined by the European Commission for inclusive growth are related to the fight against poverty and social exclusion, according to United Nations (2010) Agenda for Sustainable Development 2030, i.e. Goal 4: "Ensure inclusive and equitable quality education and promote lifelong learning, opportunities for all".

This will "set a dynamic framework for action to ensure social and territorial cohesion, so that the benefits of growth and jobs are shared across the European Union, and enables people experiencing poverty and social exclusion to live in dignity and participate actively in society". Poverty and exclusion of the population in a long time of vulnerable groups are stated: children, the elderly, Roma, social exclusion due to financial exclusion, homelessness, and disability. People with disabilities belong to the more difficult category of the vulnerable population because they have great difficulties in accessing and using web applications, the Internet, or e-government. Persons with impaired vision; or people with hearing impairments will not be able to access audio or video content on the Internet (UN, 2020b). Digital literacy in vulnerable countries may increase the introduction of certain programs that would increase the number of enrolled who are out of school. The backwardness of the female population can be eliminated if attention is paid to combating digital differences in the male group. A significant number of those out of school in vulnerable countries are due to a lack of resources, teachers, or infrastructure. Unequal access of children to secondary schools is unequal due to material deprivation and poverty, as shown in Figure 1

Figure 1. Education inequality of poor and rich children
Source: Walker et al., 2019.

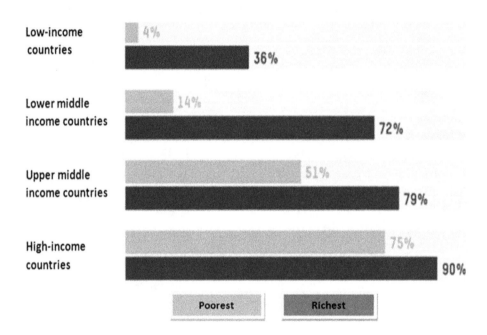

According to Walker et al. (2019), children of wealthier families from high developing countries are more likely to complete secondary school than children from the poorest families and lower developing countries. Most of them are children from the poorest, i.e. the most vulnerable families in low-income countries, only 4% completed school, then the richest, 35%; from lower-middle-income only 14%, from the poorest, and 72% from the richest, from upper-middle-income countries, only 51% from the poorest, and 79% from the richest families completed the school. Inequality is the lowest in high-income countries, where 72% of children are from the poorest and only 90% of children are from the richest families completed secondary school. High tuition costs, travel costs, etc. are an obstacle to enrolling students who are out of school. There is a direct connection between enrolling in high school, using the Internet, and overall socio-economic benefits, indicating that education is equal for all, one of the main priorities is to combat the social exclusion of vulnerable groups and vulnerable countries (Broadband Commission, 2020).

Digital Inclusion for Vulnerable Groups and Transformation

According to the UN (2012), the main reasons which contribute to the digital exclusion of vulnerable groups are: infrastructure, access to computers, internet devices, modems, telephone lines, and Internet connections, and especially insufficient use of e-government services by citizens. One of the possible partial solutions to insufficiently developed (digital) infrastructure and insufficient access to ICT has been proposed, by finding a way to reduce the prices of public access from providers, i.e. subsidies to users of digital access. The main obstacles to e-inclusion and e-government are: 1. Language and Literacy, 2. Abilities and Capacities, 3. Gender and Income, and 4. Location and Age. Also, it is pointed out that is very important to overcome social and digital inclusion with special attention to the socially vulnerable, to enable the implementation of world governments regulations of international organizations to respect equal rights for all citizens, and to enable world governments to "ensure sustainable development" (UN, 2012).

Digital Divide and Inequality

The term "digital divide" refers to the gap between individuals, households, businesses, and geographic areas at different socio-economic levels concerning both their opportunities to access information and communication technologies (ICTs) and to their use of the Internet for a wide variety of activities.

The digital divide reflects differences among and within countries (OECD, 2001). According to Dijk (2017), the digital divide is defined as the gap between people who have and those who do not have access to ICT (primarily access to the Internet, computers, smart phones, or other digital devices), which indicates social and information inequality, i.e. social exclusion. The digital divide is the difference in the access of individuals, information in terms of their quality and quantity via the Internet, as well as in terms of different acquisition of knowledge and education through ICT. The modernization of society is characterized by growing digital disparities leading to social inequality and social vulnerability (Elboj-Saso et al., 2021). The COVID-19 pandemic has brought about changes and new aspects of the crisis, not only in terms of interpersonal relationships, schooling, and professional activities but also in all areas of life. In such conditions, the need arose to use technological equipment, computers, to provide access to ICT, teleworking, online education, telemedicine.

According to Noll et al. (2001), the vulnerable population is expressed in rural areas, where they are mostly with lower incomes and lower levels of education in households. To reduce the number of vulnerable, measures are needed to reduce the digital divide, in the form of subsidies for the purchase of computers and access to the Internet, ie "targeted increase in ownership of computers". Education is a very important factor in favor of digital efficiency and the social effect of digital inclusion. Children do not have the opportunity to finance the purchase of computers in their name and on their account, nor to invest in information technology. However, the education of children and youth ICT is possible with an adequate educational policy where it is possible to implement ICT education with the use of computers (and teacher competence), during formal education (Noll et al., 2001). Although all Internet portals are mostly in English, more than 80%, only one-third of users worldwide speak English as their mother tongue. The materially disadvantaged and with a lower level of education in poor areas do not have the means to learn a foreign English language, which is the biggest obstacle to digital inclusion (UN, 2012). The growing penetration of ICT in all spheres of modern life and all social sectors such as: 1. ICT penetration or supply (technology, government policy), 2. ICT take-up or demand (access, usage), and 3. ICT environment (social-political-economic factors), provides opportunities for the necessary application of ICT in both developed and to the same extent underdeveloped countries in the world (UN, 2012). At a time of dynamic global innovation associated with changes in national revenues, policymakers face major challenges. During research and analysis of Welfens (2015), a more complex model is presented in the context of the Cobb-Douglas production function. The model presents the size of the R&D sector, which has a positive effect on elastic capital, and further shows that the share of capital income in the real gross domestic product will also increase. The basic value in the model is the macroeconomic production function, in which only a share of 1-ß' of workers produce final production – output, while ß' is the share of workers active in the research and development sector. Research and development activities can raise the level of knowledge, according to the simple function of (technological) progress. The progress function contains parameters: a parameter of productivity", and 2. the innovation efficiency parameter v, koji determines the rate of accumulation of knowledge (except for the rate of depreciation'). It is further pointed out that applying a modified neoclassical growth model explains the increased degree of income inequality (social exclusion and vulnerability) in a more innovative (technologically progressive society), that the growth of the share of capital income in the real social product can be increased. Also, it is explained that in the context of the analysis of the so-called "golden rule" can also be reported by the optimal size of the research and development sector.

Based on the research of Welfens (2015), it is not recommended to reduce the size of the research and development (R&D) sector to combat and "prevent" income inequality or to "prevent" capital income. On the contrary, the participation of workers (i.e. human capital) in the equity of the company should be taken into account. The author found an innovative version of Cobb-Douglas's production function because it is more complex and realistic; the focus is on the workforce (ie human capital) which is the input for new knowledge in the R&D sector. Examples of new forms of participation of employees in the equity of the company are in some countries, in the USA, Sweden, Great Britain, Netherlands, for many years. Besides, it is concluded that it is necessary to take into account the research of technological progress with microeconomic aspects. In addition, empirical analysis is important to gain insight into how realistic and relevant theoretical innovations are. Author Welfens explained that for specific parameter settings, the neoclassical growth model is equivalent to the modern growth theory. The advantage of a suitably modified neoclassical growth model is that it allows to easily accommodating a broad range of issues and problems in a simple way, to show critical implications in a straightforward way (Welfens, 2015).

The multidimensional character of social exclusion creates opportunities for observing measurements, relevant metrics monitoring, and comparative analysis of countries. The new NRI (Network Readiness Index) model, as the relevant metrics monitor, index of the development of the digital economy is valid and "powerful". Key effects of NRI and digital transformation are: 1. redefining global goals, 2. innovative digital devices, 3. security and trust, 4. achieving the goals of SDGs, 5. the COVID-19 as an accelerator of digital transformation; 6. education and re-skilling (Dutta and Lanvin (2020). According to the NRI (Network Readiness Index) in 2019 Serbia ranked 52nd out of a total of 121 ranked countries, behind countries in the region of the EU: Slovenia 27, Hungary 38, Croatia 44, Romania, 47, Bulgaria 49. Such a higher rank compared to the previous period is thanks to the infrastructure category, Connectivity, which among other categories is necessary for digital, social, and economic inclusion.

TECHNOLOGY, DIGITIZATION, TRANSFORMATION

Delivering universal public education for all is an investment. As the World Bank and others have noted, investment in human capital is integral to driving sustainable and equitable economic growth. Many governments recognize this and have dramatically increased their funding for education. To alleviate social inequality, it is necessary to take measures to make public services accessible to all the socially disadvantaged. This primarily refers to education services, which must be free and universal (Walker et al., 2019). It is further emphasized that most countries are making great efforts to allocate budget funds for education, but in contrast, lower-income countries allocate about half as much funding as they need for education. According to Raja and Nagasubramani (2018), the positive effects of technology on student education are: 1. better teaching, 2. globalization (video conferencing), 3. Without geographical restrictions, and 4. Distance learning, which is largely present today. According to Diermeier and Goecke (2017), ICT technologies imply subgroups: 1. infrastructural preconditions, 2. application of digital technologies by companies, and 3. application of digital technologies by individuals. Subgroups that contribute to the strengthening of information and communication technology companies are subgroups that apply digital technology in companies and by individuals. The authors analyzed the interconnectedness of: digitization, productivity, and technological trend, over a certain period. It also examines the preconditions for technology acceptance and implications for productivity and penetration rate i of each technology for all observed countries, j. The penetration rate of each technology – is $[\![$ pen $]\!]\_i$ and it is defined in the equation:

$$pen_i = \frac{\left(\sum_{j=1}^{j=1} tech_{i,j}\right)/\left(N-1\right)}{tech_{i,front}} \tag{1}$$

The arithmetic average of all standardized (e.g. per capita) technology use for all j countries, represent the amount of countries sorted by the intensity of technology use, but the frontier country in the peak year is divided by the technology usage in the frontier country and peak year" (Diermeier and Goecke). Regarding the penetration rate, large deviations were found in comparable samples that refer only to EU countries and only one subcategory - "digitization technologies"; and the penetration rate of the "infrastructure" subcategory is more than 80%. The selected countries in the sample have the appropriate preconditions for the development of complementary innovations (and technological progress), with a combination of all relevant subcategory parameters, ie with a high level of technology distribution. Technology penetration rates applied in the subcategories: a) enterprises and b) individuals, which are lower and scattered, range between 40 and 80 percent. In addition, they are in border countries, with much lower penetration rates and lower intensity of technology use. It is found that there are high penetration rates in Europe in terms of "digitization infrastructure".

However, digitization technologies applied by companies and individuals are not widespread enough. Large companies should apply digitalization technology due to further technological progress, which is measured on a macro scale, given that digitalization is the driving force of future productivity (Diermeier and Goecke, 2017). Three regulatory elements are important for digital transformation in countries with 3G and 4G levels of digital connection, to achieve transformation into 5G: 1. Collaboration is the dominant element attention is focused on the government, government institutions, government agencies for consumer protection, Internet management, finance, energy, etc. 2. High-level principles – the principles for forming a certain policy for collaborative regulation that applies an innovative approach to regulation, taking into account the broader economic and political context, and 3. G5 regulatory toolbox - it is necessary to apply a new perspective with the application of similar tools for the digital transformation of countries that have taken the leading place in the level of 5G digital connection (ITU, 2020).

Digital Inclusion and DESI – Comparative Case Study

The comparisons enable the identification of the digital gap between the performance and capabilities of each country, ie a total of 45 observed countries: 27 EU member states, and 18 candidate countries. The DESI International Overview allows comparison and identification of areas where additional measures and actions of the government of each country are needed to achieve comparative advantages over the best ranked and most successful countries in Europe. Based on the level of digital progress, it monitors how and to what extent the national and European digital strategy for 2020 is supported, with the aim of sustainable development, and gives recommendations to international organizations and researchers for further progress. DESI indicator contains the five dimensions: 1. Connectivity (fixed broadband take-up, fixed broadband coverage, mobile broadband, and broadband prices), 2. Human Capital (Internet user skills and advanced skills), 3. Use of the Internet (citizens' use of internet services and online transactions, 4. Integration of Digital Technology (business digitization and e-commerce), and 5. Digital Public Services (e-Government) (EC, 2020). The structure of the four dimensions of DESI in 2020: Connectivity, Human Capital, Internet Use, Integration of Digital Technology, and Digital Public Service, in EU countries, and selected countries (Denmark, Greece, and Serbia), is shown in Figure 2:

Figure 2. 2019 DESI scores of the EU countries and Serbia, by dimensions*
Source for EU countries: https://digital-agenda-data.eu/charts/desi-composite, 2020, (based on 2019 data)
Source for Serbia: RATEL, 2020 (based on 2019 data).
Note: *Values for Serbia and the EU countries are not fully comparable since the overview of the EU countries is based on the new methodology published in June 2020, which did not include indicators, such as: "Use of Internet" and "Digital Public Services".

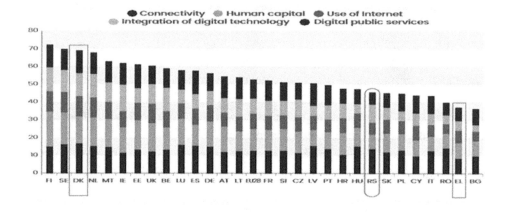

The DESI indicators show in Figure 2, that the greatest progress in the digital economy in 2019 was made by EU countries Finland, Sweden, and Denmark, but Bulgaria, Greece, and Romania are lagging behind the most. Serbia has the lowest value of the sub-index "Human Capital" among the observed countries, because a large number of people, especially the socially vulnerable population, have never used the Internet, bought or sold online services, or electronic banking (Internet indicator). Sub-dimension

"Integration of DigitalTechnology" is an important driver of economic growth. By applying aspects of digital technology companies create conditions for business efficiency, cost reduction, and competitiveness. Serbia is ranked in this sub-dimension above average, due to better results and due to the application of the latest technology. The "Digital Public Service" dimension is an indicator of digital technologies that are in the function of citizens because it is applied to improve communication between citizens, public and state enterprises, and e-government. Serbia is the least successful country in the EU, due to the low values of e-government indicators and low rates of online health services (RATEL, 2020). To highlight the digital divide and make suggestions for improving performance in the coming period, a case study of three countries further was given: Denmark, Greece, and Serbia, based on data 2019.

Denmark

According to Danish Agency for Digitization (2016), in the previous period, Denmark introduced information technology into the public sector promptly, which had effects on very high quality and unique electronic high-quality data. Thanks to the successful digital transition and the formed secure and robust digital infrastructure, e-access to the public sector via the Internet has been facilitated. Digital competencies are appropriate with a high level of education, which is reflected in companies that apply a high level of technology. Traditionally, there has been strong interaction between government, public and private companies, to innovate business and solve business problems. The system of social protection of the socially endangered is built on "widespread" trust, as well as on the trust of the public sector, where digital protection is safe and secure for all individuals, ie for the whole Danish society. One of the priority goals of digitalization is that "security and trust must be in focus at all times". It is emphasized that it is necessary to create conditions for digital inclusion, such as: establishing a clear legal framework for e-government, automatic business reporting, efficient data exchange, thus paving the cohesive paths for the well-being of all citizens. It is necessary to encourage the development of digital skills for children and youth, to provide better data on disabled and marginalized people, because, with the completion of information, appropriate social assistance is provided to the vulnerable. For sustainable inclusive development, it is of special importance to pay attention to vulnerable groups, unemployed young people in the labor market, individuals with low levels of education, people with reduced working abilities and disabilities, according to the recommendation of the European Commission, 2019. The interaction of public and private companies with NGOs also contributes to the transition creating the preconditions for a strong digital state in Denmark (Danish Agency for Digitization, 2016). Besides, Denmark has a high-tech system related to robotics and drones, which are applied in the form of automated solutions in 290 companies across the country. At the time of the COVID-19 pandemic, innovative digital technology is making a great contribution to solving problems in the health system. With advanced video consultations, online communication is established between healthcare workers and patients, as well as the use of work in the sterilization of the hospital with UV lamps. Denmark is ranked third among EU countries and is an example of good practice and a good way in which "citizens can take - directly or indirectly - ownership of their technological future" (DESI, 2020).

Greece

According to the latest overall Digital Economy and Society Index (DESI, 2020), Greece ranked second last in the EU, based on 2019 data. The country is facing large and difficult tasks due to the acceleration of technological transformation, the COVID-19 pandemic and insufficient "technological maturity". For these reasons, urgent action is needed to follow the guidelines of the adopted Digital Transformation Strategy 2020-2025. The main guidelines of the digital strategy are: 1. Safe, fast and reliable Internet access for all. 2. Creating a digital state and better digital services for all life events, 3. Developing digital skills for all citizens. 4. Transformation and digitalization of enterprises. 5. Support and strengthening digital innovation. 6. Integration of digital technologies in all economic sectors. For the future digital transformation and digital inclusion of Greece, the recommendations according to the European Commission Staff Working Document, "Analysis of the recovery and resilience plan of Greece", 2021, are given necessary measures and actions to develop digital skills, also the availability of open data. Digital inclusion should also be included equal participation of women, older people, and vulnerable groups in the digital age. These measures are aimed at improving Greece in the EU in the area of connectivity and broadband coverage, and overall digital performance.

Serbia

Serbia has a low value of the DESI and is in 22nd place, below the EU average based on 2019 data, mainly because Serbia lacks fixed broadband access, according to the IPA – Interreg – CBS (2021) study. In the study is pointed out that in the conducted household survey, in Serbia in 2020, 81% of households had an Internet connection. Besides, despite a slight increase in Internet access, by 0.9 percent compared to the previous year, the survey showed that Serbia ranks 29th in the price of broadband Internet, at 18.24 USD. The following shortcomings have been identified: 1. budget funds are allocated insufficiently, about 0.9% of GDP, 2. a small number of technological patents, 3. Inadequate interaction between the research sector and enterprises, 4. insufficient financial resources for technological innovation, 5. lack of additional risk capital models, 6. lifelong learning has not been applied adequately, 6. education is not in line with the needs of the labor market. 9. e-government is not yet in line with EU requirements, nor is it sufficiently transparent to the public (IPA – Interreg – CBS, 2021). The Government of Serbia should pay special attention to the possession of digital skills of human capital because the possession of greater digital education has a positive effect on the inclusion of socially vulnerable populations. In this way, all citizens would have greater opportunities to actively participate in digital education and digital society and use digital products and services (RATEL, 2020). Despite the increase in living standards and the trend of economic recovery, poverty, and social exclusion are still present in certain groups in Serbia, among children, young people, and the elderly population. Upcoming economic reforms according to the government program " Economic Reform – Programme for the period 2021-2023 are intended to improve the social and material status of vulnerable groups in Serbia and ensure social inclusion. For that reason, the plan is to digitalize the social system, to establish a single online information system, a "social map", in which all centers in Serbia for social work will be digitally connected. To alleviate and combat digital exclusion and the gap, the EU and UNICEF provided financial support in the field of education for the most endangered children in Serbia in the form of resources and technical equipment. The EU has provided funding for a 2m-euro project for vulnerable children in 30 local governments in Serbia (UNICEF (2020).

DISCUSSION

During the functioning of the global ICT network in the dynamic process of digitalization, different ways of access by individuals and institutions are emerging, which is causing increasing inequalities, and various challenges and problems are emerging. Digital inequality arises for many reasons: because individuals are of different ages, do different jobs, come from different urban or rural areas, have or do not have the technological skills to work on computers and the Internet, or have different levels of literacy or education, or because of the social exclusion of poverty (Neagu et al., 2021). According to Badiuzzaman (2021), during the COVID-19 pandemic that triggered the digital divide, the number of socially vulnerable individuals, and students from rural areas who could not attend online classes online, increased compared to students from cities. However, students' ability to use ICT and solve individuals' business problems through technology is insufficient and "often overestimated" (Murray and Perez, 2014).

According to Vassilakopoulou and Hustad, 2020, although digital technologies have been around for decades, the elderly population still has no possibility for digital access to digital devices and mobile phones. One of the reasons for the limited use of web specialized services by the elderly in the era of widespread use of smartphones is the probability that they were in workplaces where the ITC was not represented. This has affected the low level of interest of seniors in web education and research, from the moment they retire. The other reasons are multiple: lower levels of digital literacy, fear of adopting digital tools, or social exclusion. Based on some research, it has been noticed that some older people often use smartphones, but to a lesser extent use online public health services (Vassilakopoulou and Hustad, 2020).

In Serbia, digital exclusion is particularly pronounced in rural areas, unlike in cities. Much of the rural population lacks basic digital skills at the time of the COVID-19 pandemic when online distance learning and digital literacy are needed. In rural settlements, 63% of the population has an Internet connection, while in cities there are 78%, and the most in Belgrade, 82%. The digital exclusion applies in particular to the elderly, the less educated, and the low-income poor population. Unlike Denmark, where 11.88 percent is represented, and Greece, where it is 20.28 percent, Serbia has 43.55 percent of the rural population, which belongs to the socially and materially endangered population. Regarding Internet connection, Serbia's obligation to provide free Internet access to the socially excluded and the poor in inaccessible areas, even at reduced prices, has not yet been regulated. To improve digital literacy and competencies of the entire population, the Digital Skills Strategy for Serbia for the period from 2019 to 2023 was made, NGO initiatives were created, international cooperation in the field of safe Internet was established, and in support of vulnerable populations. The strategy focused on the mechanisms by which would be with existing infrastructure made possible by digital and services equally accessible to all users in Serbia (Social Inclusion and Poverty Reduction Team, 2019).

SOLUTIONS AND RECOMMENDATIONS

Technology will continue to have a negative impact on increasing the gaps and inequalities if effective measures are not taken to combat inequalities. Technological risks will increase as the level of the socially vulnerable and socially excluded increases due to the COVID-19 pandemic. Besides, a strategy to address inclusiveness and ICT is needed. The view that inclusive education at the time of COVID-19 requires a long-term digital and social approach is widely accepted, but not sufficiently considered how it will be implemented. To bridge digital exclusion in a comprehensive, strategic and efficient way, it is very important to apply an inclusive approach to children's rights and young people, to ensure inclusion for all (UK Committee for UNICEF, 2021). Further, is suggested that the long-term digital strategy of digital inclusion of children and youth during the COVID-19 pandemic should include the following activities: 1. define the ambitions and visions of digital inclusion, 2. determine clear departmental responsibilities and the manner of its measurement, 3. foster partnerships with children, youth, families, teachers, and digital inclusion organizations, 4. engagement appropriate digital infrastructure, 5. align the strategy with the education strategy and the poverty reduction strategy 6. anticipate resource costs and provide financial support (UK Committee for UNICEF, 2021).

According to Djoric, (2020), for the efficient global digital transformation of Serbia, the digital equality that needs to be achieved is important, and it refers to the digital gap between the highly ranked developed EU countries and the countries in transition, it is important to bridge the gap between urban and rural areas, as well as between large and small enterprises. Savic and Radojicic (2011) pointed out that instruments for overcoming digital inequality are: 1. rightful state policy, 2. well-balanced development strategy, 3. systematic monitoring of information society development, 4. investments in ICT infrastructure, 5. effective use of ICT for stimulating the development of the critical sector, 6. monitoring and evaluating of ICT use in critical sectors, and 7. strengthening of human resources through strategic investments in education, as is shown in Figure 3:

Figure 3. Instruments for overcoming digital inequality
Source: Savic, & Radojicic (2011).

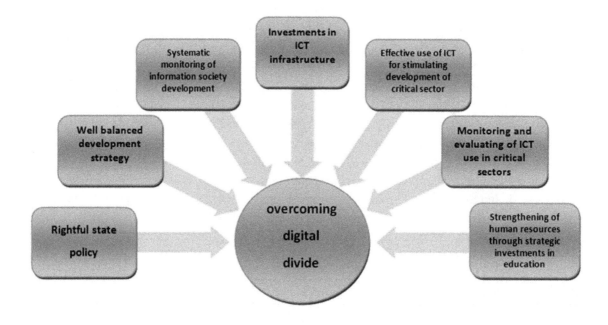

Savic and Radojicic found that it is important to emphasize the key role of human resources that can carry out the entire process of transition to the information society. To boost the human potential for a successful digital transition strengthening human capital plays a crucial role. To this end, attention should

Digital Inclusion for Vulnerable Groups and Transformation

be paid to strategic investments in education, which is a prerequisite for more efficient e-participation (digital inclusion) in economic, social, and political life. It is highlighted that for this reason, developing countries (and Serbia) must be included in the following activities: 1. implementation of institutional and social reforms that support e-participation of citizens, 2. strengthening information literacy, information culture, and critical thinking, 3. promotion and development of the lifelong learning process within the educational process. Therefore, indicators of the level of development of the information or society, ie. ICT, which aims to cover all aspects of development, must, in addition to the contained indicators, it should also contain a set of indicators that show the degree of readiness of the population for ICT (Savic and Radojicic, 2011). This indicates the importance of the overall readiness from the social, technological, political (and health) aspects of a country for the acceptance of new technology and its u innovative transition.

FUTURE RESEARCH DIRECTIONS

Badiuzzaman et al., (2021) found and suggest that relevant stakeholders should consider the level of Internet costs and reduce the price for November with active policy action. Also, it is necessary to improve the mobile network in rural areas. Decision-makers and the government should have an understanding of comprehensive problem-solving. It's necessary to examine educational inequalities rigorously and prevent digital division among students (Badiuzzaman et al., 2021). Besides the digital divide, there are many risks. According to Delloitte (2021), in the experts report "Future of risk in digital era: transformative change: disruptive risk", there is a growing appeal to digital services that are following ethical principles, fair and just, in their approach, which "promote physical and mental health. " Purposeful use of digital technology, aimed at the entire social community, encourages social and digital inclusion. "Digital adopters" following ethical principles should adopt technologies that are not harmful, but which are safe and secure without "mistakes" because it is a chance for the common good with the trust of all interested parties. Algorithms, botnets, the Internet of Things (IoT), cloud computing are the target of attacks, so fast and sophisticated defense is necessary, in all dimensions against them. For digital technologies to be able to adequately affect digital inclusion, special attention needs to be paid to cyber vulnerability (Delloite, 2021), and all other technological risks. The challenges for poorer and less developed countries are related to costs, as there is a different levels of literacy, technological readiness for transformation, and introduction of new technology. Besides, a revolution in technological innovation causes a lack of sufficient evidence to what extent the most developed and richest countries have progressed nor how nanotechnology works, artificial intelligence, robotics, 5G networks, and especially their application in medicine. In technology, and transformation are many risks and challenges, such as how to protect private data, during Internet communication or cross-border data exchange, etc.

CONCLUSION

The accelerated pace of development of information and communication technology and the digital transformation requires the attention of the international communities, stakeholders, governments of all countries, institutions, to reach an agreement following an effective regulatory approach in the digital order. The regulatory approach implies the activities of the governments of all countries, also Denmark,

Greece to pursue an adequate policy that would ensure social and digital inclusion of all marginalized and socially vulnerable individuals. Children in rural areas of Serbia are at a disadvantage because they are excluded from Internet access, deprived of computer equipment, which has negative effects on digital learning and deepens the digital divide in terms of children from rural areas and cities. The rural population does not have opportunities for online public services such as health, e-government, online education which is why the government and all stakeholders need to provide adequate financial resources for all poor populations and the socially excluded. In the future, the emphasis of the Government of Serbia should be on equal access of all residents to digital technology, education, and on increasing the number of fixed broadband access to the public Internet in all parts of Serbia.

In this consensus between organizations, governments, and stakeholders, it is necessary to establish an appropriate balance between social, economic, and technological goals, ie priority should be given to the social aspect, under international regulations. In the future, adequate strategies for solving the problem of digital and social inclusion should be adopted based on international cooperation between national governments and institutions. One way is to promote the education and high level of knowledge and experience of the country with the best practice and to explore ways to protect the privacy and security of personal integrity and cross-border personal data. Following the example of Denmark, Serbia should have a high level of unified communication between local and state institutions that together contribute to the common goals of improving information technologies. Institutional cooperation should be continuously continued and expanded with the application of digital technology and social inclusion. The government has a decisive role in implementing the goals of sustainable development, and one of those goals is social and digital inclusion. As highlighted in the policy documents, government projects, and strategies, achieving digital inclusion is central to embracing the opportunities and imperatives of this rapidly evolving world. The government of each country, and Serbia has a significant role to play in promoting the inclusion of the socially disadvantaged, combating vulnerability, and improving the quality of life of all people, in line with inclusive sustainable development. Global science-based data contributes to the complete decision-making process, encourages global investment, innovation, and inclusion, which is important for the social and digital inclusion of all inhabitants of the planet and the well-being of humanity.

ACKNOWLEDGMENT

This research received no specific grant from any funding agency in the public, commercial, or not-for-profit sectors.

REFERENCES

Abah, J. (2019). Theoretical and Conceptual Framework for Digital Inclusion among Mathematics Education Students in Nigeria: chapter six. In M. J. Adejoh, M. J., Obinne, A. D. E., & Wombo, A. B. (Eds.), Global Perspectives on Educational Issues. Makurdi. College of Agricultural and Science Education, Federal University of Agriculture.

Adam, I. O., & Alhassan, M. D. (2020). Bridging the global digital divide through digital inclusion: the role of ICT access and ICT use. *Transforming Government: People, Process and Policy.* . doi:10.1108/TG-06-2020-0114

Badiuzzaman, M., Rafiquzzaman, M., Rabby, M. I. I., & Rahman, M. M. (2021). The Latent Digital Divide and Its Drivers in E-Learning among Bangladeshi Students during the COVID-19 Pandemic. *Information (Basel)*, *12*(287), 287. Advance online publication. doi:10.3390/info12080287

Bellini, C. G. P. (2018). The ABCs of Effectiveness in the Digital Society. *Communications of the ACM*, *61*(7), 84–91. doi:10.1145/3205945

Broadband Commission. (2020). *Closing the digital divide: Supporting vulnerable countries.* https://www.broadbandcommission.org/insight/closing-the-digital-divide-supporting-vulnerable-countries/

Danish Agency for Digitization. (2016). *A Stronger and more secure digital Denmark: Digital Strategy 2016-2020.* https://en.digst.dk/policy-and-strategy/digital-strategy/

Deloitte. (2021). *Future of risk in the digital era: transformative change: Disruptive risk.* https://www2.deloitte.com/content/dam/Deloitte/us/Documents/finance/us-rfa-future-of-risk-in-the-digital-era-report.pdf

Diermeier, M., & Goecke, H. (2017). Productivity, Technology Diffusion, and Digitization. *CESifo Forum*, *18*(1), 1-32. https://www.ifo.de/DocDL/CESifo-Forum-2017-1-diermeier-goecke-digitalization-march.pdf

Djoric, Z. (2020). Digital Economy – Basic Aspects and the Case of Serbia. *Economic Views, 22*(2), 73-96. https://scindeks-clanci.ceon.rs/data/pdf/1450-7951/2020/1450-79512002073Q.pdf

Dutta, S., & Lanvin, B. (Eds.). (2020). The Network Readiness Index: Accelerating Digital Transformation in a post-COVID Global Economy. Portulans Institute.

EC (European Commission). (2020). *Digital Economy and Society Index (DESI) 2020: Thematic chapters.* https://digital-strategy.ec.europa.eu/

Elboj-Saso, C., Cortés-Pascual, A., Íñiguez-Berrozpe, T., Lozano-Blasco, R., & Quílez-Robres, A. (2021). Emotional and Educational Accompaniment through Dialogic Literary Gatherings: A Volunteer Project for Families Who Suffer Digital Exclusion in the Context of COVID-19. *Sustainability*, *13*(1206), 1–16. doi:10.3390/su13031206

Gómez-Mejía, A. (2017). The Concept of Technology in the History of Economic Thought. From the Classics to Schumpeter, Evolutionism and today. *Revista Libre Empresa*, *14*(2), 199–214. doi:10.18041/libemp.2017.v14n2.28210

Helsper, E. (2014). Digital Inclusion in Europe: Evaluating Policy and Practice. In *Harnessing ICT for social action, a digital volunteering program. Discussion Paper.* European Commission, Directorate-General for Employment, Social Affairs, and Inclusion. http://eprints.lse.ac.uk/59998/

IPA – Interreg – CBS (2021). *Territorial and socio-economic analysis of the programme area.* Interreg IPA Programme 2021-2021.

ITU. (2021). Towards building inclusive digital communities: ITU toolkit and self-assessment for ICT. *Accessibility Implementation, 3*. https://www.itu.int/pub/D-PHCB-TOOLKIT.01-2021

ITU (International Telecommunication Union). (2020). Global ICT Regulatory Outlook 2020: pointing the way forward to collaborative regulation. ITU Publications.

Jaeger, P. T., Thompson, K. M., Katz, S., M., & Decoster, E. J. (2012). The Intersection of Public Policy and Public Access: Digital Divides, Digital Literacy, Digital Inclusion, and Public Libraries. *Public Library Quarterly, 31*(1), 1-20. . doi:10.1080/01616846.2012.654728

Khan, S. (2012). *Topic Guide on Social Exclusion*. International Development Department, University of Birmingham. www.gsdrc.org

Martin, A. (2005). DigEuLit – A European Framework for Digital Literacy: A Progress Report. *Journal of e-Literacy, 2*, 130-136.

Martin, A., & Grudziecki, J. (2006). DigEuLit: Concepts and Tools for Digital Literacy Development. *Innovation in Teaching and Learning in Information and Computer Sciences*, *5*(4), 249–267. doi:10.11120/ital.2006.05040249

Muddiman, D. (2000). Theories of Social Exclusion and The Public Library: the chapter. In *Open to All?* (pp. 1–15). The Public Library and Social Exclusion. https://core.ac.uk/download/pdf/11879329.pdf

Murray, M. C., & Perez, J. (2014). Unraveling the digital literacy paradox: How higher education fails at the fourth literacy. *Issues in Informing Science and Information Technology*, *11*, 85–100. doi:10.28945/1982

NDIA (National Digital Inclusion Alliance). (2021). *Digital Inclusion: Definition*. https://www.digital-inclusion.org/definitions/

Neagu, G., Berigel, M., & Lendzhova, V. (2021). How Digital Inclusion Increase Opportunities for Young People: Case of NEETs from Bulgaria, Romania, and Turkey. *Sustainability*, *13*(7894), 7894. Advance online publication. doi:10.3390u13147894

Noll, G., Older-Aguilar, D., Gregory Rosston, G., & Ross, R. R. (2001). The Digital Divide: Definitions, Measurement, and Policy Issues. Bridging the Digital Divide, 1-28.

OECD. (2001). *Understanding the Digital Divide*. https://www.oecd.org/digital/ieconomy/1888451.pdf

Perez, C. (2002). *Technological Revolutions and Financial Capital: The Dynamics of Bubbles and Golden Ages*. Edward Elgar Editorial. doi:10.4337/9781781005323

Raja, E., & Nagasubramani, P. C. (2018). Impact of modern technology in education. *Journal of Applied and Advanced Research*, *3*(1). Advance online publication. doi:10.21839/jaar.2018.v3S1.165

RATEL (Regulatory Agency for Electronic Communications and Postal Services). (2020). *An Overview of the Telecom and Postal Services Markets in the Republic of Serbia in 2019*. Author.

Sapic, J. (2021). *Digital Inclusion 101: A Two-Fac Story*. https://socijalnoukljucivanje.gov.rs/sr

Savic, N., & Radojicic, Z. (2011). Digital Divide in the Population of Serbia. *Issues in Informing Science and Information Technology, 8*. http://iisit.org/Vol8/IISITv8p245-258Savic293.pdf

Social Inclusion and Poverty Reduction Team. (2019). *Report on digital inclusion in the Republic of Serbia for the period from 2014 to 2018*. https://socijalnoukljucivanje.gov.rs/wp-content/uploads/2019/07/Izvestaj_o_digitalnoj_ukljucenosti_RS_2014-2018_lat.pdf

UK Committee for UNICEF. (2021). *Closing the Digital Divide for Good: an end to the digital exclusion of children and young people in the UK*. https://apo.org.au/sites/default/files/resource-files/2021-06/apo-nid312856.pdf

UN. (2020a). *World Summit on Information Society (WSIS)*. https://publicadministration.un.org/en/Themes/ICT-for-Development/World-Summit-on-Information-Society

UN (United Nations). (2012). *Bridging the digital divide by reaching out to vulnerable populations 5 Chapter Five. United Nations E-Government Survey*. Author.

UN (United Nations). (2020b). *E-Government Survey 2020*. UN.

UNICEF. (2020). *Bridging the Digital Divide in Serbia For the Most Vulnerable Children, Education is important*. UNICEF. https://www.unicef.org

Van Dijk, J. G. M. (2017). Digital Divide: Impact of Access. In P. Rossler, C. A. Hoffner, & V. Z. L. V. Liesbet (Eds.), *The International Encyclopedia of Media Effects* (pp. 1–11). John Wiley & Sons. doi:10.1002/9781118783764.wbieme0043

Vassilakopoulou, P., & Hustad, E. (2020). Bridging Digital Divides: A Literature Review and Research Agenda for Information Systems Research. *Information Systems Frontiers*. Advance online publication. doi:10.100710796-020-10096-3 PMID:33424421

Walker, A. (1997). Introduction: the strategy of inequality. In A. Walker & C. Walker (Eds.), *Britain divided: the growth of social exclusion in the 1980s and 1990s*. Child Poverty Action Group.

Walker, J., Pearce, C., Boe, K., & Lawson, M. (2019). *The Power of Education to fight Inequality: How increasing educational equality and quality is crucial to fighting economic and gender inequality. Oxfam Briefing Paper*. Oxfam International.

Welfens, J. J. P. (2015). Innovation, Inequality and a Golden Rule for Growth in an Economy with Cobb-Douglas Function and an R&D Sector. *IZA DP, 8996*. https://ftp.iza.org/dp8996.pdf

ADDITIONAL READING

Andriopoulou, E., Kanavitsa, H. E., & Tsakloglou, P. (2021). Distributional Changes in Turbulent Times: Greece 2007-2016. In *36th IARIW Virtual General Conference*. https://iariw.org/wp-content/uploads/2021/08/Andriopoulou_Redistribution_Greece_paper.pdf

Borg, K., Boulet, M., Smith, S., & Bragge, P. (2019). Digital Inclusion & Health Communication: A Rapid Review of Literature. *Health Communication, 34*(11), 1320–1328. doi:10.1080/10410236.2018.1485077 PMID:29889560

Fallon, G. (2020). From digital literacy to digital competence: The teacher digital competency (TDC) framework. *Education Tech Research*, *68*(5), 2449–2472. doi:10.100711423-020-09767-4

Jaeger, P. T., Bertot, J. C., Thompson, K. M., Sarah, M., Katz, S. M., & DeCoster, E. J. (2012). The Intersection of Public Policy and Public Access: Digital Divides, Digital Literacy, Digital Inclusion, and Public Libraries. *Public Library Quarterly*, *31*(1), 1–20. doi:10.1080/01616846.2012.654728

Lips, M., & Eppel, E. (2021). *Effects of COVID-19 on digital public services*. Final Paper. https://www.wgtn.ac.nz/__data/assets/pdf_file/0010/1929448/Effects-of-Covid-19-on-digital-public-services-Final-Paper.pdf

Qu, J., Simes, R., & O'Mahony, J. (2016). *How Do Digital Technologies Drive Economic Growth?* Research Outline. https://esacentral.org.au/images/QuJSimesROMahonyJ.pdf

Reisdorf, B., & Rhinesmith, C. (2020). Digital Inclusion as a Core Component of Social Inclusion. *Social Inclusion (Lisboa)*, *8*(2), 132–137. doi:10.17645i.v8i2.3184

KEY TERMS AND DEFINITIONS

DESI (Digital Economy and Society Index): Is a composite index that summarizes relevant indicators on Europe's digital performance and tracks the evolution of EU member states across five main dimensions: Connectivity, Human Capital, Use of the Internet, Integration of Digital Technology, Digital Public Services.

Digital Divide: Refers to the gap between individuals, households, businesses, and geographic areas at different socio-economic levels concerning both their opportunities to access information and communication technologies (ICTs) and to their use of the internet for a wide variety of activities.

Digital Inclusion: Is a growing technology in modern life that is of great importance for access to all in areas such as employment, government, education, civic participation, socialization and include elements: 1. Digital division (gap in terms of socio-economic status), 2. Digital literacy, which includes digital knowledge, and 3. Promotional policy for the development of digital education.

Digital Transformation: Is a process that aims to improve an entity by triggering significant changes to its properties through combinations of information, computing, communication, and connectivity technologies is generally taking place in all spheres of our life and affects everyone from babies to the elderly; for sure, it is not confined only to organizations and the workplace anymore.

E-Government: Is the use of technological communications devices, to provide public services to citizens and other persons in a country or region. E-government offers new opportunities for more direct and convenient citizen access to government, and government provision of services directly to citizens.

ICT Development: Is the level of ICT infrastructure. Using, adopting, and adapting frontier technologies require sufficient ICT infrastructure, especially since AI, IoT, big data, and blockchain are internet-based technologies.

Social Exclusion: Is a dynamic process in which an individual is excluded from any economic, political, social, and cultural social events: feels partially or completely closed in the social system that determines the status of the individual in society; unlike the concept of poverty, social exclusion implies systematic multiple deprivations over a longer time.

Chapter 3
Education Quality and Offerings Intersection Post Pandemic for Inclusive Development:
A Case Study

Booysen Sabeho Tubulingane

Namibia University of Science and Technology, Namibia & University of Giessen, Germany & UNICAF, Cyprus

Simon T. Angombe

University of Namibia, Namibia

ABSTRACT

Contact learning and teaching was suspended in 2020 at many universities globally, including in Namibia, to counter the spread of COVID-19 transmission. The study assessed the impact of the COVID-19 outbreak on student academic performance per respective offering type (online and contact) using quantitative inferential statistical regression analysis. Data from a total of 20770 student population for 2019 and 2020 academic years was applied in the study. The study established that online rather than contact education offering is associated with improved student academic performance at the Namibian university. However, Namibian students do not benefit from online education equally due to socio-economic inequality. A correlation between internet access and online student academic performance was established. The study has also demonstrated the importance of equality in student offering modes in upholding the quality of higher education. An academic research directed at evaluating the level of plagiarism associated with online and contact offering at the Namibian university needs to be conducted.

DOI: 10.4018/978-1-6684-2448-3.ch003

Copyright © 2022, IGI Global. Copying or distributing in print or electronic forms without written permission of IGI Global is prohibited.

INTRODUCTION

COVID-19 (coronavirus) has dramatically reshaped the way global education is delivered. Millions of students were affected by educational institution closures due to the pandemic. COVID-19 has resulted in the largest online movement in the history of education (El Said, 2021). Face-to-face learning and teaching were suspended to counter the spread of COVID-19 transmission. This was also the case in Namibia, as the outbreak of COVID-19 forced universities in Namibia to move away from face-to-face lectures and examinations to virtual mode. During the 2019 academic year, students were taught face-to-face and in the year 2020 most of the learning, teaching, and assessment undertaking were shifted to online. When it comes to performance, students enrolled in face-to-face mode are more likely to perform significantly better than students enrolled in online classes in terms of the examination average and improvement in post-test lecture questions (Arias et al., 2018, p. 16). Though, Paul and Jefferson (2019, p. 1) persist that there is no significant difference in academic performance between online and face-to-face students, with respect to gender, or with respect to class rank. The move of continuous assessments and final examinations to a virtual form has arguably raised the most critical academic integrity issues among administrators, faculty members, and students (Champagne & Granja, 2021). This is because the online mode of student assessments is likely not to meet government(s) set standards for student attainment (as detecting any cheating would be significantly challenging), in terms of the knowledge and skills students are expected to have attained at different stages of their education (Gamage et al., 2020; Paulo et al., 2009). Although, Spaulding (2009) found that academic dishonesty was the same in online and traditional (contact) classrooms. This infers that in a normal education setup academic cheating by students occurs at the same level, irrespective of the mode (virtual/contact) of education offering.

The COVID-19 pandemic has created the largest disruption of education systems in history, affecting nearly 1.6 billion students in more than 190 countries and all continents (United Nations [UN], 2020). Moreover, closures of universities and other learning spaces have impacted 94 percent of the world's student population, up to 99 percent in low- and middle-income countries. This indicates that higher education systems of developing countries such as Namibia have been highly affected by the pandemic outbreak compared to developed countries. Nonetheless, the COVID-19 pandemic has also deepened the impact of disparities in developed countries. For example, McKie (2020) revealed that almost three-quarters of English students experienced a lack of access to quiet spaces to study and more than half said they were unable to access digital course materials following the switch to online learning. Moreover, due to 'digital poverty' there was inability by some students in England to access higher education from home, which likely resulted in such students being left behind in their education. According to Alsoud and Harasis (2021), during the national lockdown due to COVID-19, university students in Jordan were suffering from several challenges, mainly the feel of anxieties, not having a device to attend the online classes, not having a separate room to study at home, and internet connectivity issues. Similarly, at public universities in the United States of America (USA), there are technological and other barriers that make it harder for students of colour to stay engaged in virtual classrooms to access and benefit from higher education (Department of Education of the United States of America [DEUSA], 2021). In addition, many institutions of higher education in the USA reported a sharp drop-off in enrollment in 2020 of students graduating from high-poverty high schools compared to pre-pandemic numbers. In the same vein, the current study analyse the relationship between student academic performance and mode of study before/after COVID-19 outbreak in Namibia. Furthermore, the study determines if regional

Education Quality and Offerings Intersection

internet connectivity is associated with student academic performance after COVID-19 outbreak when mode of learning and teaching was moved to online.

The study research objectives were achieved by following a quantitative cross-sectional inferential methodological approach, as characteristics (examination results) of a population (26770) of students for the academic years 2019 and 2020 was examined in relation to the learning environment factors such as area internet connectivity in order to describe the relationships between the latter stated variables. Student results per academic year (2019 and 2020), mode of study and segregated per region of school completion was obtained from the Namibian university under study. The Shapefile depicting Namibia's regional administrative boundaries was downloaded from the Namibia Statistics Agency (NSA) (2021) website (http://geofind.nsa.org.na/) and applied during the analyses. Actual internet connection statistics per region was derived from Namibia's 2011 Census Report (NSA, 2012). Linear regression technic using SPSS and Geographic Weighted Regression (GWR) in ArcGIS was performed to analyse the overall and spatial relationship between student academic performance and regional internet connectivity. The analyses were done to achieve the study's specific research objectives as follows:

- To analyse the relationship between student academic performance and mode of study before/after COVID-19 outbreak
- To determine if regional internet connectivity is associated with student academic performance after COVID-19 outbreak-

Regression in SPSS assessed the relationship between student performance and offering type at national/country level while GWR in ArcGIS examined the correlation between student performance and regional (local) internet connectivity. GWR was appropriate as factors considered in the study are non-stationary variables and GWR modelled the local/regional relationships (based on location and internet connectivity) and student performance (Columbia Public Health, 2021). Therefore, this study is based on quantitative research design where secondary quantitative data was analysed to address the latter stated research objectives. Ethical issues considered before and during the undertaking of the research included but not limited to obtaining permission from the management of the university under study. The name of the university under study is not to be named, as per the request from the university management, reasons for not revealing the name has to do with countering competitors (competitors must not use their weaknesses, strength/information to advance than the university understudy). Dataset containing student academic results was also anonymised to protect the privacy of the students. Results were produced at aggregated level as a summary of student academic performance as affected by change of offering type and internet connectivity.

BACKGROUND

The current COVID-19 crisis has forced many universities around the world to adopt alternatives to face-to-face teaching and learning (Organisation for Economic Co-operation and Development [OECD], 2020b). Consequently, online education has been adopted by many universities to upset the spread of COVID-19 due to academic activities. The internet is a crucial component for online classes to be successful, as it is a media on which teaching, and learning takes place. Also, student assessments for online classes are conducted virtually using the internet. The shift of the mode of teaching and learning from contact (face-to-face) to online/virtual classes due to COVID-19 is accompanied by hindrances which affects students' academic performance. This is because, online than contact classes are faced with challenges associated with technical setup, institutional teaching methodological barriers, and individual student/lecturer behavioral characteristics (Khalil et al., 2020). Moreover, the absence of non-verbal clues in online classes negatively effects the quality of teaching and learning. Equally, Gherheş et al. (2021) discovered that, students in online classes are more likely to experienced technical problems during internet connection which in some cases can lead to lack of student concentration during lessons. These are some of the factors which contributes to students attaining poor academic results, as poor internet connectivity can pose a big challenge to students' online learning (Asio et al., 2021). Similarly, Mässing (2017, p. 40) discovered that, online classes can be impacted by factors such as outlined below,

- Access: Bandwidth; Connectivity; Devices; Downloadable resources; Mobile data connection; Satellite campuses.
- User motivation, attitude and awareness: Change the staff's behavior; Motivation to participate in e-learning related activities.
- Transforming the education: Inequality; Low computer literacy; Conflicting views of the situation for ICTs in the context; Conflicting views of focus.

Challenges associated with online education are crosscutting. For instance, it is argued that many lecturers have minimal experience in preparing for online examinations while students, especially those with limited access to the internet, fear that they would be at a disadvantage in online learning and assessments (Champagne & Granja, 2021). This indicate that, some students are likely to fail, not because they did not gain the required subject knowledge, but due to the experienced internet connectivity challenges. This indicates that, internet connectivity can be one of the determinant variables for student academic performance in online classes. However, during the COVID-19 pandemic, e-learning as a distance learning strategy in Jordan enabled universities to use a variety of online learning platforms that allowed faculty members to build competencies in the ability to use media and virtual collaboration (Alsoud & Harasis, 2021). In addition, lecturers were also able to provide students easy access to teaching materials and answer questions in a more interactive manner all via the internet connection. According to RSWEBSOLS (2021),

The internet is a fundamental subject area in the improvement of information technology. It has become a crucial instrument and a requirement of the knowledge-based society we have today as well as a vital means to present current and up-to-date information has become a form of effortless communication for everyone anywhere, and especially for research and learning. Students will find it beneficial if there is advancement in the development, access, as well as advancement in technology, the internet, and information, is present.

MAIN FOCUS OF THE CHAPTER

Internet Connectivity in Namibia

Namibia's technology sector is hindered by a lack of affordable access, and poor-quality service (Gervasius, 2020; Tubulingane, 2018). Moreover, Namibia is ranked 84 out of 100 countries, with a score of 41.2% for availability and 54.8% for affordability indicators respectively. This implies that, 58.8% and 45.2% of students are likely not to have access and afford quality internet services respectively. This signifies that without government and other stakeholders support online learning and teaching could not be a success at Namibian universities, as most of the students were likely not to afford quality internet services to access online learning. One of the long-term solutions to ensure internet access and affordability in Namibia was the introduction of a National Broadband Policy in early 2020 with the aim of achieving reliable and affordable broadband access services for all (Gervasius, 2020). Even if all Namibian university students will have equal access to internet services, the benefit of the service will still vary based on the social status of the student. For instance, Cahyo et al. (2020) discovered a difference effect of internet usage on student's academic performance between students from high and low socio-economic status. It was found that, students from the high social economic status group, their academic performance was mainly impacted by general internet usage than professional or academic usage. But, in lower social economic status group, professional usage gave greater prediction than general internet usage. However, the effect of internet usage on student's academic performance were both significant and positive among higher and lower social economic status group (Cahyo et al., 2020). The finding in higher social economic status group is not in line with other studies which suggest that activities related to professional use such as searching information, reading school subject material, and online learning have a higher impact on student's academic performance than general use ((Leung & Lee, 2012; Ritzhaupt et. al., 2013; Harris et.al., 2017) as cited in Cahyo et al., 2020, p. 21). This does not mean that, the higher social status group students did not use internet for learning purposes at all but used the internet mainly for socialising and other general use than for academic purposes. Also, those students likely could afford to have private academic tutors to assist them learn at home or at private tutoring centres, which led to them articulating improved performance at pair with lower social status group.

Namibia's National Broadband initiative is expected to help the lower and higher education sectors in future as the universal response to school and higher education institutions closure due to COVID-19 outbreak has been the creation of online learning and teaching platforms to support students and lecturers. Though, as outlined above that, not all students will have the same access to information and communication technologies (ICTs), the situation which persists in many countries around the world (OECD, 2020). For instance, access to broadband internet has been spreading in the United States but the Federal Communications Commission (FCC) revealed that there were still 19 million Americans without access to this type of service in year 2012 (Kingston, 2013). When it comes to Namibian universities transition to online education, where there is unequal access to ICTs service among students, which did not hinder the Namibian government to enforced (in April 2020) e-learning countrywide as a response to the COVID-19 pandemic (Gervasius, 2020). A decision which was criticised as the country has a low internet connectivity, as at the time only 30% of schools had access to the internet. This indicates that, internet connectivity is a challenge to many Namibians to access and participate in the new virtual education system equally. The challenge will be more intensive with university students, as they will still be faced with obstacles to access online university libraries and journals which in many cases requires quality stable internet connections. Also, many students are likely still faced with social economic challenges as most higher education students resides in informal urban areas characterised with no to fewer basic services such as electricity, safe drinking water and poor sanitation.

Internet availability is not a guarantee to many Namibian university students, as the internet service providers in Namibia has not yet covered the whole country with network. And where the network is available, is of poor quality in many cases (Tubulingane, 2018). According to the Namibia Statistics Agency (NSA) (2012), in year 2011 only 7% of the Namibian population had internet connections, and the great majority of these were in urban areas. Table 1 below, reveals that, the Khomas region, Namibia's highly urbanised region (hosts the national capital city, Windhoek), had the highest number of people connected to the internet, while Ohangwena and Omusati regions articulated the lowest number. According to Digital Namibia (2021), 34% of the people in the Khomas region are expected to be connected to the internet in year 2020. The Erongo and Ohangwena regions' internet connectivity rates are expected to be 23% and 3% respectively. Majority of Namibian university students with access to the internet resides in low-income areas of Windhoek (where accommodation and cost of life is cheap), however such areas are typically characterised with a high level of dissatisfaction with internet services compared to middle- and high-income areas (Tubulingane, 2018). Although, the high internet connectivity in the Khomas region where most university students in Namibia are based made it possible for online learning to take place through online platforms. Still, the Namibian university understudy, during the 2020 academic year had to postponed learning and teaching for laboratory-based engineering courses due to the lack of information technology (IT) infrastructure for both students and lecturers to complete virtual science experiments using online interactive laboratory (UN, 2020). Practical learning and assessments period for engineering students had to be extended, as students had to be divided into small groups for contact practical lectures and examinations. The social sciences students had all their learning, teaching and assessments conducted online, as no special ICT infrastructures were required to remotely attend classes or complete assessments.

Table 1. Internet penetration rate in Namibia

Region Name	Population 2011	# Of people with access to internet in 2011	Internet penetration rate (%) in 2011	Internet penetration rate (%) in 2019/2020 (Estimated)
Erongo	137361	21339	16	23
Hardap	72465	4849	7	10
Karas	70946	8059	11	16
Kavango East	100400	2741	3	4
Kavango West	100552	2740	3	4
Khomas	314943	77702	24	34
Kunene	76638	2654	3	4
Ohangwena	221705	5656	2	3
Omaheke	64500	3288	5	7
Omusati	222661	5682	2	3
Oshana	160869	13203	8	11
Oshikoto	165526	6386	4	6
Otjozondjupa	129188	10664	8	11
Zambezi	81684	3038	4	6
Total	**1919438**	**168001**		

Source: NSA (2012), Digital Namibia (2021)

Student Academic Performance and Offering Type

Online learning is regarded as an active discussion and interaction platform for effective learning and teaching of students (Shuja et al., 2019). Some authors have derived advantages of taking courses online than on face-to-face offering mode. According to Mather and Sarkans (2018), students taking online courses emphasize that flexibility, accessibility, convenience of balancing personal, professional, and academic life and their desire to experience a new way of learning are core factors that informed their decision to enrol for online courses. Similarly, Paechter and Maier (2010, p. 292) recognized that, students appreciate online learning for its potential in providing a clear and coherent structure of the learning material, in supporting self-regulated learning, and in distributing information from both students and lecturers. This has led to online program/course offerings in higher education becoming an integral part of educational delivery for post-secondary institutions (Mather & Sarkans, 2018). Due to the massive growth of web technology, more educational organisations and business schools has taken crucial moves in utilising increasingly immersive e-learning methods to improve student performance (Zolochevskaya et al., 2021). However, students who are currently participating in the Namibian higher education sector are faced with two digital divides. First-order divide refers to students having inequality of access to the internet and ICT devices while the second-order divide is in terms of inequality in the user ability to interact in meaningful ways with the internet and ICT towards learning (Dewan et al., 2005 as cited in Kingston, 2013). This is because, most of students, particularly first years from a rural set-up, tend to possess low level of internet and computer literacy skills to efficiently and effectively participate in online classes. On the other hand, students from urban centres are well prepared for online leaning as in many cases they were exposed pre-university to the use of the internet and computers at their former high schools and in their home environments. This is supported as indicated in the case of Namibia that, urban areas tend to be associated with a much higher internet connectivity rates than rural or remote areas.

Students who prefer contact learning is mainly for communication purposes in which a shared understanding must be derived or in which interpersonal relations are to be established (Paechter & Maier, 2010). Moreover, face-to-face learning is pursued when conceptual knowledge in the subject matter or skills in the application of one's knowledge are to be acquired while online learning is sought when skills in self-regulated learning are to be acquired. Students enrolled on face-to-face mode, benefits from classroom interaction with peers, faculty members, and have easy access to course materials (Mather & Sarkans, 2018). Thus, students enrolled in face-to-face classes are more likely to perform better than students in online classes where learning is characterised by lack of one-to-one interaction between lecturers and students. Also, online classes are characterised by lack of opportunity for discussion and feedback to aid improved student academic performance. Similarly, Frantzen (2014) established that online learning based on a technology-intensive curriculum alone does not significantly improve student performance. Thus, technology-based online courses need to be accompanied by interactions (from both students and lecturers) to enhance learning for online students (Frantzen, 2014). This is because, online classes not based on participant learning style are likely to be associated with lower student academic performance (Nursen et al., 2018). This is supported by Fischer et al. (2020) that online students are more likely to performance lower than students enrolled in face-to-face courses.

Researchers have also revealed that, students enrolled in online interactive classes are more likely to perform better than students in hybrid and face-to-face or contact courses. For illustrate, Johnson et al. (2000) argues that students in the face-to-face courses have a positive perception about the lecturers and overall course(s) quality. However, those positive perceptions of face-to-face students does not advantage them to perform better than online students. Comparably, Shen et al. (2007) state that, students enrolled in face-to-face classes are likely to achieve slightly better performance in examinations in comparison with students in online classes. Nevertheless, the differences in overall performance between the students are not statistically significant. In summary, the central issue which affects student academic performance in online and contact classes is the level, structure and types of interactions which occurs between students and lecturers. When well structured, and curriculum informed discussions geared towards learning and teaching takes place, student academic performance is more likely to improve regardless of the offering type (contact or online mode).

Different education offering types, whether online or contact mode, have different ways of accessing student learning outcomes. However, the assessment to be given to students need to be effective in evaluating if student learning has taken place. Effective assessment needs to include direct evidence of student learning, what skills, abilities, knowledge, and attributes students' exhibits as a result of participating in the program or module (Jimaa, 2011). Additionally, there can be a combination of direct and indirect evidence, which is typically measured by certain techniques such as homework or an exit examination towards the end of the study period. The method of assessment can affect student academic performance. For example, Joyce (2018) discovered that, the formative quiz score performance of the online students is significantly more related to summative test performance than that of the pencil and paper group. This indicates that, completion of the online homework was more beneficial to evaluate student progress than undertaking the traditional style formative homework. However, Anakwe (2008) revealed that, the use of computer-based tests instead of paper-based tests does not affects students' traditional test scores in examinations. This suggests that student academic performance is more likely to be impacted by other factors such as effectiveness of the teaching and issues with regards to plagiarism. For instance, in the latter case of comparison between academic performance of online and pencil and paper groups. The pencil and paper group are more likely not to complete the homework by themselves while the online group was required to learn and complete the assignment instantly online, which might aid them to perform better than the pencil and paper group in the course summative test assessments.

Internet Connectivity and Online Student Performance

The online academic environment constitutes of the internet and other ICT devices such as smartphones, software and computers (e-learning platforms) at many universities around the world. As a result, internet connectivity and access to ICT impacts student academic performance. This is because, students continuously and extensively use the internet to interact online, search for information, and perform specific tasks and activities. Additionally, the use of the internet implicates positive and negative effects on university students' academic performance (Chang et al. 2019 as cited in Maqableh et al., 2021). Equally, Cahyo et al. (2020) state that internet usage can have a negative or positive effects on student's academic performance depending on the level of engagement with online educational activities.

Online learning has experienced unprecedented growth in recent years (RSWEBSOLS, 2021). However, in many parts of the world, particularly in Namibia, online data and accessibility remain minimal, thus quantifying the impact of online education on student academic performance becomes challenging. This is because, student academic performance can be impacted by three elements, namely, parents (family causal factors), teachers (academic causal factors), and students (personal causal factors). Though the influence of those factors on student academic performance varies from one academic environment to another, from one set of students to the next, and indeed from one cultural setting to another (Diaz, 2003 as cited from Olufemi et al., 2018, p. 52).

Numerous researchers have revealed positive and negative impact of online education offering on university student academic performance. For instance, Zolochevskaya et al. (2021) established that, ICT has a major statistically favourable effect on the academic success of university students in e-learning/online classes. Shahibi and Ku Rusli (2017) revealed that, online media usage for education helps students in improving their academic achievement. According to RSWEBSOLS (2021) access to information via the internet can influence the academic performance of students. Equally, Ivwighreghweta and Igere (2014) state that, students who use the internet to retrieve relevant academic materials, such as E-journals and E-books are better prepared for their examinations than their counterparts who do not use e-resources. Likewise, Torres-Díaz- et al. (2016) established that, students who tend to interact more and use educational materials are less likely to fail than students whose main academic activity is to search for none-academic information. This is because the use of internet technology makes it easier for people to obtain several and latest information quickly and effectively (Shahibi & Ku Rusli, 2017). The internet has made it possible for students to access online university libraries across the globe in a more efficient and effective manner. The access and utilisation of relevant academic materials have in many cases contributed to improved student academic performance at many universities, including at the Namibian university.

Although, online learning is associated with many benefits to students. There are still some challenges associated with online education particularly for students who are unable to use technology. Moreover, in online education offering students are in many cases likely to receive late feedback and communication from their lecturers (Mather & Sarkans, 2018). This occurs in cases where lecturers struggle to use e-learning platforms, mainly when they did not receive comprehensive training on how to utilise e-learning for effective teaching. Also, some old fashion lecturers might be resistant to change as they are not used to online teaching, and consequently prefer to provide feedback to students during contact classes. Other concerns are around differences in student access to digital learning resources while at home, many students in the developing countries such as Namibia, do not have access to high quality broadband connectivity (Tubulingane, 2018). This variation in internet connectivity may impact the type of online/blended model that faculty members can deliver or constrain student engagement with online content (Cullinan et al., 2021, p. 1). Students with poor quality internet services at home are likely to performance poorly in their academic work, as they do not participate in classroom discussions at the same rate as students connected to high quality internet services. This is supported by Kaisara and Bwalya (2020) who established that, most Namibian students access e-learning platforms using mobile smartphones within their home environments which in many cases are not conducive for learning, due to poor internet connections. Challenges experienced by Namibian students are like what Nigerian university students encountered in terms of unavailable effective internet access for academic purposes (Ivwighreghweta & Igere, 2014).

Higher education e-learning platforms are negatively affected by power outage (more common in developing countries), slow internet speed, lack of computer terminals, too many hits or information overload and insufficient computer. Fischer et al. (2020) argue that, in some cases at-risk university student populations (low-income students with no or less access to quality mobile internet services) are likely to perform at pair (in online courses) with students characterised with high income and connected to quality mobile internet services. This is due to mobile smart devices providing a flexible and discussion-oriented learning to students which leads to improved academic performance (Shuja et al.,

2019). This is possible in situations where universities have created mobile e-learning platforms, supported by stable quality internet services and adequate e-learning resources for effective learning and teaching.

SOLUTIONS AND RECOMMENDATIONS

Student Academic Performance and Offering Type

Table 2 below highlight the linear regression results which indicates that, 12.4% (Adjusted R Square) of the change in the student academic performance is explained by varying 2019 regional internet penetration rates. A unit increase in the internet penetration will led to a 0.438 increase in the academic performance of students at the Namibian university during 2019 academic year. This stipulates a positive insignificant (at 0.05 alpha) association between internet access and student academic performance as P-value (Sig.) in Table 2 is > 0.05. This result is contrary to Zolochevskaya et al. (2021) who established that, ICT has a major statistically favourable effect on the academic success of university students. This is because Namibian students were still mainly enrolled in contact or face-to-face classes in 2019, and they likely benefited more from in person classroom interaction with peers, faculty members, and had easy access to course materials, as the lecturers could early handover academic materials during lessons (Mather & Sarkans, 2018). This indicates that, student engagement was the mediating variable between students' academic learning and academic achievement, particularly for first year students (Ribeiro et al., 2019). Contact classes enabled student to take advantage of the physical presence of lecturers and fellow students to enhance learning leading to the successful completion of their academic tasks. The impact of internet access and utilization is not strong in terms of influencing student academic performance during 2019 academic year. This means that, there is no relationship between, internet access and the academic performance of students at the Namibian university during the 2019 academic year when contact learning was still norm at the university. Students mainly relied on the physical presence of lecturers and their counterparts to learn and acquire knowledge needed for the completion of their modules. Also, the assessments were done physically at the university, thus students had opportunity to ask for clarity before completing assessments.

Education Quality and Offerings Intersection

Table 2. Linear Regression, 2019 student academic performance and internet penetration rate

Variables Entered/Removed[a]			
Model	Variables Entered	Variables Removed	Method
1	Internet_penetration_rate_2019	.	Enter
a. Dependent Variable: 2019_Average_Final_Mark			
b. All requested variables entered.			

Model Summary				
Model	R	R Square	Adjusted R Square	Std. Error of the Estimate
1	.438[a]	.191	.124	2.524331517546118
a. Predictors: (Constant), Internet_penetration_rate_2019				

ANOVA[a]						
Model		Sum of Squares	df	Mean Square	F	Sig.
1	Regression	18.110	1	18.110	2.842	.118[b]
	Residual	76.467	12	6.372		
	Total	94.577	13			
a. Dependent Variable: 2019_Average_Final_Mark						
b. Predictors: (Constant), Internet_penetration_rate_2019						

Coefficients[a]						
Model		Unstandardized Coefficients		Standardized Coefficients	t	Sig.
		B	Std. Error	Beta		
1	(Constant)	54.323	1.047		51.901	.000
	Internet_penetration_rate_2019	.133	.079	.438	1.686	.118
a. Dependent Variable: 2019 Average_Final_Mark						

The unplanned and rapid shift to online classes at the time of pandemic (during the 2020 academic year) did not result in a poor learning experience as was expected at the Namibian university (El Said, 2021). The opposite was experienced as the switch from face-to-face to online assessments positively impacted the academic performance of the Namibian university students as revealed in Table 3 below. The student pass-rate improved from 68% in 2019 to 78% in year 2020. This is in line with Joyce (2018) who revealed that, online assessments positive aid student academic performance. Though, Anakwe (2008) discovered that, online assessments are at pair with face-to-face assessments in terms of improving student academic performance. Similarly, at an Egyptian university, no significant difference was revealed in students' grades between contact and online teaching modes of the same course taught during COVID-19 lockdown semester and the semester before (El Said, 2021). This was achieved after controlling variables related to learning and teaching activities, (e.g., students were taught by the same lecturer and learning was evaluated using the same assessment academic materials for both online and the contact group).

Results in Table 3 was contrary to Mather and Sarkans (2018), as no major challenges were experienced by the Namibian students in terms of not able to use the internet or online learning platforms. However, the high pass-rate experienced at the Namibian university raised the most critical academic integrity issues among some administrators and faculty members (Champagne & Granja, 2021). This is because during the 2020 online assessments, it was difficult to detect cheating among students. Although, Spaulding (2009) argues that even if academic cheating was involved during the 2020 online student assessments, it is likely to be at the same level with the plagiarism of contact assessments during the 2019 academic year. This infers that, student academic performance was mainly positively impacted by the online mode of study than academic cheating. It is surprising how the students adapted quickly to online education as most of them had little previous experience with online education (Almendingen et al., 2021). Also, challenges experienced by the Namibian students may include, lack of social interaction, a feeling of being alone in their studies, unfit housing situations for home learning purposes, including insufficient data bandwidth, and a sense of reduced motivation (Almendingen et al., 2021). However, online learning might have been a good experience particularly to introvert students. Likewise, the working student population likely benefited as they could easily attend lectures even at their work offices, with no travelling cost incurred, for instance there was no need for physical submission of academic work at the university premises.

Table 3. Student academic performance, 2019 and 2020

Academic year	2019	2020	Grand Total	Pass-rate 2019	Pass-rate 2020
# of students who failed semester 1	3787	2787	6574	68% (8931/ (8931+3787)	78% (10635/ (10635+2787)
# of students who passed semester 1	8931	10635	19566		
Students with no results (blank)	358	272	630		
Grand Total	**13076**	**13694**	**26770**		

Table 4 below highlight the linear regression results based on 2020 student academic performance (when learning and teaching activities were moved to online mode at the Namibian university) and the internet penetration for period 2020. The results stipulate that, 36.4% (Adjusted R Square) of the change in the student academic performance is explained by the varying regional internet penetration rates. A unit increase in the internet penetration will led to a 0.642 increase in the academic performance of students at the Namibian university during the 2020 academic year. This stipulates a positive significant (at 0.05 alpha) association between internet access and student academic performance as P-value (Sig.) in Table 4 is < 0.05. This result is in line with (Shahibi & Ku Rusli, 2017; Ivwighreghweta & Igere, 2014) that, internet usage for academic purposes can help students improve their academic achievements. This is because access to e-resources and e-learning, better prepares students for examinations. Results in Table 4 are contrary to Kaisara and Bwalya (2020), this is because most of the Namibian students access e-learning platforms using mobile smartphones within their home environments which in many cases are not conducive for learning, due to poor internet services available. This indicates that, such students are likely part of the 22% of students who failed their 2020 assessments, as they likely did not have a favorable online learning experience due to poor internet access on their mobile devices.

Education Quality and Offerings Intersection

The experienced high rate (78%) of student academic performance is also due to efforts of the Namibian government, as a programme was roll out in early 2020 to provide free internet access to students at tertiary institutions for them to learn remotely amid COVID-19 (XINHUANET, 2020). Though, online learning in Namibia was still associated with challenges particularly for first year students who were unable to use the internet effectively (Mather & Sarkans, 2018). The Namibian university also has a computer literacy course for first time or year students. The course orients students how to use computers and internet for academic purposes. This might also explain why students easily adapted to online learning during early stages of COVID-19 in early 2020. The improved student academic performance as aided by internet connectivity might be an encouragement to many students who performanced well in 2020 online classes than in face-to-face classes during 2019 academic year to advocate for online education in future. However, the true benefit of online education to the Namibian students must be evaluated based on whether learning outcomes were achieved in all respective online courses offered, so that fit for purpose graduates are produced by the university. The Namibian university is required to produce knowledgeable and competent graduates to work in various industries in Namibia or internationally.

Table 4. Linear regression, 2020 student academic performance and internet penetration rate

Variables Entered/Removed[a]			
Model	**Variables Entered**	**Variables Removed**	**Method**
1	Internet_penetration_rate_2020[b]	.	Enter

a. Dependent Variable: 2020_Average_Final Mark

b. All requested variables entered.

Model Summary			
Model	R	R Square	Adjusted R Square	Std. Error of the Estimate
1	.642[a]	.413	.364	2.394868994448596

a. Predictors: (Constant), Internet_penetration_rate_2020

ANOVA[a]					
Model		Sum of Squares	df	Mean Square	F	Sig.
1	Regression	48.361	1	48.361	8.432	.013[b]
	Residual	68.825	12	5.735		
	Total	117.186	13			

a. Dependent Variable: 2020_Average_Final Mark

b. Predictors: (Constant), Internet_penetration_rate_2020

Coefficients[a]						
Model		Unstandardized Coefficients		Standardized Coefficients	t	Sig.
		B	Std. Error	Beta		
1	(Constant)	56.191	.993		56.588	.000
	Internet_penetration_rate_2020	.217	.075	.642	2.904	.013

a. Dependent Variable: 2020 Average_Final Mark

51

Regional Internet Connectivity and Student Academic Performance

The exposure to the internet and ICT devices has a strong influence on online student academic performance. Hence, Figure 1 below was developed to demonstrate the influence of internet on student academic performance. Moreover, Figure 1 provides the Geographically Weighted Regression (GWR) map results based on the internet penetration rate and student academic performance per region of Namibia. The internet is a strong factor which positively influences student academic performance in the following regions, Ohangwena, Kavango East, Otjozondjupa, Erongo and Hardap. This is because, student academic performance is higher than the average student performance reported in regions such as Omusati and Zambezi. Furthermore, the internet was found to be a weak predictor of student academic performance in Omaheke, Kavango West, Kunene, !karas, and Khomas regions. This is because those regions' internet connectivity results in students articulating a lower-than-average academic performance. This indicates that, COVID-19 pandemic has deepened disparities as there is no regional equal access to the internet and other ICTs. Students in regions such as Omaheke are likely to find it hard to stay engaged in virtual classrooms to access and benefit from higher education (DEUSA, 2021). When students are not engaged in learning activities due to internet disruptions, they are more likely to articulate a lower academic performance than students connected to stable internet access. The study finding also reveals that, students from Ohangwena, Kavango East, Otjozondjupa, Erongo and Hardap likely use the internet to perform interactive activities with peers and lecturers to have more academic successes than those who only seeks information (Torres-Díaz et al., 2016). This stipulates that internet connectivity alone does not affect the academic performance of students, but access and academic usage of the internet does positively impact the performance of students at the Namibian university.

Results in Figure 1 are contrary to Alsoud and Harasis (2021), where it was established that, students from remote and disadvantaged areas are more likely to face enormous challenges such as technological accessibility, poor internet connectivity, and harsh study environments. Such challenges experienced by disadvantaged students are likely to lead to poor academic performance. Nevertheless, current study results in Figure 1 stipulates that, students from remote regions such as Ohangwena, likely had access to the right or recommended academic e-materials by their lecturers, which led to them articulating improved academic performance during the 2020 academic year.

Education Quality and Offerings Intersection

Figure 1. Internet and student academic performance per region

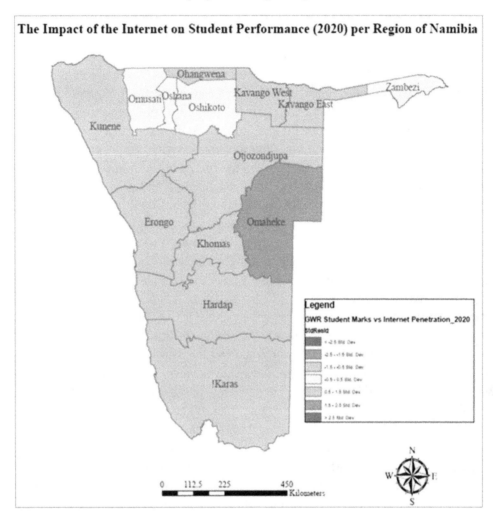

FUTURE RESEARCH DIRECTIONS

The study assessed the impact of COVID-19 outbreak on student academic performance per respective offering type (online and contact). It was found that online than contact education offering is associated with improved academic performance of students at the Namibian university. The study has also demonstrated the importance of equality in student offering modes (online versus face-to-face) in upholding the quality of higher education in Namibia. This is based on study results which revealed that online than contact education offering at the Namibian university is associated with much higher student academic performance. Thus, further academic research to be directed at evaluating the level of plagiarism associated with online and contact offerings at the Namibian university. This is needed as the pass-rate at the university for previous five years before COVID-19 outbreak has averaged between 60 and 69% when contact teaching and learning was the norm at the university. But when a switch to online was done due to COVID-19, the student academic performance jumped to 78%. The recommended plagiarism research will assist to determine whether to disregard the theory that, online than contact education offering at the university is associated with higher rate of plagiarism, which is suspected to have aided student academic performance.

Internet access and utilisation does not have a significant effect on student academic performance, when the mode of education offering is contact (face-to-face). This is because, students at the university likely benefit more from the physical presence of peers and lecturers during discussion or lessons. This conclusion is supported by various researchers (Mather & Sarkans, 2018; Frantzen, 2014; Nursen et al., 2018). There is a need to conduct a satisfaction study to evaluate the preference of students and lecturers in terms of the main education offering mode to be adopted at the university.

The study has quantified the contribution of internet connectivity to student academic performance in online classrooms. As a strong correlation between internet access for academic utilisation and online student academic performance was established. This conclusion is endorsed by researchers (Shahibi & Ku Rusli, 2017; Ivwighreghweta & Igere, 2014). Although, there is still a disparity in terms of equal access and participation in higher education by students using e-learning platforms which has led to some students failing their 2020 online assessments. Thus, a need to assist the most vulnerable (with low or no source of income) to access digital learning resources to aid online academic performance of those students. The Namibian government and civil society organisations are encouraged to further provide vulnerable students with mobile smart devices as well as quality stable internet access, or have organised teaching through television, print media or radio (OECD, 2020).

The internet is a strong factor which positively influences student academic performance in regions, Ohangwena, Kavango East, Otjozondjupa, Erongo and Hardap. However, the internet has less influence on the academic performance of students from Omaheke, Kavango West, Kunene, !karas, and Khomas regions. Moderate influence of the internet on the academic performance of students was recorded from the Zambezi, Oshikoto, Omusati and Oshana regions. This indicates that, regional internet connectivity affect student academic performance differently, and prior high exposure to the internet does not directly impact student academic performance. This is so as students from the Khomas region with the highest internet penetration rate articulated lower academic performances compared to regions with much lower internet penetration such as Kavango East. A academic study geared towards evaluating internet access and types of usage and student academic performance is encouraged. Such a study will provide a comprehensive picture of why regions with higher internet penetration rates are associated with lower online student academic performance.

REFERENCES

Almendingen, K., Morseth, M. S., Gjølstad, E., Brevik, A., & Tørris, C. (2021). Student's experiences with online teaching following COVID-19 lockdown: A mixed methods explorative study. *PLoS One*, *16*(8), e0250378. Advance online publication. doi:10.1371/journal.pone.0250378 PMID:34464386

Alsoud, A. R., & Harasis, A. A. (2021). The impact of COVID-19 pandemic on student's e-Learning experience in Jordan. *Journal of Theoretical and Applied Electronic Commerce Research*, *16*(5), 1404–1414. doi:10.3390/jtaer16050079

Anakwe, B. (2008). Comparison of student performance in paper-based versus computer-based testing. *Journal of Education for Business*, *84*(1), 13–17. doi:10.3200/JOEB.84.1.13-17

Arias, J. J., Swinton, J., & Anderson, K. (2018). Online vs. face-to-face: A comparison of student outcomes with random assignment. *E-Journal of Business Education & Scholarship of Teaching, 12*(2), 1–23.

Asio, J. M. R., Gadia, E., Abarintos, E., Paguio, D., & Balce, M. (2021). Internet Connection and Learning Device Availability of College Students: Basis for Institutionalizing Flexible Learning in the New Normal. *Studies in Humanities and Education, 2*(1), 56–69. doi:10.48185he.v2i1.224

Cahyo, S. D., Al Fariz, A. B., & Lestari, C. A. (2020). Does internet usage frequency give impact to student's academic performance? *Indonesian Journal of Educational Assessment, 3*(1), 16–23. doi:10.26499/ijea.v3i1.57

Champagne, E., & Granja, A. D. (2021). *How the COVID-19 pandemic may have changed university teaching and testing for good.* Retrieved July 18, 2021 from https://theconversation.com/how-the-covid-19-pandemic-may-have-changed-university-teaching-and-testing-for-good-158342

Columbia Public Health. (2021). *Population health methods: geographically weighted regression.* Retrieved July 10, 2021 from https://www.publichealth.columbia.edu/research/population-health-methods/geographically-weighted-regression

Cullinan, J., Flannery, D., Harold, J., Lyons, S., & Palcic, D. (2021). The disconnected: COVID-19 and disparities in access to quality broadband for higher education students. *International Journal of Educational Technology in Higher Education*, 1-21. doi:10.1186/s41239-021-00262-1

Department of Education of the United States of America (DEUSA). (2021). *Education in a pandemic: the disparate impacts of COVID-19 on America's students.* https://www2.ed.gov/about/offices/list/ocr/docs/20210608-impacts-of-covid19.pdf

Digital Namibia. (2021). *Internet users in Namibia.* Retrieved September 18, 2021 from https://datareportal.com/reports/digital-2021-namibia

El Said, G. R. (2021). How did the covid-19 pandemic affect higher education learning experience? an empirical investigation of learners' academic performance at a university in a developing country. *Hindawi -. Advances in Human-Computer Interaction, 2021*, 1–10. doi:10.1155/2021/6649524

Fischer, C., Xu, D., Rodriguez, F., Denaro, K., & Warschauer, M. (2020). Effects of course modality in summer session: enrollment patterns and student performance in face-to-face and online classes. *The Internet and Higher Education, 45*(April). doi:10.1016/j.iheduc.2019.100710

Frantzen, D. (2014). Is technology a one-size-fits-all solution to improving student performance? A comparison of online, hybrid and face-to-face courses. *Journal of Public Affairs Education, 20*(4), 565–578. doi:10.1080/15236803.2014.12001808

Gamage, K. A. A., de Silva, E. K., & Gunawardhana, N. (2020). Online delivery and assessment during COVID-19: Safeguarding academic integrity. *Education Sciences, 10*(11), 1–24. doi:10.3390/educsci10110301

Gervasius, N. (2020). *Namibia digital rights and inclusion: a paradigm initiative publication.* https://paradigmhq.org/wp-content/uploads/2021/05/lr-Namibia-Digital-Rights-Inclusion-2020-Report.pdf

Gherheş, V., Stoian, C. E., Fărcaşiu, M. A., & Stanici, M. (2021). E-learning vs. Face-to-face learning: Analyzing students' preferences and behaviors. *Sustainability (Switzerland), 13*(8), 4381. Advance online publication. doi:10.3390u13084381

Ivwighreghweta, O., & Igere, M. A. (2014). Impact of the internet on academic performance of students in tertiary institutions in Nigeria. *Journal of Information and Knowledge Management, 5*(6), 47–56.

Jimaa, S. (2011). The impact of assessment on students learning. *Procedia: Social and Behavioral Sciences, 28*, 718–721. doi:10.1016/j.sbspro.2011.11.133

Johnson, S. D., Aragon, S. R., Shaik, N., & Palma-Rivas, N. (2000). Comparative analysis of learner satisfaction and learning outcomes in online and face-to-face learning environments. *Journal of Interactive Learning Research, 11*(1), 29–49.

Joyce, P. (2018). The effectiveness of online and paper-based formative assessment in the learning of English as a second language. *PASAA, 55.* https://files.eric.ed.gov/fulltext/EJ1191739.pdf

Kaisara, G., & Bwalya, K. J. (2020). Investigating the e-learning challenges faced by students during Covid-19 in Namibia. *International Journal of Higher Education, 10*(1), 308. doi:10.5430/ijhe.v10n1p308

Khalil, R., Mansour, A. E., Fadda, W. A., Almisnid, K., Aldamegh, M., Al-Nafeesah, A., Alkhalifah, A., & Al-Wutayd, O. (2020). The sudden transition to synchronized online learning during the COVID-19 pandemic in Saudi Arabia: A qualitative study exploring medical students' perspectives. *BMC Medical Education, 20*(1), 1–10. doi:10.118612909-020-02208-z PMID:32859188

Kingston, K. J. (2013). *The impact of high-speed internet connectivity at home on eighth-grade student achievement* [Doctoral dissertation, University of Nebraska]. https://digitalcommons.unomaha.edu/cgi/viewcontent.cgi?article=1050&context=studentwork

Kothari, C. R. (2004). *Research methodology: Methods and technics* (2nd revised edition). New Age International Publishers.

Maqableh, M., Jaradat, M., & Azzam, A. (2021). Exploring the determinants of students' academic performance at university level: The mediating role of internet usage continuance intention. *Education and Information Technologies, 26*(4), 4003–4025. doi:10.100710639-021-10453-y PMID:33584119

Mässing, C. (2017). *Success factors and challenges for E-learning Technologies in the Namibian Higher Education System: A case study of the University of Namibia* [Bachelor's thesis, University of Skövde]. https://www.diva-portal.org/smash/get/diva2:1111480/FULLTEXT01.pdf

Mather, M., & Sarkans, A. (2018). Student perceptions of online and face-to-face learning. *International Journal of Curriculum and Instruction, 10*(2), 61–76.

McKie, A. (2020). *Lack of study space and poor connections hinder online learning.* Retrieved October 11, 2021, from https://www.timeshighereducation.com/news/lack-study-space-and-poor-connections-hinder-online-learning

Namibia Statistics Agency (NSA). (2012). *Namibia 2011 population and housing census main report.* https://cms.my.na/assets/documents/p19dmn58guram30ttun89rdrp1.pdf

NSA. (2021). *NSDI metadata browser.* http://geofind.nsa.org.na/

Nursen, İ., Tomruk, M., Sevi, S., Karadibak, D., & Savc, S. (2018). The relationship between learning styles and academic performance in TURKISH physiotherapy students. *BMC Medical Education*, *18*(291), 1–8. doi:10.118612909-018-1400-2 PMID:30514280

OECD. (2020). *Strengthening online learning when schools are closed - The role of families and teachers in supporting students during the COVID-19 crisis.* OECD. https://read.oecd-ilibrary.org/view/?ref=136_136615-o13x4bkowa&title=Strengthening-online-learning-when-schools-are-closed

Olufemi, O. T., Adediran, A. A., & Oyediran, W. O. (2018). Factors affecting students' academic performance in colleges of education in southwest, Nigeria. *Brock Journal of Education*, *6*(10), 43–56.

Organisation for Economic Co-operation and Development (OECD). (2020). *The impact of COVID-19 on student equity and inclusion: supporting vulnerable students during school closures and school re-openings.* https://www.oecd.org/coronavirus/policy-responses/the-impact-of-covid-19-on-student-equity-and-inclusion-supporting-vulnerable-students-during-school-closures-and-school-re-openings-d593b5c8/

Paechter, M., & Maier, B. (2010). Internet and higher education online or face-to-face? students' experiences and preferences in e-learning. *The Internet and Higher Education*, *13*(4), 292–297. doi:10.1016/j.iheduc.2010.09.004

Paul, J., & Jefferson, F. (2019). A comparative analysis of student performance in an online vs. face-to-face environmental science course from 2009 to 2016. *Frontiers of Computer Science*, *1*(November), 7. Advance online publication. doi:10.3389/fcomp.2019.00007

Paulo, S., Shewbridge, C., Nusche, D., & Herzog, H. D. (2009). Evaluation and assessment frameworks for improving school outcomes: common policy challenges. *Education and Training Policy, 21*, 1–10. https://www.oecd.org/education/school/46927511.pdf

Ribeiro, L., Rosário, P., Núñez, J. C., Gaeta, M., & Fuentes, S. (2019). First-year students background and academic achievement: The mediating role of student engagement. *Frontiers in Psychology*, *10*, 2669. Advance online publication. doi:10.3389/fpsyg.2019.02669 PMID:31920775

RSWEBSOLS. (2021). *Internet connectivity and its impact on students in Australia.* Retrieved October 12, 2021 from https://www.rswebsols.com/tutorials/internet/internet-connectivity-impact-students-australia

Shahibi, M. S., & Ku Rusli, N. K. K. (2017). The influence of internet usage on student's academic performance. *International Journal of Academic Research in Business & Social Sciences*, *7*(8), 873–887. doi:10.6007/IJARBSS/v7-i8/3301

Shen, Q., Chung, J. K. H., Challis, D., & Cheung, R. C. T. (2007). A comparative study of student performance in traditional mode and online mode of learning. *Computer Applications in Engineering Education*, *15*(1), 30–40. doi:10.1002/cae.20092

Shuja, A., Qureshi, A. I., Schaeffer, D. M., & Zareen, M. (2019). Effect of m- learning on students' academic performance mediated by facilitation discourse and flexibility. *Knowledge Management & E-Learning*, *11*(2), 158–200.

Spaulding, M. (2009). Perceptions of academic honesty in online vs. face-to-face classrooms. *Journal of Interactive Online Learning*, *8*(3), 183–198.

Torres-Díaz, J., Duart, J.M., Gómez-Alvarado, H.F., Marín-Gutiérrez, I., & Segarra-Faggioni, V. (2016). Internet use and academic success in university students. *Media Education Research Journal*, 61-70. doi:10.3916/C48-2016-06

Tubulingane, S. B. (2018). *Analysis of the impact of demographic and economic factors on internet services satisfaction levels in Windhoek, Namibia* [Masters Dissertation, University of Namibia]. https://repository.unam.edu.na/bitstream/handle/11070/2304/tubulingane_2018.pdf?sequence=1&isAllowed=y

United Nations. (2020). *Policy brief: education during Covid-19 and beyond.* https://www.un.org/development/desa/dspd/wp-content/uploads/sites/22/2020/08/sg_policy_brief_covid-19_and_education_august_2020.pdf

XINHUANET. (2020). *Namibia to provide laptops, internet access to help college students learn amid COVID-19.* Retrieved October 10, 2021, from http://www.xinhuanet.com/english/2020-06/08/c_139123647.htm

Zolochevskaya, E. Y., Zubanova, S. G., Fedorova, N. V, & Yana, E. (2021). *Education policy: the impact of e-learning on academic performance.* E3S Web of Conferences. doi:10.1051/e3sconf/202124411024

ADDITIONAL READING

Alturki, U., & Aldraiweesh, A. (2021). Application of learning management system (LMS) during the COVID-19 pandemic: A sustainable acceptance model of the expansion technology approach. *Sustainability*, *13*(19), 10991. doi:10.3390u131910991

Belay, D. G. (2020). COVID-19, distance learning and educational inequality in rural Ethiopia. *Pedagogical Research*, *5*(4), em0082. Advance online publication. doi:10.29333/pr/9133

Bunescu, L., & Canham, A. R. (2021). *The impact of COVID-19 on access to online and offline education in the EaP countries.* https://eap-csf.eu/wp-content/uploads/The-impact-of-COVID-19-on-access-to-online-and-offline-education.pdf

Fagbamigbe, A. F., Faris, M. E., França, T., González-Fernández, B., Gonzalez-Robledo, L. M., Inasius, F., Kar, S. K., & Aristovnik, A. (2021). Academic student satisfaction and perceived performance in the e-learning environment during the COVID-19 pandemic: Evidence across ten countries. *PLoS One*, *16*(10), e0258807. Advance online publication. doi:10.1371/journal.pone.0258807 PMID:34669757

Giusti, L., Mammarella, S., Salza, A., Vecchio, S. D., Ussorio, D., Casacchia, M., & Roncone, R. (2021). Predictors of academic performance during the covid-19 outbreak: Impact of distance education on mental health, social cognition and memory abilities in an Italian university student sample. *BMC Psychology*, *9*(1), 142. doi:10.118640359-021-00649-9 PMID:34526153

Gonzalez, T., de la Rubia, M. A., Hincz, K. P., Comas-Lopez, M., Subirats, L., Fort, S., & Sacha, G. M. (2020). Influence of COVID-19 confinement on students' performance in higher education. *PLoS One*, *15*(10), e0239490. Advance online publication. doi:10.1371/journal.pone.0239490 PMID:33035228

Lilian, N., & Chukwuere, J. (2020). *The attitude of students towards plagiarism in online learning: A narrative literature review*. Ife Centre for Psychological Studies/Services.

KEY TERMS AND DEFINITIONS

Academic Performance: The measurement of students' achievement at the end of the academic year.
Contact Learning: Face-to-face classes or learning by students physically on the university campus.
E-Learning: Learning conducted via electronic media, typically on the internet using ICT devices.
Equality: Ensuring that every student has an equal opportunity to improve their academic performance.
Faculty: A group of university departments concerned with a major division of knowledge.
Internet: A global computer network providing a variety of information and communication facilities, consisting of interconnected networks using standardized communication protocols.
Student Social Status: The relative rank that a student holds, with attendant rights, duties, and lifestyle, in a society.

Chapter 4
Entrepreneurship:
Higher Education and Gender – Equity and Access for Inclusive Development

Teresa Dieguez

https://orcid.org/0000-0002-4886-1446

Polytechnic Institute of Cávado and Ave, Portugal

ABSTRACT

Sustainable development has become a buzzword in all fields and domains. Since the Brundtland Report, several attempts to exactly define the meaning of it appeared, even if not always consensual, inclusive, or convergent. However, SD is a holistic notion, encompassing economic, social, cultural, political, and environmental dimensions. Inclusive development is one of the 17 central elements of the Sustainable Development Goals. It follows the United Nations Development Programme's human development approach and joins in the standards and values of human rights. The chapter aims to reflect on the gender inequality problematic and explore how higher education can have an important role on this ongoing process. After a literature review, a co-creation project in IPCA, Portugal is presented. Conclusion seems to point out that education for entrepreneurship, namely through active learning methodologies, can develop the needed 21st century skills, especially if learned in active entrepreneurial education systems and oriented to reach inclusive sustainable development.

INTRODUCTION

Sustainable Development (SD) has become a buzzword in all fields and domains of our daily life (Dieguez, Amador & Porfirio, 2012). Since the Brundtland Report, a publication released in 1987 by the World Commission on Environment and Development (WCED), several attempts to exactly define the meaning of it appeared, even if not always consensual, inclusive, or convergent (Dieguez, 2018). SD is a core concept within global development policy and agenda (Cerin, 2006; Abubakar, 2017), a development paradigm and a thought that calls for improving living standards without risking the earth's ecosystems or causing environmental challenges (Browning & Rigolon, 2019; Mensah& Casadevall,

DOI: 10.4018/978-1-6684-2448-3.ch004

Copyright © 2022, IGI Global. Copying or distributing in print or electronic forms without written permission of IGI Global is prohibited.

Entrepreneurship

2019). It is a holistic notion, encompassing economic, social, cultural, political, and environmental dimensions (Arts, 2017).

Inclusive Development (ID) is one of the 17th central elements of the Sustainable Development Goals (SDGs), kernel keys of the global United Nations (UN) development agenda for the period 2016–2030. ID follows the United Nations Development Programme's (UNDP) human development approach and join in the standards and values of human rights: participation, non-discrimination, and accountability (UNDP, 2021). This relation has been long discussed (Fukuda-Parr, 2004; Darrow, 2012; Sen, 2014) and its dynamics are not fully clear (Fedderke & Klitgaard, 2013; Lettinga & van Troost, 2015). Nonetheless, the awareness that human rights' matter in development efforts is evident (Marks, 2005; Piron & O'Neil, 2016), even if those efforts remain weak in what concerns inequality, discrimination, social exclusion, and marginalization (Arts, 2017). Reports by the UNDP and the annual State of the World's Children reports by UNICEF encourage critical reflexion to confront inequality - e.g., based on age (Dornan, & Woodhead, 2015), disability (Bukola, 2011; Lord, Raja & Blanck, 2013), ethnicity (UNICEF, 2015), sexual orientation or geography (Adepoju, Gberevbie & Ibhawoh, 2021), and gender (Cornwall & Rivas, 2015) - and pursuing inclusive development (Langford, Sumner & Yamin, 2013).

However, in Social Sciences, the term gender is used to describe the social differentiation between women and men (Weeks, 2000; Santos, 2014). From this perspective, labelling someone as a man or woman, male or female (according to a binary view of gender) is a social decision that is related to our beliefs about gender (Nunes, 2016). Additionally, gender is therefore something that is socially constructed, and its understanding varies over time and according to the historical context in which each person is inserted (Connell, 2002; Alexander, John, Hammond & Lahey, 2021). Transsexuality is still a tabu (Merhi, 2021) and this fact is a strong barrier to achieving the human rights. This is mostly because transsexuality is considered a mental disorder (Divan, Cortez, Smelyanskaya & Keatley, 2016) which means that a sustainable solution is needed.

Reflection about these problematics and critical thinking about how Higher Education may have an important and develop strategies to greater inclusion and greater advocacy for human rights. The theme of transsexuality is procedural and therefore needs to be constantly discussed incorporating new contributions. The subject arouses countless debates within different social segments, among which: LGBT militancy groups, NGOs, students, intellectuals, journalists, religious communities and, particularly, among artists (Vianna, 2018). There are several studies that reveals discrimination and harassment trans students experience during their experiences at school (James et al., 2016; Grant et al., 2017). Conversely, there is also research on the ability of university to reinforce the gendered and transphobic treatment that many students have already experienced in school and society, leading to poor academic and psychosocial outcomes: There is also evidence that universities can support and empower these students (who already show signs of resilience to the extent that they have completed high school and enrolled in college), thereby improving academic and personal success. For students who were not in High school as trans, the university can play an important role in facilitating gender identity exploration - for example, by providing the necessary supports and resources to enable students to navigate this process while remaining in university (Goldberg, 2018).

The present chapter aims to reflect about these problematics and explore how Higher Education can have an important role on this ongoing process. In fact, empowerment through entrepreneurship and entrepreneurial education can be excellent tools to help overcome these challenges. After a literature review, one good practice from a co-creation project in IPCA, Portugal is presented, as well as shared an experience of a student who developed a digital worldwide show to survive during Covid-19 and to present its abilities to the world without preconceptions. Conclusion seems to point out that education for entrepreneurship, namely through active learning methodologies, can help the development of the needed 21st century skills, especially if learned in active entrepreneurial education system and oriented to reach the inclusive sustainable development.

LITERATURE REVIEW

Transgender People, Gender Identity, and Gender Expression

Transgender is an umbrella word for persons whose gender identity, gender expression, or behavior does not match to that typically associated with the sex to which they were assigned at birth. Gender identity refers to a person's internal feeling of being male, female, or something else; gender expression refers to the way a person communicates gender identity to others through behavior, clothing, hairstyles, voice, or body characteristics. "Trans" is sometimes used as shorthand for "transgender." While transgender is generally a good term to use, not everyone whose appearance or behavior is gender nonconforming will identify as a transgender person. The ways in which transgender people are talked about in popular culture, academia, and science are constantly changing, particularly as individuals' awareness, knowledge, and openness about transgender people and their experiences grow (APA, 2021).

Gender diversity and its expressions have revealed themselves across different eras and cultures, and the possibility that both biological forces and social evolution may play a part seems to be the reason for it. The diversity of transgender expression and experiences argues against any simple or unitary explanation, seeming to be a biological basis to at least some forms of gender diversity, and a possible genetic component within that. Many experts believe that biological factors such as genetic influences and prenatal hormone levels, early experiences, and experiences later in adolescence or adulthood may all contribute to the development of transgender identities. Where genetics does play a part, the phenotypic expression of any individual is also likely to be influenced greatly by social and other environmental factors. (Wren et al, 2019).

Gender Dysphoria

As previous seen, the terms sex and gender are increasingly controversial and have generated a proliferation of terms whose meanings have varied over time and across disciplines (de Araújo Ribeiro, & de Oliveira, 2021). Gender dysphoria is a cognitive dissatisfaction with one's assigned gender, usually accompanied by dissatisfaction with physical appearance and a negative body image, with a higher incidence among transgender women. It refers to the distress that accompanies the incongruence between experienced and expressed gender and assigned gender. Although not all individuals experience this feeling because of such incongruity, many are distressed if hormonal or surgical intervention processes are not available when attempting the desired physical change. Additionally, in comparison to the general population, individuals with gender dysphoria have higher psychiatric morbidity, improving after initiation of treatment (Dhejne, Van Vlerken, Heylens & Arcelus, 2016).

From this perspective, two concepts emerge: Transgender and Transsexual. Transgender then refers to an individual who, on an ongoing or occasional basis, identifies with a gender other than their birth gender. It is a term for people whose identity, expression or behaviour does not conform to what is gen-

Entrepreneurship

erally associated with the sex they were born into, in the place where they were born. It includes people who consider themselves gender non-identity, multi-gender, androgynous, third gender, concepts without exact definitions, which vary from person to person, but each includes a blending or alternating of the binary concepts of masculinity and femininity (Zucker, Lawrence & Kreukels, 2016). Transsexual, in turn, denotes an individual who seeks, or has undergone, a social transition from male to female or female to male, which in many cases, but not all, also involves a somatic alteration with hormone treatment and genital surgery (sex reassignment surgery). Despite this transition, transsexuals are unable to change their genetic make-up and consequently cannot acquire the reproductive abilities of the sex to which they transition. There are three types of transsexuals: 1) Post-op: an individual who has undergone sexual reassignment surgery (SRS) and is on hormones; 2) Pre-op: an individual who will undergo SRS and is on hormones and 3) Non-op: an individual who does not intend to undergo surgery and is not on hormones (de Oliveira Reis et al, 2021).

Functional Consequences of Gender Dysphoria

Dysphoria can develop at all ages after the first 2 to 3 years of childhood and often interferes with daily activities. In older children, it does not happen so often. From the beginning, problems such as isolation at school, difficulty communicating with others, as well as refusal to attend school because of teasing and harassment or even pressure to dress in clothes associated with their assigned gender rather than the gender they feel comfortable in, arise. In adolescents and adults, the same concern regarding the feeling of "displacement" of self and the desire to be of another gender usually interferes with daily activities, and relationship difficulties then arise, including problems with sexual relationships, or simple school or work interactions, becoming detrimental to the individual (Steensma et al, 2011).

Gender dysphoria, along with expression atypia, is associated with high levels of stigmatisation, discrimination, and victimisation, leading to negative self-concept, increased rates of mental disorder comorbidity, school dropout and economic marginalisation, including unemployment, with high social and mental health risks, especially in individuals from poor families. In addition, these individuals' access to health and mental health services may be impeded by structural barriers, such as institutional discomfort or inexperience in working with this patient population, which ultimately causes more and greater problems for the individual (de Oliveira Reis et al, 2021).

Sexual Reassignment Surgery and its Advantages for the Individual

Sexual Reassignment Surgery (SRS) is the complex surgical procedure by which an individual's birth sex/genital characteristics are changed to those socially associated with the gender with which they identify. This includes not only genital procedures such as vaginoplasty, clitorolabioplasty, penectomy and orchidectomy in male-to-female transsexuals, and penile and scrotal reconstruction in female-to-male transsexuals, but also non-genital procedures such as breast augmentation, mastectomy, facial feminisation surgery, vocal surgery and other masculinisation and feminisation procedures. All patients should be informed about the benefits and risks of surgery and anaesthesia, as well as non-surgical alternatives, to provide informed consent (Fitzgibbons, 2016).

A surgeon should always be guided by two parameters: determining the patient's 'best interests' and 'do no harm'. As such, he or she must always consider whether transgender patients understand the social risks of gender transition surgery, whether the proposed surgery is realistic, and assess and understand whether the patient seems competent to make the decision to have surgery. This surgery can bring advantages to the individual, such as, relief from gender dysphoria symptoms, greater mental stability, increased self-esteem and increased sexual satisfaction, factors that are essential to social and personal stability (Rolle, 2015). Sexual Reassignment, besides surgery, also involves psychotherapy and hormone therapy. It has been shown to be the most effective treatment for patients affected by gender dysphoria (or gender identity disorder), in which patients are not identify with their own gender (sexual identity), the one that is compatible with their genetics.

SRS interventions have, overall, a positive effect on depressive symptoms and may have a protective effect on the individual's mental health. They are reported to be associated with lower rates of psychopathology and, when combined with social support, whether from friends, family or even health professionals, result in a dramatic decrease in the suicide rate in these individuals. It was also described that anxiety and depression are frequent at the beginning of treatment and that better social support was associated with lower intensity of depression. Finally, it was reported that, after surgery, the domain with the greatest improvement was interpersonal relationships. These interactions and improvements in social functioning are mainly associated with the individual's acceptance by others and the individual's own perception that acceptance by others would be easier after surgery, which may also be a reason for the improvement in psychopathology after surgery (Selvaggi & Bellringer, 2011; Lindqvist et al, 2017; Yildizhan et al, 2018).

Entrepreneurship Higher Education and Entrepreneurial Mindset

Entrepreneurship is a crucial element to contest in a worldwide knowledge market (Penco, Ivaldi, Bruzzi & Musso, 2020), as well as creativity (Belitski & Desai, 2016), and innovation (Schumpeter, 2000). The concept is complex (Donaldson, 2021), has no meaning (Pradhan, Arvin, Nair & Bennett, 2020) and has been developing over time (Hisrich, Peters & Shepherd, 2017). In a wider evaluation, entrepreneurship is linked with personal development, creativity, self-confidence, initiative, and action orientation (Lackéus, 2020). In this sense, the meaning and the method used will intensely affect, among others, the objectives of education, the target audience, the courses' content, the teaching method, and the evaluation procedures (Mwasalwiba, 2010).

Higher Education plays an important role in this challenging on-going process (Lans, Blok & Wesselink, 2014), developing competencies that go beyond disciplinary knowledge and encompass skills, knowledge and attitudes oriented towards a holistic and sustainability-driven approach (Wals, 2010). Students are the primary recipients of the entrepreneurship education system and the origin of the human capital development with the required skills for the 21st century (Ghafar, 2020). They are the future leaders of tomorrow, playing a vital role in supporting organizations to outperform their peers, both in terms of competitiveness and sustainability (OECD, 2016).

Entrepreneurship and 21st Century Skills

In a context of globalization and changing, reinforced by huge restrictions due Covid-19 pandemic, Human Capital is more than ever the most powerful key indicator in achieving organizational goals and competitiveness. Graduates must be well prepared with the needed 21st century skills to find solutions, to secure and sustain their career progressions. These skills include creativity, critical thinking, collaboration, leadership, perseverance, and social skills combined with performing effectively as part

Entrepreneurship

of a team (Ghafar, 2020). These are the skills which are embedded in entrepreneurship education that, with its focus on innovation, may create jobs (Komarkova, Conrads & Collado, 2015) and develop entrepreneurial mindsets (Sinkovec & Cizelj, 2013).

The world is changing as well as workplaces, especially due to digital transformation. Individuals must apply knowledge everywhere and at any context. They must deal with dynamic issues and problem solving. They must know how to research and get fluent information in a digital and complex context (Crosling, Nair & Vaithilingam, 2015). Different sources, quick changes, and improvable events among others, demand quick decisions and better ideas (Silva, 2009). Data advocates that young people with a scarce level of skills further restrict equitable economic growth and social cohesion (UNESCO, 2012). And this one of the reasons why the European Commission argue that HEIs should restructure entrepreneurship education to promote the accomplishment and improvement of transversal competencies, as they are more probable to generate social, economic, and environmental value (Komarkova et al., 2015).

However, traditional entrepreneurial education has been commonly associated to operate on a chronologically based methodology, usually linked in current entrepreneurship curricula with a commercial opportunity and following a possible business model (Kuratko & Morris, 2018). A most usual practice in entrepreneurial education is where the arena of entrepreneurship is viewed and taught as an expected science as opposed to the applied discipline (Neck & Greene, 2011). However, recent researchers argue that entrepreneurship embodies the development and transformation of behavioral change that leads to knowledge creation (Mwasalwiba, Dahles & Wakkee, 2012; Yesufu, 2018). Anyhow, it is important to note that when defining entrepreneurship education, one must avoid the "tendencies to apply entrepreneurship based on the mindset that it is distinctive from the status quo and provide a feasible framework to create innovative solutions to any given issue situated in the realm of social and economic dilemma" (Kuratko & Morris, 2018, pg. 14).

Higher Education Institutions and Sustainable Development

There is a unanimity among researchers that HEI play a crucial role in gathering the challenges of sustainable development through education (Dziminsk, Fijałkowska & Sułkowski, 2020). They are perceived as transformational players in many subjects embracing sustainability mindfulness (Mochizuki & Fadeeva, 2010), including soft skills. HEI foster adult skills such as "problem solving, critical thinking, ability to cooperate, creativity, computational thinking, self-regulation, which are more essential than ever before in our quickly changing society" (Council of the European Union 2018, p. 2). Nevertheless, the main difficulty in sustainability education ends from the multidisciplinary context, obliging new approaches (Eizaguirre, García-Feijoo & Laka, 2019). Entrepreneurial competencies and social competencies are both important when graduates want to be more competitive and find job (Lackéus, 2015), as well as professional business ethics and social responsibility (PRME, 2018). HEI contributes to the development of sustainability competencies through both formal (curricular education) and non-formal education (extracurricular activities) (European Commission, 2012).

Education for Sustainable Development is a complex process and demanding a holistic education process attentive on searching for correlations, presenting an intelligible image of the world, and preparing to operate within it (Dziminsk, Fijałkowska & Sułkowski, 2020). For this reason, teaching for sustainable development must be supported by undertaking specific activities that translate into the functioning of the university and its relations with the environment (Kalinowska & Batorczak, 2017). Expectations of the labor market and current socio-economic and civilizational challenges must be presented when curricula are designed. In addition, these demand dialogue between academia and business. In this sense, it is mandatory to support the implementation of sustainability in curricula to accomplish more positive perceptions, change mindsets, and form values and attitudes (Brito, Rodriguez & Aparicio, 2018). Universities' actions may have a positive impact on shaping competencies relevant for solving social and environmental problems (Dieguez, 2021).

Entrepreneurship Entrepreneurial Mindset and Inclusive Development

The world is moving and Covid19 is becoming the particle accelerator of one of the most disruptive workplace changes in latest years (Carnevale & Hatak, 2020). It brought new rules and behaviours, sometimes harmful feelings, and unhappiness (Cacioppo & Hawkley, 2009), but other times generated positive types of behaviour, such as the developing of new skills, new knowledge, and more interaction with one's surroundings (Donthu & Gustafsson, 2020). The forthcoming is indeterminate, and entrepreneurship is a means of transitioning from living to succeeding (Devece, Peris-Ortiz & Rueda-Armengot, 2016; Obschonka, 2016). In this sense, HEI are not only responsible for developing employability attributes that empower lifelong learning and promote it, but also deliver a full range of possible improvements correlated to entrepreneurship education (Barnett, 2017).

Nevertheless, the main goal of most entrepreneurship education rests on the development of entrepreneurial skills (Dieguez, 2017; Dieguez, 2020) which, according to Lans, Blok, & Wesselink (2014), is based on opportunity, social relationship, management, industry specificity and self-efficacy. Active methodologies are recommended to be applied in curricular and extra-curricular units that demand, above all, challenging solutions, and critical and prospective thinking. These kinds of methodologies, by demanding characteristics related to an innovative dynamic, will enhance adaptability, agility, and the capacity to initiate change (Dieguez, Au-Yong-Oliveira, Sobral & Jacquinet, 2021). A transformative mindset is created, reducing the stigma of failure, promoting measured and informed risk-taking, while creating an inclusive environment. In addition, the curricula should lecture gender identity, and explicitly trans identities and experiences (Goldberg, 2018). Students should be provided with education/training to increase their empathetic and acceptance of gender diversity, including nonbinary gender identities (Cohen-Filipic & Flores, 2014).

Training student leaders (e.g., resident advisors; officers of student organizations) is particularly significant, so that these leaders can help to transform campus climate and create respectful spaces for all students (Goldberg, 2018). Faculty/staff (e.g., campus security, dining services, financial aid, and residential life staff) should have mandatory training and resources to generate a more inclusive campus (Goldberg, Beemyn & Smith, 2019). Empowerment through entrepreneurship and entrepreneurial education can be excellent tools to help overcome these challenges (Krüger & David, 2020). As entrepreneurial competences are transversal, they are important not only for those who want to start or run a business, but also for those "who want to achieve change in the individual and collective economic and social environment by expanding their own competences and their ideas in all areas of life" (Krüger & David, 2020, p. 3). Entrepreneurial education can improve entrepreneurial skills not only designed at increasing the number of self-employed, start-ups or companies in general, but in the sense of self-empowerment, helping people to be able to act self-determined in all life situations like an entrepreneur (David, Terstriep & Barwinska-Malajowicz, 2019), including awareness of changes as opportunities, enlarging networking skills, recognising one's own potential, adapting it to the local needs of the respective target regions, and finding alternatives if Plan A does not match with its goals (Krüger & David, 2020).

Entrepreneurship

CASE STUDY

The purpose of this chapter is to reflect about entrepreneurship education and methodologies able to better reduce inequality, discrimination, social exclusion, and marginalization in Higher Education. The aim is to encourage critical reflexion to confront inequality based on gender and following inclusive development. It also seeks to share a good practice from someone who develop a digital worldwide show to survive during Covid-19 and to present its abilities to the world without preconceptions.

Methodology

This chapter presents the co-creation model (students, facilitator, and company) carried out by the Polytechnic Institute of Cávado and Ave (IPCA), in Portugal, among its teachers and students, from all study cycles (CTeSP – short cycles, Bachelor and Master) under the LinkMeUp initiative. Privileging partnerships with the surrounding community, 11 business challenges were accepted, and multidisciplinary teams were formed, with 66 students. Starting in March 2021, in a co-creation context, for 8 weeks and with future-oriented organizations, the students, accompanied by their teachers, identified, and developed complex challenges. This study also exposes some of the main used active and innovative learning methodologies, namely Design Thinking, Double Diamond, Collaborative Learning, Peer Learning, and Challenge-based learning experience, among others.

At the end of the project, three questionnaires were distributed among all those involved (teachers/facilitators, students, and companies) to evaluate mainly the obtained results and the developed skills. As the relation between facilitators and students was very close, it was also possible to do an interview to a transgender student who helped us to understand how these active learning methodologies can, reinforce the equity and the access for gender inclusive development through education for entrepreneurship.

Innovative Co-Creation Project/Process

Based on a holistic approach, the project is characterized by a fusing of active methodologies in a co-creation environment, where participants can develop with greater focus some of the needed skills for the 21st century, namely: improving pedagogical practices, explore the co-creation process, close the gap between academy and market, improve communication and collaboration, as well as solving real challenges with teams of students and members of external organizations. Having always in mind the interest of stimulate students into having reflective thinking and a scientific spirit, the project also triggers bases of entrepreneurial mindset development, providing all participants with transversal skills, essential for successful collaborative work in the workplace market. Based on the proximity between the Polytechnic Institute of Cávado and Ave (IPCA) and the local community, a pool is created (companies and non-profit organizations), where all the challenges (economic and societal with a focus on future megatrends) that institutions make to the educational community are placed. Additionally, an opportunity is opened for students to apply to the project and choose the challenges with which they most identify. After a selection based on pre-defined and rigorous criteria, students are selected according to their background and profile. The motivation letter is one of the most important elements in the process, and communication in English is required. The teams should be multidisciplinary and from various study cycles. The desirable number of students per team is 5 to 6 elements.

After selecting the students, an IPCA Teacher and the representative of the institution that posed the challenge become the Facilitators of the co-creation project. Starting with a meeting where all the elements of the team get to know each other, the institution launches the challenge and presents the problem it intends to overcome. An agenda is agreed among all partners, normally in defined in short weekly periods, for quick briefings and critical thinking on the work developed so far. Instructions are given on the methodology and objectives to be achieved each week. Regarding the students' role, a greater involvement is sought, estimated at an average of 8 to 10 hours per week. Students should start by making a personal mind map and a mind map about their understanding of the challenge, followed by a PESTLE analysis. The genesis of the co-creation project lies in the understanding of the phenomenon, its context, and the people in it. In this sense, the mapping of stakeholders, the research design, and the collection of insights are done. Through interviews, an attempt is made to identify the motivation for people's behaviours, namely regarding intention, values, and attitudes, as well as driving forces that move the selected groups. With observations, students identify some details that were not mentioned in the interviews. In doing general research, through benchmarking exercises and reading online industry reports, they gain inspiration for a more holistic approach. In the following stages, students try to identify the megatrends and signals that are likely to condition the industry/activity they are analysing, to construct/shape a long-term solution that is proactive rather than reactive. Scenarios are built with possible solutions, the results are discussed, and a report is written. The results of all co-creation projects are also presented in a final pitch session to share best practices, getting community near to Higher Education and build new mindsets.

Evaluation and Discussion of Results

This project using active methodologies has managed to capture the attention of the involved students and institutions that pose the challenges to the IPCA universe.

Direct and Visible Outputs

Outputs from the co-creation project resulted in 11 business challenges, 11 multidisciplinary teams, involving a total of 66 students, 11 companies and 11 Teachers/facilitators. All those involved were very enthusiastic about the discovery process and the new perspectives that were opening. Using a lot of visual registering, the development of the solution was always done in a collaborative way, preferably on the platform "Miro" (miro.com), Teams and Discord. At the end of this Project, students were able to: i) communicate information, ideas, problems and solutions to specialized and non-specialized audiences with clarity; ii) identify meaningful insights from noise; iii) apply critical thinking; iv) propose solutions to real societal problems and challenges that require innovation and a diverse set of skills; v) work in multidisciplinary and co-creation environments; vi) work on a creative problem solving concepts, design thinking models and tools to solve learning challenges and vii) identify and define complex problems and understand the value chains in different solutions.

For teachers/facilitators, the project also contributed to: i) develop and enhance the skills and interconnection between teachers; ii) improve the communication and collaboration, as well as interaction with external entities; iii) experiment and introduce pedagogical practices, namely through new tools and methods, interaction and cooperation; iv) solve real challenges with teams of students and members of an external organization (company, unit, etc.); v) contribute to the continuous improvement of the

Entrepreneurship

teaching-learning process and exploring the co-creation process: as facilitators and co-creators; vi) iv) work autonomously while strengthening the soft skills of critical thinking, communication, teamwork and collaboration.

Results from Questionnaires

Results from questionnaires allow drafting a summary of the main obtained conclusions. In this sense, in what concerns:

- Teachers/facilitators: 60% of the respondents agree that their experience in the project expanded the benefit of developing a new type of teaching and learning environment as well as new opportunities for cooperation. All of them agree that their participation boosts the improvement of training skills and teaching methods. 70% of them agree that participation in the project expands cooperation with the business market and the community.

When asked about the perceived benefit of their participation in the project, the main ideas are reflected upon the following illustrative sentences:

- "In personal terms it reinforced my positive perception of this type of methodology. In professional terms, it has increased team spirit"
- "Possibility of multidisciplinary interaction, inter-school cooperation as a way of establishing new connections and the challenge of solving an identified problem together with business entities"
- "The opportunity to bring together an interdisciplinary team, making communicate my knowledge and pedagogy to other training areas"
- "Knowing innovative methods of value creation. Openness to new analysis techniques. Promoting teamwork. Contact with companies and their search for innovation. Promote in students' greater openness to other learning methods"
- "Participation in the project was another opportunity to test and validate processes"
- "Pedagogical innovation"
- "Critical thinking"
- "Creative and dynamic"
- "Participation in the project gave me a new perspective of learning that is, being a teacher, I am used to controlling what students should learn and in what way. In this project, the teacher's role is different: that of a facilitator. This transition from teacher to facilitator requires a change of mentality on my part. This change of mentality requires reflection, which obviously makes me question in which situations in my teaching practice I can integrate this new way of guiding students towards learning. Being a mathematics teacher, a subject that requires a lot of structuring in knowledge, it is not always easy or possible. But at least I am forced to reflect on the matter"
- Companies: 40% of the respondents strongly agree that participation in the project expands the benefit associated with professional support in a fully facilitated environment for an innovation model based on co-creation. All agree that they have access to new knowledge, new perspectives, and new ideas. 40% of them report having the advantage of access to talent for possible hiring.

69

Entrepreneurship

When asked about the perceived benefit of their participation in the project, the main ideas are reflected upon the following illustrative sentences:

- "Knowledge sharing and methodological approach"
- "Interaction with the university"
- "Contacts with other training entities".
- "Access to talent for possible employment".
- "Networking
- Students: 87.5% of the respondents consider their participation in the project very productive and 62.5% of them believe that the change of attitude towards new challenges after participation in the project was very productive, as well as the emergence of new business ideas. Is very productive, 75% consider that the contribution of co-creation enhancing the ability to work in a multidisciplinary and multicultural team as well as the development of creativity skills. Nevertheless, only 62.5% of the participants consider having developed technical skills. All recommend the co-creation experience to friends and colleague.

When asked about the perceived benefit of their participation in the project, the main ideas are reflected upon the following illustrative sentences:

- "Networking and critical thinking"
- "New methodologies, techniques and tools#
- "Creativity development and access to design thinking methodologies"
- "English skills improvement"
- "Teamwork in an multidisciplinary environment"
- "Better communication with colleagues, teachers and companies'"
- "Possibility of present my ideas and thoughts without ties and constrains"
- "Possibility of think and communicate my ideas without barriers"
- "Vision about future"
- "Awareness of our power as citizen able to shape the desired future"

Experience Shares from Specific Interview Post Project

During the co-creation project, some students had the opportunity to work closer and to find business opportunities. Fruit of their research and necessary fieldwork to solve the problem posed by the companies, students needed to work at least 8 to 10 h a week. Being multidisciplinary teams, all participants had to use their talents and skills to come up with innovative and different solutions. In what concern their motivation to participate in the co-creation project, the reasons were very diverse, including issues related to financial aspects (those who participated won a scholarship), curiosity, the desire to learn new things and desire to travel, among others. One of the obligatory weekly exercises was to do brainstorming, exercises that by nature do not contemplate barriers or include criticism. In addition, it allows individuals to expose themselves and, as they participate, a greater team spirit and sense of belonging is created. From the student survey responses, all felt it was worthwhile participating and would recommend their participation to friends and family. As these are multidisciplinary teams, sometimes more basic techniques in their areas of specialisation are highly valued by peers from other areas of knowledge. In

70

Entrepreneurship

addition, these situations often help individuals to create self-esteem and to realise that they can do and create very interesting and differentiating projects.

One student participating in the project discovered how "cool" and communicative he was when he built solutions and had interesting ideas and insights for the co-creation project. His team then convinced him to use his talent and promote it on social networks. Why not to do small shows, using streaming sessions, where he could reach out more and take a message of joy and positivity, to people whom, due to the confinement caused by Covid-19, were isolated. At first, the student thought the challenge was a joke because they were already working in a good team environment and did not leave their place of comfort. However, as the process of co-creation progressed, he investigated and realised how the world was changing and that perhaps the challenge set by these colleagues was something achievable and doable after all. Why not to use his technical skills and its soft skills to give joy and maybe get money? In addition, this is what happened. In fact, the student opened a YouTube channel and nowadays has 50.000 followers and is presented in Facebook, Instagram, and Twitter. He is someone from arts (performative) and have an online business where he sell product for the activity, namely make up and customs.

When inquired about its success nowadays, he says that the participation in the co-creation project is was definitively the big trigger as it gave him wings and mind set to follow his dreams, to believe in his self-efficacy, in his critical thinking and detection of opportunities. He also believes that he acquired respect from his peers, because he was evaluated not because of his gender or figure, but because of his expertise and his empowerment in the project. He strongly believes that entrepreneurship education can truly help citizen feel more included and happier. However, he is aware of the barriers and difficulties that exist on Higher Education Institutions, and those barriers come from the traditional way of teaching entrepreneurship and the way society see people different from typical norms. A long journey is needed, but it is important that Higher Education feel its key role in the changing process.

SOLUTIONS AND RECOMMENDATIONS

Higher Education Institutions still don´t really face how important is for trans students social and emotional well-being to have *curricula* addressed to gender identity, and specifically trans identities and experiences. Students, teachers, and staff should be provided with education/training to enhance their understanding and acceptance of gender diversity-including nonbinary gender identities. Students should be able to have the option to change their gender marker on campus records and documents without having to change their gender marker first on legal documents.

FUTURE RESEARCH DIRECTIONS

Transgender's students are often a marginalized or complete ignored voice in the broader Higher Education and student affairs literature. Future studies may try to understand the different perceptions that the diverse actors within HEIs have on this issue. It would also be interesting to survey the policies that are already implemented and thought out in HEIs, as well as to try to understand whether the country's/ region culture is a determining factor in the development process.

CONCLUSION

The future is uncertain and the collaboration between Higher Education Institutions (HEI) and the local business community is crucial for the development of the region and the well-being of the people. The challenges are very significant, and success is strongly dependent on the quality of the human capital that goes out into the market. HEIs, through these co-creation projects, can make a very valid and highly differentiating contribution. They can develop new active learning methodologies, able to include students in real problems to find solutions. New skills are needed today because the world is changing too much and too quick. Critical thinking, problem solving, creativity, innovation empathy and social skills are, more than ever, needed. Students must be prepared for future workplace but also having a proactive role in their community. Inclusion, Human rights, equity, opportunity, ethics, and sustainable development are thematic that should be though in universities. The future depends on the present and the way HEI faces entrepreneurship education can be determinant. Active methodologies can also be applied in curricular and extra-curricular units that demand, above all, challenging solutions, and critical and prospective thinking. This methodology, by demanding characteristics related to an innovative dynamic, will enhance adaptability, agility, and the capacity to initiate change, namely in what concerns gender equity and access for inclusive development. A transformative mindset is created, reducing the stigma of failure, and promoting measured and informed risk-taking.

REFERENCES

Abubakar, I. R. (2017). Access to sanitation facilities among Nigerian households: Determinants and sustainability implications. *Sustainability*, *9*(4), 547. doi:10.3390u9040547

Adepoju, O. A., Gberevbie, D. E., & Ibhawoh, B. (2021). Culture and women participation in peacebuilding in Africa: Perspectiva of national culture and social roles theories. *Academy of Strategic Management Journal*, *20*(3), 1–8.

Alexander, G. M., John, K., Hammond, T., & Lahey, J. (2021). Living Up to a Name: Gender Role Behavior Varies with Forename Gender Typicality. *Frontiers in Psychology*, *11*, 4038. doi:10.3389/fpsyg.2020.604848 PMID:33551916

American Psychological Association. (2006). *Answers to Your Questions about Transgender People, Gender identity, and Gender expression*. Retrieved from https://www.apa.org/topics/lgbtq/transgender.pdf

Arts, K. (2017). Inclusive sustainable development: A human rights perspective. *Current Opinion in Environmental Sustainability*, *24*, 58–62. doi:10.1016/j.cosust.2017.02.001

Barnett, R. (2017). *The Ecological University a Feasible Utopia*. Routledge. doi:10.4324/9781315194899

Belitski, M., & Desai, S. (2016). Creativity, entrepreneurship and economic development: City-level evidence on creativity spillover of entrepreneurship. *The Journal of Technology Transfer*, *41*(6), 1354–1376. doi:10.100710961-015-9446-3

Brito, R. M., Rodriguez, C., & Aparicio, J. L. (2018). Sustainability in Teaching: An Evaluation of University Teachers and Students. *Sustainability*, *10*(2), 439. doi:10.3390u10020439

Entrepreneurship

Browning, M. H., & Rigolon, A. (2019). School green space and its impact on academic performance: A systematic literature review. *International Journal of Environmental Research and Public Health*, *16*(3), 429. doi:10.3390/ijerph16030429 PMID:30717301

Bukola, R. A. (2011). Poverty and the realization of the millennium development goals in Nigeria: Disability rights the missing link. *East African Journal of Peace and Human Rights*, *17*(2), 532–550.

Cacioppo, J. T., & Hawkley, L. C. (2009). Perceived social isolation and cognition. *Trends in Cognitive Sciences*, *13*(10), 447–454. doi:10.1016/j.tics.2009.06.005 PMID:19726219

Carnevale, J. B., & Hatak, I. (2020). Employee adjustment and well-being in the era of COVID-19: Implications for human resource management. *Journal of Business Research*, *116*, 183–187. doi:10.1016/j.jbusres.2020.05.037 PMID:32501303

Cerin, P. (2006). Bringing economic opportunity into line with environmental influence: A discussion on the Coase theorem and the Porter and van der Linde hypothesis. *Ecological Economics*, *56*(2), 209–225. doi:10.1016/j.ecolecon.2005.01.016

Cohen-Filipic, J., & Flores, L. Y. (2014). Best practices in providing effective supervision to students with values conflicts. *Psychology of Sexual Orientation and Gender Diversity*, *1*(4), 302–309. doi:10.1037gd0000073

Connell, R. W. (2002). *Gender*. Polity Press.

Cornwall, A., & Rivas, A. M. (2015). From 'gender equality and 'women's empowerment' to global justice: Reclaiming a transformative agenda for gender and development. *Third World Quarterly*, *36*(2), 396–415. doi:10.1080/01436597.2015.1013341

Council of the European Union. (2018). Annex to the council recommendation of 22 May 2018 on key competences for lifelong learning: Key competences for lifelong learning, a European reference framework. *Official Journal of the European Union*, *189*, 7–13.

Crosling, G., Nair, M., & Vaithilingam, S. (2015). A creative learning ecosystem, quality of education and innovative capacity: A perspective from higher education. *Studies in Higher Education*, *40*(7), 1147–1163. doi:10.1080/03075079.2014.881342

Darrow, M. (2012). The millennium development goals: Milestones or millstones-human rights priorities for the post-2015 development agenda. *Yale Human Rights and Development Law Journal*, *15*, 55.

David, A., Terstriep, J., & Barwinska-Malajowicz, A. (2019b). Brexit und seine folgen für die europäische migration: empowerment als mögliche antwort? eine reflexion. In A. David, M. Evans, I. Hamburg, & J. Terstriep (Eds.), *Migration und Arbeit: Herausforderungen, Problemlagen und Gestaltungsinstrumente* (pp. 359–386). Verlag Barbara Budrich. doi:10.2307/j.ctvg5bt77.18

de Araújo Ribeiro, É. F., & de Oliveira, E. G. (2021). Transfobia na educação: O olhar da estudante transgênero feminino. *Research. Social Development*, *10*(4), e34310414272–e34310414272. doi:10.33448/rsd-v10i4.14272 de Oliveira Reis, P. S., das Neves, A. L. M., Therense, M., Sant, E. J., Honorato, A., & Teixeira, E. (2021). Veiled transphobia: nurses-created meanings vis-à-vis the user embracement of transvestites and transgenders [Transfobia velada: sentidos produzidos por enfermeiros (as) sobre o acolhimento de travestis e transexuais]. *Revista de Pesquisa: Cuidado é Fundamental Online, 13*, 80-85.

Devece, C., Peris-Ortiz, M., & Rueda-Armengot, C. (2016). Entrepreneurship during economic crisis: Success factors and paths to failure. *Journal of Business Research, 69*(11), 5366–5370. doi:10.1016/j.jbusres.2016.04.139

Dhejne, C., Van Vlerken, R., Heylens, G., & Arcelus, J. (2016). Mental health and gender dysphoria: A review of the literature. *International Review of Psychiatry (Abingdon, England), 28*(1), 44–57. doi:10.3109/09540261.2015.1115753 PMID:26835611

Dieguez, T. (2017). Empowering Hub. In N. Baporikar (Ed.), Handbook of Knowledge Integration Strategies for Entrepreneurship and Sustainability. Academic Press.

Dieguez, T. (2018). Growth or Development? A Sustainable Approach. *Economic Research Journal, 2*(8), 38–46.

Dieguez, T. (2020). Operationalization of Circular Economy: A Conceptual Model. In *Handbook of Research on Entrepreneurship Development and Opportunities in Circular Economy* (pp. 38–60). IGI Global. doi:10.4018/978-1-7998-5116-5.ch003

Dieguez, T. (2021). Collective Approach and Best Practices to Develop Skills for the Post-COVID Era. In *Handbook of Research on Strategies and Interventions to Mitigate COVID-19 Impact on SMEs* (pp. 23–47). IGI Global. doi:10.4018/978-1-7998-7436-2.ch002

Dieguez, T., Amador, F., & Porfirio, J. (2012). The balance between the supply of the Portuguese Higher Education Institutions and the emerging challenges of sustainable development: the case of automotive suppliers' industry. In *Proceedings of ICERI2012 (Fifth International Conference of Education, Research and Innovation)* (pp. 3485-3496). Academic Press.

Dieguez, T., Au-Yong-Oliveira, M., Sobral, T., & Jacquinet, M. (2021). Entrepreneurship and Changing Mindsets: a success story. In *International Conference on Applied Management Advances in the 21st Century (AMA21)*. International Association for Development of the Information Society.

Divan, V., Cortez, C., Smelyanskaya, M., & Keatley, J. (2016). Transgender social inclusion and equality: A pivotal path to development. *Journal of the International AIDS Society, 19*, 20803. doi:10.7448/IAS.19.3.20803 PMID:27431473

Donaldson, C. (2021). Culture in the entrepreneurial ecosystem: A conceptual framing. *The International Entrepreneurship and Management Journal, 17*(1), 289–319. doi:10.100711365-020-00692-9

Donthu, N., & Gustafsson, A. (2020). Effects of COVID-19 on business and research. *Journal of Business Research, 117*(September), 284–289. doi:10.1016/j.jbusres.2020.06.008 PMID:32536736

Dornan, P., & Woodhead, M. (2015). *How inequalities develop through childhood: Life-course evidence from young lives cohort study*. Academic Press.

Entrepreneurship

Dziminsk, M., Fijałkowska, J., & Sułkowski, L. (2020). A Conceptual Model Proposal: Universities as Culture Change Agents for Sustainable Development. *Sustainability, 12*(11), 4635. doi:10.3390u12114635

Eizaguirre, A., García-Feijoo, M., & Laka, J. P. (2019). Defining sustainability core competencies in business and management studies based on multinational stakeholders' perceptions. *Sustainability, 11*(8), 2303. doi:10.3390u11082303

European Commission. (2012). *Proposal for a Council Recommendation on the Validation of Non-Formal and Informal Learning*. European Commission.

Fedderke, J., & Klitgaard, R. (2013). How much do rights matter? *World Development, 51*, 187–206. doi:10.1016/j.worlddev.2013.05.009

Fitzgibbons, R. P. (2016). Transsexual attractions and sexual reassignment surgery: Risks and potential risks. *The Linacre Quarterly, 83*(2), 337–350. doi:10.1080/00243639.2015.1125574a PMID:26997675

Fukuda-Parr, S. (2004). *Human development report 2004: Cultural liberty in today's diverse world*. Human Development Report.

Ghafar, A. (2020). Convergence between 21st century skills and entrepreneurship education in higher education institutes. *International Journal of Higher Education, 9*(1), 218–229. doi:10.5430/ijhe.v9n1p218

Goldberg, A. E. (2018). *Transgender students in higher education*. Accessed on 7 August 2021, through https://williamsinstitute.law.ucla.edu/publications/trans-students-higher-education/

Goldberg, A. E., Beemyn, G., & Smith, J. Z. (2019). What is needed, what is valued: Trans students' perspectives on trans-inclusive policies and practices in higher education. *Journal of Educational & Psychological Consultation, 29*(1), 27–67. doi:10.1080/10474412.2018.1480376

Grant, J., Mottet, L., Tanis, J., Harrison, J., Herman, J., & Keisling, M. (2011). *Injustice at every turn: A Report of the National Transgender Discrimination Survey*. National Center for Transgender Equality and National Gay and Lesbian Task Force.

Hisrich, R. D., Peters, M. P., & Shepherd, D. A. (2017). *Entrepreneurship*. McGraw-Hill Education.

James, S., Herman, J., Rankin, S., Keisling, M., Mottet, L., & Anaf, M. (2016). *The report of the 2015 US Transgender Survey*. National Center for Transgender Equality.

Kabir, M. N. (2019). *Knowledge-Based Social Entrepreneurship: Understanding Knowledge Economy, Innovation, and the Future of Social Entrepreneurship*. Springer. doi:10.1057/978-1-137-34809-8

Kalinowska, A., & Batorczak, A. (2017). Uczelnie wyˊzsze wobec wyzwaˊn celów zrównowaˊzonego rozwoju. Zeszyty Naukowe Politechniki Slˌaskiej. *Organizacja i Zarzˌadzaniez, 104*, 281–290.

Komarkova, I., Conrads, J., & Collado, A. (2015). *Entrepreneurship Competence: An Overview of Existing Concepts. Policies and Initiatives*. JRC Science Hub.

Krüger, D., & David, A. (2020, February). Entrepreneurial education for persons with disabilities—a social innovation approach for inclusive ecosystems. Frontiers in Education, 5, 3.

Kuratko, D. F., & Morris, M. H. (2018). Examining the future trajectory of entrepreneurship. *Journal of Small Business Management, 56*(1), 11–23. doi:10.1111/jsbm.12364

Lackéus, M. (2015). Entrepreneurship in Education: What, Why, When, How. *Long Range Planning, 48*, 215–227.

Lackéus, M. (2020). Comparing the impact of three different experiential approaches to entrepreneurship in education. *International Journal of Entrepreneurial Behaviour & Research, 26*(5), 937–971. doi:10.1108/IJEBR-04-2018-0236

Langford, M., Sumner, A., & Yamin, A. E. (Eds.). (2013). *The Millennium Development Goals and Human Rights: Past, Present and Future.* Cambridge University Press. doi:10.1017/CBO9781139410892

Lans, T., Blok, V., & Wesselink, R. (2014). Learning apart and together: Towards an integrated competence framework for sustainable entrepreneurship in higher education. *Journal of Cleaner Production, 62*, 37–47. doi:10.1016/j.jclepro.2013.03.036

Lettinga, D., & van Troost, L. (Eds.). (2015). *Can Human Rights Bring Social Justice?: Twelve Essays.* Amnesty International Netherlands.

Lindqvist, E., Sigurjonsson, H., Möllermark, C., Rinder, J., Farnebo, F., & Lundgren, T. (2017, June). Quality of life improves early after gender reassignment surgery in transgender women. *European Journal of Plastic Surgery, 40*(3), 223–226. doi:10.100700238-016-1252-0 PMID:28603386

Lord, J. E., Raja, D. S., & Blanck, P. (2013). Beyond the orthodoxy of rule of law and justice sector reform: A framework for legal empowerment and innovation through the convention on the rights of persons with disabilities. *World Bank Legal Review, 4*, 45.

Marks, S.P. (2005). The human rights framework for development: Seven approaches. *Reflections on the Right to Development*, 23-60.

Mensah, J., & Casadevall, S. R. (2019). Sustainable development: Meaning, history, principles, pillars, and implications for human action: Literature review. *Cogent Social Sciences, 5*(1), 1653531. doi:10.1080/23311886.2019.1653531

Merhi, T. E. T. C. (2021). Transexualidade na atenção primária de saúde: Um relato de experiência em uma unidade de uma cidade em Goiás. *Brazilian Journal of Development, 7*(1), 7074–7082. doi:10.34117/bjdv7n1-479

Mochizuki, Y., & Fadeeva, Z. (2010). Competences for sustainable development and sustainability: Significance and challenges for ESD. *International Journal of Sustainability in Higher Education, 11*(4), 391–403. doi:10.1108/14676371011077603

Mwasalwiba, E., Dahles, H., & Wakkee, I. (2012). Graduate Entrepreneurship in Tanzania: Contextual Enablers and Hindrances. *European Journal of Scientific Research, 76*, 386–402.

Mwasalwiba, E. S. (2010). Entrepreneurship education: A review of its objectives, teaching methods, and impact indicators. *Education + Training, 52*(1), 20–47. doi:10.1108/00400911011017663

Entrepreneurship

Neck, H. M., & Greene, P. G. (2011). Entrepreneurship education: Known worlds and new Frontiers. *Journal of Small Business Management, 49*(1), 55–70. doi:10.1111/j.1540-627X.2010.00314.x

Nunes, L. R. (2016). *Metamorfoses: identidades e papéis de género. Um estudo com Transhomens* [Master's thesis]. Universidade de Évora, Portugal.

Obschonka, M., Stuetzer, M., Audretsch, D. B., Rentfrow, P. J., Potter, J., & Gosling, S. D. (2016). Macropsychological Factors Predict Regional Economic Resilience during a Major Economic Crisis. *Social Psychological & Personality Science, 7*(2), 95–104. doi:10.1177/1948550615608402

OECD. (2016). *Innovating Education and Educating for Innovation: The Power of Digital Technologies and Skills.* OECD Publishing. doi:10.1787/9789264265097-

Penco, L., Ivaldi, E., Bruzzi, C., & Musso, E. (2020). Knowledge-based urban environments and entrepreneurship: Inside EU cities. *Cities (London, England), 96*, 102443. doi:10.1016/j.cities.2019.102443

Piron, L. H., & O'Neil, T. (2016). Integrating human rights into development: donor approaches, experiences and challenges (No. 111914). The World Bank.

Pradhan, R. P., Arvin, M. B., Nair, M., & Bennett, S. E. (2020). Sustainable economic growth in the European Union: The role of ICT, venture capital, and innovation. *Review of Financial Economics, 38*(1), 34–62. doi:10.1002/rfe.1064

PRME. (2018). *Search Participants.* Principles for Responsible Management Education. Available online: http: //www.unprme.org/participation/index.php

Rolle, L., Ceruti, C., Timpano, M., Falcone, M., & Frea, B. (2015). Quality of life after sexual reassignment surgery. In *Management of Gender Dysphoria* (pp. 193–203). Springer. doi:10.1007/978-88-470-5696-1_23

Santos, W. S. (2014). Uma reflexão pós-crítica sobre corpo, gênero, sexualidade no ambiente educacional. *Revista Sem Aspas, 3*(1), 7.

Schumpeter, J.A. (2000). Entrepreneurship as innovation. *Entrepreneurship: The social science view,* 51-75.

Selvaggi, G., & Bellringer, J. (2011). Gender reassignment surgery: An overview. *Nature Reviews. Urology, 8*(5), 274–282. doi:10.1038/nrurol.2011.46 PMID:21487386

Sen, A. (2014). Development as freedom (1999). *The globalization and development reader: Perspectives on development and global change,* 525.

Silva, E. (2009). Measuring skills for 21st century learning. *Phi Delta Kappan, 90*(9), 630–634. doi:10.1177/003172170909000905

Sinkovec, B., & Cizelj, B. (2013). *Entrepreneurial Education & Innovation: Developing Entrepreneurial Mindset for knowledge Economy.* University of Wolverhampton, Knowledge Economy Network (KEN). Retrieved from https://www.knowledge-economy.net/uploads/documents/2013/workshops/wolverhampton/Wolverhampton%20Workshop%20-%20Analytical%20Compendium.pdf

Steensma, T. D., Biemond, R., de Boer, F., & Cohen-Kettenis, P. T. (2011). Desisting and persisting gender dysphoria after childhood: A qualitative follow-up study. *Clinical Child Psychology and Psychiatry*, *16*(4), 499–516. doi:10.1177/1359104510378303 PMID:21216800

UNDP. (2017). *Inclusive Development*. Accessed on 15th July 2021, through http://www.undp.org/content/undp/en/home/ourwork/povertyreduction/focus_areas/focus_inclusive_development.html

UNESCO. (2012). *Youth and skills: Putting education to work*. Retrieved from https://unesdoc.unesco.org/ark:/48223/pf0000218003

UNICEF. (2015). *For every child, a fair chance: The promise of equity*. UNICEF.

Vianna, C. (2018). *Políticas de educação, gênero e diversidade sexual: Breve história de lutas, danos e resistências*. Autêntica.

Wals, A. E. (2010). Mirroring, Gestaltswitching and transformative social learning: Stepping stones for developing sustainability competence. *International Journal of Sustainability in Higher Education*, *11*(4), 380–390. doi:10.1108/14676371011077595

Weeks, J. (2000). O Corpo e a sexualidade. In G. L. Louro (Ed.), *O corpo educado* (pp. 35–82). Autêntica.

Wren, B., Launer, J., Reiss, M. J., Swanepoel, A., & Music, G. (2019). Can evolutionary thinking shed light on gender diversity? *BJPsych Advances*, *25*(6), 351–362. doi:10.1192/bja.2019.35

Yesufu, L. O. (2018). Motives and Measures of Higher Education Internationalisation: A Case Study of a Canadian University. *International Journal of Higher Education*, *7*(2), 155–168. doi:10.5430/ijhe.v7n2p155

Yildizhan, B. Ö., Yüksel, Ş., Avayu, M., Noyan, H., & Yildizhan, E. (2018). Effects of Gender Reassignment on Quality of Life and Mental Health in People with Gender Dysphoria. *Türk Psikiyatri Dergisi*, *29*(1). PMID:29730870

Zucker, K. J., Lawrence, A. A., & Kreukels, B. P. (2016). Gender dysphoria in adults. *Annual Review of Clinical Psychology*, *12*(1), 217–247. doi:10.1146/annurev-clinpsy-021815-093034 PMID:26788901

ADDITIONAL READING

Asumah, S. N., & Nagel, M. (Eds.). (2014). *Diversity, social justice, and inclusive excellence: Transdisciplinary and global perspectives*. SUNY Press.

Stewart, A. J., & Valian, V. (2018). *An inclusive academy: Achieving diversity and excellence*. Mit Press. doi:10.7551/mitpress/9766.001.0001

Tarantino, S. (2021). Empowering Entrepreneurship. In Under Pressure (pp. 125-132). Routledge. doi:10.4324/9781003038375-15

Vijeyarasa, R. (Ed.). (2021). *International Women's Rights Law and Gender Equality: Making the Law Work for Women*. Routledge. doi:10.4324/9781003091257

Entrepreneurship

KEY TERMS AND DEFINITIONS

Culture: Is a social pattern that is heritage within a society. It determines what is important and unimportant, right, and wrong, acceptable, and unacceptable. Culture includes explicit and tacit values, norms, attitudes, beliefs, behaviors and assumptions.

Entrepreneurship: It is a way of thinking, reasoning, and acting that is obsessed in opportunity, all-inclusive in method and where leadership is connected to create and retain value.

Gender Equality: Is the absence of discrimination based on a person's sex in opportunities, the allocation of resources and benefits, or access to services.

Gender Equity: Refers to the fairness and justice in the distribution of benefits and responsibilities between women and men. The concept recognizes that women and men have different needs and power, and that these differences should be identified and addressed in a manner that rectifies the imbalance between the sexes.

Human Rights: Rights inherent to all human beings, regardless of race, sex, nationality, ethnicity, language, religion, or any other status. Human rights include the right to life and liberty, freedom from slavery and torture, freedom of opinion and expression, the right to work and education, and many more. Everyone is entitled to these rights, without discrimination.

Inclusive Development: Development that includes marginalized people, sectors and countries in social, political and economic processes for increased human well-being, social and environmental sustainability, and empowerment. Inclusive development is an adaptive learning process, which responds to change and new risks of exclusion and marginalization.

Inclusive Growth: Growth that not only creates new economic opportunities, but also one that ensures equal access to the opportunities created for all segments of society, particularly for the poor.

Sustainable Development: Development that meets the needs of the present without compromising the ability of future generations to meet their own needs.

Sustainable Entrepreneurship: SUSTAINABLE entrepreneurship is a business strategy focused on increasing value for society, the environment and the company or business.

Transgender: A person whose gender identity differs from the sex the person had or was identified as having at birth.

Chapter 5

Exploring Ethical Consumption for Equity and Inclusiveness:
Bridging Thoughts and Action of Consumers

Sneha Kadyan
O. P. Jindal Global University, India

Jagbir Singh Kadyan
https://orcid.org/0000-0002-1882-0643
Swami Shraddhanand College, University of Delhi, India

ABSTRACT

This chapter is directed at examining this gap in everyday practices and is a step towards bridging thoughts and action of consumers towards sustainable social change. Utilizing a qualitative approach, purchasing practices of consumers with strong beliefs about ethical consumption are critically assessed to examine how individuals think and act with respect to their purchasing decisions. The findings of this chapter suggest that transparency and communication of the ethical investment of consumers in purchasing and consuming ethical products needs to be more pronounced for thoughts to reflect in ethical conscious practices.

INTRODUCTION

Production for economic growth and profit is the force driving global economic production across the world. As the economy has opened with liberalization, export and global transactions are giving rise to global production networks around the world. However, the economy functions from within a socio-cultural and political system spanning across, regions, countries, cultures, and traditions. As stated by Berndt and Boeckler (2009:536), "markets do not simply fall out of thin air but are continually produced and constructed socially with the help of actors who are interlinked in dense and extensive webs of

DOI: 10.4018/978-1-6684-2448-3.ch005

Exploring Ethical Consumption for Equity and Inclusiveness

social relations" In this paper, attention will be given to the consumption aspect of the global economic processes as well as to how it functions as a cardinal structure upon which the whole system operates.

Specifically focusing upon the organization of consumption is of significance as it becomes the major determinant of global manufacturing patterns that sustain and are responsible for such thriving production processes across the world. In the present age of high mass consumption, consumption beliefs, attitudes and practices have profound implications for quality of life for present and future generations (Kilbourne et al. 1997, Harrison et al. 2005). Its ever-growing importance can even be seen by the rise in alternative market movements in the 1970s such as Fairtrade that rely on significantly on ethical consumerism where profits are not made at the expense of marginalized producers. However, despite this relevance there is lack of evidence as to how consumption patterns empirically sustain such practices, especially at the level of individual consumers in everyday life settings.

By leveraging consumer ethics, the authors aim to open the debate for a more inclusive and socially informed approach towards ethically conscious consumption and practices. The objectives of the chapter center on examining how consumers construct an appropriate ethic regarding shopping behavior, what role does personal identity play in ethical consumerism and what are some of the challenges and negotiations in the process.

BACKGROUND

Ethical consumption literature has a long and consistent history in outlining the necessity of including ethics-based principles and morality in business decisions and economic arrangements. It has strongly presented itself to counter the inequities and power imbalances in market systems. Historically, the debate gained momentum and strength with the spread of global capitalism. As economic globalization spread across the world coupled with modern means of communication, it increasingly brought in focus the inequalities in these systems of exchange and the need to reform capitalism to allow for its flourishing and continued expansion to different parts of the world. The rapid industrialization and mass production with its drive for profits led to the relevance and introduction of conversations around consumerism with a rising movement towards it during the industrial revolution (Berend, 2015; Cowan et al., 2009).

With such developments, understanding consumption practices and what drives them became imperative for steering production and creating new markets for consumers. Transformations of lifestyles, changes in attitudes, choices in buying behavior became significant for the survival, continuity and spread of capitalism (Lim, 2017, Yani de Soriano and Slater, 2009). It is now well accepted that understanding consumer behavior is a critical point of navigation in business practices and strategies. As the literature and findings on consumption practices developed further, the application of this knowledge expanded to focus beyond economic enterprises and specifically on how businesses impact consumers for their own ends. The renewed focus on consumers as the vulnerable and marginalized group against powerful players of the industry allowed ethical consumption debates to build a movement for ethics in businesses. Yet, a pressing point in this literature remains with bridging the thoughts and actions of consumers. While there may be awareness and consciousness of ethical issues (Carrigan et al. 2004; Low and Davenport 2007), it seldom translates into action for consumers (Carrigan and Attalla 2001; Carrigan et al. 2011; d' Astous and Legendre 2009; Papaoikonomou et al. 2012). It is startling to find that the solution to such a persistent issue does not lie in providing more information to consumers as the latter has not been successful in changing consumer practices and behavior (Moser and Dilling, 2007).

Recent literature suggests that there is a gap between the desire and intentions of consumers and their actual purchasing behavior and practices referred to as the ethical consumption gap or the failure to "walk the talk" (Auger and Devinney, 2007; Belk et al., 2005; Szmigin et al., 2009, Chatzidakis et al., 2007; Connolly and Prothero, 2008; Davies et al. 2012). Thus, while consumers may be conscious of the negative impact of economic production across the globe, they are most often unable to translate this knowledge into good practices. There remains lack of a better understanding for how to bridge the thoughts and actions of consumers.

In this direction, the literature review reveals the following gaps. Firstly, the scholarly analysis reveals that while ethical consumerism and its relationship to capitalism has been covered extensively, the exact nature of the issues and the solutions needs to be further advanced by examining the "how" consumers and markets respond to ethics and fair practices. Secondly, the complicated paradox for consumers that lies between being aware of ethical issues and practicing them through conscious meaningful engagements and action remains (Rafi-Ul-Shan et al., 2018). Thirdly therefore, it requires more empirical investigation towards this end. Notwithstanding their important contributions, this current literature therefore, falls short of understanding the relationship between consumption practices and market rationalities and neoliberal capitalist processes that require a re-examination of everyday practices of consumption for a more thorough analysis for their impact and potential for broader social change.

To address these gaps, this chapter situates ethical consumerism within the context of Fairtrade. Fairtrade is a voluntary market-based movement that employs a market-based multi-stakeholder approach towards alternative trade that is more socially, economically, and environmentally just (Raynolds and Bennett 2015:3). It is aimed at reforming the inequities in international trade through keeping ethics and fair principles of business at the center of such transactions and trade. Recent studies on ethical consumption suggest that while the market exerts the dominant influence on how consumption practices are shaped, ethical consumerism is developing powerful challenges to it with an increasing role played by consumers and their specific choices (Carrigan & Attalla, 2001; Crane et al., 2004; Shaw et al., 2000). Since the late 1900s and early 2000s, researchers have emphasized the rise of 'alternative consumerism' which focuses on ethical domains of social and ecological thought, going beyond the economic ones (Khan et al 2016; Creyer& Ross, 1997; Shaw & Clarke, 1999; Shaw, et al., 2000; Carrigan & Attalla, 2001). While there are many alternative movements and quests for ethical trade, we focus on the one that is most prominent for its emphasis on social aspects, which is Fairtrade.

Through its voluntary certification initiatives, Fairtrade certifies products that meet its standards of social sustainability. The Fairtrade label on the products communicates to the consumers that these products have been produced using fair and just practices. Recently, with the rise in ethical consumption, Fairtrade has expanded to expand its reach to big retails and producers expanding its market since last two decades. It is now evident that the market is responding favorably to drivers of ethical consumption in the present world as evident in the rise of corporate social responsibility by paying more attention to ethical ways of doing business (Harrison et al. 2005; Niinimäki 2007). Economic system is responding by making social justice and ethical arrangements as its guiding principles through acceptance of private certification standards thereby investing in what is known as "reputational capital" as a "risk- reduction strategy" (Fombrun 1996 in Bartley 2007). Although ethical consumerism is gaining importance and is growing with much needed organizational support as evident in the rise of Fairtrade and active engagement with corporate social responsibility, there remains a lack of literature on assessing its impact by transformations in people's attitudes and culture.

The objectives of the chapter are therefore the following:

Exploring Ethical Consumption for Equity and Inclusiveness

Firstly, how do consumers construct an appropriate ethic regarding shopping behaviour? Secondly, what is the role of personal identity in ethical consumerism? Finally, what are the challenges and negotiation processes in ethical consumerism?

Adopting a critical lens to ethical consumerism, the chapter examines consumption beliefs and practices and lifestyle through making particular and specific consumption choices over others using a qualitative approach to analysis as part of an exploratory study on ethical consumption. It is central to understand why the gap persists in how consumers think and act with respect to their purchasing decisions. This direction is imperative for uncovering the processes through which consumers construct and appropriate consumer ethics related to purchasing behavior. It opens the debate to the role of personal identity and sense making in ethical consumerism as well as the challenges and processes of negotiations in such deliberations.

Using an interpretive grounded approach to conceptually frame this study, we focus on the subjective meaning assigned by individuals to their reality which includes their beliefs, values, actions, behavior and social relationships with respect to the social phenomena under examination (Lincoln & Guba 1985; Edmondson & McManus, 2007; Glasser & Strauss, 1967). With a focus on Charmaz's (2005) social constructionist approach to grounded theory, the study is directed towards building a theory inductively through a flexible approach towards successive stages of data analysis and conceptual development.

The ethical consumerism research weighs heavily on quantitative analysis especially using self-reported surveys (Auger & Devinney, 2007). This emphasis on surveys though provides valuable insights; it compromises on empirical richness that relates to consumer experiences and practices. Thus, a qualitative inquiry adopted in this research can make important contributions to the study and findings on ethical consumerism as already advanced by quantitative analysis. This focus and emphasis upon the confluence on the two methodological approaches is in the interest of their combined interpretive power as in agreement with Becker (2001:328), "qualitative and quantitative research may have different philosophies of science, but they really just work in different situations and ask different questions".

Beginning at the level of data collection, the authors start at the lowest level by collecting data for this exploratory research since it enables us to understand the multidimensional nature of ethical consumerism and opens the scope for a broader level of analysis. The authors place a critical eye on the various issues that come to the fore with thoughtful attention to inconsistencies by assessing negative explanations to make sure the research is headed in the right direction.

As part of this study on consumption practices of consumers, the authors have chosen participants by adopting inclusion criteria that enhances the depth we can achieve depending on the scope, limitations, and constraints of this study. A *mix of heterogeneous and homogenous inclusion* criteria has been selected (as reflected in Table1) for the sampling universe that includes demographic homogeneity in design by selecting all women with *independent incomes* within the *age group* of 25 to 35 years. The rationale behind this strategy is to focus on the specific experiences of a defined group as it allows us to examine the experiences among a bounded group of individuals with certain common characteristics. In addition, there is a homogenous sampling universe in terms of educational and occupational background with an intentional emphasis on experience with marginalized groups or socially sensitive research to assess the extent of embrace given to ethical consumerism by those who have experienced and witnessed it most closely. Thus, the first participant conducts research on Fair Trade and food systems, the second participant has field experience on maternal nutrition and rights of women workers, the third participant manages museum partnerships and content for Google Arts and Culture with background and first-hand experience witnessing weaving and making of handicrafts by artisans while the final participant is working on various issues as they relate to the situation of domestic workers in India. The authors have chosen heterogeneity in sampling universe to the extent of studying a respondent from a different country to assess the cross-cultural variation between participants of different cultures that may reveal comparable insights as they relate to ethical consumerism among those closest to the economic and those that are closest to the socio-cultural world.

Table 1. Sampling universe of participants

Participants	Country	Gender	Age	Educational Background	Occupation
Participant 1(P1)	United States	Female	26 years	Social Sciences	Graduate Student
Participant 2 (P2)	India	Female	29 years	Social Sciences	User Experience Researcher (Google) as well as Social Researcher (Centre for Knowledge Societies)
Participant 3 (P3)	India	Female	32 years	Fine Arts and Visual Arts	Project Manager (Google Arts and Culture)
Participant 4(P4)	India	Female	30 years	Social Sciences	Graduate Student. (PhD)

Source: Primary Data

Since the study is based on a grounded approach it is well-suited to a flexible format for sample size as and when the data requires a change in it (Glaser 1978). Moreover, justification for a smaller sample size is presented by the fact that since the research is focused on understanding the discrepancy between internal and external states of consumers, a qualitative study may have a much smaller sample than an ambitious quantitative survey (Weiss 1994).

The *selection of participants* has been undertaken using convenience sampling at first by choosing participants that were conveniently accessible for this study and met the required criteria. As the study progressed, *snowball sampling* was also adopted by choosing participants that were referred by other participants of the study.

In line with *ethics and sensitivity* to this study, there was communication of the aims and purpose of the research to all participants of the study who agreed to take part in this research endeavor on a voluntary basis with anonymity protected. Voluntary recruitment, however, will reflect a "self-selection bias" (Costigan and Cox 2001) in which participants will be different from those who do not volunteer to participate. Yet, it is not possible to avoid this bias on grounds of voluntary ethical participation in qualitative research. In addition, participants gave informed consent. Moreover, the research was conducted with an orientation to *co-learning* perspective between the researcher and the participants in which both parties gained from research insights as the authors promised to share information on relevant literature as well as the findings of this project on completion with all the participants.

Participant observation and writing in field research constitute the core of ethnographic research. As Emerson et al (2011:3) state, "ethnographers seek to do field research by doing and becoming" in a continuous process of interaction and interpretation while emphasizing that what is observed and recorded is inseparable from the observational process.

Focusing on the strategic skill of observing, recording and writing field notes as a participant observer, the authors visited a Fairtrade certified store, Ten Thousand Villages as a customer located in the city

Exploring Ethical Consumption for Equity and Inclusiveness

of Fort Collins, Colorado. The site was chosen as it operates on the principles of ethical consumerism and provided an opportunity to observe people who visit and shop at stores that have ethical business practices as a foundational principle of their operations and organizational set up.

In the role of an observer and participant, authors used Emerson et al's (2011) strategy of taking jottings since jottings can capture bits of talk and action from which the fieldworker can begin to sketch social scenes, recurring incidents, and local expressions. These jottings were then developed and transformed into full field notes at a later stage. In this "text producing mode, the ethnographer tries to 'get it down' as accurately and as completely as possible, avoiding too much self-consciousness about the writing process itself". But the ethnographer also adopts a "reading mode to reflect on how these accounts are products of his own, often implicit decisions about how to participate in and describe events" (Emerson et al 2011:86). In this direction, writing in process memos allowed me to develop these insights early in the fieldwork.

Keeping in mind the focus of the study which is to get detailed and holistic description of consumption practices, the authors followed Weiss (1994)'s advice to opt for a form of fixed question open response interviewing for a systematic collection of data with fuller and deep responses with the purpose of integrating multiple perspectives and inter-subjectivities which makes it more generalizable by following the same ordering of questions and by asking the same questions to all the respondents. However, such compromises are at the expense of the strength of qualitative interviewing in terms of richness of information gained from each respondent. The participants in the research having identified in the research design were selected through consistent effort utilizing a variety of tools such as a promotional flyer with a personalized recruitment letter giving the details of the study as well as telephone calls and messaging to coordinate, serve as reminders and connect with the participants.

Secondly, scope was provided to interviewee's in their answers by offering broad orienting questions first and more detailed specific questions afterward that tap the knowledge and experience of the participants such as mini tours that explore smaller parts of a bigger picture. Thirdly, posing related questions in a sequence helped elicit richer responses. In addition, all the questions were accompanied by probes (attention, conversational management, and credibility probes) for managing, interpreting and clarifying the conversation during the course of the interview. Saturation was achieved when no new information could be obtained in spite of follow up questions and probing. Since the sample size was small and only four, the transcription of the interview was undertaken personally that allowed us to get closer to the data.

Data analysis is a central aspect of research. A key component of this process is the search for patterns in the data that has been collected as part of the research. The systematic search for such patterns in the data for this study was undertaken by following the analytical technique of coding. According to Saldana (2016), in qualitative data analysis, a code can be described as a construct created by the researcher that symbolizes or translates data by attributing meaning to each individual datum for pattern detection, categorization, assertion or propositional development, theory building and analytical processes. Following Charmaz (2008) suggestion, authors conducted detailed line by line coding of the data that enhanced the trustworthiness of the data by reducing the likelihood of imposition of our own personal thoughts onto my respondent's in the data collected. As this process was undertaken, a pattern that was repetitive, frequent and consistent emerged that captured the essential elements of the data culminating in categories leading to the generation of 12 codes that led to the emergence of themes. The interviews and field notes were coded building with detailed memos of the process that documented the examination and interpretation of data at every step of the process. This step was achieved by importing the data into software package NVivo 12 developed by QSR International (2018). As new themes started emerging, new participants were interviewed to contribute to the data till no further insights were revealed. The study used the strategy of constant comparison for refining themes and analysis by identifying the differences in the data from different participants. Since the study adopted a grounded approach for this research that emphasizes developing theory from participant's own words, authors selected In Vivo, descriptive and process coding methods for data analysis from among a varied range of diverse methods (Saldana 2016). During the process of coding, code weaving was undertaken to ensure that codes generated were subsumed into broader themes. After every interview, a review of the generated codes was done to develop meta memos through continuous analysis of data to strategically summarize and integrate the insights from the analysis.

As stated, "documents are 'social products' that must be examined critically because they reflect the interests and perspectives of their authors" (Hammersley and Atkinson 2007). The agency of the researcher cannot be ignored since data collection and analysis require scrutiny and filtration of information by a researcher. Since data can never be exhausted for its full richness, a researcher makes conscious well thought out decisions at every step of the research journey that influence the findings and narrow down its focus to the subject of inquiry.

Since the authors decided to study the thoughts and practices behind the motivations for ethical consumerism in individuals, they have adopted this lens to measure and account for participant experiences through the analysis. The whole research is oriented to this end and therefore is reflected in the results and findings of the study. In addition, the author's cultural identity as an Indian was helpful in communicating and understanding the perspective of the participants from India, more than that of the first participant who is from United States. It made the authors subscribe to the idea that matching researcher with research participants is indeed a useful strategy and practice, especially for research on sensitive topics and subjects. However, as a researcher the authors *can also never be a full member of the society we are studying.* This unique position as Emerson et al (2011) points out has *two important consequences* for writing which culminates in *many kinds of field descriptions* as well as analysis that frame not only what is written but also how it is written emphasizing different features while ignoring and marginalizing others through the very *writing choices ethnographers as well as researchers make.* Developing inter-coder reliability would have been a useful strategy to manage research and afford it reliability and validity; however, it was beyond the scope of this study.

The main focus of this chapter is to bring out the key themes that address the many facets of the objectives of this study. The authors have developed these themes after carefully scrutinizing the qualitative data, outlined in the previous section. This chapter discusses these issues in the following section.

IDENTITY AS A CONSUMER

Mindful Consumer

Participant 1 describes oneself as a "mindful consumer.. a firm believer of what you eat, you are" (Participant 1). Being mindful is closely associated with eating organic produce because of its personal health benefits. Thus, the consumer's attitude prioritizes individual benefits of being mindful of consumption and then describes its social implications as "I am supporting farms that do not use pesticides so the workers who work on these farms are not ingesting pesticides at least". In terms of consumption of clothing too, the participant feels it is not part of daily life as much as food as it does not affect the participant directly and the participant acknowledges the fact that the participant places personal returns foremost over societal concerns.

"Umm, I guess.....in a *selfish sense* (emphasis added) because I am not consuming the clothes so it is not directly affecting me but also availability and just like overall like mentioning it so you do not go into a store and say oh this is Fair trade you know…it's not, in my daily life it is not there" (Participant 1). Moreover, in buying considerations, price is an important criterion as the participant mentions words related to price such as being expensive/cheap/poor multiple times with a frequency of 11.

The Need-Based Shopper

"I'm a need based shopper but also splurge when my pocket allows..." (Participant 2)

For participant 2, consumer identity is closely associated with a need-based identity which is described as being against a shopaholic tendency requiring careful consideration about purchases before spending.

When a product is really needed, the participant purchases irrespective of its price giving price a secondary consideration. Yet, describing oneself as a "shopper" rather than a "consumer" presents critical clues for further analysis that may reveal what word choices emphasize about an individual's thought process. Emphasis on being a shopper may reveal an unconscious price assessment in buying practices and may hold relevance much more than consumption. As stated by the participant, as the participant's buying capacity increased after employment, the participant has found that the participant finds herself spending beyond what is necessary to stay in line with what is in trend and in fashion.

Thus, price is a consideration as one becomes financially independent. Being a shopper therefore emphasizes the buying experience over the consumption aspect for the individual. In addition, fashion for the participant is dependent upon what is new in the market and goes out of trend as soon the participant realizes everyone is wearing it. Trend based shopping is described as "the *need* to stay updated" while "*need based shopping*" is focused on "comfort not trends". Critical to note however is the fact that both are described as "need".

"If I see a lot of people already wearing it.. I might discard it.. or maybe try re using by mix and match" (Participant 2)

The focus upon what others are wearing is a key insight into how consumers determine their buying and purchasing choices. The individual identity is therefore found to be functioning not in isolation but in conjunction with a more socially oriented identity. This identity seems to weigh heavily the purchasing side of consumption and accords it prime importance in talking about consumption behaviour and practices.

What is central here is that the participant puts forth a strategy of mix and match after talking about discarding the garment. It is an interesting revelation that there is a tendency to avoid complete disposal of a product and reorient it for reuse through mixing and matching. This tendency and inclination to not to waste is a strong one and should be tapped for its potential as it is seen harbouring in the minds of many consumers who wish to subscribe to what is new and latest but also feel uncomfortable discarding a product that still has use and value for them.

The Comfort over Style Consumer

For participant 3, consumption is an embodied experience described as "anything that you can see, touch, use, 'intake' hear. Anything that invigorates the senses... It leaves an impact on you, whether as something memorable or something that reveals some insight about you. It gets you thinking."

In this highly impactful journey, the participant believes that there are not that many choices available for women who wish to choose comfort over style. Fashion trends and projections create an ideal image of a thin woman which consumers are enticed into accepting and embracing. The participant however, detests it and in fact shops from the men's section where the participant can find clothes that are "loose" rather than "stretchy" on the participant's body. Moreover, while the participant considers price as important, size is a definite criterion for the purchase of a product.

The Cautious Consumer

For participant 4, clothing and apparel are of keen interest and consumption is a carefully thought-out process in which wastage is not appreciated at all and there is emphasis on donation and recycling to mitigate it. Not subscribing to fashion and media projections, daily life is considered different where the purpose that clothing serves is not to develop a certain image but to be dressed in something that is ideal according to weather conditions and is long lasting.

Moreover, by wearing Indian cotton the participant believes the participant is also backing rich Indian culture and the artisans which are important enough to be paying slightly more than what the participant would pay for the slightly cheaper western clothes. "I always believe in maintaining clothes well, and for as long as they can last. Unworn clothes or those which do not fit anymore are thereafter donated to a local Delhi NGO instead of simply being thrown. So yes, as a consumer for clothes, I'd say that I do take an active interest! Cautious to never overspend or accumulate the unnecessary...I don't need to look like I'm walking the ramp and therefore don't need to keep changing outfits incessantly!

.....With this rigid market system in place, there is no going back as most economists have anyway stated about capitalism, but what we can do is to be slightly mindful in ways in which we can be".

""Machine made, in my experience, and which is although slightly cheaper than handmade, tends to have a mix in fabric like terry-cot or polyester which don't suit the skin during the summer months. Pure cotton is something which is essential for me to avoid itchy skin excess sweat and of course, in backing the artisans and the rich Indian culture of hand work, which in fact is very affordable as well. Western garments are all mostly machine made with standard styles!" (Participant 4)

Exploring Ethical Consumption for Equity and Inclusiveness

Table 2. Comparative table for review of findings

	Summary	Ethical Consciousness	Price Criterion
The Mindful Consumer	Supports ethical and organic initiatives for mindful consumption of food	Sees a stronger connection to food that is ingested, relative to clothing that is externally worn.	Price is important in purchasing decisions
The Need Based Shopper	Careful consideration given to purchasing practices. Emphasis on what is needed.	Strong inclination towards re-using products that go out of trend.	Price is secondary for need-based shopping; but does factor it in for trend-based products
Comfort Over Style	Consumption is an embodied experience	Detests binary division of clothing where women's clothing caters to an ideal type	Comfort takes precedence over price considerations.
The Cautious Consumer	Strong emphasis on life of product through re-use, recycling, and no wastage.	Does not subscribe to media projections. Challenges market pull.	Supports local and traditional crafts and is willing to pay more for it.

Source: Primary Data

SOLUTIONS AND RECOMMENDATIONS

The Influence of Culture

For self-defined need-based consumer (participant 2), there is a strong influence of culture that is determined by the fact that the participant lives in a developing country where "there is morecompetition and less resources" (Participant 2). The participant accords importance to the social and cultural milieu in which how you dress has considerable impact on your life outcomes. In this context, survival is essential. However, survival practices and behavior reflect differently in different contexts for the participant as in student life the participant gave utmost priority to quality and longevity of the products purchased while in college and work life, the participant felt the *need* to follow latest fashion trends resulting in a desire for more choices facilitated by increase in buying capacity that is afforded by independent earnings through employment.

The needs identified by the participant seem to change with context and different phases of life where clothes as a product perform a different purpose and fulfill a different need. The participant uses them as a resource to navigate through life. The participant revelations point to the fact that consumers may be better studied according to age groups as they may be revealing of patterns as and when individuals transition into different phases of life.

The cultural theme is pronounced for participant 4 as well who sees Indian and western cultures as different with western throw away culture catching up in India. Both participant 2 and 4 believe social media boost and advertisements are primarily responsible for this takeover. For participant 4 especially who is "passionate" about Indian wear, India has a tradition of understanding the value of products purchased from "hard-earned money" that brings along an "ethic of repairing" before discarding which is however fast disappearing under western influence.

Interestingly for participant 1, who is from the western culture, it is critical to note that the participant too believes in recycling stating evidence of recycling stores in United States such as Savers described as "gold mine" and has had a family tradition of shopping second hand during festivals such as Halloween which require costumes that were worn specifically on the day of the festival and therefore may not have much use in future. Such insights from these interviews are instrumental in highlighting the need to assess the culture of consumption and whose culture, is it? From the evidence presented in this study, the western and eastern culture of consumption as described by the participants share similar practices and concerns and there may be more similarities than differences.

Importance of Relationships: Gender

Since the study is focused only on women, it does not consider the experiences of men which is a stated limitation of the chapter. But in terms at looking at the selected sample of participants, it is important to note that for 3 out of 5 women, mothers were considered to play an important role in consumption practices and behavior.

For participant 2, the participant's mother "depends on her and they can be considered alike. We are more like friends at this age consult each other and also share our purchases..I mean exchange clothes. She wears mine and I hers occasionally".

For participant 3, the mother has been instrumental in defining the participant behaviour's as the participant states, "my mother has also always had the set-up of donating clothes, curtains, etc. - being sensitive is always an important thing and the ethic of keeping what you own well and buy only when you must/need!"

Interpersonal communication and socialization practices may therefore be an avenue for further analysis as mother and daughters seem to be following similar behaviour and thought patterns with respect to consumption. Tapping into such mindset may therefore open the possibility for widespread change as women using their communication and training skills may be able to pass down information inter-generationally as well as intra-generationally through their close associations, relationships and networks with one another.

Challenges to Ethical Consumerism

All the participants of this study feel that they need more information on the products that they purchase. While the majorities (4 out of 5) were aware of environmental hazards, poor labour conditions in production, they felt too distant from the hazardous circumstances in which production take place. It is important to note that they felt most strongly about those aspects of ethical consumption that they had real in person experience with, these were the experiences that motivated them to act and practice what they felt in spite of challenges and hurdles. For instance, for participant 2, first-hand field experience in dealing with maternal rights of marginalized women workers made the participant passionate about the cause making her use the word "obvious" while describing them. It has made the participant feel a continued desire to work towards making a change by feeling a sense of responsibility for domestic workers at home long after the field experience has been over.

"*Obviously* (emphasis added) you become more compassionate, understanding and caring towards marginal groups. You get a passion to work for them and their overall development" (Participant 2)

For participant 3 as well what the participant witnessed made the participant appreciate what the participant saw in the market. While education and more information are needed (describing the weaving class as cumbersome), visually seeing the craftspeople at work, is what really was impactful for the participant.

Exploring Ethical Consumption for Equity and Inclusiveness

"Toil and hard work and number of hours put in making a garment have left a lasting impact the craftsperson sits for 6-8 hrs a day and is only able to make 6 inches worth of shawl or sari. They prepare silk on their thighs; they may still be using outdated machinery and tools. Also, I had one class on weaving in my college. I never finished it.. It was just too *cumbersome*. Then in Crafts Museum, I saw them sitting and making inch after inch of weave. And also the Dastkaar fair which is challenging this mall culture and mainstream market by holding fairs and exhibitions in which producers, handicraft workers come together with consumers for sale of their products. I think it is a great platform to know how clothes are made, who is making them and who is selling this finished products. *When you see this, you really appreciate any handmade items you get in the market*". (Participant 3)

Therefore, in terms of the future of ethical consumerism, participant 1 believes the major hurdle in the way will be negotiating the price as well as tackling the mind set of consumers in a culture that remains unaware from most aspects of ethical consumerism. With more research and sharing of information, change can be forthcoming and will have to be a joint effort between NGOs, markets with further research and education on the subject. For participant 2 and 4 felt that creation of stricter laws and their forced implementation could work in India in a slow process of change. For participant 3, change is already happening gradually with some businesses engaging in corporate social responsibility through more ethical ways of production and retail but for wider appeal and practice, products will have to be made more affordable.

Figure 1. Message on Clothing
Source: Primary Data
Source: *https://encrypted-tbn0.gstatic.com/images?q=tbn:ANd9GcRI7SWo85bpHHuWJZwE-n9KxVv2vjcMKxdBfQ&usqp=CAU*

Exploring Ethical Consumption for Equity and Inclusiveness

When asked about what message they would want to convey to people with their clothing as presented in figure 1, themes associated with culture, information on how the product is made and who makes it with consideration to comfort over style came up. It emphasizes the production and supply chain with the most marginalized groups, the workers along with support and respect for culture and traditional skills. The choice of words such as "support", "respect" and "pick" emphasizes the individual's role and responsibility in such messages.

Figure 2. Message on clothing
Source: Primary Data
Source: *https://encrypted-tbn0.gstatic.com/images?q=tbn:ANd9GcSLyh-gXDEFIN_jSfhphNFX0HnF7PeZAkAYBw&usqp=CAU*

Figure 2 represents what the participants felt was an ethical product to them. The word cloud above depicts environmental concerns to be the most important concern with labour and humane treatment of workers following next along with ethics related authenticity through original designs and fair price for the product. These considerations may be critical in the future of ethical consumption in terms of garnering the support and interests of what consumers find ethical and desirable in a product.

Exploring Ethical Consumption for Equity and Inclusiveness

Figure 3. Meaning of fair trade
Source: Primary Data
Source: https://encrypted- tbn0.gstatic.com/images?q=tbn: *ANd9GcTP20BjQI19C B6WNRV1 avtkv2gdDWGHTCy Jsw&usqp=CAU*

Figure 3 represents a word cloud of all the words that were used to describe an understanding of what is fair according to the participants. Reciprocal clear and honest relationships with no exploitation with integrity to effort with equality and justice were some of the overarchingthoughts about fairness in the cognitive maps of the individuals interviewed in this study. It will be revealing to see if participants will be able to overcome some of the challenges to ethical consumption to uphold some of these values from their own end- even going to the extent of paying more.

In terms of identity, it is important to realize that individual and social concerns were felt to be important by all the participants with varying emphasis. While for some, consumption practices felt like an embodied experience for others, being in trend with what is latest was central while some felt that clothing specifically did not affect them directly. In addition, price was a central criterion in purchasing decisions for all the participants who were willing to pay more for a product only if it supported traditional crafts and skills or if the product was a necessary item. Other important considerations while purchasing and consuming a product were related to comfort, fabric quality, size and fit as well as durability and longevity with a desire to develop ways to reuse products that were out of fashion trends.

Hence, wastage and disposal were recurring ideas with respect to use of products purchased and consumed and all the participants followed some form of putting the products to their full use and value by buying second hand, sharing with family members or donating them to charity. A further interesting insight was the use of clothing as a survival strategy to fit into different social and cultural worlds. They were resources that were channeled to present a certain image according to changing contexts and cultures.

FUTURE RESEARCH DIRECTIONS

In future, the authors emphasize more empirical qualitative research as that would allow for a much more thorough analysis going beyond an exploratory framework. The results of this preliminary research will be used to further refine and inform this advanced stage of investigation and examination of ethical consumer practices. Combining participant observation and interviewing with ethnography will be especially helpful since it will provide insights into understanding meanings of words through observing their use in context "through continuous interviewing of their implications and nuances, and the use of them under the scrutiny of capable speakers of the language" (Becker and Geer 1957:29) while participant observation makes it possible to check description against fact (Becker and Geer 1957). Thus, Emerson et al (2011) asserts that localized knowledge can be discerned not simply based on people's talk but through their "talk in interaction".

CONCLUSION

Thus concluding the chapter, as the literature review suggested there is a definite gap in terms of what people think and what they do with respect to consumption practices and behaviour. The tension is pronounced in statements where the participants are importantly *themselves aware* of this obstacle and struggle with it describing feeling like a hypocrite and questioning their own self-image.

"I do not eat a lot of dairy but sometimes I do and it kind of makes me *feel like a hypocrite* (emphasis added) because I know the dairy industry is like more brutal than beef and chickens so definitely the labour component is a big part of me, especially since all the work I have done on farm workers". (Participant 1)

"They're the most capitalist-driven and exploitative brands of the world which run only on cheap, third world labour. Yes I am aware of that. And now that *doesn't make me look very good, does it (emphasis added)*. like I mentioned, I do shop at these brands as much as I probably shop in local or export-reject markets which have much the same variety and prices when it comes to western wear...I myself feel I *feed into the system* at times. And not only regarding clothes, it's also got to do with electronics, the food industry, etc. So, there is a gap in terms of having knowledge and being able to use it for change in practices" (Participant 4).

Since the sampling universe was of participants who are well versed with these issues, what this chapter seeks to bring to prominence is the fact that education and information though valuable and much needed, need to be accompanied with direct experience. Those who are most informed about exploitation and unethical production and consumption themselves find it hard to live by what they believe in putting intense pressure on themselves. For thought to reflect in actions, challenges need to be overcome. At an individual everyday level this means that individuals who form the consumer base need to be provided with alternative solutions where hesitancy needs to be replaced by what is happening with their purchase and consumption of a product. Transparency and communication of their investment along the lines of what they desire for themselves and for society and the world needs to be more forthcoming and pronounced in the products they purchase. How one might conceptualize such a product is facilitated by this chapter with inputs into key characteristics described by participants along with clarity on what is considered a fair and ethical product. Channeling these thoughts and ideas from the consumers themselves, may be more appealing and rewarding to translate into ethically conscious consumption practices and behaviour.

Exploring Ethical Consumption for Equity and Inclusiveness

REFERENCES

Augur, P., & Devinney, T. M. (2007). Do what consumers say matter? The misalignment of preferences with unconstrained ethical intention. *Journal of Business Ethics, 76*(4), 361–383. doi:10.100710551-006-9287-y

Bartley, T. (2007). Institutional Emergence in an Era of Globalization: The Rise of Transnational Private Regulation of Labor and Environmental Conditions. *American Journal of Sociology, 113*(2), 297–351. doi:10.1086/518871

Becker, H. S. (1986). *Writing for social scientists: How to start and finish your thesis, book or article.* University of Chicago Press.

Becker, H. S., & Geer, B. (1957). Participant observation and interviewing: A comparison. *Human Organization, 16*(3), 28–32. doi:10.17730/humo.16.3.k687822132323013

Belk, R., Devinney, T. M., & Eckhart, G. (2005). Consumer ethics across cultures. *Consumption Markets & Culture, 8*(3), 275–289. doi:10.1080/10253860500160411

Bennett, E. A. (2015). Fair-trade International governance. In L. T. Raynolds & E. A. Bennett (Eds.), *Handbook of Research on Fair-trade.* Edward Elgar Publishing.

Berend, I. T. (2015). Capitalism. International encyclopedia. *Social Behavioral Sciences, 3*, 94–98.

Carrigan, M., & Attala, A. (2001). The myth of the ethical consumer. Do ethics matter in purchase behavior. *Journal of Consumer Marketing, 18*(7), 560–577. doi:10.1108/07363760110410263

Carspecken, P. (1996). *Critical ethnography in educational research: A theoretical and practical guide.* Routledge.

Castells, M. (2000). Network society. In The globaltransformations reader. Polity Press.

Charmaz, K. (2014). *Constructing grounded theory.* Sage Publications.

Chatzidakis, A., Hilbert, S., & Smith, A. P. (2007). Why people don't take their Fair Trade to the supermarket: The role of neutralization. *Journal of Business Ethics, 74*(1), 7489–100. doi:10.100710551-006-9222-2

Costigan, C. L., & Cox, M. J. (2001). Fathers' participation in family research:Is there a self- selection bias? *Journal of Family Psychology, 15*(4), 706–720. doi:10.1037/0893-3200.15.4.706 PMID:11770476

Crane, A., & Matten, D. (2004). *Business ethics: A European perspective.* Oxford UniversityPress.

Creyer, E. H., & Ross, W. T. (1997). The Impact of firm behavior on purchase intention: Do consumers really care about business ethics? *Journal of Consumer Marketing, 14*(6), 421–432. doi:10.1108/07363769710185999

Davies, I., Lee, Z., & Ahonkhai, I. (2012). Do consumers care about ethical- luxury? *Journal of Business Ethics, 106*(1), 37–51. doi:10.100710551-011-1071-y

Emerson, R. M., Fretz, R. I., & Shaw, L. L. (2011). *Writing ethnographic fieldnotes* (2nd ed.). The University of Chicago Press. doi:10.7208/chicago/9780226206868.001.0001

Fair Trade International Annual Report. (2016-2017). https://annualreport16-17.fairtrade.net/en/

Gereffi, G. (1994). The organization of buyer-driven global commodity chains. In G. Gereffi & M. Korzeniewicz (Eds.), *Commodity chains and global capitalism*. Praeger.

Glaser, B., & Strauss, A. (1967). *The discovery of grounded theory*. Aldine Publishing.

Harrison, R., Newholm, T., & Shaw, D. (2005). Introduction. In RThe ethical consumer. London: Sage Publications.

Held, D. (2005). At the global crossroads: The end of the Washington Consensus andthe rise of global social democracy? *Globalizations*, *2*(1), 95–113. doi:10.1080/14747730500085122

Held, D., & McGrew, A. (2008). *Globalization / anti-globalization: Beyond the greatdivide* (2nd ed.). Polity Press.

Henderson, J., Dicken, P., Hess, M., Coe, N., & Wai-Chung Yeung, H. (2002). Globalproduction networks and the analysis of economic development. *Review of International Political Economy*, *9*(3), 436–464. doi:10.1080/09692290210150842

Khan, Z. R., Rodrigues, G., & Balasubramanian, S. (2016, January). *Ethical consumerism and apparel industry-towards a New Factor Model* [Paper presentation]. 33rd International Business Research Conference, Dubai, UAE.

Kilbourne, W., McDonagh, P. P., & Prothero, A. (1997). Sustainable consumption and the quality of life: A micromarketing challenge to the dominant social paradigm. *Journal of Macromarketing*, *17*(1), 4–21. doi:10.1177/027614679701700103

Lim, W. M. (2017). Inside the sustainable consumption theoretical toolbox: Critical concepts for sustainability, consumption, and marketing. *Journal of Business Research*, *78*, 69–80. doi:10.1016/j.jbusres.2017.05.001

Mason, J. (2002). *Qualitative researching*. Sage.

Murray & Raynolds. (2007). Globalization and its antimonies: Negotiating a FairTrade Movement. In Fair Trade: The challenges in transforming globalization. Routledge.

Niinimäki, K. (2007). *Eettisenkuluttamisentulevaisuuskuvia. Futura*, *4*, 58–75.

Pookulangara, S., Shephard, A., & Mestres, J. (2011). University community's perception of sweat-shops: A mixed method data collection. *International Journal of Consumer Studies*, *35*(4), 476–483. doi:10.1111/j.1470-6431.2010.00950.x

Raynolds, D. L., & Long, M. A. (2007). Fair/Alternative Trade: Historical and empirical dimensions. In L. T. Raynolds, D. L. Murray, & J. Wilkinson (Eds.), *Fair Trade: Thechallenges in transforming globalization*. Routledge. doi:10.4324/9780203933534

Raynolds, L., Douglas, M., & Heller, A. (2007). Regulating sustainability in the coffeesector: A comparative analysis of third-party environmental and social certification initiatives. *Agriculture and Human Values, 24*(2), 147–163. doi:10.100710460-006-9047-8

Raynolds, L. T. (2012). Fair Trade: Social regulation in global food markets. *Journal of Rural Studies, 28*(3), 276–287. doi:10.1016/j.jrurstud.2012.03.004

Raynolds, L. T., & Greenfield, N. (2015). Fair Trade: Movements and markets. In L. T. Raynolds & E. A. Bennett (Eds.), *Handbook of Research on Fair Trade*. Edward Elgar Publishing. doi:10.4337/9781783474622.00010

Robinson, O. (2014). Sampling in interview-based qualitative research: A theoretical and practical guide. *Qualitative Research in Psychology, 11*(1), 25–41. doi:10.1080/14780887.2013.801543

Rossi, A. (2013). Does Economic Upgrading Lead to Social Upgrading in Global Production Networks? Evidence from Morocco. *World Development, 46*, 223–233. doi:10.1016/j.worlddev.2013.02.002

Saldana, J. (2016). *The coding manual for qualitative researchers* (3rd ed.). Sage Publications.

Shaw, D., & Clarke, I. (1999). Belief formation in ethical consumer groups: An exploratory study. *Marketing Intelligence & Planning, 17*(2), 109–119. doi:10.1108/02634509910260968

Shaw, D., Shiu, E., & Clarke, I. (2000). The contribution of Ethical Obligation and Self identity to the theory of planned behaviour: An exploration of ethical consumers. *Journal of Marketing Management, 16*(8), 879–894. doi:10.1362/026725700784683672

Smith, J. A., Flowers, P., & Larkin, M. (2009). *Interpretative phenomenological analysis: Theory, method and research*. Sage.

Steger, M. (2013). Globalization: A very short introduction. Oxford. doi:10.1093/actrade/9780199662661.001.0001

Szmigin, I., Carrigan, M., & McEachern, M. G. (2009). The conscious consumer: Taking the flexible approach to ethical behavior. *International Journal of Consumer Studies, 33*(2), 224–231. doi:10.1111/j.1470-6431.2009.00750.x

Trost, J. A. (1986). Statistically non-representative stratified sampling: A sampling technique for qualitative studies. *Qualitative Sociology, 9*(1), 54–57. doi:10.1007/BF00988249

Weiss, R. S. (1994). *Learning from strangers: The art and method of qualitative interview studies*. The Free Press.

Yani-de-Soriano, M., & Slater, S. (2009). Revisiting Drucker's theory: Has consumerism led to the overuse of marketing? *Journal of Management History, 15*(4), 452–466. doi:10.1108/17511340910987347

KEY TERMS AND DEFINITIONS

Alternative Consumerism: Focusing on social and ecological concerns in consumption, and not solely the economic ones.

Ethical Consumption: Making socially informed choices about consumption and purchasing behavior.

Fair Trade: A movement that is aimed at reforming the inequities in international trade through keeping ethics and fair principles of business at the center of trade.

Gender: A binary social construction that socially aligns all male bodied individuals into masculine identity and all female-bodied into feminine identity. All that is male, is not female and all that is female, is not male.

Qualitative Research: Understanding social logic through deep analysis of people's own words and communication.

Reputational Capital: The reputation of an organization is also one of its strong assets in present times. Reputation is an important investment and a source of profit for business organizations.

Social Sustainability: Addressing the concerns and needs of a society and culture including social equity and justice for more inclusive socio-economic arrangements for conducting business and trade.

Sociology: Examination of human societies and cultures to discern patterns in thoughts and action of consumers.

Chapter 6

Global Institutional Role to Promote Achievement of the Sustainable Development Goals in Zimbabwe

Mufaro Dzingirai
https://orcid.org/0000-0002-1518-8275
Midlands State University, Zimbabwe

Rodgers Ndava
https://orcid.org/0000-0002-0070-1830
Midlands State University, Zimbabwe

ABSTRACT

The role of institutions in development discourse when it comes to inclusive development is hotly debated in recent years. Nonetheless, little is known about the role of global institutions in achieving the Sustainable Development Goals in the context of the global pandemic widely known as the COVID-19 pandemic. Given this information, this chapter will focus on the role of global institutions in promoting the achievement of sustainable development goals in Zimbabwe. This study establishes that global institutions play an enabling role when it comes to the achievement of SDGs in Zimbabwe through developmental policy advocacy and guidance, sensitization and dissemination of information, capacity building, and financing developmental programs. Based on these findings, a plethora of recommendations has been proposed that includes expansion of collaboration, improvement of governance systems and practices, improvement on international co-operation, and unlocking of international finance.

INTRODUCTION

It is widely known that global institutions play a vital role in promoting socio-economic transformations around the world (Fleiss, 2021). In this regard, it is salient to observe that accountable, effective, efficient,

DOI: 10.4018/978-1-6684-2448-3.ch006

Copyright © 2022, IGI Global. Copying or distributing in print or electronic forms without written permission of IGI Global is prohibited.

and inclusive institutions can contribute significantly when it comes to the attainment of the Sustainable Development Goals (SDGs). This is supported by the fact that many governments are working towards achieving inclusive development agenda (Fleiss, 2021; Pineda, Valencia, & Andrian, 2020; World Bank, 2013). In an attempt to achieve this important agenda, many countries are guided by the SDGs. One of these crucial sustainable development goals is SDG16 ("Goal 16 aims to promote peaceful and inclusive societies for sustainable development, provide access to justice for all and build effective, accountable and inclusive institutions at all levels") (United Nations, 2015). More interestingly, the 2030 Agenda for Sustainable Development captures the prime importance of institutions in achieving sustainable development. There is no doubt about the importance of institutions in sustainable development given that sustainable development must be inclusive in nature (Fleiss, 2021; Meuleman & Niestroy, 2015, United Nations, 2016a). Every stakeholder has a special role to play when it comes to inclusive development.

In pursuit of inclusive development, there is a growing consensus on the fact that nobody must lag behind. This means that inclusive sustainable development should not exclude the marginalized people in the community such as women, youths, elderly people, poor people, and disabled people. With this in mind, it is in the public domain that the global institutions such as International Monetary Fund (IMF), World Bank, United Nations (UN), World Trade Organization (WTO), and International Labour Organisation (ILO) are driving and promoting the agenda of making inclusive development a reality in many countries across the world (Fleiss, 2021; Pineda et al., 2020). Notably, the contribution of these global institutions is hotly debated in the current development discourse. This debate provides the basis for expanding our understanding of the role of global institutions, especially from developing countries' perspectives. However, very little is known about the role of global institutions in promoting the achievement of SGDs in Zimbabwe especially in the face of the COVID-19 pandemic (Humphrey, 2020; Pineda et al., 2020). Therefore, this study aims to examine the role of global institutions in promoting the achievement of SDGs in Zimbabwe.

Global institutions' contribution or impact on development is ardently contested but in the 21st century, only a few doubt their contribution to the achievement of Millennium Development Goals (MDGs) among other developmental initiatives. This research seeks to enquire about the contribution of global institutions in promoting the achievement of sustainable development in Zimbabwe. There is no doubt that the Zimbabwean government is facing numerous challenges such as high poverty levels and a sharp increase in youth unemployment (Dzingirai, 2020). Extended arrears of the country on external debt makes it impossible to access more financing despite the expression of interests by the government's commitment to reengagement with external sources of finance or the international community. The first step would be to clear the outstanding and long overdue arrears with the World Bank, IMF, European Investment Bank, and the African Development Bank among other lenders. However, IDA & IMF (2020) reported that there is no consensus concerning the roadmap to debt clearance sustainability and the probable reconciliation creditor agreement (World Bank, 2020; IFA & IMF 2020). The objectives of this study are to capture the worldwide practices and controversies related to global institutions and sustainable development goals, to assess the challenges faced by global institutions in promoting inclusive development, to examine the development challenges faced by global institutions during the global pandemic, and to analyze the contribution of global institutions to inclusive sustainable development in Zimbabwe as well as to ascertain the role of global institutions in promoting the achievement of SDGs in Zimbabwe.

Global Institutional Role

BACKGROUND

Sustainable development emerged in the 70s and then the first global environmental summit was held in Rio de Janeiro in 1992. SDGs is a term that is considered to be the replacement for the MDGs since the year 2015 when the World Bank and the IMF engaged in an endeavor to support the Global Agenda. It is well-documented that the member states of the United Nations (UN) unanimously agreed on the 2030 Agenda for Sustainable Development in September 2015. This Agenda is clear evidence of the international commitment to the achievement of the 17 SDGs as well as 169 targets which capture different aspects from economic, environmental, and social domains (United Nations, 2015a). Although sustainable development is a complex concept, there is a general consensus that it mainly focuses on three major issues of sustainability, that is, social, economic, and environmental (Bochanczyk-Kupka & Peciak, 2015). However, it is worth mentioning that the institutional framework dimension is gaining more momentum in recent years when it comes to sustainable development discourse.

The emergence of globalization driven by the advancement in technology has accelerated the already existing socio-economic problems that necessitate the need to intensify the activities and programs of global institutions like ILO, WTO, WHO, and IMF. Some political problems are emerging on a global scale such as terrorism and international political conflicts. These problems can act as stumbling blocks to the achievement of SDGs if they are not effectively managed. Going forward, the economic problems can not also escape our attention since it is well known that there is economic instability and challenges related to the internationalization of markets. These challenges are linked to the globalization process where there is no fairness when it comes to the distribution of resources among people, organizations, countries, and regions (Bochanczyk-Kupka & Peciak, 2015).

It is also public knowledge that globalization has affected the environment since there are urgent problems linked to climate changes, exploitation of natural resources, environmental degradation, and environmental pollution (Apergis, Gozgor, & Lau, 2021; Balsalobre-Lorente, Driha, Shahbaz, & Sinha, 2021; Johnstone, 2021). These environmental problems know no borders and they can cause unprecedented negative effects across the globe. This state of affairs then forces one to interrogate the role of global institutions in trying to combat these environmental challenges on a global scale. On the other hand, the social challenges are also intensified by the globalization process (Johnstone, 2021). This issue can be dissected by scrutinizing migratory movements of people on a global scale, illegal migrants, aging societies, youth unemployment, women exploitation, poverty, international crimes, and cultural distortions. All these issues necessitate the urgent need for executing sustainable development strategies that allow the governments to achieve the 17 SDGs by 2030.

Despite the importance of governments in achieving SDGs, the role of institutions in the development agenda is gaining momentum in recent years. Many scholars are starting to unpack the importance or the role of institutions in the sustainable development process. By definition, institutions are organizations that influence the choice of actions at a local, regional or global level (Bochanczyk-Kupka & Peciak, 2015). As such, these organizations have an impact on the development process as they can affect how individuals or groups of actors in the community behave and contribute to their respective communities. With this in mind, it is interesting to scrutinize the role of global institutions like the United Nations, World Bank, IMF, and ILO as well as WTO since we are living in a global village. It is salient to observe that these international institutions have a big role to play in the achievement of the SDGs.

It is of great importance to note that there are some controversies linked to the contribution of institutions to sustainable development (Fleiss, 2021). Notably, sustainable development is a multi-faceted concept that has been defined in various ways by numerous scholars. As such, the conceptualization of sustainable development in various ways makes it difficult to measure the impact of global institutions on sustainable development (Newig, Vob, & Monstadt, 2007). This means there is a need for more studies on the interaction between global institutions and sustainable development in an effort to enlarge the current development discourse. Moreover, there are issues and controversies in the current development discourse when it comes to how the COVID-19 pandemic has redefined the development projects, and interventions of global institutions such as IMF and World Bank (Fleiss, 2021; Pineda et al., 2020). Despite many calls for understanding the role of institutions in sustainable development, not much has been done to probe the role of global institutions in promoting the achievement of SDGs, especially in Zimbabwe. Therefore, this study aims to examine the role of global institutions in promoting the achievement of SDGs in Zimbabwe.

The Need for Global Institutions in Implementing the 2030 Development Agenda

Recently, the need for inclusive development has gained potency in the development discourse. The main reason for such an increase in interest can be attributed to the fact that effective development must incorporate all social and economic actors (Ministry of Public Service, Labour, and Social Welfare, 2020). This means that even the economic and social institutions must be critically scrutinized when it comes to their roles in the achievement of SDGs especially the global institutions like World Bank, WTO, WHO, ILO, and IMF (Fleiss, 2021). It is important to note that global institutions are playing a significant role when it comes to the achievement of 17 SDGs by 2030. Firstly, global institutions such as World Bank are playing a significant role in achieving the SDGs through the implementation of capacity-building initiatives on a global scale. In this regard, according to the World Bank (2018), capacity building is one of the most difficult areas yet necessary for any development initiative to yield the expected results. As such, over the years the World Bank has remained committed to implementing capacity-building initiatives for economic transformation as well as social transformation for many economies around the globe including developing countries in Africa. Huge amounts of investment have over the years been invested in capacity building. For instance, the African Capacity Building project financed by many global institutions including the Multi-Donor Trust Fund disbursed US$119 million investment (World Bank, 2018).

According to the UN (2016b), world economies formally commenced implementation of what they called the 2030 Agenda for Sustainable Development and the plan of execution includes 17 SDGs. Sibanda (2016) and United Nations (2015) reported that despite the challenges faced in African countries the achievement of MDGs in the region has made remarkable progress especially on the provision of primary school education, infant mortality rate, the inclusion of women in politics and administration as well as bridging the gender gap. The framework for capacity building and cooperation by the World Bank and IMF continues to exist and is becoming a routine. Strengthening the involvement of the society in development initiatives is becoming a common practice and the two global institutions continue to collaborate through joint participation to assist both developing and developed countries (IDA & IMF, 2020; World Bank, 2020).

Secondly, global institutions like IMF and World Bank have a big role, as the biggest international financial institutions, in financing the sustainable development programs of many countries across the globe. In this respect, The World Bank and the IMF continue to work together in an effort to reduce the

Global Institutional Role

external debt burdens in many developing countries that are usually considered to be poor countries. The Multilateral Debt Relief Initiative and the Heavily Indebted Poor Countries (HIPC) are the most common and recent collaborations of the World Bank and the IMF to reduce the external debt burdens for poor or heavily indebted countries. Reducing the debt burden does not only help to reduce poverty and eliminate hunger but the achievement of many SDGs depends upon the debt relief or burden of that particular country. For instance, heavily indebted countries may not have enough funds to invest in education, health, and climate change initiatives hence the achievement of many SDGs depends on the debt burden of the central government. The efforts of the World Bank and the IMF are worth mentioning when it comes to the efforts to reduce the debt burden and the achievement of SDGs (IDA & IMF, 2020; Ravalion, 2016; World Bank, 2016).

Going forward, most global institutions such as the World Bank, UN, and the IMF were created for the purpose of creating international economic cooperation between world economies. For instance, the World Bank and the IMF were created way back in the year 1944 in the United States at an international conference in Bretton Woods for the purpose of establishing economic cooperation between economies of the world. These institutions, therefore, work hand in hand with central administrations of many countries as well as engaging the private sector for the purpose of addressing economic challenges in many countries and ensuring remarkable progress of development initiatives, interventions or programs (World Bank, 2020; IDA & IMF 2020).

One of the most crucial goals of the IMF is to promote monetary cooperation, capacity building, and offering advice and financial assistance so as to ensure the success of developmental interventions in many counties. In this regard, the IMF offers both short-term and long-term financial assistance through grants and loans. Many global institutions including the IMF are well known for providing loans that are aimed at helping countries to redesign policy programs for the purposes of helping the struggling economies to improve their balance of payments. The macroeconomic or financial policies are a major issue of concern by IMF, World Bank are considered crucial in any financial or economic decisions hence these institutions provide outstanding support and assistance when it comes to sustainable development goals achieved by world economies (Humphrey, 2020; World Bank, 2018).

Going forward, the mandate of the World Bank is to promote long-term economic development, provide financial assistance as well as technical support for the purpose of reducing poverty. As such, this is one of the most important SDGs that every government wishes to achieve. To achieve economic development in the long term and achieve poverty reduction, the World Bank has embarked on a number of projects and interventions related to the provision of clean water, healthcare services, construction of schools, provision of electricity, and protection of the environment. The financial muscle of the World Bank like other international institutions makes it possible for the institution to implement multiple projects and activities that are aimed at improving the welfare of many marginalized people in developing countries at the same time maintaining or accelerating the growth prospects of other developed countries (World Bank, 2016; Muhumed & Sayid, 2016).

Thirdly, global institutions like United Nations are promoting the sensitizations of the SDGs at a global level. These global institutions sensitize the issues related to poverty, hunger, education, health, gender equality, legal, and climate change. In fact, the international institutions have always been committed to supporting member countries to reach the SDGs by working together with them in joint operations (IDA & IMF, 2020). The World Bank reported that about 7.9 million people living in Zimbabwe live under extreme poverty earning less than US$30 per month. According to the World Bank (2020) and Ministry of Public Service, Labour and Social Welfare (2020), extreme poverty in the country is worsened by the outbreak of Coronavirus. The pandemic outbreak increased extreme poverty to 49% by the end of the year 2020. Not only the pandemic increased poverty but also disrupted the provision of public services such as education, health, and other social services. According to the World Bank (2020), nearly 500 000 Zimbabwean households have at least one or more family members or relatives who lost their job due to the pandemic outbreak sending the families into the poverty bracket worsening the already pitiable conditions that the families have endured due to economic hardships.

With escalating unemployment levels, food security also deteriorated forcing many families to survive on one meal a day as food becomes expensive for the families, there is a dire need for developmental interventions or programs. Attainment of SDG goal number 1, that is, to eradicate extreme hunger and poverty becomes a challenge (Ministry of Public Service, Labour and Social Welfare, 2020). The Zimbabwean government has struggled for years and now decades to eradicate extreme hunger and poverty (Dzingirai, 2021). Despite lucrative plans and blueprints by the government over the years to achieve SDG1 the country has continued to struggle and credit is given to global institutions, UN, IMF, World Bank, WHO, USAID, EU, and other non-governmental organizations that have been providing food, clothing and sanitary (World Bank, 2021; WHO, 2020; UN, 2020).

Going forward, there is also a need to capture the contribution of the WHO in the development process. No doubt that global institutions play a pivotal role in complementing the efforts by the Zimbabwean government to achieve the SDGs. Take for instance, the intervention of the international community and global institutions when the 2019 cyclone crisis hit the eastern side of the country. Not only the 2019 cyclone crisis got the attention of the global institutions but as well the current coronavirus pandemic outbreak witnessed the World Bank, WHO, and the UN among other global giants extending their help to save humanity in Zimbabwe. According to the UN (2016c), Africa has struggled for years to achieve SDGs but considerable progress has been made despite the impeding obstacles including governance challenges and brain drain. Credit is given to global institutions and some developed countries' contribution towards improvement in the provision of primary school education facilities, bridging the gender gap and healthcare facilities notably efforts to reduce HVI/AIDS infections (Sibanda, 2016). The provision of health facilities has always commanded a higher priority among other SDGs hence the goal is a priority even during the coronavirus pandemic outbreak (World Bank, 2021). The WHO among other global institutions thus extended its help through the provision of protective necessitates such as face masks, sanitizers, and medication for the purpose of preserving human lives in this unprecedented pandemic outbreak. Even before the pandemic outbreak, the WHO, UN, and other global health institutions have always extended their assistance to struggling economies including Zimbabwe with health facilities in countless efforts to help the country and the world to achieve SDG 4,5 and 6 as these goals all consider the health wellbeing of humanity (World Bank, 2021; WHO, 2020; UN, 2020).

Fourthly, global institutions are important when it comes to the promotion of quality education which is another pillar of sustainable development. According to the UN (2015), developing countries mostly in Africa have taken considerable steps to achieve SDGs with the assistance of international organizations since these organizations advocate for effective implementation of the global development initiatives. Collaborations between national, regional, and global organizations have been outstanding in ensuring that both developed and developing nations achieve SDGs. For instance, the United Nations Economic Commission for Africa, the African Development Bank, and the African Union Commission harmonized collaborations for SDGs. According to the United Nations (2015), there is steady progress on the achievement of SDG 2 in Africa, that is, to achieve universal primary education but about a third of the pupils fail to reach the last stage of the primary. The completion rate of around 67 percent of primary

Global Institutional Role

education in Africa is worrisome and barely 20 percent of the African countries managed to reach the target by the year 2012 (United Nations, 2015). Regression in some parts of the continent is largely attributed to political squabbles and unrest or conflicts and poor quality of education.

However, some countries in the continent including Ghana, Morocco, Zimbabwe, and Tanzania recorded the fastest progress between the years 2000 and 2012, and much credit is given to international institutions' collaborations with the national governments of respective countries. United Nations (2015) reported that the youth population literacy rate between 15- and 24-years has improved significantly in general over the past two decades, especially from the year 2000. However, some African countries were still lagging behind. For instance, Chad and Ivory Coast recorded less than 50 percent literacy rate while the majority of African countries achieved at least 75 percent literacy rate for the youth. Some countries recorded outstanding youth literacy exceeding 95 percent and these include Tunisia, Swaziland, Libya, and South Africa among other countries (World Bank, 2016; Muhumed & Sayid, 2016; IDA & IMF, 2020).

Fifthly, it is worth mentioning that global institutions like the United Nations promote gender equality which is another key pillar of sustainable development. United Nations advocating for gender equality among other global institutions and national governments has produced a positive spiral change in terms of equality initiatives. According to the UN (2015), there is a marked improvement in education enrolment education for girls as compared to the previous decades and globally the gender parity has increased significantly as international organizations and national governments collaborate to promote gender equality even in terms of access to education and opportunities. Gender-responsive interventions by global institutions and the central administrations around the globe are a stepping stone for women and the girl child to break the longstanding glass ceiling. UN (2015) reported that the African continent is leading as far as women representation in parliaments is concerned with Rwanda recording an outstanding percentage of women representation in the national parliament. By the year 2014, the average global women representation had risen to 22 percent from 14 percent in the year 2000 with Africa leading the way followed by the Caribbean and Latin America registered 11 percent.

Lastly, global institutions are supporting climate change initiatives in promoting sustainable development on a global scale. It is considered to be one of the most threatening issues hence in April 2016, 175 nations signed the historic agreement well known as the Paris Agreement which heralds the efforts to combat climate change (UN, 2016). The World Bank and IMF have embarked on a number of projects that help to combat climate change as SDG number 13 and these initiatives include the introduction of a pilot basis by the World Bank and IMF in 2017 well known as the IMF-World Bank Climate Change Policy Assessments (CCPA). The CCPA provides overarching assessments of preparedness, financing, and adaptation strategies for developing and capacity-constrained countries and many of these countries are in Africa. Achieving SDG13 is not an event but a continuous process that needs not only global institutions but the support of central administrations as well (World Bank, 2016; Muhumed & Sayid, 2016).

CHALLENGES FACED BY GLOBAL INSTITUTIONS AND THE CENTRAL GOVERNMENT IN PROMOTING THE ACHIEVEMENT OF SDGs

The institutional capacity of global institutions is undermined by a number of challenges despite the efforts of these institutions to contribute towards the achievement of SDGs. These challenges include governance challenges, human capital flight, and trade flow challenges among other things. These issues are discussed below:

Governance Challenges

Despite numerous efforts of global institutions to ensure that SDGs are achieved, governance challenges always found their way to impede the strategic plans and efforts to achieve SDGs. Not only does Zimbabwe faces governance challenges but many developing countries within the continent. Stakeholder involvement in governance issues and transparency is much needed in national development as well as accountability (Biermann et al., 2017). Despite the quantities and amounts of financial and non-financial assistance offered by global institutions to developing countries, achieving SDGs remains a challenge. This clearly shows that the problem is not with the financial aspects alone but governance practices and structures in developing countries including Zimbabwe (World Bank, 2016; Muhumed & Sayid, 2016).

Good governance is undoubtedly an important ingredient for the achievement of SDGs in any economy and the improvement of governance practices in Zimbabwe just like elsewhere is a prerequisite for the achievement of development goals. The 21st century has witnessed numerous governance scandals in many countries including Zimbabwe and these scandals hinder the achievement of SDGs since corruption and fraud lead to inefficient allocation of resources initially intended for development purposes. Newspaper headlines continue to parade unethical practices in companies and government departments making it difficult for development initiatives to be fully and efficiently implemented. Despite the funding of my national projects by global institutions targeted at development and human sustenance-related activities, these development-oriented interventions are derailed by poor governance systems and practices (Biermann et al., 2017).

Human Capital Flight Challenge

Brain drain is considered one of the major development impediments in Zimbabwe just like elsewhere in developing countries. Despite the countless efforts by developed countries and global institutions on funding education and training in Zimbabwe and other developing countries, the knowledge gap continues to exist as the educated and trained individuals continue to leave the country in search of greener pastures. The situation is exacerbated by the economic hardships and political tussles between the two main political rivals in the country, persistent economic woes and plagues that continue to rock the country for decades now make it difficult for the graduates to stay in the country in anticipation of changes in economic and employment conditions. As such, most graduates leave the country for neighboring countries and even go as far as overseas in search of job opportunities. According to the UNDP (2020), there are more foreign practicing doctors in America than ever before and this composition of doctors includes a greater proportion of African doctors. The social, economic, and political environments are the chief principal reasons behind the brain drain (Fleiss, 2021; Pineda et al., 2020, UN, 2018).

COVID 19 Pandemic Outbreak

Despite the efforts of global institutions to achieve SDGs, the outbreak of the COVID-19 pandemic has caused devastating effects on all economies around the globe making it difficult to achieve the predetermined goals. The COVID-19 pandemic has affected many sectors of the Zimbabwe economy through a decline in tourists arrival, supply-chain disruptions, a decline in commodity prices, diversion of government's limited resources towards combating COVID-19 pandemic, disruptions in trade flow and decline in direct foreign investment (Ministry of Public Service, Labour and Social Welfare, 2020).

Global Institutional Role

This deadly disease has negatively affected the implementation of SDGs in Zimbabwe due to lockdown restrictions. These outstanding efforts by global institutions underscore the relevance not only in the achievement of SDGs but in all aspects of development (Humphrey, 2020).

Trade Flow Challenge

It has been noted with great concern that the lockdown measures due to the emergence of coronavirus have negatively affected the trade flow in Zimbabwe (Ministry of Public Service, Labour and Social Welfare, 2020). The efforts of global institutions towards the achievement of SDGs in Zimbabwe are appreciated but the trade negotiations between the country and the international community have not been going on very well for about two decades. It has been observed with great concern that the poor relationships between Zimbabwe and western countries are acting as the stumbling block to effective trade flow which is substantiated by a serious deterioration of the balance of payment (Ministry of Foreign Affairs and International Trade, 2019). This makes it difficult for the effort of both the central government and the global institutions to be appreciated as far as development is concerned (Humphrey, 2020; IDA &IMF, 2020). This state of affairs has a negative implication of the achievement of the 17 SDGs in Zimbabwe since the attainment of these SDGs requires inclusive participation.

Debt Sustainability

Restoring debt sustainability in the case of Zimbabwe requires the sustained collaboration of the government and global institutions implementation of fiscal consolidation and comprehensive efforts since the debts accumulated over a long period of time and the arrears have escalated beyond the imaginable level (IDA & IMF, 2020). According to IDA and IMF (2020), Zimbabwe is considered to be in debt distress with untenable public debt and external arrears. The country owes huge amounts to international financial institutions as well as commercial creditors and these long-standing debts continue to thwart the possibility of improving economic activities. Domestic debts continue to escalate as a result of fiscal deficits, inflation, and insignificant access to external finance. IDA& IMF (2020) reported that Zimbabwe's external debts, arrears, and economic crisis requires comprehensive efforts and collaboration of the country and the international community to restore the debt sustainability of the country. No doubt that the international community includes influential and financially stable global institutions such as the IMF, World Bank, UN, WHO, African Development Bank, OECD, and other numerous institutions that are so much concerned with the development initiatives in both developed and developing countries. Not only do global institutions participate in the achievement of SGS in developing countries but developed countries as well contribute significantly through aid and other developmental initiatives.

However, IDA and IMF (2020) reported that establishing absolute debt sustainability for Zimbabwe is not an easy task but rather challenging and uncertain due to the uncertainties surrounding the macro-economic statistics, political squabbles and economic turbulence of the country. Reengagement of the country with the international community especially the western countries and the USA among other countries is not so easy despite the efforts of global institutions and regional entities such as the African Union, SADC, OECD, and the ADB to mention but a few (Biermann et al., 2017; UN, 2016d).

SUCCESS STORIES IN IMPLEMENTING SDGs IN ZIMBABWE

Despite the existence of acute challenges that are acting as stumbling blocks to the execution of SDGs in Zimbabwe, it is important to note that the Zimbabwean government has shown its commitment and dedication to the achievement of SDGs by 2030. The government has learned from past mistakes as it failed to achieve some of the MDGs (Sibanda, 2016). With this in mind, the government managed to prioritize the achievement of the SDGs as from 2016 to 2030. Currently, there are some notable milestones that have been attained in pursuit of the attainment of the 2030 Agenda.

Firstly, the Zimbabwean government managed to come up with a clear institutional framework that promotes the achievement of the 2030 Agenda for Sustainable Development in the country (Ministry of Public Service, Labour and Social Welfare, 2020). In this respect, the coordinating ministry is the Ministry of Public Service, Labour and Social Welfare which is spearheading the achievement of the 2030 Agenda under the supervision of the Office of the President and Cabinet. Secondly, the Zimbabwean government has incorporated the SDGs in National Vision 2030 and the National Budget in an effort to speed up the achievement of the SDGs through inclusive and active participation of all citizens and organizations. Moreover, the government has started to implement National Development Strategy 1 (NDS1) for 2021-2025 which is informed by the SDGs and Africa Agenda 2063 (National Development Strategy 1, 2020). Thirdly, the role of Civil Society Organisations (CSOs) has been widely acknowledged by the Zimbabwean government since these organizations have proved to be effective in advocating for the achievement of SDGs in Zimbabwe as they are embarking on various activities that promote inclusive development (Ministry of Public Service, Labour and Social Welfare, 2020). For example, the Zimbabwean government permitted the formation of the Zimbabwe CSOs Reference Group in 2017. This commendable development creates a conducive platform for dialogue on SDGs among CSOs in Zimbabwe and then these CSOs can also engage and advise the government in relation to SDGs.

METHODOLOGY

This study adopted a systematic literature review methodology on the role of global institutions in promoting the achievement of SDGs in Zimbabwe. This methodology permits a comprehensive analysis of the existing fragmented literature when it comes to the linkage between global institutions and inclusive development. To promote rigor, a literature search strategy in various databases such as Emerald and Google Scholar was adopted as suggested by Page (2008). Systematic review gathers and analyses secondary data available concerning the subject matter. This data was then synthesized and relevant evidence was used to make analyses and interpretations. According to Philips & Barker (2021), systematic review differs from other common types of literature review as it requires accurate and transparent methodology concerning the criteria employed in the research. This form of methodology originated from healthcare and medical although it is now being borrowed by other disciplines. Although the process of reviewing the literature is time-consuming, it was worth the time spent as it brings credible and understandable results from the analysis (Haradhan, 2018). Thematic content analysis was used to analyze data and information gathered from a systematic review. The inclusion criteria were used where articles written in English were employed to narrow down the scope of the research and investigate the relevance of global institutions in the achievement of SDGs in Zimbabwe. Moreover, the analysis spans from 2010 up to the present day where everyone is struggling to deal with the disruptions of the COVID-19 pandemic.

RESULTS AND DISCUSSIONS

This part focuses on the results and discussion related to the role of global institutions in promoting the achievement of SDGs in line with inclusive development tenets. The themes emerged from the analysis of data are captured and discussed as follows:

Alignment and Integration of Development Programs

It emerged that global institutions were playing an enabling role in promoting the achievement of SDGs in Zimbabwe through aligning and integrating the development programs or interventions. The global institutions are committed to the achievement of SDGs in Zimbabwe as well as other countries as they take gradual and coordinated processes for smooth integration of development initiatives. According to IMF (2015), it is important to have monitoring processes for development initiatives in 1-2 years on how developing countries are responding to evolving needs in developing nations. Planned programs of the World Bank, the IMF, and other institutions need pilot studies so that initiatives are aligned to the central administration's approaches towards the achievement of SDGs.

Despite the numerous arguments for and against global institutions as well as their criticism, the positive contributions by these institutions are significant. A point to take note of in the argument about the contribution of global institutions like the IMF and the World Bank is that the systems and structures of these institutions which are dominated by the western countries were designed to serve the west and not intended to serve the less developed countries many of which fall in the African continent and some parts of Asia (Ravallion, 2016; Muhumed & Sayid, 2016).

Developmental Policy Advocacy and Guidance

Another emerged theme was related to the role of global institutions in promoting the achievement of SDGs is developmental policy advocacy and guidance in Zimbabwe. It is within this context that the government of Zimbabwe acknowledged the role of global institutions especially the UN when it comes to developmental policy advocacy and guidance (Ministry of Public Service, Labour and Social Welfare, 2020; Sibanda, 2016). The IMF as well as the World Bank among other international institutions help struggling economies to come up with sound financial and economic regulatory policies and these help in the management of debt sustainability and public financial management (IMF, 2020).

Global institutions provide financial assistance as well as policy guidelines for struggling economies. For years the IMF has been focusing on assisting Zimbabwe in terms of financial policies that can stimulate sustainable development as the country find it difficult to pay back the dues accumulating from borrowing (IMF, 2015). The Debt Sustainability Analysis (DSA) framework, for instance, is considered to be one of the most effective panaceas or diagnostic tools that are recommended by IMF to monitor debt vulnerability. The IMF policy guidance also provides struggling economies with greater flexibility on how to finance development projects or investments at the same time containing risks. The World Bank together with the IMF has been working together for decades now to provide technical assistance to developing countries on debt management through what is known as the Debt Management Facility. The Debt Management Facility also provides financial assistance on capacity-building projects (Humphrey, 2020; IMF, 2020; World Bank, 2017). Besides policy guidance, the World Bank and IMF perform diagnostic activities and analyses on how debt vulnerabilities in developing countries have evolved and accumulated over the years. In this regard, the international institutions know what they are dealing with, what to address, and come up with proper recommendations on policy changes and implementation (IMF 2016).

According to Muhumed & Sayid (2016), the World Bank and IMF's contribution to developing countries can be traced way back to the early 1960s providing both financial and technical assistance to less developed countries in the region. However, the generosity of the global institutions is castigated and questioned with some claims that the international institutions are actually assisting the already developed countries despite the extreme marginalization of developing countries. Decision-making by global institutions seems to be made on the basis of creating loopholes that exploit resources from developing countries in favor of the developed economies hence the policy recommendations by the global institutions are contested (Milner, 2005). Global institutions are also accused of providing destructive technical and financial support aimed at retarding the less developed economies for the benefit of developed countries who need the market of their products and services.

Sensitization and Dissemination of Developmental Information

Sensitization and dissemination of developmental information emerged as another enabling role of global institutions in promoting the achievement of SDGs in Zimbabwe. According to IMF (2015), international institutions continue to lead the way as far as strengthening statistical data dissemination or knowledge sharing is concerned. The IMF, World Bank, and other international institutions promote knowledge sharing by leveraging technology and data exchange platforms such as the Enhanced General Data Dissemination System (e-GDDS) including the cloud-based systems and the Open Data Platforms (IMF, 2016). The e-GDDS is much applauded and appreciated for its role in improving production capacity as well as data dissemination and monitoring SDGs that are considered relevant for the work of the IMF. More so, the IMF and the World Bank systems such as Open Data Platforms and the e-GDDS provides stimulus for data transparency as these systems address the impediments to data dissemination such as incipient technical expertise and inadequate resource allocation for SDGs related activities (IMF,2016; World Bank, 2020; Pineda et al., 2020).

Despite the claims by the global institutions such as the IMF and the World Bank that they are concerned with the achievement of SDGs of all countries including developing countries, international institutions are criticized for practicing bad governance crafting and recommending biased policies, and protecting the interests of the western economies (Muhumed & Sayid, 2016; Elsayid, 2016).

Capacity Building on Developmental Programs

It is worth mentioning that capacity building on developmental programs also emerged as one of the enabling roles of global institutions in the achievement of SDGs in Zimbabwe. The outstanding performance of international organizations to capacity building as well as sustainable development is uncontested. For instance, ILO and UN contribution to fair labor practices awareness campaigns and fair representation enhances capacity building as well in Zimbabwe. Global Public Policies advocated for by the United Nations and the international community is actually one of the most prevalent issues on the global scenario getting attention not only from the international institutions but central administrations as well (Sibanda, 2016). Evidence from the literature confirms that the IMF, World Bank, African Development Bank Group, and other partners strive to advance capacity-building initiatives in Zimbabwe just like everywhere

Global Institutional Role

globally as a way of enhancing development initiatives and ensuring community participation and inclusion in development programs (African Development Bank Group, 2018). Capacity-building efforts of the global institutions do not only improve community participation in development initiatives but also build states and institutions with an investment culture and environment hence improving the GDP and per capita income as well as reducing the unemployment rate among other things.

Financing Inclusive Developmental Programs

Contribution by the World Bank, the IMF, and other global institutions on financial assistance to Zimbabwe and other developing countries is undoubtedly appreciated although there are some controversial arguments against the motive behind the provision of financial aid and technical assistance. Policy recommendations by the World Bank and the IMF for instance, strengthen revenue mobilization for developing countries with developed countries as case studies that are followed. However international institutions do not provide enough of the much-needed financial aid due to the creditworthiness of the countries in need of financial assistance in terms of loans and other financial requirements. Zimbabwe has accumulated huge amounts of debt from the international organizations and can no longer continue to accrue more loans unless other economic turnaround developments can convince the international community about the creditworthiness of the country (World Bank, 2016; World Bank 2020; IDA & IMF, 2020).

Despite the challenges witnessed over the past two decades, global institutions continue to offer financial assistance to Zimbabwe but reports continue to hit the front pages of the newspapers that development or even relief aid from the international institutions is being diverted to other non-related expenditures by the central government (Dugger, 2008; Gagne-Acoulon, 2020). Hence political and economic reforms are much needed if the country is to witness the achievement of SDGs despite the countless efforts of the international institutions.

SOLUTIONS AND RECOMMENDATIONS

The recommendations are offered in light of the results related to the role of global institutions in promoting the achievement of the SDGs in Zimbabwe. These recommendations are as follows:

Unlocking International Finance: The global financial institutions such as World Bank, IMF and African Development Bank Group should unconditionally unlock access to finance by the Zimbabwean government. The international funds can then be channeled towards the implementation of SDGs in Zimbabwe. Management of the financial aid provided by the international institutions does not only entail the use of the money for its intended use but also includes improvement as far as the circular flow of national income and the finance-related issues. Financial reforms can include such frameworks as the Debt Sustainability Analysis advocated for by the IMF in many countries as a way of monitoring the debt vulnerabilities.

Collaborations and Partnerships: The global institutions should also work hand in hand with the local development partners so as to promote the effective implementation of SDGs through inclusive and active participation of the citizens. Moreover, collaborations of global institutions and the central government can be expanded so as to improve the resources and ideas from different institutions. Collaborations of the World Bank and IMF are the most common collaborations and these can be expanded by incorporating other regional and global institutions.

Political Will: The government should display a high level of political will with respect to the achievement of SDGs. Based on the results, it is clear that the leaders of the country play an important role in inclusive development.

Improvement of Governance Systems and Practices: It is evident that the length of SDGs achievement and efforts of the international institutions is affected by the policies and development programs as well as political governance. Therefore, the Zimbabwean government should enhance systems and practices related to governance so as to reduce corruption and nepotism when it comes to the implementation of programs designed to realize SDGs. For instance, there were corruption scandals in the country surrounding the COVID-19 funds received from global institutions.

Improving International Co-operation: Some financial impediments obstructing the success of development initiatives by global institutions are related to the poor relations between the government of Zimbabwe and the western economies who happen to have an influence on the disposal of financial assistance to the global scenario. Therefore, the government should re-engage with the western economies so as to unlock international finance for funding development intervention in line with the SDGs. It is high time the longstanding feud between the country and the western economies be resolved as this affects ordinary citizens more than the public office bearers.

FUTURE RESEARCH DIRECTIONS

This study focused on a systematic literature review on the role of global institutions in promoting the achievement of SDGs in Zimbabwe. In this respect, it is recommended that future developmental studies can focus on the collection of empirical evidence in Zimbabwe. Notably, comparative studies among African countries are welcomed which focus on the challenges faced by global institutions in promoting the achievement of SDGs in African countries. Moreover, a quantitative impact assessment study on the role of global institutions in promoting SGDs is recommended.

CONCLUSION

This study focused on the role of global institutions in promoting the achievement of SDGs in Zimbabwe. This inquiry adds value to an under-researched subject of inclusive sustainable development with special emphasis on global institutions. The contribution of these global institutions is hotly debated in the current development discourse. This debate provides the basis for expanding our understanding of the role of global institutions, especially from the perspective of developing countries. However, very little is known about the role of global institutions in promoting the achievement of SGDs in Zimbabwe especially in the face of the COVID-19 pandemic. Therefore, this study examines the role of global institutions in promoting the achievement of SDGs in Zimbabwe. This study establishes that global institutions play an enabling role when it comes to the achievement of SDGs in Zimbabwe through developmental policy advocacy and guidance, sensitization and dissemination of information, capacity building, and financing developmental programs. Based on these findings, a plethora of recommendations has been proposed which include expansion of the collaboration, improvement of governance systems and practices, improving international cooperation, and fiscal revenue reforms. Notably, comparative research among African countries is welcomed when it comes to challenges faced by global institutions in promoting the achievement of SDGs in African countries.

REFERENCES

African Development Bank Group. (2018). *Zimbabwe - Governance and Institutional Strengthening Project*. Retrieved September 15, 2021, from https://projectsportal.afdb.org/dataportal/VProject/show/P-ZW-KF0-005

Apergis, N., Gozgor, G., & Lau, C. K. M. (2021). Globalization and environmental problems in developing countries. *Environmental Science and Pollution Research International, 28*(26), 33719–33721. doi:10.100711356-021-14105-z PMID:33945090

Balsalobre-Lorente, D., Driha, O. M., Shahbaz, M., & Sinha, A. (2020). The effects of tourism and globalization over environmental degradation in developed countries. *Environmental Science and Pollution Research International, 27*(7), 7130–7144. doi:10.100711356-019-07372-4 PMID:31879881

Biermann, F., Kanie, N., & Kim, R.E., (2017). Global governance by goal-setting: the novel approach of the UN Sustainable Development Goals. *Current Opinion on Environment Sustainability, 26-27*, 26-31.

Bochańczyk-Kupka, D., & Pęciak, R. (2015). Institutions in the context of sustainable development. *A Multidisciplinary Journal of Global Macro Trends, 4*(5), 29-41.

Dugger, C. W. (2008). *Aid group says Zimbabwe misused $7.3 million*. Retrieved March 27, 2022, from https://www.nytimes.com/2008/11/03/world/africa/03zimbabwe.html

Dzingirai, M. (2020). Demographic determinants of youth entrepreneurial success. *International Journal of Sustainable Entrepreneurship and Corporate Social Responsibility, 5*(2), 1–16. doi:10.4018/IJSECSR.2020070101

Dzingirai, M. (2021). The role of entrepreneurship in reducing poverty in agricultural communities. *Journal of Enterprising Communities: People and Places in the Global Economy*. doi:10.1108/JEC-01-2021-0016

Elsayid, E. (2016). *The Hidden Role of WB and IMF in Developing Countries. Egypt, Malaysia and Turkey*. AV Akademikerverlag.

Fleiss, P. (2021). Multilateral development banks in Latin America: recent trends, the response to the pandemic, and the forthcoming role. Economic Commission for Latin America and the Caribbean (ECLAC).

Gagne-Acoulon, S. (2020). *Zimbabwe's health minister charged for COVID-19 corruption*. Retrieved March 27, 2022, from https://www.occrp.org/en/daily/12594-zimbabwe-s-health-minister-charged-for-covid-19-corruption

Glass, L. M., & Newig, J. (2019). Governance for achieving the Sustainable Development Goals: How important are participation, policy coherence, reflexivity, adaptation and democratic institutions? *Earth System Governance, 2*, 100031. doi:10.1016/j.esg.2019.100031

Haradhan, M. (2018). Qualitative Research Methodology in Social Sciences and Related Subjects. *Journal of Economic Development. Environment and People*, *7*(1), 23–48.

Humphrey, C. (2020). *All Hands on Deck: How to Scale Up Multilateral Financing to Face the COVID-19 Crisis.* ODI Emerging Analysis and Ideas.

IDA & IMF. (2020). *Joint World Bank-IMF Debt Sustainability Analysis.* Retrieved September 15, 2021, from https://www.imf.org/en/About/Factsheets/Sheets/2016/08/01/16/39/Debt-Sustainability-Framework-for-Low-Income-Countries

International Monetary Fund. (2015a). *Financing for Development: Revisiting the Monterrey Consensus.* Retrieved September 10, 2021, from https://www.imf.org/en/Publications/Policy-Papers/Issues/2016/12/31/Financing-For-Development-Revisiting-the-Monterrey-Consensus-PP4966

International Monetary Fund. (2015b). *Financing for Development: Enhancing the Financial Safety Net for Developing Countries.* Retrieved September 10, 2021, from https://www.imf.org/en/Publications/Policy-Papers/Issues/2016/12/31/Financing-for-Development-Enhancing-the-Financial-Safety-Net-for-Developing-Countries-PP4965

Johnstone, I. (2021). The G20, climate change and COVID-19: Critical juncture or critical wound? *Fulbright Review of Economics and Policy*, *1*(2), 227–245. doi:10.1108/FREP-05-2021-0031

Meuleman, L., & Niestroy, I. (2015). Common but differentiated governance: A meta governance approach to make the SDGs work. *Sustainability*, *7*, 12295-12321.

Milner, H. V. (2005). Globalization, Development, and International Institutions: Normative and Positive Perspectives. *Perspectives on Politics*, *3*(4), 833–854. doi:10.1017/S1537592705050474

Ministry of Foreign Affairs and International Trade. (2019). *Impact on Zimbabwe and the region of the unilateral sanctions imposed by the United States of America and the European Union.* Retrieved September 20, 2021 from http://www.zimfa.gov.zw/index.php/component/k2/item/49-impact-on-zimbabwe-and-the-region-of-the-unilateral-sanctions-imposed-by-the-united-states-of-america-and-the-european-union

Ministry of Public Service, Labour and Social Service. (2020). *Zimbabwe Progress Review Report of Sustainable Development Goals (SDGs).* Retrieved September 10, 2021, from https://www.mpslsw.gov.zw/download/zimbabwe-sdgs-progress-report-december-2020-pdf/

Muhumed, M. M., & Sayid, A. G. (2016). The World Bank and IMF in Developing Countries: Helping or Hindering? *International Journal of African and Asian Studies*, *28*, 39–49.

National Development Strategy 1. (2020). *National Development Strategy 1- January 2021 – December 2025: Towards a prosperous & empowered upper middle income society by 2030.* Retrieved September 1, 2021, from https://www.veritaszim.net/sites/veritas_d/files/NDS.pdf

Newig, J., Vob, J.P., & Monstadt, J. (2007). Governance for sustainable development in the face of ambivalence, uncertainty and distributed power: An introduction. *Journal of Environment Policy Plan*, *9,* 185-192.

Page, D. (2008). Systematic literature searching and the bibliographic database haystack. *Electronic Journal of Business Research Methods*, *6*(2), 171–180.

Global Institutional Role

Phillips, V., & Barker, E. (2021). Systematic reviews: Structure, form and content. *Journal of Perioperative Practice*, *31*(9), 349–353. doi:10.1177/1750458921994693 PMID:34228554

Pineda, E., Valencia, O., & Andrian, L. (2020). *Possible macro-fiscal consequences of COVID-19 in Latin America*. Inter-American Development Bank.

Ravallion, M. (2016). The World Bank: Why it is still needed and why it still disappoints. *The Journal of Economic Perspectives*, *30*(1), 77–94. doi:10.1257/jep.30.1.77

Sibanda, D. M. (2016). *Zimbabwe position paper on Sustainable Development Goals (SDGs)*. Retrieved September 10, 2021, from https://www.scribd.com/document/510783065/Sibanda-SDG-Position-Paper-Presentation-11-May-2016-1

Sundaram, J. K. (2015). *Pathways Through Financial Crisis: Argentina Pathways through Financial Crisis*. Retrieved September 15, 2021 from https://law-journals-books.vlex.com/vid/pathways-through-financial-crisis-argentina-56822020

United Nations. (2015). *Millennium Development Goals Report, Lessons Learned in Implementing the MDGs: Assessing Progress in Africa toward the Millennium Development Goals. Economic Commission for Africa, Addis Ababa, Ethiopia*. Retrieved September 20, 2021, from https://www.afdb.org/fileadmin/uploads/afdb/Documents/Publications/MDG_Report_2015.pdf

United Nations. (2016a). *The Sustainable Development Goals Report 2016*. Author.

United Nations. (2016b). *The changing political economy of globalization: Multilateral Institutions and the 2030 Agenda*. Retrieved July 20, 2021, from https://www.un.org/ecosoc/sites/www.un.org.ecosoc/files/files/en/2016doc/2016-globalization-mtg-bcknote.pdf

United Nations. (2016c). *The Sustainable Development Goals Report 2016*. United Nations Publications Department of Economic and Social Affairs (DESA). Retrieved September 10, 2021, from https://www.un.org/development/desa/publications/sustainable-development-goals-report-2016.html

World Bank. (2013). *Inclusion matters: The foundation for shared prosperity*. World Bank.

World Bank. (2016d). *World Bank Annual Report 2016*. World Bank.

World Bank. (2018). *AFCC2/RI-ACBF Regional Capacity Building Project (P122478)*. Retrieved September 20, 2021, from https://projects.worldbank.org/en/projects-operations/project-detail/P122478

World Bank. (2021). *Zimbabwe Economic Update: COVID-19 Further complicates Zimbabwe's economic and social conditions*. Retrieved September 1, 2021, from https://www.worldbank.org/en/country/zimbabwe/publication/zimbabwe-economic-update-covid-19-further-complicates-zimbabwe-s-economic-and-social-conditions

ADDITIONAL READING

Allen, C., Metternicht, G., & Wiedmann, T. (2018). Initial progress in implementing the sustainable development goals (SDGs): A review of evidence from countries. *Sustainability Science, 13*(5), 1453–1467. doi:10.100711625-018-0572-3

Assuad, C. S. A. (2020). Understanding rationality in sustainable development decision-making: Unfolding the motivations for action. *Journal of the Knowledge Economy, 11*(3), 1086–1119. doi:10.100713132-019-0585-x

Barbier, E. B., & Burgess, J. C. (2020). Sustainability and development after COVID-19. *World Development, 135*, 105082. doi:10.1016/j.worlddev.2020.105082 PMID:32834381

Ivanova, M. (2013). Reforming the Institutional Framework for Environment and Sustainable Development: Rio+20's Subtle but Significant Impact. *International Journal of Technology Management & Sustainable Development, 12*(3), 211–231. doi:10.1386/tmsd.12.3.211_1

Mukarram, M. (2020). Impact of covid-19 on the UN sustainable development goals (SDGs). *Strategic Analysis, 44*(3), 253–258. doi:10.1080/09700161.2020.1788363

Nerini, F. F., Sovacool, B., Hughes, N., Cozzi, L., Cosgrave, E., Howells, M., Tavoni, M., Tomei, J., Zerriffi, H., & Milligan, B. (2019). Connecting climate action with other sustainable development goals. *Nature Sustainability, 2*(8), 674–680. doi:10.103841893-019-0334-y

Pham-Truffert, M., Metz, F., Fischer, M., Rueff, H., & Messerli, P. (2020). Interactions among sustainable development goals: Knowledge for identifying multipliers and virtuous cycles. *Sustainable Development, 28*(5), 1236–1250. doi:10.1002d.2073

Popovic, B., Soja, S. J., Paunovic, T., & Maletic, R. (2019). Evaluation of sustainable development management in EU countries. *Sustainability, 11*(24), 7140. doi:10.3390u11247140

Razzaq, S., Chaudhry, K., Tabassum, R., Kunwal, N., Najafizada, S. A. M., Acharya, S. S., Ellepola, Y., Chowdhury, M. E., Neupane, S., Kumar, B. C. R., & ... . (2020). National level preparedness for implementing the health-related sustainable development goals (SDGs) in seven South Asian countries: Afghanistan, Bangladesh, Bhutan, India, Pakistan, Nepal and Sri Lanka. *Global Policy, 11*(1), 191–201. doi:10.1111/1758-5899.12753

KEY TERMS AND DEFINITIONS

COVID-19 Pandemic: A deadly disease that is caused by a coronavirus.

Development: A process whereby the country enhances its economic and social status through the implementation of various programs.

Global Institutions: These are international organizations that are composed of many countries across the globe.

Globalization: A process whereby people, organizations, and governments interact and integrate across the world.

Inclusive Development: A process whereby all people and organizations are given the opportunities to participate in the development process.

National Development Strategy 1: It is a 5-year Zimbabwean Mid-Term Plan that is aimed at attaining the country's vision 2030 and the global aspirations of the SDGs as well as a well-thought Africa Agenda 2063.

Sustainable Development: A process of meeting the present needs of the people without compromising the ability of the future generation to meet its social, economic, and environmental needs.

Chapter 7
Global Institutional Roles in Access to Inclusive Education:
Comparison of Serbia and Europe

Biljana Stojan Ilic
https://orcid.org/0000-0001-6137-8478
Megatrend University of Belgrade, Serbia

Gordana P. Djukic
https://orcid.org/0000-0001-5419-0725
Faculty of Economics, The University of Belgrade, Serbia

Tatjana Cvetkovski
Megatrend University in Belgrade, Serbia

ABSTRACT

The aim of the chapter is to point the importance of global institutions and their role in access to inclusive education. Globalization as a world phenomenon has brought great changes both in the way of doing business and in other social spheres. First of all, a positive attitude towards the acceptance of diversity among people is the key word concerning at the social component. The modern world is facing great changes and the most important issues can be solved by education for sustainable growth and development. The authors will emphasize the comparison of Serbia and one developed European country in terms of inclusive education to highlight good practice and to apply it in Serbia.

INTRODUCTION

The key arguments for supporting inclusion are not just educational - they involve a variety of ethical and social factors. In defining the concept of inclusion, the existence of different and often conflicting opinions means that the term is controversial - inclusion refers at the same time to the individual values, but also social and educational values. Inclusive education is a concept, a movement, a process, a phi-

DOI: 10.4018/978-1-6684-2448-3.ch007

Copyright © 2022, IGI Global. Copying or distributing in print or electronic forms without written permission of IGI Global is prohibited.

Global Institutional Roles in Access to Inclusive Education

losophy, and educational practice but also a policy. To make certain terms easier for understanding, and to explain them, there is a noticeable inconsistency, ie in practice - the existence of misunderstandings and contradictions. What has caused the application of inclusion and how is inclusion a part of Globalization? Preparing for final unification, in the mid-1990s, Europe affirmed the principle of recognizing and accepting diversity as one of the guiding principles in the formation of European economic and political power (Jovanovic, 2004). Diversity was considered a major catalyst for scientific, technological, and innovative development.

The diffusion of knowledge and technology was supposed to enable strong cross-cultural and cross-regional cooperation that would satisfy the needs not only of the most developed but also of other European countries. New forms of education and training staff were considered strategic goals in the development process, the so-called learning organizations that were supposed to respond to the diverse needs of peoples of different origins and different cultures living in Europe. Mixing and knowing national cultures was desirable knowledge for the successful functioning of a united Europe multiracial concept, multiculturalism. The creation of a new and united Europe depended on the success of the transnational and transcultural intersection of knowledge and cultures. (Jovanovic and Langovic, 2009).

Old Europe has moved towards a new Europe based on cultural regions, thus building new mechanisms for external relations but also internal cohesion. The new Europe has become much more than a common market and economic competition. It was built on social democracy, women's law, equality and equal opportunities for all inhabitants, multilingualism, multiracial concept, multiculturalism (Ilic, Mihajlovic and Karabasevic, 2016). To make it easier to understand the concept of national culture, it is necessary to define it as a system of values, assumptions, beliefs, norms, and attitudes that members of a nation have to key issues and problems that are specific to the historical past of the nation. Consequently, national culture is an essential determinant of management styles in different social spheres (Ilic et al., 2021). Because, from the assumptions, attitudes, and ways in which members of a nation are perceived by people, their behavior and human values, depending on how it will deal with them and whether they will accept their differences (Vasilic and Brkovic, 2017).

It is the inclusion that is involving and recognizing people who are different from traditional stereotypes, ie the majority. There is no shame to be different, but it is inexcusable not to accept that someone is different from us. Education is a broad term and may refer to the general knowledge of an individual or group, as well as to technical and professional education. By educating people to learn to acquire knowledge, creating a new knowledge base, and enriching its upgraded same values. When education is mentioned, it refers mainly to institutions that transfer knowledge to young generations and enable them for further development and progress - both personal and social. Educational institutions, therefore, represent a bridge between the youth, energy, and the development of the necessary knowledge, which in turn contribute to creating better and more educated, primarily - mature people (Djukic and Ilic, 2020).

Education begins from the earliest childhood, ie from the family that has the initial role in the upbringing of the child, and then continues in schools and other educational institutions. What kind of education do international institutions and initiatives strive for? International initiatives aimed at inclusive education related to the education of all children. The ultimate goal of these initiatives is not only quality education but also more inclusive societies. Inclusion is usually broadly defined as a program in which children with disabilities and their peers without disabilities, jointly participate in program content and activities.

It is emphasized that activities take place not only in the classroom but also outside the school, within the community in which the children live (Guralnick, 2001; Odom, 2002). The key arguments for supporting inclusion are not exclusively educational but also include significant ethical and social factors.

119

Inclusive education takes a more inclusive society through the changes that are organized at the school level, which are the first organized form of society that children encounter (Sretenov, 2008).

The authors will also point out the important features of inclusive education, which are defined both on children's rights and on equality and providing a chance to a certain group of children, ie people with special needs, for quality education. To arrive at the last information on the degree of inclusive education in Serbia, the previous studies of authors and experts will be used in this field, and then through interviews, provided the latest information on inclusive education in Serbia - authors will talk with teachers from certain schools of Eastern Serbia, trying to show how much progress has been made in Serbia, towards inclusive education and what attitudes teachers have about this process.

The paper aims to point out good practices from European countries with a tendency to apply them in Serbia. The authors will, in addition to interviews (with teaching staff in some regional - school institutions of Serbia) compare the extent to which inclusion is included in Serbian society and the extent to which it is included in educational institutions in one of the most developed European countries (the example of Finland).

BACKGROUND

Key ideas about inclusion occur in mid last century in the context of different social movements that indicate the need for all human beings has the same rights. Based on these initiatives, strategic guidelines and standard rules for equalizing the position of marginalized groups, ie persons with special needs (with developmental difficulties) have been formulated, especially concerning exercising the right to education. Inclusion implies a networked, flexible system in which it is assumed that all children or persons can learn and mutually accept differences in terms of interests, abilities, ethnic origin, previous experiences, and knowledge (Grenot-Scheyer et.al., 1996).

With the development of the idea of inclusion - the rights of persons with disabilities, over time, have become the subject of interest of the United Nations and other international organizations. Numerous international documents have appeared, which have considered the mentioned problems of both children and adults with developmental disabilities. These problems were considered from the point of children's rights, but also from equal opportunities for all - not only in terms of education but also in terms of inclusion in community activities, from which such persons were until then mostly excluded. In these documents, the idea of inclusive education had a positive connotation in terms of the impact on the realization of children and the rights of the elderly, namely: the right to non-discrimination, the right to survival and development, the right to live in their families, the right to quality education -the right to have their opinion heard and respected.

According to some authors (Shea and Bauer, 1997), inclusion implies that people with special needs (especially children), regardless of ability, should belong to the regular education system. According to Stubss (1998), inclusive education is a strategy whose ultimate goal is to promote an inclusive society where children and adults, regardless of gender, age, abilities, ethnicity, and difficulty, are enabled to participate and educate according to their abilities.

An inclusive society is characterized by a reduction in inequality, a balance between the rights and obligations of the individual, and an increase in social cohesion (Center for Economic and Social Inclusion, 2002). According to Pasalic-Kreso, inclusion - as an idea, a movement - even today as a practice, has emerged from four important sources, which are a large number of studies that have indicated inequalities in education; postulates of critical theories of society, upbringing, and education whose teachings have contributed to the initiation of their reforms; the latest scientific research and achievements on individual differences, types of intelligence, brain functions, emotional and social intelligence, and the provisions of the Declaration of Human Rights, the provisions of the Convention on the Rights of the Child, affirming the value of every human being and child(Pasalic-Kreso, 2003).

Explaining inclusion through individual-society relations, according to Ceric and Alic, the term - social inclusion is introduced and the following dependent dimensions are stated: (a) spatial: social inclusion as close social and economic distance; (b) respectively: social inclusion as a sense of belonging and acceptance (positive interactions, being valued, having useful social roles, participation), and (c) functional: social inclusion as increasing opportunities, abilities and competencies (Ceric and Alic, 2005). The essence and value is respect for diversity among people, which should be used to spread knowledge, enrich experiences and develop positive personality traits. In the context of education, this would mean that everyone has an equal right to be educated according to their abilities. Equality understood in this way contributes to the reduction and eradication of all forms of division, isolation, and discrimination.

According to Hawawini (2011), educational institutions need to be interconnected in the global world to have a credible educational experience and relevant learning experience. Through institutions, employees in the education sector should be continuously educated, attend innovative courses, to be informed about standards, programs, and research topics related to modern education at the national and global level. In this way, knowledge of the international/intercultural dimension in education/learning, research, and functional services of institutions would be united (Hawawini, 2011). Political and educational decisions are needed for countries to adequately and inclusively face the challenges in educational institutions - with curricula, programs, professional and educated staff, that all together affect the entire educational process (Cabezudo et al., 2019).

Global Institution Importance for Inclusive Education

The term globalization comes from the word globe or global, which means „wholeness". It is a relatively new term for some old processes that were previously called differently. Synonyms for the term globalization are "universalization", "internationalization". Its origin can be traced to the French word "global", which also refers to integrity and totality (Venables, 1999). The term is defined and understood differently - it has positive and dark sides. According to the first definition, it is defined as an optimistic process that brings the development of technology, acceptance of inequality, market expansion, higher profits, easier life, scientific progress, the collapse of dictatorial regimes, and the enjoyment of consumption (hence the need to connect the world without national borders). On the dark side, globalization is also understood as a necessary evil, the dominance of the USA and the EU in all aspects of life: economy, politics, culture (thus as a form of colonialism and imperialism over small nations) (Vladimirov, 2001). Some authors about globalization say that interdependence is a basic feature of current social life and the state of countries (Wiener, 1950).

According to Madzar, globalization is a process of territorial expansion of economic activities that, besides inevitable changes in the structure of demand, has changes in technology - as its fundamental cause and basic driver. It is also the basis for the formulation of the property that proves to be crucial in globalization: it is the impossibility of predicting numerous and multi-intertwined currents of globalization. Therefore, the proposition that it is certainly an unmanageable process can be accepted as a starting platform in understanding globalization without much risk (Madzar, 2015). "Globalization means

- turning the world into a single space. In the economic sphere, globalization is primarily the expansion of the market. In addition to the prominent geographical expansion, as well as the expansion resulting from technological progress, among other things, globalization is manifested as a rapid increase in the number of different goods and different varieties within (quality, location, delivery conditions, after-sales service). A special form of market expansion also occurs, caused by the spectacular development of information systems - resulting in strong increasing of information" (Drasković and Jovovic, 2008).

The activities of multinational companies on the world market, which have developed to unprecedented proportions in the last thirty years, have been unique - called by many authors as globalization (Pejovic, 2008; Sekulovic, 2004; Stojanovic, 2005). The World Trade Organization also contributed to the process of globalization, ie the increase of international trade, by reducing customs rates and removing other restrictions that hindered dynamic development - the International Development Association and other international and regional organizations (Movius, 2010).

The globalization process carries with it certain negativeness that affects the expression of inequality and instability, low level of social justice, unified tastes and customs, the easier the operation of terrorist and other criminal groups and other social groups, the easier the transfer of a variety of diseases and vice, a negative effect on the environment, etc. Inequality is most often manifested in very large differences in wages between employees with and without qualifications."Globalization does not recognize that people are born with unequal abilities, but it does acknowledge that they have the same desires for life in a welfare state (Amadi and Agena 2015).

Globalization can be defined as the intensification of social relations that connect distant places in such a way that local events are shaped by events that took place miles away and vice versa (Gidens, 2003). Globalization means all those processes by which people all over the world are incorporated into one-world society, that is, a global society. „Globalization is simply an intensification of global inter-connectedness" (Vuletic, 2003). Globalization is one powerful myth in the full sense of the word, one powerful discourse, one strong idea, which has a social force that achieves belief. This is the main weapon in the struggle against the achievements of the welfare state (Krais, 1999). International organizations Council of Europe, UNESCO, United Nations, through the promotion of inclusive education have raised awareness that governments, individuals, and organizations need to develop and accept interdependence and cooperation. At the 1994 World Conference on Special Educational Needs, UNESCO stressed that all schools should be adapted to children regardless of their physical, intellectual, social, emotional, linguistic, or other condition, as regular inclusive schooling can effectively build an inclusive society and achieve equality in education (UNESCO, 2022; Rakonic Leskovar, 2018).

By the Declaration on Global Education in Maastricht, from 15 to 17 November 2002, from a holistic point of view, global education is defined as "education that opens people's eyes and minds to the reality of the world and movement to create a world of greater justice, fairness and human rights for all ". Such education has global dimensions, it implies human rights, sustainability, peace and conflict prevention, and intercultural education for all citizens. The defined goals of the program of the Center for Global Education North-South of the Council of Europe are following the UNESCO Decade of Education for Sustainable Development of the United Nations. The goals of the Program are to achieve partnership, networking, and dialogue between experts, policy-makers, and civil society, "between peoples, culture and religion at the micro and macro levels" (Cabezudo et al., 2008).

According to UNICEF's definition, inclusive quality education is an educational process in which services are provided to each school to "work for each child" to realize each child's full potential. In addition to promotional activities, UNICEF supported the concept of CFS, according to which inclusive education should be directed towards children who have the right to learn in a healthy, stimulating, and safe environment, with competent teachers, appropriate educational resources, and social learning conditions. CFS includes, in addition to educational activities, other services in the "package" such as health, nutrition, water, sanitation, etc. to maximize improvements in education, and the quality of knowledge and learning.

The main principles of CFS are: 1. Focus on children: during the educational process, the primary protection is the interests of the child; 2. Democratic participation: children as right holders have the right to speak in the education process; 3. Inclusion: It is the responsibility of every society to ensure that all children have the right to education; 4. Protection: children have the right to be protected from "being hurt and mistreated, physically and mentally" (Farkas, 2014). UNICEF's activities are aimed at developing a survey model for households. Survey models provide households with data on children with disabilities to perform a statistical assessment of children's disabilities; provides literature in the form of a disability assessment manual, a guide for teachers to disability education management information systems, and accessible learning literature for children with disabilities (Farkas, 2014). The international and European organizations have accepted the guidelines of the United Nations Sustainable Development Agenda. In the conditions of the COVID-19 pandemic, a global economic crisis arose. The pandemic had negative consequences for the global educational system, and on global economic development goals (SDGs): SDG-3: health and well-being, SDG-1: inequalities and poverty, SDG-2: food supply food insecurity, SDG-7-9, SDG-11-15: environmental sustainability, SDG-4: inclusive and equitable to education was limited, with a projection that more than 200 million children will still be out of education by 2030 (Popesku, 2021).

The international organizations, as well as the Council of Europe, have cooperation based on the acquis and the goals of global sustainable development. In doing so, the Council of Europe contributes to EU countries and member states in the form of a multilateral approach to the education crisis due to the COVID-19 pandemic (Council of Europe, 2020). Given that the COVID-19 pandemic had negative effects on the education system, it is necessary to examine in the forthcoming future the priorities of innovative action related to inclusive education, in accordance with certain principles: 1. responding to learners' (students have the right to appropriate information and legally on o participation in all hearings and decisions regarding their education), 2. active participation of learners (learners are entitled to be active participants in the life of the school and community); 3. positive teacher attitudes (teachers should have positive attitudes towards all learners and will work collaboratively with colleagues); 4. effective teacher skills (all teachers should develop the skills to meet the diverse needs of all learners); 5. visionary school leadership (school leaders should value diversity among staff as well as learners, encourage collegiality and support innovation), and 6. coherent interdisciplinary services (every school should have access to the support of interdisciplinary community services) (European Agency, 2011).

INCLUSION AND EDUCATION

The first association for the term inclusion is the inclusion of children with disabilities in the regular educational system, which is the true meaning of the word today. Inclusion, however, is a broader concept that is not only related to the educational system but also involves the inclusion of a child or individual in social life at all levels. This means that the first step of inclusion is acceptance of persons with disabilities within the family, practically at birth. A second step is a quality place in society. Followed by education and assimilation of skills for independent life and work in the community. The independence and dignity of adults with disabilities is the outcome of full inclusion - means the degree of society, and respect for human rights that apply to all members of society.

The basic principle in working with children and adults with disabilities is respect for and the indivisibility of human rights. Some of the important principles in working with children and adults with disabilities are shown in Figure 1. The figure represents the balance between the process of full participation in decision-making and the ability to choose services and service providers. These two sides are realized through the following sub-processes: *comprehensive* consideration needs and satisfaction, *the availability* and variety of services, at the same time *encouraging* independence through *living* in a natural environment.

Figure 1. Principles of operation with people with special needs – children and
Source: Beker, et al., 2020.

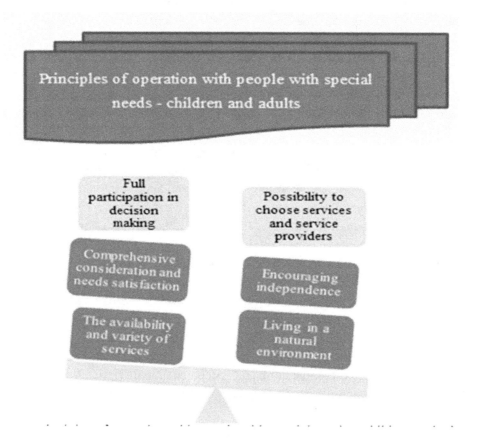

A developed inclusive society implies the creation of a "school tailored to the child", ie to enable all children to realize their full potential. It is necessary to adapt the school curriculum to the child's individual needs and create a tolerant, democratic society based on respect for human rights and respect for diversity. An inclusive model of education is often treated as a problem. A child with developmental disabilities is included in the educational system without trying to "fix" and adapt to that system. The

Global Institutional Roles in Access to Inclusive Education

child should go to a school that he/she would attend if there were no developmental disabilities, but the program and methods of work should be adapted to his/her needs.

Teachers must be able to engage in the process of learning all children with different individual needs, that environment is less restrictive and better adapted to the needs of all children, and that there is no organized support. This model is long-term sustainable and the cheapest options for the involvement of children in all school activities are maximally uniform. Within this model, children's rights to education have been recognized and conditions have been created for the realization of that right. Social inclusion, in other words, the movement for social inclusion as a basic problem emphasizes the attitude of society towards diversity (intellectual, physical, cultural, linguistic…) (Document: Big and Small, 2003). Fear, prejudice, and ignorance cause the exclusion of those who are different.Attitudes change through inter-action and living together. Therefore, in the social model, the emphasis is on creating these conditions in society, and not on a different person. So, those who are different do not need to be "cured", but it is necessary to "cure" society (Beker et al, 2020). Educational inclusion is a topic that is relevant for the pedagogical and social context, and especially for modern educational reforms. Inclusion is a request that is conceptually called education for all. In a broader sense, educational inclusion refers to the inclusion of children and adults who, because of psychological and physical, social, cultural, educational oppor-tunities, ethnic and other differences are subject to social exclusion, exposed to social marginalization, and thus disenfranchised and vulnerable. In a narrower sense, inclusion is a requirement that emphasizes that every child has the right to education under their abilities.

The Declaration of Human Rights of 1948 proclaims and sets the condition for the realization of the fundamental human right, which is the right to free primary education for all children. The countries of Europe and the world emphasize the importance of inclusion in education at all levels of the educational system through national curricula and other educational policy documents. Educational inclusion is a requirement that expands and deepens the educational model of integration of children with disabilities into regular schooling (Karamatic and Brcic, 2011). Inclusion in education as well as a theoretical and practical concept has been widely accepted and is a common feature of the practice of the functioning of modern school systems, as well as the content of the global policy and national education policies . In modern school systems in recent decades, reform processes are being implemented to develop the practice of inclusive education, but with different levels of success. In addition to changes in the teach-ing practice and schoolwork, the successful practical implementation of inclusion in education requires changes in the content and structure of the school and the functioning of the school system (Takala et al., 2009). Inclusive practice must develop in parallel with the development of inclusive politics and culture, and this is possible only in an inclusive-oriented school and social system (Ratkovic et al, 2017).

Examples of Good Practices – Europe (Finland) versus Serbia

The inclusion of education - as part of a broader process of social inclusion, can be successfully applied in practice only in inclusive societies, i.e. societies oriented towards inclusion. Socio-Political inclusive orientation (Ivancic and Stancic, 2013), involves a developed and appropriate system of values, common beliefs, and worldview (Charema, 2010; Fielding et al., 2005) which is based on the idea of equal rights for all, the need to respect diversity, as well as the importance of ensuring well-being for all. If society as a whole is not inclusive and oriented to inclusion, it is difficult to expect rapid and positive changes in practice and school work easy and simple way of segregation, through integration to inclusion in education (Kavkler et al., 2015). As an illustration of the previously exposed remarks below will give a brief overview of the current course and results of the implementation of inclusion in education in European countries: Finland, Sweden, and Germany. Applications of inclusion in education in Finland are an example of good practice. The Finnish school system is highly developed, efficient, and effective, as evidenced by the results of international tests results of school work expressed in the category of educational achievements of students. In addition, it is a system that is organized and operates on the principles of equality and equity in education (Jahnukainen, 2011). Education policy in Finland is based on the concept of inclusion, which is a result of the fact that it is also a broader social context widely accepted that all children/students should be provided with quality education (Farina et al., 2007). Practical application of inclusion in education began in Finland in the mid-80s of the last century (Halinen anf Jarvinen, 2008) and it is still continuously and systematically developed in inclusive education practices based on political and strategic reform processes and activities (Santtu and Salminen, 2015). The Finnish school system is a very functional system of teacher education and thus achieved significant results to prepare teachers for the practical implementation of educational inclusion. Starting from the premise that teachers or their competence, are a key success factor in the practical implementation of inclusion in education (Kivirauma and Ruoho, 2007), great attention is paid to the education and professional development of teachers of regular and special schools. Both effective and special education have been developed in Finland. Education of students with disabilities takes place in regular institutions where occasional special education is organized, and for children/students with a higher degree of disabilities and multiple disabilities - in special schools (Halinen and Jarvinen, 2008). This solution enables additional support to students in regular institutions in various ways - not only as an integral segment of the learning and teaching process, but also by including students with lower disabilities in occasional special education programs that usually last a month or two, and which realized by special educators independently or in cooperation with teachers at the school.

What is the approach to inclusive education in Serbia? In the past few decades, important international documents (UN Convention on the Rights of the Child, 1989; UN - Salamanca Statement and Framework education, 1994) have been adopted and accepted in Serbia, as well as national documents advocating that the right to education is one of the inalienable rights of every child (Law on the Fundamentals of the Education System, Official Gazette of RS, No. 72/2009). To create opportunities for a child with disabilities to fulfill his/her needs, it is necessary to include him/her in the community at an early age and provide him/her the opportunity to actively participate in all spheres of social life. At the preschool and primary school age, the success of inclusion depends primarily on the teachers who work with children, ie on educators, but also the willingness of other children and their parents (Avramidis et al., 2000; Reusen, et al., 2001). Why are teachers so important? They are seen as a key factor for change, and their sense of inadequacy, lack of self-confidence can be a significant barrier to inclusive education. Teachers are key support and help for a child with disabilities to face the challenges of attending regular school, starting from physical and academic, to social and emotional, which are an obstacle to achieving the primary goals of schooling. The existence of such support contributes to the development of the personality of a child with special needs, as well as to the development of the whole society.Teachers' attitudes towards inclusive education and to children with disabilities depend on their involvement, the quality of relationships that will establish how the child is both his parents, as well as the attitude of "typical" peers and their parents towards a child with developmental disabilities. For children in this developmental period, peer opinion, acceptance and a sense of belonging to the group are extremely important. The person who works with children represents a behavioral model for children and thus influences the formation of a value system, which is a prerequisite for creating a climate of acceptance and tolerance in the classroom

Global Institutional Roles in Access to Inclusive Education

(Rajovic and Jovanovic, 2010). Previous studies of attitudes towards inclusive education of children with special needs show that teachers in regular schools are „reluctant's" accept children with special needs, citing the fact that they do not feel competent enough to work with them. Research from three decades ago shows that as many as 50% of educators have a negative attitude towards people with special needs (Hrnjica, 1997). Twenty years later obtained similar results, NGOs Large and Small (2002) reports that 40% of teachers do not want to have children with special needs in classes and preschool groups, while research conducted in 2003 by Save the Children shows that only 24% of teachers believe that schooling is an inalienable right of every child. The latest results show that no significant progress has been made in terms of teachers' attitudes towards the school. Thus, in a survey conducted in 2009, within the project "School tailored to the child 2", 25.9% of teachers agreed with the statement that schooling is an inalienable right of every child (Hrnjica et al, 2009). The authors Rajovic and Jovanovic contributed to the research in the field of Inclusive Education in Serbia - by comparing the impact of private and professional experience of teachers with people with disabilities about the formation of their attitude towards inclusion. The surveys were conducted in 2010 and included 105 teachers from five regular primary schools in the territory of Belgrade (capital of Serbia).

The results of the engagement of the authors Rajovic and Jovanovic on the project "Psychological problems in the context of social change" (whose implementation was supported by the RS Ministry of Science) show that the attitudes of regular school teachers towards inclusion were extremely homogeneous and slightly positive. Although this result was an improvement compared to the previous survey (Mittler, 2004; Hrnjica et al, 2009), however, suggested that teachers were not ready for inclusion and that such conditions were unsatisfactory for the inclusion of children with special needs in regular schools. The research showed that people who have a private experience with people with disabilities showed more agreement with the philosophy of inclusion, better knowledge of the effects of inclusion of all participants, a greater willingness to adapt, training and involvement in implementing the inclusive model, and that they felt more competent to work with children from this category. Teachers in Serbia, due to the sense of incompetence, lack of knowledge on this subject, as well as the lack of continued support by the system and its segments (32.7% assess their knowledge on inclusive education of children with special needs as not) have a fear of professional failure, or have already experienced it, and have negative expectations that act as a self-fulfilling prophecy (Rajovic and Jovanovic, 2010). In order for the authors of the chapter to contribute to the review of information that is more recent, they followed the previous research of their colleagues and examined the opinions and attitudes of the teaching staff in the local environment in which they live.

Namely, the authors got in touch with primary school teachers in the summer period of 2021 and, using the technique of small interviews, came up with answers to three questions.It is examined 75 teachers in seven elementary schools in Eastern Serbia (Zajecar District) to the following issues: Are children or adults with special needs included in schools?; How many children with special needs are included in classes?; What is the attitude of teachers about inclusive education, i.e. is it necessary, effective, and how expedient? The answer to the first question was given by all respondents and they answered that in all primary schools covered by the research, children with special needs were included. The answer to the second question came to the data that 3 to 5 pupils with special needs were included in the classes from the first to the eighth grade. On the question of the attitude teachers have towards inclusion in education and whether they feel that the inclusion of effective enough in schools, responses were divided into two groups.Two-thirds of respondents believe that teachers are not competent to work with „special children" and think it would be best for the children to work with teachers who have been educated for that kind of job. One third of the teachers expressed the desire and need for additional seminars and training, which would be provided by the state or the school institution in which they are employed. This smaller number believes that the effect of education on children with special needs would be greater and the effect much better if teachers were able to approach in a better way. This better way of approaching children with special needs could be acquired through additional education. So, the authors' research results (talking to teachers in primary schools in Eastern Serbia - Zajecar District), lead to the conclusion that there is still a teachers' desire to acquire the necessary competencies for personal education. However, the majority of teachers believe that it is necessary to engage people with special education.

In Finland, according to UNESCO (2021), there are significant differences by gender (gender gap) in terms of the number of unenrolled (children-out-of-school). The number of unenrolled females from 2011 to 2013 was by a higher share of male children; from 2014 to 2018, the ratio has been opposite, because of a higher number of unenrolled males concerning female children. In Serbia, there were significant differences by gender (gap) in terms of the number of unenrolled children, children-out-of school. The number of unenrolled children in the period from 2011 to 2017 is with a higher share of unenrolled males, compared to female children, while in 2018, the number of unenrolled females was higher compared to male children, as is shown in Table 1:

Table 1. Participation children out-of-school in education in Finland and Serbia (2011-2018), (in thousands)

Finland Out-of-school children	2011	2012	2013	2014	2015	2016	2017	2018
Total	**4015**	**2196**	**2407**	**1356**	**2192**	**2612**	**4187**	**4885**
Female	2169	1295	1219	437	1074	1186	1900	2086
Male	1846	901	1188	919	1118	1426	2287	2799
Serbia Out-of-school children	2011	2012	2013	2014	2015	2016	2017	2018
Total	**7458**	**10495**	**10006**	**3423**	**2187**	**2253**	**2752**	**3815**
Female	3434	4830	4381	1283	934	1026	1250	1625
Male	4024	5665	5625	2140	1253	1227	1502	2190

Source: UNESCO, 2020., and according to the author's assessment.

A comparative overview of participation in education children out-of-school, Finland and Serbia, is given in Figure 2:

Global Institutional Roles in Access to Inclusive Education

Figure 2. Participation children out-of-school in education in Finland nd Serbia (2011-2018), (in thousands)
Source: UNESCO, 2020.

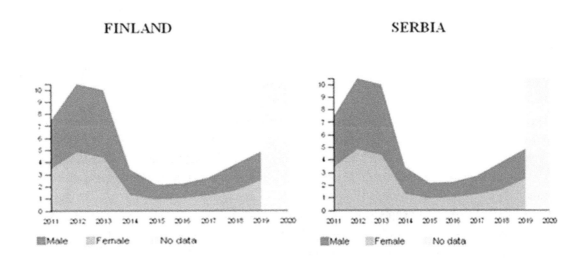

The results of the Global Gender Gap Index (which contains four sub-indexes: education attainment, economic opportunities, health, and political leadership) indicate that in the conditions of the COVID-19 pandemic, it is necessary to take urgent measures related to the economic recession and inclusion in the education system (WEF, 2021). WEF experts estimate that progress is slow and that it will take 14.2 years to bridge the gender gap in the global education system. The global Education Attainment Sub-Index shows there are no significant differences and that the oscillations are relatively low. Out of 156 countries, Finland is among the first countries in the world with the smallest gender gap, ranking 1st, while Serbia ranks 52nd, a score of 0,998 (WEF, 2021).

DISCUSSION

Education in Serbia is subject that needs structural and content changes because the Serbian economy is also changing in the direction of a market-oriented economy. This means that the aspiration of Serbia as a state is to strengthen its economy, increase economic competitiveness, and socially direct it towards higher productivity and efficiency. That is why education in Serbia is increasingly seen as a service to achieve economic development, prosperity, and the process of development of human intellectual capital. This position focuses on the quality of school education, but above all on educational outcomes, which are expressed in the category of achieved academic achievements. The results of schooling according to such a way of assessment (academic achievements), represent the quality of work of schools as educational institutions (Zajda, 2010). To improve the school system in Serbia, it was necessary to introduce two groups of reforms. The first group of school institutional reforms was aimed at ensuring and improving the quality of school education. The second group of school system reforms was focused on improving the efficiency of school work. Reforms of school institutions and education in Serbia were necessary for economic reasons, to reduce or rationalize public spending on education. It was necessary to allocate funds in a way that would ensure better results for the school system.

However, the results of reform processes depend on numerous, mutually conditioned factors, political decisions, social action. Merely making government decisions to reform the school system is not enough in itself (Aguerondo, 2003). It is necessary to provide several preconditions for the successful implementation of the reform of the school system, which is largely related to the readiness of the bearers of change to face different types of difficulties. The difficulties encountered in the process of reforming the school system and the assumptions of the success of this process can be seen as a kind of challenge faced by the creators and implementers of changes in the field of education (Hebib, 2013). One of the main challenges in implementing school system reforms is the question of whether and how the basic values promoted by accepting globally dominant orientations in the development of education can be achieved with the specifics of existing school practice and the functioning of different school systems? These specifics should not be ignored, because otherwise the "reform model" that is being promoted could be successfully applied in the practice of some schools, while in other schools and school systems it encounters a number of difficulties (Finan, 2000). The reform of the school system in Serbia, ie the implementation of certain concepts, such as the concept of inclusive education, has put the performers of the teaching process, ie teachers, in an awkward position. The theory and desire to achieve and move towards the creation of an inclusive society, regardless of the best intentions, has practically encountered some obstacles. Namely, inclusive education in a certain culture and society requires change and development of consciousness, modification of behavior, as well as through the preparation of the teaching staff to implement this process in the best way. Inclusion is a process with the humanitarian goal of including certain vulnerable and marginalized groups (children or adults with special needs) in normal life flows (education is certainly one of those flows). However, society and the main actors in the inclusion process must, first of all, ask themselves how much the environment is ready to accept "what is different" and slow down its development a little, and how vulnerable groups (children with special needs) are ready to follow the speed their environment is evolving! This attitude is a major controversy when it comes to inclusive education. However, there remains a glimmer of hope that the awareness of people and the entire community will be raised to a higher level, and that new ways may be found, as well as new means that would facilitate inclusive education as a process.

SOLUTIONS AND RECOMMENDATIONS

The concept of inclusion in education is being developed and practically applied as part of a broader process of social inclusion. In achieving the democratization and development of a society oriented to the needs of the individual - societies that are characterized by the active participation of all persons in economic, social, political, and cultural social life are developing. Regardless of gender, race, ability, national or religious origin, socio-economic status, and health status, each individual has the right to participate in social flows, according to his/her abilities. Educational inclusion can be defined as a process that responds to the diverse needs of all children and students through prominent participation in the learning process, educational and cultural activities, and community life through the reduction of exclusion in education (UNESCO, 2005). On the other hand, the majority of studies show that the impact of professional experience in the attitudes of teachers towards inclusion, significant realized in countries with a long tradition of inclusive practice and, therefore, creating the education of future teachers, the existence of support services, means of motivation, set standards of good inclusive practice, as well as legislation. In such an environment, teachers feel prepared, competent, motivated to work with children with special needs. However, what has proven to be significant for the attitudes of teachers (Serbia) towards inclusion is the private experience with people with special needs. Private experience is also in other similar research (Stanimirovic, 1986; Strohmer et al., 1984), according to Parasuram (2006), proved to be a significant factor influencing the formation of positive attitudes towards people with special needs.

For the successful application of inclusion in education, it is very important to reconsider beliefs about: care for children and youth and what is good for their development; roles and responsibilities of adults for learning and development of children and youth; characteristics of good teaching and school practice (Finnan, 2000). Parasuram (2006) in his research also finds that the existence of private experience distinguishes teachers in terms of their attitude towards inclusion. Zaromatidis (1999, according to Parasuram, 2006) argues that the importance of private experience for forming and changing attitudes towards inclusion depends on the socio-cultural context. Zaromatidis explains this by the position of a certain culture on the dimension of individualism-collectivism. Numerous school systems do not achieve the expected and desirable results in the practical application of inclusion in education, because a new concept of education is practiced without re-examining, changing and, developing attitudes and beliefs.

FUTURE RESEARCH DIRECTIONS

From the aspect of development based on social justice, society must be based on universal solidarity, in which all people have the right to inclusive knowledge and education. The extent to which efforts are made to enable persons with disabilities to be included depends on each country (Algermissen et al., 2015) with specific characteristics of the education system. According to Andrushchenko and Nesterenko (2015) "different national systems can converge into common approaches, standards, rules of the educational process". In the conditions of significant differences in the development of the educational system in the world, there is a conceptual unity in terms of attitudes: 1) that the educational environment is uneven and heterogeneous; 2) there is no alternative or unique principle for inclusive education regardless of different cultural, ethnic, physiological characteristics or socioeconomic status. Even though the original education system has been incorporated on all continents, a single position has been generally accepted to respect basic human rights. values such as: humanism, humanity, justice, equality, peace, tolerance, the self-worth of each individual (Andrushchenko and Nesterenko, 2015). According to Schuelka (2018), the most important identified factors for the successful implementation of inclusive education are: adequate policy and legal support (with the application of international law, conventions, and standards); appropriate school resources and facilities; adequate specialized teaching staff; adequate teacher training on inclusive thinking and techniques; active pedagogical techniques; modern curriculum and adequate school management; appropriate socio-cultural attitudes about schools and disability, which is important for future directions of inclusive education. The increasing application of online learning and access to virtual education is necessary for pandemic COVID-19 conditions. Given that students are exposed to great risk on the Internet and misinformation on social networks, educators with their competencies should make efforts to ensure student protection and avoid cyber risks and promote safe virtual learning. The application of modern technologies responsibly and safely like Artificial Intelligence could also contribute to fostering more inclusive teaching and learning (Council of the EU, 2021).

CONCLUSION

Conclusions regarding the link between inclusive education and social inclusion in compulsory education and higher education observed theoretically and partly through practice (in Serbia) indicate that inclusive education increases opportunities for interaction with peers and the formation of close friendships between pupils/students with disabilities and without them. Although social relationships are complex to be measured, social interactions that occur in inclusive settings are a prerequisite for the development of friendships, social and communication skills, support networks, feelings of belonging, and positive behavioral outcomes. To achieve social interactions and friendships within inclusive environments, it is necessary to pay special attention to several elements that enhance student/pupil participation (ie approach, cooperation, recognition, and acceptance). Social inclusion of students/pupils with disabilities is not achieved when their participation is prevented due to negative attitudes towards developmental disabilities and exclusionary school structures. Students/pupils with disabilities who were educated in inclusive environments can function better academically and socially than students/pupils who were educated in segregated environments. The probability of enrollment in higher education is increasing participation and receiving assistance under the environment for inclusive education. However, the authors point to the „factual situation", ie the situation in primary schools and the conclusions they reached from conversations with teachers are from practice. Although inclusive education is conceived and implemented for extremely humane reasons, the fact that children in schools are not always ready to fully accept their friends with special needs, regardless of mutual desire, is still emphasized. The children are extremely honest! Because of the different levels of development, if we look at children with special needs in whom every progress is much slower than in children who do not have developmental delays, a so-called gap is created between these sensitive categories. The entire community must develop and raise the awareness to a higher level, that the youngest generations can be included in the process of inclusion, ie to accept the differences and humanely overcome them. The authors believe that in Serbian society, although inclusive education is still in so-called"infancy", Serbia is on the right path and that in a certain sense it generally does not lag behind the countries of the Western Balkans. The acceptance of Serbia by the European Union, ie its entry into this "Alliance", would greatly contribute to the development of awareness and opportunities for inclusion and inclusive education. Certainly, good practice from advanced and socio-economically more developed European countries could be applied in Serbia as well - the desire exists!!!

ACKNOWLEDGMENT

This research received no specific grant from any funding agency in the public, commercial, or not-for profit sectors.

REFERENCES

Aguerrondo, I. (2003). Decentralization May Not Be Enough. In *Organization of Ministries of Education* (pp. 65–76). UNESCO.

Algermissen, U., Behrensen, B., & Graumann, O. (2015). Inclusion in Germany: a traditional education system in difficult conversion. In Inclusive Education in Different East and West European Countries. Progetto grafico di Eurilink.

Amadi, L., & Agena, J. E. (2015). Globalization, Culture mutation and new identity: Implication for the Igbo cultural heritage. *African Journal of History and Culture*, *1*(4).

Andrushchenko, V., & Nesterenko, G. (2015). Values decourse of diversity education: dialogue of Eastern and Western European countries. In Inclusive Education in Different East and West European countries. Progetto grafico di Eurilink.

Avramidis, E., Bayliss, P., & Burden, R. (2000). A Survey into mainstream teachers' attitudes towards the inclusion of children with special educational needs in the ordinary school in one local education authority. *Educational Psychology*, *20*(2), 191–211. doi:10.1080/713663717

Beker, K., Boskovic, D., Vlahovic, E., Ignjatovic, T., & Iles, M. (2020). *Handbook for teachers of civic education in the Gymnasium* [Priručnik za nastavnike gradjanskog vaspitanja u gimnaziji]. OEBS, ZUOV. https://zuov.gov.rs/wp-content/uploads/2020/12/gradjansko-srednja-skola.pdf

Cabezudo, A., Cicala, F., Bivar Black, M. L., & Carvalho da Silva, M. (2019). *Global Education Guidelines: concepts and methodologies on global education for educators and policy makers*. North-South Centre of the Council of Europe.

Ceric, H., & Alic, A. (2005). *Basic starting points of inclusive education*. Hijatus.

Charema, J. (2010). Inclusive Education in Developing Countries in the Sub Saharan Africa: From Theory to Practice. *International Journal of Special Education*, *25*(1), 87–93.

Council of Europe. (2020*). Making the right to education a reality in times of COVID-19: A Roadmap for Action on the Council of Europe education response to COVID-19*. https://rm.coe.int/making-the-right-to-education-a-reality-in-times-of-covid-19-a-roadmap/16809fee7b

Council of the EU. (2021). *Council Conclusions on equity and inclusion in education and training in order to promote educational success for all: meeting*, 7985/21. https://www.consilium.europa.eu/media/49660/st08693-en21-002.pdf

Djukic, G., & Ilic, B. (2020). Sustainability in higher education - a comparison of the Asia-Pacific region and Serbia. *Business Trends*, *8*(1), 9-21.

Draskovic, V., & Jovovic, R. (2008). Knowledge Processes Innovation – Dynamic Approach to Changes of Enterprise in the Knowledge Economy. *Montenegrin Journal of Economics*, *7*(4), 35–46.

European Agency for Development in Special Needs Education. (2011). *Key principles for promoting quality in inclusive education: Recommendations for Practice European Agency for Development in Special Needs Education*. https://www.european-agency.org/sites/default/files/Key-Principles-2011-EN.pdf

Farina, M. C., Opertti, M. R., Ji, M. L., & Sasu, M. N. (2007*). Regional Preparatory Workshop on Inclusive Education Eastern and Southeastern. Europe*. http://www.ibe.unesco.org/sites/default/files/Sinaia_Final_Report.pdf

Farkas, A. (2014). Conceptualizing Inclusive Education and Contextualizing it within the UNICEF Mission. UNICEF.

Fielding, M., Bragg, S., Craig, J., Cunningham, I., Eraut, M., Gillinson, S., Horne, M., Robinson, C., & Thorp, J. (2005). *Factors Influencing the Transfer of Good Practice*. University of Sussex, Department for Education and Skills.

Finnan, C. (2000). Implementing School Reform Models: Why Is It So Hard for Some Schools and Easy for Others? In *Annual Meeting of the American Educational Research Association*. American Educational Research Association. Retrieved June 25, 2021, from the World Wide Web. https://files.eric.ed.gov/fulltext/ED446356.pdf

Gidens, E. (2003). A world that eludes us. In Globalization myth or reality. Institute for Textbooks and Teaching Aids.

Grenot-Scheyer, M., Jubala, K. A., Bishop, K. D., & Coots, J. J. (1996). The inclusive classroom. Westminster: Teacher Created Materials. Centre for Economic & Social inclusion.

Guralnick, M. J. (2001). A Framework for change in early childhood inclusion. In M. J. Guralnich (Ed.), *Early Childhood inclusion: Focus on change* (pp. 3–35). Brookes.

Halinen, I., & Jarvinen, R. (2008). Towards Inclusive Education: The Case of Finland. *Prospects*, *38*(1), 77–97. doi:10.100711125-008-9061-2

Hawawini, G. (2011). *The Internationalization of Higher Education Institutions: A Critical Review and a Radical Proposal*. Faculty & INSEAD Research Working Paper. The Business School for the World. https://sites.insead.edu/facultyresearch/research/doc.cfm?did=48726

Hebib, E. (2013). How to develop a school - development and reform processes in the field of school education. Institute of Pedagogy and Andragogy, Faculty of Philosophy, University of Belgrade.

Hrnjica, S. (1997). A Child with Developmental Disabilities in Elementary School. The School of Pedagogy.

Hrnjica, S., Rajovic, V., Colin, T., Krstic, K., & Kopunovic, D. (2009). *Tailor-made school: Handbook for ad with regular school students who have developmental difficulties*. Save the Children UK, Program for Serbia.

Ilic, B., Djukic, G., & Todosijevic, J. (2021). Cultural dimensions - the impact of differences and similarities on business in the COVID-19 era. *Proceedings of the 11th International Symposium on Natural Resources Management*, *11*, 169-176.

Ilic, B., Mihajlovic, D., & Karabasevic, D. (2016). Social component of sustainable development and quality of life in Serbia. *Srpska Nauka Danas*, *1*(1), 413–423.

Ivancic, D. & Stancic, Z. (2013). Creating an inclusive school culture. *Croatian Journal of Rehabilitation Research*, *49*(2), 139-157.

Global Institutional Roles in Access to Inclusive Education

Jahnukainen, M. (2011). Different Strategies, Different Outcomes? The History and Trends of the Inclusive and Special Education in Alberta (Canada) and in Finland. *Scandinavian Journal of Educational Research, 55*(5), 489–502. doi:10.1080/00313831.2010.537689

Jovanovic, B. M., & Langovic, A. (2009). Intercultural Challenges of Globalization. Megatrend University.

Jovanovic, M. (2004). *Intercultural Management*. Megatrend University of Belgrade.

Karamatic-Brcic, M. (2011). Purpose and goal of inclusive education. University of Zadar, Croatia [Svrha i cilj inkluzivnog obrazovanja. Sveučilište u Zadru, Hrvatska]. *Acta Iadertina, 8*(1). https://hrcak.srce.hr/19009

Kavkler, M., Babuder, M. K., & Magajna, L. (2015). Inclusive Education for Children with Specific Learning Difficulties: Analysis of Opportunities and Barriers in Inclusive Education in Slovenia. *CEPS Journal, 5*(1), 31–52. doi:10.26529/cepsj.152

Kivirauma, J., & Ruoho, K. (2007). Excellence through Special Education? Lessons from the Finnish School Reform. *International Review of Education, 53*(3), 283–302. doi:10.100711159-007-9044-1

Krais, B. (1999). On Pierre Bourdieu's Masculine Domination. *Travail, Genre et Sociétés, 1*(1), 214–221. doi:10.3917/tgs.001.0214

Law on the Fundamentals of the Education System. (2009). *Official Gazette of RS, 72.*

Madzar, Lj. (2015). Economic effects of the interactions of globalization and culture. In *Globalization and Culture* (pp. 20–32). Institute of Social Sciences, Center for Economic Research. https://www.idn.org.rs/biblioteka/Ekonomisti2015.pdf

Mittler, P. (2004). *Working towards Inclusive Education*. David Fulton Publishers Ltd.

Movius, L. (2010). Cultural Globalisation and Challenges to traditional communication Theories. *Journal of Media and Communication, 2*(1). https://www.researchgate.net/publication/267254633_Cultural_Globalisation_and_ChallenGes_to_traditional_CommuniCation_theories

Odom, S. L. (2002). Learning about the barriers to facilitators of inclusion for young children with disabilities. In S. L. Odom (Ed.), *Widening the circle: Including children with disabilities in preschool programs* (pp. 1–9). Teachers' college Press.

Parasuram, K. (2006). Variables that affect teachers' attitudes towards disability and inclusive education in Mumbai, India. *Disability & Society, 21*(3), 231–242. doi:10.1080/09687590600617352

Pasalic-Kreso, A. (2003). The Genesis of the maturation of the idea of inclusion or inclusion in the function of reducing inequality in education. In A. Pasalic-Kreso (Ed.), *Inclusion in Education of Bosnia and Herzegovina* (pp. 2–24). Department of Pedagogy, Faculty of Philosophy in Sarajevo.

Pejovich, S. (2008). *Law, Informal Rules and Economic Efficiency – The Case for Common Law*. Edward Elgar. http://www.fintp.hr/upload/files/ftp/2009/1/badjun2.pdf

Popesku, C. (Ed.). (2021). *The Impact of COVID-19 on Inclusive Education at the European Level*. European Agency for Special Needs and Inclusive Education. https://www.european-agency.org/sites/default/files/COVID-19-Impact-Literature-Review.pdf

Rajovic, V., & Jovanovic, O. (2010). Professional and private experience with people with special needs and attitudes of regular school teachers towards inclusion. *Psychological Research, 13*(1), 91-106.

Rakonic Leskovar, I. (2018). School librarian in inclusive education. *Librarianship* [in Croatian. *Knjižničarstvo, 22*(1-2), 29–44.

Ratkovic, M. S., Hebib, E. D., & Saljic, Z. S. (2017). Inclusion in education as a goal and content of reforms of modern school systems, *Teaching and Education, 66*(3), 437–450.

Santti, J., & Salminen, J. (2015). Development of Teacher Education in Finland 1945-2015. *Hungarian Educational Research Journal, 5*(3), 1–18.

Save the children. (2003). *Annual report.* Retrieved, July 2021. https://www.savethechildren.org/content/dam/usa/reports/annual-report/annual-report/sc-2003-annualreport.pdf

Schuelka, M. J. (2018). Implementing inclusive education. In *Helpdesk Report: Knowledge, evidence and learning for development.* University of Birmingham. https://assets.publishing.service.gov.uk/media/5c6eb77340f0b647b214c599/374_Implementing_Inclusive_Education.pdf

Sekulovic, M. (2004). *Essays on transition.* Faculty of Economics in Nis.

Shea, T. M., & Bauer, A. M. (1997). *An Introduction to special education: A social systems perspective.* Brown & Benchmark.

Sretenov, D. (2008). *Creating an inclusive kindergarten.* Center for Applied Psychology.

Stanimirovic, D. (1986). Attitudes of visually impaired people towards the blind. *Psychology, 19,* 104–119.

Stojanovic, B. (2005). *Game theory - elements and application.* PE Official Gazette and Institute for European Studies.

Strohmer, D. C., Grand, S. A., & Purcell, M. J. (1984). Attitudes toward persons with disability: An examination of demographic factors, social context and specific disability. *Rehabilitation Psychology, 29,* 131–145.

Stubbs, S. (1998). *What is Inclusive Education? Concept Sheet.* Enabling Education Network (EENET). Retrieved 16 October 2003. www.eenet.org.uk/theory_practice/whatisit.shtml

Takala, M., Pirttimaa, R., & Tormanen, M. (2009). Inclusive Special Education: The Role of Special Education Teachers in Finland. *British Journal of Special Education, 36*(3), 162–172. doi:10.1111/j.1467-8578.2009.00432.x

UN (United Nations). (1994). Salamanca Statement and Framework for Action on Special Needs. *Education World Conference on Special Needs Education: Access and Quality.* https://www.european-agency.org/sites/default/files/salamanca-statement-and-framework.pdf

UNESCO. (2005). *Guidelines for Inclusion: Ensuring Access to Education for All.* http://www.ibe.unesco.org/sites/default/files/Guidelines_for_Inclusion_UNESCO_2006.pdf

UNESCO. (2020). *Participation in Education: Children out-of-school in education (Finland and Serbia).* http://uis.unesco.org/en/country/fi?theme=education-and-literacy

UNESCO. (2021). *Participation in Education.* http://uis.unesco.org/en/country/fi?theme=education-and-literacy

UNESCO. (2022). *UNESCO – Inclusive education.* http://www.unesco.org/education/sne/

Van Reusen, A. K., Shoho, A. R., & Barker, K. S. (2001). High School Teacher Attitudes toward Inclusion. *High School Journal, 84,* 7–20.

Vasilic, N., & Brkovic, P. (2017). *National Culture as a Determinant of Attitudes About Leadership Styles.* School of Business. http://www.vps.ns.ac.rs/SB/2017/2.3.pdf

Venables, A. (1999). *Regional integration agreements: a force for convergence and divergence?* Annual World Bank Conference on Development Economics. Working paper 2260.

Viener, J. (1950). *The Customs Union Issue.* Carnegie Endowment for International Peace.

Vladimirova, I. G. (2001). Globalization of World Economy: Challenges and Implications. *Corporate Management, 3*(1). https://www.cfin.ru/press/management/2001-3/10.shtml

Vujacic, M., & Djevic, R. (2013). Inclusive education: conceptual definition, principles and characteristics. *Topics, 2*(37), 753-768.

Vuletic, V. (2003). *Globalization - Myth or Dread.* http://velikimali.org/wp-content/uploads/2017/03/biltenvelikimali_3.pdf

WEF (Global Economic Forum). (2021). *Global Gender Gap Report 2021.* https://www3.weforum.org/docs/WEF_GGGR_2021.pdf

Zajda, J. (2010). Globalization and the Politics of Education Reform. In The Politics of Education Reforms. Springer.

Zaromatidis, K., Papadaki, A., & Glide, A. (1999). Cross-cultural comparison of attitudes toward persons with disabilities: Greeks and Greek-Americans. *Psychological Reports, 84*(3_suppl), 1189–1196. doi:10.2466/pr0.1999.84.3c.1189 PMID:10477938

ADDITIONAL READING

Azmanova, A. (2011). After the Left–Right (Dis) continuum: Globalization and the Remaking of Europe's Ideological Geography. *International Political Sociology, 5*(4), 384–407. doi:10.1111/j.1749-5687.2011.00141.x

Bhardwaj, A., Dietz, J., & Beamish, P. W. (2007). Host Country Cultural Influences on Foreign Direct Investment. *Management International Review, 47*(1), 29–50. doi:10.100711575-007-0003-7

Schewel, K. (2019). Understanding immobility: Moving beyond the mobility bias in migration studies. *The International Migration Review, 54*(2), 328–355. doi:10.1177/0197918319831952

Thompson, A., Rebecca, M. T., Kate, S., & Sarah, A. (2019). Blue and Óscar Misael Hernández, 'Reconceptualising agency in migrant children from Central America and Mexico. *Journal of Ethnic and Migration Studies*, *45*(2), 235–252. doi:10.1080/1369183X.2017.1404258

KEY TERMS AND DEFINITIONS

Disability: Is any medical condition that makes it more difficult for a person to do certain activities or effectively interact with the world around them (socially or materially).

Global Education: Is a process of individual and collective growth that allows for transformation and self-transformation. It is a social practice, a permanent preparation for life, in which the acquisition of operative and emotional competencies for analyzing and thinking critically about reality, empowers educators and learners to become active social agents.

Global Institutions: Is a stable set of norms and rules of international institutions meant to govern the behavior of states and other actors in the international system.

Globalization: Is a term that may be used broadly to mean doing things as distant people do them, or more narrowly to mean complying with global standards in the economy, politics, culture, education, environment, or other matters. It describes the way countries and people of the world interact and integrate.

Inclusive Education: Is a process of addressing and responding to the diversity of needs of all learners through increasing participation in learning, cultures, and communities, and reducing exclusion within and from education.

UNESCO: (United Nations Education, Scientific, and Cultural Organization): Is a special agency of the United Nations founded in 1946.

Chapter 8

Global Institutions and ESG Integration to Accelerate SME Development and Sustainability

Meng Kui Hu
https://orcid.org/0000-0001-5009-1105
Universiti Sains Malaysia, Malaysia

Daisy Mui Hung Kee
https://orcid.org/0000-0002-7748-8230
Universiti Sains Malaysia, Malaysia

ABSTRACT

Since the adoption of the Sustainable Development Goals (SDGs) by the United Nations in 2015, all its 193 member states committed themselves to implementation at the national, regional, and international levels. In particular, the private sector is called upon to play an active role in driving the integration of environmental, social, and governance (ESG) principles among businesses, including SMEs. Armed with adequate resources, global institutions can influence SMEs and lead the way in educating and providing them with sound guidance towards ESG adoption. In collaboration with the local government, global institutions can intensify their efforts in promoting ESG adoption among SMEs. This chapter looks at how SMEs can leverage global institutions for guidance, support, and good practices in charting ESG integration in their business operations, enabling them to achieve business sustainability in the long term. Moreover, this chapter will specifically draw on experiences of ESG integration by Malaysian SMEs.

INTRODUCTION

Environmental, social and governance (ESG) measures and disclosure have become increasingly important for businesses, underpinned by growing interest from investors at both the international and domestic levels, particularly large corporations, over the last few years (Mohammad & Wasiuzzaman, 2021). Numerous stakeholders, from government agencies to corporate investors to general consumers, have

DOI: 10.4018/978-1-6684-2448-3.ch008

Copyright © 2022, IGI Global. Copying or distributing in print or electronic forms without written permission of IGI Global is prohibited.

gained a broader knowledge of ESG and its importance to future generations. With this, the stakeholders expect to see progressive development on the implementation of ESG principles by businesses. This expectation has exerted pressure for companies, particularly those exposed to the developed nations, to emphasise ESG integration in their companies. SMEs that are dealing with multi-national corporations face systemic pressure in accelerating ESG integration into their businesses too. SMEs' implementation of ESG principles is critical in driving the company to sustainable value creation in the long term (Hu & Kee, 2021). This action will lead to the eventual attainment of the sustainable development goals (SDGs), spearheaded by the United Nations. Though SDGs are more thematic than corporate-centric, they can help SMEs align their company-specific ESG principles with broader societal and environmental goals. However, the traction among SMEs has been slow due to various reasons. Although many SMEs claimed to possess adequate awareness about ESG and its significance to businesses, most have not embarked on concrete ESG integration plans. Many SMEs do not see the urgency of such a matter. Many SMEs cited incremental costs, lack of awareness and inadequate resources for such implementation (Sommer, 2017)

The Covid-19 pandemic, nevertheless, has raised the awareness of the significance of ESG for more businesses, including SMEs. As the world continues to battle the fourth or fifth waves of the pandemic, many SMEs are making working from home a viable option and a sustainable means of operation. Working from home can boost employees' productivity and contribute to healthier employees who are less likely to take sick days. While the many benefits from working from home are apparent many SMEs faced unprecedented challenges, including difficulties in maintaining the safety and well-being of employees. When employees work from home amid the pandemic, SMEs are concerned about fading staff engagements due to a lack of face-to-face interactions that could impact productivity levels. The lack of direct interaction with the customers can also affect the overall customer relationships. Conspicuously, SMEs have encroached into ESG factors, some without knowing it. Moving forward, SMEs must engage more profoundly in ESG by leveraging option, supports and assistance from various stakeholders, including global institutions.

The primary objective of this chapter is to raise SME awareness on the significance of ESG adoption, enabling them to pursue business sustainability in the long term. This chapter discusses the hindrances faced by SMEs in implementing ESG strategy in their companies. It also elaborates the benefits SMEs can derive from ESG integration that motivates them to embark and accelerate their active involvement in ESG standards. This chapter will also deliberate how SMEs can leverage global institutions for guidance and support in charting ESG integration in their business operations. With the profound initiatives, SMEs can then implement their plans and accelerate their ESG journey. Here, the right approach in implementing the right ESG strategy is discussed for optimised results. This chapter will specifically draw on experiences of ESG integration by SMEs operating in Malaysia.

BACKGROUND

Despite the significance of ESG, SMEs are slow in adopting ESG principles in their businesses. The lack of in-depth understanding of the ESG approach partly explained that over two-thirds of companies are at a very early stage of the journey (51%) or are only planning to start the journey over the next one to two years (16%). Most companies consider ESG to be very much driven by government policy and regulation (79%) and watchdog and industry regulators (27%) (Ward & MacKenzie, 2020). Having such reservations, many SMEs would wait for the external stakeholders to force ESG implementation in

Global Institutions and ESG Integration

their business operations. Until then, SMEs will take it easy and wait. In Malaysia, the lack of integrity and transparency in institutions, public and private sectors, more so during a crisis, will impact the nation's economic growth. Datuk Seri Mustapa Mohamed, minister of the Prime Minister Department of Malaysia, added that public and private sectors must maintain good governance and ethical practices to achieve future prosperity (The Star, 2021). This is consistent with the fact that SMEs generally lack in terms of ESG implementation. Only 35% of family businesses in Malaysia, mainly comprising SMEs, have a developed and communicated sustainability strategy. Only 6% of the family businesses aim to reduce their carbon footprint, with another 12% plan to increase social responsibility in the next two years. Overall, most Malaysian family businesses place low priorities on ESG principles (PwC Malaysia, 2021). This traditional approach in conducting business without adequate emphasis on ESG integration is not sustainable in the long run. Moreover, there is consistent evidence that an increase in ESG disclosure by one unit will increase firm performance by approximately 4 percent in Malaysia (Mohammad & Wasiuzzaman, 2021). Therefore, businesses, including SMEs, must be ESG compliant when dealing with multi-national companies and businesses operate out of developed nations in the future.

Moving forward, SMEs need to step up and leverage large corporations and global institutions to integrate ESG best practices in their business operations. Management and disclosure of ESG issues, if not handled professionally, can become financially material, affecting corporate profitability and valuation (Freiberg et al., 2019). With limited resources, SMEs are handicapped in spending, knowledge, and skills to implement ESG principles in their business. Nevertheless, they need to leverage available assistance first to gain an in-depth understanding of ESG and its significance to business sustainability and then work on sustainability strategies before systematically executing them. However, it is easier said than done. The entire process of ESG adoption can be challenging for most SMEs. How could SMEs plan and work on their sustainability strategy? Who can they look upon for guidance and assistance? Can the global institutions guide SMEs in this area? Separately, what do SMEs need to do more and better in accelerating the process towards ESG compliance? How about SMEs operating in Malaysia? Can they rely upon global institutions' guidance in achieving business sustainability goals? This chapter aims to address these questions for the benefit of SMEs and readers.

METHODOLOGY

The resource-based view of the firm (Barney, 1991) is used to explain how SMEs perceive ESG and integrate ESG principles in their business operations, leading to sustainable competitive advantage in the new normal. The resource-based theory focuses on the link between strategy and firm internal resources. Drawing from the resource-based view of the firm, internal analysis of the resources that are regarded as sources of competitive advantage controlled by the SMEs is imperative in today's business environment. A narrative analysis is applied on information gathered from literature reviews and the author's observations. This paper focuses on the way SMEs can leverage global institutions in ESG adoption, leading to business sustainability in the long term. The reflection in this chapter involves a discussion of findings from secondary research and deliberation on practical measures SMEs can take to integrate ESG principles in their businesses. More so, with the guidance rendered by global institutions. In addition, this chapter also includes the author's extensive practical experiences and the authors' opinions and interpretation on the impacts caused by various crises faced by the SMEs, with a specific focus on SMEs operating in Malaysia.

Figure 1. Global institution's influence on ESG in SME development and sustainability

IMPLICATIONS OF ESG

ESG integration in businesses has become more prominent in the last decade. The adoption of ESG standards in businesses was accelerated during the Covid-19 pandemic. The general stakeholders like shareholders, investors, customers, suppliers, and employees are getting more informed about ESG and its significance. Consequently, large corporations, in particular, have been investing resources in deepening the engagement of ESG for their businesses. These corporations are increasingly using various instruments, tools, and channels to communicate their ESG reports to stakeholders. In Malaysia, public listed companies that were given a Bloomberg ESG rating over 2005 to 2018 recorded lower cost of capital by 1.2%, while Tobin's Q increases by 31.9% upon receiving an ESG rating. These findings demonstrate the benefits of securing ESG certifications (Wong et al., 2021). Tobin's Q is widely used in relevant research on firm value. This indicator reflects the current company's profitability and its future development potential. These research outcomes were consistent with evidence that an increase in ESG disclosure by one unit will increase firm performance by approximately 4% in Malaysia (Mohammad & Wasiuzzaman, 2021).

On the contrary, the progress of ESG integration among SMEs has been slow. The social and environmental practices are grossly neglected in SMEs, more specifically in emerging markets of Asia (Ng et al., 2020). While SMEs do take up some kind of sustainability practices but in most cases, they are occasional, informal, unstructured, and are not managed as part of their business strategy. SMEs also do not communicate their social and environmental activities clearly to their employees and related stakeholders. Sustainability activities are generally more focused on social issues than ecological concerns (Das et al., 2020). Although ESG integration is slow among SMEs at this juncture, its significance cannot be ignored. In the long run, ESG is impactful to the overall business community, more so for SMEs. As ESG practices become more intense, particularly among the large corporations in developed nations, SMEs dealing with such corporations must also adhere to ESG compliance soon. Consequently, fulfilling ESG

Global Institutions and ESG Integration

requirements is critical for SMEs to remain relevant and continue their dealing with large corporations. Following are elaborations of ESG and its implications on SME businesses:

Environmental

Climate change, conservation, energy decarbonisation, green agenda, and environmental protection are the common primary components often raised in ecological issues. These are big words with diverse implications for different people from different sectors. For the business community, including SMEs, the environmental principle extends broadly from the use of environment-friendly materials to the methods used to treat industrial wastes and consumption of renewable energy. Environment factors are also actively discussed due to the broad interest in climate finance (Broadstock et al., 2020). According to United Nations (2019), energy use for electricity generation, heat production, and transport relies heavily on fossil fuels and together accounts for roughly 70% of global greenhouse gas emissions. Trends in energy-related greenhouse gas emission reductions are far from being on track to meet the Paris Agreement objectives. If current demand trends continue, the rate of decarbonisation needs to triple to reach the 2°C targets and quintuple to reach the 1.5°C targets by 2050. A profound effort across every sector is crucial to bridge the foreseeable gaps in carbon intensity. SMEs can contribute to this aspect by focusing more intensely on environment-related areas. They need to improve the use of their natural resources, conservation efforts, and recycling and sustainability. SMEs must also evaluate their carbon footprint and energy use. If the business involves chemicals, the company might determine if there is a more environmentally friendly option. SMEs must place adequate priorities in the green agenda for business sustainability and resilience.

Social

Social criteria encompass business relationships with the employees, suppliers, partners, shareholders, and the overall community. The scope of coverage is broad, involving wage and labour issues, philanthropy, workplace safety, diversity, equity, and inclusion. Social problems require evaluation of the company's diversity and inclusion efforts from the boardroom to entry-level employees. During the Covid-19 pandemic, the social factor experienced an enormous shift, particularly in occupational health and safety, employee protection, social security measures, and the domains of supply chain resilience and longevity. These events had been put on a test with the commencement of the global health crisis (Zumente & Bistrova, 2021). Wellness programs and work environments must be evaluated to assure that employees are treated fairly and can work safely and without harassment. Companies should also consider their social impact opportunities to make the world a better, safer, and more just place where all people can thrive. Businesses, including SMEs, must invest adequately to improve the well-being of their employees. In the future, a business must recognise that protecting the health, well-being, and jobs of their employees and contractors is central to long-term resilience, as human capital is one of the most important capitals for company development. It guarantees adaptability and an ability to innovate. During the Covid-19 pandemic, the simultaneous move to remote working experienced by large populations of white-collar workers was unprecedented and unplanned. It demonstrated that extensive change could be managed quickly when necessary (World Business Council for Sustainable Development, 2020). Therefore, SMEs must prepare to invest more in accelerating human capital development by tapping into the positive vibe and resourcefulness of their employees, who keep the wheels of the firm moving. In short, business is no longer confined to just making profits but also covering a broader scope of staff welfare and community relations. SMEs must realise that ESG is not equal to corporate social responsibility (CSR) but is more comprehensive than this.

Governance

Governance involves how a company is run: from board practices to transparency in shareholder communications to the ethics of its leadership. The governance efficiency depends on how a company's leadership guides the company to operate above board and not engage in illegal activities. This includes how decisions are made and their effectiveness, how companies comply with the law, and how the needs of external stakeholders are met (Jeavons & Thandi, 2021). Governance includes evaluating the board, executive, and management composition for diversity and inclusion. It also focuses on equity in compensation, transparency with investors and other stakeholders, and integrity. Thus, when executed properly, corporate governance practices lead companies, including SMEs, toward improved business performances (Umrani et al., 2015). In different words, governance, if not enforced, can cause numerous problems to businesses. Certain breaches can be severely offensive in law that could land the leadership team and board members in trouble. For instance, companies engaging in illegal activities will be reprimanded by the authorities for further investigations. Therefore, businesses mustn't take governance lightly. Consequently, SMEs need to reform government towards greater transparency and enhanced business operations, leading to sustainability in the long term.

As many SMEs do not spend much attention on ESG now, it does not mean they can continue ignoring it in the near future. Like it or not, ESG is here to stay, and businesses will have to comply with ESG requirements to remain relevant in the future regardless of their sizes and nature. On this basis, SMEs must start to spend time and resources to understand ESG better. They need to overcome the challenges they face, enabling them to integrate ESG principles into their business in the near term.

SMEs CHALLENGES

Although ESG has gained much traction, mainly among the large corporations in the last decade, SMEs have been progressing slowly in this area. Unlike larger firms, SMEs are currently not required to disclose non-financial information on their ESG performance (Barbagila et al., 2021). As such, there is no urgency for them to adopt ESG in their business operations. Many prefer to wait and see what would happen next. Separately, most SMEs lack resources, experience, and incentives to implement sustainability in their daily management, but their potential contribution to sustainable development is enormous (Sommer, 2017). In general, tools to link the SDGs with the business processes of SMEs do not exist (Verboven & Vanherck, 2016). Without proper and easily accessible tools, SMEs find ESG integration even more difficult. Consequently, there is a lack of motivation and pressure for SMEs to integrate ESG principles into their business operations. Although many SMEs may claim they have adequate knowledge about ESG principles, most do not practically incorporate them in their businesses. They have misconceived the real meaning of ESG adoption in companies. Many SMEs equate ESG to corporate social responsibility (CSR), where they implement from time to time. This equation, however, is incorrect. ESG covers much broader areas than CSR that represent only the "S" of ESG. SMEs also need to address the "E" and "G" of the equation. What are the critical challenges obstructing or delaying the implementation of ESG

Global Institutions and ESG Integration

among SMEs? How can these obstacles be handled effectively by SMEs in their pursuit of achieving business sustainability? A good understanding of these challenges can be helpful for SMEs to manage ESG better in the future. Following are the challenges faced by SMEs in their path on ESG journey:

Lack of Knowledge

Without prioritising ESG, many SMEs lack awareness and knowledge of ESG related matters (Lee, 2021). They do not see ESG as essential components in delivering success to their business performances. Many felt ESG are only relevant and confined to the large corporations. They reckoned that SMEs are simply too small to care about ESG. With such a mentality, most SMEs do not bother to spend time and resources finding out and understanding ESG and its implication to their businesses. Without the proper knowledge, SMEs do not even know where to begin their ESG journey. Separately, many SMEs often lack information about the costs and benefits of relevant ESG practices and have limited capacity to understand environmental requirements and low awareness of the need to address their environmental impacts. In simple terms, SMEs do not fully acknowledge the significance of ESG in driving business sustainability. The lack of knowledge will not augur well for SMEs in their ESG adoption process in the long term. They will find it even tougher to implement ESG standards in their businesses when the requirement becomes more critical in the future. Consequently, SMEs will miss out on the opportunity due to failure to recognise the benefits of ESG integration.

Misconceptions

Although many SMEs claim to understand ESG adequately, many equate ESG with corporate social responsibility (CSR) activities. While CSR forms part of ESG, many other areas need to be considered and carried out when integrating ESG into business operations. This misconception led many SMEs to think of ESG compliance as CSR performance (Lee, 2021). However, CSR alone is not sufficient. Most CSR efforts are random, hence do not address the overall negative impact the business is causing. Separately, Ward and MacKenzie (2020) found that many mid-sized companies have misconceptions about ESG, thinking they know what constitutes ESG. In reality, they do not have the correct sense of ESG. Separately, some SMEs presume the practice of 3R (reduce, reuse, recycle) as construed to ESG. The other common area when SMEs miss out is related to employee welfare, corporate governance. With misconception on the fundamental of ESG, many SMEs thought they were already embracing ESG in their businesses, hence would not bother to explore further on this subject. This results in a lack of ESG integration work in their business operations. If this misconception is prolonged, SMEs will face more significant hurdles in embracing ESG in their business in the near term.

Inadequate Resources

One pertinent reason hindering SMEs from ESG adoption is due to inadequate resources (Sommer, 2017). By implementing ESG principles, they need to incur set-up and compliance costs. They also need to engage a specific human resource to manage this initiative. Although the implementation of ESG disclosure can raise the company value and performance, affordability theory suggests that without sufficient resources, ESG disclosures may not be materialised for small and growing firms (Ren et al., 2020). Many SMEs have limited capacity to implement the changes required to improve the overall ESG

145

integration. As such, they could not incorporate ESG principles in their business planning. This situation is similar for SMEs in Malaysia, where most of them lack resources to implement the environmental disclosures. Specifically, financial capability and talents are the primary resources that SMEs are lacking that prevent them from driving ESG principles more aggressively in their businesses. SMEs need to look out for financial assistance, mainly from governments, to execute their ESG strategy.

Incomplete Data and Quality

Another common problem cited by businesses, including SMEs, when addressing the obstacles in ESG implementation in the investment evaluation process is data availability and quality (Zumente & Bistrova, 2021). Data inconsistency creates challenges in proper data evaluation. Without clean and quality data, it is difficult for SMEs to gauge the level of ESG engagement, making it challenging to rate their ESG performances. This frustrates SMEs and demotivates them to drive ESG integration further until they can access quality data in the future. In addition, the diverse and differing requirements of ESG criteria from different buyers, financial institutions, and other business partners add further burden to SMEs. Due to a lack of harmonisation in this aspect, SMEs face parallel procedures of implementation, documentation, and multiple certifications, which shoots up compliance costs. As such, SMEs have to invest time and resources to collect and analyse relevant information to decide whether to implement ESG standards for their businesses.

Having deliberated on the challenges, SMEs must not be deterred from pursuing ESG goals. It is a matter of time that SMEs are required to adhere to ESG standards, particularly those dealing with large corporations and companies operating from developed nations. They need to create new measures to handle the situation. They must also understand the benefits of integrating ESG in their businesses. By leveraging such knowledge, SMEs will be more receptive and engaging in ensuring the success of ESG integration. Strategically, SMEs need to strive to overcome the challenges, enabling them to accelerate their ESG integration journey. At the same time, they should reap the benefits that ESG integration can offer to the business.

BENEFITS OF ESG INTEGRATION

Although there are challenges in ESG integration, this should not stave off SMEs from allocating adequate efforts and resources in incorporating ESG principles in their businesses. There are ample benefits that SMEs can leverage from ESG integration. Failure to recognise the benefits of ESG integration would hinder SMEs from lifting their business to new heights. Friede et al. (2015) examine more than 2000 empirical studies on ESG disclosures and firm performance and find that 90% of the studies report a positive association between ESG and performance. Therefore, SMEs need first to understand and appreciate the benefits of ESG. They will then find the reasons and motivation to achieve the ESG agenda. Consequently, they will be able to reap the following benefits:

Improved Profitability

There is a growing body of evidence highlighting improved company performance associated with better ESG practices. In research conducted by Deutsche Bank and the University of Hamburg that examined over 2,000 empirical studies relating to ESG integration and corporate performances, they found that ESG integration did not adversely affect investment returns in 90% of cases. Indeed, ESG added value in most cases, with 63% of studies finding a positive correlation (Jeavons & Thandi, 2021). Separately, ESG can enhance the brand image of companies, leading to the improvement of the bottom line. ESG can lead a company to new markets and business opportunities with an enhanced reputation since consumers may seek companies dedicated to ESG (Sommer, 2017). While there was already evidence that strong company performance on ESG yields better financial results, the COVID-19 pandemic has provided a new opportunity to examine the relationship between sustainability leadership, financial performance, and resilience.

Effective Cost Management

The escalating cost could be an issue to SMEs in the early stages of ESG adoption. In the long term, when ESG is effectively implemented, it can lead to significant cost savings. The use of renewable energy, recycling activities, and energy conservation resulted in costs reduction and helped the environment over time. SMEs should promote clean, reliable, and modern energy sources, including harnessing the potential of decentralised renewable energy solutions. In Malaysia, solar energy is getting popular, supported by the government's initiative to drive better energy efficiency while saving the environment. Following the Covid-19 pandemic, some SMEs adopt a hybrid-work style where part of the staff force will be asked to work from home. If this new arrangement is carefully implemented, productivity can be maintained, and the companies can save costs related to workspace and utilities. In the long run, the savings in operational cost from ESG adoption is translated to enhanced financial performances for SMEs, allowing them to have more effective cost management and enable value-creation in the mid and long term (Lee, 2021).

Value Creation

In addition to working from home, the emphasis on other areas of the social aspect of ESG can help create a diverse workforce where employees are valued and treated fairly, which will attract top talent, improve morale, and reduce turnover. Employees treated well and who enjoy a workplace free of discrimination and harassment are likely to be more productive and less likely to leave their jobs. Moreover, employees who are treated fairly are less likely to leave their jobs (Ansari, Kee, & Aafaqi, 2000) or file regulatory complaints. Studies have shown that ESG integration into a firm's valuation model improves its non-financial indicators such as consumer satisfaction, market acceptance, lower cost of debt, and the societal values it brings to its stakeholders. Hence, a firm's competitive advantage may grow over the years of its operation (Schramade & Schoenmaker, 2018). Separately, when SMEs implement ESG and provide ESG data to bankers, it helps improve transparency, allowing the banks to understand the company better, precisely their sustainability policies. All these ESG related activities that promote positive social and environmental externalities lead to value creation and enhancement for the business, contributing to long-term sustainable growth and SDGs.

Greater Resilience to Risk

One of the primary functions of ESG integration involves risks management of diversified issues, including climate change, diversity, cybersecurity and company reputation. The pressure is intensifying from investors and other stakeholders to identify and mitigate ESG risks quickly and effectively. A combination of robust risk controls, strong compliance standards, and embedded planning to deal with current, medium- and long-term ESG risks allows high ESG-rated companies, including SMEs, to embrace ESG integration in their business operations. By doing so, SMEs can lower the risks of severe incidents, such as fraud, litigation and environmental or corporate governance issues (Jeavons & Thandi, 2021). Although SMEs may find it challenging to cope with demand from stakeholders for a tighter risk management system, they will gain in the long term. Established risks management helps SMEs to strengthen their business resilience that is crucial during turbulent periods. They will become more prepared to face any untoward incidences in the future.

Whilst SMEs may view compliance with sustainable practices as an additional cost, governments should extend financial incentives for SMEs to reduce their carbon footprint and implement best practice models. Some governments have already offered various aids to SMEs in the form of industry grants, allowing SMEs to embark on energy-efficient processes and equipment. Timely attention to these matters in strategic management would help SMEs to ensure long-term competitiveness. SMEs that acknowledge the benefits from ESG adoption will become more proactive and more willing to implement policies in integrating ESG into their business. By doing so, they will capitalise on opportunities in growing the business sustainably in the future.

LEVERAGING GLOBAL INSTITUTIONS

Global institutions are regulatory bodies worldwide like World Bank, International Monetary Fund (IMF), United Nations (UN), International Labour Organisation (ILO), Association of Southeast Asian Nations (ASEAN), Organisation for Economic Co-operation and Development (OECD), and Asian Development Bank (ADB), among others. They are here to ensure that all nations are supported for growth and national development. Sustainability that includes the adoption of ESG principles among businesses is one of the primary initiatives actively driven by these global institutions. Consequently, SMEs must understand how these global institutions can assist them in the ESG aspect. By leveraging the global institutions, SMEs can seek guidance and work on accelerating ESG adoption. Following are the key measures SMEs can leverage on global institutions in their pursuit of achieving business sustainability through ESG:

Raising Awareness

Global institutions provide vast information and training that can be valuable to SMEs in understanding ESG and related matters. For instance, ESCAP maintains a comprehensive website (https://www.unescap.org/learning-training) with numerous learning and training programmes. Although these programmes aim to assist governments in developing technical, managerial, and institutional capacities to plan and deliver more effective policies and programmes in support of inclusive and sustainable development, SMEs can benefit from these programmes. By reviewing the information on this platform, SMEs can

Global Institutions and ESG Integration

learn and appreciate ESG better. Separately, ADB offers a wide range of e-learning courses for interested parties (https://elearning-adbi.org/courses). SMEs can sign up and learn from these online lecture series. In the wake of the Covid-19 pandemic, a new window of learning opportunity was opened when SMEs could participate in some of the virtual programmes organised by these global institutions. With this, SMEs could listen directly to the experts on various subjects related to ESG. In Malaysia, the Economic Planning Unit of the Prime Minister's Department (https://www.epu.gov.my/en/sustainable-development-goals) is the focal point for sustainable development and coordinates agency on the related initiatives, including the Sustainable Development Goals (SDGs). This website illustrates the progress and alignment of SDGs in the National Development Plan, allowing SMEs to understand SDGs from the national perspectives thoroughly. Hence, there is ample avenue for SMEs to learn and understand more about ESG and its significance on nations and businesses. By acquiring such a level of awareness, SMEs will become more receptive to ESG implementation. SMEs just need to get committed and spend adequate resources to understand what is lacking in them.

Riding on Incentives

Global institutions and national governments have piloted multiple approaches to guide and assist SMEs in embracing ESG principles in their businesses. The governments are also enacting concrete measures to prompt ESG issues (Ng, 2021). Governments have provided various incentives to SMEs through loan subsidies and credit guarantee mechanisms, enabling SMEs to accelerate their ESG integration processes. Additional innovative measures are being piloted, such as credit bureaus, collateral registers, and psychometric credit scoring, all of which would expand the basis of usable collateral for SMEs to secure additional financial resources. UNICEF has established a venture fund supporting innovative SME growth. Global institutions have significantly influenced governments to take on a more aggressive stance in promoting ESG among businesses. Following these initiatives, governments have provided various incentives to SMEs in driving ESG adoption, and the common ones include government grants to implement ESG and tax incentives. For instance, a government guarantee for green financing is offered to businesses as an enabler to implement environmentally friendly business operations (Mustaffa et al., 2021). During the Covid-19 pandemic, the Malaysian government provided wage subsidies to businesses, including SMEs, as financial aids to preserve employment within the companies. This initiative is essential to ensure the livelihood of the people while keeping businesses afloat. According to the Finance Minister of Malaysia, RM12.945 billion (US$2.95 billion) of wage subsidies was channelled to 322,177 employers as of 1st October 2021 to continue operating and maintaining employment for 2.64 million workers (Malay Mail, 2021). This government assistance has helped SMEs in addressing the social aspect of their staff force. During the Covid-19 pandemic, governments have granted SME wage subsidies, allowing them to keep the staff force.

Adopting the Best Practices

There are ample avenues for SMEs to review, understand and adopt some of the best practices regarding ESG integration from global institutions. The development community provides robust platforms to bring together stakeholders from diverse industries in different countries to foster the exchange of good practices on SME growth for the SDGs. SMEs from developing countries like Malaysia can learn from their peers in developed nations. Most global institutions offer training programmes on sustainability where SMEs can be benefited. SMEs can also leverage the tools devised by the International Labour Organization (ILO), namely Enabling Environment for Sustainable Enterprises (EESE). This unique tool that provides evidence-based recommendations on improving the business-enabling environment focuses on the political, economic, social, and environmental aspects of doing business. The actual evidence generated enables ILO constituents to identify priorities and make specific proposals for business environment reforms (International Labour Organization (ILO, 2014). Leveraging the expertise and guidance of global institutions, SMEs can develop ESG roadmaps to guide them in their ESG journey. This roadmap is essential to SMEs as it provides clear direction and dynamic execution plans for ESG implementation.

Although there are limitations for SMEs to gain direct access to most global institutions for financial assistance, this should not deter SMEs from seeking guidance from the relevant global institutions. Most global institutions provide massive information and guidelines on their websites, which is an excellent reference point. Furthermore, global institutions are liaising with governments on policies in driving ESG standards among SMEs in the respective countries. Hence, SMEs can approach their respective government agencies assigned to oversee the development and progress of SDGs for guidance. SMEs should leverage on incentives granted by governments, allowing them to accelerate their ESG integration process.

ESG FOR THE LONG TERM

ESG integration is a long-haul measure. As highlighted earlier, ESG adoption by businesses, including SMEs, is not an option but will soon become an integral part of the business. It will form part and parcel of business in the future. When the business community and people, in general, become more alert about climate changes and the workforce's well-being, ESG will be inevitable for SMEs. Companies that are not adhering to ESG will find it challenging to hire and retain talents. As such, SMEs must start their ESG journey without delay. SMEs can begin in a small way by investing in cleaner and efficient energy to reduce their carbon footprint in their business operations. They can then expand their ESG adoption to the other components. Moving forward, SMEs must put the system in place and, importantly, ensure compliance with the set ESG policies. To succeed in their pursuit of integrating ESG in their business operation, SMEs must have the determination, stamina, and drive to ensure the proper execution of plans. Following are the critical imperatives that will bring SMEs success in their ESG journey in the long term:

Leadership Commitment

Change must start from the top - an ordinary reality for businesses. When the senior leadership team is determined in making changes to specific policies, the chances of success will be greater. Similarly, leadership commitment is crucial for SMEs to initiate the ESG journey. The management needs to take on a mindset shift and proactive steps to embed ESG practices. In this context, transformational leadership is deemed suitable and relevant for SMEs in driving their businesses towards ESG implementation. Transformational leaders are leaders who bring change in the individuals and the organisational structure. They increase the motivation, morale, and performance of the followers. Transformational managers usually create a high-performance workforce, which engages their peers to do activities outside the job role and encourages them in taking risks. Being the role model and front runner of the team, they put

Global Institutions and ESG Integration

their team's priorities and requirements first to make them feel more confident, thereby understanding the strength and weaknesses of the teammates (Bass & Avolio, 1994). The transformational leaders must create the motivation and convince the entire staff force of the company to agree with the ESG roadmap and be ready to strive for it. The changes relating to ESG implementation must also be measurable and communicated to the broader stakeholder group to get buy-in (Lee, 2021). Implementing ESG measures is a team effort.

Congruent Direction

Setting business improvement goals is a continuous process for organisations. But the success of the goals depends on various critical success factors. One of the essential factors involves clear communication on the impending changes with the internal stakeholders. Likewise, the plan to integrate ESG principles into the business needs to be communicated with the entire staff force. Realistically, this approach makes sense that the workforce will be more driven with a better understanding of the initiatives. With the information, they will be more receptive to change. Lückmann and Feldmann (2017) reiterated the importance and need for all key stakeholders to be involved early during any business process improvement like ESG integration to ensure visibility and transparency. The goals related to ESG implementation, benefits, and early successes need to be highlighted to the stakeholders as early as possible. Goal congruence in this context is critical and can be achieved by striving for win-win solutions. By acknowledging congruent goals, the entire staff force of the company is convinced and put their mind towards the attainment of the common goals. It is through collective effort that ESG strategy can be implemented smoothly and effectively.

Resource Allocation

As most SMEs operate with limited resources, allocating adequate resources for ESG activities can be the most formidable challenge to overcome. Every business function wants a higher operational budget to perform its tasks. Even if SMEs want to reallocate their resources to address some ESG issues, they face challenges. With resources thinly spread across various functions, many SMEs do not have the flexibility to realign their resources. Furthermore, many SMEs are accustomed to their current allocation of resources and hence do not see the need to change. Why change when things are going on well? However, Freiberg et al. (2019) reiterated that a company could disrupt an industry through innovating and developing a competitive advantage, forcing competing firms to improve their performance on specific issues or develop new capabilities to compete with the innovating firm. For instance, the introduction of electric vehicles as a viable alternative to internal combustion engine vehicles to lower carbon emissions in the transportation industry and mitigate the effects of climate change. Indeed, technology can generate solutions to many of the challenges relating to the SDGs. While pursuing further research, scaling up applications of existing scientific knowledge and technological innovation – in both the natural and social sciences – can enable shifts away from business-as-usual actions and address development challenges across many sectors. SMEs may not have an abundance of resources to be aggressively reallocated for ESG matters. They need to start the process now. Taking a small step in reallocating resources is crucial for SMEs to charge forward and successfully integrate ESG principles in their businesses.

Integrated Reporting

SMEs may see integrated reporting as something far-fetched that applies only to large companies. This could be true now, but SMEs better rethink and start acknowledging the significance of integrated reporting that will soon be imposed upon SMEs, particularly those dealing with large and international firms. An integrated report is a concise communication highlighting the organisation's strategy, governance, performance, and prospects, in the context of the external environment, towards creating value in the short, medium, and long term. In short, it is safe to say that integrated reporting will somehow be imposed on SMEs in the future. Therefore, it is sensible for SMEs to start exploring the requirements and ways to implement this reporting. SMEs can initiate the move by first strengthening the core leadership team with adequate knowledge on integrated reporting. The core team should be educated and trained about ESG and its significance to business in the future. With this, SMEs can then strive to adopt a systematic approach to identifying and addressing risks related to ESG. Management of ESG-related risks is critical for integrated reporting. This part could be challenging to most SMEs due to limited resources and people with the right skills. The following steps involve the development of an ESG framework that would guide proper implementation of strategy towards ESG integration, thus integrated reporting. Lastly, it is critical to set targets and manage the overall performance of the entire exercise. Most SMEs may not be ready to implement the above measures now. However, by thinking through integrating ESG in their business operations, it can be helpful to SMEs. The thought process would put SMEs in the right frame of mind about ESG integrating and integrated reporting. With this, they will be able to launch the whole exercise of ESG integration at the right time.

Putting ESG to work within an organisation is challenging for SMEs with a lack of knowledge and resources. Despite the challenges, SMEs should not walk away from ESG but work harder to reap the benefits and opportunities associated with the implementation. They need to remain persistent and driven in garnering success in their ESG journey. ESG integration is inevitable and will be a driving force towards business sustainability for SMEs in the future.

CONCLUSION AND RECOMMENDATIONS

ESG integration in businesses, including SMEs, has become increasingly important over the last few years. The Covid-19 pandemic has further aggravated the need for imminent ESG adoption among SMEs. When business performances were affected amid the pandemic, many SMEs were compelled to leverage government assistance through wage subsidy schemes to retain employment for the workforce. By doing so, SMEs were embracing the social aspect of ESG, some without knowing it. This is true that SMEs, in general, lack knowledge about ESG and its principles. Many often have a misconception of ESG altogether. Other than this, ESG integration has not been easy for SMEs due to the lack of resources and incomplete data for decision making. As SMEs are not required to comply with ESG standards, they lack the motivation and drive to push this initiative through. However, this should not be an excuse for SMEs to delay the implementation of ESG standards in their businesses. They need to find ways to overcome the challenges of ESG integration. Consequently, SMEs must understand and acknowledge the benefits of ESG implementation, providing them with the drive and reasons to push forward their ESG agenda. Based on studies, ESG adoption can improve SME performances through effective cost management and value creation. Improved business resilience in the long term can also help SMEs towards business sustainability. Moving forward, SMEs can leverage the support of global institutions to accelerate ESG integration. Global institutions offer massive information and knowledge about ESG, clearing SMEs doubt on ESG and its integration process. SMEs can also benefit from various incentives granted by governments to fund the implementation of ESG standards. By adopting the best practices already executed by other companies would simplify and shorten the ESG journey for most SMEs. With the right leadership, clear ESG strategy, and resource allocation, SMEs will encroach ESG adoption systematically in the near future.

FUTURE RESEARCH DIRECTIONS

Narrowing down the contributions from global institutions, there could be other effective avenues in the domestic front where SMEs can leverage to accelerate ESG adoption. The local government agencies, non-governmental organisations (NGOs), and trade associations are essential entities that can support SMEs in adopting ESG principles and practices in their business operations. In the 2021 Banking and Finance Summit in Malaysia, the author reiterated the significance of banks in guiding and supporting SMEs in ESG related matters. Closer to SMEs, the local entities can complement the drives and actions from global institutions in guiding SMEs towards business sustainability in the future. With this, there is scope for future research to assess the capabilities and effectiveness of domestic entities in driving ESG adoption among SMEs. This future research should identify profound measures that can help SMEs in their journey towards sustainable business in the long term.

REFERENCES

Ansari, M. A., Kee, D. M. H., & Aafaqi, R. (2000). Fairness of human resource management practices, leader-member exchange and intention to quit. *Journal of International Business and Entrepreneurship*, *8*, 1–19.

Barbagila, M., Buttice, V., Giudici, G., Mendy, J., Sarker, T., Sharma, G. D., Thomas, A., & Zutchi, A. (2021). Supporting SMEs in sustainable strategy development post-Covid-19 : Challenges and policy agenda for the G20. *G20 Insight*, 1-12.

Barney, J. (1991). Firm resources and sustained competitive advantage. *Journal of Management*, *17*(1), 99–120. doi:10.1177/014920639101700108

Bass, B. M., & Avolio, B. J. (1994). Transformational leadership, organizational culture. *International Journal of Public Administration*, *17*(3-4), 541–554. Advance online publication. doi:10.1080/01900699408524907

Broadstock, D. C., Chan, K., Cheng, L. T., & Wang, X. (2020). *The role of ESG performance during times of financial crisis: Evidence from Covid-19 in China*. Academic Press.

Das, M., Rangarajan, K., & Dutta, G. (2020). Corporate sustainability in SMEs: An Asian perspective. *Journal of Asia Business Studies*, *14*(1), 109–138. doi:10.1108/JABS-10-2017-0176

Freiberg, D., Rogers, J., & Serafeim, G. (2019). How ESG issues become financially material to corporations and their investors. Harvard Business School. doi:10.2139srn.3482546

Friede, G., Busch, T., & Bassen, A. (2015). ESG and financial performance: Aggregated evidence from more than 2000 empirical studies. *Journal of Sustainable Finance and Investment, 5*(4), 210–233. doi: 10.1080/20430795.2015.1118917

Hu, M. K., & Kee, D. M. H. (2021). Strategic measures and tactical interventions for COVID-19 impact relief on SMEs. In N. Baporikar (Ed.), *Handbook of research on strategies and interventions to mitigate COVID-19 impact on SMEs* (1st ed., pp. 522–541). IGI Global. doi:10.4018/978-1-7998-7436-2.ch026

International Labour Organization (ILO). (2014). *An enabling environment for sustainable enterprises.* https://www.ilo.org/wcmsp5/groups/public/---ed_emp/---emp_ent/---ifp_seed/documents/publication/wcms_175476.pdf

Jeavons, M., & Thandi, J. (2021). *AA view: The benefits of ESG.* https://insights-north-america.aon.com/responsible-investing/aon-the-benefits-of-esg-integration-report

Lee, J. (2021, September 25). ESG boost for small businesses. *The Star Malaysia*, 1–8. https://www.thestar.com.my/business/business-news/2021/09/25/esg-boost-for-small-businesses

Lückmann, P., & Feldmann, C. (2017). Success factors for business process improvement projects in small and medium sized enterprises - Empirical evidence. *Procedia Computer Science, 121*, 439–445. doi:10.1016/j.procs.2017.11.059

Malay Mail. (2021, October 15). Finance minister: Wage subsidy programme applications hit RM12.94b as at Oct 1. *Malay Mail Malaysia*, p. 5. https://www.malaymail.com/news/malaysia/2021/10/15/finance-minister-wage-subsidy-programme-applications-hit-rm12.94b-as-at-oct/2013687

Mohammad, W. M. W., & Wasiuzzaman, S. (2021, June). Environmental, social and governance (ESG) disclosure, competitive advantage and performance of firms in Malaysia. *Cleaner Environmental Systems, 2*, 1–11. doi:10.1016/j.cesys.2021.100015

Mustaffa, A. H., Ahmad, N., & Bahrudin, N. Z. (2021). A systematic literature review on barriers to green financing participation worldwide. *Global Business and Management Research, 13*(4), 66–79.

Ng, E. (2021). What is ESG and why does it matter for business and investors? *South China Morning Post.* https://www.scmp.com/business/companies/article/3132470/what-esg-and-why-does-it-matter-businesses-and-investors

Ng, T. H., Lye, C. T., Chan, K. H., Lim, Y. Z., & Lim, Y. S. (2020). Sustainability in Asia: The roles of financial development in environmental, social and governance (ESG) performance. *Social Indicators Research, 150*(1), 17–44. doi:10.100711205-020-02288-w

PwC Malaysia. (2021). *Family business survey 2021: The Malaysian chapter.* https://www.pwc.de/de/mittelstand/family-business-survey/pwc-intes-family-business-survey-2021.pdf

Ren, S., Wei, W., Sun, H., Xu, Q., Hu, Y., & Chen, X. (2020). Can mandatory environmental information disclosure achieve a win-win for a firm's environmental and economic performance? *Journal of Cleaner Production, 250*, 119530. doi:10.1016/j.jclepro.2019.119530

Schramade, W., & Schoenmaker, D. (2018). *Royal Philips: A sustainable finance case.* Rotterdam School of Management Erasmus University.

Sommer, C. (2017). *Drivers and constraints for adopting sustainability standards in small and medium-sized enterprises (SMEs).* Discussion paper. Deutsches Institut fur Entwicklungspolitik (DIE). https://www.econstor.eu/bitstream/10419/199511/1/die-dp-2017-21.pdf

The Star. (2021, July 29). Mustapa: Lack of integrity detrimental. *The Star*, 1–7.

Umrani, A. I., Johl, S. K., & Ibrahim, M. Y. (2015). Corporate governance practices and problems faced by SMEs in Malaysia. *Global Business and Management Research*, 7(2), 71–77.

United Nations. (2019). *Global sustainable development report: The future is now - Science for achieving sustainable development.* https://sustainabledevelopment.un.org/globalsdreport/2019

Verboven, H., & Vanherck, L. (2016). Sustainability management of SMEs and the UN sustainable development goals. *Uwf UmweltWirtschaftsForum*, 24(2–3), 165–178. doi:10.100700550-016-0407-6

Ward, T., & MacKenzie, J. (2020). ESG in small and mid-sized quoted companies : Perceptions, myths and realities. Quoted Companies Alliance.

Wong, W. C., Batten, J. A., Ahmad, A. H., Mohamed-Arshad, S. B., Nordin, S., & Adzis, A. A. (2021). Does ESG certification add firm value? *Finance Research Letters*, 39(April), 101593. doi:10.1016/j.frl.2020.101593

World Business Council for Sustainable Development. (2020). *Building long-term business resilience.* https://docs.wbcsd.org/2020/09/WBCSD_Vision_2050_Building_longterm_business_resilience

Zumente, I., & Bistrova, J. (2021). Do Baltic investors care about environmental, social and governance (ESG)? *Entrepreneurship and Sustainability Issues*, 8(4), 349–362. doi:10.9770/jesi.2021.8.4(20)

ADDITIONAL READING

Hu, M. K., & Kee, D. M. H. (2021). Advancing SME sustainability: Rising above the atrocities of crisis. In S. Stephens (Ed.), *Cases on small business economics and development during economic crisis* (1st ed., pp. 159–178). IGI Global. doi:10.4018/978-1-7998-7657-1.ch008

Kikeri, S., Kenyon, T., & Palmade, V. (2006). Reforming the investment climate: Lessons for practitioners. *World Bank/IFC.* doi:10.1596/978-0-8213-6837-4

KPMG. (2020). *Integrating ESG into your business.* https://home.kpmg/cn/en/home/insights/2020/01/integrating-esg-into-your-business.html

PwC. (2021) *Risk and regulatory outlook 2021.* https://www.pwc.com/sg/en/insights/assets/docs/risk-regulatory-outlook-2021-esg.pdf

Stephenson, M., Hamid, M. F. S., Peter, A., Sauvant, K. P., Seric, A., & Tajoli, L. (2021). More and better investment now! How unlocking sustainable and digital investment flows can help achieve the SDGs. *Journal of International Business Policy*, 4(1), 152–165. doi:10.105742214-020-00094-2

KEY TERMS AND DEFINITIONS

Best Practices: A procedure that has been shown by research and experience to produce optimal results and generally accepted for widespread adoption.

Business Sustainability: Refers to SME capability to continue its business operations for an indefinite period, sustain itself in a rapidly changing world and market by balancing economic, social, and environmental impact.

ESG Integration: The process of starting to use ESG principles in business operations.

ESG Principles: An accepted rule of conduct guiding businesses in ESG adoption.

Global Institutions: Multigovernmental institutions in which all, or the vast majority, of the world's governments, take part.

Small and Medium Enterprises (SMEs): Business enterprises that are smallish by capital, business turnover, and the number of employees and operate in various industries. The quantum of each criterion varies by country globally.

Sustainable Development Goals (SDGs): Comprising a collection of 17 interlinked global goals designed to be a blueprint for achieving a better and more sustainable future for all people and the world by 2030.

Chapter 9
Institutional Transformation of Participatory Governance

José G. Vargas-Hernández
 https://orcid.org/0000-0003-0938-4197
Instituto Tecnológico Mario Molina, Zapopan

ABSTRACT

This chapter is aimed to analyze the institutional transformation of participatory governance from the socio-intercultural perspective and interethnic relationships. The analysis of the public culture is based on the assumption that socio-intercultural and interethnic relations are a broader social field considered in the context of the analysis of the institutions of governance to understand the social institutions and events. The method used is reflective analytical based on the literature review and empirical study. It is concluded that these institutional transformations of participatory governance have been sourced and evolved into governance structures to govern the behaviors of the communities, organizations, leadership, and members.

INTRODUCTION

In this time of pandemic crisis, the health care systems around the world are being transforming their institutional governance at all levels by the market orthodoxy whereby the multilateral authority of the nation state is being supplanted by new socio-political actors, economic agents, and other multi-stakeholder governance arrangement systems (Dentico, 2020). The institutional transformation of participatory governance behaviors and structures must be based on the principle of maintaining the integrity of ecosystems.

The word governance was used in the 12th Century in France to designate the administration of a bailliage while in England designated the method of feudal power and organization (de Alcantara, 1998; Kooiman, 2003; and Plumptre and Graham, 1999). The term governance derives from the Latin gubernare with the meaning of rudder conveying the action of steering a ship. Governance is the set of "the interactions among structures, processes and traditions that determine how power and responsibilities are exercised, how decisions are taken, and how citizens or other stakeholders have their say" (Graham, et al. 2003, ii).

DOI: 10.4018/978-1-6684-2448-3.ch009

Copyright © 2022, IGI Global. Copying or distributing in print or electronic forms without written permission of IGI Global is prohibited.

Governance is a multi-dimensional concept that moves between several layers of discourses, institutions, governments, policy structures, bureaucracies, localities, activities, etc., which need to be real and tangible for people who are potentially concerned to facilitate change and opening a space for dialogue. The concept of governance is descriptive, normative, and analytical approaches of institutions, motivations, behaviors, cultural values, norms, and so on of a system, structure, policy, political environment, and processes perspectives.

The conceptualizations of governance translate into the organizational environment meaning that the conceptualizations of other communities may be totally different context of the organization (Morphy, 2007) or may form a cultural match (Cornell and Begay, 2004). The collective analyses of governance arise some theoretical propositions. Afterwards, this analysis concentrates on the relevant roles that play. Governance assumes conditions and features of uncertainty and open-endedness (Stoker, 1998) affecting the distribution of power, decision making and engagement in a distinction way that conventional government.

Institutional transformation is related to structures of power, institutional governance of culture, socio-interculturalism in governance, and cultures of governance, which are beyond the term good governance pushed of some governments. Organizational socio-interculturality is sometimes perceived as a museum of cultures problematic for good governance. Good governance is being perceived as a vague concept (Baron, 2003, Gaudin, 2002, Simoulin, 2003) linked to corporate governance with a managerial connotation. Its origins are French and adopted by Great Britain and United States (Le Roy, 2005).

Institutionalized practices of co-determination in functional conversion (Thelen, 2000) are becoming transformed to re-establish complementarity with the corporate governance system (Hoepner, 2001; and Hoepner and Jackson, 2001). The institutional structure changes to negotiate on issues that support efficiency, although the shareholders, agents and actors adapt their demands diversify quality production and new complementarity (Streeck 2001; and Beyer and Hassel 2002).

Governing socio-intercultural inter-organization relationships requires awareness of socio-intercultural activities and practices in the governance structure. The internal governance structures and standards should be focused on procedures to avoid debates on the contents. Social contacts foster socio-interculturalism (Morgan, 2005; Bagwell and Evans 2012). Creation of socio-intercultural spaces is an attractive place for people with diverse backgrounds to encounter each other, recognize and engage with cultural and human values without xenophobia. The membership in an association or organization in any constituency of a settler society is a bounded category and artefact of socio-intercultural space that make cause dynamic governance tensions between the influence of dominant groups.

The socio-intercultural pluralism dialogue open to alterity and complexity in a global perspective is the core of good governance. The governance approach selected implicates a process referred as plural selectivity (Bagshaw, 1977: 27). Socio-interculturalism is related to the knowledge systems of two cultures that are working together (Marika, Ngurruwutthun, & White, 1992, p. 28), and therefore the analysis of acquiring knowledge applies to others as much as to oneself (Abdallah-Pretceille, 2006, p. 477).

A multi-level governance system needs gateways and platforms for socio-intercultural dialogue to develop into socio-intercultural societies based on mutual respect, partnership, and cooperation among all the governance levels. The lower levels of governance have more opportunities to provide input into other higher levels of decision making. Multilevel partnerships governance arrangements are appropriate to coordinate the governmental responsibility in the solution of problems. Organizations may deliver collaborative good governance arrangements designed and implemented in multilevel institutions to achieve intended outcomes guided by value-based standards (Howlett and Rayner, 2006).

Institutional Transformation of Participatory Governance

Devolved governance at multilevel systems occurs in tasks undertaken at decentralized level represented by all legitimized governing actors exercising their authority in conditions of integrity which provides the governance legitimacy which is consistent with communicative rationality (Habermas, 1981). Communicative rationality applies in contexts of governance where policy depends on trust developed between the participation of shareholders (Selman, 2001; Stratford and Davidson, 2002). An instrumental rational governance is based on a functional interconnectivity to build interdependencies across all the government, territory and policy scales and levels of (Dovers, 2005).

Institutional transformation of participatory governance is relevant in institutionalization theory that helps to understand the institutional environment through the historical, rational choice and sociological institutionalism. Institutional design is the normative perspective of institutional transformation that use the institutional-agent interactions as the media and tools in agency, governance, and coordination (Alexander, 1995). The institutional transformation of governance is part of the socio-cultural field (Gluckman, 1968). A socio-intercultural governance is based on the encouragement of innovation and risk associated in a socio-intercultural organizational system. The fields of socio-intercultural governance are constituted by deeply interwoven by similarities and differences of socio-cultural forms of thought, personhood, institutions, and actions leading to mutual exposure of engagements and transformations (Smith 2007; Gluckman, 1968).

The socio-intercultural space institutions, also known as the border zone, are sites of contestation for good governance, not always comfortable and untenable for effective and conducive governance arrangements. A hybrid socio-intercultural institutional and economy framework strengthens the institutional transformational adaptive capacities to manage governance for difference instead of governance for sameness. Hybrid and socio-intercultural form of governance operates in an increasingly creative and adaptive changing environment continuously addressing re-alignment challenges posed by the competing context influenced by the aboriginal and western forms of governance and social norms. These competing social norms must be managed and negotiated.

The analysis of the public culture based on socio-intercultural and interethnic relations as a broader social field must be considered in the context of the analysis of governance to understand the social institutions and events (Gluckman, 1968; Smith, 2007; Sullivan, 2005). These institutional transformations have been sourced and evolved into a participatory governance structure to govern the behaviors of the communities, organizations, leaderships, and members.

The analysis starts giving some background in this introductory note to continue analyzing the institutional dimensions of governance. Afterwards, the analysis concentrates on the relevant roles that play the socio-political actors and economic agents in the participative mechanisms. At this point, the analysis focuses on some of the conceptual, theoretical, and methodological issues related to contract governance and transaction costs to be able to highlight the implications of policy decision making and strategic governance. The theoretical treatment of institutional transformation of participatory governance has a significance beyond any specific single case. Finally, some concluding remarks are presented to wrap up this analysis

INSTITUTIONAL DIMENSIONS OF GOVERNANCE

Governance lies in institutions as the rules of the game as the glue for the way how things must be done to be considered as legitimating the practices (Cornell and Kalt, 2000; Kesteven and Smith 1984; Smith,

2007). Institutional building capacity is centered around the notion of institutions as the rules of the game, behavioral, socially, and culturally legitimate expectations. The rules of the game are the organizing processes and tools for governance. New institutional transformations of participatory governance acquire legitimacy through its outcomes produced by a consensuenced vision of its leadership (Newman, et al. 2004). The alliances based on socio-intercultural matches may support the governance legitimacy and effectiveness through some socio-cultural forms to match the local and indigenous control (Hunt and Smith, 2006: 18).

Socio-intercultural scale can be the basis to legitimate the dynamic structure and processes of the formal transformation institutions interwoven with the regional and local field of participatory governance. Formal and informal rules as governance institutions are generated by a transitional rule of innovation attempted to create workable solutions for challenging cultures of governance problems. Externally generated rules can easily undermine the institutional transformational culture of participatory governance and have less cognitive flexibility.

The long-lasting organizational and institutional dimensions activate the influential behaviors in determining the extent of local indigenous governance arrangements. These governance arrangements may be accommodated between formal and informal indigenous sociopolitical values. Cross (2008) investigates the contemporary indigenous governances in local authorities, institutions, relationships, and values that are opposed by the state governments and agencies. The institutional transformation strength must be developed from the individuals' choice of local indigenous people. Governments, indigenous local groups, and their agents may find and use appropriate governance institutions, values, processes and practices, related policies, and funding frameworks. The United Kingdom developed a standard for government and nongovernment agencies using public funding (TICGG, 2004).

The normative approach of global governance of organizations and intergovernmental organizations are supported by transnational rule-making organizations and related to institutional values such as accountability, transparency, inclusiveness, deliberativeness, etc., shaping and enacting their own identity. Accountability is a central notion to good governance. Governance accountability refers to the acceptance and allocations of responsibilities for decisions taken and actions in essential contexts for the credibility and authority, which may be distributed in vertical and horizontal accountability (Rosenau, 2000). Governance inclusiveness is referred to opportunities available for actors and stakeholders can engage in governance processes to participate in decision making processes.

A bidirectional accountability is a universal arrangement of good governance (Morphy, 2007). The accountability of the state to citizens is vertical while the horizontal accountability is by the state to the public institutions of accountability (O'Donnell,1999, Schedler, 1999, Schacter, 2000). Institutional horizontal accountability binds institutions of government buttressed by vertical accountability (Schacter, 2000) allowing the citizens to punish when they fail.

Global governance organizations and institutions are changing their normative frameworks to include more socio-intercultural inclusive organizational fields and broader organizational structures to meet the social environments. Institutions and organizations need to develop good governance and anti-corruption policies supported by the normative and rulemaking dynamics of transnational governance schemes and organizations to include public, stakeholders and experts' consultations and deliberations despite the increase in the governance costs and the decrease of organizational autonomy. There are some organizational fields and issue areas that are more enthusiastic to accept the support of transnational governance while others issue areas are not able to accept transnational governance features such as the labor issues.

Institutional Transformation of Participatory Governance

Power-based theories may serve to design and create governance models able to identify and regulate the power of agents and actors who are driving the international organizations to obtain concrete benefits form more participatory communication and decision-making processes, consultation, and deliberation among the different stakeholders. Power, norms, and interests are crucial factors for inner and transnational governance in the emergence and functioning of international institutions and organizations (Hasenclever, et al., 1997).

Power, economic, and political interests defined in terms of ideologies are factors relevant to transnational governance to norm the interactions and develop the governance rulemaking and modeling in institutional and organizational structures and processes. Colonists perceived local indigenous groups and unruly, lawless, and acephalous, but colonists were political, institutional, and social alien hieroglyph, enigmatic and incomprehensible symbols for local indigenous governance.

The western democratic concepts, governance institutions and structures have been imposed through the incorporation of social groups using hard and soft power mechanisms, authority, responsibilities and functions of the state, policy and legislative frameworks, diverse democratic systems of collective decision-making rights and individual citizenship and newly created legal categories of people. There is a cross cultural incongruity (Bagshaw, 1977: 69) between Western and Aboriginal forms and notions of governance. To maintain socio-intercultural checks and balances between Western mode of governance and customary aboriginal mode of governance and social norms must be mediated.

State power and bureaucratic institutions may assert through policy implementation processes to negotiate space for the regionalization of governance to reassert governance institutions and values. Certainty and security are built on the exercise of inclusive power and control. Local indigenous governance has been under state control and surveillance. Power dependence and institutional inequalities in the state identifies different types of governance as forms of construction of identity and institutional power, policy design, decision making, negotiation and contestation.

Thus, governance is seen like the states being supportive of authority and treated as *gubernare nullius* a kind of a *tabula rasa* with statecraft and control liberal institutions and norms. Good governance in liberal democracy does not give relevance to equality and fairness considering that people are not created equal, and leaders are not always elected under democratic principles. In some socio-intercultural contexts, women are taking power and authority positions in some activities, such as education.

The designing of transformational participatory governance institutions and organizations by members of a team making consensus decisions may develop a strong commitment to share visions, developing a sense of trust on self-governance and enabling them to be able to provide advice on government policy demands. Cultural collective shared views enhance workability enforcement and legitimacy of governance policies and rules and governing institutions. The state uses bureaucratic and statutory institutions, policy and regulations to govern their different systems of culturally based-institutions' culture of governance and governance culture to reassert the decision-making theory their legitimacy of governance arrangements.

Local cultural geographies strategically reinforce governance institutional transformational arrangements, structures, solutions and to resist externally imposed governmental institutions. The governance of culture is a symbiotic concept with cultures of governance both considered as tools to analyses the nature of engagements and interactions between different local and indigenous cultures farmed by institutional practices of government, communities, organizations, etc. The governance of cultures is an interrelated concept with cultures of governance to assert cultural geographies into a regionalization of governance trough the institutions inserting decision making processes to elucidate the nature of interactions and contestation between groups, communities, organizations, and the state.

Institutional transformation of government's culture of local participatory governance has implications on the government processes which may lead to government policy reversals an erratic form of governance of government. Culture of governance in local affairs is based on institutionalized policies, programs and funding's supported by financial compliance, transparency and accountability, technical, administrative, and financial reviews and audits as tools activated by government committees and agencies.

There are successful and outstanding local transformations of participatory governance capacities and institutions while others are dysfunctional having failed to deliver the basic rights to the represented population. Legitimacy of local governance and state nation governance may be inextricably linked through the institutions, norms, priorities, and so on. A policy of legitimate governance facilitates the institutional transformations and imperative designing of participatory governance innovation. Multiple agreements between public and private transformations of institutions can be used to deal complex issues of participatory governance and regimes aimed to give answers to the differing interests of stakeholder and states through comprehensive international agreements or bottom-up approach based on national initiatives (Hulme, 2010; Keohane and Victor, 2011). The implementation of this strategy has advantages in governance culture, diversification and structural flexibility, accountability, diverse institutional capital, and leadership. Institutional capital is the result of the interacting cognitive, regulative, and normative components (Hunt and Smith, 2007; Oliver, 1997; Bresser and Millonig, 2003: 225–2; and Scott, 1995: 35–9).

PARTICIPATIVE MECHANISMS

The organizational interactions are identified in global governance by the dynamics and shapes of the organizational fields as the structures and processes and their effects on all the involved stakeholders. Organizations are the subject of potential and significant economic component between the interests of involved agents that may derive in conflict to become the subject of an increasing element of contestation to the governance arrangements of local people.

Global governance stresses innovative forms of cooperation among the interactions between the different economic, social, and political agents, actors and stakeholders accepting core norms and gaining legitimacy (Dingwerth, and Pattberg, 2009). Of course, the interactions between these actors and agents are not exempt of functional and dysfunctional tensions, disputes, and conflicts of the pre-existing conditions in organizational operations at the different scales of the indigenous governance. The tensions between the orientations market-based governance and western and indigenous kin-based governance show that there is structural incongruence tracing towards adaptation of creative organizations.

Transnational rulemaking of organizational fields is understood as global governance organizations is an element of global governance that interact with other specific elements of intergovernmental governance organizations. The organizational fields micro-level dynamics should be incorporated into the analytical models to explain transnational regulation in the processes of global governance. Debilitated local governance need to develop a structure and process to rebuild their governance arrangements, to develop local capacities and articulate a strong governance model identified by external agents in its context. Organizational interactions lead to the adoption of social norms in accordance with the collective identity and expectations for the proper behavior of actors (Katzenstein, 1996: 5).

Different types of actors with disparities of power require the formation of a nation state and transnational rule-making organizational forces for private governance to regulate the interests among the

Institutional Transformation of Participatory Governance

actors. Their interrelationships may be contested despite the inherent complexities for the articulation of roles between regional and local organizations and the roles of the state government agencies. Local authorities and government are democratic when they have downward accountability to their communities, constituencies and people (Ribot, 2002).

Private governance emerges in areas of limited statehood, and in transnational contexts where there is vacuum of the states where the market retailers, consumers and other actors demand for governance non-state market driven (Börzel, and Risse, 2010; Cashore, Auld, Bernstein, and McDermott, 2007). Institutional transformation of corporate governance has been most pronounced in coordinated market economies with an impetus for and advocacy of change from the West economies, mainly from US (Lane, 2004; O'Sullivan 2000).

The structural relationship between the organizations related to governance should represent the socio-intercultural spaces along a continuum of exclusion – inclusion of the different political actors and economic agents. The socio-intercultural organizational structure of a different governance for the different populations tends to blend and accommodate indigenous social norms, codes of behavior and accountability with the western governance approach.

Indigenous and aboriginal populations actively involved in suitable organizational governance may invest in governance training for their bureaucrats due to their high turnover and because training has not been locally available before. The existence of other cultures as part of a socio-intercultural spaces of local organizations are incorporated in the vertical hierarchy of the state system including some features of governance arrangements taking more holistic approaches.

A hierarchical, command and control style governance (Davis and Rhodes 2000; Rhodes 2005) reverses self-determination for local indigenous people more aligned with collaborative partnership approaches. The unintended consequences of self-determination policy are the formation of western style advisers depending on partnerships with local aboriginal people. The informal and formal conditions of indigenous regional and local fields of governance are increasingly interweaving across the various scales and resulting in the ability of active and formal relationships of governance confirming the styles of indigenous sociopolitical governance. The enacted regional and local aboriginal forms of governance may be closely tied between the different involved stakeholders across the communities and the associated land ownership system.

International governance organizations and intermediaries working thorough their own channels, can cumulate more influence. Public regulators and regulated public and private agents engaged in direct relationship under the framework of old global relationship. The government´s regulatory scrutiny undermines the resilience of governance rather than enabling it while focusing on the fulfillment of external and financial compliance and responsibilities.

The context of governance must facilitate the collective participation with immediate practical use able to adapt to the changing governance needs. Good governance paradigm emerges through the participative, democratic, and interactive approaches between actors and stakeholders. The organizational dynamics embedded in broader social contexts, theoretically draws on appropriate global governance foundations on public-private partnerships and multi-stakeholder governance models. Mixed public–private system can be enhanced as a decentralized system to embed agreements, coherent architecture, decentralized initiatives, and leadership for private schemes filling the gaps of public governance. Good public governance requires compliance with legislation, standards, codes, etc., to have conformity with internal and external audits, as well as reporting requirements.

Larger regional aggregations may develop legitimacy, generate capacity, and respect indigenous local governance autonomy. A relative autonomy framework for socio-intercultural organizations such as the sites so called border zones as the places that create the hybrid and socio-intercultural interactive and meeting behaviors and forms (Clifford, 1997; Mattingly, 2006: 495) and cultural matches (Cornell and Begay, 2004).

The public–private governance is problematic when the authority is not well localized and is deeply entangle (Porter, 2009), although the distinction is crucial in social life (Pattberg and Stripple, 2008). The stakeholder participation norm in trans and international governance contributes to the diffusion of multi-sectoral partnerships. Governance issues can be treated, negotiated, and enforced according to the existing ecological norms and the cooperation of all the stakeholders and actors involved, such as in the case of land use. The institutional transformation of participatory governance should be sustained on the principle of maintaining the integrity of ecosystems.

Regulatory cooperation and orchestration schemes are mechanisms in which international governance organizations engage with other stakeholders such as private partners, business and industries groups and other intermediaries to influence their behavior toward the achievement of their targets (Abbot et al. 2010). Regulatory cooperation and orchestration as governance mechanisms strengthen centralized coordination of international governance organizations opposing to the current decentralized practices. The orchestration mechanism supporting existing or new schemes of the intermediaries and stakeholders can be used to advance and adopt public goals, policies, structures, and endorsement, facilitating formation and material assistance. However, despite that orchestration has some sovereignty costs it is a low-cost strategy with stronger actions and less resistance.

Orchestration efforts are used for biofuel governance by public regulators taking measures in the European Union actively supported by nation states and international organizations. However, there is little empirical evidence of the complications and benefits provided. Therefore, orchestration bonds third parties into governance arrangements (Abbott, *et al.* 2010, p. 1).

CONTRACT GOVERNANCE AND TRANSACTION COSTS

Contract governance is a new form of governance that has the potential to connect local socio-intercultural norms of a diverse partners. Contract and relational governance have an effective role on relationship commitment and performance between organizations which is used to govern interorganizational collaboration, although the impact is not well known. Relational governance supports information exchange and maintenance of the collaboration relationships to promote cooperation and potentially mitigating differences and conflicts. Contract governance effectiveness is related to the level of organization cultural intelligence capabilities which plays a relevant role in the implementation of collaboration. Effectiveness contract governance mechanism of organizations are being evaluated in terms of the detailed contract, coordination, information, and decision-making.

The interorganizational relationships, such as in the case of supply chains has relied on contract and relational governance leading to the fulfillments of joint and common objectives. The interorganizational relationship also needs collaboration and contract governance which are affected by the national culture and cultural intelligence as the moderating influence. Contract governance promotes cooperation and commitment to a partnership leading to fulfill joint objectives. The meta-cognitive and motivational cultural intelligence have positive effects on contract governance effectiveness for collaboration. Behavioral

Institutional Transformation of Participatory Governance

and motivational components of cultural intelligence moderate the relationships between collaboration and contract relational governance.

Cultural intelligence logics in contract governance is relevant in emerging economies where the political uncertainty is high, the transformation of the institutional environment and the rule of law are weak. Cultural intelligence is expressed in the behavioral flexibility and adaptability influencing the relationship between contract governance, collaboration, and social performance. Governance mechanism effectiveness of organizations is dependent on organization age and size (Zhu et al. 2012), the industry type and the experience of employers affect the social performance (Hair et al. 2010). Organizational governance performance information on all decisions should be transparent, accessible and available to all the stakeholders and anyone interested (Davidson and Stratford, 2000).

National culture and organizational culture have a contingent effect on the effectiveness of governance mechanisms and interorganizational cooperation (Handley, & Angst, 2015). The formal contract governance is associated with performance of collaboration. Activities and operations of organizations involved in contract governance benefit from collaborative knowledge and solutions. The legal bonds are laid out by the rights and obligations of parties involved in the relationship to safeguard the transactions. The contract governance should specify roles, obligations, expectations, and constraining opportunism of parties involved in interorganizational relational governance, incorporating legal bonds to foster commitment and improve performance.

The contract governance in interorganizational cooperation relationships is related to be more administrative effective in terms of transaction costs economics (Williamson, 2008, 1996, 1991) under conditions of cultural intelligence. The contract governance is based on transaction cost economics theory to promote the relational mechanisms governing exchanges though shared behavioral expectations of mutual control or understanding between the parties. Contract governance is interconnected to cultural intelligence capabilities to be able to promote socio-intercultural collaboration and cooperation between the partner's entities.

More administrative efficient organizations, from the transaction costs perspective (Williamson, 1996), is conducive to contract governance has positive effects leading to develop relationships of collaboration by decreasing behavioral opportunism. From the perspective of transactional costs economy, the high levels of meta-cognitive and motivational cultural intelligence enhance the socio-intercultural interactions and improves collaboration at the lower information exchange cost.

Cultural intelligence has effects on governance mechanism of the interorganizational relationships and cooperation. The dimensions of cognition, metacognition, behavioral, and motivational of cultural intelligence affect differently the socio-intercultural interactions and their impact on contract governance and collaboration relationships. Contract governance has a moderating effect with metacognition of cultural intelligence and more significant relationship for the collaboration, and the differences in metacognition of cultural intelligence are related with the level of collaboration and contract governance.

Cultural intelligence has effects on the relationship between contract-relational governance and collaboration (Ang and Inkpen, 2008) Cultural intelligence has a motivational component that leads to more cooperative behavior and socio-intercultural negotiations between members of different cultures while at same time moderates contract governance and collaboration. Metacognition of cultural intelligence has a moderating effect on contract governance and collaboration whose differences are associated with the levels of collaboration and contract governance.

Stakeholders should develop cultural intelligence capabilities as a source aimed to improve their relationship through contract governance to align their collaboration practices and activities. Some of these capabilities are the analytical and critical discussion, communicative and inspirational skills, as well as the capabilities to develop synergies through various methods for teamwork, learning and reflection.

POLICY DECISION MAKING AND STRATEGIC GOVERNANCE

Developing governance solutions may be an active process of innovation and adaptation of policy and decision making involving elected representatives and bureaucratic managers. The social organization nodes of highly decentralized governance systems enable decision making of nodal leadership and organizations that constitute the circuitry of authority and governing. Socio-intercultural leadership has emerged as a counterpoint of the colonial domination leadership providing a more culturally oriented and informed idea which proposes a cultural encounter considering all the fundamental characteristics of each specific and individual cultural (Coll, 2004, p. 27).

There is always a need to make decisions on the identity related to self-governance (Hunt and Smith 2006). Governance is about the politics of socio-interculturality and cultural identities more oriented towards local autonomy at the scales of cultural geography. Cultural geography focuses on indigenous and local governance, negotiation and contestation occurring in its boundaries, changing scales, and so on in the collective self in governance arrangements between and within governments and communities. These local aboriginal organizations extend the complexities of the governance styles including the aboriginal identity forms, localized population, types of land ownership, etc. Contemporary local indigenous governances have ontological frameworks components that are ignored or diminished in relevance by analysts (O'Malley, 1998, Christie, 2007, Howitt, 2001) or erased from its formal administrative structures and processes (Muller, 2008).

There is a wider regional level of connectedness related to indigenous governance structural and procedural arrangements which have implications on politicized and contested identity.

The disabling of these governance arrangements may have analytical and practical implications. This regional indigenous domain is located within the complexity of dimensions of a field governance environment. These dimensions or layers have been identified by Hunt and Smith (2006:76) as the individual, entity, inter-relationships, and environment.

The principles of governance have the tendency towards crossing boundaries and open-ended situations subject to negotiations (Williams, 1982) and values adhered. The governance principles are the platform to develop the governance, monitoring and evaluating instruments to apply in self-assessments and audits. These governance principles can be used to design and implement the institutional transformation of governance that must be legitimate, inclusive, transparent, accountable, fair, functional, structurally integrated, adaptable, capable, etc. A corporate governance principle has proposed for an evaluation of governance arrangements at Australian regional NRM organizations (Turnbull, 2005).

The common assumption that indigenous local cultures across the diverse settings of nation states are different that common design principles underpinning governance cannot infer needs to be rectify (Hunt and Smith 2007). The designing of these principles is a critical factor in strengthening indigenous local governance.

The existence of complex diversity and several different governance cultures operating in a broad field of governance such as the contested state governance. Organizations may embed the governance culture by promoting the norms and values such as fairness, respect, accountability, commitment, teamwork, autonomy, etc., which reinforce the legitimate collective governance. All these values and quali-

Institutional Transformation of Participatory Governance

ties are regarded as the collective support for the organizational cultural identity (Armstrong, 2007: 75, 2003) emphasized by members to maintain a style of governance. The governance culture is a process of building transformative institutional capital supported not only by deliberative leadership but also by the extended family organizations.

This governance socio-interculturality is required to attend the diversity of cultures. Socio-intercultural communication agency supported by local media can raise awareness of cultural diversity and socio-intercultural dialogue and the benefits practicing a cultural pluralism approach. Socio-intercultural dialogue challenges assumptions confronting different values, knowledge, worldviews, and beliefs, as well as exploring visions and aspirations of people to bring new and creative possibilities of living (UNESCO, 2008c) and providing an experiential opportunity to forge cultural links and knowledge exchanges. The socio-intercultural dialogue is valued for shaping social and cultural change processes (UNESCO, 2008a, 2008b).

Formal governance solutions must be included in an official document previously gained agreement. Forms of global governance have an impact on organizational strategies and therefore on the evolution of social norms and interactions at micro and private governance levels beyond the ideology, power, and efficiency of the nation-states. Socio-interculturality embraces the differences tolerated by the nation state by reducing the power asymmetries promoted by socio-intercultural projects determined by political and ideological frameworks. The state must make decisions on the value and benefits of resolving complex governance issues to facilitate the design and implementation of innovative strategies and policies. Governance was shunted aside when public bureaucrats at local governments took over it with extraordinary powers (Siewart 2007) after the implemented strategies of government reforms (Smith, 2004).

Local indigenous governance has been in continued policy complexity and contestation to the nation state that has not been able to deal with the indigenous identity and their political consequences on treating and control the affairs (Arabena, 2005: 28). The socio-intercultural process changes in complex multi-sited governance systems. Since the colonial times, indigenous local governance has been considered underdeveloped, unknowable, and invisible.

Transparent governance may facilitate early detection and correction of any policy mistakes and misallocations, an approach that may be demanding and time inefficient, it is expected that bureaucrats commit to this governance mechanism. A counterproductive policy implementation to the achievement of legitimate governance sometimes is maintained either by self-interest of negligence by policy makers or officials. When local government authorities are in organizational bankruptcy and perceived in parlous state constituting a stark crisis of governance (Behrendt, et al. 2007, Sanders, 2003, 2004 and Smith1995, 1996, 2007).

In a norm-based approach of organizational governance, the converging model may involve high costs of transnational regulations driven by ideological macro-social foundations of a transnational governance imposed on micro foundations of a sociological approach (Bernstein and Cashore, 2007). Organizational governance has formal and informal components, but informal governance is at the individual level working through the behavioral processes of conflicts, appeals, rewards, sanctions, etc., personal style, individual and collective identities, decision making, etc. Organizational governance also calls repeatedly for better evaluation of effectiveness despite the experiencing of internal tensions and the presence of complexity and uncertainty.

The improvement of the internal organizational governance arrangements can be the result of a negotiating empowering governance system in socio-intercultural spaces. The construction of values and

DISCUSSION

This study is based on the analysis focusing on the conceptual, theoretical, and methodological issues related to contract governance and transaction costs to be able to highlight the implications of policy decision making and strategic governance. 90 conceptual and theoretical research papers were analyzed based on the variables of the research, institutional transformation, and participatory governance. Out of these analyses, a reflective process leads to the following tendencies:

The spatial resources used by associations and organizations in participatory governance to advocate the reconstruction of spaces and development of a model of governance and public-civil partnership, that as users of spaces invest in the transformation into contemporary socio intercultural institutional governance. Institutional participatory governance is based on the interactions between public actors, organizations, and civil society, enabling the citizens to build their capacities to be used as democratic instruments for decision making to transform and improve the democratic quality of institutions.

Participation in institutional development governance faces structural, cultural, and transformative challenges. Cultural participation is a conceptual, operational, and interpretative foundations of cultural human rights based on institutional participatory governance policies such as the encouragement of social inclusive transformation. Social and cultural capital frameworks are fundamental resources for creation and development of settings based on institutional participatory governance, transforming territorial and locational communities.

The new institutions and innovations in public policies have transformative potential. Transformation of institutional participatory governance functions is remedied by operational functioning and established to the different actors and stakeholders involved in the non-institutional and institutional existing positions. Socio-intercultural participatory governance implies a critical awareness and respect for other cultural values that reflect diversity in the public transformations of public policies, institutions, public spaces, and civic culture that enable initiative and projects.

Policy scholarly agendas can help to understand the potential of institutions of participatory governance to transform the economic, social, and sustainable environment in which they are embedded. Policy making and activism are concerned about the specific contexts that better suite participatory governance to reframe process of transformation, although there is lack of knowledge about types of institutions given the limited resources available for institutional building.

CONCLUSION

This analysis concludes that the institutional transformations of participatory governance have been sourced and evolved into a governance structure to govern the behaviors of the communities, organizations, leaderships, and members. It is needed more robust institutional participatory governance arrangements to cope with this time of pandemic crisis around the world. The traditional governance arrangements need to be transformed at all levels in such a way that the multilateral authority of the nation state is be-

Institutional Transformation of Participatory Governance

ing supplanted by new socio-political actors, economic agents, and other multi-stakeholder governance arrangement systems.

The institutional transformations of participatory governance have been sourced and evolved into a structures to govern the behaviors of the governments at all levels, communities, organizations, leaderships and members The practice of organizational governance should have to be more open to compromise and capacity building enable to create and develop more trust and autonomy to outweigh the benefits of outcomes performed by the synergetic support between the stakeholders, organizations and governments.

A broader organizational governance review may require including various local government agencies that may lead to make generalized recommendations that may not respond to clarify specific nature of the problems and the possible solutions to rectify them. Imposition of governance solutions to internal bodies because the organization had received funding to carry out the review may bring more problems than solutions and the outcomes may have limited traction (Hunt and Smith 2007: xvi).

REFERENCES

Abbott, K. W., Genschel, P., Snidal, D., & Zangl, B. (2010) *IOs as Orchestrators*. Paper presented at the 7th Pan-European Conference on International Relations, Stockholm, Sweden.

Abdallah-Pretceille, M. (2006). Socio-interculturalism as a paradigm for thinking about diversity. *Socio-intercultural Education, 17*(5), 475–483. doi:10.1080/14675980601065764

Alexander, E. R. (1995). *How Organizations Act Together: Interorganizational Coordination in Theory and Practice*. Gordon & Breach.

Ang, S., & Inkpen, A. C. (2008). Cultural intelligence and offshore outsourcing success: A framework of organization-level socio-intercultural capability. *Decision Sciences, 2008*(39), 337–358. doi:10.1111/j.1540-5915.2008.00195.x

Arabena, K. (2005). *Not fit for modern Australian society. Aboriginal and Torres Strait Island people and the new arrangements for the administration of Indigenous Affairs*. Research Discussion Paper No. 16. AIATSIS.

Armstrong, L. (2003). *Financial management and business systems: the backbone of an effectively resourced capacity for governance*. Unpublished paper presented to the Building Effective Indigenous Governance Conference. Available at http://www.nt.gov.au/cdsca/indigenous conference/web/html/papers.html

Armstrong, L. (2007). Finding Australia's soul: rebuilding our Indigenous communities. *The Circle, 1*, 74–6. Available at https://www.socialventures.com.au/files/pdf/TC%20mag%20Leah%20Armstrong.pdf

Bagshaw, G. (1977). *Analysis of Local Government in a Multi-Clan Community* (BA Dissertation). Department of Anthropology, The University of Adelaide.

Bagwell, S., & Evans, G. (2012). Public Space Management, report to the socio-intercultural cities programme Council of Europe Publishing, socio-intercultural cities step by step socio-intercultural cities. *Newsletter*. www.coe.int/socio-interculturaLcitiezs

Baron, C. (2003). La gouvernance: Débats autour d'un concept polysémique. *Droit Social*, (54), 329–351. doi:10.3917/drs.054.0329

Behrendt, L., McCausland, R., Williams, G., Reilly, A., & McMillan, M. (2007). The promise of regional governance for Aboriginal and Torres Strait Islander communities. *Ngiya: Talk the Law, Governance in Indigenous Communities, 1*, 126–166.

Bernstein, S., & Cashore, B. (2007). Can Non-State Global Governance be Legitimate? *Regulation & Governance, 1*(4), 347–371. doi:10.1111/j.1748-5991.2007.00021.x

Beyer, J., & Hassel, A. (2002). The market for corporate control and financial internationalization of German firms. *Economy and Society*, 31.

Börzel, T., & Risse, T. (2010). Governance without a state: can it work? *Regulation and Governance, 4*(2), 113–34.

Bresser, R., & Millonig, K. (2003). Institutional capital: Competitive advantage considering the new institutionalism in organisational theory. *Schmalenbach Business Review, 55*(3), 220–241. doi:10.1007/BF03396675

Cashore, B., Auld, G., Bernstein, S., & McDermott, C. (2007). Can non-state governance "ratchet up" global environmental standards? Lessons from the forest sector. *Review of European Community, and International Environmental Law, 16*(2), 158–72.

Christie, M. (2007). Knowledge management and natural resource management. In M. K. Luckert, B. Campbell, & J. T. Gorman (Eds.), *Investing in indigenous natural resource management* (pp. 86–90). Charles Darwin University Press.

Clifford, J. (1997). *Routes: Travel and Translation in the Twentieth Century*. Harvard University Press.

Coll, A. C. (2004). *The socio-intercultural challenge*. Pipal Tree.

Cornell, S., & Begay, M. (2004). *What is cultural match and why is it so important? Lessons from 14 years of the Harvard Project*. Paper presented at the Building Effective Governance Conference.

Cornell, S., & Kalt, J. P. (2000). Where's the glue? Institutional and cultural foundations of American Indian economic development. *Journal of Socio-Economics, 29*(5), 443–470. doi:10.1016/S1053-5357(00)00080-9

Cross, S. (2008). *The Scale Politics of Reconciliation* (PhD. Dissertation). Department of Human Geography, Macquarie University.

Davidson, J., & Stratford, E. (2000). *Building the knowledge base of the social and institutional dimensions of natural resource management*. Land and Water Resources Research and Development Corporation.

Davis, G., & Rhodes, R. A. W. (2000). From hierarchy to contracts and back again: reforming the Australian public service. In Institutions on the Edge? Capacity for Governance. Allen & Unwin.

de Alcantara, C. H. (1998). Uses and abuses of the concept of governance. *International Social Science Journal, 155*(155), 105–113. doi:10.1111/1468-2451.00113

Dentico, N. (2020). Editorial: The Vital Pedagogy of the New Coronavirus. *Development*, *63*(2-4), 145–149. doi:10.105741301-020-00279-5 PMID:33311953

Dingwerth, K., & Pattberg, P. (2009). World Politics and Organizational Fields: The Case of Transnational Sustainability Governance. *European Journal of International Relations*, *15*(4), 707–743. doi:10.1177/1354066109345056

Gaudin, J.-P. (2002). *Pourquoi la gouvernance?* Presses de Sciences Po. doi:10.3917cpo.gaudi.2002.01

Gluckman, M. (1968). The utility of the equilibrium model in the study of social change. *American Anthropologist*, *70*(2), 219–237. doi:10.1525/aa.1968.70.2.02a00010

Graham, J., Amos, B., & Plumptre, T. (2003). *Governance principles for protected areas in the 21st century*. Institute on Governance, Parks Canada, and the Canadian International Development Agency.

Habermas, J. (1981). *The theory of communicative action: Reason and the rationalization of society*. Beacon Press.

Hair, J. F. J., Black, W. C., Babin, B. J., & Anderson, R. E. (2010). *Multivariate Data Analysis* (7th ed.). Prentice Hall.

Handley, S. M., & Angst, C. M. (2015). The impact of culture on the relationship between governance and opportunism in outsourcing relationships. *Strategic Management Journal*, *2015*(36), 1412–1434. doi:10.1002mj.2300

Hasenclever, A., Mayer, P., & Rittberger, V. (1997). *Theories of International Regimes*. Cambridge University Press. doi:10.1017/CBO9780511521720

Hoepner, M. (2001). *Corporate governance in transition: ten empirical findings on shareholder value and industrial relations*. Discussion Paper 01/5. Max-Planck-Institut für Gesellschaftsforschung.

Hoepner, M., & Jackson, G. (2001). *An emergent market for corporate control? The Mannesmann takeover and German corporate governance*. MPIfG Discussion Paper 01/4. Cologne: MPIf.G.

Howitt, R. (2001). *Rethinking resource management: Justice, sustainability, and indigenous peoples*. Routledge.

Howlett, M., & Rayner, J. (2006). Convergence and divergence in 'new governance' arrangements: Evidence from European integrated natural resource strategies. *Journal of Public Policy*, *26*(2), 167–189. doi:10.1017/S0143814X06000511

Hulme, M. (2010). Moving beyond climate change. *Environment*, *52*(3), 15–19.

Hunt, J., & Smith, D. (2006). *Building Indigenous community governance in Australia: preliminary research findings*. CAEPR Working Paper No. 31, CAEPR, ANU.

Hunt, J., & Smith, D. E. (2007). *Indigenous Community Governance Project: Year two research findings*. CAEPR Working Paper No. 36, CAEPR, CASS, ANU.

Katzenstein, P. J. (1996). Introduction: Alternative Perspectives on National Security. In P. J. Katzenstein (Ed.), *The Culture of National Security* (pp. 1–32). Columbia University Press.

Keohane, R.O., & Victor, D. (2011). The regime complex for climate change. *Perspectives on Politics, 9*(1), 7–23.

Kesteven, S., & Smith, D. E. (1984). Contemporary Land-Tenure in Western Arnhem Land: An Investigation of Traditional Ownership, Resource Development and Royalties. Report to the Australian Institute of Aboriginal Studies and the Northern Land Council.

Kooiman, J. (2003). *Governing as Governance*. Sage Publications.

Lane, C. (2004). *Institutional transformation and system change: changes in corporate governance of Germancorporations* (Reihe Soziologie / Institut für Höhere Studien, Abt. Soziologie, 65). Wien: Institut für Höhere Studien (IHS). https://nbn-resolving.org/urn:nbn:de:0168-ssoar-220637

LeRoy, G. (2005). *The Great American Jobs Scam: Corporate Tax Dodgingand the Myth of Job Creation*. Berrett-Koehler Publishers.

Marika, R., Ngurruwutthun, D., & White, L. (1992). Always together, yaka gäna: Participatory research at Yirrkala as part of the development of a Yolngu education. *Convergence (Toronto), 25*, 23–39.

Mattingly, C. (2006). Pocahontas goes to the clinic: Popular culture as lingua franca in a cultural borderland. *American Anthropologist, 108*(3), 494–501. doi:10.1525/aa.2006.108.3.494 PMID:20706562

Morgan, G., Rocha, G., & Poynting, S. (2005). Grafting Cultures: Longing and Belonging in Immigrants' Ottaviano G.I.P., G. Peri (2005), Cities and cultures. *Journal of Urban Economics, 58*, 304–337.

Morphy, H. (2007). *Becoming Art: Exploring Cross-Cultural Categories*. Berg.

Muller, S. (2008). Accountability constructions, contestations, and implications: Insights from working in a yolngu cross-cultural institution, Australia. *Geography Compass, 2*(2), 1–19. doi:10.1111/j.1749-8198.2007.00087.x

Newman, J., Barnes, M., Sullivan, H., & Knops, A. (2004). Public participation and collaborative governance. *Journal of Social Policy, 33*(2), 203–223. doi:10.1017/S0047279403007499

O'Donnell, G. (1999). Horizontal accountability in new democracies. In A. Schedler, L. Diamond, & M. F. Plattner (Eds.), *The Self-Restraining State: Power and Accountability in the New Democracies*. Lynne Rienner Publishers.

O'Malley, P. (1998). Indigenous governances. In M. Dean & B. Hindess (Eds.), *Governing Australia: Studies in contemporary rationalities of government* (pp. 156–172). Cambridge University Press.

O'Sullivan, M. A. (2000). *Contests for Corporate Control. Corporate governance and economic performance in the United States and Germany*. Oxford University Press.

Oliver, C. (1997). Sustainable competitive advantage: Combining institutional and resource-based views. *Strategic Management Journal, 18*(9), 697–713. doi:10.1002/(SICI)1097-0266(199710)18:9<697::AID-SMJ909>3.0.CO;2-C

Pattberg, P., & Stripple, J. (2008). Beyond the public and private divide: Remapping transnational climate governance in the 21st century. *International Environmental Agreements: Politics, Law and Economics, 84*(4), 367–88.

Institutional Transformation of Participatory Governance

Plumptre, T., & Graham, J. (1999). *Governance and Good Governance: International and Aboriginal Perspectives*. Institute on Governance.

Porter, T. (2009). Global governance as configurations of state/non-state activity. In J. Whitman (Ed.), *Palgrave advances in global governance*. Palgrave Macmillan. doi:10.1057/9780230245310_5

Rhodes, R. (2005). The unholy trinity of governance. The Blake Dawson Waldron Lecture, National Museum of Australia.

Ribot, J. C. (2002). *Democratic decentralization of natural resources: Institutionalizing popular participation*. World Resources Institute.

Rosenau, J. N. (2000). Change, complexity, and governance in globalizing space. In J. Pierre (Ed.), *Debating governance* (pp. 167–200). Oxford University Press.

Sanders, W. (2003). *Participation and representation in the 2002 ATSIC elections*. CAEPR Discussion Paper No. 252, CAEPR, ANU.

Sanders, W. (2004). *Thinking about Indigenous community governance*. CAEPR Discussion Paper No. 262, CAEPR, ANU.

Schacter, M. (2000). *When accountability fails: A framework for diagnosis and action. Policy Brief No. 9*. Institute on Governance.

Schedler, A. (1999). Restraining the state: conflicts and agents of accountability. In A. Schedler, L. Diamond, & M. F. Plattner (Eds.), *The Self-Restraining State: Power and Accountability in the New Democracies*. Lynne Rienner Publishers.

Scott, J. C. (1998). *Seeing Like a State: How Certain Schemes to Improve the Human Condition Have Failed*. Yale University Press.

Selman, P. (2001). Social capital, sustainability, and environmental planning. *Planning Theory & Practice, 2*(1), 13–30. doi:10.1080/14649350122850

Siewart, R. (2007). *Ministerial powers to seize assets of service providers in prescribed areas within the Northern Territory*. Background Briefing, Parliament House. Available at <http://www.rachelsiewert.org.au/files/campaigns/extras/Briefing_on_NT_seizure_powers.pdf>

Simoulin, V. (2003). La gouvernance et l'action publique: Le succès d'une forme simmélienne. *Droit Social*, (54), 307–328. doi:10.3917/drs.054.0307

Smith, D. E. (1995). Representative politics and the new wave of native title organisations. In J. Finlayson & D. E. Smith (Eds.), Native Title: Emerging Issues for Research, Policy and Practice. CAEPR Research Monograph No. 10. CAEPR, ANU.

Smith, D. E. (1996). From cultural diversity to regionalism: The political culture of difference in ATSIC. In P. Sullivan (Ed.), Shooting the Banker: Essays on ATSIC and Self-determination. North Australia Research Unit, ANU.

Smith, D. E. (2004). *From Gove to governance: Reshaping Indigenous governance in the Northern Territory*. CAEPR Discussion Paper No. 265, CAEPR, ANU.

Smith, D. E. (2007). Networked governance: Issues of process, policy, and power in a West Arnhem Land regional initiative. *Ngiya: Talk the Law. Governance in Indigenous Communities, 1*, 24–52.

Stoker, G. (1998). Governance as theory: Five propositions. *International Social Science Journal, 155*(155), 17–28. doi:10.1111/1468-2451.00106

Stratford, E., & Davidson, J. (2002). Capital assets and intercultural borderlands: Socio-cultural challenges for natural resource management. *Journal of Environmental Management, 66*(4), 429–440. doi:10.1006/jema.2002.0597 PMID:12503497

Streeck, W. (2001). *The transformation of corporate organization in Europe: an overview.* MPIfG Working Paper 01/8, December 2001. MPIfG/Cologne/Germany.

Sullivan, P. (2005). Searching for the socio-intercultural, searching for the culture, in The Independent Commission for Good Governance in Public Services (TICGG). *The good governance standard for public services.* http://www.opm.co.uk/icggps/download_upload/Standard.pdf

Thelen, K. (2000). Timing and temporality in the analysis of institutional evolution and change. *Studies in American Political Development, 14*(1), 101–108. doi:10.1017/S0898588X00213035

Turnbull, W. (2005). *Evaluation of current governance arrangements to support regional investment under the NHT and NAP.* Canberra, Australia: Departments of Environment and Heritage and Agriculture, Fisheries and Forestry.

United Nations Educational, Scientific and Cultural Organization (UNESCO). (2008a). Background Note. A Review of Education for Sustainable Development (ESD) Policies from a Cultural Diversity and socio-intercultural Dialogue Perspective. Unpublished document. UNESCO/CLT/CPD/CPO20/11/2008. Paris: UNESCO.

United Nations Educational, Scientific and Cultural Organization (UNESCO). (2008b). UNESCO Concept Note. Towards a New Cultural Policy Profile. UNESCO/CLT/CPD 01/08/2008. Paris: UNESCO.

United Nations Educational, Scientific and Cultural Organization (UNESCO). (2008c). ESD Lens, version 2, draft 1: Comments from a cultural diversity perspective. Unpublished document. Paris: UNESCO.

Williams, N. M. (1982). A boundary is to cross observations on Yolngu boundaries and permission. In N. M. Williams & E. S. Hunn (Eds.), *Resource Managers: North American and Australian Hunter-Gatherers.* Australian Institute of Aboriginal Studies Press.

Williamson, O. E. (1991). Comparative economic organization: The analysis of discrete structural alternatives. *Administrative Science Quarterly, 1991*(2), 269–296. doi:10.2307/2393356

Williamson, O. E. (1996). *The Mechanisms of Governance.* Oxford University Press.

Williamson, O. E. (2008). Outsourcing: Transaction cost economics and supply chain management. *The Journal of Supply Chain Management, 2008*(44), 5–16. doi:10.1111/j.1745-493X.2008.00051.x

Zhu, Q., Sarkis, J., & Lai, K.-H. (2012). Examining the effects of green supply chain management practices and their mediations on performance improvements. *International Journal of Production Research, 2012*(50), 1377–1394. doi:10.1080/00207543.2011.571937

Chapter 10
Integrated Reporting for Inclusive and Sustainable Global Capitalism

Isaac Okoth Randa

https://orcid.org/0000-0001-7370-3864

Namibia University of Science and Technology, Namibia

ABSTRACT

There is growing universal agreement that neoliberalism, a form of political economy governance, has under-delivered for a majority of people over many years. This is exhibited in the extent of job losses, reduced tax revenues, dwindling overall savings, and so on. Whereas several contributory factors are identifiable, fundamentally these policy ambiguities are issues of failing global governance. This chapter analytically describes the influence of integrated reporting as an instrument for embedding corporate transparency, accountability, and responsibility, hence inclusive corporate governance for the common good in emerging economies. This investigation identified three channels through which integrated reporting connects with sustainable and inclusive capitalism, transparency and adequate disclosures in capital markets, stakeholder engagement, and corporate legitimacy. Integrated reporting provides the required cultural shift in corporate management by emphasising multi-capital long-term value creation, which ultimately promotes long-term behaviour in capital markets.

INTRODUCTION

Under the guise of free market globalization, multi-national corporations transfer money around the world searching for places with cheap labour and relaxed environmental and industrial laws for their enterprises (Watts & Hodgson, 2019). Consequently, capitalism as practiced today has resulted in exportation of millions of jobs to destinations where labour is cheaper and relaxed environmental regulations (Henry Jackson Initiative, 2012). The results are many displaced employees ill prepared for the residual high-skilled jobs; the situation is even worse for youths as the number of entry-level job opportunities have significantly dwindled. Additionally, the ensuing financial scandals as corporations seek for more profits

DOI: 10.4018/978-1-6684-2448-3.ch010

Copyright © 2022, IGI Global. Copying or distributing in print or electronic forms without written permission of IGI Global is prohibited.

have also generated awareness that the contemporary shareholders' profit maximization governance model, especially in the short-run, does not improve the wellness for either the firms or society in the long run (Brunelli & Di Carlo, 2020). Consequently, inclusive capitalism as a concept and policy movement is attempting to improve business governance and hence the society by addressing the growing income and wealth inequality in the predominantly Western capitalistic systems. Inclusive capitalism is an argument that if private enterprise is encouraged through suitable policy interventions; then it can create more jobs for low-income people as well as provide underprivileged people with access to financial capital for business (Randa & Atiku, 2021). Arguably, inclusive capitalism has the potential for enabling poor people to purchase a variety of goods and services thus increasing their welfare.

The market short-termism, partly driven by today's short term-focused financial markets; compels managements to focus more on short-term financial profits rather than sustainable long-term business development (Henry Jackson Initiative, 2012). For example, recently Chief Executive Officers (CEOs) and boards tend to manage their companies against quarterly targets aimed at generating highest returns now, neglecting their companies' long-term needs. All this is happening within the context of rules-based national and global surveillance systems; the argument is that what have gone wrong did not involve illegal activities. There is clear manifestation that complex global phenomena ranging from financial to ecological processes determine the fate of communities across the world. Additionally, the problem-solving capacity of the existing systems of global institutions in many areas are losing effectiveness, accountability, or responsiveness in resolving these global dilemmas. For example, the ensuing neoliberal policies have compelled workers to be more flexible, mobile and adaptable given the rapidly changing and uncertain labour markets characterised by casual, part-time and contract work (Watts & Hodgson, 2019), adds to the present instability. According to Gertz and Kharas (2019), there is a rising agreement that neoliberalism; a form of political-economy governance model has under-delivered for a majority of people over many years in many areas. Arguably, the extent of job losses, reduced tax revenues, dwindling overall private savings and so on underscore this phenomenon. Several reasons for the persistence of these problems can be articulated; but at the most fundamental level, these policy inconsistencies are arguably issues of failing global governance systems requiring systemic institutional reforms (Held & Young, 2009). Debatably, corporate sustainability initiatives promise alternatives to the dominant traditional, short-term profit-oriented approaches to firm management by balancing economic, environmental, and social forces not only for the present and but also for future generations (Lozano, Carpenter & Huisingh, 2015).

BACKGROUND

Emerging economies (EEs), a term with several interpretations such as emerging markets, developing markets/economies/ countries, as well as the BRICs countries to mention a few have become increasingly relevant to the world economy (Saviano & Carrubbo, 2014). Arguably, EEs gross domestic product will permanently surpass that of all advanced economies by 2035 (Sheth, 2011). Similarly, EEs is home to more than two-thirds of the world's population (Prahalad & Hart, 2002; Kayser & Budinich, 2015) making them a formidable force as consumers. Whereas, multinational corporations have already acknowledged this untapped market potential, their involvement with EE's poverty reduction initiatives have not been effective (Karnani, 2011). Their perception of emerging economies have mainly been understood from two perspectives: firstly, they view EE's as new markets purely from the traditional marketing concept; secondly, they view them as handicapped countries requiring foreign aid for poverty alleviation mainly through charity. These conceptions seem to suggest a continuation of the status quo. However, an emerging third perspective, a view mainly promoted by Prahalad (2002) sees EEs through the lens of inclusive partnerships where inclusive business is possible. Sustainable global enterprises concept represents a new form of private sector-based development paradigm that creates profitable businesses and employment. Sustainable global enterprises therefore not only promise to raise the quality of life for the world's poor, but also respects cultural diversity and conserves the ecological integrity of the planet for future generations (Hart, 2005).

The continuing desire to solve contemporary global challenges threatening public life has never been so urgent. Amongst others, these include efficiently delivering quality services, collaborating effectively with the private and non-profit sectors, championing widespread and equitable economic growth and opportunities, besides coping proactively with transnational threats among others (Brinkerhoff, & Brinkerhoff, 2015). Arguably, at the centre of the present global dilemma is neoliberalism, an economic governance model and a social philosophy that emerged in the 1970s, which defines human relationships in terms of competition, choice and individualism (Monbiot, 2016). Harvey (2007) sees neoliberalism as a political-economic theory proposing that human well-being is best advanced by liberating individual entrepreneurship and skills within an institutional framework characterized by strong private property rights, free markets and free trade. This dominant policy approach, also called the financial market theory of development suggests that providing access to capital through local financial markets potentially generates entrepreneurship motives and hence economic growth, while at the same time providing a mechanism for disciplining businesses (Davis, 2010). The theory echoed in the World Bank's World Development Report for the 2000s, suggests that creation of well-functioning financial markets open to foreign investors promises the surest and shortest route to rapid economic development for emerging economies. In this development model, financial development and economic growth have been perceived to be strongly correlated according to financial liberalisation theory championed by the International Monetary Fund (IMF) (McKinnon, 1989). Consequently, in the 90s financial liberalisation theory was applied in a number of developing and emerging countries. Supposedly, the establishment of robust financial institutions would benefit from foreign capital inflows and together with competition among local banks and financial institutions foster economic efficiency (Glen & Singh, 2005); however, these financial inflows arising from interest rate liberalisation caused massive financial and trade instability in these countries (Tajudeen, Olusola & Ademola, 2017). In this context, the role of the state was majorly limited to creation and preservation of an institutional framework appropriate for market operations. As already suggested neoliberalism sees citizens as consumers, exercising their democratic choices by buying and selling goods, a process that rewards merit and punishes inefficiency. Its central premise is that "the market" delivers benefits that are unachievable by any system of centrally planned economic activities (Gertz & Kharas, 2019). Whereas the market development paradigm promises wealth, prosperity and a better life for many, it delivers these unevenly leading to severe detrimental human and ecological well-being disasters. The coronavirus (COVID-19) pandemic has shown considerable governance failures not only at the national level but also at the global level. Wider shifts towards neoliberalism are evident; "governments" have largely been replaced by "governance". Consequently, public resources, authority and responsibility have been dispersed to different public and private actors, while central state managers have withdrawn to a mere "regulatory role" for steering these actors in largely favoured directions (Jones & Hameiri, 2021). Neoliberalism has depleted public services, converted education and healthcare into profit-driven businesses, amassed profits at the expense of the working class, and aggravated inequalities between people and countries.

A further scrutiny of neoliberalism suggests its roots were strengthened in the 1970's, a period that coincided with Margaret Thatcher and Ronald Reagan as heads of governments in the UK and US respectively. This period witnessed massive tax cuts for the rich, the crushing of trade unions, deregulation, privatisation, outsourcing and competition in the provision of public services. Through the International Monetary Fund (IMF), the World Bank, and the World Trade Organisation (WTO); neoliberal policies have been imposed on much of the developing world often without democratic consent within the context of structural adjustment policies (Monbiot, 2016). This notwithstanding, there is no denying of the many sophistications and complexities that the term capitalism and subsequently neoliberalism have evolved to the present day. Neoliberalism represents the incarnation of capitalism, its ability to adapt and reshape under new and different fronts have invariably been referred to as monetarism, post-Fordism, and globalisation (Watts & Hodgson, 2019). Neoliberalism represents the later phase in the capitalistic development paradigm reinforcing exploitation, greed, inequality, and capital accumulation practices championed by the economic elite (Harvey, 2007). Hall and Soskices (2001) as cited in Vervaart (2018) pioneering work "Varieties of Capitalism (VoC)" presents a new system of classifying economic systems that centrally situate firms or businesses as main actors in their analysis of varieties of capitalism. In their view, firms engage with different actors in multiple ways within the economic systems and depending on how these actors are coordinating with other agents within that system, firms' either succeed or fail. Economic systems tend to operate under distinct institutional and political-economical frameworks, which generate systematic differences in corporate strategies reminiscence of either Liberal Market Economies (LMEs) or Coordinated Market Economies (CMEs) models. Hall and Gingerich (2009), claim that such coordination tend to involve five different institutional factors featuring industrial relations; vocational training and education; corporate governance; inter-firm relations; and relations with employees. The CMEs also referred to as the stakeholder-oriented approach to capitalism, permits various players in and around the organization an opportunity to negotiate over allocation and distribution of resources. This mode of economic governance generally contrasts with the shareholder-oriented approach; the Anglo-Saxon model featuring Economics of Extraction or the Liberal Market Economy (LME) in which financial capital dominates all other types of capital (de Jong, 2021). In a nutshell, LMEs tend to share an emphasis on short-term orientation of company finances, deregulated labour markets, preference for general education, and strong inter-company competition. In the case of CMEs, readily available long-term industrial finances, co-operative industrial relations, high levels of vocational training, and cooperation in technology and standards setting across companies (Vervaart, 2018) characterize them. Soskice (1999), argues that each of these institutional domains tend to have a reinforcing dependence on each other for effective functioning.

Currently the dominant corporate governance model, the Anglo-Saxon based on short-term profit maximisation itself an offspring of the free market system governed by price mechanism still commands much recognition. This view is central for the Liberal Market Economies (LMEs), seen as economic governance systems combining private ownership of productive enterprises with competition between them in pursuit of short-term profits. This articulation picks out three characteristics generally accepted as defining features of contemporary market capitalist systems. These are private ownership, competition and the profit motive (Nwanji & Howell, 2007). Under this, predominantly shareholder finance model of corporate governance, the aim is to ensure that shareholders' stipulated objectives govern corporations and all their actions and agents. However, this dominant view has recently been under attack by factors

Integrated Reporting for Inclusive and Sustainable Global Capitalism

such as globalisation of capital markets, increase participation of institutional investors, greater share-holders' activism, wider stakeholders' expectations and the growing importance of corporate governance (Benson & Davidson, 2010). In the context of Shareholder Model, corporate governance is about two things – accountability and communication. Accountability is about how the company management are accountable to shareholders and other providers of finance. The second aspect, communication is how the company communicates elements of accountability to the wider constituencies such as shareholders; potential investors; employees; regulators; and other groups with a legitimate interest in its affairs (Pricewaterhousecoopers, 2003)

Arguably, companies and individuals have worked together in a bid to make the capitalist system more inclusive and therefore more sustainable. From its very inception, the concept of capitalism has undergone sea changes spanning labour, government, investor, managerial, and entrepreneurial capitalism each privileging the rights of one group over the others (Freeman, Martin & Parmar, 2007). However, visible in its absence is the concept of sustainability. Sustainability as a business concept comes in several formats, variously expressed as "stakeholder capitalism", "enlighten shareholder model" or just as the "triple bottom-line", is not new. This notion of stakeholder capitalism represents a shift in mind-set, where corporations focus on meeting the needs of all stakeholders: customers, employees, partners, the community, and society as a whole (Grove, Clouse & Xu, 2020). Corporate responsibility reminiscence of this movement regardless of the label has become the dominant philosophy underlying corporate social responsibility centred on creating "shared values", Rangan, Chase and Karim (2012). It represents a continuum from corporate conformance to corporate performance covering corporate financial reporting (CFR) and corporate governance (CG) responsibilities in addition to potential corporate social responsibility (CSR) reporting and stakeholder value creation (SVC) (Bhimani & Soonawalla, 2005). The goal is to mainstream metrics and tools for assessing core business activities and performance that capture inclusive economic approaches away from erstwhile paradigms centred on philanthropy and corporate social responsibility (CSR) per see. Arguably, according to the inclusive business model, itself an extension of stakeholder inclusivity model; the role of business is to create value for its shareholders but in ways that also create value for society, thereby manifesting a win-win proposition for all. Inclusive capitalism encompasses a wide and growing range of initiatives. For example, it is about creating new assets that create new jobs rather than merely transacting existing assets at continuously, spiralling prices from one market to another. Inclusive capitalism has emerged as a means for solving inherent market or policy failures precipitated by the highly financialised market structures, the darling of the World Bank (WB) and International Monetary Fund (IMF) (Davis, 2010). Whereas a number of approaches may be feasible for companies and institutions to execute this responsibility, the three crucial areas are (a) pursuing education for employment, (b) supporting the growth and development of small and medium-sized enterprises (SMEs), and (c) improvements in corporate management and governance for achieving long term sustainability (Henry Jackson Initiative, 2012). It is fundamental that for companies to play an active role in building a more inclusive and sustainable capitalism, they need an integrated, multi-stakeholder governance approach that focuses their operations and management on long-term value creation. Therefore, through the provision of relevant and integrated insights on all material aspects of values creation processes articulated under the integrated reporting framework (International Integrated Reporting Council [IIRC], (2016a); Chief Finance Officers (CFOs) and their teams stand a better chance in facilitating the shift of corporate mind-set from the current inherently short-term shareholder value capture models to a long-term stakeholder values creation and protection model.

179

Additionally, there are increasing evidence that the assets covered by contemporary financial reports continuously reflect a diminishing emphasis on certain components of shareholder value. For example, in 2015 research found that net assets of S&P 500 companies represented only 16% of their total market capitalisation, compared to 83% in 1975 (Demirel & Erol, 2016), pointing to the urgent need for the adoption of integrated reports. Besides, recent global economic crises have prompted regulatory bodies to question the relevance and reliability of the contemporary conceptual framework upon which contemporary financial reporting is based (Ivan, 2018). Integrated reporting (IR), which combines traditional financial reporting, sustainability reporting and corporate governance disclosures; potentially enhances the decision usefulness of modern corporate reporting. It has emerged as a key instrument for management control and stakeholder relations management in view of market increasing demands for non-financial reporting information after the financial crisis of 2008/2009 (Velte & Stawinoga, 2017; Gatti, Chiucchi & Montemari, 2018). Integrated reporting has come to represent a more holistic view of corporate activity through the combination of previously separate elements of corporate reporting such as the sustainability/CSR report and the annual report (Rowbottom & Locke, 2016). Arguably, the recurrent financial crises in the global economy have exposed corporations to be viewed more from the dominant narrow financial perspective. Recurrent financial crises have created the need for a more integrated and holistic approach to corporate reporting (Rowbottom & Locke, 2016). As a consequence, the International Integrated Reporting Council (IIRC) formed in 2010 has adopted a principle-based conceptual framework for integrated reporting (IR) (IIRC, 2013). The requirement for an integrated presentation of both financial and non-financial information (Oliver et al., 2016), provides a holistic approach to business transparency and accountability reporting framework. The International Integrated Reporting Council (IIRC) integrates reporting guidelines and standards developed by the Global Reporting Initiative (GRI), Accounting for Sustainability (A4S), the World Intellectual Capital Initiative (WICI), the Enhanced Business Reporting Consortium, the Carbon Disclosure Project, the International Corporate Governance Network, the Sustainability Reporting Standards Board and the Climate Disclosure Standards Board (Rowbottom & Locke, 2016). IR represents the contemporary frontier in corporate reporting and introduces an alternative perspective to the traditional economic notion of shareholder value maximization. IR therefore promotes an alternative framework for assessing corporate success based on an organization's ability to create sustainable value based on all potential sources of capital in-put (De Villiers et al., 2017).

The origins of IR is linked and represents the evolution of corporate governance practices that increasingly demands corporate leadership to focus more on the sustainability, strategic management, organisational performance and risk management amongst others (Samans & Nelson, 2020). This is a consequence of increased incidences of environmental disasters, financial crises and rising corporate scandals (Roxana-Ioana & Petru, 2017). In South Africa where the integrated report has roots, the King III Code of Corporate Governance Principles formally introduced the term 'integrated reporting' as a re-conception of the triple bottom-line reporting framework (Institute of Directors in Southern Africa [IDSA], 2012). In the light of 2007-08 global financial crisis that prompted greater emphasis for social and environmental value within the overall framework of economic and capital market decision-making, the idea of inclusive Capitalism has taken a centre stage. In other quarters, it is also referred to as stakeholder capitalism, which is an integration of shareholder primacy and corporate responsibility culminating in integrated governance with great promises for both shareholders and society at large (Samans & Nelson, 2020). Inclusive capitalism represents a viable opportunity for examining how capitalism can be made more inclusive through the recognition of various types of capitals and how they are controlled and

Integrated Reporting for Inclusive and Sustainable Global Capitalism

managed (de Jong, 2021). In this line of argument, the IIRC's six capitals represent not only an overall framework for understanding, measuring and articulating broader dimensions of human, economic and social progress within organizations but also an overall measurement framework of the well-being of nations (Bray & Prescott, 2020).

Arguably, the contemporary dominant corporate governance model supported by global institutions is increasingly associated with the need to maximise short-term shareholder returns and therefore the genesis of the widening gap between the rich and the poor globally. This model, reminiscence of traditional capitalism is encumbered with notions of competition, limited resources, and a winner-take-all mind-set as central to business and economic activity. Concomitantly, financial markets are increasingly becoming more complex, highly intermediated, and similarly short-termism in nature, with shares increasingly traded for short-term value accumulation rather than held for long-term investments in sound businesses that create inclusive value (McCann & Berry, 2017). In this context, the objectives of this chapter are first to descriptively analyse the influence of Integrated reporting as an instrument for imbedding corporate transparency, accountability, fairness, and responsibility, and hence inclusivity in corporate management for the common good in emerging economies. Secondly, the chapter proposes to identify a suitable framework for implanting inclusive capitalism and thereby contributing to the ongoing debate for an inclusive global financial architecture.

Going forward following the introduction and background, section two covers the study methodology, which includes the study design and sampling strategy as well as issues of validity and reliability. Similarly, section three delves into the pertinent literature on the issue providing the foundation of this study and covers inclusive capitalism, corporate governance models and mechanisms, integrated corporate reporting and its theoretical foundations, and finally a conceptual framework for understanding integrated reporting, inclusive capitalism and sustainable value creation. Section four covers the study findings and discussions, being the product of secondary desk-top research and assessments of inclusive capitalism and resilient emerging economies. Subsequently the remaining sections provide conclusions, recommendations and directions for future studies on stakeholder inclusivity in emerging economies.

METHODOLOGY

This chapter is based on constructive conceptual analysis strategy, aimed at achieving analytical generalizability by reflecting on linkages between integrated reporting and inclusive capitalism in emerging economies. This approach supports the twin objectives of this chapter as earlier articulated, which includes firstly a descriptive analysis of the influence of Integrated reporting as an instrument for imbedding corporate transparency, accountability, fairness, and responsibility, and hence inclusivity in corporate management. Secondly, the chapter proposes to identify a suitable framework for promoting inclusive capitalism in the emerging economies with particular reference to sub-Sahara Africa. Since the purpose is to explore and capture a deeper understanding and clarity of required public policy proposals for corporations in emerging economies for stimulating widespread and equitable economic growth and opportunity, the constructive conceptual analysis, aligned to qualitative research is considered appropriate (Baldwin & Rose, 2009). Similarly, because the study aims to identify a suitable framework for embedding sustainable and inclusive capitalism as the new foundation for the global financial system architecture; a theoretical sampling strategy is deemed appropriate. Theoretical sampling supports building interpretative theories from emerging information on prior sources and selection of new documentary materials for further examination and elaboration based on emerging ideas and information as the study progresses (Marshall, 1996).

Sustainable and inclusive capitalism practices presume the existence of exclusionary institutional approaches and practices by the financial system's governance framework as well as regulatory gaps that prevent inclusive participation, sharing and building of wealth. Conceptually, therefore from integrated governance perspective, the stakeholder approaches embedded within the integrated reporting literature promises overarching solutions. The implied constructive analysis purports to expand the conceptual theory of inclusive capitalism, either by postulating new relationships or suggesting that some relationships already known seem to hold among previously perceived disparate parts of the discourse (Kosterec, 2016).

The study therefore adopts an interpretivist research perspective employing mainly analytical research strategy using secondary documentary data to explore the role of integrated reporting on sustainable and inclusive capitalism in emerging economies aimed at determining fruitful and possible interventions for implementation. Therefore using scholarly databases including ABI Inform Complete (ProQuest), Business Source Complete (EBSCO), Scopus and other related sources; resources on inclusive and sustainable capitalism were downloaded and the three terminologies integrated reporting, integrated governance and inclusive capitalism were comprehensively analysed, compared and interpreted.

LITERATURE REVIEW

Kahn (1995) argues that sustainable development paradigm described in Agenda 21 of the United Nations, rests on three conceptual pillars of economic, social and environmental sustainability. Economically, sustainability is conceptualised in terms of growth, development, and productivity; socially it is equity, empowerment, accessibility, participation, sharing, cultural identity, and institutional stability. While environmentally, it is about maintaining an ecosystem's integrity, carrying capacity and biodiversity (Dhahri, & Omri, 2018). Integrated reporting borrows sustainable development concept of capital and expands development's emphasis beyond monetary capital to consider natural, social and human capitals (Basiago, 1998). This articulation agrees with Freeman (2004) concept of firm performance as a reflection of the totality of value created by firms through their activities, which is the entire utility created for each of a firm's legitimate stakeholders. Sustainability has become a crucial perspective in the management of firms via a holistic approach embedding simultaneously economic, environmental and social dimensions of firms. With the rising significance of sustainable development discourse, theories linking sustainability to firms' operations have evolved from Corporate Social Responsibility, Stakeholder Theory, Corporate Sustainability, and lately Green Economics (Chang, et al., 2017). In accounting literature, the phrase environmental and social accounting research have slowly become known as sustainability reporting signifying the integrated nature of such reports.

Further according to de Villiers et al. (2014), accounting, accountability systems and reporting on corporations' financial and non-financial performances have occasioned the development of four reporting frameworks; the Balanced Scorecard, Triple Bottom Line, Sustainability Reporting, and Integrated Reporting. Integrated reporting as a mechanism for managing, measuring and reporting the three elements of an organisation's social, environmental and economic impacts is traceable to the work of Elkington's (1997). Its first adoption as tool for reporting on corporate sustainability links to the first King Report on Corporate Governance, which represents a milestone in the evolution of corporate reporting (Dumay, Bernardi, Guthrie & Demartini, 2016). Integrated Reporting strategy relates an organization's strategy, governance, performance and forecasts in the context of its external environment resulting in the creation of overall organisational values (Thomson, 2015). As an overarching concept in corporate reporting, integrated reporting helps businesses in taking more sustainable decisions and enables investors and other stakeholders in comprehending how an organization is really performing. Integrated reporting is about building and maintaining trust with investors, which to date remains the cardinal goal of corporate reporting. Whereas disclosing financial performance has served for long as a conduit for corporate reporting, its continued relevance in today's world has become not only questionable, but also suspect. Investors progressively have come to appreciate the connection between company performance on a range of environmental, social and governance factors and their ability to deliver profits over the long-term (IIRC & Kirchhoff, 2020). Integrated reporting concepts and principles are therefore critical in bridging current corporate reporting gaps and building linkages between financial reporting and additional information considered relevant to the broader enterprise value creation process (Veltri & Silvestri, 2020). Integrated reporting is therefore not only a reporting framework but also an effective corporate management system (Setia et al., 2015) that communicates benefits to the organization and its stakeholders; it integrates different streams of information spanning corporate governance, accounting, and sustainability. Consequently, integrated reporting represents a comprehensive framework that companies can use to provide not only investors, but also all stakeholders with information they need to make better investment and engagement decisions.

Whereas in managing modern organisations several philosophical orientations or perspectives can be available, two of these are dominant: the shareholder and the stakeholder capitalism perspectives. For instance if a manager chooses shareholder capitalism perspective, then it is that manager's duty to maximize the amount of money that goes back to the initial financial capital investment contribution. Alternatively, if stakeholder capitalism is the preferred choice, then it is that manager's duty to bring together all the resources necessary to create and redistribute greater value from those same resources (Ingerson et al., 2015). According to Ahmad and Omar (2016), models of corporate governance span the Anglo-Saxon, Continental European, Value-based, Islamic model and Family Business Organizations (FBOs). Integrated reporting framework is more attuned to the values-based model of corporate governance. This is reminiscence of the four schools of thought in CSR reflecting moral obligation, sustainability, corporate reputation, and license to operate (Boesso, Kumar & Michelon, 2013). The CSR as a corporate reporting framework for sustainability is supported by a number of organisational theories, which also appear relevant in understanding the advent of Integrated Reporting. For example, Berndt, Bilolo, and Müller (2014) and da Costa Tavares and Dias (2018) have presented a comprehensive overview of the theoretical framework of corporate reporting. In their case, three principal research domains are relevant for understanding integrated corporate reporting and sustainability. These include the role of disclosures in capital markets with emphasis on information asymmetry and the agency problem; the stakeholder theory; the legitimacy and the political cost theories as theoretical lenses for understanding sustainability and CSR reporting.

Financial Disclosure Theory

Underlying the financial disclosure theory also called the shareholder theory is the concept of information asymmetry arising mainly due to organisational agency problems. Since shareholders are not directly involved in the daily operations of a company, periodically relevant information is required as a mechanism for monitoring and evaluating the performance of the manager agent (Adhariani & Sciulli, 2020). In this context, corporate reporting plays an important role in reducing information asymmetry. Agency theory has therefore emerged as a tool for solving the problem of information asymmetry; a situation where one party has more or better information than the others in a transaction leading to problems such as adverse selection and moral hazards. It is for these reasons that corporate disclosures is instrumental in reducing information asymmetry and therefore agency costs, while reconciling the interests of shareholders and managers (Farvaque et al., 2011). Whereas shareholder value creation orientation still remains significant in corporate management; it needs to be balanced with other stakeholders' interests, a position referred to as an enlightened approach to shareholder value maximization (O'Connell & Ward, 2020). Enlightened approach to shareholder value maintains that effective corporate social responsibility management is not incompatible with shareholder value (Andreadakis, 2012); instead having wider interests can in fact be instrumental to sustainable long-term financial performance.

Stakeholder Theory

Central to stakeholder theory, is the conviction that corporations should not be managed to maximize shareholder wealth, instead they should optimize wealth and value creation for all stakeholders (Venkataraman, 2019). The concept of integrated thinking embedded within Integrated Reporting (IR) combines traditional financial reporting concept with sustainability and corporate governance related measures, which consequently enhance the decision usefulness of modern business reporting (Velte & Stawinoga, 2017). Voluntary disclosure practices by corporations for sustaining a positive relationship with the stakeholders and gaining their support for its strategy demonstrates stakeholder theory (Magnagh & Aprile, 2014). Stakeholder theory provides for social and environmental reporting by companies as a reflection of their accountability and responsibility to all the stakeholders including employees, suppliers, regulators, governments, customers and society at large (Nakib & Dey, 2018). It provides a new narrative for understanding and remedying three interconnected modern business problems involving: understanding how value is created and traded, connecting ethics and capitalism, and helping managers think about management in a way that addresses the first two problems (Parmar, et.al, 2010).

Stakeholder theory has been variously advanced and debated in literature, for example Donaldson and Preston's (1995) three-way classification: instrumental, descriptive and normative articulation continues to serve as a useful framework for comprehending the multiple approaches for considering stakeholder theory (Venkataraman, 2019). The instrumental approach maintains that adopting a stakeholder approach to managing a business is self-fulfilling because firms adopting such an approach tend to facilitate their own competitive advantage and long-term successes, leading to improved corporate performance (Donaldson & Preston, 1995). Similarly, descriptive approaches tend to focus on outlining and ordering who qualify as stakeholders, under the presumption that a firm may not have necessary resources to satisfy all actors who could potentially stake claim under the stakeholder label. Lastly, normative approaches support businesses in engaging and managing stakeholders for ethical or moral reasons; in a manner, which largely aligns with sustainability principles. Normative approaches are generally seen as the ultimate justification for the existence of business (Collins et al., 2005). Stakeholder theory therefore views all users of corporate reports as consumers of corporate reporting. Hence, their need for information should be reflected in the company's reports, i.e., by providing both shareholders and other stakeholders with relevant and timely information (Adhariani & Sciulli, 2020).

Integrated Reporting for Inclusive and Sustainable Global Capitalism

Legitimacy and Political Cost Theory

Legitimacy theory provides another explanatory channel through which corporations are compelled to disclose their financial and non-financial information by arguing that in order to be legitimate in their operating environment; a company must develop alignment between its social impacts with the norms of acceptable behaviour within the larger social system (Cho & Patten, 2007). Implicitly an organization has a social contract with the society in which it operates motivating its compliance with a society's specific values, norms and boundaries. Thus, an organisation's requirement for going concern and long-term survival is a subject of its ability to meet the society's expectations through suitable systematic adjustments and alignments (Velte & Stawinoga, 2017). In instances where legitimacy gaps arise or are perceived; organizations are motivated to adopt legitimating strategies for compliance (Fernando & Lawrence 2014). Therefore, through legitimization strategies, organizations improve their access to resources, image and customer, employee and investor relationships, which subsequently enhance their competitive positions (Velte & Stawinoga, 2017). Similarly, the social responsibility activities of a corporation is another channel providing an avenue for effectively reducing its political attention (Van Staden & Cahan, 2011). Political attention, which relates to political cost theory, suggests that organisations voluntarily disclose information to reduce political costs (e.g. taxes, fees) and to obtain certain benefits, such as subsidies or continue attracting government actions in their favour (Idowu & Baldo, 2019). Arguably, this means companies in countries with higher levels of regulations; nationalisation and confiscation tendencies tend to disclose more information to reduce political costs.

Institutional Theory

Institutional theory, compliments both stakeholder and legitimacy theories and clarifies how firms respond to events in their institutional and operating environments. Arguably, stakeholders such as governments, regulatory authorities, non-governmental organisations (NGOs), and organisations within the supply chain can exert their influence on any business (Camilleri, 2019). According to DiMaggio and Powell (1983), as cited in Speziale, (2019), political, financial, educational, cultural, and economic institutional systems can exert pressure on companies (i.e., economic units) through three types of institutionalisation mechanisms: coercive isomorphisms, normative pressures, and mimetic processes (Randa, 2021). Coercive isomorphisms generally based on regulatory mechanisms are concerned with setting rules, norms or laws, monitoring their application, and finally giving rewards and punishment. Similarly, normative institutional pressures relate to non-imposed values and norms and to the impact that educational or professional authorities have on companies by setting operating standards. Lastly, mimetic processes involve imitating successful organisations or competitors' strategies regarded as best practice in the industry.

CONCEPTUAL FRAMEWORK

Researchers tend to use the terms theoretical and conceptual frameworks interchangeably (Savin-Baden, Cousin, & Major, 2010; Imenda, 2014), however, there is a growing realisation that *conceptual* frameworks reflect the need to use multiple theoretical frameworks as a basis for creating new knowledge. Similarly, Parahoo (2006) suggests that theoretical framework should be used when research is underpinned by a single theory; whereas conceptual frameworks tend to draw on concepts from various theories and research findings to guide a study. It is an overarching statement of theoretical principles and concepts forming a frame of reference for a particular field of study (Davies, Paterson, & Wilson, 1997). This study is underpinned by agency, stakeholder, legitimacy and institutional theories; therefore it is relevant to talk of its conceptual framework rather than theoretical framework.

This chapter argues that sustainability corporate reporting is influenced by institutional factors together with stakeholders' pressures. Therefore, it is underpinned by institutional theory, stakeholder, legitimacy and agency theories operating at different levels, all providing different perspectives for examining sustainable reporting (Herold, 2018). Arguing from agency perspective, full disclosure helps firms to reduce information asymmetry, which in turn increases awareness about a firm's existence and its investor base (Bellalah & Bouy, 2005). Hence, quality disclosures enhance operating cash flows and reduce the cost of financing together leading to increased shareholder value. Further, stakeholder theory maintains that a firm should take care of its owners as well as the society, economy, and the environment in which the firm operates (Hussain, Rigoni & Orij, 2018). Similarly, from legitimacy perspective, corporations engage in activities that project them as responsible citizens. legitimacy is seen as a tool for obtaining approval to operate in the society thereby avoiding negative campaigns from pressure groups (Cavezzali, Hussain & Rigoni, 2016). In terms of institutional theory, organizations are intertwined with the broader political, economic, financial, educational, and cultural systems that wield institutional pressures on them. Institutional theory therefore provides complementary perspectives on legitimacy theory and stakeholder theory (Speziale, 2019). In accordance with neo-institutional theory, three types of isomorphisms exist: coercive, normative, and mimetic. They occur due to both formal and informal pressures created by other organizations that rely on them, besides cultural expectations of the society also influence organizations behaviour. Therefore, one can conclude that while integrated reporting increases accountability through the provision of concise and complete disclosure of a company's social, environmental, and financial performance (Steyn, 2014); it potentially achieves sustainability by balancing the cooperative and competitive interests of stakeholders.

Figure 1. Conceptual framework

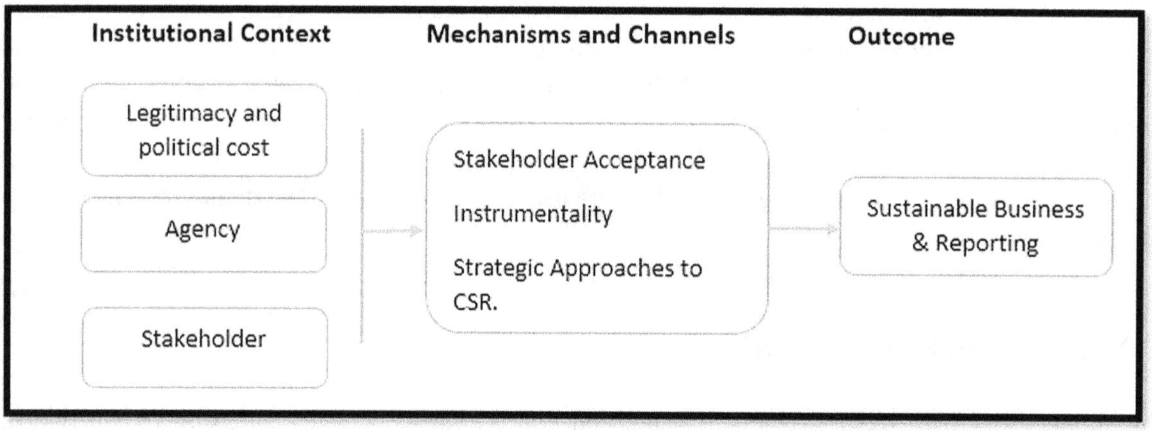

Integrated Reporting for Inclusive and Sustainable Global Capitalism

FINDINGS AND DISCUSSION

This chapter was driven by two objectives, firstly to provide a descriptive analysis on how integrated reporting can be instrumental for imbedding corporate transparency, accountability, fairness, and responsibility, and hence inclusivity in corporate management. Secondly, it proposed to identify a suitable governance framework for implanting inclusive capitalism in the global financial system.

In line with Henry Jackson Initiative (2012), achieving an inclusive capitalistic system requires companies and institutions to adopt approaches and interventions in three critical areas spanning the pursuit of education for employment, sustaining the growth and development of small and medium-sized enterprises (SMEs), and progressively adopting corporate management and governance systems for long-term sustainability. Findings in this chapter expand on the last strategy, which is about advancements in corporate management and governance for long-term sustainability. Any solution aimed at improving corporate management and governance centres on the company's operating business model. Arguably, the business model controls and directs every aspect of what a company does, it therefore needs to be embedded in high standards of corporate governance. Furthermore, it needs to be underpinned by unquestionable ethical values that drive the right organisational culture and behaviours. Based on this premise, the success of a company overtime is seem in terms of a company's successful adoption of a values based business model that draws effectively on the financial, human and other sources of capital. This understanding and articulation seem to support the increasing adoption of integrated reporting and its multi-capitals' framework. The integrated reporting model gives the same weight to human, natural, intellectual and social information, which traditionally had mainly been given to financial information. Hence, findings are presented in line with key conceptual mechanisms and channels in figure 1; which include stakeholder acceptance operating through legitimacy, instrumentality through enlighten shareholder theory and strategic approaches to CSR embedded in ethical leadership and organisational culture.

In the context of legitimacy, businesses will need to demonstrate that their operations are useful to the target community and operating environment. This is aimed at building socially responsible image through continuous improvement in transparency and credibility not only amongst public authorities, but also in non-government organisations (NGOs). These initiatives are perceived as crucial elements of business success. Implicitly organizations have social contracts with the society in which they operate. This motivates their continued relevance and compliance with the society's specific values, norms and boundaries' requirements (Velte & Stawinoga, 2017). Therefore, through the adoption of a system for integrated communication to a broad group of constituencies, businesses will proactively address concerns about their production processes and product safety as well as emphasise self-regulation on environmental principles.

Similarly, from the context of shareholder agency perspective, value creation is increasingly conceptualised more broadly than the accretion of financial capital regardless whether a corporation openly says its reports are in line with the Integrated Reporting Framework. There is evidence that in the development and adoption of the Integrated Reporting Framework; companies tend to align their social investment activities with their business strategy and long-term notions of value creation (Adams et al, 2016). Instrumental CSR under the agency theory views social and environmental spending as necessary costs that increase shareholder value and therefore remains a means for increasing business accountability as these types of investments drive long-term value creation. The Enlighted shareholder value sees CSR as a shareholder value driver and a rallying point for a win-win situation for all stakeholders through establishment of intangibles, risk management strategies, shareholder value priority, and strategic investments.

Under the instrumental strategy, businesses present their social responsibility efforts as supporting their core strategy, with the underlying assumption of building stronger stakeholder–shareholder relations.

Turning to Stakeholder theory, CSR represents a planning guideline. In this context, integrated reporting involves communicating business activities aimed at minimising social and environmental impacts. These are seen as integral business development plans that benefit not only the company but also all its key stakeholders. Central to stakeholder theory, is the conviction that corporations should not be managed to maximize shareholders wealth, instead they should strive to optimize wealth and value creation for all stakeholders (Venkataraman, 2019). This position agrees with the central theme of stakeholders' approach which is the achievement of maximum cooperation and hence inclusivity among the stakeholder groups and the corporation into decision-making processes. Strategic CSR is an attempt to send signals to socially responsible investors regarding CSR practices aimed at reducing information asymmetries, thereby distinguishing a particular business from its competitors. Strategic CSR includes two approaches: firstly, it stresses a strategic approach to CSR and second it emphasises leadership in optimising financing costs and through that increase in business value. Besides, integrated reporting can also be instrumental for governments in identifying and measuring their national wealth comprising natural capital, human capital, produced capital, social and institutional capital, intellectual property and net foreign assets (Bray & Prescott, 2020).

Arguably, the current global financial architecture comprises three interlocking components working in concert: an economic model, which directs international financial relations and flows; an institutional arrangement of networks for managing these relations; and a system for distributing decision-making powers among individual member countries (Crockett, 2009; Schinasi &Truman, 2010). Overtime, this arrangement has failed to deliver. Previous global financial crisis have demonstrated the downside of the system as currently constituted revealing a range of systemic vulnerabilities such as problems of adverse selection, moral hazard, monitoring failure, herding effects, contagions etc. (Akyüz, 2002). Major joint and collaborative efforts are urgently required to address the ensuing systematic loss of public trust and confidence in the ability of the financial system to deliver value to the real economy. Collaborative efforts for rapid and unparalleled transformation in financial services together with removal of significant barriers to access affordable financial products for the under-served populations globally are required. According to Maimbo and Zadek (2017), a sustainable global financial system is inclusive, stable and creates, values, and transacts financial assets in ways that influence and shape real wealth to serve the long-term needs of a sustainable and inclusive global economy. This position conjures with Prahalad (2002) who looks at sustainable global enterprises as drivers of a new form of private sector-based development paradigm. Through their ability to create profitable businesses, sustainable global enterprises not only raise the quality of life for the world's poor, but also respect cultural diversity and therefore conserve the ecological integrity of the planet for future generations (2005).

RECOMMENDATIONS

This chapter therefore recommends business adoption of integrated reporting. It argues that the success of a company overtime is seem in terms of a company's successful adoption of a values based business model that draws effectively on the financial, human and other sources of capital. The integrated reporting model underpinned by integrated governance gives the same weight to human, natural, intellectual and social information, which traditionally had been ignored in the traditional financial reporting model.

Integrated Reporting for Inclusive and Sustainable Global Capitalism

The adoption of integrated reporting hopefully will encourage businesses to report holistically their value creating activities.

Arguably, the business model embedded within high standards of corporate governance, underpinned by unquestionable ethical values controls and directs every aspect of what a company needs to be and drives the right organisational culture and behaviours. Inclusive business models are therefore central in the integrated reporting narrative.

In the context of legitimacy, businesses need to demonstrate that their operations are useful to the target community and operating environment. As such, adoption of an integrated communication mechanism focusing on a broad group of constituencies, will proactively enable businesses to address concerns about their production processes and product safety in addition to emphasising self-regulation on environmental matters.

Similarly, in the context of shareholder agency perspective, value creation is increasingly conceptualised more broadly than the short-termism accretion of financial capital. Therefore, by integrating financial and non-financial information, integrated reporting is a means of combating the short-termism behaviour in contemporary financial and capital markets, the source of many evils.

Turning to Stakeholder theory, CSR represents a set of planning guidelines for inclusive engagement among various stakeholders. This position agrees with the central tenets of stakeholders' approach, which is the achievement of maximum cooperation and hence inclusivity among the stakeholder groups and corporations in decision-making processes.

And lastly, the emergence of systematic loss of public trust and confidence in the ability of the financial system to deliver value to the real economy; coupled with rapid and unparalleled transformation in financial services; and removal of significant barriers to access affordable financial products for the under-served populations globally; requires a paradigm shift in the system. A sustainable global financial system is inclusive, stable and creates, values, and transacts financial assets in ways that influence and shape real wealth in serving the long-term needs of a sustainable and inclusive economy.

FUTURE RESEARCH DIRECTIONS

Based on archival research strategy using documentary and secondary data, this chapter aimed at achieving analytical generalizability reflecting on existing connections between integrated reporting, integrated governance and inclusive capitalism. Through this strategy, the investigation identified three channels through which integrated reporting connects with sustainable and inclusive capitalism. However, further exploration is required to determine which of these three mechanisms offers a better policy intervention and therefore leads to conservation of resources. Similarly, this research grappled with the issue of sustainable and inclusive capitalism from the integrated reporting perspective, which puts emphasis on integrated corporate management and governance interventions. Arguably there are other perspectives for example pursuit of education for employment, supporting the growth and development of small and medium-sized enterprises (SMEs) that could be studied together to offer better insights on sustainable and inclusive capitalism.

CONCLUSION

Inclusive capitalism maintains that encouraging private enterprise through suitable policy interventions creates more jobs for low-income people; provides access to business finance for the underprivileged and in so doing enables poor people the opportunity to purchase a variety of goods and services. This chapter argues that integrated reporting addresses the limitations of traditional corporate reporting practices that are backward looking, fragmented and therefore fails to communicate sources of future business sustainable performance and ensuing risks. Integrated reporting provides the much needed glue and required cultural shift in corporate management by emphasising long-term value creation, which ultimately promotes long-term behaviour in capital markets. In recent years, various institutions including corporations have experienced severe decline in trust caused primarily by their behaviour and decisions often perceived to compromise society and the environment for the short-term benefit. Integrated reporting frames holistic value creation in organisations through its multi-capitals reporting framework. Therefore, integrated reporting framework is more attuned to the values-based model of corporate governance. Value based corporate governance as a tool for crafting a firm's vision, building leadership and resilient organisation culture has never been so important; by building these bridges, it connects various stakeholders and creates a structure for inclusive decision-making.

For organisations that pursue shareholder's value, managers increase transparency and disclosure by expanding the information content and quality contained in their reports to prevent conflicts with stakeholders. Through the provision of a holistic picture of an organisational capacity to create value from multiple capitals over time; integrated reports are capable of alleviating information asymmetry problems and thereby reduce agency costs. Further in order to close the legitimacy gap; businesses strive to increase and maintain consensus among stakeholders. Arguably, obtaining consensus among stakeholders is a prerequisite for operational effectiveness and therefore a means for obtaining social legitimization and stakeholder approval.

The concept of inclusive capitalism gained traction in response to 2007-08 global financial crisis; since then the idea has evolved, giving greater weight to the inclusion of social and environmental value within the overall framework of economic and capital market decision-making models. Integrated reporting broadly offers a picture for enhancing our understanding of both societal and human progress through the measurement and reporting of various capitals. Integrated reporting supports major global trends covering ideas such as global interconnectedness, inclusive capitalism, governance and stewardship, sustainable development, technological change, long-termism etc.

In a nutshell, by linking strategy, governance, performance and organisational prospects through a multi-capital lens, integrated reporting underscores the importance of a holistic approach to measuring, managing and expressing business value creation. Further, through its emphasis on business strategy, resource allocation and value creation, integrated reporting promotes long-term thinking and sustainable business models. In addition, by its stronger focus on long-term investments and a more holistic view of value creation, integrated reporting provides platforms for understanding business strategy, performance, and prospects through the multi-capital lens.

REFERENCES

Adams, C. A., Potter, B., Singh, P. J., & York, J. (2016). Exploring the implications of integrated reporting for social investment (disclosures). *The British Accounting Review*, *48*(3), 283–296. doi:10.1016/j.bar.2016.05.002

Adhariani, D., & Sciulli, N. (2020). The future of integrated reporting in an emerging market: An analysis of the disclosure conformity level. *Asian Review of Accounting*, *28*(4), 619–634. doi:10.1108/ARA-02-2019-0045

Ahmad, S., & Omar, R. (2016). Basic corporate governance models: A systematic review. *International Journal of Law and Management*, *58*(1), 73–107. doi:10.1108/IJLMA-10-2014-0057

Akyüz, Y. (2002). *Towards Reform of the International Financial Architecture: Which Way Forward?* Reforming the Global Financial Architecture, Issues and Proposals.

Andreadakis, S. (2012). Enlightened Shareholder Value: Is It the New Modus Operandi for Modern Companies? In *Corporate governance* (pp. 415–432). Springer. doi:10.1007/978-3-642-31579-4_18

Basiago, A. D. (1998). Economic, social, and environmental sustainability in development theory and urban planning practice. *The Environmentalist*, *19*(2), 145–161. doi:10.1023/A:1006697118620

Bellalah, M., & Bouy, C. (2005). On Portfolio Analysis, Market Equilibrium and Corporation Finance with Incomplete Information. *International Journal of Business*, *10*(2), 133.

Benson, B. W., & Davidson, W. N. (2010). The relation between stakeholder management, firm value, and CEO compensation: A test of enlightened value maximization. *Financial Management*, *39*(3), 929–964. doi:10.1111/j.1755-053X.2010.01100.x

Bhimani, A., & Soonawalla, K. (2005). From conformance to performance: The corporate responsibilities continuum. *Journal of Accounting and Public Policy*, *24*(3), 165–174. doi:10.1016/j.jaccpubpol.2005.03.001

Boesso, G., Kumar, K., & Michelon, G. (2013). Descriptive, instrumental and strategic approaches to corporate social responsibility: Do they drive the financial performance of companies differently? *Accounting, Auditing & Accountability Journal*, *26*(3), 399–422. doi:10.1108/09513571311311874

Bray, M., & Prescott, L. (2020). The International Integrated Reporting Council's agenda of moving integrated reporting towards global adoption by 2025. In *The Routledge Handbook of Integrated Reporting* (pp. 17–36). Routledge. doi:10.4324/9780429279621-2

Brinkerhoff, D. W., & Brinkerhoff, J. M. (2015). Public sector management reform in developing countries: Perspectives beyond NPM orthodoxy. *Public Administration and Development*, *35*(4), 222–237. doi:10.1002/pad.1739

Brunelli, S., & Di Carlo, E. (2020). Accountability, ethics and sustainability of organizations. *Accounting, Finance, Sustainability, Governance and Fraud, Theory and Application*, *4*, 82–123.

Camilleri, M. A. (2019). Theoretical insights on integrated reporting: Valuing the financial, social and sustainability disclosures. Integrated Reporting, 61-76.

Capitalism, I. (n.d.). *Oxymoron Or The Perfect Balance*. Retrieved from https://www.forbes.com/sites/nigelwilson/2018/07/29

Cavezzali, E., Hussain, N., & Rigoni, U. (2016). The integrated reporting and the conference calls content. In *Integrated Reporting* (pp. 231–252). Palgrave Macmillan. doi:10.1057/978-1-137-55149-8_12

Chang, R. D., Zuo, J., Zhao, Z. Y., Zillante, G., Gan, X. L., & Soebarto, V. (2017). Evolving theories of sustainability and firms: History, future directions and implications for renewable energy research. *Renewable & Sustainable Energy Reviews*, *72*, 48–56. doi:10.1016/j.rser.2017.01.029

Cho, C. H., & Patten, D. M. (2007). The role of environmental disclosures as tools of legitimacy: A research note. *Accounting, Organizations and Society*, *32*(7), 639–647. doi:10.1016/j.aos.2006.09.009

Collins, E., Kearins, K., & Roper, J. (2005). The risks in relying on stakeholder engagement for the achievement of sustainability. *Electronic Journal of Radical Organisation Theory*, *9*(1), 81.

Crockett, A. (2009). Reforming the global financial architecture. In *Asia Economic Policy Conference; Asia and the Global Financial Crisis, Santa Barbara, California* (pp. 191-201). Academic Press.

da Costa Tavares, M. D. C., & Dias, A. P. (2018). Theoretical Perspectives on Sustainability Reporting: A Literature Review. *Accounting from a Cross-Cultural Perspective*. https://scholar.google.com

Davies, M., Paterson, R., & Wilson, A. (1997). The quest for a conceptual framework for financial reporting. In *UK GAAP* (pp. 39–128). Palgrave Macmillan. doi:10.1007/978-1-349-13819-7_2

Davis, G. F. (2010). Is shareholder capitalism a defunct model for financing development? *Review of Market Integration*, *2*(2-3), 317–331. doi:10.1177/097492921000200306

de Jong, M. (2021). Inclusive capitalism: The emergence of a new purpose paradigm in economics and business administration and its implications for public policy. *Global Public Policy and Governance*, 1-16.

De Villiers, C., Venter, E. R., & Hsiao, P. C. K. (2017). Integrated reporting: Background, measurement issues, approaches and an agenda for future research. *Accounting and Finance*, *57*(4), 937–959. Advance online publication. doi:10.1111/acfi.12246

Demirel, B., & Erol, I. (2016). Investigation of integrated reporting as a new approach of corporate reporting. *International Journal of Business and Social Research*, *6*(10), 32–46. doi:10.18533/ijbsr.v6i10.1002

Dhahri, S., & Omri, A. (2018). Entrepreneurship contribution to the three pillars of sustainable development: What does the evidence really say? *World Development*, *106*, 64–77. doi:10.1016/j.worlddev.2018.01.008

Donaldson, T., & Preston, L. E. (1995). The stakeholder theory of the corporation: Concepts, evidence, and implications. *Academy of Management Review*, *20*(1), 65–91. doi:10.2307/258887

Dumay, J., Bernardi, C., Guthrie, J., & Demartini, P. (2016, September). Integrated reporting: A structured literature review. *Accounting Forum*, *40*(3), 166–185. doi:10.1016/j.accfor.2016.06.001

Elkington, J. (1997). *Cannibals with forks: The triple bottom line of 21st century business*. Capstone Publishers.

Farvaque, E., Refait-Alexandre, C., & Saïdane, D. (2011). Corporate disclosure: A review of its (direct and indirect) benefits and costs. *International Economics, 128*, 5–31. doi: (13)60001-3 doi:10.1016/S2110-7017

Freeman, R. E. (2004). The stakeholder approach revisited. *Zeitschrift für wirtschafts-und unternehmensethik, 5*(3), 228-254.

Freeman, R. E., Martin, K., & Parmar, B. (2007). Stakeholder capitalism. *Journal of Business Ethics, 74*(4), 303–314. doi:10.100710551-007-9517-y

Gatti, M., Chiucchi, M. S., & Montemari, M. (2018). Management control systems and integrated reporting: Which relationships? The case of the Azienda Ospedaliero Universitaria Ospedali Riuniti Ancona. *International Journal of Business and Management, 13*(9), 169–181. doi:10.5539/ijbm.v13n9p169

Gertz, G., & Kharas, H. (2019). *Beyond Neoliberalism: Insights from Emerging Markets*. The Brookings Institution.

Glen, J., & Singh, A. (2005). Corporate governance, competition and finance: Rethinking lessons from the Asian crisis. *Eastern Economic Journal, 31*(2), 219–243.

Grove, H., Clouse, M., & Xu, T. (2020). Stakeholder capitalism strategies and opportunities for corporate governance. *Journal of Governance & Regulation, 9*(4), 59–68. doi:10.22495/jgrv9i4art5

Hall, P., & Gingerich, D. (2009). Varieties of capitalism and institutional complementarities in the political economy: An empirical analysis. *British Journal of Political Science, 39*(3), 449–482. doi:10.1017/S0007123409000672

Hall, P., & Soskice, D. (2001). *Varieties of capitalism: The institutional foundations of comparative advantage*. Oxford University Press. doi:10.1093/0199247757.001.0001

Hart, S. L. (2005). *Capitalism at the crossroads: The unlimited business opportunities in solving the world's most difficult problems*. Wharton School.

Harvey, D. (2007). *A brief history of neoliberalism*. Oxford University Press.

Held, D., & Young, K. (2009). The world crisis: global financial governance: principles of reform (No. 43602). London School of Economics and Political Science, LSE Library.

Henry Jackson Initiative. (2012). *Towards a more inclusive capitalism*. The Henry Jackson Foundation Initiative.

Herold, M. H. (2018). Demystifying the link between institutional theory and stakeholder theory in sustainability reporting. *Economics. Management and Sustainability, 3*(2), 6–19. doi:10.14254/jems.2018.3-2.1

Hussain, N., Rigoni, U., & Orij, R. P. (2018). Corporate governance and sustainability performance: Analysis of triple bottom line performance. *Journal of Business Ethics, 149*(2), 411–432. doi:10.100710551-016-3099-5

Idowu, S. O., & Baldo, M. D. (2019). *Integrated Reporting*. Springer. doi:10.1007/978-3-030-01719-4

IIRC. (2013). *The International IR Framework*. International Integrated Reporting Council. http:// www. theiirc.org/wp-content/uploads/2013/12/13-12-08-THE-INTERNATIONAL-IR-FRAMEWORK-2-1.pdf

IIRC & Kirchhoff. (2020). Closing the gap: the role of integrated reporting in communicating a company's value creation to investors. Investor Research Report.

Imenda, S. (2014). Is there a conceptual difference between theoretical and conceptual frameworks? *Journal of social sciences, 38*(2), 185–195. doi:10.1080/09718923.2014.11893249

Ingerson, M. C., Donaldson, T., Harris, J. D., Keevil, A., Phillips, R. A., Agle, B. R., ... Mitchell, R. K. (2015). Normative Stakeholder Capitalism: Getting from Here to There. *Business & Professional Ethics Journal, 34*(3), 377–406.

Institute of Directors in Southern Africa. (2012). Practice Notes: King III Chapter 9. = Institute of Directors in Southern Africa.

International Integrated Reporting Council (IIRC). (2016a). *Creating Value. The Cyclical Power of Integrated Thinking and Reporting*. International Integrated Reporting Council.

Ivan, O. R. (2018). Integrated Reporting in the Context of Corporate Governance. Case study on the Adoption of Integrated Reporting of Romanian Companies listed on BSE. *Valahian Journal of Economic Studies, 9*(2), 127–138. doi:10.2478/vjes-2018-0024

Jones, L., & Hameiri, S. (2021). COVID-19 and the failure of the neoliberal regulatory state. *Review of International Political Economy*, 1–25. doi:10.1080/09692290.2021.1892798

Kahn, M. (1995). Concepts, definitions, and key issues in sustainable development: the outlook for the future. *Proceedings of the 1995 International Sustainable Development Research Conference*, 2-13.

Karnani, A. (2011). *Fighting Poverty Together*. Palgrave MacMillan. doi:10.1057/9780230120235

Kayser, O., & Budinich, V. (2015). *Scaling up business solutions to social problems: A practical guide for social and corporate entrepreneurs*. Springer. doi:10.1057/9781137466549

Lozano, R., Carpenter, A., & Huisingh, D. (2015). A review of 'theories of the firm and their contributions to Corporate Sustainability. *Journal of Cleaner Production, 106*, 430–442. doi:10.1016/j.jclepro.2014.05.007

Maimbo, S. M., & Zadek, S. (2017). *Roadmap for a sustainable financial system*. Retrieved from http://unepinquiry.org/publication/roadmap-for-a-sustainable-financial-system/

McCann, D., & Berry, C. (2017). *Shareholder Capitalism, System Crisis*. New Economics Foundation.

McKinnon, R. I. (1989). Financial liberalization and economic development: A reassessment of interest-rate policies in Asia and Latin America. *Oxford Review of Economic Policy, 5*(4), 29–54. doi:10.1093/oxrep/5.4.29

Monbiot, G. (2016). *How did we get into this mess? Politics, equality, nature*. Verso Books.

Nakib, M., & Dey, P. K. (2018). The journey towards integrated reporting in Bangladesh. *Asian Economic and Financial Review, 8*(7), 894–913. doi:10.18488/journal.aefr.2018.87.894.913

Nwanji, T. I., & Howell, K. E. (2007). A review of the two main competing models of corporate governance: The shareholdership model versus the stakeholdership model. *Corporate Ownership and Control*, *5*(1), 9–23. doi:10.22495/cocv5i1p1

O'Connell, M., & Ward, A. M. (2020). Shareholder Theory/Shareholder Value. Encyclopedia of Sustainable Management, 1-7.

Oliver, J., Vesty, G., & Brooks, A. (2016). Conceptualising integrated thinking in practice. *Managerial Auditing Journal*, *31*(2), 228–248. doi:10.1108/MAJ-10-2015-1253

Parahoo, K. (2006). *Nursing research: Principles, process and issues*. Palgrave Macmillan.

Parmar, B. L., Freeman, R. E., Harrison, J. S., Wicks, A. C., Purnell, L., & De Colle, S. (2010). Stakeholder theory: The state of the art. *The Academy of Management Annals*, *4*(1), 403–445. doi:10.5465/19416520.2010.495581

Prahalad, C. K., & Hart, S. L. (2002). Strategy and business. *The Fortune at the Bottom of the Pyramid*, *26*, 2–14.

Pricewaterhousecooper, L. (2003). *Shareholders' Questions: Questions That May Be Asked At 2003 Shareholders' Meetings*. Pricewaterhouse Cooper.

Randa, I. O. (2021). Corporate Social Responsibility Interventions for Namibia's Post-COVID-19 Sustainable Banking Sector. In Handbook of Research on Strategies and Interventions to Mitigate COVID-19 Impact on SMEs (pp. 48-73). IGI Global. doi:10.4018/978-1-7998-7436-2.ch003

Randa, I. O., & Atiku, S. O. (2021). SME Financial Inclusivity for Sustainable Entrepreneurship in Namibia During COVID-19. In Handbook of Research on Sustaining SMEs and Entrepreneurial Innovation in the Post-COVID-19 Era (pp. 373-396). IGI Global. doi:10.4018/978-1-7998-6632-9.ch018

Rangan, K., Chase, L., & Karim, S. (2012). *Why every company needs a CSR strategy and how to build it*. Harvard Business School Working Paper No. 12–088.

Rowbottom, N., & Locke, J. (2016). The emergence of Integrated Reporting. *Accounting and Business Research*, *46*(1), 83–115. doi:10.1080/00014788.2015.1029867

Roxana-Ioana, B., & Petru, S. (2017). Integrated Reporting for a Good Corporate Governance. *Ovidius University Annals. Economic Sciences Series*, *17*(1), 424–428.

Samans, R., & Nelson, J. (2020*). Integrated Corporate Governance: A Practical Guide to Stakeholder Capitalism for Boards of Directors*. Geneva: World Economic Forum.

Saviano, J. P. S. B. M., & Carrubbo, F. P. L. (2014). The contribution of VSA and SDL perspectives to strategic thinking in emerging economies. *Managing Service Quality*, *24*(6), 565–591. doi:10.1108/MSQ-09-2013-0199

Savin-Baden, M., Cousin, G., & Major, C. H. (2010). *New approaches to qualitative research: wisdom and uncertainty*. Routledge. doi:10.4324/9780203849873

Schinasi, G. J., & Truman, E. M. (2010). *Reform of the global financial architecture*. Bruegel Working Paper, No. 2010/05, Bruegel.

Setia, N., Abhayawansa, S., Joshi, M., & Huynh, A. V. (2015). Integrated reporting in South Africa: Some initial evidence. *Sustainability Accounting, Management and Policy Journal, 6*(3), 397–424. doi:10.1108/SAMPJ-03-2014-0018

Sheth, J. N. (2011). Impact of emerging markets on marketing: Rethinking existing perspectives and practices. *Journal of Marketing, 75*(4), 166–182. doi:10.1509/jmkg.75.4.166

Soskice, D. (1999). Divergent production regimes: coordinated and uncoordinated market economies in the 1980s and 1990s. *Continuity and Change in Contemporary Capitalism, 38*, 101-134.

Speziale, M. T. (2019). Theoretical perspectives on purposes and users of integrated reporting: a literature review. *Integrated Reporting*, 13-60.

Steyn, M. (2014). Organisational benefits and implementation challenges of mandatory integrated reporting: Perspectives of senior executives at South African listed companies. *Sustainability Accounting, Management and Policy Journal, 5*(4), 476–503. doi:10.1108/SAMPJ-11-2013-0052

Tajudeen, E., Olusola, A. T., & Ademola, B. A. G. (2017). Interest rate liberalization, financial development and economic growth in Sub-Saharan African economies. *African Journal of Economic Review, 5*(2), 109–129.

Thomson, I. (2015). 'But does sustainability need capitalism or an integrated report' a commentary on 'The International Integrated Reporting Council: A story of failure. *J. Critical Perspectives on Accounting, 27*, 18–22. doi:10.1016/j.cpa.2014.07.003

Velte, P., & Stawinoga, M. (2017). Integrated reporting: The current state of empirical research, limitations and future research implications. *Journal of Management Control, 28*(3), 275–320. doi:10.100700187-016-0235-4

Veltri, S., & Silvestri, A. (2020). The value relevance of corporate financial and non-financial information provided by the integrated report: A systematic review. *Business Strategy and the Environment, 29*(8), 3038–3054. doi:10.1002/bse.2556

Venkataraman, S. (2019). *Stakeholder approach to corporate sustainability: A review.* Indian Institute of Management Kozhikode Working Papers, (319).

Vervaart, B. (2018). *Varieties of Capitalism Revisited: Empirical Testing of Country Cluster Classifications and the Implications for Other Empirical Work* [Doctoral dissertation]. Hertie School of Governance.

Watts, L., & Hodgson, D. (2019). *Social Justice Theory and Practice for Social Work: Critical and Philosophical Perspectives.* Springer. doi:10.1007/978-981-13-3621-8

KEY TERMS AND DEFINITIONS

Emerging Economies: Refers to a country that is in the process of developing its economy, generates low to middle per capita income and is rapidly expanding due to high production levels and significant industrialization in their transition to become more advanced.

Financialisation: Represents the continuous growth in prominence of financial markets, financial innovations, financial institutions, and financial elites in the operations of an economic system and its governing institutions, both at the national and international levels.

Governance: Represents structures, functions, processes, and organizational traditions put in place within the context of a programmes' or organisational authorizing environment for ensuring the achievement of its objectives in an effective and transparent manner.

Inclusive Capitalism: As a concept and policy movement attempts to improve business governance and hence the society by addressing the growing income and wealth inequality in the predominantly western capitalistic systems.

Integrated Corporate Governance: Views stakeholder interests holistically by systematically internalizing environmental, social, governance and data stewardship (ESG&D) considerations into the firm's strategy, resource allocation, risk management, performance evaluation and reporting policies and processes.

Integrated Reporting: Is the amalgamation of traditional financial reporting, sustainability reporting and corporate governance disclosures aimed at enhancing the decision usefulness of modern corporate reporting.

Neoliberalism: Neoliberalism is a political-economy policy model and ideology that seeks to transfer the control of economic factors from the public sector to the private sector.

Shareholders Capitalism: Represents an economic system characterised by a dominant corporate form, which are legally independent companies capable of independently pooling capital from many shareholders with limited liability, complemented by an open stock market to trade these shares freely.

Stakeholder Capitalism: A form of capitalism in which businesses do not only optimize short-term profits for shareholders, instead seek long-term value creation, by taking into consideration the needs of all their stakeholders, and society at large.

Chapter 11
International Financial Organizations:
Russian Experience of Cooperation for Three Decades

Elena Viktorovna Burdenko
https://orcid.org/0000-0001-5073-5062
Plekhanov Russian University of Economics, Russia

ABSTRACT

The chapter examines Russia's cooperation with international financial organizations for the period from 1992 to 2021. Attention is paid to cooperation programs with the International Monetary Fund and projects implemented jointly with the International Bank for Reconstruction and Development, the Multilateral Investment Guarantee Agency, and the International Finance Corporation. The participation of Russia in the projects of the International Development Association is shown. The chapter analyzes the problems of Russia's cooperation with "old" international organizations.

INTRODUCTION

The history of the creation, development and effectiveness of international organizations is relevant for all countries across the world. The Second World War, the development and enhancement of integration between countries, expanding activities of multinational corporations resulted in a stronger interconnection between all countries of the world.

To facilitate the recovery after World War II and promote the economic development of European countries that have chosen the socialist path, in 1949, an intergovernmental economic organization, the Council for Mutual Economic Assistance (Comecon) was established (Sheinis, 2022). Within Comecon, economic integration between the socialist countries developed and countries cooperated in the scientific and technical field. The 1973 energy crisis gave impetus to crisis developments in the economic cooperation among Comecon countries. The organization was disbanded on June 28, 1991 by a decision

DOI: 10.4018/978-1-6684-2448-3.ch011

Copyright © 2022, IGI Global. Copying or distributing in print or electronic forms without written permission of IGI Global is prohibited.

International Financial Organizations

made at the 46th meeting of the Council session. Collapse of the socialist system and the disintegration of the USSR in 1991 preceded Russia's cooperation with international organizations (Shakhray, 2016). The USSR voluntarily dismantled the socialist system, and within the country limits it did not prevent the exit of the union republics from the state. At the same time, the transformation of the economic and political system began. The transition from a planned economy to a market economy was announced. As a result, production, financial and economic ties were cut, which led to a crisis in all sectors of the economy. In 1991, the number of employed decreased by 9.9 million people and the first unemployed appeared. (Holotik et al., 2002). Its cooperation with international organizations that began in 1992 was aggravated by political and economic problems. The majority of the international organizations functioning in 2021 were established in the 20th century. The development of processes and technology laid the technical foundation for fast interaction between representatives of different countries. Amid expanding foreign economic activity, cooperation among countries within international organizations is becoming one of the most relevant issues.

The purpose of this chapter is to carry out a retrospective analysis of the establishment of international organizations and Russia's cooperation with international organizations. As part of a research on Russia's cooperation with international financial organizations from 1992 to 2021, an attempt was made to objectively analyze the problems of interaction. The objective was to show the role and impact of international financial organizations on the economic reforms carried out in the period 1992-2000, as well as further cooperation in the 21st century. Special attention is paid to cooperation programs with the International Monetary Fund (IMF), as well as projects implemented jointly with the International Bank for Reconstruction and Development (IBRD), the Multilateral Investment Guarantee Agency (MIGA) and the International Finance Corporation (IFC). Moreover, steps aimed at Russia's interaction with the Organization for Economic Cooperation and Development (OECD) were shown. To conduct a comprehensive study, it was necessary to focus on cooperation within the framework of the BRICS intergovernmental organization and the creation of the New Development Bank (NDB). When studying Russia's cooperation with international organizations, information provided on the official websites of the United Nations, the World Bank Group, the International Monetary Fund, the Organization for Economic Cooperation and Development, the New Development Bank, BRICS, the Ministry of Foreign Affairs of the Russian Federation, the Central Bank of the Russian Federation was used (*History of BRICS*, 2021; *Russia's cooperation with the World Bank*, 2016; *World Bank Group | Bank of Russia*, 2021).

BACKGROUND

More than 2000 studies are devoted to the research of the development, functioning of international organizations and their impact on the economies of different countries across the world. Let us review some of them.

The history of the creation of the World Bank, its management and financing is studied in the works of Mason and Asher (1973), Williams and Young (1994), Gilbert et al. (2000), Woods (2006), Çelik et al. (2014). The study of the authority of international organizations was made by Hooghe and Marks (2014). Delegation allows you to reduce the transaction costs of cooperation. The research showed that the structure of an international organization should be based on clear and understandable decisions. Such global trends as an increase in the share of the world economy, more accessible technologies in the field of communications, positive shifts in global cooperation in meeting basic human needs, and

199

others had an impact on the development and functioning of international organizations since the 1990s. McArthur and Werker (2016) mention factors that have a serious impact on the behavior and nature of international organizations.

One of the factors that has a serious impact on the outcomes of an international organization is the personality of its leader. A study by Hall and Woods (2018) highlighted three different limitations faced by executive directors of international organizations: political and legal, resource and bureaucratic ones. These limitations will affect the result of the activities of the international organization. The legitimacy of international organizations' activities in global governance, which is a relevant issue today, is studied by Tallberg and Zürn (2019). Legitimacy influences the efforts of states to coordinate actions to solve global problems. An example of declining legitimacy of an international organization is the withdrawal of the UK from the European Union, known as Brexit. Moreover, legitimacy affects the ability of international organizations to enforce international rules and regulations. The policies of international organizations have an impact on national policies within the country. At the same time, international organizations, being open systems, have to adapt to new challenges in order to continue participating in the development of global policy. These problems are studied using the example of the global pension reform, in the article by Heneghan and Orenstein (2019).

Despite the fact that the participation of countries in international organizations became common as part of international cooperation in the 20th century, will this trend continue in the twenty-first century? Von Borzyskowski and Vabulas (2019) in their article answer the question: "When do states withdraw from international organizations?". To find the reasons for the withdrawal of countries from international organizations, statistical data from 1945 are used. Analysis of confirmed information from 495 intergovernmental organizations identified 200 cases of countries refusing to participate in such organizations.

A study by Vreeland (2019) focuses on the problem of corruption in such global organizations as the International Monetary Fund (IMF), the World Bank, and the United Nations (UN). The article shows that the main shareholders (mainly the United States), using their influence, direct financial resources of international organizations in the countries strategically beneficial for them. The partnership between the European Union (EU) and international organizations is studied by Petrov et al. (2019) and Tatar (2020).

The changing landscape of international cooperation is associated with an increase in the representation of developing countries such as Brazil, Russia, India and China (BRICS) in international organizations. The article by Parizek and Stephen (2020) showed that although developing countries send their representatives to the UN, WTO, IMF, they are still poorly represented in international organizations. The interaction between Russia and international financial institutions is the subject of research by Andronova et al. (2007), Proka (2017), Pakova et al. (2017) and other scholars.

METHODOLOGY

To conduct a study of Russia's cooperation with international organizations from 1992 to 2021, a retrospective analysis of IMF lending, as well as joint projects conducted by the IBRD, MIGA, IFC, and the NDB, was made. To present data on IMF loans, the SDR was converted into dollars. When providing information on changes in Russia's GDP from 1990 to 2000, the GDP growth rate by 1990 is calculated, which is taken as the base year. The provided information allows assessing the dynamics of GDP. The historical and logical method, synthesis, comparative factor analysis, as well as a systemic and statistical approach were used for the research.

International Financial Organizations

Cooperation of Russia with International Financial Institutions

One of the main problems that countries face in terms of foreign trade activities is the regulation of the exchange rate. That is why, at the end of World War II, in 1944, a conference was held in the United States in Bretton Woods (New Hampshire) which hosted representatives of top industrial countries, including the USSR. Following the conference, the Bretton Woods monetary system, which restored fixed exchange rates pegged to the US dollar freely convertible to gold, was established. To maintain and implement the Bretton Woods system, special international organizations were created:

1. The International Monetary Fund (IMF),
2. The International Bank for Reconstruction and Development (World Bank).

Cooperation between the International Monetary Fund and Russia

The USSR was not part of the IMF, which was connected with both the economic characteristics of the planned economy and ideological reasons. Following the collapse of the USSR, Russia became the successor. It got all the debts of the union republics, since President B. Yeltsin signed the zero option agreement (*Russia's cooperation with the World Bank*, 2016).

Russia joined the IMF in June 1992. The fund began to influence the domestic economic policy of the country through recommendations to the Government and the Central Bank of the Russian Federation. In 1992, Russia applied for financial assistance (Table 1). An agreement was reached to provide a loan in the amount of SDR 25.8 billion. All settlements in the IMF since 1972 have been carried out in SDR (Special Drawing Rights). In SDR, only non-cash loans are issued. The SDR rate is floating. Since 2016, the SDR rate has been pegged to a basket of 5 currencies: US dollar – 41.73%; euro – 30.93%; Chinese yuan – 10.92%; Japanese yen – 8.33%; pound sterling – 8.09% (*IMF Launches New SDR Basket Including Chinese Renminbi, Determines New Currency Amounts*, 2016). The loan was paid in tranches if Russia met the conditions set.

Table 1. IMF loans to Russia in the period from 1992 to 2005 (thousand SDR)

Year	Amount of IMF loan		Amount of IMF loan repayment (without interest)		Amount of interest paid to IMF	
	Thousand SDR	Thousand Dollars	Thousand SDR	Thousand Dollars	Thousand SDR	Thousand Dollars
1992	719 000	1006966	-	-	-	-
1993	1 078 275	1510134	-	-	56 082	78543
1994	1 078 275	1510134	-	-	122 264	171232
1995	3 594 250	5033781	-	-	193 954	271634
1996	2 587 861	3624323	359 500	503483	323 568	453160
1997	1 467 252	2054900	359 500	503483	423 093	592546
1998	4 600 000	6442343	673 921	943833	528 876	740696
1999	471 429	660241	3 101 139	4343174	528 470	740127
2000	-		2 189 497	3066411	523 542	733225
2001	-		2 997 938	4198640	398 106	557551
2002	-		1 147 587	1607206	161 638	226376
2003	-		1 356 066	1899183	100 707	141041
2004	-		1 117 424	1564963	75 830	106201
2005	-		2 293 770	3212446	18 065	25300
Всего	15 596 342	21842822	15 596 342	21 842 822	3 454 195	4 837 632

Source: compiled by the author based on the data of the Central Bank of the Russian Federation, for recalculation, the rate of 1 SDR = 1.4 US dollars was taken (Central Bank of Russia, 2004)

Cooperation between the Fund and Russia was carried out through regular programs, which fixed the obligations of the Russian side to carry out a specific macroeconomic policy and the volume of the loan provided. From 1992 to 2004, the following programs were carried out:

- The first program was implemented in 1992-1993, with a condition that the budget deficit should not exceed 5% of GDP, and the inflation rate should not exceed 10%. In 1992, prices increased 30 times, 40% of the country's population found themselves below the poverty line (Holotik et al., 2002), GDP amounted to $91.625 billion, and the GDP growth rate compared to 1990 was 12.6% (Table 2). In 1993, the IMF Commission was not satisfied with the results of the macroeconomic policy and changes in the composition of the Russian Government. Therefore, only the first tranche was provided, and the second tranche was not paid.
- The second program was approved in July 1993 for 1993-1994. Within this program, 2 tranches were allocated. Since 1993, Russia began to pay interest on the loan.
- The third program was adapted from 1994 to 1997. It was decided to tighten monetary policy and reduce inflation. The economic policy pursued proved to be effective, and during this period the IMF provided tranches to Russia. Since 1996, Russia paid not only interest on the loan, but began paying off the bulk of the debt.
- The fourth program was designed for 1998. It suggested lending in exchange for economic reforms, economic liberalization, reducing the budget deficit to 2% of GDP, keeping inflation at

International Financial Organizations

6.9% per year. The proposed recommendations proved to be effective in industrialized countries. The IMF decided to increase the creditor agreement by SDR 6.3 billion. However, on August 17, 1998, Russia experienced a default. A 90-day moratorium was introduced on payments on external obligations of commercial banks and the devaluation of the ruble. Therefore, only a part of the tranche was paid, while the IMF did not transfer over SDR 7 billion. At this time, Russia was the largest borrower of the IMF.

- The fifth program was implemented from 1999 to 2004. It was decided to continue lending to Russia in 1999-2000, and 1 tranche was transferred. However, later, Russia voluntarily turned down lending in 2000. This was also due to the improvement in macroeconomic conditions.

Table 2. Russia's GDP from 1990 to 2000

Year	GDP (Billion Dollars)	GDP Growth Rate by 1990 (%)
1990	1187.9	-
1991	1166.1	-1,8
1992	1019.3	-12,6
1993	953	-19,8
1994	851	-28,4
1995	832.9	-30
1996	817.5	-31,2
1997	843.1	-29
1998	807	-32
1999	870.7	-25
2000	1000.6	-16

Source: compiled by the author on the basis of IMF data (GDP, Current Prices, 2022)

Russia was actually given a loan of SDR 15.6 billion at a low interest rate (in 1992 - 6.6%), which then decreased. The loan was repaid between 1996 and 2005. Russia no longer applied for financial assistance from the IMF. The early repayment of the IMF loan made it possible for Russia to become one of the fund's members, whose funds are used in the financial operations of the IMF. In 2016, the Russian Federation's quota in the IMF was increased from 9945 to 12903.7 million SDRs. Today, Russia ranks 8th by quota size (2.7%).

In 2021, Russia is represented in the IMF by:

1. The Manager from Russia in the IMF is the Minister of Finance of the Russian Federation A.G. Siluanov;
2. The Deputy Governor from Russia in the IMF is the Chairman of the Bank of Russia E.S. Nabiullina;
3. The Executive Director from Russia in the IMF is A.V. Mozhin.

Cooperation between the IMF and Russia continues and is consistent. New Arrangements to Borrow (NAB) and bilateral arrangements to borrow are being prolonged on terms proposed by the IMF. As part of cooperation, the IMF provides consulting and technical support. The Bank of Russia is the

International Financial Organizations

depositary of the IMF funds in Russian rubles. The Bank of Russia representatives participate in sessions and annual meetings of the Fund, as experts in working groups during working meetings, consultations and videoconferences. The Russian financial sector is now part of the global financial system and is of global importance. Therefore, since 2010, an assessment of the Russian financial sector has been carried out as part of the Financial Sector Assessment Program (FSAR). This Program is implemented together by the IMF and the World Bank. The Bank of Russia participates in assessing compliance with international standards and monetary policy codes, banking supervision and corporate governance. In accordance with the Special Data Dissemination Standard (SDDS), the IMF receives information on the balance of payments, external debt, and the dynamics of foreign exchange reserves. The Bank of Russia participates in the analytical and research activities of the IMF.

International Bank for Reconstruction and Development (World Bank)

To restore the economies of countries devastated by World War II, in 1944, the International Bank for Reconstruction and Development was established and later renamed into the World Bank. The World Bank is currently a specialized agency of the United Nations. It includes 189 member countries with its headquarters located in the USA, Washington.

The main objective of the World Bank is to support the comprehensive and sustainable development of all countries in the world, reduce poverty, and improve living standards. Today, it features the following 5 organizations, which are called the World Bank Group:

1. International Bank for Reconstruction and Development (IBRD), organized in 1944;
2. International Development Association (IDA), established in 1960;
3. International Finance Corporation (IFC), organized in 1956;
4. Multilateral Investment Guarantee Agency (MIGA), established in 1985;
5. International Center for Settlement of Investment Disputes (ICSID), organized in 1966.

The World Bank provides loans to developing countries through the IBRD and IDA. Financial aid is provided through low-interest or interest-free loans, in the form of grants. Loans amount to tens of billions of US dollars per year.

Each member country in the World Bank is represented by the Minister of Finance, who is on the Board of Governors. Once a year the Board of Governors holds the meeting, known as the Annual Meetings of the Boards of Governors of the World Bank Group and the International Monetary Fund. The Board of Directors, which includes the President of the World Bank and 25 executive directors, is in charge of operational activities. Only a US citizen can become the President of the World Bank, as this country is the largest shareholder. The Board of Directors meets twice a week and carries out general management of the bank, approves all loans, and makes political decisions. In 2021, the World Bank has more than 120 offices around the world, employing more than 10,000 people.

Russia joined the World Bank Group in June 1992. In December 1992 it joined the MIGA, and in 1993 it began cooperation with the IFC (*Russia's cooperation with the World Bank*, 2016). In 2021, Russia is represented at the World Bank by:

1. The Manager from the Russian Federation in the World Bank is the Minister of Finance of the Russian Federation A.G. Siluanov;

International Financial Organizations

2. The Deputy Governor from Russia in the World Bank is the Minister of Economic Development of the Russian Federation M.S. Oreshkin;
3. The Executive Director from Russia – A.S. Lushin.

Cooperation of the International Bank for Reconstruction and Development with Russia

The key structure of the World Bank is the International Bank for Reconstruction and Development. From 1992 to 2014, the IBRD approved 71 loans for Russia with a total value of $14.35 billion (*IFC PROJECT INFORMATION & DATA PORTAL*, 2021a). The largest share of financing was provided in the first years of Russia's membership in the IBRD. The share of loans received by Russia from the WB from 1992 to 1999 was 87% of the total volume of funds obtained by the country from the IBRD for the entire period of its membership in the organization. During this period, 42 projects were funded. In 2014, due to the economic sanctions against Russia, the IBRD stopped financing. Table 3 lists 10 projects with a total value of $697.1 million that were in the pipeline in 2014. Cooperation on these projects continued. As of November 27, 2021, 4 projects remain in the active stage of implementation: the Development of the State Statistics System, the Development of the System of Housing and Utilities Services; the Russian Cultural Heritage – 2, the Modernization of the Hydrometeorological Services Sector.

Table 3. Projects financed by the IBRD in Russia from 2003 to 2013

Nº	Name of project	Date of project approval	Date of project completion	Amount of financing (million dollars)
1.	Economic development of St. Petersburg	May 15, 2003	April 29, 2021	161.1
2.	Supporting judicial reform	February 15, 2007	July 12, 2018	50
3.	Development of the state statistics system	June 28, 2007	December 31, 2021	10
4.	Development of the system of housing and utilities services	February 26, 2008	December 31, 2021	200
5.	Financial education and financial literacy	December 7, 2010	July 24, 2021	25
6.	Russian cultural heritage – 2	December 7, 2010	June 30, 2022	100
7.	Fighting forest fires	September 20, 2012	July 25, 2019	40
8.	Technical Assistance in Public Financial Management	September 13, 2013	April 2, 2018	50
9.	Modernization of the hydrometeorological services sector	September 17, 2013	December 31, 2022	60
10.	Promotion of the potential of youth in the North Caucasus	September 18, 2013	November 03, 2016	1
	Total			697.1

Source: compiled by the author based on data from the World Bank (IFC PROJECT INFORMATION & DATA PORTAL, 2021b).

Before September 2014, 10 more projects with a total value of $1,547.9 million were under consideration; however, they were not approved.

205

In 2011, the World Bank Group developed and adopted the Partnership Strategy with Russia for the period from 2012 to 2016 *(World Bank: Projects in Russia, 2021)*. The following areas of cooperation were identified, where assistance was provided:

1. Accelerating the growth and diversification of the economy;
2. Development of human capital by advanced training of the workforce and enhancing the social security system;
3. Enhancing the global and regional role of Russia;
4. Improving the quality and transparency of public administration.

In 2015, the World Bank Group developed a new Partnership Strategy. However, due to the economic sanctions, it was not submitted for consideration to the Board of Directors.

Cooperation of the Multilateral Investment Guarantee Agency with Russia

The agency started its operations in 1988 with an initial capital of $1 billion. It included 29 member countries. In 1991, the number of participating countries increased to over 100. The main activity of the MIGA is to insure creditors and investors against political risks in developing countries. In 2009, the Agency provided guarantees for $1.2 billion to support the economies of Europe and Central Asia after the global financial crisis. The MIGA experts have extensive experience in political risk insurance and have excellent knowledge of banking, capital markets, environmental and social sustainability, project finance, international law and dispute resolution. The MIGA provides guarantees for a long period (15-20 years). Insurance against the following risks is possible:

1. Currency Transfer;
2. Expropriation;
3. Violation of the Contract;
4. War and Civil Disobedience.

Today Russia ranks 4th in terms of the volume of MIGA guarantees provided for the period of cooperation. Table 4 features active projects on which cooperation between the Agency and Russia continues in November 2021.

International Financial Organizations

Table 4. MIGA projects in Russia on which cooperation continues in 2021

Nº	Project name	Date of project approval	Amount of financing (million dollars)	Brief description of project
1.	OOO Ken-Pak Zavod Upakovki	July 29, 2014	61.8	Provision of guarantees to OOO Ken-Pak Zavod Upakovki for the construction of a plant producing aluminum cans for drinks in Volokolamsk.
2.	Linxtelecom Module 5 and Skytrade Data Centers	November 22, 2010	10.1	Provision of guarantees for the construction and operation of data storage and processing centers in Moscow and St. Petersburg
3.	OOO SUNTY	April 13, 2009	30.2	Providing guarantees to the Cypriot company Campestres Holdings Limited for investment in the Russian coffee and tea producer OOO Sunty.
4.	OOO Raiffeisen Leasing	May 26, 2008	70.8	Provision of guarantees for two equity loans issued by Raiffeisen Zentralbank sterreich AG to the Russian subsidiary OOO Raiffeisen Leasing

Source: compiled by the author based on MIGA data (Projects | Multilateral Investment Guarantee Agency | World Bank Group, 2021)

Cooperation between the International Finance Corporation and Russia

The main activity of the International Finance Corporation is to support private entrepreneurship in developing countries. Today, the IFC features 185 member countries. The Board of Governors and the Board of Directors have been established to manage the IFC. The Board of Governors consists of 1 Governor and 1 Deputy Governor from each member country. The Board of Directors consists of 25 executive directors representing one country or group of countries.

Support for private entrepreneurship in developing countries is carried out in 3 areas:

1. Investing in companies through the provision of loans, participation in the authorized capital, providing long-term securities and guarantees.
2. Raising capital from other lenders.
3. Consulting enterprises and governments.

Since Russia's accession to the IFC in 1993, 296 projects have been supported. The main areas in which IFC funds were raised are:

1. Financial Services,
2. Infrastructure,
3. Manufacturing Industry,
4. Oil and Gas and Mining Sector,
5. Telecommunications,
6. Retail Trade,
7. Healthcare.

In 2021, there are 30 active IFC projects, on which cooperation with Russia continues. Table 5 presents 5 projects as an example.

Table 5. Examples of IFC projects in Russia, on which cooperation continues in 2021

Nº	Project name	Date of project approval	Amount of financing (million dollars)	Brief description of project
1.	RUSSKIE BASHNI, ZAO	March 7, 2012	20	Equity investment in a company that is building a nationwide network of telecommunications towers.
2.	KuAZ	July 19, 2013	150	Providing a loan to KuAZ company for the modernization of the production of cyclohexanone, nitric acid.
3.	PAO CCS GROUP	September 11, 2021	25	Improving the efficiency of the company providing space heating and hot water in the Tula and Kemerovo regions of Russia.
4.	TRIVON AG	February 15, 2012	25	Funding for a company providing broadband access through wireless and fiber optic solutions.
5.	KULON UGROS, ZAO	July 6, 2009	7.5	Construction and operation of warehouses near Mineralnye Vody, Stavropol Krai of Russia

Source: compiled by the author based on IFC data (IFC PROJECT INFORMATION & DATA PORTAL, 2021a).

Due to the introduction of economic sanctions against Russia in 2014, IFC's investment activities in the country have been completely suspended. Since May 2014, the IFC has not approved projects in the country.

Cooperation of the International Development Association with Russia

Russia has been a partner of the International Development Association since 1997. The association was established as part of the World Bank to provide aid to the poorest countries in the world with a per capita GDP of less than $1,165. Today, this group includes 74 countries with 500 million people. The IDA also provides loans to countries whose GDP per capita is more than $1,165, but they cannot use the IBRD loans.

The activities of the Association are financed by contributions from richer member countries. Moreover, additional funds come from the income of the IBRD, IFC and through the repayment of previously issued IDA loans by borrowers. Partners meet every 3 years to replenish funds and review IDA policies. The outcomes are recorded and called Replenishments (for example, IDA20 Replenishment).

Russia promotes international development at the regional and global level. The priority areas of official aid for development are:

- Healthcare,
- Food Security,
- Agriculture,
- Human Development,
- Education,
- Strengthening Institutional Capacity.

Starting from 2004, the volume of Russian aid has been increasing annually. If in 2004 about $100 million was contributed, then in 2017 the sum amounted to $1,188 million. As part of international

International Financial Organizations

development assistance, Russia made financial donations to 22 IDA / IBRD trust funds, 14 of which are operating in 2021 (table 6).

Table 6. Operating Russia-funded IDA trust funds (2021)

N°	Name of fund	Amount, thousand dollars
1.	Trust Fund for the Recovery of Countries Affected by the Ebola Virus	3 000
2.	Social Security Rapid Response Program in the Labor Market Considering Nutritional Aspects	2 500
3.	Debt Management Facility (Phase II) in Africa	500
4.	Trade Transparency	1 500
5.	Building the Capacity of Statistical Offices in Europe and Central Asia	15 000
6.	Capacity Development Program in Europe and Central Asia	19 500
7.	Regional Program for Strengthening Public Financial Management Systems in Europe and Central Asia	18 000
8.	Public Expenditure Management Peer Assisted Learning Program in Europe and Central Asia	8 400
9.	South-South Experience Sharing Mechanism	1 500
10.	Reconstruction of Afghanistan	4 000
11.	Rapid Social Response Program	50 000
12.	Energy SME support in Sub-Saharan Africa (Mali, Tanzania, Rwanda, Senegal, Kenya, Botswana)	30 000
13.	Russia Education Aid for Development (Read II) (Armenia, Cambodia, India / South Asia, Kyrgyz Republic, Mongolia, Nepal, Tajikistan, Vietnam)	6 000
14.	Financial Education for All-Fast Track Initiative	10 000
	Total	169 900

Source: compiled by the author based on data from the World Bank (World Bank Group, 2018).

Starting from 2004, Russia has been actively developing a model of cooperation in the field of assistance to international development. This is reflected in the following documents approved by the President of the Russian Federation:

1. The Concept of Russia's Participation in International Development Assistance, June 2007;
2. The Concept of the Russian Federation's State Policy in the Area of International Development Assistance, April 2014.

The following areas of Russian policy contributing to international development at the regional and global level can be identified:

- Support for improving the efficiency of public administration systems, improving the conditions of trade and investment in aid recipient countries;
- Developing industrial and innovation potential in the poorest countries;
- Boost of economic activity in aid recipient countries;
- Strengthening government measures to combat organized crime and terrorism;

209

- Consolidation and restoration of peace in countries after military conflicts;
- Implementation of socio-economic projects in the poorest countries across the world.

Russia, together with other donor countries, took part in the following important global initiatives: debt relief to countries with large public debt, in the fight against AIDS, tuberculosis and malaria. Despite the economic sanctions imposed in 2014, Russia is still open to international cooperation, participates in meetings and maintains a dialogue with all members of the World Bank Group.

In June 2021, as part of cooperation with the World Bank Group, the Knowledge Exchange Program, and 2021-2024. Leveraging Russia's Potential as a Global Development Partner strategic document was adopted. This document lays the foundation for a new stage of cooperation.

Organization for European Economic Cooperation: History of Creation and Interaction with Russia

The Organization for European Economic Cooperation (OEEC) was established in April 1948. The OEEC was created to coordinate the actions of European states for economic recovery after World War II on the basis of the Marshall Plan (1948-1951). One of the main objectives of the organization was the integration and development of economic cooperation between the member countries. After the completion of the European economic reconstruction program in the late 1950s, OEECD had to adapt to the new conditions. It was decided that the accumulated positive experience of interaction between European countries as part of the OEECD would be further used. To continue cooperation, on December 14, 1960, representatives of twenty countries in Paris signed the Convention on the transformation of the Organization for European Economic Cooperation (OEECD) into the Organization for Economic Cooperation and Development (OECD). In the new organization, the number of participating countries increased with the addition of the USA and Canada.

By now, the OECD has actually become an organization for the coordination of socio-economic policies of the developed countries. Within the OECD, practically all the most important issues of global development are regulated, trends in the development of countries are analyzed and predicted, theoretical and practical approaches to solving world economic problems are being developed, which are then codified in international agreements and treaties. The highest political governing bodies of the OECD are the Committees, consisting of representatives of the member countries of the organization and countries with observer status. Today, the OECD has more than 20 Committees in different areas.

The OECD is funded through two sources. The bulk of the funding that supports the work of the Secretariat and the staff of Directorates and Project Committees is provided through mandatory contributions of the member countries. The size of the annual contribution is determined by the share of the country's GDP in total GDP – the aggregate product of the OECD countries. The second part of the funding is formed up by voluntary contributions from member countries and partner countries for participation in projects and programs of Committees.

As of November 2021, the OECD includes 38 countries with developed democratic institutions and market economies. The OECD maintains active partnerships with more than 70 non-member countries, of which 24 countries regularly participate in the activities of various OECD Committees as observers. In general, the OECD countries account for 17.7% of the world's population and over 60% of world GDP. As of November 2021, the OECD is made up of 38 countries with developed democratic institutions and market economies. The OECD maintains an active partnership with more than 70 non-member

International Financial Organizations

countries, of which 24 countries regularly participate in the activities of OECD Committees as observers. Overall, the OECD countries account for 17.7% of the world's population and over 60% of world GDP.

Cooperation between the OECD and Russia

Cooperation between the OECD and Russia began in the first half of the 1990s. For this purpose, in 1990, the OECD established the Center for Cooperation with Countries with Economies in Transition, which, among other things, started to coordinate the interaction of the OECD with Russia. Table 7 presents in chronological order the activities aimed at Russia's accession to the OECD over the period 1993-2021.

Table 7. Chronology of the development of cooperation between the OECD and Russia over the period from 1993 to 2021

Date	Description of steps
June 1993	The OECD decided to expand cooperation with developing countries.
June 8, 1994	The Declaration on Cooperation between Russia and the OECD was signed.
1995	The first Working Cooperation Program between Russia and the OECD was approved.
May 16, 2007	The OECD Council decided to invite the Russian Federation to start official negotiations on joining the organization.
November 2007	The OECD Council approved the Roadmap for the Accession of the Russian Federation to the organization.
June 2009	At the meeting of the OECD Council, the Russian side presented the Initial Memorandum on the Position of the Russian Federation on OECD Legal Acts. The beginning of the negotiation process to agree on the terms of Russia's accession to the OECD. The Russian government has developed a "Plan of Legislative Work to Harmonize Russian Legislation with OECD Standards."
2009-2013	The issues of Russia's accession were discussed in all key OECD Committees. Most of the Committees gave a positive opinion on Russia's readiness to join the OECD.
March 12, 2014 - 2021	The OECD suspended activities related to the accession process of the Russian Federation for an indefinite period.

Source: compiled by the author based on OECD data (Russia and the Organization for Economic Cooperation and Development (OECD), 2016).

Despite the temporary suspension of the Russian application consideration, Russia retains its official status of an acceding country and continues to participate in the working bodies of the OECD at the expert level. At the same time, political contacts were not completely frozen either. Over this period, about 180 representatives of the Russian Federation from more than 30 bodies and organizations took part in OECD events at the expert level. The practice of sending messages to Russian ministers by the OECD Secretary-General featuring the main results of the OECD's work in various fields with the presentation of documents has become common.

Problems of Cooperation between Russia and the "Old" International Organizations

Russia's cooperation with international organizations has faced a number of problems. Funding is required to support the activities of any international organization. The sources of funds are the contributions

211

(quotas) of the member countries. The United States were most active in the creation and financing of the IMF, a group of the WB organizations, and the OECD. Today, the United States has the largest quota in these international organizations of all the participating countries and, therefore, the largest number of votes (Table 8). For example, in the IMF a quota of 15% allows you to block almost any important decision.

Table 8. Russian and US quota in international organizations

Name of international organization	Size of quota	
	Russia	US
International Monetary Fund	2.7%	16.1%
International Bank for Reconstruction and Development (IBRD)	2.98%	15.7%
Multilateral Investment Guarantee Agency (MIGA)	3.13%	58.4%
International Finance Corporation (IFC)	4.1%	19.62%
International Development Association	0.31%	9.92%
Organization for European Economic Cooperation	none	20.5%

Source: compiled by the author based on data from the World Bank, OECD

When international organizations were being established, the USSR did not participate in them. Russia, having joined international organizations in 1992, received an insignificant quota, and, consequently, votes. Other developing countries that had joined international organizations found themselves in the same situation. They needed to establish a new intergovernmental organization to represent their interests. The idea of uniting Brazil, Russia, India and China emerged in 2006 at the session of the UN General Assembly (New York, USA) and the new intergovernmental organization was named BRIC (*History of BRICS*, 2021). The first official meeting of the BRIC Foreign Ministers took place in 2008 in Russia (Yekaterinburg). With the accession of South Africa in 2010, the abbreviation changed to BRICS. The BRICS countries generate about 30% of the world's gross product and 42% of the world's population live in these countries.

The actively developing BRICS economies need financial resources to implement projects in their countries, and the IMF could not meet their needs. Therefore, in 2014, the summit in Fortaleza (Brazil), expressed an idea of creating a new international financial organization. It was named the New Development Bank (NDB) and was organized in 2015. UN member states can become a member of the NDB. The authorized capital of the NDB is $100 billion. The initial subscribed capital of the NDB is $50 billion. In 2021, 2 countries joined the NDB: the United Arab Emirates, Bangladesh.

The bank was created to complement existing financial institutions and is not a competitor to the IMF and the World Bank. The purpose of the Bank is to support infrastructure projects of the member countries to ensure sustainable development and promote environmental protection. Table 9 shows 13 projects approved by the NDB, totaling $4,455 million, which are being implemented in 2021 in Russia.

International Financial Organizations

Table 9. Projects approved by the NDB for Russia, in the process of implementation in 2021

Nº	Project name	Date of project approval	Amount of funding (million dollars)	Project content
1.	Affordable Housing and Urban Development Program	March 19, 2021	300	Financing of the Affordable Housing Program outside the cities of Moscow, St. Petersburg and Kazan
2.	COVID-19 Emergency Program Loan for Supporting Russia's Healthcare Response	March 25, 2021	1000	The program features payments to healthcare professionals providing medical care for the diagnosis and treatment of COVID-19 (doctors, nurses, paramedics)
3.	Cellular Network and Cloud Services Expansion Project	March 9, 2020	300	The project is carried out in 2 areas: 1. Modernization of the existing cellular infrastructure, construction of new cell towers 2. Creation of infrastructure of cloud services
4.	Small Historic Cities Development Project Phase II	March 17, 2020	205	Restoration of cultural heritage to create tourist hubs
5.	Russian Maritime Sector Support Program	April 10, 2020	100	Support for seaports, sea vessels, including river vessels, which will facilitate the development of trade
6.	Toll Road Program in Russia	May 12, 2020	100	The project focuses on construction of new toll roads and upgrading of existing toll roads.
7.	Water Supply and Sanitation Program in Russia	May 12, 2020	100	Financing of subprojects for the modernization and renovation of existing water supply and sanitation systems.
8.	Development of Renewable Energy Sector in Russia	September 12, 2019	300	Investment in Renewable Energy Plants.
9.	Locomotive Fleet Renewal Program	November 8, 2019	550	The program is intended for the purchase of 3,500 new locomotives over the period 2019-2025.
10.	Development of Educational Infrastructure for Highly Skilled Workforce	December 24, 2019	500	Within the project, about 30 Russian universities will create advanced training schools to train graduates with advanced engineering skills.
11.	Small Historic Cities Development Project	May 28, 2018	220	Development of tourism infrastructure while preserving and developing cultural heritage and urban services. Support for sustainable socio-economic development in small historical cities of Russia.

Continued on following page

Table 9. Continued

Nº	Project name	Date of project approval	Amount of funding (million dollars)	Project content
12.	Volga	May 28, 2018	320	Modernization of water supply and sewerage systems in 5 cities of the Volga river basin.
13.	Judicial System Support Project	August 30, 2017	460	Improving the protection of the rights and legitimate interests of citizens and organizations through the development of the judicial infrastructure and the introduction of modern information and communication technologies.
14.	Total		4455	

Source: compiled by the author based on NBR data (List of All Projects, 2021).

Participation in international organizations has become mandatory for countries. National governments are influenced through consultations and funding. An example is the introduction of economic sanctions against Russia from 2014 until today, which changes the humanitarian direction of the activities of international organizations to punitive. The recommendations and forecasts of the IMF, which do not always take into account the national specifics of the country, may be erroneous or result in catastrophic events, are criticized a lot. The more countries are included in an international organization, the more complex the structure of the organization itself is, the more time it takes to negotiate agreements and bureaucratic procedures.

SOLUTIONS AND RECOMMENDATIONS

The positive experience of cooperation between countries as part of international organizations has to be preserved. The development of global integration, the functioning of world markets is impossible without the development of common rules and coordination of actions. Changes in the global economy, active economic growth in developing countries present challenges for the activities of many international organizations. Flexible, quick response and reform, as a response to external challenges, will make international organizations more stable and resilient.

FUTURE RESEARCH DIRECTIONS

As part of this research, an analysis of Russia's cooperation with certain global international organizations was carried out. The activities of international organizations are not limited only to the provision of economic aid. By gaining access to the domestic market of the country, foreign companies participating in projects of international organizations have an impact on other spheres of life, such as culture, customs, language, education, religion and others. The union republics that were part of the USSR became new

International Financial Organizations

independent states, and each country had to choose its own development path. The countries of Eastern Europe, which were part of the socialist camp, faced the same problem. Everyone had to transform the economic and political systems. In future research, it is possible to analyze the cooperation of these countries with international organizations and study how countries solved economic problems.

CONCLUSION

International organizations, established in the twentieth century with the aim of economic recovery of European countries that suffered during World War II, proved to be effective. The UN established the IMF, the World Bank Group for the functioning and maintenance of the stability of the financial system. After the completion of the European economy's recovery, it was decided to use the accumulated positive experience. Therefore, the direction of international organizations activities is changing. They are more focused on providing financial assistance to developing countries using various lending options.

Russia's cooperation with the IMF and the World Bank Group was not limited to providing only financial assistance. Moreover, a range of expert and consulting services was provided, which is still criticized a lot and is assessed differently by Russian scholars. However, in general, it led to the development of a market economy in the country. From 1992 to 2021, Russia transformed the country's economy, moving from a planned to a market economic system. If at the beginning of cooperation with international organizations it acted as a borrower of financial resources, then active interaction made it possible to change the economic situation in the country and repay the loan issued by the IMF in a short time. In the 21st century, Russia is already acting as a creditor and partner in many international projects and initiatives carried out by international organizations. From 2000 to 2019, GNI per capita in Russia increased from \$1,710 to \$11,260. Economic growth, which began in 2000, made it possible to double GDP by 2016. The share of the population living below the poverty line decreased from 29% in 2000 to 12.1% in 2020 (*The World Bank in Russia*, 2021). Russia's cooperation with the World Bank Group from 1992 to the present covered the following areas:

1. Energy efficiency.
2. Development of public-private partnerships.
3. Employment.
4. Anti-crisis policy.

Joint projects have given impetus to Russia's economic growth and are focused on supporting and developing private entrepreneurship. Since 2014, due to the sanctions against Russia, the approval of new projects was suspended. Cooperation with the IMF, the World Bank Group continues only on previously approved projects. Cooperation between Russia and the OECD was the most complicated. Despite the fact that from 1993 to 2013 a lot of work was done to join the OECD, nevertheless, the consideration of the Russian application was suspended. Difficulties and problems of cooperation of developing countries with international financial institutions led to the formation of a new economic intergovernmental union – BRICS. A financial organization was created within it – the New Development Bank. Today, the NDB can only be viewed as a regional financial institution that serves only the BRICS countries.

215

ACKNOWLEDGMENT

The study was supported by Plekhanov Russian University of Economics.

REFERENCES

Çelik, I. E., Dinçer, H., Hacıoğlu, Ü., & Dinçer, H. (2014). The Role of World Bank in Global Development. In H. Dinçer & Ü. Hacioğlu (Eds.), *Global Strategies in Banking and Finance* (pp. 56–64). IGI Global. doi:10.4018/978-1-4666-4635-3.ch004

Central Bank of Russia. (2004). *Bulletin of Banking Statistics* (No. 3). CJSC "AEI "Prime, TASS". http://www.cbr.ru/collection/collection/file/36863/bbs0403r.pdf

GDP, current prices. (2022, February 9). *International Monetary Fund*. Retrieved February 9, 2022, from https://www.imf.org/external/datamapper/NGDPD@WEO/RUS?year=2022

Gilbert, C. L., Vines, D., & Powell, A. (Eds.). (2000). *The World Bank: Structure and policies*. Cambridge University Press. doi:10.1017/CBO9780511560002

Hall, N., & Woods, N. (2018). Theorizing the role of executive heads in international organizations. *European Journal of International Relations*, *24*(4), 865–886. doi:10.1177/1354066117741676

Heneghan, M., & Orenstein, M. A. (2019). Organizing for impact: International organizations and global pension policy. *Global Social Policy*, *19*(1–2), 65–86. doi:10.1177/1468018119834730

History of BRICS. (2021). *BRICS*. https://infobrics.org/

Holotik, S. I., Eliseeva, N. V., & Karpenko, S. V. (2002). Russia in 1992 - 2000: Economy, Power and society. *New Historical Bulletin*, *8*, 164–203.

Hooghe, L., & Marks, G. (2014). Delegation and pooling in international organizations. *The Review of International Organizations*, *10*(3), 305–328. doi:10.100711558-014-9194-4

IFC Project Information & Data Portal. (2021a*). IFC | International Finance Corporation | World Bank Group*. https://disclosures.ifc.org/enterprise-search-results-home?f_region_description=ECAREG

IFC Project Information & Data Portal. (2021b, November 27). *International Finance Corporation*. https://disclosures.ifc.org/enterprise-search-results-home?f_region_description=ECAREG

IMF Launches New SDR Basket Including Chinese Renminbi, Determines New Currency Amounts. (2016, September 30). *International Monetary Fund*. https://www.imf.org/ru/News/Articles/2016/09/30/AM16-PR16440-IMF-Launches-New-SDR-Basket-Including-Chinese-Renminbi

List of All Projects. (2021, June 24). *New Development Bank*. https://www.ndb.int/projects/list-of-all-projects/?country_name=4&status_name=1

International Financial Organizations

Mason, E. S., & Asher, R. E. (1973). The World Bank since Bretton Woods; the origins, policies, operations, and impact of the International Bank for Reconstruction and Development and the other members of the World Bank group: the International Finance Corporation, the International Development Association [and] the International Centre for Settlement of Investment Disputes. Brookings Institution Press.

McArthur, J. W., & Werker, E. (2016). Developing countries and international organizations: Introduction to the special issue. *The Review of International Organizations*, *11*(2), 155–169. doi:10.100711558-016-9251-2

Parizek, M., & Stephen, M. D. (2020). The long march through the institutions: Emerging powers and the staffing of international organizations. *Cooperation and Conflict*, *56*(2), 204–223. doi:10.1177/0010836720966017

Petrov, P., Dijkstra, H., Đokić, K., Zartsdahl, P. H., & Mahr, E. (2019). All hands on deck: Levels of dependence between the EU and other international organizations in peacebuilding. *journal of European Integration*, *41*(8), 1027–1043. doi:10.1080/07036337.2019.1622542

Projects | Multilateral Investment Guarantee Agency | World Bank Group. (2021). *MIGA*. https://www.miga.org/projects?host_country%5B%5D=495&project_status=All&env_category=All&project_type=All&board_date%5Bmin%5D=&board_date%5Bmax%5D=&title=&project_id=

Projects. (2021). *World Bank*. https://projects.vsemirnyjbank.org/ru/projects-operations/projects-list?countrycode_exact=RU&os=0

Russia and the Organization for Economic Cooperation and Development (OECD). (2016, November 2). *The Ministry of Foreign Affairs of the Russian Federation*. https://www.mid.ru/organizacia-ekonomiceskogo-sotrudnicestva-i-razvitia-oesr-/-/asset_publisher/km9HkaXMTium/content/id/2511808

Russia's cooperation with the World Bank. (2016, November 1). *The Ministry of Foreign Affairs of the Russian Federation*. https://www.mid.ru/vsemirnyj-bank-vb-/-/asset_publisher/km9HkaXMTium/content/id/2511066

Shakhray, S. M. (Ed.). (2016). *The Collapse of the USSR: Documents and Facts (1986–1992)*. Kuchkovo Field. http://www.fa.ru/org/div/museum/SiteAssets/Pages/1917-2017/%D0%A8%D0%B0%D1%85%D1%80%D0%B0%D0%B9%20%D0%A1.%D0%9C.%20%D0%A0%D0%B0%D1%81%D0%BF%D0%B0%D0%B4%20%D0%A1%D0%A1%D0%A1%D0%A0.%20%D0%94-%D0%BE%D0%BA%D1%83%D0%BC%D0%B5%D0%BD%D1%82%D1%8B%20%D0%B8%20%D1%84%D0%B0%D0%BA%D1%82%D1%8B.pdf

Sheinis, E. Y. (2022, February 8). *Council of Mutual Economic Assistance*. The Great Russian Encyclopedia. https://bigenc.ru/domestic_history/text/3589191

Tallberg, J., & Zürn, M. (2019). The legitimacy and legitimation of international organizations: Introduction and framework. *The Review of International Organizations*, *14*(4), 581–606. doi:10.100711558-018-9330-7

Tatar, H. E. (2020). IMF, World Bank, and the European Union With the Perspective of New Institutional Economics. In I. Akansel (Ed.), *Comparative Approaches to Old and New Institutional Economics* (pp. 217–238). IGI Global. doi:10.4018/978-1-7998-0333-1.ch013

The World Bank in Russia. (2021). *World Bank*. https://www.vsemirnyjbank.org/ru/country/russia

von Borzyskowski, I., & Vabulas, F. (2019). Hello, goodbye: When do states withdraw from international organizations? *The Review of International Organizations, 14*(2), 335–366. doi:10.100711558-019-09352-2

Voting Powers. (2021, November 27). *The World Bank*. https://www.worldbank.org/en/about/leadership/votingpowers

Vreeland, J. R. (2019). Corrupting International Organizations. *Annual Review of Political Science, 22*(1), 205–222. doi:10.1146/annurev-polisci-050317-071031

Williams, D., & Young, T. (1994). Governance, the World Bank and Liberal Theory. *Political Studies, 42*(1), 84–100. doi:10.1111/j.1467-9248.1994.tb01675.x

Woods, N. (2006). *The globalizers: The IMF, the World Bank and their borrowers*. Cornell University.

World Bank Group. (2018, October 2). *Russia and the World Bank: International Development Assistance*. World Bank. https://www.worldbank.org/en/country/russia/brief/international-development

World Bank Group | Bank of Russia. (2021). *Bank of Russia*. http://www.cbr.ru/today/ms/smo/wb/#highlight=%D0%B2%D1%81%D0%B5%D0%BC%D0%B8%D1%80%D0%BD%D0%BE%D0%B3%D0%BE%7C%D0%B1%D0%B0%D0%BD%D0%BA%D0%B0

World Bank: projects in Russia. (2021, November 27). *The World Bank*. https://projects.worldbank.org/en/projects-operations/projects-list?countrycode_exact=RU&os=0

ADDITIONAL READING

Andronova, I. V., Daniltsev, V. V., & Zuev, V. N. (2007). *Problems of efficiency and reform of the system of international multilateral institutions*. TEIS.

Organization for Economic Cooperation and Development. (2021, November 5). *Humanitarian Portal*. https://gtmarket.ru/organizations/oecd

Pakova, O. N., Yarykova, Z. R., Bayramov, M. R., & Bitlev, K. G. (2017). Modern realities and prospects for the development of relations between Russia and the leading financial and credit institutions of the UN. *Economics and Management: Problems. Solutions, 7*(9), 27–31.

Proka, K. (2017). *Russia's Interaction with International Financial Institutions: A Background Review*. Center for Strategic Research.

Williams, D., & Young, T. (1994). Governance, the World Bank and Liberal Theory. *Political Studies, 42*(1), 84–100. doi:10.1111/j.1467-9248.1994.tb01675.x

International Financial Organizations

KEY TERMS AND DEFINITIONS

Concessional Lending: Is used to support low-income IMF member countries. Is issued to reduce poverty and stimulate economic growth in the country. The new lending terms have been used since 2010. The extended credit facility (ECF) is used for lending. Financial assets under the ECF are issued at a zero interest rate, for a period of up to 5.5 years, the full maturity is 10 years.

Extended Fund Facility (EFF): Was created to help countries overcome significant balance of payments problems. Fundamental economic reforms are required to solve the problems. The usual loan term is 3 years. The maximum loan term is 4 years. The maturity period is 4.5 - 10 years from the date of the actual provision of funds. Used since 1974.

Flexible Credit Line (FCL): Is a form of lending to IMF member countries with stable economies and good economic performance. If the economic indicators of the country meet the criteria of the IMF, then access to the financial resources of the IMF is granted immediately. The period of validity of the FCL is 1 or 2 years. The maturity period is 3.5-5 years.

Precautionary and Liquidity Line (PLL): Is a form of lending to IMF member countries with sound economic performance. May be granted if the country does not meet the criteria for the provision of the FCL. Issued for a period from 6 months to 2 years. There are restrictions on the amount of funds provided: 1. For 6 months, an amount of no more than 250% of the quota is provided. In exceptional cases, it can be increased up to 500% of the quota. 2. A limit of 500% of the quota is set for 1-2 years. The maturity period is 3.5-5 years.

Stand-By (SBA): Is a loan that is provided to the member countries of the IMF under certain conditions. The purpose of obtaining a loan has to be approved. The bank reserves the approved amount by a certain date, and the client uses it in full or in part. The SBA is designed to overcome short-term balance of payments problems. It is issued for a period of 12 to 24 months. The loan repayment period is 3.5 - 5 years from the date of actual receipt of funds. Such a loan has been issued since 1952.

Chapter 12
International Organizations' Aid for Educational Transformation and Inclusive Development

Kannan Rajagopal

Symbiosis Centre for Management and Human Resource Development, Symbiosis International University, Pune, India

Vaishali Mahajan

iD https://orcid.org/0000-0002-1958-5809

Symbiosis Centre for Management and Human Resource Development, Symbiosis International University, Pune, India

ABSTRACT

There has been several research studies and articles on foreign aid for education which predominantly deliberates on the aspects that really works effectively in favor of aid and on the points which indicate the main reasons for the failures of such education aid initiatives. In fact, studies have abundantly shown that these foreign aids for education have made positive contributions to the education aid-recipient nations specifically in terms of enhancing the enrolment percentages under the basic education levels. However, there is also strong evidence on the existence of a wide gap on what the aid does to the nation and what it is intended to possibly achieve specifically in terms of the quality of education anticipated to be achieved. Overall findings of the research studies suggest that interventions are more effective at improving student performance and learning when social norms and intertemporal choices are factored in the design of educational policies and when two or more drivers of change are combined.

INTRODUCTION

The education is considered to be one of the largest sectors of the current era, education includes products (books, reading material, writing material, computer software and hardware, and teaching aids) comprises of various programs (Curricula, academic systems, procedures and processes which helps in attaining a Degree or an academic certificate). Education embraces services (such as examinations, tests, laboratory

DOI: 10.4018/978-1-6684-2448-3.ch012

Copyright © 2022, IGI Global. Copying or distributing in print or electronic forms without written permission of IGI Global is prohibited.

International Organizations' Aid

and practical courses, research, mentoring, counselling teaching and consulting). The combination of all leading to employment and successful career. Hence the education sector is considered as one among the largest service sector which serves as a pillar for development of the country and its citizens. In this context International aid for education has taken a prime position in helping the developing and under-developed nations to attain their set goals on education effectiveness and excellence. (Heyneman, 2001).

Imparting education to an individual has monetary and non-monetary influences, higher level of education an individual attains, lesser are the chances of they being poverty stricken and unemployed. The education not only works positively towards the individual's betterment, it also impacts the growth and prosperity of the community and Nation where the educated individual hails from. The non-monetary impact of education enhances health, personal safety and hygiene, nutritive food intake practices, and on a whole improves individual wellbeing and quality of life. In this changing economy, education leading to knowledge and wisdom is acquired through formal system of school, college and university as an institution. This gets transformed to the next generation through systematic incorporation and transformation of the assimilated new knowledge and skills acquired over a lifetime period (Schultz, 1982; McMahon, 1999).

The concept of foreign assistance for education is more visible since 1960 onwards. In the early periods, the focus of educational aid and assistance was more towards imparting work-related skills, engineering education and technology related education with utmost thrust on assisting vocational training and development. By the start of 1980's the emphasis of foreign aid moved towards extending support and assistance to primary and secondary school education, professional course education, education research and moving ahead towards social sciences discipline of education in addition to the technical and engineering field.

The priority of the International aid is much more focused on the development of the infrastructure like roads, specifically highways, bridges, railway tracks, dams, agricultural and Industrial developments. However, to man these Infrastructure projects and to maintain these projects the need for skilled and knowledgeable manpower was identified as the important requirement which is the need of the hour. Thus, the focus of the International aid on education started moving towards enhancing the locally available manpower's skills and knowledge to manage the Infrastructural and technical projects. (Heyneman,2004).

The return on investment was very high when the investment of financial aid is made on the primary education. Therefore, the shift from international funding for the higher education to primary education has been visibly seen, further the higher education funding has been generated through collecting higher additional tuition fees (Psacharopoulos et al., 1986). This approach was further followed by the model adopted universally called the "education for all" of course with a prime focus placed by the International aid Organizations' on the primary education (Heyneman, 2009, 2010, 2012a).

Though aid for education has direct and indirect impacts on the growth and economy of the country plus its impact on poverty alleviation and individual empowerment has been profusely discussed about in the research literature reviews. Thus, Education in general and the Primary education in specific has been of major focus and manifestly listed in the Millennium Development Goals (MDGs). The World Education Forum (2000) laid more importance on the quality of education through the Dakar frame work of action. Further in the year 2015 precisely in the month of September the Sustainable Development Goals (SDGs) which had taken the place of the Millennium Development Goals (MDGs) overtly supported and emphasized the education quality aspect and stressed upon the importance of bringing up "inclusive and equitable quality education" through the SDG (Goal 4). 103 million youth universally are

221

deprived of basic literacy skills, more than 60 percent are women, according to the UNDP data. Correct support if received will help improve learning to a great extent in difficult situations also.

Figure 1 shows the Top 10 international organizations who are dedicated in providing worldwide access to eminence edification and lifelong education opportunities. Considering the number of employees working and the impact these are the largest organizations covering extensive array of countries and beneficiaries.

Figure 1. Top 10 international organizations in education sector
Source: Developmental Aid, 2021

Organizations	Number of employees	Territory coverage	Impact
UNESCO	5,001-10,000	worldwide	millions of beneficiaries
Room to Read	1,001-5,000	worldwide	over 18 million children
Education Development Trust	1,001-5,000	worldwide	2.3 million learners
Pearson	1,001 - 5,000	70 countries	millions of teachers and learners
World Learning, Inc	1,001-5,000	162 countries	19.000 participants in active programs
Education Development Center	1,001-5,000	50 U.S. states & 22 countries	millions of individuals
American Institutes for Research	1,001-5,000	31 U.S. & international office locations	millions of beneficiaries
TAFE Queensland	1,001-5,000	more than 50 locations in Australia	110,000
British Council	501-1,000	100 countries	100 million learners and teachers during 2018 - 2019
Creative Associates International Incorporated	501-1,000	more than 20 countries	millions of children and teachers

Besides the above top 10 organizations, Development Aid cumulates information about 742 organizations with more than 500 employees, which represent 57% from the total number of organizations working in the education sector registered on our web platform. All these organizations have access to almost 300 grants for the educational sectors' programs. The change in education sector became an imminent condition under the circumstances of COVID-19 crisis. The leading organizations have got involved in redressing the situation and mitigating the negative effects. A lot of them provide significant support and advice during COVID-19.

BACKGROUND

The International aid assistance program ensures flow of financial assistance from the developed donor countries to the recipient countries including the developing and under developed countries and the countries which are in the process of transition. The financial assistance in various forms such as assistance in the form of financial loans, funding offered to enhance trade and business, extending assistance of funds for the purpose of military support, alleviate poverty, enhance health and well-being, upgrade educational

International Organizations' Aid

levels and offering political and security aid. The International aid in different form is aimed at fighting the misery, infirmity, hunger, lack of shelter and overcome all the other dire caused by the natural disasters. The aid is offered to the developing countries to assist these countries to become self-reliant and help the countries to advance and develop their resource so as to create sustainable development.

The International aid and its effectiveness are viewed in varied perspectives, the prime being the growth and development of the individual, upgradation of the skills, knowledge, and wisdom when exposed to a formal education. Going ahead what more can be gained for the betterment of life beyond the classrooms precisely out of the schools, college and Universities. The support required for education and its upliftment is classified into first order primary requirements and other secondary requirements. In the first order requirement includes the basic infrastructural requirements such as clean and organized class rooms with rudimentary and essential furniture like chairs and tables for the students to sit and learn, teaching aids like boards and other instructional support materials, and the teacher who imparts education.

The outcome of education is intensely influenced by various factors which are measurable and some that could not be measured so easily such as curriculum and its profound nature. Other factors like the training of teachers and their effectiveness, the relevance and correctness of the teaching and learning materials used, the geographical location of the educational institutions and its impact on education, the amenities of the schools, the educational mentors, teachers in leadership positions. Furthermore factors such as the respect adored by the society in general and community in particular on the schools and teachers and its involvement in the activities of the educational institutions are also some of the factors which have a strong influence on the outcome of education.

The International aid towards education though focuses and contributes majorly towards the upgraded standards of learning, the crux of the focus is enhancing the number of student's enrollment in the primary levels, assessment of the progress with respect to the universal enrolment (which is part of the MDGs and SDGs). In addition to the above the strong concentration also remains firmly on to ensure the teaching and learning offered through various pedagogy in the schools and colleges are carried forward to lead rewarding and prosperous life ahead in the future beyond the confined frame of school and college education system.

Amidst this multifaceted background the International Aid Organizations' supporting towards the cause of better education focus to report about the number of enrolments made as a point of success rather than on the counting on the effectiveness of the aid in terms of development.

There are certain International Aid Organization such as Global Partnership for Education (GPE) make strong claims that countries availing education aid from them are performing better in terms of primary education than the countries which are not receiving any educational aid from GPE. Thus, GPE strongly affirms that their aid to Education is far more productive and superior than the others alike.

LITERATURE REVIEW

Education plays a vital role in contemporary and industrialized world. The need of the general public is to have a good education system for survival. The requirement for a better education system has been recognized by the society for the betterment of the future generations to come. Many countries have recognized the need for quality education and are investing lots of money towards education. These are given in terms of scholarship for obtaining higher education. For the betterment and a secured future, the people need to possess higher education.

In the past era's foreign educational aid has been receiving greater attention in spite of donor's aid being increased. The major issue is that the policy makers often overlook the classrooms. To fight the poverty education is a critical tool. Economic success can be gained by a literate population. Aid received for international organizations is not easy to handle. Education aid would easily run into politics during implementation with indigenous communities. According to Abby Riddell, what works and the absence of evidence of it is a greatest issue. It would take years to measure the learning as it is vague and not possible to measure the impact accurately. To receive fund and gain results in a shorter duration many agencies focus on Millennium Development Goals (MDGs) by enabling supplies to schools, increasing the attendance percentage and literacy rates. Aim of MDGs' is to achieve primary education worldwide. Most of the programs fail to deliver extensive solutions as the curriculum of the schools are outdated. Kazim Bacchus, states that many developing countries still have curriculums which were developed years ago and which cannot be transferred in the day to day lives. Financial report shared by the world bank shows that in spite of huge attendance there has been a very little learning achieved in the female children of Cambodia. There have been great initiatives like granting scholarship to female students, construction of classrooms, distributing school materials.

With the increasing concerns of state of education, in response to growing concerns to the state of education, alternate curriculums are endeavoring to reinforce the association amid community and schools. Epstein recommends the new programs should enable students to just not focus on academics but the emphasis should be on learn tools and techniques which would make a positive impact on the community. Deaton's suggestion is to diminish the role of aid inside governments, which will impact the school curriculums if the accountability is within the system.

Aid from Foreign countries is an imposition of established countries on underdeveloped countries as a criterion for economic development Rostow (1990). On the other hand, Hayter, (1971) observations of aid received from foreign as modern imperialism which may not lead to predicted economic benefits. This has led to a regular flow of capital received for developing to the developed countries in effort to decrease the gap while overpowering their issues. There are no noteworthy changes to the destinies, after receiving foreign aid for several eras in African countries Andrews (2009). The rate of development in these countries is very slow. Even though there was wide flow of aids from the foreign for the purpose of extensive empirical work and developing nations for years on the aid-growth link, the assistance efficiency literature rests debatable. Main objective of the aid is to improve the economic development and well-being of less established countries, which is measured basis the impact on economic growth. In spite of years transferring aid to developing countries, many studies reveal the relationship between aid and economic development not able to achieve the objectives, Durbarryet al., (1998). A study on African countries, between 1970 to 1997 revealed that aid was ineffective. According to Tarp & Director (2009) aids are vital in the growth of the underdeveloped countries, which Girmaet al. (2005) considers the access to certain services such as food security, education and health which are significant for the economic growth of the country. Influence of Aid on human development was observed in education and health which exhibit a significant correlation among human development in underdeveloped countries.

Developing countries are receiving educational aids, in spite of this the poverty still seems to be enormous and underdevelopment still prevails which concludes that there is no strong evidence as to aid affecting the growth of the country Dreher et al. (2015). On the other hand, Alemu and Lee (2015) in their study on comparative analysis showing the impact of foreign aid on Middle and Low-Income countries in African determined that aid has significant positive impact on low-income countries disagreeing that criticisms of foreign aid is flawed. Galiani et al. (2014) also jagged that foreign aid has a substantial

International Organizations' Aid

optimistic consequence on economic growth. Adeyeye (2013) pointed out that stealing and misuse of development aids are flourishing, too. The government are not taking these issues seriously to bring such people under the legal system by appropriate examination. Education aid may be unsuccessful to help the endangered, as aid money can be wrenched Oshewolo (2011). In 2010 foreign educational aid of 26.9% was mainly used for administration Adewole (2014). Similarly, 9.4% of the aid was allocated to energy and mining, 5.4% of to agriculture, 6.8% to transportation and 1.9% to industry and trade.

Numerous study has methodically reviewed and tried to uncover implications for education policies from the studies of randomized control trials, quasi-experiments/natural experiments (Kremer and Holla, 2009, Glewwe, 2002; Nino-Zarazua, 2015, Glewwe and Kremer, 2006 and Glewwe et al., 2014). Decreasing cost of education and providing health programs for school saw an increase in the school participation (Kremer and Holla, 2009). According to (Masino and Nino-Zarazua, 2015) studied the supply-side interventions were establishing to be fruitless in improving the quality of education and be largely efficient when they are complemented with community participation or incentive programs. Result from meta-analysis on the whole too show similar program though with some interventions contain diverse evidence to draw conclusion (Krishnaratne et al., 2013; Petrosino et al., 2012; McEwan, 2014). To increase the participation of students in school, new schools and infrastructure building interventions, conditional cash transfer programs and school feeding programs had positive effect (Krishnaratne et al 2013, Petrosino et al., 2012). Good infrastructure facilities provided a positive influence on increasing learning outcomes and the attendance of students. Yet, another analyses exhibited that interventions made to decrease school fees and subsidy programs necessarily did not improve learning outcomes of students (McEwan, 2014, Krishnaratne et al., 2013). Education resources such as extra teachers and computer-based education were most effective on learning outcomes (Krishnaratne et al., 2013; McEwan, 2014). Additional interventions like school-based management, merit-based scholarships, information to parents on schooling could have an optimistic influence on learning outcomes but evidence was not strong (Krishnaratne et al., 2013).

In future the research can be focused on areas where the educational aid can have a direct effect in the long term. Subsequently, there are concerns about the educational quality and their outcomes, there should a focus on the underdeveloped countries. Students are able to complete their primary schooling without becoming literate (UNESCO, 2012). Hence the need arises for the measurement of learning outcomes. Further it is observed that empirical studies are required for observing and assessing aid projects and for forthcoming policymaking Banerjee and He, 2008.

Methodology

The Objective of the chapter is to make a review and learn how International aid for education has been functioning to bring changes in the education and betterment. The chapter aims at understanding how aid effectiveness is evolving and improving to attain sustainable outcomes in the domain of education. The chapter attempts to define and address the unresolved problems and challenges encountered rather than prescribing answers to the explicit problems.

The chapter is segregated into sub sections to explain the 1. International aid's impact on the education reviewing the pertinent studies undertaken previously. This section is followed by the 2. discussion on the aid-modalities adopted by the International Aid Organizations to support education. 3.The factors that impede the effective implementation and its success is dealt in the subsequent section. 4.The challenges faced by the International aid organizations in terms of budgetary assistance, governmental and other partnership supports, capacity utilization and development aspects. The last section is on the conclusion.

Institutional Architecture of International Aid

Though foreign aid began for the revitalization, political influence and more for philanthropic purpose during the World war two. The United states Marshall Plan to support the reconstruction of European Nations specifically the 14 Nation with a transfer of sizeable funds of 13 Billion Dollars in the year 1948 focused to aid the education. The chief inspiration was to develop Technology based schools, televised education, uplift folk development colleges, diversified educational arena, and to promote bi-lingual education (Heyneman, 2006a). The focus of Government, private Foundation Organization and the Non-Governmental Organizations had their own Agenda points in terms of elevating the education paradigm. Foundations such as Ford and as well the Foundations of Carnegie had strenuous emphasis on the higher education, on the other side the Soros Foundation was working to assist and uplift the primary secondary educations, plus substantial focus on the civic educational aspects through their financial aid and assistance. The Multilevel funding organizations extending huge financial aid for augmenting education across the globe includes UNICEF (United Nations Children's Fund), UNESCO (United Nations Educational, Scientific and Cultural Organization), World Bank, world Health Organization (WHO) (Moyo,2009, Singh,2011). Along with these Multilateral International funding Organizations, the other Organizations such as the Asian Development Bank, Japan International Cooperation Agency (JICA), Inter-American Development Bank, Department of International Development, UK(DFID) and U.S Agency for International Development (USAID) perform a laudable role in inspiring the education of the world Nations through their consistent International aid and financial support mechanism.

The source of International aid for education flows predominantly through bilateral Organizations to an extent to 75% flows from bilateral Funding Organizations. The balance percentage funds are through multilateral organizations. The major contribution towards education from multilateral Organization is made by the World Bank followed by the European Union, the Inter-American and the Asian Development Banks also makes considerably high contribution to the Education assistance program.

The emphasis of education aid of Bilateral Organizations is more based on the domestic interests of the funds receiving nations. The interest areas include bilingual language promotion, diversified education program and technical schools and college packaged program. Though the all-time priority of International education aid is always towards basic primary education, the International aid funding is diverted towards other vivid significances such as adult literacy program, woman education, training of trainers specifically teachers, higher education, vocational education, technical education and as well science education events and programs.

The International aid to education looks similar but there are certain subtle differences based on the mission of the Organizations providing the financial aid. For instance, the organizations which is related to the Agriculture and Food focuses on funding the rural education, the funds diverted by the World Health Organization is more towards the Health and education allied with the Health and hygiene.

International Aid to Education: What Works and What does not Work

Several ongoing research studies have shared their findings stating that evaluation of the impact of International aid on improving the health interventions are much more perceptible than the impact on the

International Organizations' Aid

education. However, while assessing the contribution the International aid has on the service delivery mechanism, the challenges experienced are much similar, be it the health sector or the education sector. The specific reason being the attributions are complicated and are of multifaceted nature in both the cases, when we specifically look at these aspects one could understand the underlying similarities and difficulties. For instance, when it comes to education, the swiftness at which the distribution of the books and learning material are made has a very strong impact on the success and efforts of the International aid program. This is similar in the case of the Health aid program where the success depends on the swiftness at which the anti-malarial bed nets and tablets for the curing the diseases are distributed. Further determining and quantifying the outcome of the international aid is very much difficult as there are many more factors that acts for and against the success of such health care and educational program alongside the International aid factor. To further ensure a wholistic and sustainable development of education is further difficult as it needs collective involvement and devotion of the economic, political, social and all the other allied sectors cooperation and synergy to make it long lasting and consistent program.

Steered Efforts to Weigh the Impact of International Aid on Education

When it is looked at the quantum of leap in the International aid for education, one could understand that there has been a huge increase from the year 1995 to 2010 and then after by a whooping percentage of 360 percent. When the stats on International aid on different levels of education indicates that in the 1995s the aid to the basic education was to an extent of 19 percentage of the total aid, close to 12 percentage for the secondary level of education and the percentage of aid to post-secondary education was much less to the tune of 1 percentage. Where as in the 2010 almost after a decade and a half the table turned around and the contribution of International aid to the post-secondary education was to the extent of 40%, the contribution of aid to the secondary level was 10 percentage and the aid to basic education grew up to 30 percentage. Whereas the recent studies on the recent past decades of the time period (Michaelowa and Birchler, 2016) states their percentage of international aid on education towards different levels keeps changing but the challenge remains in assessing the impact the International aid has made on education and the underlying outcomes. Though it has been reported that impact of the International aid has been laying more focus on the rate of enrollment at the basic level than concentrating on to evaluate and measure the improvement achieved in terms of the quality of education due to the International aid mechanism.

In the recent past this limitation of measuring the outcome of the impact of the International aid on education has been rectified by way of creating the scientific indicators through various measures. Some of the initiatives includes the PISA measure which is Program for International student assessment, PIRLs-Progress in International Reading Literacy study initiatives, TIMSS which refers to the Trends in International Mathematics and Science Study, other regional studies such as the SACMEQ refers to the Southern and Eastern African Consortium for Monitoring Educational Quality and yet another analysis which is commonly referred to in African countries as PASEC -Program on the Analysis of Education Systems of the Conference of Ministers of Education of Francophone Africa.

However, the International Aid Organization strongly focuses still on the attainment of the Millennium Development Goals (MDGs) and Sustainable Development Goals (SDGs). More thrust is rested on the feeding of the school children, girl child education through scholarship provisions to ensure pre-mature school dropouts, constructions of schools and specifically class rooms, educational and training of the teachers, extending assistance in developing and up grading the school curriculum through expert panels are some of the focus areas of aid program of the International Organizations.

Longitudinal study conducted by (Dreher et al.2008) attempts to evaluate the International aid's impact on education by applying production function approach. The study is conducted over a period of time (between 1970 to 2000) involving 96 middle- and lower-income nations. The results of the study imply the impact of the International aid has enhanced the enrolment of the primary education by an overall range of 2.5 to 5 percent. There have been several studies performed to gauge the impact of International educational aid on the school effectiveness with regard the increase in the quantum of school enrolment and impact on the teaching and learning outcomes.

International Aid for Education and School Effectiveness Research

The early research conducted by the donor countries on their contribution made in the form of aid towards the education betterment of the underdeveloped countries identified that though the aid helps in enhancing the school enrolment numbers, its impact on the quality of education was not evidences. However, the research conducted by the recipient under developed country researchers proved that the factors such as the family background, support and guidance proved to be more impactful on attaining learning achievement than the impact of the International aid and assistance. However, the research conclusions were challenged by the other contemporary researchers since 1989 and then after (Riddell, 1989, 2008). However, the school effectiveness research is continued to explore more on the learning assessments and the educational quality attributes connected to the International aid process. (Wagner, 2011)

Research Trials with Randomized Controlled Efforts

The research conducted by the donors have taken a different focus on the objective of research in recent times, the focus is more on understanding the results and impact of the International aid and assistance provided and the expenditure incurred by way of conducting randomized controlled trials research (RCTs). The focus on the educational policy perspective, and educational methodology and processes which were the focal point of earlier research were now found to lose its priority and importance.

The study conducted in Cambodia (Ferreira et al., 2009) on the poor students living in the rural areas of Cambodia indicates that the conditional cash transfer (CCT) program has a strong impact on the attendance of children than on their learning effectiveness. The eighteen months' study did not show any evidence in terms of their marks in the subjects like Mathematics' and English vocabulary compared to the control group of students taken up for the study. This leads to a glaring and obvious conclusion that the aid just ensures students to attend the educational institution but have not made any impact in the marks they score and the assimilation of the subject knowledge. The study conducted on the education assistance in the form of scholarship offering to the children of Bogota, Colombia reveals that the rate of enrolment and pass percentage of the children has gone up at the graduation and matriculation school level because of the scholarships assistance offered to them. (Barrera-Osorio, 2008).

The study conducted by Nin-O-Zarazu'a and Masino (2016) deploying both experimental and Quasi-experimental research on to understand what actually works in favor of augmenting educational quality. The results of the study indicated that the educational policy is the core aspect and when these policies are well implemented taking other interventions alongside with the policy, which will prove to be more successful in providing quality and holistic education.

International Organizations' Aid

It is obvious from the research conducted through randomized control trials (RCT) or through effective school research that no single approach can be formulated to say that this is the best approach and a wholistic approach that would provide us the success formulae for education. The research results of Glewwe and Kremer (2005) aimed at studying the impact of the educational outcomes availing International assistance divulges that providing financial aid towards education through International sources have very minimum impact on the learning and development and all the other allied interventions and factors needs to be given utmost importance as these factors in some form or the other impacts the education considerably.

Inter-Linkages between International Aid's Specific Contribution and Overall Impact on Education

With the advent of technology and innovative planning has helped to establish the linkages between the specific contributions made by the International funding sources for education and the overall impact the international aid has made on the education in particular and other facets of education in general.

The International aid system for the betterment of education are well knitted with the Government ministries of education, NGOs and other regional department of the nation's predominantly. This enable systematic and logical planning of the funds management and development of the information management systems (EMIS) related to the education. Formulating and executing the plans based on the EMIS by itself forms a major part of the International aid to education. The strong and robust data derived out of the International aid helps ineffective planning and addressing of the problems related to enrollment of the students, expansion of the schools, assistance to the teachers to upgrade their skills and knowledge through training. If the data collection and data storage efforts had not been done scientifically through the aid, it would be very difficult to identify the gaps that exists in the education provisions. For instance, the data on the student teacher ratio, students and number of class rooms requirements, standard text books supply required and for that matter even the number of washrooms and bathrooms required for a given population of students helps the planners to determine where from they need to start the development initiatives. Therefore, such mapping of the needs has helped to determine the success of the educational reforms which are funded through the International aid. With the help of the data of EMIS generated through the education aid has evidently proved that gender inequality issues and school dropout instances could be brought down through the Scholarships offered specifically to the girl children in many nations. The success of the aid to education of course depends on the successful planning initiative, but the real success of these aid program depends on how defectively the planned programs are culminating and bringing positive and better educational outcomes (Bray and Varghese, 2011; Riddell, 2009).

Factors Limiting the Effectiveness of the International Aid on Education

Overlap and Duplications of the Program: The purpose of the funds deployed by multiple International Organizations to assists education of a nation may have a duplication effect. For instance, when we look at the efforts and assistance rendered by Asian Development Bank and the World Bank's to provide textbooks to the children of Kyrgyzstan at the same period of time ended up offering two sets of same text books to the children pointlessly. One set of textbooks offered through World Bank aid project and the other set of same text book offered from the Asian Development Bank.

Capabilities to Collect and Retrieve Pertinent Data on the Education System: To channelize the International education aid, the countries should be able to hold authentic data on the current situation of their education system. However, there is an inability among the nations to collect the pertinent data by way of conducting scientific research, resulting in non-availability of vital data and appropriate information on their country's education system on age wise break of students, data points on their academic achievements, and expenditures made on the education of the nation. This naturally would mis guide the International funding agencies who would not be able to gauge the impact of their aid on the education, post and pre-instance scenario.

Fluctuation and Shortfall of the Funds: Though budget of UNESCO is substantially high towards education upliftment when compared to the US research funds of the university it is substantially low and only accounts for 50 percentage of the US University research funds. The point is the fund allocation to the countries has to be planned only based on the available budget in hand with UNESCO. Many a times the needs and requirements of the recipient countries are much more than the funds available with UNESCO. This leads to a situation of shortfall and inadequacy now and then. The year on year fund allocation of World Bank towards education has not changed and has not seen any steep rise, this also proves to be demotivating factor for the recipient countries who are craving for funds to enhance the standard of education. Instances of corruptions, misappropriation of the funds meant for education, occasions where educational aid funds get diverted to other priority activities related to commercial crisis of the nations and for military and defense emergencies of the country.

Contradiction and Discrepancy in Funds and Budget Management: Certain developing nations who are more or less self-reliant and capable of managing their educational expenses on their own funds seek for International aid from other developed countries with their domestic funds and resources. When these countries deploy huge amount of their funds to space research, spend more on defense revival and nuclear arsenals why is not possible to for them to re-budget their educational budgets effectively by rationalizing their domestic urgencies meticulously.

Reliance on International Aid for Education: Most of the African countries are exhibiting their dependency towards the International aid for the education program is again is definitely a matter of concern. These countries rely and depend on International aid to an extent of 50 to 70 percentage of their educational budgets which is again a pitiable situation.

TYPES OF INTERNATIONAL AID

The principal type of International aid is Multilateral aid, Bilateral aid, Military aid and humanitarian aid. The major form of International aid aimed at business and commercial outcomes is Foreign direct investment (FDI). This includes the asset in the form of equity holding by the nonresident (donors) in a foreign recipient country. Instances of American companies having equity holding in Nigerian or any other African company is a good example of FDI. The Global FDI has reached a peak of 1.7 trillion dollars in 2019.

The second most important type of International aid provided by the Governmental, Non-Governmental and nonprofit organizations to fight against the menace of poverty and allied problems of the nation. These initiatives of helping the developing and underdeveloped countries is primarily done by economically well to do and wealthier countries who are part of OECD (Organization for Economic Co-operation and Development). The OECD countries keep spending 100 billion dollars to 150 billion

International Organizations' Aid

dollars every year and the spending figures reached a whooping height of 162 billion dollars due to the Covid -19 pandemic across the globe.

The next important type is foreign trade, which is relatively larger and is the single pointer indicating the development and growth of the poor nations. These free trade policies go along well hand in hand with the political stability and economic freedom of the countries mutually involved.

Features of Bilateral International Aid

The Bilateral International aid is a state-run and managed aid. In this form of aid the transaction of the aid is made directly from the donor country's government to the recipient country. The focus of these Bilateral aids is towards the growth of the recipient country's economic status, education, poverty alleviation. The limitation or the demerit of this type of aid is, this predominantly involves cash transfers from the donor nation to the recipient country. The possibilities and instances of corruptions, and diversion of funds for other purposes such as military and defense. Sometimes directing of funds towards education programs where there is scope for the Government to make propaganda and promotion of their achievement which would help them to win political elections also happens very often.

Military Aid as a Form of International Aid

Another common form of International aid is the Military aid provided by the donor country to the recipient country. This normally happens in the form of the recipient country buys the arms and ammunitions from the donor country for which assistance is extended or the defense contracts for buying arms are signed by both the receiving and donating nations. The best example for this aid the support and transactions that happens between the United states of America and Israel, for this year 2020, 3.3 billion transaction of arm deal has materialized.

Norms of the Multilateral Aid

There is not much difference between the Multilateral and the bilateral banks, the prime difference is instead of flow of funds from one Government of the nation the money gets pooled from many Governments and then get transferred to the needy nations in the form of Multilateral aid. These multilateral aids are pooled by world Bank and the aid is directed towards various forms of welfare and developmental programs of the recipient nation.

Humanitarian Aid Assistances Features

This is yet another form of Bilateral aid which is focused more towards short-term aids and assistance extended to the recipient nations. The best example of this types of aid is the assistance that was extended by the wealthy nations to the Countries in the South Asian Coastal regions when there was an earth Quake which had 9.0 Richter which triggered a Tsunami which lead to the sad death of 20,000 lives. Humanitarian aids by and large receive more private funding when compared to the other forms of findings.

World Bank's Aid for Education

The World Bank has ramped up the support to 62 countries specifically to support the entire gamut of education form basic level to the higher education levels. The world bank's overall commitment towards education upliftment across the globe in the financial year ending was 2020, US$5.3 Billion, which is considered to be the highest assistance aid offered towards education in the recent times. The Bank is likely to provide additional funds to the tune of 6.2 billion US$ in the year 2021. The World Banks has given the directive to its aid recipients to have a three-phase agenda during the pre and post pandemic situation. The first phase is to focus on the coping mechanism to restore the education to its normalcy level, the second phase is to manage the continuity and sustainability of the educational standards, and the third phase is to improve and accelerate the education pace so as to cope up with the lost opportunity of knowledge acquisition and assimilation of the students.

The world Bank has been able provide policy advisory assistance to 65 countries by leveraging partnership with UNICEF, University of Harvard, University of John Hopkins, University of Oxford, UNESCO, OECD and others alike). In the process the services and aid are being extended to 400 million students and 16 million teachers from the list of countries the bank is serving currently.

Approaches for Providing International Aid for Education

The two approaches or the modes that are commonly seen in providing the International aid for education to the recipient countries are the Sector -wide approach (SWAp), Program-based approach (PBAs) and Budget support. These approaches had come into play from 1990s and primarily tried in the health and education domain and was tested in Africa first and then was extended to the other countries later.

The Program based approach came into practice as the certain agencies which were involved in the development pursuit of education did not want their resources to be controlled by the government and they were preferring to channelize their resources and funds through Non -Governmental Organizations (NGOs) and Civil Society Organizations (CSOs) working in the education filed directly who may or may not want to be encompassed with the "SWAp" donors (UNESCO,2007)

Role of SWAps and PBAs in the Upliftment of Education

The main purpose of comprehending SWAps is to take care and address the stand-alone project's subtle weaknesses and also to reap the benefit of donors who are working jointly to serve the countries receiving the International Aid. Over a period of time as SWAps were able to get established well in a greater number of countries. SWAps formulated and incorporated aid procedures and modalities of operation which could also enable the inclusion of the project aid which were capable of offering sustainable and were able to contribute substantially contributing towards the growth and development of education domain and build local capacities. The international aid offered through the SWAps has been consistently growing year on year as per the data of EFA Global Monitoring Report, this has been consistently growing since 2000 onwards at varied percentages ranging between 31 percentages to 54 percentages.

Budget Support

In the recent times, directing the International aid through the national budget has become a very common phenomenon. Though the percentage and quantum of aid is quite small in some of the countries it has encompassed to an extent of 30 percentage of the formal and official international aid. In the countries like Uganda, Ethiopia, Burkina Faso and Tanzania (Advisory Board for Irish Aid report, 2008). An intricate step by step evaluation of General Budget support was done on a very large scale (IDD and Associates,2006) involving seven countries. The results of the study have revealed that with the increase in the expenditure and with enhanced expenditure on the education resulting out of the PGBS (Partnership General Budget Support) indicates that though there is substantial expansions' have been evident the expansion has been done at the cost of compromising the quality. Similar opinions have been indicated in the study conducted on Budget support at Rwanda and Mali (Williamson and Dom,2010). The study results speak extensively upon the un-professional way of functioning of the donor staff of the in-country. It is also indicated the department of Policy and Planning Department comprises of personnel with economics and finance backgrounds. Though they have the expertise in their field of specialization, they absolutely have no understanding on how to discuss with the service providers who are always in the frontline operations of the project. The core discussion of this department always surmounts around the budgeting and planning of the project than on subjects related to service delivery and implementation which is the most vital part. Such situation not only has impact on the weakened communications and dialogues with the ministries of education but also has a strong impact on the initiation and conduct of the research related to the policy aspect on education on behalf of the ministries of education.

LESSONS LEARNT RE INTERNATIONAL AID'S INFLUENCE ON EDUCATION

There are a greater number of examples of research conducted in the developing countries to illustrate the impact of the International aid on education however it has not been scaled up further. Glewwe and Kremer (2005) draw he importance of looking at the results at a wider prospect and to contextualize the interventions appropriately. Further the research draws the importance of contextualization and also cautions that instead of just looking at following the best practices suggested by the studies and working on the cost control measures one should focus more on the growth and evolution of the Education system per say and on its sustainable and continuous improvement. The study conducted by Pritchett (2008) indicates three major consideration to be made while conducting the International aid impact studies, the first and foremost point being consideration of the schools at the same platform whether it is public or private, the second is research conducted engaging the policy makers should lay equal concentration on disseminating the findings and results of the conducted research. And the third point is to be conscious that they research should focus on how to scale the innovative results identified.

The experiences shared by The European Commission (2010) on the Impact of International aid on education shares the experiences had with specifically the developing nations. The most significant lesson learnt is the importance of conducting a wholistic study from the primary level to lifelong learning, further adds that education has to looked at beyond and specifically the impact it makes on one's Profession and employment attained after the formal education. The next important lesson indicates the underlying linkages between the quality aspect of quality education, inclusive and sustainable education. For example, the linkages between the compensation offered to the teachers and quality of education. The research on International aid for the education has drawn valuable points helped to strategize and implement the decentralization in the domain of education management in various nations. The limitation of encouraging the decentralization is they may experience the difficulty of getting resourced poorly. The international donor agencies do not recommend the usage of the aid for the payment of the salary of the teachers directly as they consider the responsibility of paying the salary and doing such allied expenditure should be responsibility of the Government of the respective recipient nation. However, one could see a change in the outlook of the funding agencies on introduction of sector-wide support initiatives.

A study was performed to establish the association and connection between the two variables, the learning scores and the outcome of education(Based on Quality and Quantity metrics) supported through International aid (Education Policy and Data Center,2018).The findings of the study on examining the data of 25 developing countries reveals that strong relationship does not exist between the learning scores of the students who have studied through the aid received out of the International funding and the students' entry rate, primary school children's attendance rate and as well the balanced and stable pupil teachers ratio. Thus, the findings obviously indicate the so-called claims and achievements and laurels of education achieved through the International aids is of pyrrhic eminence and possibly making the ordeal to win not worth it.

Technical Collaboration, Knowledge Transfer, Skills-Capacity Development

The biggest problem which is being encountered by the International Organizations' while funding for the education project is the blind spot related to the capacity building of the team which is supposed to implement and execute the Project formulated. The issue is not that the capacity building is not given much importance, on the contrary every donor looks at this aspect with utmost importance and gives priority. The reality is there is great problem in terms of how the capacity building process is approached, in fact huge sum of money and time is spent in capacity building process (European Commission,2006).

There are very good principles and lessons developed by projects on the best practices related to capacity development, worth mentioning is the Agenda of Action (2018) Project lays emphasis on the importance of proper planning, effective management and high caliber co-ordination as the important traits of capacity building. Further the capacity development process also encompasses the training aspects of the individuals involved in the project not only to upgrade their skills and knowledge but also improve their understanding on the governance and enhance their skills on efficient management of project. (OECD,2016).

Extensive research carried out by UNESCO's sub division unit on education known as IIEP (International Institute for Education Planning) on capacity development specifically in the education sector states on the existence of high influence of the donors on capacity building. The examples referred in the research includes the two cases where the capacity development in education planning project which were conducted at Bangladesh and Guyana (Riddell,2011).

Approaches Related to "Transferability" of International Aid Assisted Educational Program

The uniqueness of these project is conceptualizing the education aid projects based on the context of the political economy of the recipient nation, plus based on the Governmental and the ministerial support received. There is always a great support solicited from the local and regional bodies who are taking

International Organizations' Aid

up these educational aid projects. The knowledge built out of studying the success and failure of the International aid for education interventions offers an indicative guidelines for taking the learning to the other projects and ensure success if some modifications are made keeping in mind the contextual and local situations of the projects undertaken. However, the success of the educational aid program predominantly depends on the effective planning and systematic implementation.

Importance of Scalability of Aid-Supported Educational Program

The most important lessons to be learnt while evaluating the effectiveness of international aid to education is to look at the project in a very holistic way and have a very systematic view of the whole project. This is mostly put across in the education sector's development plans of the nations. The biggest challenge which has been attributed in terms of scaling up the education aid project is effective and proper documentation; this was also indicated in the study conducted by Samoff et al (2011). This study points out on the lack of documentation of the pilot education reforms of Africa if the documentation of the successful pilot projects is made effectively than this documentation would have supported in scaling up the lessons of the successful pilot projects initiatives up to the national levels. The findings draw the importance of involving local leadership, bringing the innovations at each of the projects as per the local demand.

The study results of Gillies (2010) on how to scale the results of the pilot projects indicates that the most important aspect to be focused is to initiate the stakeholder concerned to take sincere ownership of the project and have leadership orientation at all the levels to bring consistency and sustainability of the project's success. Word Bank keeps guiding and giving directives related to the modalities of International aid periodically. The guidelines for the recipient countries includes the following: the commitment shown by the nation to improve and bring in educational policy changes, effective management and governance of the projects, establishing strong policies and inculcate dedication and involvement of the leadership team towards the project specifically at the country level and generally at all the levels.

Similarly, the World Bank directives for the donors to enable the program to scale up was given on the following parameters: providing external support to bring in changes and ensure capacity building, provide adequate financial resources for scaling up of the project, enable the Government and people in authority to see the value for money aspect while the scaling of the project is done

EFFECTIVENESS OF THE INTERNATIONAL AID FOR EDUCATION

The general notions on the International aid for education works well i) if the aid and support is extended to very poor nations ii) the education aid works well if the support is extended to the country which has very strong policy backup and well managed systems in place iii) the nation which has effective allocation mechanism of the project funding is considered to be more effective in utilizing the International aid (Klein and Harford: 2005: 36-7).

Yet another issue in the measuring of the international aid effectiveness is, measuring the effectiveness of the aid is a very difficult task (Cullen, 2008: 24). The evaluation may be towards a particular problem or a program, but the evaluation is not done on a wholistic manner and hence the results claimed to be success may not be a successful one in real terms. Here are cases were the effectiveness of the education aid is differentiated in terms of giving importance to the project implementation parameters. Wherein

International Organizations' Aid

countries like UK give utmost importance to this parameter of project implementation and connects it strongly with the aid effectiveness aspect and on the contrary Norway and the United States gives less importance while relating the implementation part to aid effectiveness aspect.

International aid towards primary education has been argued to have been moderately effective (Birchler and Michaelowa 2013) in terms of the enrollments but when it comes to Improved learning there is no strong evidence to prove this effectiveness. There have been several arguments to state that the effectiveness of education aid cannot be evaluated that easily for several reasons. The problem of "reverse Causality" has been identified by Michaelowa and Birchler, to enhance the enrollment rate more aid is required. The other challenge encountered in the aid effectiveness studies is the inter-sub- sector or level- complementarities. Though stakeholders concerned will not agree that the there is inter linkages between the educational levels (Primary, secondary and higher levels). However, the recent experiences have indicated that the aid which is used for supporting the education at the higher level has increased the performance of the students at the lower level.

Steps for Improving the International Aid Utilization in Education

Bases on the constant efforts made by the donors and the recipients to overcome the problems related to the aid utilization, there has been lot of recommendations received from different part of the funding fraternity for improvement of the system. The EFA goals to help the education has recommended to the donor countries to consider specific targets and work towards the same to attain the set targets (UNU-WIDER,2014). There has been a strong suggestion towards the aid for the welfare of the community and social sector projects. There is firm recommendation made to ensure the continuity and consistency maintained while supporting International aid for the cause of health, sanitation, hygiene, social protection and more importantly education. Based on meticulous implementation of this recommendation have enabled the school enrollments have increased from 57 to 78% for boys and 50 to 74% for the girls in the African nations in a span of two decades (UNU-WIDER,2014).

The recent innovations made in the designing of the International aid program is the advent of the Results-Based-Aid (RBA). As per this modulated aid approach the targeted results, the recipient nation of the International aid should be prepared to make the reallocation of their own resources so as to attain the set objectives and goals. (Savedoff, 2015). The advantages of this aid system are of multifold. The first point is i) every recipient nation is made accountable for the international aid and assistance they receive. ii) the linkages between the objective and purpose of receiving the aid and the outcome and results to be achieved out of the assistance is made very clear to the recipient Nation's Government, administrators and others concerned iii) The Transparent nature of the RBA in facts make the recipient more accountable, in a way it is made aware to the beneficiaries of the project on what is to be expected and if they don't get what has been projected they can even hold the authorities concerned for the non-deliverable outcomes. iv) Flexibility allowed by the aid agencies to the recipients to have their own discretions in terms of implementation of the project based on the availability of the local knowledge, innovation, capability and resources (Perakis and Savedoff, 2015).

The Organizations like UNESCO which has explicit mandates regarding the education upliftment should reiterate the aspect of intra and inter dependency of the educational subsectors of the private and the public institutions. The Organization also has a strong mandate to discuss, propagate the problems and challenges encountered by them during the process of extending educational aid across the globe.

International Organizations' Aid

This would be an eye opener for donor and the recipient nations and as well speak with the developed and wealthy country like US, Industrial democratic countries and European nations.

Further, the International agencies engaged in the pursuit of funding the educational projects also need to have an in-depth understanding of the changes that are taking place in the education policies of different recipient nations. Further provisions to be made in the aid for the collection of pertinent data through research which are of both primary and secondary in nature. The word Bank in its directive (made in 2012) apportioned sizable funds towards collection and consolidation of the data pertaining to education.

The recommendations made by Meltzer commission (2000) directs that world Bank to take up the responsibility of making a thorough analysis of the problems related to the developmental issues related to the Education aid projects. The commission also suggests the involvement of the regional banks like New Asian Infrastructure Investment Bank (AIIB) to identify, manage and finance the Projects. This will help in much effective implementation of the education aid projects and as well help in de-linking the customary analytical tasks out of the lending agencies and ensure the check and control measures to be undertaken within the country level. When the analytical authority is vested on to the regional banks there is an added advantage for these banks to independently take decisions on what aspect of the aid project that needs to be analyzed and by whom and when these analyses have to be performed. Such measure will ensure the avoidance of monopolistic behavior world Bank in terms of having both the lending and the analytical powers. Plus, this initiative will make the professional agencies within the country to not look at the aid impact on education based on the efficiency but can look the progress of the program even more beyond on a wholistic perspective.

FUTURE RESEARCH DIRECTIONS

The shift in the focus of education aid is moving from the aspect of basic education to higher levels of education, from gender equity to concentrate on holistic growth and development of both the gender's educational needs and from the infrastructural support to offering support towards improvement in quality of education and improvement in standard of education. Therefore, the future research should be focused towards the above mentioned aspects. The capacity development of the recipient nation's staff and other stakeholder is also an important agenda for the donors, however only concentrating on the capacity development will not give a complete improvement of the operation of the projects and its system, this is a real matter of concern to be looked at seriously by both the donors and the recipients of the aid which also requires in-depth research and study.

CONCLUSION

The impact of the International aid on the education of any nation is considered to be very significant and is gaining much importance in the recent times. The controversy in terms of servicing is relatively less compared to the other sectors like banking, agriculture, tourism and manufacturing. The controversy is less as the education sector clearly demarcates the service offerings and responsibilities between private and Government organizations' very clearly.

The aid and investments in the education offers substantial benefits both monetary and non-monetary ones to the individuals in particular and for the nation in general. When it comes to individual benefits, there is direct relationship between better employment opportunity and carrier for the individuals who are educated, their status in the society is elevated because of the education and knowledge acquired out of education, their understanding on the health, hygiene, savings, economic status and overall wellbeing is improved because of the one's education. The benefit derived out education by the nation or the community is enhanced productivity, increased participation of educated citizens in the political and economic pursuits of the country, and overall a social solidarity is attained.

The Education sector as like other sectors also encounters the problems of international development aid problems like undue dependence of financial aid for development and growth of the sector, governmental lobbying during the receipt of international funds and while utilization, problems and menace of corruptions, and lack of institutional building issues.

There is a considerable tilt in the attention of the donor organization towards the quality of education component, there is also evidence that these agencies look at funding the development of Education management Information System, and invest in the tools to access EGRA (Early Grade reading Assessment). However, the point is these measures will not bring about or lead to the improvement of the education system. This has to be seriously viewed and constructive measure should be taken to lay focus on the improvement of the core aspect of education.

Several studies, observations, and experiences have helped the donors and recipients of the international aid for education to identify and understand the problems that lead to the inactiveness of the aid program, but the biggest challenge is the lessons learnt are remaining as lessons learnt, the solutions derived are not implemented in the future project instances.

In the future days to come utmost focus has to be laid on joint and partnership approach of both the donors and recipients. Both the funding agencies and aid receiving countries has the responsibility of working along with the regional partners to address the educational domestic needs and demands of the recipient nation and re allocating the funds according to their local priorities.

In the new era after the pandemic every country will have similar expectations in terms of managing and upholding the health and educational needs of their citizens, so the focus of the international funding organizations should also modulate their objectives and priorities to full fill the needs in a wholistic manner.

Finally, with the advent of technology and new era digitalization measures it is easy to assess the impact of international aid on Health care and education. However, the impact has to be evaluated on a long-term basis. If the aid recipient nation is looking forward to attain a sustainable educational outcome they should not only concentrate on the short-term individual projects but the emphasis should be more on the long-term projects that would redefine the educational system and will have long lasting impacts and bearing on the education in total.

REFERENCES

Addison, T., Niño-Zarazúa, M., & Tarp, F. (2015). Aid, social policy and development. *Journal of International Development*, *27*(8), 1351–1365. doi:10.1002/jid.3187

Alemu, A. M., & Lee, J. S. (2015). Foreign aid on economic growth in Africa: A comparison of low and middle-income countries. *Suid-Afrikaanse Tydskrif vir Ekonomiese en Bestuurswetenskappe, 18*(4), 449–462. doi:10.4102ajems.v18i4.737

Ashtekar, A., & Singh, P. (2011). Loop quantum cosmology: A status report. *Classical and Quantum Gravity, 28*(21), 213001. doi:10.1088/0264-9381/28/21/213001

Banerjee, A., Merugu, S., Dhillon, I. S., Ghosh, J., & Lafferty, J. (2005). Clustering with Bregman divergences. *Journal of Machine Learning Research, 6*(10).

Birchler, K., Limpach, S., & Michaelowa, K. (2016). Aid modalities matter: The impact of different World Bank and IMF programs on democratization in developing countries. *International Studies Quarterly, 60*(3), 427–439. doi:10.1093/isqqw014

Birchler, K., & Michaelowa, K. (2016). Making aid work for education in developing countries: An analysis of aid effectiveness for primary education coverage and quality. *International Journal of Educational Development, 48*, 37–52. doi:10.1016/j.ijedudev.2015.11.008

Blunden, J., & Arndt, D. S. (2012). State of the climate in 2011. *Bulletin of the American Meteorological Society, 93*(7), S1–S282. doi:10.1175/2012BAMSStateoftheClimate.1

Bray, M., & Varghese, N. V. (Eds.). (2011). *Directions in educational planning: International experiences and perspectives.* UNESCO Pub.

Bretzel, F., & Calderisi, M. (2006). Metal contamination in urban soils of coastal Tuscany (Italy). *Environmental Monitoring and Assessment, 118*(1), 319–335. doi:10.100710661-006-1495-5 PMID:16897548

Brod, G., & Breitwieser, J. (2019). Lighting the wick in the candle of learning: Generating a prediction stimulates curiosity. *NPJ Science of Learning, 4*(1), 1–7. doi:10.103841539-019-0056-y PMID:31646002

Brookings, C., Goldmeier, D., & Sadeghi-Nejad, H. (2013). Sexually transmitted infections and sexual function in relation to male fertility. *Korean Journal of Urology, 54*(3), 149–156. doi:10.4111/kju.2013.54.3.149 PMID:23526114

Brus, D. J., Kempen, B., & Heuvelink, G. B. M. (2011). Sampling for validation of digital soil maps. *European Journal of Soil Science, 62*(3), 394–407. doi:10.1111/j.1365-2389.2011.01364.x

Christensen, D. L., Braun, K. V. N., Baio, J., Bilder, D., Charles, J., Constantino, J. N., Daniels, J., Durkin, M. S., Fitzgerald, R. T., Kurzius-Spencer, M., Lee, L.-C., Pettygrove, S., Robinson, C., Schulz, E., Wells, C., Wingate, M. S., Zahorodny, W., & Yeargin-Allsopp, M. (2018). Prevalence and characteristics of autism spectrum disorder among children aged 8 years—Autism and developmental disabilities monitoring network, 11 sites, United States, 2012. *MMWR. Surveillance Summaries, 65*(13), 1–23. doi:10.15585/mmwr.ss6513a1 PMID:30439868

Christensen, L. B., Johnson, B., Turner, L. A., & Christensen, L. B. (2011). Research methods, design, and analysis.

Coelho, J. S., Santos, N. D., Napoleão, T. H., Gomes, F. S., Ferreira, R. S., Zingali, R. B., Coelho, L. C. B. B., Leite, S. P., Navarro, D. M. A. F., & Paiva, P. M. (2009). Effect of Moringa oleifera lectin on development and mortality of Aedes aegypti larvae. *Chemosphere*, *77*(7), 934–938. doi:10.1016/j.chemosphere.2009.08.022 PMID:19747711

Collier, J., & Esteban, R. (2007). Corporate social responsibility and employee commitment. *Business Ethics (Oxford, England)*, *16*(1), 19–33. doi:10.1111/j.1467-8608.2006.00466.x

Denny, L., Adewole, I., Anorlu, R., Dreyer, G., Moodley, M., Smith, T., Snyman, L., Wiredu, E., Molijn, A., Quint, W., Ramakrishnan, G., & Schmidt, J. (2014). Human papillomavirus prevalence and type distribution in invasive cervical cancer in sub-Saharan Africa. *International Journal of Cancer*, *134*(6), 1389–1398. doi:10.1002/ijc.28425 PMID:23929250

Ding, J., & Adeyeye, A. O. (2013). Binary ferromagnetic nanostructures: Fabrication, static and dynamic properties. *Advanced Functional Materials*, *23*(13), 1684–1691. doi:10.1002/adfm.201201432

Dreher, A., & Gaston, N. (2008). Has globalization increased inequality? *Review of International Economics*, *16*(3), 516–536. doi:10.1111/j.1467-9396.2008.00743.x

Dreher, A., Gaston, N., & Martens, P. (2008). Measuring globalisation. In Gauging its Consequences. Springer.

Dreher, A., & Lohmann, S. (2015). Aid and growth at the regional level. *Oxford Review of Economic Policy*, *31*(3-4), 420–446. doi:10.1093/oxrep/grv026

Duflo, E. (2001). Schooling and labor market consequences of school construction in Indonesia: Evidence from an unusual policy experiment. *The American Economic Review*, *91*(4), 795–813. doi:10.1257/aer.91.4.795

Fiszbein, A., & Schady, N. R. (2009). *Conditional cash transfers: reducing present and future poverty*. World Bank Publications. doi:10.1596/978-0-8213-7352-1

Galiani, S., Gertler, P., Ajzenman, N., & Orsola-Vidal, A. (2016). Promoting handwashing behavior: The effects of large-scale community and school-level interventions. *Health Economics*, *25*(12), 1545–1559. doi:10.1002/hec.3273 PMID:26461811

Glewwe, P. (2002). Schools and skills in developing countries: Education policies and socioeconomic outcomes. *Journal of Economic Literature*, *40*(2), 436–482. doi:10.1257/jel.40.2.436

Glewwe, P., & Kremer, M. (2006). Schools, teachers, and education outcomes in developing countries. Handbook of the Economics of Education, 2, 945-1017.

Glewwe, P., Maiga, E., & Zheng, H. (2014). The contribution of education to economic growth: A review of the evidence, with special attention and an application to Sub-Saharan Africa. *World Development*, *59*, 379–393. doi:10.1016/j.worlddev.2014.01.021

Greenaway, D., Gullstrand, J., & Kneller, R. (2005). Exporting may not always boost firm productivity. *Review of World Economics*, *141*(4), 561–582. doi:10.100710290-005-0045-5

International Organizations' Aid

Gyimah-Brempong, K., & Aziedu, E. (2008, November). *Aid and human capital formation: some evidence*. African Development Bank/UNECA Conference on Globalization, Institutions and Economic Development in Africa.

Haenggi, M., Andrews, J. G., Baccelli, F., Dousse, O., & Franceschetti, M. (2009). Stochastic geometry and random graphs for the analysis and design of wireless networks. *IEEE Journal on Selected Areas in Communications, 27*(7), 1029–1046. doi:10.1109/JSAC.2009.090902

Hansen, H., & Tarp, F. (2000). Aid effectiveness disputed. *Journal of International Development, 12*(3), 375–398. doi:10.1002/(SICI)1099-1328(200004)12:3<375::AID-JID657>3.0.CO;2-M

Hanushek, E. A. (1981). Throwing money at schools. *Journal of Policy Analysis and Management, 1*(1), 19–41. doi:10.2307/3324107

Harford, T., & Klein, M. (2005). *Aid and the Resource Curse: How Can Aid Be Designed to Preserve Institutions*. Academic Press.

Hayter, T. (1971). *Aid as imperialism*. Academic Press.

Heyneman, S. P. (2001). The growing international commercial market for educational goods and services. *International Journal of Educational Development, 21*(4), 345–359. doi:10.1016/S0738-0593(00)00056-0

Heyneman, S. P. (2004). Education and corruption. *International Journal of Educational Development, 24*(6), 637–648. doi:10.1016/j.ijedudev.2004.02.005

Heyneman, S. P. (2009). The failure of education for all as political strategy. *Prospects, 39*(1), 5–10. doi:10.100711125-009-9107-0

Heyneman, S. P. (2010). A comment on the changes in higher education in the former Soviet Union. *European Education, 42*(1), 76–87. doi:10.2753/EUE1056-4934420104

Heyneman, S. P. (2012). When models become monopolies: The making of education policy at the World Bank. In *Education strategy in the developing world: Revising the World Bank's education policy*. Emerald Group Publishing Limited. doi:10.1108/S1479-3679(2012)0000016007

Heyneman, S. P., & De Young, A. J. (Eds.). (2006). *The challenges of education in Central Asia*. IAP.

Kremer, M., & Holla, A. (2009). Improving education in the developing world: What have we learned from randomized evaluations? *Annual Review of Economics, 1*(1), 513–542. doi:10.1146/annurev.economics.050708.143323 PMID:23946865

Krishnaratne, S., & White, H. (2013). *Quality education for all children? What works in education in developing countries*. International Initiative for Impact Evaluation (3ie).

Masino, S., & Niño-Zarazúa, M. (2016). What works to improve the quality of student learning in developing countries? *International Journal of Educational Development, 48*, 53–65. doi:10.1016/j.ijedudev.2015.11.012

Methé, B. A., Nelson, K. E., Pop, M., Creasy, H. H., Giglio, M. G., Huttenhower, C., ... Mannon, P. J. (2012). A framework for human microbiome research. *Nature, 486*(7402), 215.

Michaelowa, K., & Weber, A. (2006). Aid effectiveness in the education sector: A dynamic panel analysis. In *Theory and practice of foreign aid*. Emerald Group Publishing Limited.

Michaelowa, K., & Weber, A. (2008). *Aid effectiveness in primary, secondary and tertiary education*. Background paper prepared for the Education for All Monitoring Report.

Moyo, D. (2009). Why foreign aid is hurting Africa. *The Wall Street Journal, 21*, 1-2.

Oshewolo, S. (2011). Poverty Reduction and the Attainment of the MDGS in Nigeria: Problems and Prospects. *Africana, 5*(2), 211–238.

Perakis, R., & Savedoff, W. (2015). Does results-based aid change anything? Pecuniary interests, attention, accountability and discretion in four case studies. *CGD Policy Paper, 52*.

Psacharopoulos, G., & Arriagada, A. M. (1986). The educational composition of the labour force: An international comparison. *Int'l Lab. Rev., 125*, 561.

Reynolds, A. D., Kadiu, I., Garg, S. K., Glanzer, J. G., Nordgren, T., Ciborowski, P., Banerjee, R., & Gendelman, H. E. (2008). Nitrated alpha-synuclein and microglial neuroregulatory activities. *Journal of Neuroimmune Pharmacology, 3*(2), 59–74. doi:10.100711481-008-9100-z PMID:18202920

Richardson, I. E. (2004). *H. 264 and MPEG-4 video compression: video coding for next-generation multimedia*. John Wiley & Sons.

Riddell, R. (2008). *Does foreign aid really work?* Oxford University Press.

Robins, H. S., Campregher, P. V., Srivastava, S. K., Wacher, A., Turtle, C. J., Kahsai, O., ... Carlson, C. S. (2009). Comprehensive assessment of T-cell receptor β-chain diversity in αβ T cells. *Blood. The Journal of the American Society of Hematology, 114*(19), 4099–4107. PMID:19706884

Rosenzweig, M. R., & Schultz, T. P. (1982). Market opportunities, genetic endowments, and intrafamily resource distribution: Child survival in rural India. *The American Economic Review, 72*(4), 803–815.

Rostow, W. W., & Rostow, W. W. (1990). *The stages of economic growth: A non-communist manifesto*. Cambridge University Press.

St-Jacques, B., Hammerschmidt, M., & McMahon, A. P. (1999). Indian hedgehog signaling regulates proliferation and differentiation of chondrocytes and is essential for bone formation. *Genes & Development, 13*(16), 2072–2086. doi:10.1101/gad.13.16.2072 PMID:10465785

Stead, R. H., Dixon, M. F., Bramwell, N. H., Riddell, R. H., & Bienenstock, J. (1989). Mast cells are closely apposed to nerves in the human gastrointestinal mucosa. *Gastroenterology, 97*(3), 575–585. doi:10.1016/0016-5085(89)90627-6 PMID:2666250

Tarp, F., & Director, U. N. U. (2009). *Aid effectiveness*. A Note Prepared Based Both on Joint Work with Channing Arndt and Sam Jones Including an Unpublished Report for NORAD and 2009 UNU-WIDER Research Paper Entitled "Aid and Growth: Have We Come Full Circle?" Dated September 2009, 1-22.

Wagner, A. (2011). *The origins of evolutionary innovations: a theory of transformative change in living systems*. OUP Oxford. doi:10.1093/acprof:oso/9780199692590.001.0001

International Organizations' Aid

Wagner, L., & D'Aiglepierre, R. D. J. (2010). *Aid and Universal Primary Education* (No. 201022). Academic Press.

Weber, M. (2008). The business case for corporate social responsibility: A company-level measurement approach for CSR. *European Management Journal*, *26*(4), 247–261. doi:10.1016/j.emj.2008.01.006

Weber, M., Hellmann, I., Stadler, M. B., Ramos, L., Pääbo, S., Rebhan, M., & Schübeler, D. (2007). Distribution, silencing potential and evolutionary impact of promoter DNA methylation in the human genome. *Nature Genetics*, *39*(4), 457–466. doi:10.1038/ng1990 PMID:17334365

Williamson, T., & Dom, C. (2010). *Sector budget support in practice. Synthesis report, Overseas Development Institute and Mokoro*. ODI.

KEY TERMS AND DEFINITIONS

MDG: The Millennium Development Goals (MDGs) were eight international development goals for the year 2015 that had been established following the Millennium Summit of the United Nations in 2000.

NGO: Stands for non-governmental organization. Typically, it is a voluntary group or institution with a social mission, which operates independently from the government.

SDG: Sustainable Development Goals (SDGs), also known as the Global Goals, were adopted by the United Nations in 2015 as a universal call to action to end poverty, protect the planet, and ensure that by 2030 all people enjoy peace and prosperity.

Chapter 13
Policy Framework and Planning in Global Institutions

Mukund Vasant Deshpande
Independent Researcher, India

ABSTRACT

Global institutions play a central role in developing nations. Each nation has its own identity, and therefore, single policy for one nation rarely matches with the other. As a result, a variety of dimensions is essentially searched while planning a policy especially in a global institution. Although policies on food, habitation, and clothing are considered as common need of people in the globe, peoples' living entirely depends upon variety of characteristics such as their philosophy, environment, and desire to make development creating heavy influence on policy making. Therefore, this chapter is planned to understand how ideas and concepts are developed amongst the policy designers and converted into policy making.

INTRODUCTION

Global Institutions, as the title suggests, play a central role in developing the nations. A nation is unique due to its upbringing history and as such, each nation has its own set of laws for better living and governance that mainly follows manmade rules. Designing the policies is frequently a complex task owing to the rise of diverse challenges. Although the base of Global Institutions by and large rely on various factors such as religions, castes, languages, environment and governance that are diverse characteristics of human life, their goal is to set policies for better living in the society and therefore their ability of developing ideas is the essence in the planning of policies. Uniform policy amongst all nations, for those reasons, is difficult to set. Other side of the challenge includes diverse geographical and environmental conditions that heavily influence the living conditions of people. As such, policy design by Global Institution for one nation occasionally matches the other. Global Institutions therefore face intricate situation to design and implement generalized policy covering all of them. The impact of global multilateral institutions (Boas Morten, 2003) such as the World Bank, UNO, and IMF have on development is severely debated, but few doubt their power and influence. Therefore, the main aim of this chapter is to examine the concepts that have powerfully influenced development policy and, more

DOI: 10.4018/978-1-6684-2448-3.ch013

Copyright © 2022, IGI Global. Copying or distributing in print or electronic forms without written permission of IGI Global is prohibited.

Policy Framework and Planning in Global Institutions

broadly, look at the role of ideas in these institutions and how they have affected current development discourse. Policy is an action that is designed for the user to operate when certain conditions evolve. The role of policy makers is important since they have to satisfy the goal of national development that comes up by addressing challenges. So far, the policy-making path has been settled to consist of Definitions, Roles and Responsibilities, Policy Development Guide and Template, Policy Approval, Implementation and Communication, Retention and Storage, Review Process, Compliance. While a policy framework is known to consist of a document that lays down a set of procedures or goals, which might be used in negotiation or decision-making to guide a more detailed set of policies, or to guide ongoing maintenance of an organization's policies. Boas Morten (2003) reports key topics such as poverty, global governance; sustainable development and the environment are closely examined, with detailed case studies of the World Bank, the WTO, the IMF, Asian Development Bank, UN Development Programme and the OECD's Development Assistance Committee.

The impact multilateral institutions such as the World Bank and IMF have on development is hotly debated, but few doubt their power and influence. This chapter examines the concepts that have powerfully influenced development policy and, more broadly, looks at the role of ideas in international development institutions and how they have affected current development discourse. The authors analyze why these institutions take up some ideas, how the ideas travel within the systems and how they are translated into policy, modified, distorted or resisted. Well-known dimensions of development are finance, economy, technology, and public administration in a nation and the role of Global Institutions like World Bank, IMF, UNO, or ILO is to assist in developing the nations. Prime challenge in a national development is its economic condition and the mindset of the governing people, which is responsible for its survival and growth whilst social and economic development relies on ideas, and concepts that come from various levels of the society. This unique chapter explores a very broad range of ideas and institutions and provides thorough and detailed case studies in the context of broader theoretical analysis. Recent research has paid growing attention to the role of policy networks—the actors involved in policy-making, their relationships with each other, and the structure formed by those relationships.

The chapter is planned and written using a method of review of literature. In the literature review process, adopt the principles of a systematic review as recommended by Jesson, Matherson and Lacy (2011). First, a research plan is developed comprising the research questions that are of interest in answering, the keywords, and a set of inclusion and exclusion criteria. Focus is directed on the status of research into Knowledge Management benefits to identify promising areas for future study.

BACKGROUND

UNDP (2021) has stated that the United Nations adopted the Sustainable Development Goals (SDGs), also known as the Global Goals, in 2015 as a universal call to action to end poverty, protect the planet, and ensure that by 2030 all people enjoy peace and prosperity. The 17 SDGs are integrated—they recognize that action in one area will affect outcomes in others, and that development must balance social, economic and environmental sustainability. Countries have committed to prioritize progress for those who are furthest behind. The SDGs are designed to end poverty, hunger, AIDS, and discrimination against women and girls. The creativity, knowhow, technology and financial resources from all of society is necessary to achieve the SDGs in every context.

245

Policy Design Logic

Peters (2018) has stated that scholars and the individuals involved in making public policy use a variety of words to describe how they actually arrive at the content of those policies. Perhaps the most commonly used word is "formulation" (see Jordan and Turnpenny, 2015), but words such as creation, innovation, and development are also used to describe the process of finding some form of intervention to confront a policy problem. The hope is always that the policy that is formulated or created will be able to "solve" the problem, and that government (and citizens) can go on to cope with the next problem that arises. When Herbert Simon (1996, 111) wrote that "everyone designs who devises courses of action aimed at changing existing situations into preferred ones", the definition was somewhat generic but was definitely speaking to policy design.

Meaning of Global Institutions

Wagg (2015) reported that Global governance refers to the way in which global affairs are managed. As there is no global government global institutions have been created to fill this role and facilitate issues arising in the living conditions of the human beings. Guay (2016) reports that the International Organization for Migration (IOM) is a worldwide organization in the field of migration that has played an increasingly important role in international migration governance. First established in 1951, the IOM finally joined the United Nations System in September 2016.The organization is inter-governmental by status, which means it represents its member states. With 166 nations as members, the IOM has offices in more than 100 countries. Its activities are broad and revolve around four areas: migration and development, facilitating migration, regulating migration and addressing forced migration. The core of the IOM's mission is to promote international cooperation alongside a 'humane and orderly management' of migration. It is committed to encouraging social and economic development through migration and to upholding the well-being and human rights of migrants.

Obama (2013) has reported that the World Bank is clearly one of the most influential global inter-governmental operators for international development assistance. In recent decades, the Bank and other agencies have invested immense technical and financial resources in a troubled and unprecedented mission of revitalizing and restructuring the development of education in Africa. A growing body of critique has emerged that articulates the failures of the revitalization mission, framing these exchange relationships as representing nothing but new patterns of embedded neocolonialism, dependency, and geopolitical asymmetry.

Activities of Global Institutions

Benedict (2001) has reported that, "Global governance is a purposeful order that emerges from institutions, processes, norms, formal agreements, and informal mechanisms that regulate action for a common good. Global governance encompasses activity at the international, transnational, and regional levels, and refers to activities in the public and private sectors that transcend national boundaries. They include keeping peace throughout the world; developing friendly relations among nations; helping nations work together to improve the lives of poor people, conquering hunger, disease and illiteracy, and encouraging respect for each other's rights and freedoms; and to be a centre for harmonizing the actions of nations to achieve these goals.

Policy Framework and Planning in Global Institutions

Areas of Work

Global Policy Forum (n.d) reports that the work programs currently focus on sustainable development and human rights, development finance and tax justice, UN reform and multilateralism, and corporate influence and accountability. The GPF thus takes a holistic approach, combining social with economic, financial and environmental issues, peace and security, and human rights and gender justice.

Organization

Global Policy forum (n.d) reports that a board and secretariat in New York, the business of GPF Europe by a separate board and secretariat in Bonn conduct the business of GPF. The programs are closely linked and are implemented by teams in Bonn and New York respectively. These teams are supported by a network of volunteer members (from GPF Europe) and consultants based in different parts of the world. BMC Public Health (2019) has reported that Public health policies sometimes have unexpected effects. Understanding how policies and interventions lead to outcomes is essential if policymakers and researchers are to intervene effectively and reduce harmful and other unintended consequences (UCs) of their actions. Yet, evaluating complex mechanisms and outcomes is challenging, even before considering how to predict assess and understand outcomes and UCs when interventions are scaled up. We aimed to explore with UK policymakers why some policies have UCs, and how researchers and policymakers should respond. Policymakers suggested UCs happen for a range of reasons: poor policy design, unclear articulation of policy mechanisms or goals, or unclear or inappropriate evidence use, including evaluation techniques. While not always avoidable, it was felt that UCs could be partially mitigated by better use of theory and evidence, better involvement of stakeholders in concurrent design and evaluation of policies, and appropriate evaluation systems.

Merton (1936) reported that public health policies, for example, sometimes evolve unexpected effects. Understanding how policies and interventions lead to outcomes is essential if policymakers and researchers are to intervene effectively and reduce harmful and other unintended consequences (UCs) of their actions. Yet, evaluating complex mechanisms and outcomes is challenging, even before considering how to predict assess and understand outcomes and UCs when interventions are scaled up. They aimed to explore with UK policymakers why some policies have UCs, and how researchers and policymakers should respond. In the social sciences, unintended consequences (sometimes-unanticipated consequences or unforeseen consequences) are outcomes of a purposeful action that are not intended or foreseen. The term was popularized in the twentieth century by American sociologist Merton.

Thus the focus of this chapter is:

- To enhance the understanding of how the ideas travel within the systems and how they are translated into policy, modified, distorted, or resisted. It is not about creating something fundamentally new, nor is it really about completely transcending the efforts of these Global Institutions.
- To examine the concepts that have powerfully influenced development policy and, more broadly, look at the role of ideas in these institutions and how they have affected current development discourse.
- To examine assorted dimensions of policy frame work such as finance, economy and technology that are used for development and the role of Global Institutions like World Bank, IMF, UNO, or ILO.

- To plan about creating effective Global Institutions at a global level, this can aid in social and economic development globally. Hence, to explore a broad range of these ideas and institutions.
- To investigate how entrepreneurs, organizations globally can develop to design policy frame work effectively and efficiently.

Global Initiatives

Its purpose was to identify specific actions to be taken by transit countries, by donor countries and institutions, and by the landlocked countries themselves in order to reduce the excessive trade transaction costs faced by the latter countries and to improve their competitiveness in the global trading environment. The programme of action sets out specific actions to be taken in five priority areas, namely:

- Fundamental transit policy issues: Actions should be taken by landlocked and transit developing countries to review and revise their transit transport regulatory frameworks in order to allow greater participation of the private sector, make transport services responsive to user demands, and increase the transparency of transit and border regulations.
- Infrastructure development and maintenance: Inadequate infrastructure was recognized as a major obstacle to establishing efficient transit transport systems in landlocked and transit developing countries. The lack of adequate infrastructure was seen to be the result of severely limited national financial resources and official development assistance for infrastructure development. Specific actions required to address this problem were identified as encouragement by development partners of private sector participation in transit transport infrastructure development through co-financing, Build-Operate-Transfer schemes and playing a catalytic role in attracting foreign direct investment, as well as in facilitating increased access to commercial bond markets.
- International trade and trade facilitation: Excessive trade transaction costs were identified as the main reason for the marginalization of landlocked developing countries in the international trading system. Because of the inextricable linkage of trade and transport, transport costs can provide either a means of access, or a barrier, to foreign markets. Cumbersome and inefficient Customs and other border crossing procedures and documentation were recognized as contributing to excessive transit costs for landlocked countries, as were costly bank transactions. Actions to reduce or eliminate these problems were seen as appropriate, as were actions on the part of development partners to achieve better market access for goods of special interest to landlocked developing countries, by supporting their accelerated accession (and that of transit developing countries) to the World Trade Organization. One of the specific actions required is that landlocked and transit developing countries should consider establishing, where appropriate, and/or strengthening existing national trade and transport boards or committees involving all major stakeholders, including the private sector.
- International support measures: It was recognized that as many of the landlocked developing countries are among the poorest of countries, the costs of establishing and maintaining efficient transit transport systems would be beyond their financial capacity and that therefore they would require assistance from the development partners. Such assistance was primarily identified in the form of increased official development assistance, and the application of innovative financing methods for transport infrastructure development. Donor countries and multilateral financial and development institutions were urged to continue their efforts to ensure effective implementation

Policy Framework and Planning in Global Institutions

of commitments reached in the Monterey Consensus. Priority areas for financial and technical assistance were identified as: provision of "missing links" in transit transport corridors; alternative cost effective routes; dry port projects; development of adjacent border posts; rehabilitation of transport infrastructure; and promotion of the implementation of agreed trade and transport facilitation measures. Finally, priority areas for technical cooperation were identified as promotion of the implementation of bilateral, sub regional, regional and international agreements; promotion of socially beneficial - 41- and market-oriented transit transport policies; implementation of privatization programmes; development and delivery of Customs training programmes; and expansion of regional data bases on road transport.

- Institute's approach in policymaking: Worth (2011) has highlighted three-prong approach to policy making. In that, he reports that attempts to defining and policy improving as the first approach, whether the approach is able to address challenges as the second while analyzing the effects produced as the third approach. He has further reported about the drive on professionalization of policy making where objective, approach and outcome are aligned to evolve professionally designed, covering process, quality, structure and politics. Policymakers suggested UCs happen for a range of reasons: poor policy design, unclear articulation of policy mechanisms or goals, or unclear or inappropriate evidence use, including evaluation techniques. While not always avoidable, it was felt that UCs could be partially mitigated by better use of theory and evidence, better involvement of stakeholders in concurrent design and evaluation of policies, and appropriate evaluation systems.

CHALLENGES

Impact of Undesired Outcome

- Policy objective is paralyzed: An objective is an aim or the target that the institution aims to achieve which is unsusceptible to any kind of personal feelings and emotions. Objectives are the specific steps that lead to the successful completion of the goals. Completion of objective results in specific, measurable outcomes that directly contribute to the achievement of the goals. SAMSHA (2017) reports that objectives are specific to understand, what will be done and who will do it. They should be measurable to understand how the action will be measured as it helps in making progress. It keeps you on track and on schedule. They should be achievable to understand that they are realistic given the realities faced in the community. Setting reasonable objectives, helps set the success. They should be relevant to understand how they make sense, that is, it fits the purpose of the grant, it fits the culture and structure of the community, and it addresses the vision of the project. They should be Time-bound and every objective has a specific timeline for completion. While designing a policy desired outcome is set as the objective. Therefore, in order to achieve the desired outcome, an approach to achieve that objective is planned and formulated using appropriate resources and processes. However, when the desired outcome is associated with unanticipated outcome, the policy is unable to perform as it will interfere or at times oppose the happening of the desired result. If this happens, it will need to modify or amend the objective. For example, good environmental policy is a global policy. The policy objective in this case becomes

249

"To maintain clean environment in the Place/City/Town" and the policy for example is written as "States to abide by the global norms for strictly maintaining clean environment." The orientation of this policy is towards achieving clean environment; therefore, it evolves controls on industrial enterprises since they are supposed to follow stringent operating norms to abate solid, liquid and gaseous pollution. Industries will therefore need to cut down on polluting components that are likely to result in closing down of certain technologies used in production. Therefore, undesired outcome is likely to result in reduction or closing down certain processes, which pose problems for the running of industries. In that case, few industries may face closure since they would be unable to abide by those norms. The approach to maintain norms would lead to loss of production of precious materials and unemployment. The objective may thus be paralyzed.

- Policy purpose is defeated: In the above-referred global policy, the purpose is to eliminate pollution. On the other hand, it would lead to loss of economy of the state if the industries are unable to adhere to the stringent norms. The purpose is therefore defeated.
- Policy faces entirely new challenges: The policy may lead to emergence of new challenge of unemployment and loss of economy, if the polluting industries are asked to close down.

Examples of Challenges

1. Policies fail to achieve the objective, of better living, due to lack of knowledge on its development
2. Evolving food policy framework up to 2050 is a challenge as the demand for food is continuously rising and will reach 60% greater than it is today.
3. Despite huge gains in global economic output, there is evidence that our current social, political and economic systems are exacerbating inequalities, rather than reducing them.
4. The scale of the employment challenge is vast. The International Labour Organization estimates that more than 61 million jobs have been lost since the start of the global economic crisis in 2008, leaving more than 200 million people unemployed globally.
5. The Earth's average land temperature has warmed nearly 1°C in the past 50 years because of human activity, global greenhouse gas emissions have grown by nearly 80% since 1970, and atmospheric concentrations of the major greenhouse gases are at their highest level in 800,000 years.
6. The global financial crisis revealed significant weaknesses in the financial system and some of the vulnerabilities that can result from having such an interconnected global market.

Analysis of Challenges

Policy designing invariably requires pre-examination of challenges / issues / problems/ existing and evolved conditions to find out right approach to address the same. The above challenges clearly indicate that conditions have evolved due to lack of knowledge and that is the essential tool to tackle them. Following is the modus operandi, the Institutions follow while planning for a policy.

- Knowledge of Input resources (e.g. machines, materials, people, time-scale) and conditions evolved, with their quality and scale.
- Competitive Approach (process, norms of processing) to addressing the challenges
- Review of the outcome.

Policy Framework and Planning in Global Institutions

Let us examine the case wherein following conditions are evolved:-

Evolving food policy framework up to 2050 is a challenge as the demand for food is continuously rising and will reach 60% greater than it is today.

Existing Knowledge and Travelling of Ideas: In the above case time scale, materials, quantity scale are prominently observed. Knowledge of data on existing yearly production is required; quantity in terms of rising demand is stated. Therefore, food policy should essentially plan establishment of higher production rate or supplement the demand with import of food. Another implied observation is that, the rising demand is linked with the rising population; therefore, knowledge of population growth rate is essential. The other observation is that the rise in agro production rate and storing requirements results into meaning of setting of additional machines, workers and materials and time as resources. Therefore, composite policy planning is essential in achieving success of the policy.

Ideas come from interactions: Scholars taking a discursive approach depart from the assumption that ideas are tools for policy actors to transfer and distribute in groups or networks. Questions of ideational change do not centre so much on the stringency or flexibility of ideas, but on questions of reconfiguration or convergence and divergence of ideas. As such, studying the effect of ideas on public policy concerns the ways in which ideas are transmitted in policy processes. Ideational research in this stream takes us to the study of policy entrepreneurs and their capacities to transmit ideas in networks, advocacy groups, and epistemic communities. The concept of policy entrepreneurs was first established by Kingdon (1984) and refers to policy actors capable of linking policy problems to policy ideas to promote policy decisions. Yet, a major challenge ahead lies in the ways in which such communicative interactions of policy entrepreneurs truly function as an explanation of policy processes.

SOLUTIONS AND RECOMMENDATIONS

Approach to Policy Planning: Global Institutions are official corporate entities located on global map, which work to contribute to the welfare of human beings, social development and share responsibility of planning policies. They are meant to address issues related to human race in the globe and for their benefit and for that matter each such institution has to present its skill and capability in professionally planning and execution of a policy. The very basic start on policymaking takes place based on following equation:

(A) Basic Approach to reach the Policy Objective
Input data+ Approach= Outcome
(B) Extended Approach to reach the Policy Objective
Input data (quality, quantity, state, characteristics) + Approach (with Process, processing norms)
= Outcome (intended & resulted)

Planning Process Described

a. Setting outcome oriented objective
b. Designing the path to reach the objective
c. Reviewing & examining the probable result of undesired side effect

d. Checking the Levels of side effect can be classified as severely undesired, moderately undesired weakly undesired side effect)
e. Altering the objective to make it result to weaken the undesired side effect
f. Define the problem, process and the user requirements not being met
g. Measure the extent of the problem by gathering data from the process, product and the users
h. Analyze the data and the process to find out what is causing the problem
i. Improve the process by eliminating the causes and building in safeguards to make sure the problem doesn't return
j. Designing the policy

Preliminary process requirements included obtaining real time data, ensuring the accuracy of the data, and correctly analyzing the data so that it was relevant to the policy objectives. It is equally important to recognize that many seemingly positive phenomena can lead to undesirable outcomes and thus fail to promote the best things.

POLICY PLANNING

Planning is a process that is composed of procedural steps linking the objective and outcome through an approach. Policy is role played by the policy user to achieve the objective.

Global Institution Works out a Plan

1. Monitoring the State of global affairs by identifying the challenges to living, social issues, problems, controversies, and peoples' rights
2. Setting Remedial objective
3. Planning the action by optimal use of resources & processes
4. Reviewing the outcome
5. Measuring the desired outcome(Scale & Time Period)
6. Measuring the undesired outcome (Scale & Time Period)
7. Balancing the objective and outcome to minimize undesired outcome

The research study has revealed that to gain insight of 'Policy Planning is on the basis of philosophy cultured by the Institution. The Global Institution invariably employs following tools / a / processes.

- Exhaustive Designer's philosophy
- Long term sustainability based on philosophy of making growth of the nation,
- Philosophy can be greatly improved through knowledge,
- Knowledge can be supplemented and improved through self-reading, learning and
- Mentor and Businesses that engage proper policy generate success and achieve
- Sustainability.
- Other variety of approaches have been recognized by the researchers in policy making

Policy Framework and Planning in Global Institutions

Role of ideas in the Institution on Policy Planning

1. Ideas & concepts generated using knowledge on the input resources, processes & their conditions evolved.

2. Ideas generated on approach to addressing the problems, their comparison, analysis to advantage & searching alternative routes

3. Ideas generated by focussing on the outcome of policy with emphasis placed on the abatement of undesired or unwanted outcome. Balancing of desired and undesired outcome

4. Orientation to Sustainability Development as majority of the countries made a choice to sustainability of policy. Over 130 countries have produced national development plans to show their priorities for achieving SDGs.

5. Motive of long term Policy. The five-year (medium term) plan is the most popular although some countries have longer term visions documents.

6. Focus on the Economy of the Nation. National Planning Commissions are back and play a lead role although Economic Ministries still dominate the process.

7. Ideas on the practicality of policy implementation. A majority of national plans lack financing strategies a factor that can affect implementation and achievement of SDGs.

Core 'Approach' to Policy Planning

A. Nation Focused Approach: - Great number of the Policy Designers consistently put into action the **"Nation** centred Approach" to sustain. This widespread, universally recognized approach is predominantly cultured to earn revenue and significantly adopted by policy designers as they have prominently targeted to the requirements of nations.

B. Sustainable Approach: - Continuity of income encourages sustainability. Therefore, each nation primarily focuses on the revenue-earning instrument to induce sustainability. Other criteria should include economic, environmental and social stability. Sustainable Approach brings stability by developing new instruments and enhancing the scale of existing instrument in an ongoing competitive process. Further aspect that is cultured is sensitivity concern for environment, justice, fair play & integrity. On social grounds increase in the suppliers, stakeholders, employment of persons is considered to impart sustainability. Any Approach that makes continuity of income encourages sustainability. Customer focused Approach being revenue earning instrument induces sustainability. Other policy aspects those need to be upheld is the long-term stability criteria based on economic, environmental and social grounds. Entrepreneurial preference would as a result go to that Approach which flawlessly contests their strengths and the long-time business opportunity that becomes accessible to them.

C. International Trade Policy: - Amongst variety of leads to developing a nation, few prominent policies invariably use international trade, the concept of selling local products on the global map in the niche segment of the demand province. This fact came to be evident based on philosophy cultured by the nations based on their technical and management skills as their strength.

Complementary or Paired 'Approaches'

1. *Operating standard (Standardization) Approach:* This Approach is the one that draws attention of the focused customer and hence it is used in pair with it and hence regarded as complementary. Majority of the Institutions have obtained certifications from the international standard organization that establishes their Approach of reliability to the quality.

2. *Joint working Approach:* Global Institutions perpetually bring into play joint working Approach to address diverse global challenges such as recurring financial needs, supply chain facility, technology up gradation and product marketing needs. This Approach positively establishes to strengthen the type, size and sustaining value of the resources.

3. *Cluster Approach:* Majority of global firms have opted cluster approach to enhance their resources in terms of sales Turn Over, competitive edge in technology, search of joint venture partners and for making effective supplies to their clientele. Area of expertise of Pune enterprises, among the other zones in India, is that they have succeeded in developing supply clusters as a component manufacturer and supplier. This Approach has brought in effectiveness and sustainability of supply chain within many industries. In the cluster-based policy for example, plenty of Institutions that produce precious materials have been benefited. Strong evidence suggests that a cluster policy brings additional positive effect particularly from the point of view of the Institutions, which are the main actors in the cluster development process, in relation to whether their performance has been improved because of cluster effects.

4. *Innovative Flexible Approach:* Greater part of the developed nations operates on the principle of innovation in technology and governance to satisfy the fresh necessities of the nations to stay safer and longer in the globe. This approach advocates continuous up gradation of existing processes. "Designing the operations on Six Sigma theory" is an illustration of this instrument that is generally demonstrated by the nations. "Designers Philosophy" positively influences the performance as it is the choice available to a nation to adopt among the core and complementary 'approaches' to living conditions. Statistical analysis of the data has exposed this significant feature. In depth view of Philosophical basis was researched to find out that the orientation of a designer mostly lies in following categories:

5. Designers' Philosophy Based Approach: Research in this area has strongly revealed the inevitability of the designers' philosophy as an instrument to the success of global institution and supports the findings of professionals. Over the years, there have been numerous attempts to define Entrepreneurship. While schools of thought are beneficial in broad sense, it is unlikely that any one school completely defines entrepreneurial behaviour. This is apparent when examining entrepreneurial characteristics as researched by academics. Taking into account, the original theories, as well as more recent literature, a modern definition of entrepreneurship has been drawn. An entrepreneur is most likely to possess the need for achievement, be independence oriented, desire personal control, seek opportunity, be innovative and assume calculated risk. These factors are perpetually interconnected to the philosophy of the entrepreneur. Many researchers have tested the relationship between entrepreneurship and business performance. While strategy and industry structure both significantly affect the performance of new venture, an entrepreneurial philosophy was found to have statistically significant influence. Results obtained through primary data strongly propose entrepreneur's philosophical Approach as new a dimension that has come up through study of cases researched. Designing a policy, is as a result a composite process, that mainly consists of

Policy Framework and Planning in Global Institutions

preparing rules for governing the enterprise and such regulations are compiled in statements form. They are the outcome of decisions taken by the management after deeply studying the business process flow called mapping. Rules are structured to satisfy the objectives of the organization. Supporting information and involvement of knowledgeable participants could only draw effective solutions based on the valuable thoughts or the philosophy of the entrepreneur. Policy makers require clarity to decide the priorities between different policy objectives and then select the set of instruments, which most efficiently promote those objectives. They are then, conceptually, two rather different sorts of choices to make. Firstly, choices about objectives; secondly, choices about which instruments to employ in order to pursue best of those objectives and which choice to make depends upon the philosophy of the entrepreneurs. Therefore, new instrument has emerged from the study called "Philosophical Approach to policy designing". Driven by the need to succeed, they rationalize that reaching their goals and going beyond the ordinary requires taking risks. The risks will be offset by the achievement of extraordinary gains. The people's philosophy which influences competitive choices invariably stand for either one or many of the traits the study reveals such as Passion for growth, Analytic mind, Resources and capability Achiever personality. Study has come out with the finding that philosophy positively influences the performance of their business, as it is entrepreneur's choice among the Core and complementary 'Approaches' to business. Statistical analysis of the data has exposed this especially significant feature. In depth, view of Philosophical basis was researched to find out that the orientation of a businessman is responsible for business success.

Balancing of Policy Objective and Undesired Outcome

Policy sustainability is said to be achievable by balancing the objective with the outcome. Policy makers require clarity to decide the priorities between different policy objectives and then select the set of instruments which most efficiently promote those objectives. They are then, conceptually, two rather different sorts of choices to make. Firstly, choices about objectives; secondly, choices about which instruments to employ in order to pursue best of those objectives and which choice to make depends upon the philosophy of the designers. Therefore new instrument has emerged from the study called "Philosophical approach of designers".

Challenge Balancing

Managing the challenges is through adoption of the state-of-the-art social logic that needs to turn out as the significant aid. The ability to gauge the challenges and take fitting arrangement within is the input to success of the policy. Challenge managing institutions can only survive and become effective as the risk-averse keep perishing. Predominance of balancing approach over other instruments has proven to be of utmost relief to the institutions from the peril of competitive and complex environment. The approach suggests balancing the external environment with the internal. The improvements to be chosen must be guided by the priorities in the operating system. For small firms having a single business it could mean the adoption of courses of action that will yield better profitability in the firm. Approach to absorb the technology and management changes is essential in building a balance within its system that will take care of all the challenges. As a result, it is meaningful for the Institutions to develop an approach that

Policy Framework and Planning in Global Institutions

works for the survival and growth of the enterprise. This approach has the ability to balancing the effect with appropriate cause.

For instance, Davis & Newstrom (1985) pointed out that a system is said to be in social equilibrium when there is a dynamic working balance among its interdependent parts. Each subsystem will adjust to any change in the other subsystems and will continue to do so until equilibrium is retained. The process of achieving equilibrium will only work if the changes happen slowly, but for rapid changes it would throw the social system into chaos, unless and until a new equilibrium can be reached. Government makes an allotment of funds to promote small and medium enterprises through a Global Institution formulated policy. However, their effects have been reported to be quite controversial. In order to manage such Government funds effectively, feedback information obtained from the rigorous evaluation procedure of Government investments needs to be utilized for future selection of new projects.

Once the responsibility arising out of challenge is assessed, the Global Institution needs to pursue for a right decision-making in managing the newly evolved state of affairs. Right decision is the one that is capable of surviving the nation. Global Institutions being small in numbers compared to the large corporate are only capable to bring in just a small change through low cost options. Survival measures would further account for the priority, urgency and triviality of action. Accordingly, step by step situation could be tuned up with the external environment through number of options that have to be identified by the Global Institutions. While making decision it is equally important that it is suitably supported by relevant and in depth information. Therefore, knowledge management is another competitive edge that is obligatory for creating correct resolution.

Extent of Undesired Outcome

a) Scale / level of effects
   The policy outcome is measured to understand its effect. It is always the objective of the policy designers that the level of desired outcome is a major percentage while undesired outcome should be nominal.
b) Time period:
   The other objective of policy designers is that policy should generate to the minimal undesired outcome and without causing failure for a long period
c) Low level debate
   Policy designers have the responsibility to formulate the policy that will give outcome without creating much debate since that is harmful for its survival.

Knowledge Management Approach

The challenge of information overload has become a real and persistent issue. The bottom line however is simple one can get as much information or access as man knowledge bases as one requires. Global Institutions invariably keep a knowledge management a cell that is capable of data mining, information search and organizing the data for use in planning policies. Data is classified into sectors, divisions; subsectors with further extension towards the evidence of cases of international presence, approach used in planning and actual implementation results. This data is usefully retrieved from the storage to make use in planning. Knowledge on objectives approaches and outcomes of various policies are retrieved.

256

Policy Framework and Planning in Global Institutions

For fresh policy designs some of the approaches could be used either individually or jointly to squash the problem into useful solutions.

Insight of Institutional Philosophy

This philosophy essentially matters for successful planning of policies. The philosophy relates to the thoughts, ideas and concepts developing skills of the group members in an Institution. Research study has further revealed that philosophy of the designers' pertains to the their attitudes like curiosity, questioning, inquiry, predictions to gain knowledge of environment and risks involved therein, Government regulations, business opportunities and survival. In addition Utility, Flexibility, Viability, and Competitiveness that needed to match with the Type, Size and Value of their resources and their capability for a prolonged subsistence. Smilor (2011), a professor at the Neeley School, USA, said what set the university's program apart from the other finalists was the emphasis placed on the philosophical approach to entrepreneurship.

POLICY FRAMEWORK

Policy framework is a structure that is composed and exhibited by nodes and links. It is prepared using the utility value of each node and link on which the policy is based. In the context of global institution, it consists of following parts:

- *Definitions:* Each policy that is going to be designed by a Global Institution should include definitions of terms, dimensions or factors in order to evolve clarity in the design.
- *Roles and Responsibilities*: Policy designers have specific roles to play and for a design project, they are grouped according to the skill of each person and bear responsibility in procuring, composing and utilizing the knowledge from the accessible data on a particular problem that the policy is expected to resolve and they are generally engaged as professionals who have the knowledge, skills and capabilities in bringing the policy to practicality and success. Global Institutions essentially hire professionals and keep them on their role. The highest administrative officer normally shares the authority of policy design. If appropriate, he might call for the next required review until his satisfaction. Skills useful in policy design are communication, articulation, ideation & conceptualization, knowledge of rules & regulation.
- *Policy Development Guide and Template:* Policy development guide is the procedure of developing the policy, where terminologies, nomenclatures and statement writing skills are given as examples for ready use while template is the format duly prepared to bring it in all the requirements and to avoid missing any important issue.
- *Policy approval*: Normally the design team heads to granting approval on policy, which conducts scrutiny / analysis to check and consider if it is fit to deliver the desired outcome.
- *Implementation & Communication:* Policy implementation is usually conducted by another group of executives or officers who have the responsibility in explaining the roles and responsibilities of policy stakeholders in an organization. The officers are well versed with the communication skills so that success while implementing the policy could be achieved in the real sense.
- *Retention and storage:* Once the policy is implemented and success is delivered by the policy, the policy so designed and formulates becomes final and is retained by the Institution for records.

257

- *Review Process:* The implementation group has the responsibility to keep monitoring the results of policy and that is usually done on a periodic review to check if it is deviating with time. Review process is therefore essentially incorporated in policy planning.
- *Compliance:* Policy compliance is said to be achieved once the policy success is repeatedly tested as that proves the reliability.

Frame Work Explanation

The study has revealed that better living conditions can be introduced and developed or brought about by the exchange of knowledge. While social and economic development can be brought about by, the ideas and concepts developed from various levels of the society. Setting the policy framework therefore plays an important role in policy designing. This framework setting is the major challenge amongst the nations. It will also aid the institutions of higher learning and educators to focus properly and help policymakers in designing and implementing policies that are more effective in the new global world order.

Global Solutions Initiative (GSI) speaks to • How to make global governance complementary with national governance in addressing global problems • the appropriate combination of top-down and bottom-up policy initiatives in multilateral climate negotiations • Devising new political settings to strengthen inclusive participatory democracy.

Brainstorming is only a first step to innovation. What matters more are execution and implementation? Gradual transformative policy change has attracted increasing attention in recent times. However, existing explanations for the evolvement of the various modes of such change do not account for the direction and content of change and have difficulty with more complex policy change processes in which several modes are employed. Ideational analysis can fill this gap, albeit most ideational research does not address gradual policy and ideational changes. Based on a process tracing of two cases from Israeli immigration policy, this article argues that a low level of discretion and a strong status quo bias are conditions that enable institutional conversion through layering. Ideational change in policy solution and problem definition ideas, and the interaction between the two, can explain this pattern and its direction. The article not only expands our knowledge of gradual transformative change, but also moves ideational research a step beyond punctuated equilibrium. The recent ideational turn in political science and public administration implies that ideas matter. Ideas are an essential explanatory concept for understanding policy changes and decision-making processes. The aim of the chapter is to specify how ideas matter as a variable in public policy research, providing students and scholars of public policy with a stock take of the current state-of-the-art literature on ideas in political science and public administration. The chapter first identifies three approaches to ideas as a variable in the policy process. It then discusses where ideas come from and the dynamics and drivers of ideational change to shed light on the ideational mechanisms underpinning policy processes. Furthermore, it taps into different research methods that can be used to study ideas. Finally, the chapter concludes with five lessons for future research endeavors on the study of ideas in public policy.

Policy Frame Work of World Bank: World Bank (2013) has reported that it has set its current environmental and social policies, split into eleven Operational Policies. Performance Standards for Private Sector Projects Supported by IBRD/IDA. The Board of Executive Directors approved adoption and application of World Bank Performance Standards to be used for Bank financing or support (e.g., Partial Risk Guarantees) which is destined to projects, or components thereof, that are owned, constructed, and/or operated by the private sector, in place of the World Bank. Technical assistance for preparatory work

Policy Framework and Planning in Global Institutions

for private sector engagement in Public-Private Partnerships would be eligible, as well as investment operations that include medium -or long-term management contracts, afterimage /leases, privatizations, concessions, and projects within the Build-Own-Transfer (BOT) family. Financial Intermediary lending also is a candidate, provided the Bank lending or guarantee to the financial intermediary is designated for subprojects implemented by the private sector or private parties.

IMF Policy Frame Work: Lower equilibrium interest rates with long term benefit has been observed in this policy. IMF (2020) reports that they intend to implement New Policy Frameworks for a "Lower-for-Longer" World. The COVID-19 pandemic is causing an unprecedented global economic contraction, leading many central banks to reduce interest rates to historically low levels and to rely more heavily on unconventional monetary policies. Amidst growing concern that policy space will be further eroded by lower equilibrium interest rates and falling inflation expectations, many central banks are reviewing their monetary policy frameworks. This event considers several key questions. Can new policy frameworks spur faster recoveries and help central banks deliver on their mandates? Are there tradeoffs between adopting a new framework versus using existing tools more aggressively? ***In addition,*** do "lower-for-longer" policies pose risks to financial stability and if so, what is needed to contain these risks?

ILO Policy Frame Work: ILO (2015) reported emphasis on Sustainable development, decent work and green jobs, in the time of ILO centenary. It includes realities, renewal and tripartite commitment, the report of the Director-General said. Conclusions were concerning the promotion of sustainable enterprises, Tripartite declaration of principles concerning multinational enterprises and social policy Promotion of Cooperatives Recommendation, Job Creation in Small and Medium-Sized Enterprises Recommendation,

UNO Policy Frame Work: Sustainable Development is the main objective observed in the policy framework of United Nations Organization. UNO (2001) reported policy framework in terms of indicators of sustainable development and methodologies. The main objective of the Commission of Sustainable Development Work Programme was to make indicators of sustainable development accessible to decision-makers at the national level, by defining them, elucidating their methodologies and providing training and other capacity building activities. At the same time, it was foreseen that indicators as used in national policies could be used in the national reports to the Commission and other intergovernmental bodies.

FUTURE RESEARCH DIRECTIONS

Sustainability of policy has been observed as the prime motive of Institutional Policy Planning. Level or the extent of sustainability is the emerging issue in the planning of the policies. Although policy makers expect hundred percent sustainability, the same is rare due to continuously changing world new issues keep evolving and emerging thereby harming the existing policies. In that case, even 70% sustainability would be welcome by the policy planners. Investigation in that direction is suggested.

CONCLUSION

UCs can be used to explore the mechanisms underpinning social change caused by public health policies. Articulating these mechanisms is essential for truly evidence-informed decision-making, to enable informed debate about policy options, and to develop evaluation techniques. Future work includes trying to develop a holistic stakeholder-led evaluation process. Broad and precise conclusions could be drawn based on the reviewed literature to highlight that nations can benefit from Knowledge that is developed through ideas and concepts with regard to success of Global Institutions.

REFERENCES

Andreeva, T., & Kianto, A. (2012). Wissens- und Informations management in kleinen und mittleren Unternehmen. Academic Press.

Beijerse, R. P. (2000). Does knowledge management really matter? Linking knowledge management practices, competitiveness and economic performance. *Journal of Knowledge Management, 16*(4), 617–636.

Bozbura, F. T. (2007). Knowledge management in small and medium-sized companies: Knowledge management for entrepreneurs. *Journal of Knowledge Management, 4*(2), 162–179.

Conditions for policy evaluation in Public Policies, debate on the role of institutionalist. (2020). *Pública, 54*(3). doi:10.1590/0034-761220190258x

Global Policy. (n.d.). https://www.globalpolicy.org

Guay. (2016). *An example of a global institution: The International Organization for Migration.* https://www.futurelearn.com/info/

ILO. (2015). *Policy Frame work.* http://www.ilo.org

IMF. (2020). *New Policy Frame Work for a Lower for Longer World.* https://www.imf.org/en/News/

Knowledge management practices in Turkish global institutions. (n.d.). *Journal of Enterprise Information Management, 20*(2), 209–221. doi:10.1108/17410390710725788

Morten. (2003). *Global Institutions and development: Framing the world?* https://www.researchgate.net

Oliver. (2019). *BMC Public Health.* https://bmcpublichealth.biomedcentral.com

Peters, B.G. (2018). *The Logic of Policy Design.* https://www.elgaronline.com/view

Samsha. (2017). *Smart Goals fact sheet.* https://www.samhsa.gov

Study on Coordination Mechanisms. (n.d.). www.unescap.org/sites/default/files/

Swinkels. (2019). *How ideas matter in public policy: A review of concepts, mechanisms, and methods.* Academic Press.

The Role of the WTO in Global Development Policy. (2004). In B. von Hoffmann (Ed.), Global Governance (pp. 101–129). Academic Press.

University of Huddersfield. (2017). *Policy Frame work. Inspiring Global Professionals.* Author.

UNO. (2001). *Indicators of Sustainable Development.* https://www.un.org/

World Bank. (2013). *Projects-Operations/Environmental-and-Social-Policies.* https://www.worldbank.org/

Chapter 14

Poverty and Poverty Indicators in the Republic of Serbia:
The Impact of Uneven Regional Development

Biljana Stojan Ilic
iD https://orcid.org/0000-0001-6137-8478
Megatrend University of Belgrade, Serbia

ABSTRACT

Poverty has become one of the most important categories of the global social and economic order and thus part of sustainability. Poverty is a product of harmful and excessive inequalities in the world as well as in almost every individual society. The aim of the chapter is to point to the importance of poverty indicators in the Republic of Serbia, as well as the impact of uneven regional development on poverty. Therefore, for Serbia, as well as for other countries in transition, it is vital to ensure sustainable and dynamic growth of real per capita income. The chapter also provides an overview of developing strategic directions for poverty alleviation.

INTRODUCTION

In modern society, the concept of poverty, as well as its occurrence, is a concept of multidimensional characteristics. Important - in other words - category standards that explain this concept can be material, such as income, consumption, and property, but it also includes health, education, as well as the dimensions of individual or social activities, such as work and other obligations. It is necessary to mention that the concept of poverty is seen through the influence of politics, social contacts, the environment, and finally - through the economic, physical security, or insecurity of citizens (Ilic et al., 2019).

The rate of economic growth and the rate at which growth is transformed into poverty reduction is not simply a matter of choice, but the product of a complex set of interactions between the initial conditions characteristic of a country, its institutions, policies, and external shocks to which it is exposed. Poverty is

DOI: 10.4018/978-1-6684-2448-3.ch014

Copyright © 2022, IGI Global. Copying or distributing in print or electronic forms without written permission of IGI Global is prohibited.

most often associated with hunger - today affects almost close to 800 million people (UN, 1995). Hunger leads to feelings of suffering, sadness, humiliation, and fear. The consequences of famine can also be seen in international financial and trade relations between countries. Industrialized countries import food worth about $ 60 billion a year from Third World countries, but most of the profits are reaped by processors, traders, and retailers. Poverty and unemployment are causal consequences. Unemployment means poverty and vice versa - the search for income most often leads men to leave home, while, on the other hand, it can cause domestic violence(Matkovic,2014) (Djukic and Ilic, 2020).

In the world, almost 1/3 of the household relies on a woman - she is the head of the family. The biggest obstacle to combating poverty is the way people think about hunger - the "fullness" does not believe in hunger (Ilic, 2019). In America, 97% of the population receives some form of social assistance, until 1/4 billion people in the world live in extreme poverty, and can hardly meet the most basic human needs. Although economic growth is crucial to combating poverty, the changes in income distribution (that accompany that growth) must not be overlooked. The effect of economic growth on poverty depends on how the additional income is distributed among the members of society (Ravallion, 2013).

If economic growth is accompanied by an increase in the distribution of income, then the income of that category of the population will grow faster than the average income and vice versa. The same goes for the poverty rate. Poverty will fall faster if the distribution of income is balanced than if it becomes more uneven (Stiglitz et al., 2009). Openness to international trade, sound monetary and fiscal policy (embodied in a moderate budget deficit and the absence of high inflation), along with a well-developed financial system, strongly contribute to increasing production. Institutional factors are also important. "The rule of law and the absence of corruption have been shown to have a positive effect on economic expansion, creating a favorable, rules-based environment for investment and economic advancement (Dollar and Kraay, 2010).Among the many causes, hyperinflation in 1993, contributed to the great impoverishment of the population and the expansion of the gray economy which became the main way for surviving a significant part of the population. The difficult economic and social situation is aggravated by the large influx of refugees and displaced persons, whose number in some years reached up to 10% of the population (Ilic and Djukic, 2021).

The standard of living of a part of the population was affected by the (temporary) impossibility of using the right to income and property from the republics of the former Yugoslavia. The number of the population with increased social needs has been growing, and the economic possibilities of the state for providing social assistance have been declining, so certain categories of the most endangered population have suffered the hardest from the consequences of the economic crisis. Serbia is characterized by uneven regional development. "On the one hand, the Western region of the country is developed, while the Eastern and Southern regions are less economically developed. Poverty is also more pronounced in these regions and poverty categories of people are more vulnerable" (Ilic and Jovanovic, 2017). In the chapter, the author will give an overview of poverty in Serbia, compare the regions of the country and point out the guidelines and directions of sustainable development, which aim to reduce poverty in the country as well as balanced regional development.

BACKGROUND

The European Union, as well as the United Nations, has categorized poverty as a multidimensional concept, accepting comprehensive and official definitions. According to these definitions, the poor are

Poverty and Poverty Indicators in the Republic of Serbia

considered to be social strata that have insufficient income as well as resources and those people are not able to provide a standard of living that is characterized as acceptable in a country (Veselinovic, 2013). Therefore, these layers are endangered and cannot be included in the normal life and social flows of a community, such as education, culture, social inclusion, and similar. Poor social strata are on the margins of social life, and often do not have the opportunity to exercise fundamental rights. Poverty, which is even more pronounced in Serbia during the transition period, cannot be explained only by the transition process, as is the case with the former socialist countries (Devetakovic et al., 2008). It is known that the transition in Serbia was quite slow, with great difficulties and delays. Therefore, the chapter emphasizes not only the causes, type, and quantitative indicators of poverty in Serbia, but also the poverty rate in rural and urban parts of the country. The analysis included the educational structure, as well as the number of household members. Measuring poverty is of great importance because it allows us to see the dimensions and understand the essence of this problem, as well as ways to alleviate or eliminate it (Stankovic, 2008). If at the very beginning poverty is observed from the national tradition, then its causes are classified into the following groups (Bogicevic et al., 2012): the fateful causes of poverty; inherited causes of poverty; personal causes of poverty; general causes of poverty. Fateful poverty is a consequence of the action of some fateful "force majeure" and its elimination is very difficult or even impossible. Whatever an individual or household does - works diligently and hard - creates - the result will always be negative. A higher power that prevents a person from escaping poverty is called misery. Inherited poverty is often a national tradition, where an individual or family changed their place of residence, got a job, educated, saved - worked hard, or went to richer environments. Personal causes of poverty are numerous in the national tradition. Irresponsibility, unemployment, laziness, as well as wastefulness, are most often the main causes of poverty. General reasons for poverty are the result of natural disasters, economic crises, or political events (wars, loss of privileges and positions, state looting). In the last decade of the twentieth century, official unemployment increased, and hidden unemployment increased because the number of employees decreased more slowly than the dramatic decline in economic activity. The most important reason for increasing poverty in Serbia was a decline in per capita income (since inequality in income distribution has not changed significantly in the last decade of the 20th century, nor the first years of the 21st century). Till the end of that period, hidden unemployment had reached a level of about a third of total unemployment. This situation in the labor market resulted in a decline in real wages and delays in payment, which generated the impoverishment of the majority of the population. However, the phenomenon of poverty can be certainly related tothe uneven regional development of the country, but also with the concept of implementing Sustainable Development and the social component as the part of this concept (in addition to the economic component), with a degree of national environmental awareness - and how is one nation is connected with its natural environment. All the listed terms have a great influence on the lifestyle of a whole society. The social component of sustainable development has the effect of reducing and increasing poverty - these two concepts are inversely proportional. The more developed the social component in the country, the greater its impact on poverty reduction and vice versa - poverty is more pronounced in countries with the less developed social component of sustainable development (Ilic and Mihajlovic, 2017).

Concept of Sustainable and Regional Development in the Republic of Serbia

The first decade of the last century was marked by progress in various spheres of social and economic "global" life - including environmental awareness, optimism, and innovation. These processes are closely linked to growing human systems - increased global inequality, major economic system failures, and worsening global environmental trends (Ramos et al., 2018). All the listed terms are included in the concept of Sustainable Development. The beginnings of sustainable development at the global level can be traced back to the 1980 World Strategy, which specified that sustainable development could not be achieved without the conservation of natural resources (United Nations Educational, Scientific and Cultural Organization, 1997). Sustainable development has emerged in response to a growing awareness of the need to balance social and economic development with the environment (Hattingh, 2002). Brundtland's report of the World Commission on Environment and Development entitled "Our Common Future" brought sustainability to the forefront in all spheres of human action and behavior (Fincham et al., 2004). Sustainability is closely linked to the quality of life and the environment in which life takes place, emphasizing the harmony of economy and ecology. According to Agbedahin: "The emergence of efficiency and eminence of this global conceptual framework includes education for sustainable development (ESD), as well as the Sustainable Development Goals (SDG) 2030" (Agbedahin, 2019). Sustainability means the balanced development of the region, both in the world - globally and in countries - locally.

What is the regional development of the Serbian state and where is Serbia concerning to the neighboring countries in Europe? Answering these questions, it is possible to find out how far Serbia has come on the path of sustainable development, ie whether the concept of sustainability is applied in the country. The trend of uneven regional development of Serbia has especially increased after the disintegration of the formerly great state of Yugoslavia (Serbia was part of the SFRY). After the wave of recession, Serbia has faced a trend of growing regional demographic decline, economic and infrastructural gaps, regional educational disparities, deteriorating fiscal position, and deepening fiscal imbalance. To have a clearer insight into where Serbia is about to certain European countries according to the GDP per capita indicator, Table 1 (European Union, Operational Budget Balance, 2018) is shown. Table 1 can also be interpreted as an indicator of Serbia's economic status in the region (and within the country's region).

Table 1. GDP per capita, EU = 100%

Country	National level	The most riched region (1)	The most poored region (2)	Relationship (1:2)
Bulgaria	45	75	27	2,8
Czech Republic	80	175	66	2,7
Hungary	66	109	40	2,7
Poland	65	97	41	2,4
Romania	49	111	29	3,8
Slovenia	84	105	72	1,5
Croatia	61	78	44	1,8
Serbia	35	60	22	2,7

Source: European Union, 2018.

Table1shows that Serbia is in last place (35%) in the EU (GDP by purchasing power), Bulgaria (47%),and Romania (49%) are approximately at the same level as the EU. A group of middle-developed

Poverty and Poverty Indicators in the Republic of Serbia

transition countries (Hungary, the Czech Republic, Poland, Croatia) are at 2/3 in the EU - Slovenia stands out with a GDP PPS above 80%.However, internal regional disparities are different: in Serbia, they are higher (2.9: 1) than economic disparities in Slovenia and Croatia (1,5: 1 and 1,8: 1), at the level of economic inequalities in Bulgaria, the Czech Republic, and Hungary. The largest regional economic differences are in Romania (3,8:1). Table 2 shows the trend of regional productivity in Serbia. It is clear that the northern part of Serbia is more productive than the southern part, i.e. the region of Belgrade is the most productive - GDP per capita is 71% above the national average, followed by the region of Vojvodina (North) with 2.9% above the Serbian average, while the other two regions - Western Serbia, especially the Southeast region - far below the national average.

Table 2. Regional productivity trend

GDP / capita (Serbia = 100)										
Regions	2009.	2010.	2011.	2012.	2013.	2014	2015	2016	2017	2018
Belgrade	179,4	177,8	172,2	171,4	170,9	164,9	166,2	166,8	168,1	170,8
Vojvodina	95,2	96,8	99,5	102,6	102,9	102,7	98,4	98,4	99,5	97,1
Sumadia and Western Serbia	71,4	69,9	67,3	67,6	67,3	70,7	72,1	71,3	67,3	69,5
South and East Serbia	63,3	63,9	63,1	63,3	62,7	64,2	65,6	65,0	65,6	63,7

Source:SORS, 2018

From the presented tables, it can be concluded that the economic lag of the state of Serbia - behind the EU average - has its regional dimension. Serbia is below the EU average (in terms of GDP/capita in terms of purchasing power), the Belgrade region is the most developed - as the richest in the country - and the least developed (poorest) regions of Southern and Eastern Serbia are the least developed regions in the country and EU. The entire area is below the EU average in terms of economic strength (Serbia's Regional Development Report, 2013).The transition has contributed to increasing regional disparities - which is transitional legality. The space for conducting an active regional development policy in Serbia is still significantly narrowed. The way out of poverty will depend mostly on building regional development institutions, respecting economic rules, and regional planning in the "long run". Regional incentives should be redirected to resources that increase employment, and in that way, the poverty rate in Serbia could be significantly reduced.

Social Component of Sustainability in Serbia

As the socio-economic inequality of Serbia and its regions is evident, it can be said that in terms of social values, two problems dominate in the country. The first is generated by excessive differences within the political and economic elite in terms of the normative framework of the new social order (Ilic et al., 2019). This situation enables the simultaneous existence of three models of social reproduction: command, market, and wild (informal).Another problem lies in the fact that approximately the same percentage of people in Serbia believe that, even at the cost of some environmental pollution and economic development. Serbia has a relatively low level of environmental awareness, so the average citizen does not have a positive attitude towards the need to act in a way to reduce pollution, rationally use energy and change attitudes towards non-renewable resources - to reduce costs and improve the environment. "Serbia is rich in natural resources and in energy resources, especially renewable ones (Renewable Energy Sources - RES). The fact is that the use of RES is currently very important for many reasons - from reducing emissions, to reducing the cost of energy use (over time). Also, the use and construction of certain facilities on the basis of RES would create new jobs and indirectly reduce unemployment..." (Stojanovic et al., 2017). A clean environment, aesthetically enriched, is a prerequisite for modern ecological culture. A large number of Serbian citizens do not represent healthy living habits. According to reports from the National Development Strategy of Serbia, almost a quarter of citizens do not have enough self-confidence, do not believe in other people's views, while in some absurd way still believe in their superiority and omniscience (Government of Republic of Serbia, 2008).Almost a quarter of Serbian citizens do not have enough trust in political attitudes, which represent the solution of certain social phenomena (for example, poverty) (Ilic, 2020). The percentage of young people who participate in the work of political parties and the work of various associations, in general, is relatively small (Ilic and Pavicevic, 2018). Young people in Serbia have little chance to build better lifestyles, due to the unresolved and unstable economic situation. In less developed areas of the country, there is almost no or little chance of young people participating in creating projects that would be economically viable (Ilic, 2019).

Today, Serbia faces two tasks, the first to eliminate contradictions that hinder the establishment of a stable social form, and the second to resolve and avoid such contradictions on a global level, and to fit into the global trend of sustainable development. Inherited economic difficulties and poverty, which exist in Serbia, affect the spread of materialistic goals, the feeling of insecurity, and the feeling of excessive risk exposure when starting any economic or social activity. There was also a great alienation of the rural population from natural resources (Kokovic, 2009). The concept of social capital emphasizes the social and cultural aspects of human behavior, ie indicates that these dimensions have economic implications (Golubovic, 2009).Older generations of citizens have more trust in old, former institutions than in new and modern ones. In terms of a better quality of life, it means freeing citizens from fear for tomorrow, the possibility of freedom of expression, protection from any threats from criminal groups, which would endanger the peaceful life and stability. The quality of life is also related to the identity of one nation, that is, to how that nation sees itself with others. Serbian national identity indicates that structural socio-economic variables, although necessary, are not sufficient for the development of civic national identity. A stable international framework is needed to build identity (Manetovic, 2016). One of the national issues is the collective identity, and the collective consciousness is still an insufficiently studied scientific issue, as well as the mentality of certain smaller or larger social groups (Radakovic, 2012).The citizens of Serbia have a diverse collective identity because it has been subject to change and influence over time. Serbia is committed to being a part of developed Europe. In recent decades, the population of Serbia has adhered to the church and religion, and thus presents itselfin a new, different light. Mass media have a significant role and great influence in the creation and acceptance of certain norms of behavior.

Employment Situation in Serbia

The labor market in Serbia has been affected by two important groups of factors since 2001. The first group of factors was related to the processes of transition and restructuring of companies, while the second group referred to the effects of the economic crisis in the period from 2008 (Jandric and Molnar, 2017). After the outbreak of the global economic crisis and recession in 2009, occasional periods of

Poverty and Poverty Indicators in the Republic of Serbia

economic recovery in Serbia were interrupted by new recessions. However, after the Serbian economy emerged from the last recession, a period of relatively moderate economic growth began.

The reaction of the labor market to changes in production (measured by the GDP growth rate) was not the same in the period before the crisis that occurred in 2008-2009 years and in periods during and after the crisis (Jandric and Molnar, 2017). Namely, the period between 2001 and 2008 can be characterized as a period in which economic growth was not adequately transferred to jobless growth. The term jobless growth refers primarily to worryingly low, but still positive values of employment elasticity, while in Serbia for a long time the values of elasticity were negative, that is, GDP growth was accompanied by a decline in employment.

The positive effects of GDP growth in that period were transmitted to the population through the growth of productivity and wages, and not through the growth of employment (Krstic and Soskic, 2016). This trend in employment relative to GDP in Serbia in the period up to 2008 was probably largely due to the transitional restructuring and layoffs of redundant employees in privatized companies. "With the beginning of the economic crisis of 2008-2009, the elasticity of employment in relation to GDP becomes positive and higher than 1 - in other words, the decline in GDP was accompanied by an even stronger decline in employment. The decline in GDP in Serbia during the crisis was accompanied by a much larger decline in employment than in many other Central and Eastern European countries" (Arandarenko and Aleksic, 2016).

The large decline in employment that occurred during the crisis was the result of the simultaneous impact of the economic crisis and other economic factors, which are primarily related to the completion of the process of transitional restructuring and privatization (Krivokapic and Mesanovic, 2016). However, according to the Labor Force Survey (LFS), the labor market in Serbia has experienced a significant recovery in the past few years (Labor Force Survey, 2014). It should be noted that one of the key sources of data on the labor market in Serbia is this Survey (LFS). The Labor Force Survey enables an overview of the situation and monitoring of changes in the labor market through internationally established indicators, including the employment rate and the unemployment rate. In addition, this survey provides an overview of the socio-demographic characteristics of the employed, unemployed, and the population outside the labor force. It is the only source of information on informal employment in Serbia (Labor Force Survey, 2014).

Given several adjustments to the LFS methodology, monitoring the situation in the labor market in Serbia has been somewhat difficult, especially for the period from 2014 to 2016. Therefore, the data on basic labor market indicators are divided into two tables (tables 3 and 4): Table 3 refers to the period 2008-2014, while Table 4 contains revised data for 2014 (according to the new methodology), as well as data for 2015 and 2016 (Arandarenko, 2011). Considering that a significant change in the methodology was made in 2015, the Statistical Office of Republic of Serbia published in 2017, and revised data for 2014 to ensure comparability (Consumption, income and living conditions, 2017).

Table 3. Movement of basic indicators of the labor market in Serbia (15-64), 2008-2014

	2008	**2009**	**2010**	**2011**	**2012**	**2013**	**2014**
Unemployment rate	14,4	16,9	20,0	23,6	24,6	47,4	19,7
Unemployment rate	53,7	50,4	47,2	45,4	45,3	47,5	49,6
Activity rate	62,7	60,6	59,0	59,4	60,1	61,6	61,8

Source: LFS, 2014; Consumption, income and living conditions, 2017

267

Table 4. Movement of basic indicators of the situation on the labor market in Serbia (15-64), 2014-2016

	2014	**2015**	**2016**
Unemployment rate	19,9	18,2	15,9
Unemployment rate	50,7	52,0	55,2
Activity rate	63,3	63,6	65,6

Source: LFS, 2014; Consumption, income and living conditions, 2017

According to the Structure of Earnings Survey, conducted in Serbia in 2016, data on employment, unemployment, and inactivity indicate a significant recovery of the Serbian labor market in the period after 2012. The unemployment rate in Serbia is in the period 2014-2016 decreased from 19.9% in 2014 to 15.9% in 2016. At the same time, activity and employment rates in Serbian society have increased (Structure of Earnings Survey, 2016). According to the same source, the employment rate increased significantly from 50.7% in 2014 to 55.2% in 2016. The author emphasizes that there are still no revised data for the years before 2014, which would be fully comparable with the data from 2015 onwards, and given the latest revision of the Labor Force Survey methodology, the chapter considers the period from 2008 to 2016 (which is in line with the time monitoring of the poverty rate in Serbia).

However, to assess the situation on the labor market, in addition to these general rates, it is necessary to take into account the structure and quality of employment. It is also important to note that, despite the improvement in the labor market in the previous period, the basic indicators - activity rate, employment rate, and unemployment rate in Serbia in 2016 were worse than the EU-28 average (Statistical Yearbook of the Republic of Serbia, 2016). The activity rate of persons aged 15-64 in Serbia in 2016 was 65.6%, which is still low compared to the EU-28 average (Structure of Earnings Survey, 2016). According to the data from the manual on measuring the quality of employment, issued by the Economic Commission for Europe, United Nations, in the group of European countries, only Italy had a lower activity rate than Serbia (Italy, 64.9%; Serbia 65.6%), while Croatia and Romania had activity rates at the same level as Serbia. The situation is similar to the employment rate. Although it has significantly increased compared to 2014, compared to other European countries, this rate in Serbia is still low and amounts to 55.2% (EU average employment rate: 66.6%) (UN, 2015). Of all the observed European countries, only in Greece, this indicator had a lower value (52%) compared to Serbia.

"For example, in Sweden, which in 2016 recorded the highest employment rate in the EU, the employment rate was as high as 76.2%. For a long time, Serbia was below the goal set in the National Employment Strategy for 2011-2020, which envisaged reaching the employment rate in Serbia of 61.4% in 2020. The unemployment rate, despite significant improvements in the labor market in Serbia, in 2016 was higher in only two countries than in Serbia: Greece and Spain" (Jandric and Molnar, 2017). Given that the chapter is based on the examination of poverty in Serbia, it is necessary to say something more about vulnerable employment as part of the category that falls under the labor force in Serbia. According to the methodology followed by the Labor Force Survey in Serbia, the total number of employees is divided into: paid employees (employees); self-employed with employees; independent (self-employed) without employees and helping household members.

"Vulnerable employment essentially means employment in precarious jobs, with low wages and low productivity, with a low level of protection at work and poor working conditions, and very often it is also informal jobs without paid basic and health insurance. It is important to note that this indicator

Poverty and Poverty Indicators in the Republic of Serbia

also has certain limitations. First of all, paid employees may find themselves in a position characterized by great insecurity, while, on the other hand, some categories of self-employed (e.g. small business owners, highly qualified professionals, doctors with private practice, etc.) may be in a really good position. Positions in the labor market, although by this definition they enter into vulnerable employment. However, the participation of this group in vulnerable employment is relatively low, except in developed countries) " (Arandarenko, 2011).The share of vulnerable employment defined in this way (as the sum of self-employed and helping household members divided by the total number of employees) practically represents the share of all types of employment except wage employment in total employment (Mannila, 2015). According to the defined indicator of vulnerable employment, its participation in Serbia in 2016 was extremely high (28.3%) compared to other European countries (the average for the EU was 15%). Table 5 shows the structure of employment in Serbia by professional status.

Table 5. Employment structure by professional status (15-64) 2014-2016)

	2014	2015	2016
Employed workers	71,3	72,5	71,7
Self-employed	21,5	20,1	21,2
Helping household members	7,2	7,3	7,1
Helping household members	28,7	27,4	28,3

Source: LFS, 2014; Consumption, income and living conditions, 2017

Table 5 shows that the share of vulnerable employment in Serbia increased slightly in 2016 compared to 2015. However, it is worrying that close to 30% of all employees were in categories related to vulnerable employment (helping household members and the self-employed).

What is the employment situation in Serbia in 2021? According to available SORS data, in the third quarter of 2021, the number of employees in Serbia was 2,924,500, and the number of unemployed was 341,500. The employment rate for the given period was 50.0%, and the unemployment rate was 10.5%. According to the LFS for the third quarter of 2021, and compared to the second quarter of 2021, the number of people aged 15 and over decreased outside the labor force (-95,600) due to an increase in the active population (+ 83,000). Within the contingent of the active population in Serbia, there was an increase in the number of employees (+93,400) and a decrease in the number of unemployed (-10,500) (Labour market dynamics in the third quarter 2021).

POVERTY RATE TRENDS IN SERBIA

Taking into account the stated facts above, it is concluded that the social components of the development of a country and its regions, but also the employment situation in Serbia are closely related to the quality of life (Ilic and Jovanovic, 2017). On the other hand, quality of life should be viewed together with the degree of poverty. Who are the poor social strata in Serbia and how is the poverty rate monitored? In Serbia, poverty is monitored and reported based on two basic methodological concepts of measuring poverty: the concept of absolute and the concept of relative poverty. Absolute poverty represents the inability to meet basic, minimum needs, while relative poverty implies the inability to achieve a standard of living that is appropriate to the society in which the individual lives. Although assessments of the financial position and living standard of the population are made with different methodological concepts, with constant improvement of the methodology and the indicators themselves, it is interesting to note that there are no significant differences in the profile of the poor according to the concept of absolute and relative poverty. The data show that the most vulnerable population include: children up to 14 years of age, young people (15-24 years), large households, residents of suburban areas, persons living in households with low levels of education, persons living in households with the carriers are unemployed or out of the labor market. The most important poverty risk factors are: education (completed or incomplete primary school), employment status (unemployed/inactive), household size (five-member and larger households), location of residence (suburban area).These categories of the population need special attention when designing social policy measures. Table 6 shows the absolute poverty rates of the most at-risk groups in Serbia, 2006–2018, expressed as a percentage. It should be noted that the absolute poverty line defined based on the food line, increased by the number of other expenditures (clothing, footwear, housing, health, education, transport, recreation, culture, other goods, and services), calculated in 2006, increased by the amount inflation (measured by the consumer price index) for each year(Government of the Republic of Serbia, 2021).

Table 6. Absolute poverty rates of the most at-risk groups in Serbia, 2006–2018, (%)

	2006	2007	2008	2009	2010	2011	2012	2013	2014	2015	2016	2017	2018
Total population - average for the Republic of Serbia	**8,8**	**8,3**	**6,1**	**6,6**	**7,6**	**6,6**	**6,3**	**7,4**	**7,6**	**7,4**	**7,3**	**7,2**	**7.1**
Residents of suburban areas	13,3	11,2	7,5	9,0	12,1	9,4	8,7	10,5	10,9	10,5	10,5	10,5	10.4
Residents of the region of Southern and Eastern Serbia	11,4	10,7	10,7	15,0	15,5	11,3	11,8	14,7	13,5	13,1	12,8	12,1	11.9
Persons living in households where the head of the household is unemployed	14,7	10,9	16,9	17,0	16,5	16,9	16,7	18,0	21,8	19,0	22,5	23,8	20,6
Persons living in households in which the head of the household is without completed primary school	21,0	18,8	9,0	17,4	14,3	16,5	15,6	20,5	18,8	21,8	19,0	18,5	21,3
Persons living in households in which the head of the household is with primary school	13,7	13,2	10,5	10,4	13,7	11,0	11,4	13,8	14,9	11,8	12,2	14,8	12,7
A family of five members	8,3	8,1	5,2	5,5	9,8	8,8	10,9	11,6	8,9	8,7	7,3	10,6	8,1
Six-member and larger family	17,3	14,4	10,0	13,7	14,3	12,7	10,1	14,0	15,4	15,8	12,1	15,2	9,8
Children up to 13 years	11,6	11,2	7,3	9,7	11,9	9,7	9,4	10,4	10,5	9,9	8,4	9,1	7,6
Children aged 14-18	11,7	8,8	6,9	8,3	7,9	9,0	9,7	8,8	9,9	10,6	8,5	10,6	8,2

Source: Mladenovic, 2017; Absolute Poverty, 2018

In the continuation of the chapter, the data for the period of 10 years of the movement of the poverty rate in Serbia (2006 to 2016) will be discussed, and then new research on this phenomenon will be pointed out, especially in the period 2020 and 2021.

The data will refer to the general trend of poverty, then to poverty in urban and rural areas, according to the educational structure of the population, as well as according to the number of household members (Mijatovic, 2017). Data on the depth (intensity) of poverty show how much the consumption of the poor is below the poverty line. In the observed period, from figure 1, which represents the graph, it can be seen that the poverty rate is pronounced, in the first year of observation (2006), 8.8 and the following year it decreases (8.3) and oscillates around 7.0 to 7 each year, 4 which shows that there is a constant reduction in the depth of poverty. In the observed period, for each year, the number of the poor was observed, ie divided by the total number of inhabitants, and in that way, the rate of the poor was obtained. The poverty line in 2016 amounted to 11,694 dinars per month per consumption unit and is a consequence of the regular annual adjustment for the amount of inflation since 2006when the line was originally constructed. Every person who had a monthly consumption below that amount belonged to the category of the poor. Within households, resource allocation and resource sharing were assumed, so that each subsequent adult in the household, according to the OECD equivalence scale, "spent" 0.7% of the amount that an adult would "spend" to live alone. A weight of 0.5 was applied to a child up to 14 years of age. For example, a household with four members (two adults and two children up to 14 years of age) in 2016 was considered poor if it had a monthly consumption of less than 31,574 Dinars (300Euros)(Serbian currency) (Mladenovic, 2017).

Figure 1. Poverty rate, lower and upper limit of 95% confidence interval, 2006-2016
Source: Mladenovic, 2017

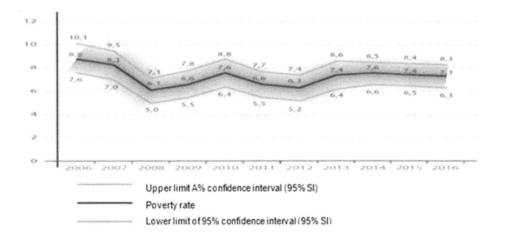

In the observed period 2006-2016 year, we cannot talk about a significant reduction in the poverty rate. In the last observed 2016, 7.3% of the population is absolutely poor, while the reductions in the absolute number of the poor are primarily due to the decline in the population. Approximately half a million inhabitants do not have enough consumption to cover basic living needs. As poverty rates are obtained based on sample, and not based on a survey of the entire population, they are discussed with a certain probability.

If the phenomenon of poverty in Serbia is observed regionally, very pronounced differences in the prevalence and poverty rates can be seen. The transition process, intensified restructuring of the economy, demographic depopulation, and inadequate educational and qualification structure, have further deepened the existing economic disparities between the regions, for the period 2006-2016. The poorest population lives in the region of Southeast Serbia, which makes up a quarter of the total number of poor, where there is an extremely high difference in poverty between urban (8.5%) and rural areas (18.7%). In this area, poverty is the deepest and most pronounced, especially for the category of unemployed persons. Poverty is twice as common in suburban areas. The regional overview indicates a significant deviation of the region of Southern and Eastern Serbia, which records the highest poverty rates in the entire observed period. The Belgrade region has a stable lowest poverty rate, and as a positive trend in the observed period can be seen the approach of the region of Vojvodina and Sumadija and Western Serbia - the Belgrade region.

Figure 2 shows a graph of the poverty rate by type of settlement, while figure three shows a graph of the poverty rate by region.

Figure 2. Poverty rate by type of settlement
Source: Mladenovic, 2017

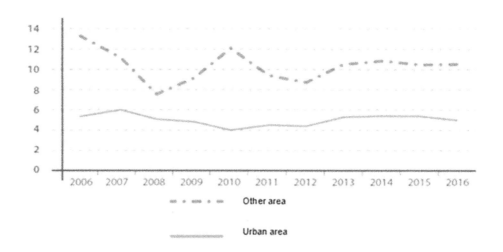

Figure 3. Poverty rate by regions
Source: Mladenovic, 2017

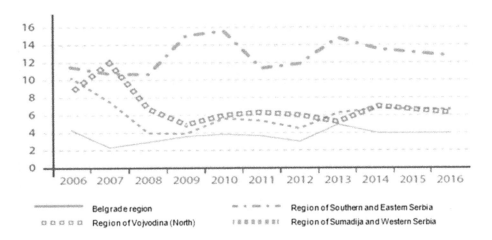

If we consider the equal distribution of consumption within households (ie, the fact that in one household there can be no one person who is poor and one who is not), the differences in poverty by gender are primarily affected by single households and households with the same sex. For this reason, it is not possible to notice significant differences in poverty by gender. Observed by age, the position of children of all observed years is much worse than the position of adults. Although there is a noticeable reduction in the differences in the poverty rates of children and adults, it is primarily a consequence of the worsening position of those aged 65 and 75.

Figure 4. Graph of Poverty rate of children and adults
Source: Mladenovic, 2017

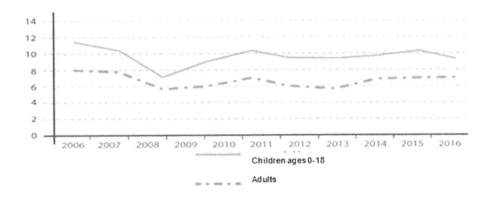

Figure 4 shows the Graph of Child and Adult Poverty Rates in Serbia. The big problem that Serbia is facing is the poverty of children and youth. As many as 9.3% of children are poor, ie. every ninth child is poor. This data is even more worrying if we take into account that child poverty in Serbia has a growing trend. Indicators of poverty in children are: malnutrition during childhood (due to malnutrition, a third of children in preschool institutions are anemic), more frequent illnesses, problems in schooling (late enrollment in school, dropout during primary school, repetition), problems in physical development (deformities, developmental delay, consequences of chronic diseases), some forms of social deviance (juvenile delinquency). These poverty indicators sometimes appear as isolated and more often as combined, even cumulative. Figure 5 shows the Graph of Poverty Rates by Age of the Population in Serbia.

Figure 5. Poverty rate by age of the population
Source: Mladenovic, 2017

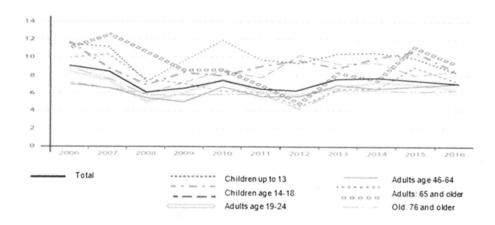

Refugees and displaced persons are in a very difficult, if not the most difficult position, who were forced to leave their homes due to the war in the former SFRY and the autonomous province of Kosovo and Metohija. According to the estimates of the Commissariat for Refugees, there are 278,000 refugees and over 200,000 displaced persons from Kosovo and Metohija living in Serbia. Of that number, as many as 18,500 refugees are housed in collective centers. Although there are no valid and precise data on the poverty of these groups. the poverty of refugees and displaced persons is estimated to be twice as high as the rest of the population. It is also interesting that almost half (49.2%) of the Roma population is poor, but only 6.4% of Roma in Serbia are extremely poor. As a rule, the poverty rate is always higher in rural areas, and not often several times. Therefore, it does not seem strange that an increasing number of people decide to leave the village to try their luck in big cities. The problems faced by the inhabitants of rural areas are either not solved or are not solved well enough, so the expressed poverty is a logical sequence of these (in) actions by the state (Veselinovic et al., 2012).

Poverty According to the Educational Structure in Serbia

Poverty status is also strongly influenced by the level of education through the labor market. People with a higher level of education have access to the labor market and high-quality jobs, but there are still significant differences between the sexes. Low levels of education remain the most significant factor in poverty. On average, poverty is more than ten times more common among people living in households where the head has not completed primary school than among those living in households where the

Poverty and Poverty Indicators in the Republic of Serbia

head has a college or university degree. Approximately 60% of all the poor live in households in which the head has the most primary school, compared to their half smaller share in the population structure. Figure 6 shows the Poverty Rate according to the level of education of household heads in Serbia.

Figure 6. Poverty rate according to the level of education of the household head
Source: Mladenovic, 2017

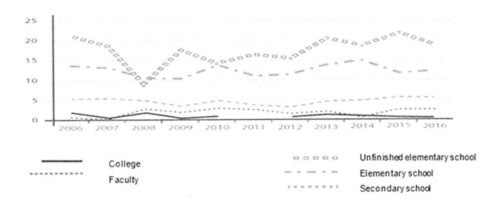

Besides education, labor market status is another decisive factor in poverty. Persons living in households where the head is unemployed and inactive are between four and five times more often poor than persons living in households where the head is employed, although employment status alone does not ensure a way out of poverty for all persons (3% of persons who live in households in which the holder is employed are poor). The most endangered are persons with incomplete primary education, as well as persons with completed primary school. The higher the level of education, the lower the risk of poverty. "This is confirmed by the fact that about a third of the poor (in the some observed countries in the Balkan region - former member states of the SFRY) have not completed primary school. As many as half of the poor population do not have a secondary education, and the least endangered are people with higher education" (Ilic, 2019). There is also a correlation between poverty and the number of household members. Thus, households with a larger number of members (with five, six, and more members) are exposed to the greatest danger of poverty. Households with six or more members are significantly above average exposed to poverty. In the total number of the poor, approximately a quarter live in households with six or more members. In recent years, there has been a trend of increasing poverty among people living in two-member and three-member households (Mladenovic, 2017). This fact is supported by data related to Serbia. According to the data, over a third of the poor come from households with five or more members. On the other hand, households with one or two members are far less poor and at risk of poverty. An important factor in explaining the poverty of extended families, i.e. multi-member households, is the degree of dependence. The degree of dependence measures the number of family members of the unproductive age (children and the elderly) that productive members must support. Large households have more children, so there is a smaller number of those who earn, while three- and four-member households are in a more favorable position (Miletic and Sovtic, 2018).

According to the official data of the SORS, the average salary (gross) calculated for February 2021 in Serbia was about 85,000Dinars (800Euros), while the average salary without taxes and contributions (net) was about 60,000 Dinars (550Euros). Growth in gross wages in the period January-February 2021, compared to the same period last year, amounted to 6.0% in nominal terms and 4.8% in real terms. Compared to the same month of the previous year, the average gross salary for February 2021 was nominally higher by 6.9% and really by 5.6%, while the average net salary was nominally higher by 7.1%, ie by 5,8% real. The median net salary for February 2021 amounted to 47,682 dinars, which means that 50% of employees earned up to the stated amount (Average earnings per employee, February,2021). If the presented data are taken into account, it can be concluded that the poverty rate in Serbia should be lower. However, this is not the case with all regions of the country, as the average at the state level is shown and calculated. The problem of underdeveloped regions of the country, South, and East, as well as sensitive categories of the population living in these areas, remains. The state must make great efforts to reduce this difference.

DISCUSSION

How to overcome inequalities in Serbia, with what goals to start? Serbia (in response to the questions), has the following development goals: intensifying market reforms, initiating economic development, creating jobs, as well as removing barriers that affect the reduction of unemployment.

Only recently, by overcoming long-term economic and political isolation, in Serbia have been created conditions for intensifying market reforms and initiating economic development on a stable basis. The fate of poverty in the process of economic reforms largely depends on economic growth, and economic growth on the way economic reforms are shaped and implemented. Job creation and all activities that will lead to employment should be at the center of economic policy and social protection. In addition to removing barriers that reduce unemployment, economic and social policy makers must pay attention to the nature of the work that the economic system creates. Activation of the able-bodied population and high employment ensure the sustainability of the welfare state, because taxes and contributions of employees, among other things, finance public expenditures for pensions, social benefits, and health, while employment increases the number of social protection beneficiaries. Regional long-term planning faces, above all, a challenge of an institutional nature. Macro regions are asymmetric and dysfunctional, the decentralization process is slow, the decision-making process is slowly approaching the citizens to make more rational.

The phenomenon of poverty in Serbia is related to the following problems: the demographic situation of the country, unfavorable migration flows of the population, low educational and personnel structure of the population, regional and social inequalities. According to the Report on Regional Development of Serbia from 2013, one of the biggest development problems of the country was demographic. Serbia has lost more than 5% of its population in the last decade, while demographic devastation has affected more than 50% of municipalities in Serbia. Eight years ago, in 2014, the number of inhabitants was lower in 146 municipalities, and higher only in 22, which is determined by the negative natural increase. In the capital of Serbia, Belgrade, the number of households increased by six percent in this period, while in southeastern Serbia, the number of households decreased by the same percentage. The territorial aspect of depopulation indicates that all municipalities have lost an average of more than 2,600 inhabitants, ie each district has lost an average of more than 15,000 inhabitants (Serbia's Regional Development Report,

Poverty and Poverty Indicators in the Republic of Serbia

2013). Unfavorable migration flows include external migrations of young, able-bodied, and most highly educated population, but also very frequent internal migrations between villages and cities. In Serbia, there is a low educational and personnel structure of the population in almost 2/3 of the municipalities, and thus a pronounced rate of ecologically less aware population. Regional and social inequalities in Serbia in the coming period will depend primarily on: the speed of transitional reforms (post-privatization restructuring, structural reforms, investments), education reforms, and regional models of endogenous growth and social inclusion.

SOLUTIONS AND RECOMMENDATIONS

Employment is the primary goal in Serbia, but numerous social and societal relations depend on the quality of work. The state must, through active employment measures, take responsibility for reducing unemployment and raising the quality of employees' work. Along with strengthening active employment measures (raising the educational level of employees, additional education and training programs, entrepreneurship development, measures to strengthen regional and social cohesion, etc.), the primary emphasis must be placed on the education system to improve the labor supply. Although Serbia set many strategic priorities for regional development policy in 2015, starting with the functional redefinition of the Institutional Model of Regional Development Policy of Serbia, then the adoption of the umbrella strategic development document in the field of regional development for the period 2015-2020, to the establishment of a new measurement methodology levels of development in Serbia, it should be noted that many measures did not materialize because at the beginning of 2020, a "state of emergency" was declared, caused by the pandemic virus COVID-19. In this situation - globally, regionally, and locally - it was necessary to focus all efforts on combating the spread of the virus and the functioning of the health system. Although Serbia had great help from China and other major countries such as Russia and even European countries, the fight against the virus put all the plans in the background. The state was focused on saving human lives and healing. Poverty as a phenomenon in Serbia was not in focus, although its existence was still evident. The health care system was quickly reorganized, comprehensive measures were introduced to suppress the spread of the infection, and the state helped the economy with various economic measures.

However, the fact is that not much could be done in the previous period regarding the country's regional inequality and in reducing the poverty (Djuric et al, 2019). Therefore, in the following period in 2021, the state undertook certain activities. The Law on the Budget of the Republic of Serbia for 2021 ("Official Gazette of the Republic of Serbia", No. 149/20) in Article 8 of the Decree of 2021, established the Program for Encouraging Regional and Local Economic Development and provided funds of 25,000.000,00 dinars. These funds are intended for the measure of co-financing the annual membership fee of local self-government units for the work and operations of accredited regional development agencies (abbreviated: ARRA). The program is implemented by the Ministry of Economy (hereinafter: the Ministry) in cooperation with the Development Agency of Serbia (hereinafter: the Development Agency). The goal of the Program is to support the regional and local development of Serbia by connecting the subjects of regional development at the national, regional, and local levels. The measure of the Program is co-financing the annual membership fee of local self-government units for work (Development Agency of Serbia, 2021). Regarding the level of development of the local self-government unit, the valid single list of development of the region and the local self-government unit at the time of submitting the re-

277

quest is applied.Co-financing of membership fees is done depending on the level of development of the local self-government unit, and under the Decree on determining the conditions, criteria, and manner of accreditation for regional development and revocation of accreditation before the expiration of the "Official Gazette of the Republic of Serbia", 2019), in ways according to the following criteria: 1) in the amount of 25% of the annual membership fee for local self-government units classified in the third group by the level of development, 2) in the amount of 50% of the annual membership fee for local self-government units classified in the fourth group 3) in the amount of 75% of the annual membership fee for local self-government units classified in devastated areas and for local self-government units from the Region of Kosovo and Metohija.

The request with the necessary documentation is submitted by the local self-government units to the Development Agency (directly or through ARRA), in two copies, no later than October 2021. The Ministry and the Development Agency are concluding an Agreement on the implementation of the measure of co-financing the annual membership fee of local self-government units for the work and operations of ARRA. The Development Agency processes and controls the submitted requests and submits to the Ministry a Proposal of the list of requests for transfer of funds for co-financing the annual membership fee of local self-government units for work and operations of ARRA with accompanying documentation by October, 2021.After the control of the proposal list of requests by the Ministry, the Minister of Economy makes a Decision on approving the co-financing of the annual membership fee of local self-government units for work and operations of ARRA. The Ministry is obliged to transfer the approved funds to the local self-government units to the prescribed accounts for the payment of public revenues. The Ministry, in cooperation with the Development Agency, should monitor the implementation of ARRA activities following this program.

FUTURE RESEARCH DIRECTIONS

The directions of Serbia's future development could be classified into the following categories - increased social inclusion, on the other hand, reduced social exclusion, and finally through an attempt to reduce poverty in the country. Social inclusion is defined as a process that enables those at risk of poverty, and social exclusion to be given the opportunity and resources necessary to participate fully in economic, social and cultural life and to achieve the standard of living and well-being considered essential in society in which they live. Social inclusion in Serbia would ensure greater participation of citizens in decision-making that affects their lives and the realization of basic rights. Serbia must take measures so that individuals and/or groups of the population are not far from various opportunities: for employment, income generation, and education opportunities, as well as to include the poor in participation in social networks and community activities. Excluded individuals and/or groups would thus gain adequate access to institutions, authorities, and decision-making processes. Poverty is defined as a multidimensional phenomenon which, in addition to insufficient income to meet living needs, includes the inability to find employment, inadequate housing conditions, and inadequate access to social protection, health, education, and utilities. Poverty reduction would realize the rights of vulnerable categories of the population to a healthy environment and natural resources. The main goals and guidelines of the economic policy of the Republic of Serbia identified in the document Fiscal Strategy for 2019 - with projections for 2020 and 2021 (Fiscal Council, 2019) are: Preservation of fiscal stability with growth support, Macro economically sustainable and inclusive economic growth reducing the country's regional inequality as well

Poverty and Poverty Indicators in the Republic of Serbia

as the EU Accession Process. Fiscal developments at the end of 2017 show a consolidated government sector surplus of 1.2% of GDP (Ministry of Finance Serbia, 2019). According to the projections set out in the Fiscal Strategy in 2018, the deficit of the consolidated government sector with the application of fiscal consolidation measures amounted to 0.7% of GDP, with a further reduction in 2019 and 2020, when they amounted to 0.5% of GDP. Thanks to fiscal consolidation measures, fiscal space was created for new policies, which in 2018 were used to increase capital investments, increase pensions and salaries in one part of the public sector and reduce the tax burden on wages. These measures and their fiscal implications are designed not to jeopardize the stability of public finances and the pace of public debt reduction, but on the other hand to raise the living standards of the population, stimulate private consumption and accelerate economic development in the long run. The goals set in 2018 and 2019 are still in the process of realization, and it can be concluded that the future sustainable growth and development of Serbia depends on the realization of these pipes.

CONCLUSION

Poverty and social exclusion have been recognized as problems that significantly burden the smooth functioning of the modern world. It is indisputable that no progress can hardly ignore the hunger and misery of man at the beginning of the 21st century. It is precisely this contradiction that makes this world less beautiful but also less understandable. The problem of poverty has not bypassed Serbia either, while at the same time it seems that its weight is based on the already present problems in the Serbian economy. The positive trends of poverty reduction were stopped by the effect of the global financial crisis, but also by the domestic crisis. This is supported by the presentation of poverty through the prism of numbers that indicate the fact that poverty in Serbia is still on the rise. Having in mind the achieved level of economic development, Serbia cannot boast of any major allocations that could be directed through social benefits to alleviate the effects of the poverty problem. Also, it cannot boast of the domestic disposal of those funds. This development inevitably had to be transferred to the poverty segment. The beginning of the third millennium seemed promising in terms of poverty reduction. At least then, it seemed that poverty was a problem whose solution was in sight soon. From year to year, the state boasted of reducing the number of poor. However, it should be emphasized that the official national data on the number of the poor were mostly unrealistic, because they did not match, and in addition, they were smaller in concerning the data of the European Union. Serbia has at least declaratively advocated for poverty reduction. The fact that the Poverty Reduction Strategy was adopted in 2003 speaks in favor of that. After more than a decade of its implementation, it can be said that it seems as if it was not applicable in the existing Serbian circumstances, and this is confirmed by the results of its implementation. Economic policy-makers are not facing the problem of poverty for the first time. To solve the problem of poverty, it is crucial to implement a broad consensus of decision-makers at all levels of decision-making in Serbia. One thing is for sure, as various international reports say, economic growth must be inclusive to ensure sustainable jobs and promote poverty reduction. Rising inequality is hampering efforts to reduce poverty. Faster poverty reduction depends on reducing inequality. High inequality reduces the effect of growth on poverty reduction, and with a higher degree of inequality, poverty reduction becomes more difficult. In contrast, if economic growth is accompanied by a reduction in inequality, growth has a greater effect on poverty reduction. Therefore, overcoming different dimensions of inequality is crucial for progress towards achieving the Sustainable Development Goals. In addressing inequality and poverty, the complexity of these phenomena should be taken into account. It is necessary to understand that the relative importance attached to the various goals related to the reduction of inequality and poverty depends on the strategic outcome that society wants to achieve.

ACKNOWLEDGMENT

This research received no specific grant from any funding agency in the public, commercial, or not-for profit sectors.

REFERENCES

Agbedahin, A. V. (2019). Sustainable development, Education for Sustainable Development, and the 2030 Agenda for Sustainable Development: Emergence, efficacy,eminence, and future. *Sustainable Development*, (1), 12.

Arandarenko, M. (2011). Labor market in Serbia: trends, institutions, policies. Center for Publishing Activities of the Faculty of Economics.

Arandarenko, M., & Aleksic, D. (2016). Not all jobs are created equal: How not to misread the labour force statistics in Serbia. *Business Economics (Cleveland, Ohio)*, *64*(3–4), 211–224.

Average earnings per employee, February. (2021). *SORS*. https://www.propisi.net/prosecne-zarade-po-zaposlenom-februar-2021/

Bogicevic, B., Krstic, G., & Mijatovic, B. (2012). Poverty in Serbia and the reform of state aid to the poor. Center for Liberal-Democratic Studies, Belgrade.

Consumption, income and living conditions. (2017). *SORS*. https://www.stat.gov.rs/sr-Latn/oblasti/potrosnja-prihodi-i-uslovi-zivota

Development Agency of Serbia (DAS). (2021). *Decree on determining the program for encouraging regional and local development in 2021*. Author.

Devetakovic, S., Jovanovic, Gavrilovic, B., & Rikalovic, G. (2008). *National Economy*. Faculty of Economics, University of Belgrade.

Djukic, G.P., & Ilic, B.S. (2020). Sustainable development, social protection and responsibility. *İzmir Sosyal Bilimler Dergisi*, *2*(2), 83-91.

Djuric, K., Cvijanovic, D., Prodanovic, R., Cavlin, M., Kuzman, B., & Lukac Bulatovic, M. (2019). Serbian Agriculture Policy: Economic Analysis Using the PSE Approach. *Sustainability*, *11*(2), 309. doi:10.3390u11020309

Dollar, D., & Kraay, A. (2010). *Growth is Good for the Poor*. World Bank.

EU. (2018). *Operating budgetary balance*. https://ec.europa.eu/info/publications/operating-budgetary-balance-gni_hr

Fincham, R., Georg, S., & Neilsen, E. (Eds.). (2004). *Sustainable developmentand the university: New strategies for research teaching and practice*. Howick, Brevitas.

Fiscal Council. (2019). Fiscal and Economic Trends in 2019 and Strategic Recommendations for Budget and Fiscal Policy in 2020. Author.

Golubovic, N. (2009). Social capital and economic-theoretical 'imperialism' [Društveni kapital i ekonomsko-teorijski 'imperijalizam']. *Proceedings of the "Matica Srpska" for Social Sciences, 128*, 63-73.

Government of the Republic of Serbia (2021). *Social Inclusion Team- Social inclusion, Poverty statistics, Who are the poor in Serbia?* [Socijalno uključivanje, Statistika siromaštva, Ko su siromašni u Srbiji?]. Author.

Hattingh, J. (2002). On the imperative of sustainable development: A philosophical and ethical appraisal. In Environmental education, ethics andaction in Southern Africa (pp. 5–16). Human Sciences Research Council.

Ilic, B., & Djukic, G. (2021). Introduction of crisis management for the purpose of positive changes in the age of COVID -19. In *Proceedings of 7th International ConferenceInnovation as the initiator of development* (Vol. 3, pp. 398–408). Faculty of Applied Management, Economics and Finance.

Ilic, B., & Jovanovic, L. (2017). Quality of Serbian life as one of the components of sustainable development. *Proceeding of the 7th International Symposium on Natural Resources Management, 7*, 272-279.

Ilic, B., & Mihajlovic, D. (2017). Motivational theories and factors of sustainable and socially responsible business. *Proceedings of 9th International Scientific Conference Social actors before information technologies challenges in search for new vision of social peace, 9*, 312-325.

Ilic, B., & Pavicevic, N. (2018). Selection of economic and ecological development rights of tourism using the method of multi-criteria decision-making-case study Gamzigradska Banja. Society of Economists, Economics (NIS, Medivest KT).

Ilic, B., Sovtic, K., & Mihajlovic, D. (2019). Economic and ecological sustainability of Serbia - a condition for raising quality and environmental protection. *Ecologica, 94*(26), 193–198.

Ilic, B. S. (2019). Renewable Energy Sources Management and Role of Ecological Parks: Improving Quality of Life for Sustainable Development. In U. Akkucuk (Ed.), *Handbook Ethical and Sustainable Supply Chain Management in a Global Context* (pp. 220–228). IGI Global. doi:10.4018/978-1-5225-8970-9.ch014

Ilic, B. S. (2020). Social Component of Sustainable Development and Quality of Life: Region of the Balkans, Eastern Serbia. In U. Akkucuk (Ed.), *Handbook of Research on Creating Sustainable Value in the Global Economy* (pp. 452–462). IGI Global. doi:10.4018/978-1-7998-1196-1.ch026

Jandric, M., & Molnar, D. (2017). *Quality of employment and labor market in Serbia*. Friedrich-Ebert Foundation, Belgrade Office.

Kokovic, D. (2009). Culture and ecological values. *Annual Review of the Faculty of Philosophy, 1/2*(34), 207–215.

Krivokapic, Dj., & Mesanovic, E. (2016). *Leasing Workers - A Guide to the Rights of Workers Temporarily Engaged through Employment Agencies*. Share Olof Palme Foundation and International Center.

Krstic, G., & Soskic, D. (2016). Economic statistics. Center for Publishing Activities of the Faculty of Economics.

Labour Force survey in Serbia. (2014). *SORS*. https://www.stat.gov.rs/sr-Latn / areas / labor-market / labor-force-survey

Labour Market dynamics in the third quarter. (2021). *SORS*. https://www.stat.gov.rs/sr-latn/vesti/20211130-anketa-o-radnoj-snazi-iii-kv-2021/?s=2400

Manetovic, E. (2016). Serbian National Identity: A Look Beyond the Modernization Paradigm. *Serbian Science Today, 1*(1), 18–29.

Mannila, S. (2015). Informal Employment and Vulnerability in Less Developed Markets. In J. Vuori, R. Blonk, & R. H. Price (Eds.), *Sustainable Working Lives*. Springer. doi:10.1007/978-94-017-9798-6_2

Matkovic, G. (2014). *Poverty Measurement-Theoretical Concept, Situation and Recommendations for the Republic of Serbia*. Team for Social Inclusion and Poverty Reduction of the Government of the Republic of Serbia.

Miletic, D., & Sovtic, K. (2018). Poverty as a national and regional problem of the Republic of Serbia [Siromaštvo kao nacionalni i regionalni problem Republike Srbije]. *Proceeding Regional Development and Border Cooperation, II International Scientific Conference*, 339-350.

Ministry of Economy Sector for Regional Development and Strategic Economic Analysis Republic of Serbia. (2013). *Serbia Regional Development Report*. Author.

Ministry of Finance Belgrade of Serbia. (2019). *Macroeconomic and Fiscal Data*. Author.

Mladenovic, B. (2017). *Poverty in the Republic of Serbia 2006-2016*. Team for Social Inclusion and Poverty Reduction of the Government of Serbia.

National Strategy for Sustainable Development of Serbia. (2008). Available at: http: / /indicator.sepa. gov.rs/slike/pdf/o-indikatorima/nacionalna-strategija-odrzivog-razvoja-srbije

Official Gazette of the Republic of Serbia, No. 149/20.

Official Gazette of the Republic of Serbia, No. 74/10, 4/12, 44/18 - State Law 69/19.

Radakovic, M. (2012). Problems in the construction of collective national identity. *Political Magazine, 11*(3), 153-169.

Ramos, T. B., Caeiro, S., Pires, S. M., & Videira, N. (2018). How are new sustainable development approaches responding to societal challenges? *Sustainable Development, 26*(2), 117–121. doi:10.1002d.1730

Ravallion, M. (2013). *The Idea of Antipoverty Policy*. NBER Working Paper Series.

Social inclusion and poverty reduction unit. (2021). *Absolute poverty*. https://socijalnoukljucivanje.gov.rs/sr/социјално-укључивање-у-рс/статистикасиромаштва/апсолутно-сиромаштво/

SORS. (2018). *Publication.* https://www.stat.gov.rs/sr-latn/publikacije/

Stankovic, B. (2008). *Living Standards Study: Serbia 2002-2007: Poverty Profile in Serbia 2002-2007.* Statistical Office of the Republic of Serbia.

Statistical Yearbook of the Republic of Serbia. (2016). SORS.

Stiglitz, J., Sen, A., & Fitoussi, J.P. (2009). *Report by the Commission on the Measurement of Economic Performance and Social Progress.* Academic Press.

Stojanovic, D., Ilic, B., & Mihajlovic, D. (2017). Sustainable development in Serbia in correlations with foreign direct investment. *21st International Scientific Conference on Economic and Social Development, 21,* 101-108.

Structure of Earnings Survey. (2016). *Eurostat Press Office.* https://ec.europa.eu/eurostat/documents/2995521/7762327/3-08122016-AP-EN.pdf/3f02c5ed-81de-49cb-a77e74396bac2467

UN. (1995). *UN Documents: Overview of Secretary-General's Reports.* https://www.securitycouncilreport.org/un-documents/document/unro-s1995-1.php

UN. (2015). *Handbook on Measuring Quality of Employment – a Statistical Framework.* United Nations Economic Commission for Europe.

UNESCO. (1997). *Education for a sustainable future: A transdisciplinary vision for concerted action.* UNESCO. https://en.unesco.org/themes/education/

Veselinovic, P. (2013). National Economy. Faculty of Economics.

Veselinovic, P., Micic, V., & Miletic, D. (2012). Serbia – zone of poverty and social exclusion. *Economics Of Agriculture, 59*(2), 305–318.

ADDITIONAL READING

Alvaredo, F., Chancel, L., Piketty, T., Saez, E., & Zucman, G. (2017). *World Inequality Report 2018.* World Inequality Lab.

Clavet, N. J., Tiberti, L., Vladisavljevic, M., Zarkovic, J., Anic, A., Krstic, G., & Randjelovic, S. (2019). Reduction of child poverty in Serbia: Benefit or employment strategy? *Economics of Transition, 27*(3), 615–645. doi:10.1111/ecot.12197

Djukic, G., Ilic, B., & Balaban, M. (2018). The role and management of renewable energy sources in the sustainable development of Serbia. *Energy, Economics, Ecology, 20,* 1–2, 451–459.

Ilic, B., Stojanovic, D., & Pavicevic, N. (2019). Management of life and environment quality in modern technologies. *Journal of Sustainable Development, 23*(9), 14–28.

Jolliffe, D. (2014). *A measured approach to ending poverty and boosting shared prosperity: concepts, data, and the twin goals.* World Bank Publications.

Nikolic, M., Vesic, T., Cogoljevic, T., & Ilic, B. (2018). Knowledge management with the aim of preventing ecological crisis. *Ecologica*, *89*, 82–85.

KEY TERMS AND DEFINITIONS

Accredited Regional Development Agencies: A regional development agency is a company or association established to perform activities or improve regional development.

Hyperinflation: Hyperinflation is extremely high or fast inflation (price growth), which causes a significant decline in the value of the national currency.

LFS: Labour force survey enables an overview of the situation and monitoring of changes in the labor market in Serbia.

Local Economic Development: Local economic development is the youngest competence of local self-government, the need and development priority of each city/municipality.

Relative Poverty: This measure does not mean the level of poverty, but the risk that the covered individual will be poor, i.e., that some person will have difficulty in providing funds for standard common in the country in which he/she lives.

SFRY: Is an abbreviation of the former state known as the Socialist Federal Republic of Yugoslavia, which was composed of 6 Republics and two Autonomous provinces. In the 1990s, the state disintegrated into smaller states, which today occupy the Western Balkans.

SORS: The Statistical Office of the Republic of Serbia (Serbian latin: Republički zavod za statistiku Srbije or RBS) is a specialized government agency of Serbia charged with collecting and disseminating official statistics.

Sustainable Development Goals: The Sustainable Development Goals, also known as global goals, are a universal call to action to eradicate poverty, protect the environment and ensure peace and prosperity for all. These 17 goals are based on the success of the Millennium Development Goals, but also include new priority areas such as climate change, economic inequalities, innovation, sustainable consumption, peace, and justice.

Third World Countries: Shortened Third World, are terms that refer to the countries that are economically underdeveloped (but that are developing). The terms originate from the time of the Cold War, when these countries are formed.

Chapter 15
Role of Global Institutions in Competency Development

Ramnath Dixit
 https://orcid.org/0000-0002-7131-5857
Symbiosis International University, Pune, India

Vinita Sinha
Symbiosis Centre for Management and Human Resource Development, Symbiosis International University, Pune, India

ABSTRACT

This chapter aims to highlight the role of global institutions in facilitating competency development for people from different nationalities spread across diverse geographies. Training and development is an essential step towards accomplishing inclusive development and is closely connected with social and economic development on a universal scale. Although multilateral institutions are taking efforts towards providing timely and regular training to people worldwide, there is ample scope for ensuring the successful implementation of knowledge and skills disseminated through various training initiatives. It is in this context that transfer of training or learning transfer gains prominence as a game changer in shaping the development initiatives driven by global institutions. This chapter thus delves deeper on the need to ensure a robust training transfer ecosystem and the significance of global institutions in facilitating the same to achieve competency development. The chapter concludes with pragmatic recommendations to enhance competency development universally.

INTRODUCTION

Institutions and organizations depend on their workforce to survive and prosper. Therefore, it is imperative that institutions continually invest in human development through training interventions. Training and development is a critical organizational task it delivers the personnel with pertinent insights on ways to perform their roles and the resources to deliver performance in their field of work (Suazo et al., 2009). Training is an indispensable component in strategic Human Resource Development (HRD) framework (Kucherov & Manokhina, 2017). According to (Wilson & Madsen, 2008) continual training of personnel

DOI: 10.4018/978-1-6684-2448-3.ch015

Copyright © 2022, IGI Global. Copying or distributing in print or electronic forms without written permission of IGI Global is prohibited.

is the most critical organizational competency. Training also contributes to norm localization, defined by Acharya (2004) as "a complex process and outcome by which norm-takers build congruence between transnational norms … and local beliefs and practices." It their research, (Sekerin et al., 2018) prove the efficacy of on-the-job training in enhancing a nation's competitive strength and building a knowledge economy. Anane (2013) rightly asserts that "in today's competitive global economy, technical/vocational education is a key element in the equation of development, because it allows people and society to unlock their potential, broaden their horizons, and adapt to changes in a dynamic world."

Competency building and measurement are becoming increasingly crucial for business success in current times of increasing flexibility, speed and globalization within the economy (Stracke, 2011). Abele & Reinhart (2011) suggest that skills and competency development must be adaptable in accordance with the following:

- New forms of learning that are adapted to the learning ability of older employees
- Changing requirements for knowledge management in the company

Furthermore, empirical investigation by proves that competence level of learners can be increased by providing them adequate training opportunities (Mohanakumari & Magesh, 2017). Research by (Dixit, 2019) clearly highlights the positive impact of competency development of workers in healthcare institutions. Similar sentiments are echoed in another study that proves training is a strategic tool to provide impetus to competency development initiatives (Dixit & Sinha, 2021). However, merely investing time, money and effort in training without ensuring its effective implementation is likely to result in loss of invaluable resources. Hence, global institutions need to assess the significance of their role both in competency development through adequate training along with ensuring successful learning transfer in the aftermath of training interventions. Multilateral institutions play a critical role in facilitating the development of Corporate Social Responsibility (CSR) (Vives, 2004). Researcher Kuruc (2018) states that institutions such as the International Monetary Fund (IMF) play a significant role in fragile states towards accomplishing macroeconomic stability along with building state capacity and institutions in the domain of its core competency. Libraries of work have commented on the role and relevance of World Bank as a leading a development institution (Barnett & Duvall, 2005; Griffin, 2006; Broad, 2007; Weaver, 2010; Vetterlein, 2012) extending project financing and intellectual output. Institutions of the stature of World Bank are becoming increasing important in every sphere of economic activity. As famously remarked by (Kramarz & Momani, 2013) "the world bank has always sold ideas, not just loans."

Transfer is central to all learning (Marini & Genereux, 1995). Transfer of training, also termed learning transfer is often the missing link that renders the training exercise futile. Nur et al. (2015), training transfer is referred to the application of acquired knowledge, skills and attitudes to assigned tasks. Global institutions perform a critical task of funding training projects that enable corporations, individuals as well as nations to compete and survive in the volatile environments. This chapter attempts to highlight the role of global institutions in competency development through a dual focus on training and the subsequent learning transfer of the training programs delivered, through adoption of a strategic approach. The key challenges impacting competency development involve the following:

1. Existing bottlenecks in the global training environment
2. Inadequacy of training transfer mechanism to drive knowledge and skills implementation
3. Absence of training transfer tools to ensure success of training interventions

Role of Global Institutions in Competency Development

4. Paucity of sufficient financial assistance to sustain training initiatives
5. Lack of measurement and accountability to evaluate competency development initiatives

BACKGROUND

The world organizations OECD and UNESCO (2001) are among the most important institutions at the global level for competencies and education. It is necessary to emphasize the fact that there is an evident growing demand for higher academic qualifications and the need for constant updating, both didactic expertise and teacher knowledge. For educational institutions, this is essential for a simple reason - the future world and future generations need to be provided with knowledge and skills that will help form a new economic and social order. The Organization for Economic Cooperation and Development (OECD), 2001, seeks to identify the competencies needed for the successful implementation of education in modern society, based its results on studies and competencies related to economics. Observing the needs of the market for educational staff, competencies are desirable in terms of the use of modern information technology, communication technology, rapid problem solving, supervision and monitoring of continuity of education.

The World Bank is amongst the most significant sources of knowledge for development (St Clair, 2006). It was the first development organization to seriously consider the implications of the increased importance of knowledge in economic and institutional growth in Organization for Economic Co-operation and Development (OECD) nations for itself and its clients (King, 2002). The World Bank officially termed as the International Bank for Reconstruction and Development (IBRD). The World Bank is an institution of prime importance and has provided development assistance to its member countries for 70 years. In that time, it has lent close to one trillion dollars in loans and credits, has published libraries worth of books, policy briefs, and working papers on a litany of subjects, and has led the mainstream practice of international development assistance (Bazbauers, 2018). The World Bank in its current mission statement mentions that "Our mission is to fight poverty with passion and professionalism for lasting results and to help people help themselves and their environment by providing resources, sharing knowledge, building capacity and forging partnerships in the public and private sectors" (World Bank, 2010). Prior to this, the (World Bank, 2009) also stated that "Knowledge is the key to development effectiveness, and the driver of a successful development institution. Without knowledge, the WBG cannot lend, it cannot advise, and it cannot convene. Knowledge is the core of our DNA." Even international training organizations such as the Joint Vienna Institute (JVI) perform a significant role in fostering socialization and driving ideational change at an individual level (Nsouli, 2003).

Teachers with very less formal training is a universal problem and unfortunately the World Bank has been complicit on this matter (Fontdevila & Verger, 2015). Researchers (Dixit & Sinha, 2020) observe that although training and development is invaluable to organizations, the training effort is often rendered futile on account on the several bottlenecks present in the organizational environment. In particular, professional training wields a powerful influence on how policy actors make sense of the environment in which they seek to act, and how they identify and diagnose the nature of the problems they seek to act upon (Chwieroth, 2008).

COMPETENCE DEVELOPMENT AND KEY CHALLENGES

In the field of teacher training, Berliner advocates a number of proposals for formal teacher education programs (Berliner, 2000), as follows:

1. Good teachers must develop pedagogical experience, but also knowledge of pedagogical content. Knowing the content of a certain teaching area is not enough. Thorough knowledge of the context of the educational process, but also of scientific matters, is the most important competence that a teacher (working in complex environments) must have.
2. Teachers need seven years to maximize performance with their students and approximately five to progress from primary to advanced level.
3. Teachers must and have the right to protect the public from poor quality training and programs offered by some providers as non-standard programs.
4. Quality teaching methods emphasize techniques and principles that facilitate the conversion of subject knowledge into cognitive structures so that knowledge is accessible to students.
5. Universities should develop teacher training programs that bridge the gap between lectures / trainings and classrooms. Talented and experienced mentors and teachers can be expected to work - together with beginner students, helping them to integrate the theoretical knowledge acquired at universities with practical knowledge.
6. It is desirable that there are general and codified principles of teaching.
7. Teachers and their trainers must be the "voice" and creators of education policy, when making laws and implementing education-related projects.
8. Teacher education, in order to better place the knowledge that will have practical application, requires hours and hours of preparation. Before that, teachers must achieve a satisfactory level in mastering curricula.

Key Challenges Affecting Competence Development

1. Existing bottlenecks in the global training environment
2. Inadequacy of training transfer mechanism to drive knowledge and skills implementation
3. Absence of training transfer tools to ensure success of training interventions
4. Paucity of sufficient financial assistance to provide and sustain training initiatives
5. Lack of measurement and accountability to evaluate competency development initiatives

1. Existing bottlenecks in the global training environment

Organizations, institutions and people at large depend on the acquisition of skill and knowledge for both social survival and economic prosperity. This consistent need to upgrade oneself demands setting-up of a dynamic training and development ecosystem that enables the populace in various nations. However, the training and development environment is riddled with numerous challenges especially for the masses in developing and third world countries. Multilateral institutions equipped with global reach are trying to focus on improving this scenario, however the efforts needed to create a sustainable change globally is no easy task and requires sustained momentum. Often organizations and nations tend to either ignore or abandon training necessities of its masses on account of several bottlenecks such as

Role of Global Institutions in Competency Development

poor training infrastructure, lack of resources, financial constraints, paucity of quality trainers and many others. Furthermore, even those nations that ensure continual training for its manpower during normal situations, tend to either postpone or cancel training provisions during times of uncertainty or economic upheavals. This gives rise to increase in global unemployment as well as greater income disparity, since a huge mass of the population continues to remain unemployable on account of skilled based training focusing on competency development. Hence, global institutions need to emphasize on ensuring skill-based competency development as its priority area.

2. Inadequacy of training transfer mechanism to drive knowledge and skills implementation

As nations and organizations gain more maturity in terms of understanding learning needs of its people, there is a definite shift towards bringing larger sections of populations under the skill development initiatives. Countries are making sustained efforts in driving competency development programs through governmental support as well as working in conjunction with organizations and institutions in the private sector. Businesses are expanding their spending in employee training based on the premise that training and development improves organizational competitiveness (Ho, 2016). A recent study shows that in the year 2015 alone, global entities have incurred a massive sum of $356 billion was invested on training intervention (Baldwin & Ford, 2017). However, merely designing and delivered training interventions is less likely to yield the desired result, either in terms of skill acquisition or behavior modification. Transfer of training is the Achilles heel of the training process (Botke et al. 2017). Previous studies also indicate that a major portion of investments in training is wasted on account of poor training transfer (Dhaka et al., 2018). Positive training transfer is widely considered to be the most important goal of training efforts, but it has shown to be a daunting task (Baldwin et al., 2017). A study by Cowman & McCarthy (2016), shows that despite massive, ever-increasing expenditures on human resources training and development programs, the rate of training/learning transfer is abysmally low at 10 percent. Therefore, it is imperative that there is a shift in focus towards practical implementation of training programs to ensure a holistic competency development. To accomplish this objective, it is quintessential that nations and organizations must work in tandem with multilateral institutions to strengthen the transfer of training at the grassroots level. For training to yield value, the acquired learning must be transferred to the workplace (Yaw, 2008). Recent studies by Hurt (2016) and Baldwin et al. (2017), have shown that training transfer is low as most learners lack the ability to transfer their newly learned knowledge and skills at workplaces. The absence or lack of training transfer mechanism often renders the training projects futile or at best provides a marginal return on the training investments. For instance, if a certain group of individuals in a particular location are imparted training on enhancing competencies that make them job ready, then there has to be a framework in place that ensures that the learners are able to apply their learnings in a post-training environment. There also needs to be a provision for learners so that they get an opportunity to practice the skills and competencies gained during the training program.

3. Absence of training transfer tools to ensure success of training interventions

Transfer of training needs to be adequately complimented with appropriate tools and techniques that facilitate transfer. Unfortunately, both organizations and governments do not have the wherewithal about the nature of transfer tools that leaners can be equipped with. The absence of relevant tools for leaners means that inspite of their willingness to implement knowledge from the training sessions, they will not in a position to apply any of those. Also, absence of transfer tools is likely to impact the motivation levels of leaners and may dissuade them from practicing the acquired competencies. A wide variety of learning transfer tools are available yet inaccessible to the training participants across various geographies and nations on account of either cost constraints, technological barriers and other such pertinent factors. Some of the tools that can be instrumental in facilitating effective transfer include one-on-one coaching, mobile learning applications, learning chat groups, augmented reality, gamification, video & audio learning clips, reading literature, live projects, e-learning etc. Also adopting the appropriate design strategy such as the andragogical instruction methodology (e.g. case study, role playing and simulation) for matured learners and pedagogical methodology (e.g. lecture methods) for immature learners can positively impact trainees' motivation towards better training transfer (Muduli et al., 2018).

4. Paucity of sufficient financial assistance to provide and sustain training initiatives

Training and development demands continual and often heavy financial investments, especially in the context of competency initiative which are national or of international stature. Multilateral organizations often find it challenging to fund the training requirements on such a massive scale. Also for instance, the International Finance Corporation (IFC), the World Bank's investment arm, consistently and aggressively funds the low-cost private educational institutions in poorer nations (Klees et al., 2019). Financial limitations coupled with resource crunch are likely to result in either complete absence of competency development programs in certain regions or are likely to result in only partial implementation at best. This can be often hamper the competency interventions in developing as well as under-developed nations. In addition to this, global events such as economic upheavals, pandemics, business slowdowns also compel institutions to curtail their spending on training interventions. This trend can be witnessed not only in poor countries but even in the most advanced nations.

5. Lack of measurement and accountability to evaluate competency development initiatives

Yet another roadblock in ensuring timely and consistent competency development is the lack of a reliable measurement and accountability system to assess the success of a training intervention. The absence of a process to evaluate the effectiveness of the undertaken competency development initiative can often result in rendering the entire intervention meaningless. Empirical data comprising results from a Turkish organization conducted by (Aycan, 2001) reveals that one of the key challenges in employee training and development is the evaluation of training effectiveness. On similar lines, Baldwin et al. (2017) advocate the expansion of measurement and reporting of transfer results. Governments that possess the financial muscle to fund training interventions aimed at achieving competency development, often struggle to accomplish the desired objectives on account of absence to monitor the effectiveness of the trainings delivered and its subsequent practical application. On the other hand, nations and governments that are grappling with financial constraints to sponsor their competency training programs, cannot afford to set aside funds for establishing an audit system to oversee the results of their initiatives, unless they are supported by multilateral institutions. Inability to create a transparent and accountable system to facilitate seamless competency development threatens not only existing training initiatives but also future interventions.

Role of Global Institutions in Competency Development

Table 1. Underlying causes for competency development bottlenecks

Competency Development Bottleneck	Underlying Causes
Existing bottlenecks in the global training environment	• Sustainable change globally is no easy task and requires sustained momentum. • Poor training infrastructure, lack of resources and financial constraints
Inadequacy of training transfer mechanism to drive knowledge and skills implementation	• Lack of awareness towards implementation of trained knowledge and skills • Absence of expertise to driver transfer efforts on a sustainable basis
Absence of training transfer tools to ensure success of training interventions	• Lack of necessary wherewithal to use training transfer tools • Lack of knowledge regarding tools that can facilitate transfer
Paucity of sufficient financial assistance to provide and sustain training initiatives	• Poor and developing nations do not have the financial muscle to sustain training efforts to accomplish competency development • Lack of public-private partnerships to fund drive training interventions and ensure subsequent implementation
Lack of measurement and accountability to evaluate competency development initiatives	• Too much emphasis on training design and delivery with negligible focus on measurement and evaluation • Lack of expertise in assessing training success and absence of measurement mechanism to evaluate transfer of learning efforts

SOLUTIONS AND RECOMMENDATIONS

Multilateral institutions need to counter the prevailing challenges in competency development through a host of measures that would ensure elimination of bottlenecks and thus pave the way for sustainable results from future training interventions on a global scale.

1. Creation and maintenance of a robust and sustainable training ecosystem

To ensure a level playing field and to build a competent workforce that can flourish in a competitive and volatile business climate, global institutions must focus on creating a training ecosystem that is both robust and sustainable. People in developing and third world nations need to be provided skill-based training opportunities on a continual basis to ensure their employability. This will be a necessary step towards ensuring higher employment generation, reducing the disparity of income and provide self-sustenance in various parts of the world. Institutions such as the International Labor Organization (ILO) and World Bank must support skill-development both for employment creation as well as to encourage micro-entrepreneurship initiatives at the grassroots level.

2. Systematic implementation of trained skills and knowledge to drive learning transfer

Transfer of training is the ultimate aim of learning (Thalheimer, 2018). Research reveals that organizations have a better opportunity of gaining superior returns on training investment provided they facilitate effective learning transfer (Nazli & Khairudin, 2018). There is also a need to promote effective and efficient transfer tools to ensure implementation of skills and knowledge at the workplace (Dixit & Sinha, 2022). Global institutions need to exercise their influence in overseeing the successful implementation of the disseminated skills and knowledge. This holds true for corporations as well as social institutions alike. Institutions such as World Bank, IMF and other international bodies that fund educational and training initiatives directly or indirectly, also need to oversee the implementation of the imparted skills and knowledge. This requires setting up systems and processes that are closely monitored at regular intervals. Learning transfer would be a defining step in the progression of competency development and should be given due priority in all knowledge driven initiatives. The Joint Vienna Institute (JVI) is an apt

291

example of a global organization that culminates theoretical economic analysis with practical hands on approach and thus focuses on training that enables immediate application by participants (Broome, 2010).

3. Leveraging appropriate tools to facilitate practical learning transfer

Often training interventions are designed and delivered effectively, however they fail to consider the most vital ingredient which is the successful application of the trained skills and knowledge in real life scenarios. Global institutions must exercise adequate caution to ensure that learning transfer or the actual implementation of trained knowledge is truly accomplished by those who underwent the training program. For instance, if a global institution funds a skill building initiative aimed at training people on customer service skills, they must ensure that the trainees are in a position to put their training knowledge to practical use post the training program. This requires facilitating the learners with appropriate tools thus ensuring practical application of the skills disseminated during the training program. Research conducted by Yaw (2008) emphasizes the need for using effective tools to ensure transfer. Burke (2001) suggests strategies for transfer that need to be implemented before, during, and after a training programme, for improving training transfer. Some of the tools that can be considered for learning or training transfer include one-on-one coaching, mobile learning application, live projects on the job, augmented reality, e-learning, etc. Modern tools such as Augmented Reality (AR) can pave the way for effective learning transfer and facilitate superior learning engagement (Dixit & Sinha, 2019). In another innovative post-training approach involving professionals from the Information Technology (IT) industry, trainees were made to write post-training letters to themselves highlighting the components involved in the training that strengthened their self-affirmation (Shantz & Latham, 2012). According to Na-nan (2010), due to the ease of access to relevant knowledge and skills, utilizing technology in training transfer will lead to continual learning. Martin (2010) emphasizes that follow-up strategies such as action plans, peer meetings and supervisor consultations enhance transfer in a post-training scenario. Similar sentiments are echoed by (Lee et al., 2014) who support the use of diverse strategies to ensure transfer, depending on the performance delivered by trainees in a pre-training scenario. Various training transfer methodologies have been proposed, depending on whether the transfer occurs before, during, or after the training intervention (Burke, 2001). In another recent study, it is identified that transfer tools such as one-one-one coaching; E-learning and Augmented Reality positively promote transfer of acquired skills and knowledge from the training program back in the real environment (Dixit, 2021). Evidence from research by Çakiroğlu & Gökoğlu (2019) proves successful transfer of behavioral concepts to real environments by deploying virtual-reality led training. A recent study by Dixit & Sinha (2022) reveals that virtual training can be effectively utilized to ensure transfer of training. Furthermore, the appropriate use of transfer tools is likely to motivate learners and as Ng & Ahmad (2018) state, motivated learners are likely to be highly successful in their transfer efforts. Furthermore, institutions such as the Economic Development Institute (EDI), formed under the World Bank also emphasize on a pragmatic approach to learning both in its content and delivery. Its courses comprise of practical tools such as group discussion, experience pooling and most importantly translating learning into actual practice (Bazbauers, 2018). It has further adopted the training-the-trainers approach to provide an impetus to the competency building activities by provisioning the skills required by learners.

The World Bank Institute (2015) discusses the use of "learning by doing" methods in the case of a leadership program featuring a five-and-a-half day intensive leadership skills course and an 11-month 'laboratory' phase to allow participants to apply their new skills through a learning-by-doing process. As Noorizan et al. (2016), rightly advocates the ability to put newly acquired knowledge to use influences motivation for training transfer. This also holds true because as time lapses, Knowledge, Skills and At-

Role of Global Institutions in Competency Development

titudes (KSAs) tend to decay and a lack of opportunity to apply the new KSAs, plans or enthusiasm to transfer may also decline (Ellington et al., 2015).

4. Providing funding support and resource allocation to ensure sustenance of training initiatives

Often training initiatives in smaller organizations, welfare institutions, and educational institutions gets adversely impacted due to paucity of financial aid. Lack of adequate funds to continue with knowledge or skill dissemination interventions can adversely affect the quality of human capital. It is therefore, quintessential that global institutions proactively participates in meeting the financial needs of training initiatives concerning skill upgradation and other knowledge driven programs. The training budgets should not only include the initial cost of design and program delivery but also the monetary requirements to sustain the training initiative, especially in a post-training scenario. Global institutions enjoy a superior social status that transcends national borders and often are in a position to act as a connecting bridge between institutions that have access to necessary resources and those that are struggling to fulfil their resource needs. Partnerships with Corporate Universities that have better reach and access towards the necessary resources, is another way of ensuring long-term sustenance of human capital development initiatives. This would be an essential step in providing a level playing field between governments as well as institutions and thus enhance social equity at all levels. There are growing instances of virtual universities such as the BAE Systems Virtual University that facilitate employee training and development through online professional courses (Lytovchenko, 2016). By providing institutional development, capacity building and training opportunities, the World Bank employs soft technical assistance (Bazbauers, 2018). For instance, International Bank for Reconstruction and Development (IBRD) extended a Technical Assistance Loan (TAL) in Uruguay to the tune of UD\$6.5 million to finance studies designed to provide frameworks for future reforms, as well as training and equipment needed for their implementation. Similar initiatives can be witnessed in the form of support to Secretariat of the National AIDS Program which financed consultant services to create and manage funding proposals, undertake regular training activities, and develop community-based monitoring capacity. The Reimbursable Advisory Service (RAS) programs also focused include the provision of policy advice, analytical and diagnostic work, donor coordination, impact evaluations, program implementation support, knowledge sharing, and training, which are reimbursed by the recipient for the costs involved in delivering the services (World Bank 2015).

The World Bank's 'teaching and learning arm" – Economic Development Institute (EDI), World Bank Institute (WBI) as well as the World Bank e-Institute play a major role in providing an impetus to the competency development initiatives. The WBI is dedicated to training, policy consultations as well as the creation and maintenance of knowledge networks (St Clair, 2006). These institutions also seek to build communities of like-minded decision-makers. Bazbauers (2018) observes that these entities operational within the World Bank framework, deeply influence the direct socialization of learners into accepting and adopting particular ways of thinking. In 2005 alone, the World Bank Institute provided more than one thousand learning products to 110,000 government officials, private sector agents, and educators, adopting a training-the-trainers approach geared towards building the capacity of graduates to teach others what they have learnt. This initiative of knowledge dissemination is further augmented by institutions such as The Global Development Network (GDN), Global Development Learning Network (GDLN), and Global Development Gateway which are prime examples of the World Bank's online knowledge-sharing initiatives.

It is commendable to note that the the WBI and its online arm—the World Bank e-Institute—through the launch of the Open Learning Campus in 2016. The Campus' activities are divided between initiatives building 'communities of practice' (connecting experts and peers globally) and delivering online e-courses via the WBI Academy (virtually facilitated and self-paced online courses), as well as uploading podcasts, videos, webinars, infographics, mobile apps, and games (World Bank 2016). Another noteworthy initiative on similar lines is the The Social Policy Reform in Transition Economies (SPRITE) training program founded in 1993 clearly illustrates the scope of EDI's collaborative endeavors. It received financial support from several bilateral donors, including the governments of Canada, Japan, the Netherlands, and South Korea, it provided training and institutional support to government officials in former Soviet economies. Similar results are found in the initiatives led by the World Bank Institute (WBI) which successfully implemented the "Learning for Development" intervention by designing 'customized programs that create opportunities for development stakeholders to acquire, share, and apply global and local knowledge and experiences' (WBI, 2008).

It is clearly evident that multilateral development institutions perform a key role in funding corporate social responsibility initiatives. They perform this role through advocacy, creation of favorable policy environment, financial support and promoting compliance, reporting and accountability (Vives, 2004). It is therefore important that they extend this sphere of responsibility by including competency development initiatives, especially in countries with lower financial strength.

Setting up Mechanisms to fix Accountability Towards Competency Development Initiatives

Lastly, global institutions must set up mechanisms to fix accountability towards competency development initiatives. There must be periodic audits to evaluate the Return on Training Investment (ROTI) for the various training initiatives being undertaken to support competency development. A study by Lim & Nowell (2014) reveals that merely 21 percent of organizations measure the level of training transfer. The audit process must focus on the quantity and quality of the training programs delivered, the practical relevance of the training initiatives, learning transfer of the trained skills and knowledge and consistent feedback gathering from diverse stakeholders such as the trainees/learners, participant governments, corporate partners and other sponsors of the project. Transfer and training needs assessment (TNA) must be related interconnected since a well-designed TNA can match trained KSAs to performance, and evidence of transfer can be used to assess the training's efficacy (Surface, 2012). There also needs to be a feedback and feedforward process set in place to ensure evaluation of past performance as well as guidance for future action plans. Feedforward is an essential tool that can be leveraged by multilateral institutions to provide appropriate directions to their member nations as well as other participating stakeholders. Research proves that feedforward is likely to strengthen learner performance and encourage a forward-looking approach towards learning interventions (Dixit & Sinha, 2021). As Dethier (2007) observes, the World Bank lending facilitates opportunities for learning about development and the key to such learning involves rigorous evaluation of programs. On similar lines, the International Management Framework (IMF) Skills and Competency Framework aims to explore and address the skills and competencies needed across diverse set of roles, enabling the industry to eliminate existing skill gaps while charting a learning pathway for the people involved in the process of developing and executing the IMF and the National Digital Twin (NDT) goal (Plummer et al., 2021).

Role of Global Institutions in Competency Development

Table 2. Recommended solutions with their expected benefits for competency development

Recommended Solution	Expected Benefit for Competency Development
Creation and maintenance of a robust and sustainable training ecosystem	• Facilitates competency development on an ongoing basis universally • Enhanced training ecosystem would help in generating employment opportunities and sustain livelihoods
Systematic implementation of trained skills and knowledge to drive learning transfer	• Ensures application of trained knowledge and skills by learners thereby making them job-ready • Logically conclusion to training intervention right from training design, delivery and finally implementation in the form of learning transfer
Leveraging appropriate tools to facilitate practical learning transfer	• Provides learners with motivation to apply and practice their learnings using appropriate tools for transfer • Develops a practical approach towards facilitating competency development
Providing funding support and resource allocation to ensure sustenance of training initiatives	• Enables consistency of competency development through appropriate and adequate training interventions • Ensures equitable and balanced growth amongst nations by funding essential training infrastructure and resource support
Setting up mechanisms to fix accountability towards competency development initiatives	• Drives ownership amongst all the stakeholders associated with the competency development initiatives • Justifies funding of competency led programs by ensuring fair Return on Training Investments (ROTI)

FUTURE RESEARCH DIRECTIONS

The future of business and sustainability is closely related to education, i.e. educational institutions and teachers, who must meet the needs of development - by placing appropriate educational content. It is necessary to supplement the knowledge, as well as the discipline of teachers in the implementation of teaching, i.e. their innovated pedagogical competence, but also the motivation of teachers to learn and cooperate with other teachers. According to Rychen (2002), the following challenges have been identified: rapid social and technological change, economic and cultural globalization, growing individual and social diversity, competition, liberalization, value changes, instability of norms and significant global inequalities, poverty in all its forms, various diseases and environmental destabilization. As these problems become more and more growing, traditional skills and competencies of education become insufficient. Thus, the development of higher level mental abilities becomes important, ie constitutive in the formation of future knowledge bases.

Broome (2010) observes that global training organizations do not possess the coercive strength and influence in the same traditional sense that is often associated with the controversial role of global governance institutions such as the IMF and the World Bank. Furthermore, Broome (2010) regards international training organizations socializing individuals as potentially leading to epistemic change. The World Bank Institute (2003) rightly posited that 'country ownership is key. There are numerous examples of successful public-private partnerships for training in nations such as Kazakhstan (Abdimomynova, 2021), Tanzania (Sirili et. al., 2019), Nigeria (Oviawe, 2018), China (Wang, 2018), etc. that indicate the need to encourage collaborative efforts in the domain of competency development.

Competency development is a matter of grave significance for institutions, governments and nations alike. The continuous dissemination of skills, knowledge and attitudinal insights is quintessential to ensure desired behavioral modification and knowledge acquisition that leads to a robust competency development framework. However, accomplishing this result requires continual support from diverse stakeholders, especially multilateral institutions that have global reach and access to adequate resources and learning infrastructure. It is therefore imperative that future researchers discuss the role of global institutions in facilitating competency development universally through training interventions with greater focus on transfer of training. Furthermore, it is also recommended that researchers delve deeper into various facets of learning including training dissemination, training transfer and audit mechanisms to measure and evaluate the success of competency development initiatives. Research needs to focus on gathering evidence through empirical investigation as well as theoretical methods to address this vital issue. This would involve research of a higher scope and magnitude and requires effective collaboration between international government agencies, global research institutions, intra-governmental entities as well as the private sector. There is need to shift the existing paradigm towards competency development that involves active participation from all stakeholders, spearheaded by global institutions of repute and significance. There is also scope for considering the involvement of International Non-governmental Organizations (INGOs) as global institutions (Teegen, 2003) in this herculean task of ensuring universal competency development. As Reimers (2009) rightly postulates "the development of global competency requires multifaceted approaches."

CONCLUSION

Institutions such as the World Bank are at the center of driving major changes in the current global education scenario. Global institutions perform a pivotal role in shaping the learning landscape in organizations and institutions across the world. However, driving competency development initiatives and ensuring sustainable results requires a collaborative effort on the global scale. Because capacity enhancement requires sustained effort over time and across sectors, because it involves networks of people, institutions, and resources within and across countries, its achievement is almost always beyond the scope of any single organization'. This further calls for public-private partnerships to strengthen competency development interventions at the grassroots levels. Given this impact, it is vital that institutions of repute actively participate in ensuring equal opportunities of competence development across geographies. Training and development is fundamental to competence building and successful training interventions need to be aiming for effective learning transfer of trained skills and knowledge to ensure sustenance and long-term viability of human development projects.

REFERENCES

Abdimomynova, A., Duzelbayeva, G., Berikbolova, U., Kim, V., & Baimakhanova, A. (2021). Entrepreneurship Education Prospects in The Public-Private Partnership System. *Montenegrin Journal of Economics*, *17*(2), 83–92. doi:10.14254/1800-5845/2021.17-2.7

Abele, E., & Reinhart, G. (2011). *Future of production. Phil Transl*. HANSER.

Acharya, A. (2004). How ideas spread: Whose norms matter? Norm localization and institutional change in Asian regionalism. *International Organization*, *58*(2), 239–275. doi:10.1017/S0020818304582024

Anane, C. A. (2013). Competency based training: Quality delivery for technical and vocational education and training (TVET) institutions. *Education Research International, 2*(2), 117–127.

Aycan, Z. (2001). Human resource management in Turkey-Current issues and future challenges. *International Journal of Manpower, 22*(3), 252–260. doi:10.1108/01437720110398347

Baldwin, T. T., Kevin Ford, J., & Blume, B. D. (2017). The state of transfer of training research: Moving toward more consumer-centric inquiry. *Human Resource Development Quarterly, 28*(1), 17–28. doi:10.1002/hrdq.21278

Barnett, M., & Duvall, R. (2005). Power in international politics. *International Organization, 59*(1), 39–75. doi:10.1017/S0020818305050010

Bazbauers, A. R. (2018). *The World Bank and Transferring Development.* International Political Economy Series. doi:10.1007/978-3-319-58160-6

Berliner, D. C. (2000). A personal response to those who bash teacher education. *Journal of Teacher Education, 51*(5), 358–371. doi:10.1177/0022487100051005004

Botke, J., Jansen, P. G., Khapova, S., & Tims, M. (2017). Transfer of soft skills training: A systematic literature review. In Academy of Management Proceedings. Academy of Management. doi:10.5465/AMBPP.2017.11483abstract

Broad, R. (2007). 'Knowledge management': A case study of the World Bank's research department. *Development in Practice, 17*(4-5), 700–708. doi:10.1080/09614520701470094

Broome, A. (2010). The Joint Vienna Institute. *New Political Economy, 15*(4), 609–624. doi:10.1080/13563460903290953

Burke, L. A. (2001). Training transfer: ensuring training gets used on the job. In L. A. Burke (Ed.), *High Impact Training Solutions* (pp. 89–116). Quorum Books.

Çakiroğlu, Ü., & Gökoğlu, S. (2019). Development of fire safety behavioral skills via virtual reality. *Computers & Education, 133*, 56–68. doi:10.1016/j.compedu.2019.01.014

Chwieroth, J. M. (2008). Normative change from within: The International Monetary Fund's approach to capital account liberalization. *International Studies Quarterly, 52*(1), 129–158. doi:10.1111/j.1468-2478.2007.00494.x

Cowman, M. C., & McCarthy, A. M. (2016). The impact of demographic and situational factors on training transfer in a health care setting. *Irish Journal of Management, 35*(2), 129–142. doi:10.1515/ijm-2016-0009

Dethier, J. J. (2007). Producing knowledge for development: Research at the World Bank. *Global Governance, 13*(4), 469–478. doi:10.1163/19426720-01304002

Dhaka, B. L., Vatta, L., & Chayal, K. (2018). Workplace Factors Affecting Training Transfer–A Meta Evaluation. *Indian Research Journal of Extension Education, 18*(2), 91–92.

Dixit, R. (2021). Facilitating Training Transfer of Patient Service Skills through Healthcare Learning Champion (HLC) Interventions. *Psychology and Education Journal, 58*(4), 4468–4474.

Dixit, R., & Sinha, V. (2019). Leveraging augmented reality for training transfer: A case of healthcare service providers in ophthalmology. *Development and Learning in Organizations*, *34*(6), 33–36. Advance online publication. doi:10.1108/DLO-09-2019-0211

Dixit, R., & Sinha, V. (2020). Addressing Training and Development Bottlenecks in HRM: Facilitating a Paradigm Shift in Building Human Capital in Global Organizations. In *Contemporary Global Issues in Human Resource Management*. Emerald Publishing Limited. doi:10.1108/978-1-80043-392-220201012

Dixit, R., & Sinha, V. (2021). Is feedforward the way forward? A case of managers in a manufacturing firm. *Development and Learning in Organizations*, *35*(2), 7–10. doi:10.1108/DLO-10-2019-0254

Dixit, R., & Sinha, V. (2021). Training as a Strategic HRM Tool to Foster Employee Development in SMEs. In *Handbook of Research on Strategies and Interventions to Mitigate COVID-19 Impact on SMEs* (pp. 609–628). IGI Global. doi:10.4018/978-1-7998-7436-2.ch030

Dixit, R., & Sinha, V. (2022). Investigating tools and techniques to promote workplace training transfer. *Journal of Workplace Learning*. Advance online publication. doi:10.1108/JWL-04-2021-0052

Dixit, R., & Sinha, V. (2022). Leveraging Virtual Learning to Facilitate Training Transfer in VUCA Times: A Case Study. *International Journal of Virtual and Personal Learning Environments*, *12*(1), 1–19. doi:10.4018/IJVPLE.295301

Dixit, R. R. (2019). Enhancing service experience through excellence in patient relationship (EPR) training programs. *Indian Journal of Public Health Research & Development*, *10*(5), 771–776. doi:10.5958/0976-5506.2019.01105.7

Ellington, J. K., Surface, E. A., Blume, B. D., & Wilson, M. A. (2015). Foreign language training transfer: Individual and contextual predictors of skill maintenance and generalization. *Military Psychology*, *27*(1), 36–51. doi:10.1037/mil0000064

Fontdevila, C., & Verger, A. (2015). *The World Bank's Doublespeak on Teachers: Analysis of Ten Years of Lending and Advice*. Education International. Available at http://download.eiie.org/Docs/WebDepot/World_Banks_Doublespeak_on_Teachers_Fontdevila_ Verger_EI.pdf

Griffin, P. (2006). The World Bank. *New Political Economy*, *11*(4), 571–581. doi:10.1080/13563460600991028

Ho, M. (2016). *Investment in learning increases for fourth straight year*. Talent and Development. https://www.td.org/Publications/Magazines/TD/TD-Archive/2016/11/Investment-in-Learning-

Hurt, K. J. (2016). A theoretical model of training and its transference: The pivotal role of top management team composition and characteristics. *Human Resource Development International*, *19*(1), 44–66. doi:10.1080/13678868.2015.1102007

Jones, P. W. (2007). *World Bank financing of education: Lending, Learning and Development*. Routledge. doi:10.4324/9780203965931

King, K. (2002). Banking on knowledge: The new knowledge projects of the World Bank. *Compare: A Journal of Comparative Education*, *32*(3), 311–326. doi:10.1080/0305792022000007472

Klees, S. J., Stromquist, N. P., Samoff, J., & Vally, S. (2019). The 2018 world development report on education: A critical analysis. *Development and Change, 50*(2), 603–620. doi:10.1111/dech.12483

Kramarz, T., & Momani, B. (2013). The World Bank as Knowledge Bank: Analyzing the Limits of a Legitimate Global Knowledge Actor. *The Review of Policy Research, 30*(4), 409–431. doi:10.1111/ropr.12028

Kucherov, D., & Manokhina, D. (2017). Evaluation of training programs in Russian manufacturing companies. *European Journal of Training and Development, 41*(2), 119–143. doi:10.1108/EJTD-10-2015-0084

Kuruc, K. (2018). *The IMF and Fragile States: Assessing Macroeconomic Outcomes. Background Papers*. Independent Evaluation Office of the IMF.

Lee, C., Lee, H., Lee, J., & Park, J. (2014). A multiple group analysis of the training transfer model: Exploring the differences between high and low performers in a Korean insurance company. *International Journal of Human Resource Management, 25*(20), 2837–2857. doi:10.1080/09585192.2014.934887

Lim, D. H., & Nowell, B. (2014). Integration for training transfer: Learning, knowledge, organizational culture, and technology. In *Transfer of Learning in Organizations* (pp. 81–98). Springer. doi:10.1007/978-3-319-02093-8_6

Lytovchenko, I. (2016). Corporate university as a form of employee training and development in American companies. *Advanced Education, 0*(5), 35–41. doi:10.20535/2410-8286.62280

Marini, A., & Genereux, R. (1995). The challenge of teaching for transfer. In A. McKeough, J. Lupart, & A. Marini (Eds.), *Teaching for Transfer: Fostering Generalization in Learning* (pp. 1–19). Lawrence Erlbaum Associates, Inc.

Martin, H. J. (2010). Improving training impact through effective follow-up: Techniques and their application. *Journal of Management Development, 29*(6), 520–534. doi:10.1108/02621711011046495

Mohanakumari, D., & Magesh, R. (2017). Competency Development through Training and Development: An Empirical Study. *Indian Journal of Scientific Research, 14*(1), 69–70.

Muduli, A., Vinita, K., & Ali, Q. (2018). Pedagogy or andragogy? – Views of Indian graduate business. *IIMB Management Review, 21*(3), 161–178.

Na-nan, K. (2010). A causal model of factors affecting transfer of training. *Journal of Education, 9*(1), 93–109.

Nazli, N. N. N. N., & Khairudin, S. M. H. S. (2018). The factors that influence transfer of training and its effect on organizational citizenship behaviour. *Journal of Workplace Learning, 30*(2), 121–146. doi:10.1108/JWL-09-2017-0080

Ng, K. H., & Ahmad, R. (2018). Personality traits, social support, and training transfer: The mediating mechanism of motivation to improve work through learning. *Personnel Review, 47*(1), 39–59. doi:10.1108/PR-08-2016-0210

Noorizan, M. M., Afzan, N. F., & Akma, A. S. (2016). The moderating effects of motivation on work environment and training transfer: A preliminary analysis. *Procedia Economics and Finance, 37*, 158–163. doi:10.1016/S2212-5671(16)30107-1

Nsouli, S. M. (2003). *The Changing Institutional Needs of the Transition Economies and the Role of the IMF*. Paper presented to the East-West Conference, Vienna, Austria.

Nur, Y. F. A., Ruhizan, M. Y., & Bekri, R. M. (2015). Learning transfer in national occupational skill standard (NOSS) system and workplace learning: How training design affect it? *Procedia: Social and Behavioral Sciences, 174*, 156–163. doi:10.1016/j.sbspro.2015.01.641

Oviawe, J. I. (2018). Revamping Technical Vocational Education and Training through Public-Private Partnerships for Skill Development. *Makerere Journal of Higher Education, 10*(1), 73–91. doi:10.4314/majohe.v10i1.5

Plummer, D., Kearney, S., Monagle, A., Collins, H., Perry, V., Moulds, A., & Lewis, C. (2021). *Skills and Competency Framework-Supporting the development and adoption of the Information Management Framework (IMF) and the National Digital Twin*. Academic Press.

Reimers, F. M. (2009). Global competency. *Harvard International Review, 30*(4), 24–27.

Sekerin, V. D., Gaisina, L. M., Shutov, N. V., Abdrakhmanov, N. K., & Valitova, N. E. (2018). Improving the quality of competence-oriented training of personnel at industrial enterprises. *Calitatea, 19*(165), 68–72.

Shantz, A., & Latham, G. P. (2012). Transfer of training: Written self-guidance to increase self-efficacy and interviewing performance of job seekers. *Human Resource Management, 51*(5), 733–746. doi:10.1002/hrm.21497

Sirili, N., Frumence, G., Kiwara, A., Mwangu, M., Goicolea, I., & Hurtig, A. K. (2019). Public private partnership in the training of doctors after the 1990s¢ health sector reforms: The case of Tanzania. *Human Resources for Health, 17*(1), 1–11. doi:10.118612960-019-0372-6 PMID:31118038

St Clair, A. L. (2006). The World Bank as a transnational expertised institution. *Global Governance, 12*(1), 77–95. doi:10.1163/19426720-01201007

Stracke, C. M. (2011). Competence Modelling, Competence Models and Competence Development-An Overview. In *Competence Modelling for Vocational Education and Training*. Innovations for Learning and Development.

Suazo, M. M., Martínez, P. G., & Sandoval, R. (2009). Creating psychological and legal contracts through human resource practices: A signaling theory perspective. *Human Resource Management Review, 19*(2), 154–166. doi:10.1016/j.hrmr.2008.11.002

Surface, E. A. (2012). Training need assessment: Aligning learning and capability with performance requirements and organizational objectives. In M. A. Wilson, W. Bennett, S. G. Gibson, & G. M. Alliger (Eds.), *The handbook of work analysis: The methods, systems, applications and science of work measurement in organizations*. Routledge.

Role of Global Institutions in Competency Development

Teegen, H. (2003). International NGOs as global institutions: Using social capital to impact multinational enterprises and governments. *Journal of International Management, 9*(3), 271–285. doi:10.1016/S1075-4253(03)00037-1

Thalheimer, W. (2018). *The learning-transfer evaluation model.* Available at: https://www.worklearning.com/wp-content/uploads/2018/02/Thalheimer-The-Learning-Transfer-Evaluation-Model-Report-for-LTEM-v11a-002.pdf

Vetterlein, A. (2012). Seeing like the World Bank on poverty. *New Political Economy, 17*(1), 35–58. doi:10.1080/13563467.2011.569023

Vives, A. (2004). The role of multilateral development institutions in fostering corporate social responsibility. *Development, 47*(3), 45–52. doi:10.1057/palgrave.development.1100065

Wang, J. S. (2018). Practice and exploration of establishing blood purification training center with ppp (Public Private Partnership) model. Academic Journal of Second Military Medical University, 19-23.

WBI. (2008). *World Bank Institute Annual Report 2008.* World Bank Institute.

WBI. (2015) *Leadership: The World Bank Institute's Leadership for Development Program.* World Bank Institute. https://wbi.worldbank.org/wbi/content/leadership-world-bankinstitute%E2%80%99s-leadership-development-program

Weaver, C. (2010). Reforming the World Bank. In J. Clapp & R. Wilkinson (Eds.), *Global Governance, Poverty, and Inequality* (pp. 112–131). Routledge.

Wilson, I., & Madsen, S. R. (2008). The influence of Maslow's humanistic views on an employee's motivation to learn. *The Journal of Applied Management and Entrepreneurship, 13*(2), 46–62.

World Bank. (2009). *Annual report.* Retrieved from http://siteresources.worldbank.org/EXTAR2009/Resources/6223977125295083187/AR09_Complete.pdf

World Bank. (2010). *About Us.* Retrieved from http://go.worldbank.org/3QT2P1GNH0

World Bank. (2015). *Reimbursable Advisory Services in Europe and Central Asia (ECA): Expanding Options for Our Clients: Global Knowledge, Strategy, and Local Solutions.* World Bank.

World Bank. (2016). *Open Learning Campus.* World Bank. https://olc.worldbank.org/

Yaw, D. C. (2008). Tools for transfer. *Industrial and Commercial Training, 40*(3), 152–155. doi:10.1108/00197850810868658

ADDITIONAL READING

Berge, Z., de Verneil, M., Berge, N., Davis, L., & Smith, D. (2002). The increasing scope of training and development competency. *Benchmarking, 9*(1), 43–61. doi:10.1108/14635770210418579

Boas, M., & McNeill, D. (Eds.). (2004). *Global institutions and development: framing the world?* Routledge. doi:10.4324/9780203496336

Kapur, D., Lewis, J. P., & Webb, R. C. (2011). *The World Bank: its first half century* (Vol. 1). Brookings Institution Press.

King, K., McGrath, S. A., & McGrath, S. (2004). *Knowledge for Development?: Comparing British, Japanese, Swedish and World Bank Aid*. Zed Books. doi:10.5040/9781350220966

Klees, S. J., Samoff, J., & Stromquist, N. P. (Eds.). (2012). *The World Bank and education: Critiques and Alternatives* (Vol. 14). Springer Science & Business Media. doi:10.1007/978-94-6091-903-9

Lebeau, Y., & Sall, E. (2011). Global institutions, higher education and development. In *Handbook on Globalization and Higher Education*. Edward Elgar Publishing. doi:10.4337/9780857936233.00017

Marshall, K. (2008). *The World Bank: From Reconstruction to Development to Equity*. Routledge. doi:10.4324/9780203967539

Van Der Wende, M. (2011). Global institutions: The organization for economic co-operation and development. In *Handbook on Globalization and Higher Education*. Edward Elgar Publishing. doi:10.4337/9780857936233.00015

Weinbauer-Heidel, I., & Ibeschitz-Manderbach, M. (2016). *What Makes Training Really Work: 12 Levers Of Transfer Effectiveness*. Institute for Transfer Effectiviness.

KEY TERMS AND DEFINITIONS

Competency Development: Competency development is a culmination of skills, knowledge and job attitude aimed at accomplishing desired workplace behavior and/or performance.

Economic Development Institute (EDI): The Economic Development Institute is a training institute operational under the World Bank, meant for the government officials. It was launched in the year 1955 as a training college to cater to the needs of senior government officials.

Epistemic Community: An epistemic community is considered to be a sociological group of people with similar thinking styles.

Global Institutions: Global institutions comprise of multilateral entities that perform humanitarian operations such as education and health initiatives on a universal scale.

International Labour Organization (ILO): The International Labour Organization is a entity formed under the United Nations agency to promote social and economic justice through establishment of international labour standards and laws.

International Monetary Fund (IMF): The International Monetary Fund is a global entity working towards providing financial stability and ensuring global monetary co-operations between member nations.

Return on Training Investment (ROTI): This refers to the approximate value, calculated in monetary terms, derived from a particular training intervention.

Training Intervention: This refers to a series of training programs designed and delivered to learners over a certain period of time.

Training Transfer: A systematic process that ensures implemented of training skills and competencies by leaners from the training classroom to actual work environment.

World Bank: The World Bank is a very reputed international financial entity that provides financial support to low and middle-income nations towards pursuing various development projects.

Chapter 16
Role of Global Institutions in Economic Development of India

Amit Uttam Jadhav
G. S. Moze College, India

Dileep B. Baragde
iD https://orcid.org/0000-0001-9112-5535
G. S. Moze College, India

ABSTRACT

The International Monetary Fund (IMF), the World Bank, and the International Trade Organisation were conceived at the Bretton Woods Conference in July, 1944 as institutions to strengthen international economic cooperation and to help create a more stable and prosperous global economy. Instead, the General Agreement on Tariffs and Trade, through successive rounds of negotiations, got transformed into what has come to be known as the World Trade Organisation. The various institutions have been set up to govern international economic relations. While all the institutions work in close coordination with each other, each of these institutions has its own specific area of responsibilities. The IMF promotes international monetary cooperation and provides member countries with policy advice, temporary loans, and technical assistance so they can establish and maintain financial stability and external viability and build and maintain strong economies. The World Bank promotes long-term economic development and poverty reduction by providing technical and financial support.

INTRODUCTION

The different foundations IMF, World Bank, GATT, WTO and ADB's have been set up to administer global monetary relations. While every one of the organizations work in close coordination with one another, every one of these foundations has its own particular area of obligations. Institutions are defined as a structure of societal features, like organizations, codes, faiths, and criteria. These features direct, empower, and restrain the activities of persons (Greif, 2000; Dixit, 2004). The IMF advances global money related collaboration and furnishes part nations with strategy exhortation, brief advances, and

DOI: 10.4018/978-1-6684-2448-3.ch016

Copyright © 2022, IGI Global. Copying or distributing in print or electronic forms without written permission of IGI Global is prohibited.

specialized help so they can lay out and keep up with monetary strength and outer reasonability and assemble and keep up with solid economies. The World Bank advances long haul monetary turn of events and destitution decrease by offering specialized and monetary help. The WTO looks to accomplish a similar goal by giving an exchange climate which labor and products might move between the countries, unreasonable by any limitations or hindrances. On a little provincial level likewise worldwide associations have been set up. Among these, the most significant for us has been the Asian Development Bank. All things being equal, the General Agreement on Tariffs and Trade (GATT) was set up in 1947. Hence, the objectives of this chapter are to understand the role of international institutions in the development process of India and reckon the significance of the different international organizations for India.

LITERATURE REVIEW

Although many studies propose that institutions are indeed vital to economic growth, they are not, however, the only cause of growth; for instance, Knack and Keefer (1995) show that the explanatory influence of the regressions is greater when indicators of political violence are involved. However, due to data restrictions, the empirical investigation of cross-country growth was constrained to a constricted investigation of the institutions' role. Many other studies were done, such as the one by Acemoglu et al. (2000), in which they discovered the presence of a solid correlation between colonial institutions and economic performance. The current review endeavors at breaking down the job of the International Financial Institutions (IFIs) to be specific the World Bank (International Bank for Reconstruction and Development and International Development Association), the Asian Development Bank (ADB) and the International Monetary Fund (IMF) in the financial improvement of South Asian economies with unique reference to Indian economy.

Todaro and Smith (2003) bring up that monetary improvement should be imagined as a multi-faceted cycle including significant changes in friendly designs, famous perspectives and public foundations, as well as the speed increase of financial development, the decrease of imbalance and the annihilation of neediness. Advancement, in its embodiment, should address the entire of array of progress by which a whole friendly framework tuned to the assorted fundamental requirements and wants of people and gatherings inside that framework. Monetary Growth and Economic Development are by and large utilized as equivalents. Financial advancement alludes to the issues of the emerging nations and monetary development to those of the created nations. By financial development, we basically mean an expansion in per capita pay or expansion in Gross National Product. In late writing, the term, monetary development alludes to supported expansion in a nation's result of labor and products, or all the more exactly, item per capita, while financial improvement infers change in the mechanical and institutional association of creation as well as in the distributive example of pay. Subsequently, cycle of improvement is undeniably broader, for example it includes development with change. Aside from an ascent in yield, it includes changes in the arrangement of the result, change in the portion of useful assets, and end or decrease of neediness, disparities and joblessness.

The World Development Report (1991) notices, "The test of advancement, in the broadest sense is to work on the personal satisfaction, particularly on the planet's unfortunate nations. A superior personal satisfaction by and large calls for higher pay, however it includes significantly more. It includes as finishes in themselves better training, better expectations of wellbeing and nourishment, less destitution, cleaner climate, greater uniformity of chance, more noteworthy individual opportunity, and a

Role of Global Institutions in Economic Development of India

more extravagant culture life any idea of rigorously monetary advancement must, at any rate, look past development in per-capita pay to the decrease of neediness and more prominent value, to advance in instruction, wellbeing and sustenance, and to the security of the climate. ''For temporary economies like that of India, there are obstacles as deficiency of capital, restricted innovation, skill and insufficiency of foundations vital for cultivating quick financial turn of events. Because of the Savings-Investment hole, Export-Import whole and Technological hole, these economies can't mobiles the expected capital for the monetary turn of events.

Hence, to accomplish the objectives of advancement these economies search for unfamiliar capital. Unfamiliar capital takes a few structures, specifically advances and awards through between legislative streams (respective streams), unfamiliar help through establishments (IFIs), unfamiliar value capital through capital market exchanges and Foreign Direct Investments (FDI). Also, there is stream of unfamiliar capital as move of innovation and specialized ability. Generally, every temporary economy utilizes any or all the above accessible choices of unfamiliar capital for accomplishing the financial turn of events. After the Second World War (1939-45), a few establishments at the worldwide level were shaped. Unmistakable among them were United Nations Organization (UNO), International Bank for Reconstruction and Development (IBRD), International Monetary Fund (IMF), World Health Organization (WHO), International Labor Organization (ILO) and so on Out of these global organizations, the IBRD and the IMF came to be known as International Financial Institutions (IFIs). IFIs allude to monetary organizations that have been laid out by more than one country. Their proprietors or investors are for the most part public states. The objective of IFIs is to lay out a structure for monetary participation and improvement that would prompt a more steady and prosperous worldwide economy. The IFIs could impact the financial improvement through a few channels, significant among them are counsel to strategy creators and cash dispensed under different projects. Among IFIs, the Bretton Woods sisters, International Bank for Reconstruction and Development (IBRD) and International Monetary Fund (IMF) were framed in the financial 1944 based on the Keynes Plan (ready by John Maynard Keynes) and the White Plan (ready by American master Harry D. White). The essential elements of these plans were melded into a typical arrangement, which was introduced at the United Nations Monetary and Financial Conference held in Bretton Woods in July 1944. Other IFIs incorporate Asian Development Bank (ADB), African Development Bank (AfDB)'', Inter-American Development Bank (IDB) and European Investment Bank (EIB) As the principle focal point of the review is with respect to breaking down the job of World Bank, ADB and IMF, beneath is the short presentation of these IFIs These take the form of contracts, codes of conduct, standardized weights and measures, disclosure agreements, and enforcement through courts and policing. Where transaction costs are small, the private enforcement of contracts may still be preferred. But as economic relations develop and become increasingly impersonal, the role of a third party to enforce compliance to rules is increasingly necessary (Shirley, 2003).

India has been the organizer individual from the Bretton Woods sisters, i.e., the World Bank and the IMF and furthermore of the ADB. Till 2008, on the combined premise, India is the biggest borrower of the World Bank loaning and the 4 biggest borrower of the ADB loaning. Throughout the long term, both the World Bank and the ADB have expanded their inclusion in India by raising and enhancing the loaning in the various areas of the economy. Both the World Bank and the ADB have given loaning by keeping in view India's Five-Year arranging needs. The current section makes an undertaking to investigate the job of IFIs in the financial advancement of Indian economy. For directing this activity, a few significant areas of Indian economy have been embraced as a mark of financial turn of events. Institutions which are conducive to development ensure greater self-expression, allow the free flow of information and encourage the formation of associations and clubs. These form prosperous social relationships, which are conducive to greater economic interaction by increasing levels of trust and wider availability of information (Putnam, 1993). They allow greater sharing of resources through democratic institutions and the use of the state to reduce the risk attached to economic activity (Bardhan, 2006, p.5).

DISCUSSION

India has been viewed as an appealing target for capital inflows and net capital inflows, due to various socio-political and financial examinations. Net capital inflows that were 1.9 percent of GDP in 2000-01 extended to 9.2 percent in 2007-08. New portfolio theory added daintiness to the Indian capital business areas. Indian corporate began powerful obtainment gorge abroad, which got reflected in the high volume of outbound direct theory streams during 2007-2009. Not with standing, the year 2008-09 was separate by opposing upgrades in the external region of the Indian economy, particularly during the last piece of the year, reflecting the impact of overall financial emergency. The threatening progressions in the worldwide money related business areas, disregarding having a banking and financial structure that had basically nothing to do with interests in coordinated financial instruments cut out of subprime gets, whose mistake had set off the chain of events completing in overall money related crisis. Emerging economies were affected in contrasting degrees depending on the level of responsiveness and the dependence on capital streams as the external environment broke down as a result of stoppage in overall premium, reversal of capital streams and lessened induction to external wellsprings of cash even with ominous overall credit monetary circumstances.

The episodes of overall crises furthermore inferred that the economy experienced absurd insecurity to the extent that instabilities in monetary trade costs, exchange rates and extension levels during a short range requiring reversal of system to oversee emerging conditions. These truths are particular badge of the negative side of openness/globalization that is making countries powerless against crisis like situation. The situation started improving consequently and in the year 2010 - 11 the worldwide or corresponding trade again started again getting.

World economy can't exist without the connections of the states and overall financial Institutions. This the truth is shown by basically advanced patterns of common blend, in which cases, the shortcoming coming from „negative" imports is changed by a colossal notwithstanding of handiness and power, drawn from overall trade. Following this arrangement, monetary straightforwardness implies trade relations with lessened or discarded obligations and non-demand trade limits with the help of International Institutions to stay aware of uniformity and security in the world business sectors. On one hand, the products show the penetration of inward things on new business areas. Their plan shows the public period of monetary development. Of course, the imports set out open ways to accumulate upper quality resources that help the economy. These improvements of product, organizations or capitals are reciprocal, provoking a sound monetary turn of events. Thusly from the above discussion it is clear that the technique of straightforwardness has direct impact over the advancement of the economy especially in the non-modern countries like India, China, Russia, etc The International Financial foundations expect an uncommonly fundamental part in the new development and improvement of these economies as the game plans of these associations are illustrated for the basic objective of the money related and social improvement in the part country. India has experienced the new turn of events and occupation of these associations has been by and large around agreed in the straightforwardness of Indian economy and re-

Role of Global Institutions in Economic Development of India

lated improvement. It is seen that straightforwardness vehemently impact money related advancement. Responsiveness is certifiably not an engine of improvement anyway goes probably as a stimulus for propelling advancement through imaginative work, more broad market access and allowing decline in progress cost.

International Monetary Fund (IMF)

Global Monetary Fund (IMF) is one of the two organizations that were laid out because of the Bretton woods Conference in 1944, the other foundation was the International Bank for Reconstruction and Development (IBRD), otherwise called the World Bank. IMF targets advancing worldwide money related participation so as to accomplish specific commonly concurred global monetary objectives. It is likewise a loan specialist of momentary assets to part nations, essentially to change equilibrium of installments shortages. The targets of IMF are to advance worldwide financial participation through a long-lasting organization this gives the hardware to conference and coordinated effort on global money related issues. To work with the extension and adjusted development of global exchange and to contribute subsequently to the advancement and support of elevated degrees of business and genuine pay and to the improvement of the useful assets of all individuals as essential targets of monetary strategy. To advance trade strength, to keep up with organized trade courses of action among individuals, and to stay away from cutthroat trade deterioration. To aid the foundation of a multilateral arrangement of installments in regard of current exchanges among individuals and in the disposal of trade limitations which hamper the development of world exchange. To give certainty to individuals by making the overall assets of the Fund briefly accessible to them under sufficient protections, accordingly, furnishing them with a chance to address maladjustments in their equilibrium of installments without turning to measures horrendous of public or worldwide success. As per the above mentioned, to abbreviate the length and decrease the level of disequilibrium in the global equilibrium of installments of individuals. Stone (2006) have referenced that, while the IMF lost its underlying mission without completely getting another job, the World Bank has likely changed better to the changing worldwide monetary climate by getting more information driven job for itself.

IMF gives impermanent help to part nations to hold over equilibrium of installments shortfalls. At the point when the nation requires unfamiliar trade, it tenders its own cash to the IMF and gets the unfamiliar trade. This is known as 'drawing' from the Fund. Whenever the BOP circumstance of the nation improves, it ought to 'repurchase' its money from the IMF and reimburse the unfamiliar exchange. Ordinarily, for a part country, a first acquiring or drawing is essentially programmed and without strings. A nation basically requires the arrival of its unique 25% offer (called the "hold tranche") paid in hard currency. After that, it might get the "principal credit tranche", another 25% with for all intents and purposes no strings. Three further credit tranches might be acquired in every one of three ensuing years, and each adding up to 25 percent of the first quantity. Toward the finish of the 5 years, the maximum furthest reaches of 125% is reached. Likewise, a part can acquire a further 90 percent of share every year for a very long time under the "augmented admittance" strategy. With the extended admittance strategy, further credits from 270 to 330 percent of amount can be gotten in a three-year time frame, notwithstanding the typical loaning. Yet, this is dependent upon a total maximum constraint of 400 to 440 percent of quota. While getting under prior credit tranches includes no commitment to embrace IMF coordinated strategy changes, acquiring under higher tranches and broadened admittance office includes such commitments. Normally, the IMF will expect as requirements for acquiring reductions in

307

spending plan shortfall including endowments to different areas of the economy, decrease in the pace of money related development, measures to limit wages and costs, degrading of an exaggerated swapping scale, and an activity to cause the value framework to reflect costs all the more precisely and some turn towards the support of commodities. These are known as contingency's that are forced on the borrowers who need to utilize IMF offices.

As organizer individual from the IMF, India was at first appointed a portion of $400 million or around 5.2 percent of the aggregate. Being the fifth biggest standard holder, India was likewise given a seat on the IMF's Executive Board. With progressive audits, be that as it may, India's amount share has dwindled. India's current portion is SDRs 4.1582 billion (1.96 percent of the aggregate, rank 13). The nation has utilized the Fund's offices various times to meet her BOP necessities. Such drawings of unfamiliar trade have empowered the country to hold over the intense unfamiliar trade emergency and to keep up with the imports of basics merchandise. India depended on drones from the IMF under the Oil Facility made in June, 1974 to meet bigger expenses for the import of oil rough. The SDRs give unequivocal liquidity since the members approach unfamiliar trade assets voluntarily. The country's participation of the IMF has qualified it for become an individual from the World Bank; as an individual from the Bank, India has gotten enormous specialized and monetary help for the different improvement projects. Credit under this office is contracted at milder terms yet there is a not kidding restriction proviso connected to it. The nation has profited the administrations of the experts in the Fund to survey the condition of the Indian economy and for planning important reports on different parts of the economy. Notwithstanding, India has been profoundly particular in moving toward the Fund. It is over 10 years now that India took more time to monetary assistance from the IMF. It was in mid 1990s that it became fundamental for India to move toward the IMF for a gigantic help to reestablish a feeling of practicality to her unfamiliar trade position. With the guide of concessional credit from the IMF in 1991 and resulting reception of adjustment and change program, India effectively defeated the BOP emergency. It prepaid this advance and has from that point forward turned into a net repurchased from the Fund, i.e., it has been repaying its advances to the Fund, as shown in Table.1.

Table 1. India's transactions with the IMF ($ millions)

Year	Repurchases	Net
1990-91	644	1214
1997-98	618	-618
1998-99	393	-393
1999-00	260	-260
2000-01	26	-26

The World Bank

The World Bank is one more of the 'Bretton woods Twin Sisters'. The World Bank, as it gets as of now, is an umbrella association, under which five distinct establishments work. These five establishments are as per the following:

Role of Global Institutions in Economic Development of India

Worldwide Bank for Reconstruction and Development (IBRD); established in 1944, is the single biggest supplier of improvement advances. Worldwide Development Association (IDA); established in 1960, helps the least fortunate nations. Worldwide Finance Corporation (IFC); upholds private endeavor in non-industrial nations. Multilateral Investment Guarantee Agency (MIGA); offers financial backers protection against non-business chance and assist emerging nation legislatures with drawing in unfamiliar speculation. Worldwide Center for the Settlement of Investment Disputes (ICSID); empowers the progression of unfamiliar venture to agricultural nations through mediation and assuagement offices.

International Bank for Reconstruction and Development (IBRD)

The principle capacity of the IBRD is of long haul capital help to its part nations for their remaking and advancement. World Bank BOP support isn't accessible without a Fund program, while a Fund program can't be finished without the earlier arrangement of BOP support from the World Bank and from respective contributors to fill the modified 'asset hole'. The reciprocal doesn't submit assets until arrangements with the World Bank have been finished up. Though the Fund sets the macroeconomic rules and focuses of a program, the World Bank forces an extensive rundown of neo-liberal miniature monetary arrangement changes on the acquiring country. To aid remaking and improvement of the domains of it part legislatures by working with venture of capital for useful purposes; To advance unfamiliar private speculation by ensures or through cooperation's in credits and different ventures of capital for useful purposes; Where private capital isn't accessible on sensible conditions, to make advances for useful purposes out of its possessed assets or out of the assets acquired by it; and To advance the long-range development of worldwide exchange and the upkeep of harmony yet to be determined of installments of individuals by empowering global venture for the useful assets of individuals. Assets of the Bank comprise of the capital and borrowings. The capital of the Bank is contributed by its 184 part nations. The five biggest investors of the Bank are: USA, Japan, Germany, Great Britain and France. India is the 6th biggest donor. The administration of the Bank is on the very lines as that of the IMF. Prior to allowing or ensuring a credit, the Bank thinks about the accompanying issues: The task for which the advance is asked has been painstakingly inspected by a skillful board as respects the value of the proposition; The borrower has sensible possibility for reimbursement; The advance is intended for useful purposes; and The advance is intended to back unfamiliar trade prerequisites of explicit undertakings of recreation and improvement. The pace of revenue on Bank not set in stone by adding a spread of ½ of 1% on the "pool rate" of exceptional acquiring of the Bank.

India is the originator financier of the Bank. For India, the Bank implies numerous things. The Bank has not been simply a loaning foundation to India yet has likewise filled in as a commendable advice whom India has drawn nearer for exhortation in troubles. India has been the single biggest borrower of the Bank. The Bank has stretched out liberal help to India in executing various improvement projects in various areas like assembling, industry, transportation - rail lines, ports, streets and airplanes - electrical power, farming, and so on The Bank has additionally been instrumental in the foundation of the India Development Forum, a consortium of giver countries to India. The enormous monetary help vowed by the consortium individuals has been the biggest guide responsibility and is a milestone throughout the entire existence of advancement help from created nations to agricultural nations. Yet, in accordance with the overall changes in the climate, India's developing inclination for value capital rather advances have brought about an undeniable fall in the inflow of help from the Bank to India, as shown below Table.2.

309

Table 2. World Bank Assistance to India ($ billions)

Year	Grants	Loans	Total
1980-81	–	175.5	175.5
1990-91	–	1217.5	1217.5
1997-98	8.0	581.9	589.9
1998-99	3.0	575.1	578.1
1999-00	5.1	646.6	651.7
2000-01	5.4	706.8	712.2
2001-02	1.5	772.8	774.3
2002-03	10.4	657.3	667.7
2003-04	13.2	902.3	915.4

India's total outstanding debt from the Bank stands at about $5 billion presently.

The Bank has granted loans for specific purposes and projects rather than for general development purposes. The Bank exercises excessive control over the expenditure on the proposed projects. The rate of interest charged by the Bank is very high. An increasingly large share of the Bank's assistance is linked to the "conditionality", i.e., to effect the changes in the economic policies as desired by the Bank.

International Development Association (IDA)

Global Development Association (IDA) is a partner of the IBRD. It was laid out in 1960 to give "delicate credits" to financially sound activities which make 'social capital' like the development of streets and scaffolds, ghetto leeway and metropolitan turn of events. The IDA gives advances to such activities sans interest and for longer periods. Accordingly, it is regularly alluded to as the 'delicate credit window' of the Bank. Only the least fortunate of the unfortunate part nations (with per capita pay underneath $895 at 1995 costs) are qualified for help.

India has tremendously profited from the IDA. It has gotten a progression of credits, ceaselessly. A large portion of the help has gone to the high improvement need projects which couldn't get finance from different sources. However, as with the IBRD, there has not been much change in the IDA assistance to India in recent years, as shown in Table 3.

Table 3. IDA Assistance to India ($ millions)

Year	Grants	Loans	Total
1980-81	24.0	000.1	684.1
1990-91	–	773.9	773.9
1997-98	2.3	825.8	828.1
1998-99	3.7	867.4	871.1
1999-00	7.0	840.1	847.1
2000-01	3.2	1063.4	1065.6
2001-02	7.3	1177.3	1184.6
2001-02	7.3	1177.3	1184.6
2002-03	5.4	900.4	905.8
2003-04	5.9	928.8	934.7

IDA assistance has also been criticized for the excessive control exercised by the IDA.

International Finance Corporation (IFC)

The IBRD credits are accessible just to part country states or with the assurance of part country legislatures. Further, IBRD can make a credit however it can't partake in the value of the funded task. IFC was laid out in 1956 with the particular reason for funding private endeavors. It is a member of the IBRD. The Board of Governors of the IBRD likewise comprise the Board of Governors of the IFC. Yet, it is a different element with reserves kept separate from those of the IBRD.

The reason for the IFC is to additional financial advancement by empowering development of private undertaking in part nations. The IFC, in this manner: Invests in private endeavor in part nations in relationship with private financial backers and without Government ensure, in situations where adequate private capital isn't accessible on sensible conditions; Seeks to unite venture open doors, private capital of both unfamiliar and homegrown beginning, and experienced administration; and Stimulates conditions helpful for the progression of private capital - homegrown and unfamiliar - into useful interests in part nations. The IFC speculation regularly doesn't surpass 40% of the all-out venture of the endeavor. In the event of its speculation by value cooperation, it doesn't surpass 25% of the offer capital. The interest charged on propels differs relying on the proposition and status of the borrower.

India has also received substantial assistance from the IFC.

Asian Development Bank (ADB)

Notwithstanding the World Bank family, there are three other global loaning organizations working just in explicit topographical region, yet run on lines like the World Bank. The Inter-American Development Bank, established in 1959. The Asian Development Bank, established in 1964, and the African Development Bank, established in 1966. Each gets on world capital business sectors and loans generally on close business conditions. ADB is an improvement bank under the aegis of ESCAP (Economic and Social Commission for Asia and Pacific). Its participation comprises of nations from Asian district as well as from different areas. ADB funds essentially explicit undertakings in the district. It might make credits to or put resources into the undertakings concerned. It might likewise ensure advances allowed to the ventures. The majority of the advances conceded are hard credits or tied advances. Be that as it may, credits from unique supports put away by the ADB upto 10% of its settled up capital are conceded under delicate advance term for which reason it has set up a different window known as the Asian Development Fund (ADF). Delicate advances are ordinarily allowed to undertakings of high improvement need requiring longer times of reimbursement with lower paces of interest. ADB ordinarily funds unfamiliar trade cost of the task and the advance is repayable in the cash in which it are made.

India has been qualified for help both under the ADB and its delicate credit window, ADF. However, India has avoided the ADF. Be that as it may, it has been getting enormous help under the ADB.

Be that as it may, India doesn't appear to be too energetic to even think about getting credits lately as reflected below in Table 4.

Table 4. ADB Assistance to India ($ millions)

Year	Amount
1990-91	212.4
1997-98	601.1
1998-99	613.9
1999-00	610.5
2000-01	470.9
2001-02	392.3
2002-03	544.7
2003-04	613.8

World Trade Organization (WTO)

The International Trade Organization (ITO), initially, was proposed to be set up alongside the World Bank and the IMF on the suggestions of the Bretton woods Conference, 1944. However, as the ITO couldn't be set up, the US, UK and a couple of different nations set up in 1947 a break association about exchange named GATT (General Agreement on Tariff and Trade). The GATT was one-sided for the created nations and was called casually as the "rich men's club". The agricultural nations demanded setting up of the ITO; the move came to be gone against by the US. To settle the issue - the UN designated a Committee in 1963. The Committee suggested as a potential option a by means of media, UNCTAD (United Nations Conference on Trade and Development). The UNCTAD was set up in 1964 based on this other option. The UNCTAD could figure out how to get a few concessions for the emerging nations, more significant among which was the GSTP (General Scheme for Trade Preferences). GATT was likewise made dynamically more liberal.The Uruguay Round of GATT tried to extend the extent of the association by including, administrations, venture and licensed innovation freedoms. The Uruguay Round recommendations were acknowledged by every one of the individuals from GATT in December, 1993. The arrangements were approved by the councils of 85 part nations by year-end 1994. On such amendment, the WTO began working from January 1, 1995. The WTO arose out of the General Agreement on Tariffs and Trade (GATT) arrangements with a command to expand and insert the worldwide commercial center, not least, through the joining of non-industrial nations (Narlikar, 2006).

Role of Global Institutions in Economic Development of India

It controls through different gatherings and boards the 29 arrangements contained in the last venture of the Uruguay Round of world exchange talks, in addition to various arrangements, remembering those for Government acquisition. It directs execution of the huge duty cuts and decrease of non-levy hindrances consented to in the exchange dealings. It is a guard dog of global exchange, consistently looking at the exchange systems or individual individuals. Individuals are expected to tell exhaustively different exchange measures and insights, which are kept up with by the WTO in a huge data set. It gives placation systems to showing up at a neighborly answer for exchange clashes among individuals. Exchange debates that can't be addressed through reciprocal discussions are arbitrated under the WTO question settlement "court". Boards of free specialists are laid out to look at debates in the illumination of WTO administers and give decisions. The harder, smoothed out methodology guarantees equivalent treatment for all exchanging accomplices and urges individuals to submit to their commitments. The WTO is an administration expert for world exchange. Its market analysts keep a nearby watch on the beat of the worldwide economy and give studies on the principle issues of the day. The WTO secretariat helps non-industrial nations in carrying out Uruguay Round outcomes through a recently settled advancement division and a reinforced specialized participation and preparing division. The WTO is a gathering where nations constantly arrange the trading of exchange concessions to exchange limitations from one side of the planet to the other. The WTO as of now has a significant plan of additional exchanges in numerous region, eminently certain administrations areas. Increasing expectations of living and earnings, guaranteeing full business, growing creation and exchange, ideal utilization of world's assets, simultaneously stretching out the targets to administrations and making them more exact. Presents the possibility of reasonable advancement comparable to the ideal utilization of world's assets, and the need to safeguard and save the climate in a way reliable with the different degrees of public financial turn of events. Perceives the requirement for positive endeavors intended to guarantee that emerging nations, particularly the most un-created ones, secure a superior portion of development in global exchange. The WTO proceeds with the dynamic practice followed under the GATT Decisions will be taken by a larger part of votes cast based on one country, one vote.

India is an organizer individual from the WTO. India has contributed essentially to the advancement of the idea of the WTO. Thus, India is as of now harvesting incredibly different advantages that can be straightforwardly or in a roundabout way connected with the WTO. India is encountering an exceptional blast in sends out, similar to the world commodities. India is soon to arrive at the commodity focus of $100 billion, up from just $33.22 billion out of 1998-99. This can be ascribed, in an enormous measure to the WTO-instigated bringing down of the exchange boundaries. India has monstrously profited from the multilateral debate settlement framework that has been set up under the WTO. Activity has been started against such strong economies as the USA on debates including India. Reception of worldwide principles in Intellectual Property Rights assurance would upgrade stream of unfamiliar venture and innovation. Indian labs occupied with research in plant assortments and seeds for tropical locales would benefit. Exchange materials and agrarian items, specifically, would get a lift. WTO has opened up new vistas in global financial relations for every one of the nations of the world. In the opened up world, the stakes of the relative multitude of nations have increased, thus has the level of contention and seriousness. India, similar to some other nation, would be alert to save its inclinations and advance them in a world which is overwhelmed with multifold potential open doors.

SOLUTIONS AND RECOMMENDATIONS

India's developing stature in international politics, particularly inside its region, has encouraged Indian policy makers to take a more energetic role in delivering key worldwide and nearby 'public goods' including poverty reduction, preventing the effect of weather exchange and contributing to international growth. Concerned that developing nations are underrepresented in the ones worldwide bodies that define global public goods and finance their provision, India goals to beautify its engagement with multilateral institutions. At the identical time there's an growing choice at the a part of other nations to have interaction more closely with India on a range of worldwide challenges, not least development. In January 2012, India extended its overseas resource programme via setting up the Development Partnership Administration (DPA), its own foreign resource company beneath the Ministry of External Affairs (MEA). With a considerable price range of $15 billion to be spent over the following five years, the DPA will oversee the management of India's distant places improvement tasks. The creation of a crucial company is a part of an attempt to streamline implementation, decrease operating fees, and cope with other demanding situations that have lengthy stymied India's worldwide improvement schedule. The DPA may even assess the impact of the Lines of Credit that India has extended to accomplice countries in current years. India has additionally improved its overseas help efforts via engaging in multilateral useful resource programmes. The IBSA Trust Fund offers an innovative approach of delivering assistance to different countries and demonstrates that India is amenable to pooling sovereignty within the provision of assistance. There is also a willingness to adopt extra considerable help programmes, visible most truly inside the Pan African E-Network undertaking. The non-public quarter plays a key role in India's usual position as an aid-giver. However, India's programme is possibly to be refined in the future. In the early years of the programme, Lines of Credit had been used to fund initiatives of questionable improvement advantage together with the construction of a presidential palace (in Ghana) and a cricket stadium (in Guyana). In latest years most projects funded have clearer cut developmental outcomes. India has long approached resource thru bilateral offers and help. However, Indian policymakers have began to look useful resource, as well as greater financial ties with other international locations, as a method of positioning India as an rising energy within the eyes of 'recipient' international locations and other donors. Traditionally, India has provided investment to a variety of United Nations and World Bank groups; it lately became a donor to the World Bank's Trust Fund for South–South learning. It has also presented assistance to different international locations through education and capacity-constructing. The Indian Technical and Economic Cooperation scheme (ITEC) was based in 1964 and changed into visible as an crucial demonstration of India's commitment to South–South cooperation within the Nineteen Sixties and Seventies. The long-status scheme has furnished for more than a few projects, inclusive of, most currently, solar-power plant life in Cuba and Costa Rica; a laptop system for the high minister of Senegal; fitting artificial limbs in Cambodia and Uzbekistan; and a vocational schooling middle for small and medium-sized companies in Zimbabwe. India increasingly more coordinates its aid efforts with other donors. India has signed the Paris Declaration on Aid Effectiveness (as a recipient instead of a donor) and joined the Nepal Development Forum, the Afghanistan Reconstruction Trust Fund and the multi-donor fund for Iraq. India, Australia, Japan and the USA together coordinated the global response to the 2004 Asian tsunami. Established in June 2003, the IBSA Dialogue Forum, concerning the IBSA grouping of India, Brazil, and South Africa, aims at stronger cooperation in regions along with agriculture, alternate, lifestyle and protection. In 2004, the IBSA grouping mounted a Trust Fund. India's contribution to the Trust Fund, even as small scale India, Brazil, and South Africa every make contributions US$1m yearly

Role of Global Institutions in Economic Development of India

suggests a potential willingness for greater pooling of sovereignty in India's aid provision. The Fund ambitions to pick out replicable and scalable initiatives that may be disseminated to involved growing international locations as examples of great practices for tackling poverty and hunger. Projects underneath the IBSA Trust Fund are achieved in collaboration and consultation with accomplice nations. Consist of a solid waste collection mission in Haiti; the introduction of recent seeds and ability building in stepped forward agricultural strategies in Guinea-Bissau; and the refurbishment of two nearby, isolated health gadgets in Cape Verde. India's participation in the BRICS emerging-kingdom bloc, made from Brazil, Russia, India, China, and South Africa, affords new opportunities for superior multilateral cooperation in worldwide improvement. At the BRICS Summit held in South Africa in March 2013, the BRICS participants introduced that the establishment of a BRICS improvement financial institution changed into viable, but the assertion fell short of suggesting precise timelines for the financial institution's establishment. The information of how this type of financial institution might paintings are nonetheless, it'd seem, being formulated. Whether the financial institution is supposed to attention in most cases at the BRICS international locations themselves, or to assist other growing nations, remains unclear. The proposed BRICS Development Bank has emerged as an alternative to Western-ruled global financial institutions. Unlike the International Monetary Fund (IMF) or the World Bank, which attach political restructuring conditions to low-interest loans, the BRICS Development Bank is predicted to offer higher-interest loans without situations. While some key logistical questions stay unresolved, inclusive of which BRICS nation ought to host the bank, which currency need to be used and the dimensions of the initial contributions, the BRICS Development Bank poses a task to existing lending institutions and alerts members states' purpose to amplify financial and trade cooperation.

CONCLUSION

This chapter explores the role of global economic institutions (GEIs) in contemporary economic governance: The International Monetary Fund (IMF), the World Bank and the World Trade Organization (WTO) etc. It discusses global governance and globalization and examine competing perspectives on international organizations. Controversies over the role of the GEIs in the global economy have focused on the economic impact of their activities and their representative nature as institutions of governance. The historical evolution of the IMF, World Bank and WTO as they adapted to the challenges of an evolving global economy. It examines competing claims concerning their competence as economic managers. Recently, the legitimacy, accountability and representative nature of GEIs have been called into question. It focuses on the debate over the democratic credentials of the GEIs. A set of different international economic organizations has been set up to ensure orderly international economic cooperation and smooth economic relations between the nations of the world. While the IMF and the World Bank were set up when the world was caught in the turmoil of the World War, the WTO has been set up when the wave of globalization and liberalization was sweeping across the globe. Both the situations called for a need to set up mutually-agreed organization, which would only prove a win-win situation for all the contracting parties. While there may be some short-term pains for a few, due to need for structural adjustment during the phase of transition, long term prospects for economic development only serve to attract more adherents to this doctrine.

REFERENCES

Acemoglu, D., Johnson, S., & Robinson, J. A. (2000). *The Colonial Origins of Comparative Development: An Empirical investigation.* National Bureau of Economic Research Working Paper Series, No. 7771.

Ben Ali, M., & Krammer, S. (2016). *The Role of Institutions in Economic Development.* . doi:10.1057/9781137480668_1

Andriamananjara, S., & Nash, J. (1997). *Have Trade Policy Reforms led to Greater Openness in Developing Countries?* World Bank Working Paper No. 1730. The World Bank.

Aron, J. (2000). Growth and Institutions, a Review of the Evidence. *The World Bank Research Observer, 15*(1), 465–490. doi:10.1093/wbro/15.1.99

Banerjee, A. V., & Duflo, E. (2011). *Poor Economics: A Radical Rethinking of the Way to Fight Global Poverty.* Public Affairs.

Bardhan, P. (2006). Institutions and Development. In D. Clark (Ed.), *The Elgar Companion to Development Studies* (pp. 2–56). Edward Elgar Publishing.

Bates, R. H. (2001). *Prosperity and Violence: The Political Economy of Development.* W.W. Norton&Company.

Bhagwati, J. (1963). Some Recent Trends in the Pure Theory of International Trade. In R. Harrod & D. Hague (Eds.), *International Trade Theory in a Developing World* (pp. 1–30). Macmillan and Co. Ltd. doi:10.1007/978-1-349-08458-6_1

Bhagwati, J. (1978). *Anatomy and Consequences of Exchange Control Regimes: Liberalisation Attempts and Consequences.* Ballinger Pub. Co.

Birdsall, N., Rodrik, D., & Subramanian, A. (2005). How to Help Poor Countries. *Foreign Affairs, 84*(July/August), 136–152. doi:10.2307/20034426

Breslin, S. (2007). *China and the Global Political Economy, Basingstoke: Palgrave. Brooks, Chris (2008), Introductory Econometrics for Finance* (2nd ed.). Cambridge University Press. doi:10.1057/9780230223943

Chang, H.-J. (2008). Under-explored Treasure Troves of Development Lessons- Lessons from the Histories of Small Rich European Countries (SRECs). In Doing Good or Doing Better – Development Policies in a Globalising World. Amsterdam University Press.

Coase, R. H. (1992). The Economic Structure of Production. *The American Economic Review, 82*(September), 713–719.

Dixit, A. (2004). *Lawlessness and Economics: Alternative Modes of Governance.* Princeton University Press.

Greif, A. (2000). The fundamental problem of exchange: A research agenda in historical institutional analysis. *European Review of Economic History, 4*(3), 251–284. doi:10.1017/S1361491600000071

Hall, R., & Jones, C. I., (1999). Why Do Some Countries Produce So Much More Output per Worker than Others? *Quarterly Journal of Economics, 114*(1), 83-116.

Keefer, P., & Stasavage, D. (2002). Checks and balances, private information, and the credibility of monetary commitments. *International Organization, 56*(4), 751–774. doi:10.1162/002081802760403766

Myrdal, G. (1992). The Equality Issue in World Development. In Nobel Lectures, Economics, 1969-1980. Singapore: World Scientific Publishing.

Narlikar & Odell. (2006). *The Strict Distributive Strategy for a Bargaining Coalition: The Like Minded Group in the World Trade Organization*. Academic Press.

North, D. C. (1990). *Institutions, Institutional Change and Economic Performance*. Cambridge University Press. doi:10.1017/CBO9780511808678

Putnam, R. (1993). *Making Democracy Work: Civic Traditions in Modern Italy*. Princeton University Press.

Rodrik, D. (2000). *Institutions for High-Quality Growth: What they are and how to acquire them*. Working Paper 7540.

Rodrik, D., Subramanian, A., & Trebbi, F. (2004). Institutions Rule: The Primacy of Institutions over Geography and Integration in Economic Development. *Journal of Economic Growth, 9*(2), 131–165. doi:10.1023/B:JOEG.0000031425.72248.85

Savoia, A., Easaw, J., & McKay, A. (2010). Inequality, Democracy, and Institutions: A Critical Review of Recent Research. *World Development, 38*(2), 142–154. doi:10.1016/j.worlddev.2009.10.009

Shirley, M. M. (2005). Institutions and Development. In C. Ménard & M. M. Shirley (Eds.), *Handbook of New Institutional Economics*. Springer. doi:10.1007/0-387-25092-1_25

Todaro, M. P., & Smith, S. C. (2003). Economic Development (8th ed.). Pearson Education Pvt. Ltd.

Chapter 17
Socio-Intercultural Organizational Development

José G. Vargas-Hernández
https://orcid.org/0000-0003-0938-4197
Instituto Tecnológico Mario Molina, Zapopan, Mexico

ABSTRACT

This chapter analyzes socio-intercultural organizational development as a novel perspective in organizational sciences. The analysis departs from the assumption that an effective socio-intercultural management and organizational long-term development based on the collaboration among all the stakeholders must be based on the cultural basic assumptions, values, and beliefs of participants involved in intercultural communication and dialogue, committed, and acting on equal basis despite the cultural differences and the challenges derived. The method employed is the transdisciplinary reflective-analytical approach. The analysis concludes that the transdisciplinary and socio-intercultural perspective of organizational development and effective management competence is based on intercultural communication and dialogue.

INTRODUCTION

This chapter aims to analyze the socio-intercultural organizational development as a novel perspective. To achieve this aim, the main objectives are to explain the concept of socio-intercultural organizations as the starting point to follow with the second objective, to conceptualize the socio-intercultural organizational development.

There is a lot of theoretical and empirical research that has been conducted on the issue of organizational development but there is a gap on research related to the socio-intercultural organizational development that this chapter intends to address. The analysis departs from the assumption that an effective socio-intercultural organizational long-term development must be supported by the collaboration among all the stakeholders and must be based on the cultural basic assumptions, values and beliefs of participants involved in intercultural communication and dialogue, committed, and acting on equal basis despite the cultural differences and the challenges derived.

DOI: 10.4018/978-1-6684-2448-3.ch017

Copyright © 2022, IGI Global. Copying or distributing in print or electronic forms without written permission of IGI Global is prohibited.

Socio-Intercultural Organizational Development

Socio-interculturalism is a category that requires a critical analysis and subjective reflexibility on the interactive different forms of world view and thinking the sociopolitical, historical, and cultural structures. The concept of socio-interculturalism is the result of understanding the effects of population growth and creating dialogue with multiethnic and multicultural communities (Костовић & Ђерманов, 2006; Göler, 2016). The development and implementation of the socio-interculturalism concept in organizational settings is a leading priority. The concept of socio-interculturalism should not only be accepted on a declarative way but must be implemented in the sociocultural circumstances of specific organizational arrangements. The organizational potential to implement and apply socio-interculturalism requires to know and practice the concept in a multicultural and pluralistic society.

The concept of socio-interculturalism in organizational settings requires of conditions for the implementation of socio-intercultural values and for the encouragement of coexistence through the interactions, interrelationships able to develop understanding and create dialogue. An adequate and proper implementation of the socio-interculturalism concept in organizations requires the transformational changes of all the aspects and individual life conditions at the workplace.

The holistic approach of the concept of socio-interculturalism supports the changing of an organizational paradigm towards a more open and integrated dialogue and communication based on knowledge and learning strategies. Creating and disseminating transdisciplinary socio-intercultural knowledge, values and functional organizational practices are some of the activities.

A transdisciplinary approach to socio-interculturalism encourages the use of metacognitive skills, reflexive discussion, development of attitudes, behaviors, values, and practices for proper actions to transform individuals, groups, communities and organizational situations, contexts, and environments through collaborative projects. In organizational contexts it is required that the members learn to be aware of the prejudices, stereotypes, biases, and discrimination emerging at the workplace and the use of transformative dialogue as a mean to overcome these problems (Oljača, 2006).

Individuals, organizations, groups, and communities need to engage and adopt the new socio-intercultural approach in such a way that all the issues, concerns and topics must be transdisciplinary examined to develop, acquire, and implement competences in real practice. Individuals and groups in organizations and communities apply transdisciplinary knowledge, skills, competences, and learning experiences to make decisions, collaborate on tasks and projects and solve specific problems in different environments. Socio-intercultural knowledge, skills and competencies acquired and applied in solving real-life organizational problems represent a step towards a better organization (Анђелковић, СтанисављевићПетровић, 2013).

The interconnections between diverse cultural values, the emerging understandings and dialogue between the members have severe consequences for the development of organizations in society. Organizational members interact in ways unthinkable in terms of demanding the right for equal opportunities, more autonomy in the self-evaluation at the workplace, equal share and rights in allocation, management and use resources, involving and blending marginalized and immigrant culturally diverse groups (Childeres & Urquhart, 1994).

The organizational development of socio-intercultural experiences and competences is a necessity in an era of a global market (Anderson, et al., 2006; Chieffo & Griffiths, 2004; Donnelly-Smith, 2009) in the context of cultural differences challenging their sense of being and with a positive impact on cross cultural understanding, interactions, and relationships for a better coexistence. The concept of socio-intercultural is an indicator of global society integration and the dialogue in favor of general assimilation of cultural diversity and against stereotypes and prejudices (Костовић & Ђерманов, 2006). The cultural differences are present in the entire world where peoples face cultural diversity in all spheres of human life. Socio-interculturalism is a concept of tolerance between the diverse cultures (Perotti, 1995; Vrcelj, 2005; Hrvatić, 2007; Marković & Prnjat, 2011).

Socio-interculturalism is assumed as a dynamic and dialogic communicative action space acknowledging a constructing reflection on cultural differences and diversity based on human rights, democracy and solidary in organizational and community development. The socio-intercultural dialogue at the organization offers civil engagement to support the development of initiatives and inspiring empowerment to the best use of skills and resources aimed to promote transformational change. Socio-interculturalism in organizations promotes challenges in interactions and exchanges between the individuals' cultural values related to diversity backgrounds, identity constructions, solidarity, etc., by direct actions such as addressing and combatting any kind of discrimination and involving citizens in human rights and participating in policymaking.

Socio-intercultural skills acquired by individuals teach to be more tolerant in the job-market, to have respect for human rights and diverse cultural identities by combating discrimination, opening more opportunities for inter-sociocultural dialogue, civil engagement in society and organizations, inspiring empowerment in a more efficient and sustainable use of organizational and natural resources and in sum to the promotion of transformative change.

Socio-intercultural organizational management should move away from antagonistic concepts prevailing in Western culture by adopting an independent perspective based on self-organizing social systems (Capra1997). The socio-intercultural organization is a meeting place for cultural dialogue and peaceful coexistence of diverse cultures, facing the internal and external challenges under the principles of socio-interculturalism. The optimal form of socio-intercultural organizational management is characterized by the deepest level of engagement, interactions, dialogue, participation and full partnership between the diverse cultural groups and stakeholders within and between the organizations.

The research emphasizes that socio-intercultural management is an empathetic approach to bridge the cultural differences in management practices (Nyambegera et al., 2016) conducted by the members of the group learning about the selves and the "others" group´s philosophies to broaden perceptions.

The research questions of this chapter, in accordance with the aim of the analysis are related to the two main objectives: What are the main characteristics, elements and attributes of the concept of socio-intercultural organizations? The second question is related to the second objective, what are the elements to conceptualize the socio-intercultural organizational development?

BACKGROUND OF SOCIO-INTERCULTURAL ORGANIZATIONS

The concept of socio-interculturalism implies among other dimensions, the sensitivity, understanding and the recognition of diversity in all conditions of human life based on equality and human rights, such as the differences in ethnicity and cultural development of individuals, organizations and communities living in diverse ways, styles and values of life, traditions, and customs, etc. which enhance and enrich the social development. The organizational socio-interculture defines the direction that the organization choses to attain the strategies of internal intercultural communication to improve the internal working environment and the intercultural social responsibility. Socio-intercultural analysis on the differences between communication styles of high and low contexts people or organizations in international environments are still in infancy age.

Socio-Intercultural Organizational Development

The concept of socio-interculturalism in organizations has become the guidelines for an organizational comprehensive and multifaceted transformation experience based on the improvement of understanding and dialogue between the members of diverse cultural background. Socio-intercultural is a dynamic term used to indicate a relation, exchange, and a set of dynamic flows of meetings between the individuals holding diverse cultural identities (Camilleri, 1992).

A globally oriented context organization is based on organizational principles of socio-culturalism and development of enough autonomy in its institutional framework to operate by its own or in partnership. The organization needs to make significant internal changes in its perspective and attitude towards the cooperation with local authorities, institutional and organizational environment, associations, and other relevant stakeholders in the community. Community, local and organizations are the spatial-time environments that have become the meeting places where people with diverse cultures, religious, ethnicities, gender, etc., can develop socio-intercultural relationships (Bedeković, 2007).

Socio-intercultural studies give orientation to some basic organizational principles to give support to organizational management which are multidisciplinary focused and developed with the assistance of trained staff and consultants while keeping autonomy in operations within its institutional frameworks.

Leading a socio-intercultural organization in new global environments where it is required an intercultural communication for the interactions between people of diverse cultures and to match with the social responsibility. A socio-intercultural responsive organization to his context has an orientation towards a more global cultural intelligence to behave differently that other multinational organizations in developing global competence and expertise.

Socio-intercultural knowledge, learning and research in organizational environments oriented toward a global non utilitarian mentality and values, can deliver the socio-intercultural organizational competencies and expertise through the means spatial and temporal real-time, the living experiences and practices. Knowledge integration to socio-intercultural organizational management is more related to adaptive co-management and shared management, social justice, and biocultural diversity.

Anthropology has proposed the notion of cultural differences approach now being challenged diffuse sources of information through popular media (Marcus and Fischer 1999: xx) leading to ethnography to regain more new opportunities for disciplinary thinking and practice in this field to reorient its core practices in the global environment based on collaborative dialogue which has a lot of implications in organizational socio-intercultural strategies and programs (Fischer and Marcus 1999: xxviii). The collaborative dialogue approach is a cooperative perspective based on socio-intercultural and transdisciplinary global framework.

The socio-intercultural dialogue requires appropriate conditions to facilitate the understanding, human freedom, tolerance, peace, rule of law, etc., between people (Lukač-Zoranić and Ivanović 2014). These appropriate conditions focus on the acceptance of human rights and its foundation of mutual respect, the acceptance of cultural diversity, inclusive policies, socio-intercultural, communications, etc. These conditions require socio-intercultural knowledge and learning in inclusive organizations and communities.

Organizational socio-interculturalism is oriented toward global intelligence involving both the world conditions and the human interactions in specific areas of economic growth, social development and sustainable environmental. Socio-intercultural organizational issues and topics can be trans disciplinarily analyzed from different approaches and perspectives recognizing the purpose and significance of knowledge and practices in the interactions and connections between individuals, groups, organizations, and communities that are culturally diverse.

Ideological, interpretive anthropological and political perspectives in a global framework must re-orient some of the valuable principles and insights in the further elaboration and conceptualization of sociocultural in organizations, such as the use of hermeneutics for the reconstruction of meanings. Is in this sense that the reconstruction of socio-interculturalism dialogue requires besides other theoretical building blocks as part of the integral elements of any socio-intercultural mentality capable of removing the deeply engrained any dysfunctional cultural background and enabling new possibilities of cultural alterities as more universally human

The socio-intercultural organizational process begins with the emergence of socio-intercultural et-noeducation contextualized in conceptual, sociohistorical, and institutional community environments. Socio-interculturalism at organizational environments is a complex and interdependent issue beyond the cultural stereotypes and reductionism to maintain an equilibrium between the cultural differences.

National and regional cultural dimensions are relevant to socio-intercultural organizations in terms of interactions focused on beliefs related to relationships, time, space, context, responsibility, duty, status, stress (Hall, 1997; Hofstede, Hofstede, and Minkov 2010; Trompenaars and Hampden-Turner, 2012; Böhm, 2013; Myers and Tan, 2003). National and regional culture influences socio-intercultural manage-rial and organizational collaboration by the perceptions of the individuals (Trompenaars & Asser, 2010).

Globalization has increased the need to develop socio-intercultural managerial and organizational skills aimed to be applied in the identification of cultural managerial differences and interpersonal and managerial interactions that affect global management. Individuals participating in organizational and managerial socio-intercultural interactions have diverse cultural backgrounds, values, and different prefer-ences (Boonstra and de Vries, 2015; House, Hanges, Dorfmanand, and Gupta, Eds. 2004; Hofstede, 2001).

Misinterpretations of perceived culture-based behaviors occur when they are judged by the perceiver´s belief and value system, which makes difficult to infer based on cultural determinations. A good example is the one explained by Köster (2010) who proposes that there is a cultural gap between the dimension of uncertainty avoidance (Hofstede, Hofstede, and Minkov 2010; Köster, 2010) and the independent cultural dimension of risk avoidance used to contrast avoiding risks and embracing risk in socio-intercultural organizational management projects.

Globalization socio-economic, political, and cultural processes and changes have led to an increase in socio-intercultural collaboration in international business organizations, communication, and conflict management (Van der Nest, 2004). In any organizational internationalization process, professionals should be able to communicate and interact with others with diverse cultural values to create value for their organizational. The different issues related to socio-intercultural organizational management in-teractions are a priority in economic globalization processes that requires the training of a multicultural personality in socio-intercultural dialogue, cooperation, and communication (Soter, 2016). The specific global competences related to socio-interculturality is linked to structure in the organizational, relational and self-knowledge dimensions

In contextualized and dynamic environments of socio-intercultural organizational collaboration support the understanding perceptions of work (Hinds et al., 2011). Socio-intercultural collaboration is often achieved through the domination of one culture by the other (Graen, Hui & Gu, 2004, p. 225) an approach that is dysfunctional, conflictive, and inadequate. Often, socio-intercultural management in less developed countries has been perceived as a challenging high conflict potential resulting from political instability, weaknesses in the rule of the law, lack of transparence, personal security, and difficult labor relations (Humphreys & Bates, 2005).

Socio-Intercultural Organizational Development

Socio-intercultural organizational management promotes the dialogue of all the involved individual from the different participating cultures challenging the ability to adapt to new global circumstances and the flexibility to establish asynchrony and asymmetrical relationships. Socio-intercultural relationships may be asymmetrical and asynchronous between the different economic and political counterparts but may not be able to impose a dominant power and culture to the dominated one and may emerge transformed by their contact and dialogue. Organizations such as communities need mechanisms for organizational and community participation, where appropriate, to generate a socio-intercultural vision to promote dialogue between all participants and between institutional systems differentiated from a dominant culture over another dominated culture.

Socio-intercultural managerial and organizational problems can cause long-term and short-term dysfunctionalities and conflicts. To avoid these organizational and managerial dysfunctionalities and conflicts a strategy should aim at a coherent management of the specific crisis situations of economic, social, and political nature in such a way that must generate added value (Constantin Șcheau and Zaharie Pop, 2020).

However, if culture is considered as the basic assumptions, values, norms (Rosinski, 2011) it has the potential for dysfunctionalities and conflict increases (Mayer & Boness, 2011; Mayer & Louw, 2012) affecting the socio-intercultural collaboration between diverse cultural parties and groups (Mayer, 2011). It has been assumed that the differences in basic assumptions, values and beliefs create different perceptions challenging the socio-intercultural collaboration. Any socio-intercultural organizational collaboration led to socio-intercultural perceptions, communications, and experiences. Socio-intercultural organizational communication and management must be trained in the context of organizational functions and activities

Socio-intercultural organizational collaboration is a challenging process in terms of perceptions and understanding each other's experiences and knowledge sharing, styles, etc., aimed to contribute to a sustainable long-term improvement of both involved working parties. Socio-intercultural managerial and organizational challenges for constructive collaboration is subject to the individuals´ awareness, perceptions, their abilities, skills and the design and implementation strategies through human resources management embracing cultural diversity.

The implementation of socio-interculturalism in an organizational setting requires to intensify efforts for an understanding and dialogue between the diversity of cultures. The role of this socio-intercultural organizational comprehensive dialogue and commitment to more common values is the development of a new democratic, diverse, and plural citizenship. This may lead to an increase in international socio-intercultural management collaboration, and conflict management (Van der Nest, 2004). Intersociocultural factors influence individual preferences concerning the type and style of socio-intercultural communication in organizations in the context of international markets.

Organizational socio-intercultural collaboration can be improved by the mutual understanding between the parties involved to work in a more equal and solidary partnerships with all internal and external organizational contexts. A socio-intercultural organizational exchange between management of different localities, regions and countries, the purpose of socio-intercultural communication is to establish partnerships between parties to create a common ground to exchange and share information and to convey the meaning, ideas, decisions, feelings, etc. (Hambrick, Davidson, Snell, Snow, 1998, p. 181).

Socio-intercultural managerial and organizational collaboration competence needs to improve to support the improvement of a sustainable international and socio-intercultural collaboration (Koehn, 2007). Individuals in organizations must be trained in socio-intercultural collaboration competences to improve the understanding of organizational relationships and contacts, reflecting on prejudices, bias and stereotypes and reinforce the self and others knowledge, basic cultural values, experiences, etc.

The knowledge management (KM) learning process is an approach proposed by Nonaka & Takeuchi (1995) based on the theory of the organizational knowledge creation and transformation from tacit to explicit in a spiral to new tacit knowledge, which is from socialization to externalization and combination before internalization again (Nonaka et. al. 1995).

To achieve these means in socio-intercultural organizational environments, multinational and transnational organizations have opportunities to use information and communication technologies. Some socio-intercultural managerial skills required by international managers of multinational and transnational organizations are related with learning foreign cultural elements and the language for a foreign country which ensures their abilities to adapt new life and working conditions more efficiently. Social interactions and exposures in different sociocultural contexts help to develop experiences in learning socio-intercultural organizational competences, knowledge acquisition and accumulation.

However, to learn socio-intercultural organizational and managerial pragmatic competences requires the support of integrated theoretical and conceptual framework as a model to be implemented. Responsible socio-intercultural organizational management model in multinational and transnational organizations demands national and local cultural perception in socio-intercultural environment to determine the influence on the interactions between the organizational and individual behavior.

A world without boundaries is an illusion for many multinational and transnational enterprises and organizations that need to take into consideration in their spatial and territorial operations and actions the role of sociocultural differences. Socio-intercultural competence is one of the essential skills of individuals, teams and organizations functioning in an international environment and exerting influence across the national borders. The socio-intercultural organizational model affects the values, norms, and beliefs, etc., on the internal intercultural communications and the social responsibility with its interactions between the national and local culture in a pristine environment.

METHOD

The method employed is the transdisciplinary reflective – analytical approach. Some of the theoretical and methodological foundations related to socio-intercultural organizations and management are the theory of socio-intercultural communication (Astafurov, 1997); the theory of self-organization, "chaos", order, nonlinearity of the "culture" system (Alefirenko, 2010; Hacken, 1995); the socio-intercultural communicative competence formation. The socio-intercultural organizational approach requires to be supported by a more dynamic and flexible institutional framework.

The principles of socio-intercultural and transdisciplinary dialogue and cooperation are the ground rules for organizational socio-intercultural management research and dialogue, contact and liminality as conceptual tools and transdisciplinary analysis, as the basic methodological tools from a glocal perspective. Organizational socio-interculturalism are based on principles, theoretical assumptions, methodologies, and practices of cultural anthropological, ethnography and literary studies oriented toward the inclusion of other transdisciplinary and knowledge fields global intelligence.

SOCIO-INTERCULTURAL ORGANIZATIONAL DEVELOPMENT

The theoretical foundations of socio-intercultural organizational development are supported by the interactions between organizational culture, internal intercultural communication, and organizational intercultural social responsibilities. Organizational culture is defined as a comprehensive system of values, norms, traditions, notions, beliefs, customs, and symbols (Rozman 2007, 2008, & 2010; Schein, 1990; Denison et al., 2012; Fullan, 2014, pp. 5–6; Verčič, Verčič & Sriramesh, 2012; Schein 2010). Socio-intercultural organizational development is a new stage in evolution of relationships between the cultural diversity of groups and stakeholders within and between organizations in meaningful participation, understanding each other and learning together in common initiatives (Pedota 2011).

Organizational culture is defined as values, beliefs, and behavior, which are visible internally and externally (Sweeney and McFarlin 2002, p. 336). Organizational culture forms the basis to formulate and manage the socio intercultural responsibilities of an organization. A pluralistic cultural approach may contribute to achieve socio-intercultural creating the conditions for the organizational development of values, attitudes, skills and abilities for cultural understanding and dialogue.

Socio-interorganizational culture differs between organizations, between principles, characteristics, and goals as some categories for the organizational analysis using the tools of intercultural communication and social responsibilities in a unique environment. Sites in organizational socio-intercultural analysis are different by their different by their independences and not for the geographical, physical, or virtual position in such a way that because a reciprocal causality relationship between the local and global, socio-interculturalism can be conducted in any location.

A more humanistic and holistic approach to organizational development is the socio-interculturalism based on a dialogue between the diverse meeting cultural backgrounds of all the members and stakeholders.

The comparative analysis of socio-intercultural communication and dialogue based on the principles of global intelligence is at the initial development stage in engaging in global. Socio-intercultural space and time of organizational development may vary between different human communities and civilizations. This socio-intercultural, transdisciplinary, and theoretical reflection and dialogue from a historical perspective can be the reference frame to be translated into space and time action at glocal level.

The socio-intercultural organizational discourse and dialogue is the direct and indirect communication between subjects of distinct cultures that has significant characteristics as a component of socio-intercultural interaction in the ability to understand each other´s participants' cultural differences. Understanding each other in the socio-intercultural organizational communication process is complex by the interpretation of verbal and non-verbal components.

Communities, organizations, and groups devoted to socio-intercultural managerial promote dialogical tolerance around the world supporting the integration an assimilation of immigrants and local people in a pristine environment (Piechota, 2014). This situation results in socio-intercultural contacts and cultural values change creating new communication groups and community types with new identities (Van Dijk 2010: 237). Socio-intercultural communication in social media displayed by diverse groups, organizations and communities promote socio-intercultural and tolerance dialogue.

The theoretical-methodological foundations for the development of socio-intercultural organizations, communities and societies are emphasized by a systematic sociological approach based on the analysis of the sociocultural relationships and interactions between people, their needs and expectations of the urban communities, their cultural and natural environments, concepts of resources and socio-intercultural public spaces, sociocultural identity, and identification.

The organizational development of understanding of cultural diversity, it is necessary to learn about diverse ways and styles of life, to understand their perceptions, motivations, expectations, etc., from another perspectives and views (Milutinović & Zuković, 2007; Prnjat, 2015).

The organizational development based on a technology-cultural synergy model has applications in the formation of socio-intercultural communicative competence by neutralizing the native identity and actualizes the situation of being foreign and becoming and extra systemic element and organizing the interactions.

Organizational development and socio-intercultural management model should match the organizational values, and the internal communication in the social responsibility when the organization is in a pristine environment and confronting diverse cultures. Socio-intercultural management and the organizational and individual behavior from diverse cultures are influenced by the national and regional culture and the communication with other cultures focusing on differences and attributes such as basic cultural assumptions, values, norms, social attributes, language, religion, etc. (Georgescu, 2016).

Colonialism has determined and marked the dynamics of socio-intercultural interactions and contacts leading to the construction of an attitudinal orientation toward the cultural otherness.

Colonialism expressed as cultural domination has produced a severe traumatic experience in the collective psyches as the result of interactions of both colonized and colonizers which require a socio-intercultural approach to heal and reconcile.

The new ethnography methodology proposes an intercultural dialogue as a grounding principle. Socio-intercultural contacts, interactions and experiences between the missions, other relevant forms of organizations and native cultures in South America during the 16th, 17th and 18th centuries are a relevant example to comprehend and understand the differences between cultures (Lima Magalhães 2011). Socio-intercultural organizational benefits in other specific areas such as health care have been demonstrated in other cultural contexts in Latin America.

The postcolonial cultural anthropology supported by van-guard ethnography based on deconstructions beyond nihilism leads toward feedback loops to create an intercultural dialogue between the theoretical and methodological practical principles to construct organizational socio-interculturalism. Other perspectives, such as experimental ethnography and imaginary ethnography offer possibilities to reproduce the socio-interculturalism interactive processes outside the realm of politics. From using these perspectives, individuals in organizations may confront experiences of otherness internal such as psychological social, cultural, sexual, etc., and external such as the same socio-interculturalism. Socio-intercultural otherness is an alterity that have engendered forms of socio-intercultural interactions and contacts based on asymmetrical and unequal relations of power.

A good theoretical and conceptual model of socio-intercultural managerial and organizational model at meta-level can provide a logical understanding and awareness of behavioral culture differences affecting the design and implementation of cultural management organizational strategies. Organizations should be aware of their socio-intercultural organizational management and corporate social responsibilities related to their environments.

SOLUTIONS AND RECOMMENDATIONS

The term socio-intercultural organizational management development refers to organizational systems, structures, behaviors, and managerial technology that entails a dialogue seeking mutual exchange of

Socio-Intercultural Organizational Development

knowledge and practices between the diversity cultures of the involved people while perceiving them as equal in status. In socio-intercultural organizational management converge the interaction of different concepts, languages, contents, and structures. The socio-intercultural initiative entails a dialogue and generates something innovative (Schroder 2006).

Development of the socio-intercultural organizational management may benefit from the theory and practice of cultural translation and interpretation, imaginary ethnography, and literary anthropology to conceive liminal spaces as the meeting places and neutral grounds for alterities for mutual learning and transformation. The organizational development of these socio-intercultural and transdisciplinary knowledge and learning environments within a framework of global intelligence can stimulate the socio-intercultural development of human beings. These actions will lead to the creation, development and adoption of socio-intercultural values and practices in the spirit of a glocal understanding and intelligence.

The content of socio-intercultural organizational development programs of competences can be enhanced by exchanging experiences of different social contexts reflecting the cultural diversity, creating knowledge, attitudes, behaviors, and skills required (Milutinović & Zuković, 2007). Socio-intercultural awareness in transdisciplinary diversity encourage from a global perspective the development of socio-intercultural competences that includes the domains of cognitive, affective, and behavioral in a holistic framework (Deardorff, 2006, King, and Baxter Magolda, 2005).

The organizational development of socio-intercultural competences of members and their active participation requires more than the transfer of knowledge, a system to create the conditions in real time and space through diverse activities to provide opportunities to discover and experience the cultural differences and similarities. The organizational development of the socio-intercultural competence is regarded as one of the essential skills of individuals in teams and organizations is highly related to international market environment.

This organizational development programs of socio-intercultural competencies give the opportunities in field workplace to gain experience, understand attitudes and behaviors, analyze, and accept other´s cultural values, beliefs, etc. in such a way that can be established cooperative behaviors and relationships to perform common tasks and assignments. The content of socio-intercultural organizational development programs for mutual cultural understanding is always conditioned by context (Anđelković & Stanisavljević Petrović, 2014).

Socio-intercultural management and organizational development´s environment is supported by the organizational culture, intercultural communication, leadership's vision, organizational strategy, socio-cultural competence social responsibility and development of the organizational and business environment, etc. (Kukovec, Mulej & Šarotar Žižek, 2018). Crystal, 1997; Muha, 2003; Wright, 1999, p. 199; Thill & Bovee, 2002, p. 165; Cateora & Graham, 2002, p. 106, et al.)

The organizational development of socio-intercultural competences enables the changes in communication styles depending on the specific circumstances, high or low context organization, preferences, and the international receivers of messages. The organizational development of socio-intercultural competence requires a knowledge and learning processes supported not only by all the modalities of education as a principle permeating all the programs but the most important is the creation of living conditions for an entire school of life to experience in real place and time and at the right created environment.

Organizational culture and knowledge influence organizational changes confronting the behaviors that block the organizational development and sharing behaviors for social responsibilities (Bhatt, 2001; Koskinen eds., 2003; Arenius eds., 2003). These socio-intercultural and transdisciplinary changes will require an organizational development of creating knowledge and developing environments to bring the

327

socio-intercultural dialogue and conversations to enable the discussion, modification, and implementation of a more global socio-intercultural. Knowledge and learning organizational programs can be oriented toward the organizational development of a more global framework leading toward less utilitarian global intelligence to instrument them as disseminators of socio-intercultural values, competences, and expertise.

Glocal socio-intercultural and transdisciplinary learning initiatives aimed to the organizational development of learning spaces where human beings can relate to each other and to the sustainable environment. With these means in mind, glocal communities must be committed to get involved in sustained efforts to redirect the digital technologies toward the shifting of human mentalities and support the organizational development of a more transdisciplinary socio-intercultural global intelligence.

Cultural identification of individuals has an influence on their socio-intercultural sensitivity and competence organizational development, their interactions, and their acculturation processes in a more dynamic global environment (Lee, & Negrelli, 2018).

DISCUSSION

The analysis concludes that the transdisciplinary and socio-intercultural perspective of organizational development and effective management competence based on intercultural communication and dialogue, is an approach to promote a more comprehensive sustainable socio-economic and environmental development, efficient use of resources, employment creation and growth to overcome poverty, social justice and inclusion, security and peace, and sustainable environment and socio-ecosystems.

The socio-intercultural model of organizational development in urban socioeconomic spaces emphasizes the selection strategy marking specific elements of the urban culture such as the multicultural values and needs (Horpynych, & Ibrahimova, 2020). The organizational development of socio-intercultural urban spaces requires activation factors to motivate the strategic design and implementation of the concept of socio-interculturalism aimed to achieve objectives in economic growth, social justice and equity of people and sustainable environment in the socio-ecology system.

A socio-intercultural managerial and organizational development competences in the context of international business requires to be supported by the development of socio-intercultural management activities in selecting and training managers (Botescuthe, 2010). The formation and development of skills are required for the implementation of socio-intercultural organizational development of management competencies to improve the organizational performance through the development of socio-intercultural spaces and the development of integrative learning. Cultural awareness, capacities and skills lead to better managerial and organizational performance collaborating with multiple clients and partners in several locations (Trompenaars, Woolliams, 2003).

The management of socio-intercultural work teams (IWT) ensuring effective cooperation may contribute to increase the organizational performance in the context of globalization process. Socio-intercultural managerial and organizational formation considers the positioning of the national cultural dimensions, which are closely related to the process of organizational development of socio-intercultural management and organizational capabilities. Socio-intercultural organizational configuration is a multidimensional constellation with distinctive characteristics occurring together (Meyer & Hathaway, 1993).

Socio-intercultural managerial competence prepares individuals for living in more heterogeneous organizations. The organizational development of socio-intercultural managerial competence is a complex activity demanding significant resources, knowledge, methods, techniques, and time to create synergies

Socio-Intercultural Organizational Development

for new opportunities. The organizational development stage of socio-intercultural managerial mindset is established before the skillset as the result of sequencing general cultural information and before specific cultural information. Socio-intercultural managerial and organizational capacities comprise leadership skills, empowering other for individual growth and maintaining ethical standards (Giles, 2016).

Organizations allocate limited time to socio-intercultural training of managerial capabilities and skills while focusing more on behaviors and attitudes to have an impact on organizational development of relationships and performance. The values and norms necessary for the performance of an organization, consider the socio inter organizational cultures within the internal intercultural communication and the social responsibilities.

Socio-intercultural competency is key for socio-intercultural organizational interaction and communication between culturally and heterogeneous and diverse teams as well as other stakeholders of the organization required for the learning targets in the advancement of organizational development. A model of socio-intercultural organizational management communication should support the development of behavioral and communicative skills to facilitate the interconnections between the components of the interactions aimed to achieve higher effectiveness in performance (Batsevych, 2007; Sadokhin, 2007).

The creation of a socio-intercultural organizational communicative competences is connected to the development of the ability to participate in the dialogic socio-intercultural promoting principles of respect and tolerance for cultural differences and engage in dialogue, empathy and freedom from prejudices, bias, discrimination, and social exclusion. Socio-intercultural organizational management communication requires complex behavioral and communicative skills to stablish human interactions achieving understanding and cooperation affecting the various aspects of the organization development. Socio-interculturalism requires the organizational development of interactive space-time learning and practice in projects that promote cooperation, understanding and dialogue in specific cultural environments.

Organizations can be more open to socio-intercultural training and development to facilitate changes of individual and group perceptions aimed to build and develop an organizational sustainable socio-intercultural collaboration. Socio-intercultural organizational training favors the development of appropriate cultural behaviors framework and the socio-intercultural competence. One of the best practices in organizational development in health delivery is the approach in socio-intercultural health care.

Health organizations have been investing in training, organizational development and research on socio-intercultural health programs aimed to improved health care practices and services to all sociocultural groups. The socio-intercultural health care approach ties local indigenous medicine practices with biomedicine which consider complementary (Gyas, 2018). Local indigenous knowledge and communication in socio-intercultural organizations and communities working across cultural collectives contributes to a decolonization process and increases the trust, efficiency, and socioecological resilience.

Socio-intercultural interactions and communication in organizations for the development of socio-intercultural managerial and organizational competence is a challenge faced by diverse and heterogeneous teams (Bouncken, Pfannstiel, Reuschl, Haupt 2015).

Socio-intercultural policy and selection policy design and implementation require de sustainable organizational environment conditions for the establishment and organizational development of the socio-intercultural public spaces for a sustained interrelationship between the citizens and the authorities.

The corporate intercultural social responsibility dimensions and activities are relevant to create the organizational development of the environment in relation to sustainable workplace in a social and environmental sustainability (Visser, 2005). Organizational sociocultural values such as openness to change and learning, adoption of values of social responsibility and ethical behavior lead to more

329

socio-intercultural organizational development (Keyton et al., 2012, pp. 13–15). Companies adopting socio-intercultural organizational values develop and environment of work organization and technology change that have an impact in the development of human resources management systems (Vetráková, Ďurian, *Seková*, and *Kaščáková*, 2016)

FUTURE RESEARCH

Future research on socio-intercultural management and organizational collaboration must focus more on mixed methods and transdisciplinary studies with emphasis on organizational psychology perspective focusing on the different organizational contexts.

CONCLUSION

Transdisciplinary and organizational socio-interculturalism can engaged any field of knowledge to participate in the analysis. The organizational development of socio-intercultural organizational communication and management is an approach to promote social interactions, comprehensive sustainable socio-economic development, efficient use of resources, employment creation and growth, social justice, and inclusion to overcome poverty and sustainable environment, security, and peace. This is the unique contribution of the analysis: A sustained socio-intercultural and transdisciplinary organizational management must be based on a historical and theoretical reflection and dialogue and participating in the creation and development of new projects within the glocal frame of reference to disseminate and amplify the socio-intercultural wisdom. Other forms of socio-intercultural sustained dialogue and related transdisciplinary cooperative activities are based on collaborative projects and other related concerns and issues on social and ethical values with implications on the time-space organizational development of glocal intelligence. The most important task to achieve is to reach a consensus on socio-intercultural values and goals.

This societal transition from traditional cultures toward more socio-intercultural society requires the institutional transformation and the creation and development of an alternative organizational and institutional framework more appropriate to glocal socio-interculturalism supported by knowledge learning and research technological platforms more oriented toward glocal intelligence. Organizational development of information and communication technologies to serve and support glocal systems of socio-intercultural values and beliefs must be grounded on a mentality of a responsive understanding and communication, culture of peace, global ethics, and sustainable development.

Organizations become a significant factor in the socio-intercultural organizational development of a harmonious and peaceful social community. All the organizational members must take an active role in the organizational development and implementation of a socio-intercultural approach. This multicultural approach of the organization requires a transformative change-minded people to enable the organizational restructuration more aligned with the environment.

REFERENCES

Костовић, С., & Ђерманов, Ј. (2006). *Изазови интеркултурализма и школа, У: Љ. Суботић (ур.), Сусрет култура, Зборник радова са 4.* Међународнох.

Alefirenko, N.F. (2010). *Linguoculturology: Values and Meaningful Spaces of Language.* Moscow: Flinta.

Anđelković, S., & Stanisavljević Petrović, Z. (2014). Nature as an Inspiration and a Context for Learning and Teaching. *Bulletin of the Serbian Geographical Society, 94*(1), 57–65. doi:10.2298/GSGD1401057A

Anderson, P. H., Lawton, L., Rexeisen, R. J., & Hubbard, A. C. (2006). Short-term study abroad and intercultural sensitivity: A pilot study. *International Journal of Intercultural Relations, 30*(4), 457–469. doi:10.1016/j.ijintrel.2005.10.004

Arenius, P., & Minniti, M. (2003). Women in entrepreneurship. The entrepreneurial advantage of nations. *First Annual Global Entrepre-neurship Symposium, 29*(1), 4-8.

Astafurova, T.N. (1997). *Linguistic aspects of socio-intercultural business communication.* Vol-gograd: Publ. House of Volgograd State University.

Batsevych, F. (2007). *Glossary of intercultural communication.* Dovira.

Bedeković, V. (2007). Interkulturalne komponente interkulturalnog odgoja i obrazovanja pripadnika nacionalnih manjina. In *Pedagogija prema cjeloživotnom obrazovanju i društvu znanja.* Zagreb: Hrvatsko pedagogijsko društvo.

Bhatt, R. M. (2001). World Englishes. *Annual Review of Anthropology, 30*(1), 527–550. doi:10.1146/annurev.anthro.30.1.527

Böhm, C. (2013). Cultural Flexibility in ICT Projects: A New Perspective on Managing Diversity in Project Teams. *Glob. J. Flex. Syst. Manag. Springer, 14*(2), 115–122. doi:10.100740171-013-0037-6

Boonstra, A., & de Vries, J. (2015). Information System Conflict: Causes and Types, International. *Journal of Information Systems and Project Management, 3*(4), 5–20. doi:10.12821/ijispm030401

Botescuthe, I. (2010, January 01). training of international managers – success factor. *International Business Management & Marketing, 8*(1), 115–120.

Bouncken, R. B., Pfannstiel, M. A., Reuschl, A. J., & Haupt, A. (2015). *Diversität managen. Wie Krankenhäuser das Beste aus personeller Vielfalt machen* (1st ed.). Kohlhammer.

Camilleri, C. (1992). *Le condizioni di base dell'socio-interculturale. Verso una societa socio-interculturale.* Celim.

Capra, F. (1997). *The web of life.* Doubleday-Anchor Book.

Cateora, P. R., & Graham, J. L. (2002). *International Marketing (11ᵗʰ ed.).* McGraw-Hill Publishing.

Chieffo, L., & Griffiths, L. (2004). Large scale assessment of student attitudes after a short-term study abroad program. *Frontiers: The Interdisciplinary Journal of Study Abroad, 18*(1), 101–118. doi:10.36366/frontiers.v10i1.140

Childers, E., & Urquhart, B. (1994). *Renewing the United Nations System*. United Nations.

Childers, E., & Urquhart, B. (1994). *Renewing the United Nations System*. United Nations.

Constantin Şcheau, M., & Zaharie Pop, S. (2020). Andreea Valentina Şoimu Migration, economic causes, and decisions. *Theoretical and Applied Economics, 27*(2), 33-50.

Crystal, D. (1997). The language that took over the world. *The Guardian, 22*(21).

Deardorff, D. K. (2006). The identification and assessment of intercultural competence as a student outcome of internationalization at institutions of higher education in the United States. *Journal of Studies in International Education, 2006*(10), 241–266. doi:10.1177/1028315306287002

Denison, D. (Ed.). (2012). *Leading culture change in global organizations: Aligning culture and strategy*. John Wiley & Sons.

Donnelly-Smith, L. (2009). Global learning through short-term study abroad. *Peer Review: Emerging Trends and Key Debates in Undergraduate Education, 11*(4), 12–15.

Fischer, M., & Marcus, G. (1999), Introduction to the Second Edition. In Anthropology as Cultural Critique: An Experimental Moment in the Human Sciences (2nd ed.). University of Chicago Press.

Fullan, M. (2014). *Leading in a culture of change personal action guide and workbook*. John Wiley & Sons.

Georgescu, R. (2016) Analysis of socio-intercultural communication in organizations. *Scientific Bulletin – Economic Sciences, 15*(2).

Giles, S. (2016). The Most Important Leadership Competencies, According to Leaders Around the World. Harvard Business Review. Retrieved fromhttps://hbr.org/2016/03/the-most-important-leadership-competencies-according-to-leaders-around-the-world

Göler, D. (2016). Elusive Migration Systems. Lessons from Europe's New Migratory Map. *Bulletin of the Serbian Geographical Society, 96*(2), 42–49. doi:10.2298/GSGD1602038G

Graen, G. B., Hui, C., & Gu, Q. L. (2004). A new approach to socio-intercultural cooperation. *LMX Leadership*, 225–246. https://www.researchgate.net/profile/George_Graen2/publication/292729391_A_NEW_APPROACH_TO_SOCIOINTERCULTURAL_COOPERATION/links/56b0dde408ae9c1968b97809.pdf

Gyas, R. M. (2018). Unmasking the Practices of Nurses and Socio-intercultural Health in Sub-Saharan Africa: A Useful Way to Improve Health Care? *Journal of Evidence-based Integrative Medicine, 23*, 1–5.

Hacken, G. (1985). *Synergetics: Hierarchy of instabilities in self-organizing systems and devices*. Moscow: Mir.

Hall, E. T. (1997). *Beyond Culture*. Random House Inc.

Hambrick, D. C., Davison, S. C., Snell, S. A., & Snow, C. C. (1998). When groups consist of multiple nationalities: Towards a new understanding of the implications. *Organization Studies, 19*(2), 181–205. doi:10.1177/017084069801900202

Hinds, P., Liu, L., & Lyon, J. (2011). Putting the global in global work: A socio-intercultural lens on the practice of cross-national collaboration. *The Academy of Management Annals, 5*(1), 135–188. doi:10.5465/19416520.2011.586108

Hofstede, G. (2001). *Culture's Consequences: Comparing Values, Behaviors, Institutions, and Organizations across Nations* (2nd ed.). SAGE Publications.

Hofstede, G., Hofstede, G. J., & Minkov, M. (2010). *Cultures and organizations: Software of the mind. Socio-intercultural cooperation and its importance for survival* (3rd ed.). McGraw-Hill.

Horpynych, O., & Ibrahimova, Z. (2020). Socio-intercultural model of the development of modern cities: A conceptual analysis. *Scientific and Theoretical Almanac Grani, 23*(4), 13–19. doi:10.15421/172036_

House, R. J., Hanges, P. J., Dorfmanand, P. W., & Gupta, V. (Eds.). (2004). *Culture, Leadership, and Organizations. The GLOBE Study of 62 Societies.* SAGE Publications, Inc.

Hrvatić, N. (2007). Interkulturalna pedagogija – nove paradigme. *Pedagogijska istraživanja, 4*(2), 241-252.

Humphreys, M., & Bates, R. (2005). Political institutions and economic policies: Lessons from Africa. *British Journal of Political Science, 35*(3), 403–428. doi:10.1017/S0007123405000232

Keyton, J. D., Ford, J., & Smith, F. L. (2012). Communication, collaboration and identification as facilitators and constraints of multiteams systems. *Multiteam Systems: An Organization Form for Dynamic and Complex Environments, 21,* 173–190.

King, P. M., & Baxter Magolda, M. B. (2005). A Developmental Model of Intercultural Maturity. *Journal of College Student Development, 2005*(46), 571–592. doi:10.1353/csd.2005.0060

Koehn, P. H. (2007). Peaceful and sustainable development? Middle-management entrepreneurship and transnational competence in China. *East Asia (Piscataway, N.J.), 24*(3), 251–263. https://doi.org/10.1007/s12140-007-9017-9

Koskinen, Y. (Ed.). (2013). *Corporate social responsibility and organization risk. Theory and empirical evidence.* Retrieved from http://www.ecgi.global/sites/default/files/working_papers/documents/SSRN-id1977053.pdf

Köster, K. (2010). *International Project Management.* SAGE Publications Ltd.

Kukovec, D., Mulej, M., & Šarotar Žižek, S. (2018). Professional Languages Alone Do Not Suffice for Successful and Socially Responsible Internal Communication between Different Cultures. *Naše gospodarstvo/Our Economy, 64*(3), 47-55. DOI: doi:10.2478/ngoe-2018-0017

Lee, J., & Negrelli, K. (2018). Cultural Identification, Acculturation, and Academic Experience Abroad: A Case of a Joint Faculty-Led Short-Term Study Abroad Program. *Journal of International Students, 8*(2), 1152–1072. https://doi.org/10.32674/jis.v8i2.138

Lima Magalhães, M. (2011). *Cleber Cristiano Prodanov Jesuítas, culturas nativas y colonos: relaciones socio-interculturales en América Latina Diálogos.* Academic Press.

Lukač-Zoranić, A. Ivanović R. A. (2014), *Interkulturalno obrazovanje: Nužnost današnjice Interkulturalno obrazovanje: Nužnost današnjice /Intercultura educationa: necessity o nowadays, Zbornik radova II Međunarodne konferencije* "Bosna i hercegovina i euroatlantske integracije - Trenutni izazovi i perspektive", god. 2, br. 2, tom II, UDK 37-01, Pravni fakultet Biha ći Centar za društvena istraživanja Internacionalnog Burč Univerziteta, Bihać, 2014, str. 1081-1999.

Marcus, G., & Fischer, M. M. J. (1999). *Anthropology and Cultural Critique: An Experimental Moment in the Human Sciences* (2nd ed.). University of Chicago Press.

Marković, Lj., & Prnjat, Z. (2011). Incorporating Socio-intercultural Communicative Competence in ESP Courses: Design of Materials and Activities for the Students of Economics, Finance and Trade. In B. Đorić-Francuski (Ed.), *Image_Identiy_Reality* (pp. 83–96). Cambridge Scholars Publishing.

Mayer, C.-H. (2011). *The meaning of sense of coherence in transcultural management*. Waxmann.

Mayer, C.-H., & Boness, C. M. (2011). Culture and conflict in urban Tanzania: Professionals' voices in educational organizations. *African Journal on Conflict Resolution, 11*(2), 59–83. https://doi.org/10.4314/ajcr.v11i2.69833

Mayer, C.-H., & Louw, L. (2012). Managing cross-cultural conflicts in organizations. *International Journals of Cross-Cultural Management, 12*(1), 3–8. doi:10.1177/1470595811413104

Meyer, S. D., & Hathaway, W. (1993). Competition and cooperation in social movement coalitions. Lobbying for peace in the 1980s. *Berkeley Journal of Sociology, 38*, 157–183.

Milutinović, J., & Zuković, S. (2007). Obrazovanje i kulturni pluralizam. *Pedagogija, 62*(1), 23–33.

Muha, A. V. (2003). Sodobni položaj nacionalnih jezikov v luči jezikovne politike [Modern position of national languages regarding to the language policy]. Ljubljana: Filozofska fakulteta

Myers, M. D., & Tan, F. B. (2003). *Beyond Models of National Culture in Information Systems Research*. IGI Global.

Nonaka, I., & Takeuchi, H. (1995). *The knowledge-creating company*. Oxford University Press.

Nyambegera, S. M., Kamoche, K., & Siebers, L. Q. (2016). Integrating Chinese and African culture into human resource management practice to enhance employee job satisfaction. *Journal of Language. Technology and Entrepreneurship in Africa, 7*(2), 118–139.

Oljača, M. (2006). Stereotipi i predrasude u vaspitno-obrazovnom procesu. In *Modeli stručnog usavršavanja nastavnika za interkulturalno vaspitanje i obrazovanje*. Filozofski fakultet.

Pedota, L. (2011). *Indigenous intercultural universities in Latin America: Interpreting interculturalism in Mexico and Bolivia* [Thesis]. Loyola University. http://ecommons.luc.edu/luc_theses/516

Perotti, A. (1995). *Interkulturalni odgoj i obrazovanje*. Educa.

Petrović i sar. (2010). Kako budući učitelji vide položaj Roma u sistemu obrazovanja? In *Socijalna pedagogija u nastajanju –traženje odgovora na probleme društveno –isključenih grupa*. Jagodina: Pedagoški fakultet.

Socio-Intercultural Organizational Development

Piechota, G. (2014). The Role of social media in Creating Socio-intercultural Dialogue and Overcoming Prejudice –a Comparative Analysis of Pilot Survey Results. *KOME – An International Journal of Pure Communication Inquiry, 2*(2), 37-63.

Prnjat, Z. (2015). Welcome to Serbia: Using Blogs in an English for Tourism Course. *Proceedings of the 2nd International Conference on Teaching English for Specific Purposes and New Language Learning Technologies,* 478-484.

Rosinski, P. (2011). Global coaching for organizational development. *The International Journal of Coaching in Organizations, 8*(2), 49–66.

Rozman, R. (2007). Pomeni in zahtevnost analiziranja za boljše odločanje [Meaning and complexity of analysis for better decision making]. In Zbornik referatov 13. Strokovnega posvetovanja o sodobnih vidikih analize poslovanja in organizacije [Collection of 13th edition of professional papers on professional consultations on modern aspects of business analysis and organization] (pp. 9-23). Portorož: Zveza ekonomistov Slovenije.

Rozman, R. (2008). Spreminjanje ulture v združbah [Changing culture in organizations]. In 9. znanstveno posvetovanje o organizaciji [9th Scientific consultation on the organization] (pp. 57-59). Ljubljana: Fakulteta za organizacijske vede.

Rozman, R. (2010). Razmerja med organizacijskimi procesi upravljanja in ravnateljevanja, koordinacije in odločanja [Relationships between organizational processes of management and governance, coordination, and decision-making]. In 11. znanstveno posvetovanje o organizaciji: Koordinacijski in komunikacijski vidiki organizacije združb [11th Scientific organizational consultation: Coordination and communication aspects of the organization entities] (pp. 15-21). Ljubljana: Fakulteta za organizacijske vede UM.

Sadokhin, A. P. (2014). *The Introduction in intercultural communication theory: study guide.* KNORUS.

Schein, E. H. (1990). Organizational culture. *American Psychologist.*

Schein, E. H. (2010). *Organizational culture and leadership.* John Wiley & Sons.

Schroder, B. (2006). Native science, intercultural education, and place-conscious education: An Ecuadorian example. *Educational Studies, 32*(3), 307–317. https://dx.doi.org/10.1080/03055690600845438

Soter, M. (2016). Theoretical Modelling of Socio-intercultural Communication Process. *Journal of Advocacy, Research and Education, 6*(2).

Sweeney, P. D., & McFarlin, D. B. (2002). *Organizational behavior, solutions for management.* McGraw-Hill.

Thill, J. V., & Bovee, C. L. (2002). *Essentials of business communication.* South End Press.

Trompenaars, F., & Asser, M. N. (2010). *The global M and A Tango: Cross-cultural dimensions of mergers and acquisitions.* McGraw-Hill.

Trompenaars, F., & Hampden-Turner, C. (2012). Riding the Waves of Culture: Understanding Cultural Diversity in Business (3rd ed.). Nicholas Brealey Publishing.

Trompenaars, F., & Woolliams, P. (2003). *Business Across Cultures.* Capstone Publishing Ltd.

van der Nest, D. (2004). *The impact of black economic empowerment on the management of small companies in South Africa.* Retrieved August 16, 2017, from https://ujdigispace.uj.ac.za/bitstream/handle/10210/319/ImpactofBEEontheMngofSMEinSouthAfrica.pdf?sequence=1

van Dijk, J. (2010). *Social Aspects of the New Media* [Społeczne aspekty nowych mediów]. Wydawnictwo Naukowe PWN.

Vercic, A. T., Verčič, D., & Sriramesh, S. (2012). Internal communication: Definition, parameters, and the future. *Public Relations Review*, *38*(2), 223–230. doi:10.1016/j.pubrev.2011.12.019

Vetráková, M., Ďurian, J., Seková, M., & Kaščáková, A. (2016). Employee Retention and Development in Pulp and Paper Companies. *BioResources*, *11*(4), 9231–9243.

Visser, W. (2005). Corporate citizenship in South Africa: A review of progress since democracy. *Journal of Corporate Citizenship*, *18*, 18–20.

https://doi.org/10.9774/GLEAF.4700.2005.su.00004

Vrcelj, S. (2005). *U potrazi za identitetom –iz perspektive komparativne pedagogije.* Rijeka: Graftrade/Hrvatsko futurološko društvo.

Wright, M. (1999). Influences on learner attitudes towards foreign language and culture. *Educational Research*, *41*(2), 197–208. https://doi.org/10.1080/0013188990410207

KEY TERMS AND DEFINITIONS

Collaboration: Action or effect of collaborating. Work done jointly with other people.

Interculturality: It refers to the relations of egalitarian exchange and communication between cultural groups that differ according to criteria such as ethnicity, religion, language, or nationality, among others.

Knowledge Management: Knowledge management is a process that follows a systematic, logical, and organized order to produce, transmit and apply knowledge.

Organization: An organization is an association of people who relate to each other and use resources of various kinds to achieve certain objectives or goals.

Organizational Development: Organizational development is the progress experienced by organizations through processes that improve their internal management.

Socio-Intercultural: It refers to the relations of egalitarian exchange and communication between cultural groups that differ according to criteria such as ethnicity, religion, language, or nationality, among others.

Compilation of References

Abah, J. (2019). Theoretical and Conceptual Framework for Digital Inclusion among Mathematics Education Students in Nigeria: chapter six. In M. J. Adejoh, M. J., Obinne, A. D. E., & Wombo, A. B. (Eds.), Global Perspectives on Educational Issues. Makurdi. College of Agricultural and Science Education, Federal University of Agriculture.

Abbott, K. W., Genschel, P., Snidal, D., & Zangl, B. (2010) *IOs as Orchestrators*. Paper presented at the 7th Pan-European Conference on International Relations, Stockholm, Sweden.

Abdallah-Pretceille, M. (2006). Socio-interculturalism as a paradigm for thinking about diversity. *Socio-intercultural Education*, *17*(5), 475–483. doi:10.1080/14675980601065764

Abdimomynova, A., Duzelbayeva, G., Berikbolova, U., Kim, V., & Baimakhanova, A. (2021). Entrepreneurship Education Prospects in The Public-Private Partnership System. *Montenegrin Journal of Economics*, *17*(2), 83–92. doi:10.14254/1800-5845/2021.17-2.7

Abele, E., & Reinhart, G. (2011). *Future of production. Phil Transl.* HANSER.

Åberg, J. H. S. (2016). A Struggle for Leadership Recognition: The AIIB, Reactive Chinese Assertiveness, and Regional Order+. *Contemporary Chinese Political Economy and Strategic Relations*, *2*(3), 1125–1171.

Abubakar, I. R. (2017). Access to sanitation facilities among Nigerian households: Determinants and sustainability implications. *Sustainability*, *9*(4), 547. doi:10.3390u9040547

Acemoglu, D., Johnson, S., & Robinson, J. A. (2000). *The Colonial Origins of Comparative Development: An Empirical investigation*. National Bureau of Economic Research Working Paper Series, No. 7771.

Acharya, A. (2004). How ideas spread: Whose norms matter? Norm localization and institutional change in Asian regionalism. *International Organization*, *58*(2), 239–275. doi:10.1017/S0020818304582024

Adam, I. O., & Alhassan, M. D. (2020). Bridging the global digital divide through digital inclusion: the role of ICT access and ICT use. *Transforming Government: People, Process and Policy.* . doi:10.1108/TG-06-2020-0114

Adam, R. G. (2020). *Brexit. Causes and Consequences*. Springer. doi:10.1007/978-3-030-22225-3

Adams, C. A., Potter, B., Singh, P. J., & York, J. (2016). Exploring the implications of integrated reporting for social investment (disclosures). *The British Accounting Review*, *48*(3), 283–296. doi:10.1016/j.bar.2016.05.002

Addison, T., Niño-Zarazúa, M., & Tarp, F. (2015). Aid, social policy and development. *Journal of International Development*, *27*(8), 1351–1365. doi:10.1002/jid.3187

Adepoju, O. A., Gberevbie, D. E., & Ibhawoh, B. (2021). Culture and women participation in peacebuilding in Africa: Perspectiva of national culture and social roles theories. *Academy of Strategic Management Journal*, *20*(3), 1–8.

Adhariani, D., & Sciulli, N. (2020). The future of integrated reporting in an emerging market: An analysis of the disclosure conformity level. *Asian Review of Accounting*, *28*(4), 619–634. doi:10.1108/ARA-02-2019-0045

African Development Bank Group. (2018). *Zimbabwe - Governance and Institutional Strengthening Project*. Retrieved September 15, 2021, from https://projectsportal.afdb.org/dataportal/VProject/show/P-ZW-KF0-005

Agbedahin, A. V. (2019). Sustainable development, Education for Sustainable Development, and the 2030 Agenda for Sustainable Development: Emergence, efficacy,eminence, and future. *Sustainable Development*, (1), 12.

Aguerrondo, I. (2003). Decentralization May Not Be Enough. In *Organization of Ministries of Education* (pp. 65–76). UNESCO.

Ahmad, S., & Omar, R. (2016). Basic corporate governance models: A systematic review. *International Journal of Law and Management*, *58*(1), 73–107. doi:10.1108/IJLMA-10-2014-0057

Akyüz, Y. (2002). *Towards Reform of the International Financial Architecture: Which Way Forward?* Reforming the Global Financial Architecture, Issues and Proposals.

Alefirenko, N.F. (2010). *Linguoculturology: Values and Meaningful Spaces of Language*. Moscow: Flinta.

Alemu, A. M., & Lee, J. S. (2015). Foreign aid on economic growth in Africa: A comparison of low and middle-income countries. *Suid-Afrikaanse Tydskrif vir Ekonomiese en Bestuurswetenskappe*, *18*(4), 449–462. doi:10.4102ajems.v18i4.737

Alexander, E. R. (1995). *How Organizations Act Together: Interorganizational Coordination in Theory and Practice*. Gordon & Breach.

Alexander, G. M., John, K., Hammond, T., & Lahey, J. (2021). Living Up to a Name: Gender Role Behavior Varies with Forename Gender Typicality. *Frontiers in Psychology*, *11*, 4038. doi:10.3389/fpsyg.2020.604848 PMID:33551916

Algermissen, U., Behrensen, B., & Graumann, O. (2015). Inclusion in Germany: a traditional education system in difficult conversion. In Inclusive Education in Different East and West European Countries. Progetto grafico di Eurilink.

Almendingen, K., Morseth, M. S., Gjølstad, E., Brevik, A., & Tørris, C. (2021). Student's experiences with online teaching following COVID-19 lockdown: A mixed methods explorative study. *PLoS One*, *16*(8), e0250378. Advance online publication. doi:10.1371/journal.pone.0250378 PMID:34464386

Alsoud, A. R., & Harasis, A. A. (2021). The impact of COVID-19 pandemic on student's e-Learning experience in Jordan. *Journal of Theoretical and Applied Electronic Commerce Research*, *16*(5), 1404–1414. doi:10.3390/jtaer16050079

Amadi, L., & Agena, J. E. (2015). Globalization, Culture mutation and new identity: Implication for the Igbo cultural heritage. *African Journal of History and Culture*, *1*(4).

American Psychological Association. (2006). *Answers to Your Questions about Transgender People, Gender identity, and Gender expression*. Retrieved from https://www.apa.org/topics/lgbtq/transgender.pdf

Anakwe, B. (2008). Comparison of student performance in paper-based versus computer-based testing. *Journal of Education for Business*, *84*(1), 13–17. doi:10.3200/JOEB.84.1.13-17

Anane, C. A. (2013). Competency based training: Quality delivery for technical and vocational education and training (TVET) institutions. *Education Research International*, *2*(2), 117–127.

Anđelković, S., & Stanisavljević Petrović, Z. (2014). Nature as an Inspiration and a Context for Learning and Teaching. *Bulletin of the Serbian Geographical Society*, *94*(1), 57–65. doi:10.2298/GSGD1401057A

Compilation of References

Anderson, P. H., Lawton, L., Rexeisen, R. J., & Hubbard, A. C. (2006). Short-term study abroad and intercultural sensitivity: A pilot study. *International Journal of Intercultural Relations*, *30*(4), 457–469. doi:10.1016/j.ijintrel.2005.10.004

Andreadakis, S. (2012). Enlightened Shareholder Value: Is It the New Modus Operandi for Modern Companies? In *Corporate governance* (pp. 415–432). Springer. doi:10.1007/978-3-642-31579-4_18

Andreeva, T., & Kianto, A. (2012). Wissens- und Informations management in kleinen und mittleren Unternehmen. Academic Press.

Andriamananjara, S., & Nash, J. (1997). *Have Trade Policy Reforms led to Greater Openness in Developing Countries?* World Bank Working Paper No. 1730. The World Bank.

Andrushchenko, V., & Nesterenko, G. (2015). Values decourse of diversity education: dialogue of Eastern and Western European countries. In Inclusive Education in Different East and West European countries. Progetto grafico di Eurilink.

Ang, S., & Inkpen, A. C. (2008). Cultural intelligence and offshore outsourcing success: A framework of organization-level socio-intercultural capability. *Decision Sciences*, *2008*(39), 337–358. doi:10.1111/j.1540-5915.2008.00195.x

Ansari, M. A., Kee, D. M. H., & Aafaqi, R. (2000). Fairness of human resource management practices, leader-member exchange and intention to quit. *Journal of International Business and Entrepreneurship*, *8*, 1–19.

Apergis, N., Gozgor, G., & Lau, C. K. M. (2021). Globalization and environmental problems in developing countries. *Environmental Science and Pollution Research International*, *28*(26), 33719–33721. doi:10.100711356-021-14105-z PMID:33945090

Arabena, K. (2005). *Not fit for modern Australian society. Aboriginal and Torres Strait Island people and the new arrangements for the administration of Indigenous Affairs.* Research Discussion Paper No. 16. AIATSIS.

Arandarenko, M. (2011). Labor market in Serbia: trends, institutions, policies. Center for Publishing Activities of the Faculty of Economics.

Arandarenko, M., & Aleksic, D. (2016). Not all jobs are created equal: How not to misread the labour force statistics in Serbia. *Business Economics (Cleveland, Ohio)*, *64*(3–4), 211–224.

Arenius, P., & Minniti, M. (2003). Women in entrepreneurship. The entrepreneurial advantage of nations. *First Annual Global Entrepre-neurship Symposium*, *29*(1), 4-8.

Arias, J. J., Swinton, J., & Anderson, K. (2018). Online vs. face-to-face: A comparison of student outcomes with random assignment. *E-Journal of Business Education & Scholarship of Teaching*, *12*(2), 1–23.

Armstrong, L. (2003). *Financial management and business systems: the backbone of an effectively resourced capacity for governance.* Unpublished paper presented to the Building Effective Indigenous Governance Conference. Available at http://www.nt.gov.au/cdsca/indigenous conference/web/html/papers.html

Armstrong, L. (2007). Finding Australia's soul: rebuilding our Indigenous communities. *The Circle*, *1*, 74–6. Available at https://www.socialventures.com.au/files/pdf/TC%20mag%20Leah%20Armstrong.pdf

Aron, J. (2000). Growth and Institutions, a Review of the Evidence. *The World Bank Research Observer*, *15*(1), 465–490. doi:10.1093/wbro/15.1.99

Arts, K. (2017). Inclusive sustainable development: A human rights perspective. *Current Opinion in Environmental Sustainability*, *24*, 58–62. doi:10.1016/j.cosust.2017.02.001

Ashtekar, A., & Singh, P. (2011). Loop quantum cosmology: A status report. *Classical and Quantum Gravity*, *28*(21), 213001. doi:10.1088/0264-9381/28/21/213001

Asio, J. M. R., Gadia, E., Abarintos, E., Paguio, D., & Balce, M. (2021). Internet Connection and Learning Device Availability of College Students: Basis for Institutionalizing Flexible Learning in the New Normal. *Studies in Humanities and Education*, 2(1), 56–69. doi:10.48185he.v2i1.224

Astafurova, T.N. (1997). *Linguistic aspects of socio-intercultural business communication*. Vol-gograd: Publ. House of Volgograd State University.

Augur, P., & Devinney, T. M. (2007). Do what consumers say matter? The misalignment of preferences with unconstrained ethical intention. *Journal of Business Ethics*, 76(4), 361–383. doi:10.100710551-006-9287-y

Average earnings per employee, February. (2021). *SORS*. https://www.propisi.net/prosecne-zarade-po-zaposlenom-februar-2021/

Avramidis, E., Bayliss, P., & Burden, R. (2000). A Survey into mainstream teachers' attitudes towards the inclusion of children with special educational needs in the ordinary school in one local education authority. *Educational Psychology*, 20(2), 191–211. doi:10.1080/713663717

Aycan, Z. (2001). Human resource management in Turkey-Current issues and future challenges. *International Journal of Manpower*, 22(3), 252–260. doi:10.1108/01437720110398347

Badiuzzaman, M., Rafiquzzaman, M., Rabby, M. I. I., & Rahman, M. M. (2021). The Latent Digital Divide and Its Drivers in E-Learning among Bangladeshi Students during the COVID-19 Pandemic. *Information (Basel)*, 12(287), 287. Advance online publication. doi:10.3390/info12080287

Bagshaw, G. (1977). *Analysis of Local Government in a Multi-Clan Community* (BA Dissertation). Department of Anthropology, The University of Adelaide.

Bagwell, S., & Evans, G. (2012). Public Space Management, report to the socio-intercultural cities programme Council of Europe Publishing, socio-intercultural cities step by step socio-intercultural cities. *Newsletter*. www.coe.int/socio-interculturaLcitiezs

Baldwin, T. T., Kevin Ford, J., & Blume, B. D. (2017). The state of transfer of training research: Moving toward more consumer-centric inquiry. *Human Resource Development Quarterly*, 28(1), 17–28. doi:10.1002/hrdq.21278

Balsalobre-Lorente, D., Driha, O. M., Shahbaz, M., & Sinha, A. (2020). The effects of tourism and globalization over environmental degradation in developed countries. *Environmental Science and Pollution Research International*, 27(7), 7130–7144. doi:10.100711356-019-07372-4 PMID:31879881

Banerjee, A. V., & Duflo, E. (2011). *Poor Economics: A Radical Rethinking of the Way to Fight Global Poverty*. Public Affairs.

Banerjee, A., Merugu, S., Dhillon, I. S., Ghosh, J., & Lafferty, J. (2005). Clustering with Bregman divergences. *Journal of Machine Learning Research*, 6(10).

Barbagila, M., Buttice, V., Giudici, G., Mendy, J., Sarker, T., Sharma, G. D., Thomas, A., & Zutchi, A. (2021). Supporting SMEs in sustainable strategy development post-Covid-19 : Challenges and policy agenda for the G20. *G20 Insight*, 1-12.

Bardhan, P. (2006). Institutions and Development. In D. Clark (Ed.), *The Elgar Companion to Development Studies* (pp. 2–56). Edward Elgar Publishing.

Barnett, M., & Duvall, R. (2005). Power in international politics. *International Organization*, 59(1), 39–75. doi:10.1017/S0020818305050010

Barnett, R. (2017). *The Ecological University a Feasible Utopia*. Routledge. doi:10.4324/9781315194899

Compilation of References

Barney, J. (1991). Firm resources and sustained competitive advantage. *Journal of Management*, *17*(1), 99–120. doi:10.1177/014920639101700108

Baron, C. (2003). La gouvernance: Débats autour d'un concept polysémique. *Droit Social*, (54), 329–351. doi:10.3917/drs.054.0329

Bartley, T. (2007). Institutional Emergence in an Era of Globalization: The Rise of Transnational Private Regulation of Labor and Environmental Conditions. *American Journal of Sociology*, *113*(2), 297–351. doi:10.1086/518871

Basiago, A. D. (1998). Economic, social, and environmental sustainability in development theory and urban planning practice. *The Environmentalist*, *19*(2), 145–161. doi:10.1023/A:1006697118620

Bass, B. M., & Avolio, B. J. (1994). Transformational leadership, organizational culture. *International Journal of Public Administration*, *17*(3-4), 541–554. Advance online publication. doi:10.1080/01900699408524907

Bates, R. H. (2001). *Prosperity and Violence: The Political Economy of Development*. W.W. Norton&Company.

Batsevych, F. (2007). *Glossary of intercultural communication*. Dovira.

Bazbauers, A. R. (2018). *The World Bank and Transferring Development*. International Political Economy Series. doi:10.1007/978-3-319-58160-6

Becker, H. S. (1986). *Writing for social scientists: How to start and finish your thesis, book or article*. University of Chicago Press.

Becker, H. S., & Geer, B. (1957). Participant observation and interviewing: A comparison. *Human Organization*, *16*(3), 28–32. doi:10.17730/humo.16.3.k687822132323013

Bedeković, V. (2007). Interkulturalne komponente interkulturalnog odgoja i obrazovanja pripadnika nacionalnih manjina. In *Pedagogija prema cjeloživotnom obrazovanju i društvu znanja*. Zagreb: Hrvatsko pedagogijsko društvo.

Behrendt, L., McCausland, R., Williams, G., Reilly, A., & McMillan, M. (2007). The promise of regional governance for Aboriginal and Torres Strait Islander communities. *Ngiya: Talk the Law, Governance in Indigenous Communities*, *1*, 126–166.

Beijerse, R. P. (2000). Does knowledge management really matter? Linking knowledge management practices, competitiveness and economic performance. *Journal of Knowledge Management*, *16*(4), 617–636.

Beker, K., Boskovic, D., Vlahovic, E., Ignjatovic, T., & Iles, M. (2020). *Handbook for teachers of civic education in the Gymnasium* [Priručnik za nastavnike gradjanskog vaspitanja u gimnaziji]. OEBS, ZUOV. https://zuov.gov.rs/wp-content/uploads/2020/12/gradjansko-srednja-skola.pdf

Belitski, M., & Desai, S. (2016). Creativity, entrepreneurship and economic development: City-level evidence on creativity spillover of entrepreneurship. *The Journal of Technology Transfer*, *41*(6), 1354–1376. doi:10.100710961-015-9446-3

Belk, R., Devinney, T. M., & Eckhart, G. (2005). Consumer ethics across cultures. *Consumption Markets & Culture*, *8*(3), 275–289. doi:10.1080/10253860500160411

Bellalah, M., & Bouy, C. (2005). On Portfolio Analysis, Market Equilibrium and Corporation Finance with Incomplete Information. *International Journal of Business*, *10*(2), 133.

Bellini, C. G. P. (2018). The ABCs of Effectiveness in the Digital Society. *Communications of the ACM*, *61*(7), 84–91. doi:10.1145/3205945

Ben Ali, M., & Krammer, S. (2016). *The Role of Institutions in Economic Development*. . doi:10.1057/9781137480668_1

Bennett, E. A. (2015). Fair-trade International governance. In L. T. Raynolds & E. A. Bennett (Eds.), *Handbook of Research on Fair-trade*. Edward Elgar Publishing.

Benson, B. W., & Davidson, W. N. (2010). The relation between stakeholder management, firm value, and CEO compensation: A test of enlightened value maximization. *Financial Management, 39*(3), 929–964. doi:10.1111/j.1755-053X.2010.01100.x

Berend, I. T. (2015). Capitalism. International encyclopedia. *Social Behavioral Sciences, 3*, 94–98.

Berglöf, E., Kunov, A., Shvets, J., & Yuaeva, K. (2003). *The New Political Economy of Russia*. The MIT Press. doi:10.7551/mitpress/5007.001.0001

Berliner, D. C. (2000). A personal response to those who bash teacher education. *Journal of Teacher Education, 51*(5), 358–371. doi:10.1177/0022487100051005004

Bernstein, S., & Cashore, B. (2007). Can Non-State Global Governance be Legitimate? *Regulation & Governance, 1*(4), 347–371. doi:10.1111/j.1748-5991.2007.00021.x

Beyer, J., & Hassel, A. (2002). The market for corporate control and financial internationalization of German firms. *Economy and Society, 31*.

Bhagwati, J. (1963). Some Recent Trends in the Pure Theory of International Trade. In R. Harrod & D. Hague (Eds.), *International Trade Theory in a Developing World* (pp. 1–30). Macmillan and Co. Ltd. doi:10.1007/978-1-349-08458-6_1

Bhagwati, J. (1978). *Anatomy and Consequences of Exchange Control Regimes: Liberalisation Attempts and Consequences*. Ballinger Pub. Co.

Bhatt, R. M. (2001). World Englishes. *Annual Review of Anthropology, 30*(1), 527–550. doi:10.1146/annurev.anthro.30.1.527

Bhimani, A., & Soonawalla, K. (2005). From conformance to performance: The corporate responsibilities continuum. *Journal of Accounting and Public Policy, 24*(3), 165–174. doi:10.1016/j.jaccpubpol.2005.03.001

Biermann, F., Kanie, N., & Kim, R.E., (2017). Global governance by goal-setting: the novel approach of the UN Sustainable Development Goals. *Current Opinion on Environment Sustainability, 26-27*, 26-31.

Birchler, K., Limpach, S., & Michaelowa, K. (2016). Aid modalities matter: The impact of different World Bank and IMF programs on democratization in developing countries. *International Studies Quarterly, 60*(3), 427–439. doi:10.1093/isqqw014

Birchler, K., & Michaelowa, K. (2016). Making aid work for education in developing countries: An analysis of aid effectiveness for primary education coverage and quality. *International Journal of Educational Development, 48*, 37–52. doi:10.1016/j.ijedudev.2015.11.008

Birdsall, N., Rodrik, D., & Subramanian, A. (2005). How to Help Poor Countries. *Foreign Affairs, 84*(July/August), 136–152. doi:10.2307/20034426

Blunden, J., & Arndt, D. S. (2012). State of the climate in 2011. *Bulletin of the American Meteorological Society, 93*(7), S1–S282. doi:10.1175/2012BAMSStateoftheClimate.1

Bochańczyk-Kupka, D., & Pęciak, R. (2015). Institutions in the context of sustainable development. *A Multidisciplinary Journal of Global Macro Trends, 4*(5), 29-41.

Boesso, G., Kumar, K., & Michelon, G. (2013). Descriptive, instrumental and strategic approaches to corporate social responsibility: Do they drive the financial performance of companies differently? *Accounting, Auditing & Accountability Journal, 26*(3), 399–422. doi:10.1108/09513571311311874

Compilation of References

Bogicevic, B., Krstic, G., & Mijatovic, B. (2012). Poverty in Serbia and the reform of state aid to the poor. Center for Liberal-Democratic Studies, Belgrade.

Böhm, C. (2013). Cultural Flexibility in ICT Projects: A New Perspective on Managing Diversity in Project Teams. *Glob. J. Flex. Syst. Manag. Springer, 14*(2), 115–122. doi:10.100740171-013-0037-6

Boonstra, A., & de Vries, J. (2015). Information System Conflict: Causes and Types, International. *Journal of Information Systems and Project Management, 3*(4), 5–20. doi:10.12821/ijispm030401

Börzel, T., & Risse, T. (2010). Governance without a state: can it work? *Regulation and Governance, 4*(2), 113–34.

Botescuthe, I. (2010, January 01). training of international managers – success factor. *International Business Management & Marketing, 8*(1), 115–120.

Botke, J., Jansen, P. G., Khapova, S., & Tims, M. (2017). Transfer of soft skills training: A systematic literature review. In Academy of Management Proceedings. Academy of Management. doi:10.5465/AMBPP.2017.11483abstract

Bouncken, R. B., Pfannstiel, M. A., Reuschl, A. J., & Haupt, A. (2015). *Diversität managen. Wie Krankenhäuser das Beste aus personeller Vielfalt machen* (1st ed.). Kohlhammer.

Bozbura, F. T. (2007). Knowledge management in small and medium-sized companies: Knowledge management for entrepreneurs. *Journal of Knowledge Management, 4*(2), 162–179.

Bray, M., & Prescott, L. (2020). The International Integrated Reporting Council's agenda of moving integrated reporting towards global adoption by 2025. In *The Routledge Handbook of Integrated Reporting* (pp. 17–36). Routledge. doi:10.4324/9780429279621-2

Bray, M., & Varghese, N. V. (Eds.). (2011). *Directions in educational planning: International experiences and perspectives*. UNESCO Pub.

Breslin, S. (2007). *China and the Global Political Economy, Basingstoke: Palgrave. Brooks, Chris (2008), Introductory Econometrics for Finance* (2nd ed.). Cambridge University Press. doi:10.1057/9780230223943

Bresser, R., & Millonig, K. (2003). Institutional capital: Competitive advantage considering the new institutionalism in organisational theory. *Schmalenbach Business Review, 55*(3), 220–241. doi:10.1007/BF03396675

Bretzel, F., & Calderisi, M. (2006). Metal contamination in urban soils of coastal Tuscany (Italy). *Environmental Monitoring and Assessment, 118*(1), 319–335. doi:10.100710661-006-1495-5 PMID:16897548

Brinkerhoff, D. W., & Brinkerhoff, J. M. (2015). Public sector management reform in developing countries: Perspectives beyond NPM orthodoxy. *Public Administration and Development, 35*(4), 222–237. doi:10.1002/pad.1739

Brito, R. M., Rodriguez, C., & Aparicio, J. L. (2018). Sustainability in Teaching: An Evaluation of University Teachers and Students. *Sustainability, 10*(2), 439. doi:10.3390u10020439

Broadband Commission. (2020). *Closing the digital divide: Supporting vulnerable countries*. https://www.broadband-commission.org/insight/closing-the-digital-divide-supporting-vulnerable-countries/

Broad, R. (2007). 'Knowledge management': A case study of the World Bank's research department. *Development in Practice, 17*(4-5), 700–708. doi:10.1080/09614520701470094

Broadstock, D. C., Chan, K., Cheng, L. T., & Wang, X. (2020). *The role of ESG performance during times of financial crisis: Evidence from Covid-19 in China*. Academic Press.

343

Brod, G., & Breitwieser, J. (2019). Lighting the wick in the candle of learning: Generating a prediction stimulates curiosity. *NPJ Science of Learning*, *4*(1), 1–7. doi:10.103841539-019-0056-y PMID:31646002

Brookings, C., Goldmeier, D., & Sadeghi-Nejad, H. (2013). Sexually transmitted infections and sexual function in relation to male fertility. *Korean Journal of Urology*, *54*(3), 149–156. doi:10.4111/kju.2013.54.3.149 PMID:23526114

Broome, A. (2010). The Joint Vienna Institute. *New Political Economy*, *15*(4), 609–624. doi:10.1080/13563460903290953

Browning, M. H., & Rigolon, A. (2019). School green space and its impact on academic performance: A systematic literature review. *International Journal of Environmental Research and Public Health*, *16*(3), 429. doi:10.3390/ijerph16030429 PMID:30717301

Brunelli, S., & Di Carlo, E. (2020). Accountability, ethics and sustainability of organizations. *Accounting, Finance, Sustainability, Governance and Fraud, Theory and Application*, *4*, 82–123.

Brus, D. J., Kempen, B., & Heuvelink, G. B. M. (2011). Sampling for validation of digital soil maps. *European Journal of Soil Science*, *62*(3), 394–407. doi:10.1111/j.1365-2389.2011.01364.x

Bukola, R. A. (2011). Poverty and the realization of the millennium development goals in Nigeria: Disability rights the missing link. *East African Journal of Peace and Human Rights*, *17*(2), 532–550.

Burke, L. A. (2001). Training transfer: ensuring training gets used on the job. In L. A. Burke (Ed.), *High Impact Training Solutions* (pp. 89–116). Quorum Books.

Bustillo, R., & Andoni, M. (2018). China, the EU and multilateralism: The Asian Infrastructure Investment Bank. *Revista Brasileira de Política Internacional*, *61*(1), e008. doi:10.1590/0034-7329201800108

Cabezudo, A., Cicala, F., Bivar Black, M. L., & Carvalho da Silva, M. (2019). *Global Education Guidelines: concepts and methodologies on global education for educators and policy makers*. North-South Centre of the Council of Europe.

Cacioppo, J. T., & Hawkley, L. C. (2009). Perceived social isolation and cognition. *Trends in Cognitive Sciences*, *13*(10), 447–454. doi:10.1016/j.tics.2009.06.005 PMID:19726219

Cahyo, S. D., Al Fariz, A. B., & Lestari, C. A. (2020). Does internet usage frequency give impact to student's academic performance? *Indonesian Journal of Educational Assessment*, *3*(1), 16–23. doi:10.26499/ijea.v3i1.57

Cai, K. G. (2018). The one belt one road and the Asian infrastructure investment bank: Beijing's new strategy of geo-economics and geopolitics. *Journal of Contemporary China*, *27*(114), 831–847. doi:10.1080/10670564.2018.1488101

Çakiroğlu, Ü., & Gökoğlu, S. (2019). Development of fire safety behavioral skills via virtual reality. *Computers & Education*, *133*, 56–68. doi:10.1016/j.compedu.2019.01.014

Camilleri, M. A. (2019). Theoretical insights on integrated reporting: Valuing the financial, social and sustainability disclosures. Integrated Reporting, 61-76.

Camilleri, C. (1992). *Le condizioni di base dell'socio-interculturale. Verso una societa socio-interculturale*. Celim.

Capitalism, I. (n.d.). *Oxymoron Or The Perfect Balance*. Retrieved from https://www.forbes.com/sites/nigelwilson/2018/07/29

Capra, F. (1997). *The web of life*. Doubleday-Anchor Book.

Carnevale, J. B., & Hatak, I. (2020). Employee adjustment and well-being in the era of COVID-19: Implications for human resource management. *Journal of Business Research*, *116*, 183–187. doi:10.1016/j.jbusres.2020.05.037 PMID:32501303

Compilation of References

Carrigan, M., & Attala, A. (2001). The myth of the ethical consumer. Do ethics matter in purchase behavior. *Journal of Consumer Marketing*, *18*(7), 560–577. doi:10.1108/07363760110410263

Carspecken, P. (1996). *Critical ethnography in educational research: A theoretical and practical guide*. Routledge.

Cashore, B., Auld, G., Bernstein, S., & McDermott, C. (2007). Can non-state governance "ratchet up" global environmental standards? Lessons from the forest sector. *Review of European Community, and International Environmental Law, 16*(2), 158–72.

Castells, M. (2000). Network society. In The globaltransformations reader. Polity Press.

Cateora, P. R., & Graham, J. L. (2002). *International Marketing (11th ed.)*. McGraw-Hill Publishing.

Cavezzali, E., Hussain, N., & Rigoni, U. (2016). The integrated reporting and the conference calls content. In *Integrated Reporting* (pp. 231–252). Palgrave Macmillan. doi:10.1057/978-1-137-55149-8_12

Çelik, I. E., Dinçer, H., Hacıoğlu, Ü., & Dinçer, H. (2014). The Role of World Bank in Global Development. In H. Dinçer & Ü. Hacioğlu (Eds.), *Global Strategies in Banking and Finance* (pp. 56–64). IGI Global. doi:10.4018/978-1-4666-4635-3.ch004

Central Bank of Russia. (2004). *Bulletin of Banking Statistics* (No. 3). CJSC "AEI "Prime, TASS". http://www.cbr.ru/collection/collection/file/36863/bbs0403r.pdf

Ceric, H., & Alic, A. (2005). *Basic starting points of inclusive education*. Hijatus.

Cerin, P. (2006). Bringing economic opportunity into line with environmental influence: A discussion on the Coase theorem and the Porter and van der Linde hypothesis. *Ecological Economics*, *56*(2), 209–225. doi:10.1016/j.ecolecon.2005.01.016

Champagne, E., & Granja, A. D. (2021). *How the COVID-19 pandemic may have changed university teaching and testing for good*. Retrieved July 18, 2021 from https://theconversation.com/how-the-covid-19-pandemic-may-have-changed-university-teaching-and-testing-for-good-158342

Chang, H.-J. (2008). Under-explored Treasure Troves of Development Lessons- Lessons from the Histories of Small Rich European Countries (SRECs). In Doing Good or Doing Better – Development Policies in a Globalising World. Amsterdam University Press.

Chang, R. D., Zuo, J., Zhao, Z. Y., Zillante, G., Gan, X. L., & Soebarto, V. (2017). Evolving theories of sustainability and firms: History, future directions and implications for renewable energy research. *Renewable & Sustainable Energy Reviews*, *72*, 48–56. doi:10.1016/j.rser.2017.01.029

Charema, J. (2010). Inclusive Education in Developing Countries in the Sub Saharan Africa: From Theory to Practice. *International Journal of Special Education*, *25*(1), 87–93.

Charmaz, K. (2014). *Constructing grounded theory*. Sage Publications.

Chatzidakis, A., Hilbert, S., & Smith, A. P. (2007). Why people don't take their Fair Trade to the supermarket: The role of neutralization. *Journal of Business Ethics*, *74*(1), 7489–100. doi:10.100710551-006-9222-2

Chieffo, L., & Griffiths, L. (2004). Large scale assessment of student attitudes after a short-term study abroad program. *Frontiers: The Interdisciplinary Journal of Study Abroad*, *18*(1), 101–118. doi:10.36366/frontiers.v10i1.140

Childers, E., & Urquhart, B. (1994). *Renewing the United Nations System*. United Nations.

Chin, G. T. (2019). The Asian Infrastructure Investment Bank – New Multilateralism: Early Development, Innovation, and Future Agendas. *Global Policy*, *10*(4), 569–581. doi:10.1111/1758-5899.12767

Cho, C. H., & Patten, D. M. (2007). The role of environmental disclosures as tools of legitimacy: A research note. *Accounting, Organizations and Society, 32*(7), 639–647. doi:10.1016/j.aos.2006.09.009

Christensen, L. B., Johnson, B., Turner, L. A., & Christensen, L. B. (2011). Research methods, design, and analysis.

Christensen, D. L., Braun, K. V. N., Baio, J., Bilder, D., Charles, J., Constantino, J. N., Daniels, J., Durkin, M. S., Fitzgerald, R. T., Kurzius-Spencer, M., Lee, L.-C., Pettygrove, S., Robinson, C., Schulz, E., Wells, C., Wingate, M. S., Zahorodny, W., & Yeargin-Allsopp, M. (2018). Prevalence and characteristics of autism spectrum disorder among children aged 8 years—Autism and developmental disabilities monitoring network, 11 sites, United States, 2012. *MMWR. Surveillance Summaries, 65*(13), 1–23. doi:10.15585/mmwr.ss6513a1 PMID:30439868

Christie, M. (2007). Knowledge management and natural resource management. In M. K. Luckert, B. Campbell, & J. T. Gorman (Eds.), *Investing in indigenous natural resource management* (pp. 86–90). Charles Darwin University Press.

Chwieroth, J. M. (2008). Normative change from within: The International Monetary Fund's approach to capital account liberalization. *International Studies Quarterly, 52*(1), 129–158. doi:10.1111/j.1468-2478.2007.00494.x

Clifford, J. (1997). *Routes: Travel and Translation in the Twentieth Century*. Harvard University Press.

Coase, R. H. (1992). The Economic Structure of Production. *The American Economic Review, 82*(September), 713–719.

Coelho, J. S., Santos, N. D., Napoleão, T. H., Gomes, F. S., Ferreira, R. S., Zingali, R. B., Coelho, L. C. B. B., Leite, S. P., Navarro, D. M. A. F., & Paiva, P. M. (2009). Effect of Moringa oleifera lectin on development and mortality of Aedes aegypti larvae. *Chemosphere, 77*(7), 934–938. doi:10.1016/j.chemosphere.2009.08.022 PMID:19747711

Cohen-Filipic, J., & Flores, L. Y. (2014). Best practices in providing effective supervision to students with values conflicts. *Psychology of Sexual Orientation and Gender Diversity, 1*(4), 302–309. doi:10.1037gd0000073

Coll, A. C. (2004). *The socio-intercultural challenge*. Pipal Tree.

Collier, J., & Esteban, R. (2007). Corporate social responsibility and employee commitment. *Business Ethics (Oxford, England), 16*(1), 19–33. doi:10.1111/j.1467-8608.2006.00466.x

Collins, E., Kearins, K., & Roper, J. (2005). The risks in relying on stakeholder engagement for the achievement of sustainability. *Electronic Journal of Radical Organisation Theory, 9*(1), 81.

Columbia Public Health. (2021). *Population health methods: geographically weighted regression*. Retrieved July 10, 2021 from https://www.publichealth.columbia.edu/research/population-health-methods/geographically-weighted-regression

Conditions for policy evaluation in Public Policies, debate on the role of institutionalist. (2020). *Pública, 54*(3). doi:10.1590/0034-761220190258x

Connell, R. W. (2002). *Gender*. Polity Press.

Constantin Şcheau, M., & Zaharie Pop, S. (2020). Andreea Valentina Şoimu Migration, economic causes, and decisions. *Theoretical and Applied Economics, 27*(2), 33-50.

Consumption, income and living conditions. (2017). *SORS*. https://www.stat.gov.rs/sr-Latn/oblasti/potrosnja-prihodi-i-uslovi-zivota

Cornell, S., & Begay, M. (2004). *What is cultural match and why is it so important? Lessons from 14 years of the Harvard Project*. Paper presented at the Building Effective Governance Conference.

Cornell, S., & Kalt, J. P. (2000). Where's the glue? Institutional and cultural foundations of American Indian economic development. *Journal of Socio-Economics, 29*(5), 443–470. doi:10.1016/S1053-5357(00)00080-9

Compilation of References

Cornwall, A., & Rivas, A. M. (2015). From 'gender equality and 'women's empowerment' to global justice: Reclaiming a transformative agenda for gender and development. *Third World Quarterly*, *36*(2), 396–415. doi:10.1080/01436597.2015.1013341

Costa, K., & Chin, G. T. (2019). The AIIB and Sustainable Infrastructure: A Hybrid Layered Approach. *Global Policy*, *10*(4), 593–603. doi:10.1111/1758-5899.12771

Costigan, C. L., & Cox, M. J. (2001). Fathers' participation in family research:Is there a self- selection bias? *Journal of Family Psychology*, *15*(4), 706–720. doi:10.1037/0893-3200.15.4.706 PMID:11770476

Council of Europe. (2020). *Making the right to education a reality in times of COVID-19: A Roadmap for Action on the Council of Europe education response to COVID-19.* https://rm.coe.int/making-the-right-to-education-a-reality-in-times-of-covid-19-a-roadmap/16809fee7b

Council of the EU. (2021). *Council Conclusions on equity and inclusion in education and training in order to promote educational success for all: meeting,* 7985/21. https://www.consilium.europa.eu/media/49660/st08693-en21-002.pdf

Council of the European Union. (2018). Annex to the council recommendation of 22 May 2018 on key competences for lifelong learning: Key competences for lifelong learning, a European reference framework. *Official Journal of the European Union*, *189*, 7–13.

Cowman, M. C., & McCarthy, A. M. (2016). The impact of demographic and situational factors on training transfer in a health care setting. *Irish Journal of Management*, *35*(2), 129–142. doi:10.1515/ijm-2016-0009

Crane, A., & Matten, D. (2004). *Business ethics: A European perspective*. Oxford UniversityPress.

Creyer, E. H., & Ross, W. T. (1997). The Impact of firm behavior on purchase intention: Do consumers really care about business ethics? *Journal of Consumer Marketing*, *14*(6), 421–432. doi:10.1108/07363769710185999

Crockett, A. (2009). Reforming the global financial architecture. In *Asia Economic Policy Conference; Asia and the Global Financial Crisis, Santa Barbara, California* (pp. 191-201). Academic Press.

Crosling, G., Nair, M., & Vaithilingam, S. (2015). A creative learning ecosystem, quality of education and innovative capacity: A perspective from higher education. *Studies in Higher Education*, *40*(7), 1147–1163. doi:10.1080/0307507 9.2014.881342

Cross, S. (2008). *The Scale Politics of Reconciliation* (PhD. Dissertation). Department of Human Geography, Macquarie University.

Crystal, D. (1997). The language that took over the world. *The Guardian*, *22*(21).

Cullinan, J., Flannery, D., Harold, J., Lyons, S., & Palcic, D. (2021). The disconnected: COVID-19 and disparities in access to quality broadband for higher education students. *International Journal of Educational Technology in Higher Education*, 1-21. doi:10.1186/s41239-021-00262-1

da Costa Tavares, M. D. C., & Dias, A. P. (2018). Theoretical Perspectives on Sustainability Reporting: A Literature Review. *Accounting from a Cross-Cultural Perspective*. https://scholar.google.com

Danish Agency for Digitization. (2016). *A Stronger and more secure digital Denmark: Digital Strategy 2016-2020.* https://en.digst.dk/policy-and-strategy/digital-strategy/

Darrow, M. (2012). The millennium development goals: Milestones or millstones-human rights priorities for the post-2015 development agenda. *Yale Human Rights and Development Law Journal*, *15*, 55.

Das, M., Rangarajan, K., & Dutta, G. (2020). Corporate sustainability in SMEs: An Asian perspective. *Journal of Asia Business Studies*, *14*(1), 109–138. doi:10.1108/JABS-10-2017-0176

David, A., Terstriep, J., & Barwinska-Malajowicz, A. (2019b). Brexit und seine folgen für die europäische migration: empowerment als mögliche antwort? eine reflexion. In A. David, M. Evans, I. Hamburg, & J. Terstriep (Eds.), *Migration und Arbeit: Herausforderungen, Problemlagen und Gestaltungsinstrumente* (pp. 359–386). Verlag Barbara Budrich. doi:10.2307/j.ctvg5bt77.18

Davidson, J., & Stratford, E. (2000). *Building the knowledge base of the social and institutional dimensions of natural resource management*. Land and Water Resources Research and Development Corporation.

Davies, I., Lee, Z., & Ahonkhai, I. (2012). Do consumers care about ethical- luxury? *Journal of Business Ethics*, *106*(1), 37–51. doi:10.100710551-011-1071-y

Davies, M., Paterson, R., & Wilson, A. (1997). The quest for a conceptual framework for financial reporting. In *UK GAAP* (pp. 39–128). Palgrave Macmillan. doi:10.1007/978-1-349-13819-7_2

Davis, G., & Rhodes, R. A. W. (2000). From hierarchy to contracts and back again: reforming the Australian public service. In Institutions on the Edge? Capacity for Governance. Allen & Unwin.

Davis, G. F. (2010). Is shareholder capitalism a defunct model for financing development? *Review of Market Integration*, *2*(2-3), 317–331. doi:10.1177/097492921000200306

de Alcantara, C. H. (1998). Uses and abuses of the concept of governance. *International Social Science Journal*, *155*(155), 105–113. doi:10.1111/1468-2451.00113

de Araújo Ribeiro, É. F., & de Oliveira, E. G. (2021). Transfobia na educação: O olhar da estudante transgênero feminino. *Research. Social Development*, *10*(4), e34310414272–e34310414272. doi:10.33448/rsd-v10i4.14272

de Jong, M. (2021). Inclusive capitalism: The emergence of a new purpose paradigm in economics and business administration and its implications for public policy. *Global Public Policy and Governance*, 1-16.

de Oliveira Reis, P. S., das Neves, A. L. M., Therense, M., Sant, E. J., Honorato, A., & Teixeira, E. (2021). Veiled transphobia: nurses-created meanings vis-à-vis the user embracement of transvestites and transgenders [Transfobia velada: sentidos produzidos por enfermeiros (as) sobre o acolhimento de travestis e transexuais]. *Revista de Pesquisa: Cuidado é Fundamental Online, 13*, 80-85.

De Villiers, C., Venter, E. R., & Hsiao, P. C. K. (2017). Integrated reporting: Background, measurement issues, approaches and an agenda for future research. *Accounting and Finance*, *57*(4), 937–959. Advance online publication. doi:10.1111/acfi.12246

Deardorff, D. K. (2006). The identification and assessment of intercultural competence as a student outcome of internationalization at institutions of higher education in the United States. *Journal of Studies in International Education*, *2006*(10), 241–266. doi:10.1177/1028315306287002

Deloitte. (2021). *Future of risk in the digital era: transformative change: Disruptive risk*. https://www2.deloitte.com/content/dam/Deloitte/us/Documents/finance/us-rfa-future-of-risk-in-the-digital-era-report.pdf

Demirel, B., & Erol, I. (2016). Investigation of integrated reporting as a new approach of corporate reporting. *International Journal of Business and Social Research*, *6*(10), 32–46. doi:10.18533/ijbsr.v6i10.1002

Denison, D. (Ed.). (2012). *Leading culture change in global organizations: Aligning culture and strategy*. John Wiley & Sons.

Compilation of References

Denny, L., Adewole, I., Anorlu, R., Dreyer, G., Moodley, M., Smith, T., Snyman, L., Wiredu, E., Molijn, A., Quint, W., Ramakrishnan, G., & Schmidt, J. (2014). Human papillomavirus prevalence and type distribution in invasive cervical cancer in sub-Saharan Africa. *International Journal of Cancer, 134*(6), 1389–1398. doi:10.1002/ijc.28425 PMID:23929250

Dentico, N. (2020). Editorial: The Vital Pedagogy of the New Coronavirus. *Development, 63*(2-4), 145–149. doi:10.105741301-020-00279-5 PMID:33311953

Department of Education of the United States of America (DEUSA). (2021). *Education in a pandemic: the disparate impacts of COVID-19 on America's students.* https://www2.ed.gov/about/offices/list/ocr/docs/20210608-impacts-of-covid19.pdf

Dethier, J. J. (2007). Producing knowledge for development: Research at the World Bank. *Global Governance, 13*(4), 469–478. doi:10.1163/19426720-01304002

Devece, C., Peris-Ortiz, M., & Rueda-Armengot, C. (2016). Entrepreneurship during economic crisis: Success factors and paths to failure. *Journal of Business Research, 69*(11), 5366–5370. doi:10.1016/j.jbusres.2016.04.139

Development Agency of Serbia (DAS). (2021). *Decree on determining the program for encouraging regional and local development in 2021.* Author.

Devetakovic, S., Jovanovic, Gavrilovic, B., & Rikalovic, G. (2008). *National Economy.* Faculty of Economics, University of Belgrade.

Dhahri, S., & Omri, A. (2018). Entrepreneurship contribution to the three pillars of sustainable development: What does the evidence really say? *World Development, 106*, 64–77. doi:10.1016/j.worlddev.2018.01.008

Dhaka, B. L., Vatta, L., & Chayal, K. (2018). Workplace Factors Affecting Training Transfer–A Meta Evaluation. *Indian Research Journal of Extension Education, 18*(2), 91–92.

Dhejne, C., Van Vlerken, R., Heylens, G., & Arcelus, J. (2016). Mental health and gender dysphoria: A review of the literature. *International Review of Psychiatry (Abingdon, England), 28*(1), 44–57. doi:10.3109/09540261.2015.11157 53 PMID:26835611

Dieguez, T. (2017). Empowering Hub. In N. Baporikar (Ed.), Handbook of Knowledge Integration Strategies for Entrepreneurship and Sustainability. Academic Press.

Dieguez, T., Amador, F., & Porfirio, J. (2012). The balance between the supply of the Portuguese Higher Education Institutions and the emerging challenges of sustainable development: the case of automotive suppliers' industry. In *Proceedings of ICERI2012 (Fifth International Conference of Education, Research and Innovation)* (pp. 3485-3496). Academic Press.

Dieguez, T., Au-Yong-Oliveira, M., Sobral, T., & Jacquinet, M. (2021). Entrepreneurship and Changing Mindsets: a success story. In *International Conference on Applied Management Advances in the 21st Century (AMA21)*. International Association for Development of the Information Society.

Dieguez, T. (2018). Growth or Development? A Sustainable Approach. *Economic Research Journal, 2*(8), 38–46.

Dieguez, T. (2020). Operationalization of Circular Economy: A Conceptual Model. In *Handbook of Research on Entrepreneurship Development and Opportunities in Circular Economy* (pp. 38–60). IGI Global. doi:10.4018/978-1-7998-5116-5.ch003

Dieguez, T. (2021). Collective Approach and Best Practices to Develop Skills for the Post-COVID Era. In *Handbook of Research on Strategies and Interventions to Mitigate COVID-19 Impact on SMEs* (pp. 23–47). IGI Global. doi:10.4018/978-1-7998-7436-2.ch002

Diermeier, M., & Goecke, H. (2017). Productivity, Technology Diffusion, and Digitization. *CESifo Forum, 18*(1), 1-32. https://www.ifo.de/DocDL/CESifo-Forum-2017-1-diermeier-goecke-digitalization-march.pdf

Digital Namibia. (2021). *Internet users in Namibia*. Retrieved September 18, 2021 from https://datareportal.com/reports/digital-2021-namibia

Ding, J., & Adeyeye, A. O. (2013). Binary ferromagnetic nanostructures: Fabrication, static and dynamic properties. *Advanced Functional Materials, 23*(13), 1684–1691. doi:10.1002/adfm.201201432

Dingwerth, K., & Pattberg, P. (2009). World Politics and Organizational Fields: The Case of Transnational Sustainability Governance. *European Journal of International Relations, 15*(4), 707–743. doi:10.1177/1354066109345056

Divan, V., Cortez, C., Smelyanskaya, M., & Keatley, J. (2016). Transgender social inclusion and equality: A pivotal path to development. *Journal of the International AIDS Society, 19*, 20803. doi:10.7448/IAS.19.3.20803 PMID:27431473

Dixit, A. (2004). *Lawlessness and Economics: Alternative Modes of Governance*. Princeton University Press.

Dixit, R. (2021). Facilitating Training Transfer of Patient Service Skills through Healthcare Learning Champion (HLC) Interventions. *Psychology and Education Journal, 58*(4), 4468–4474.

Dixit, R. R. (2019). Enhancing service experience through excellence in patient relationship (EPR) training programs. *Indian Journal of Public Health Research & Development, 10*(5), 771–776. doi:10.5958/0976-5506.2019.01105.7

Dixit, R., & Sinha, V. (2019). Leveraging augmented reality for training transfer: A case of healthcare service providers in ophthalmology. *Development and Learning in Organizations, 34*(6), 33–36. Advance online publication. doi:10.1108/DLO-09-2019-0211

Dixit, R., & Sinha, V. (2020). Addressing Training and Development Bottlenecks in HRM: Facilitating a Paradigm Shift in Building Human Capital in Global Organizations. In *Contemporary Global Issues in Human Resource Management*. Emerald Publishing Limited. doi:10.1108/978-1-80043-392-220201012

Dixit, R., & Sinha, V. (2021). Is feedforward the way forward? A case of managers in a manufacturing firm. *Development and Learning in Organizations, 35*(2), 7–10. doi:10.1108/DLO-10-2019-0254

Dixit, R., & Sinha, V. (2021). Training as a Strategic HRM Tool to Foster Employee Development in SMEs. In *Handbook of Research on Strategies and Interventions to Mitigate COVID-19 Impact on SMEs* (pp. 609–628). IGI Global. doi:10.4018/978-1-7998-7436-2.ch030

Dixit, R., & Sinha, V. (2022). Investigating tools and techniques to promote workplace training transfer. *Journal of Workplace Learning*. Advance online publication. doi:10.1108/JWL-04-2021-0052

Dixit, R., & Sinha, V. (2022). Leveraging Virtual Learning to Facilitate Training Transfer in VUCA Times: A Case Study. *International Journal of Virtual and Personal Learning Environments, 12*(1), 1–19. doi:10.4018/IJVPLE.295301

Djoric, Z. (2020). Digital Economy – Basic Aspects and the Case of Serbia. *Economic Views, 22*(2), 73-96. https://scindeks-clanci.ceon.rs/data/pdf/1450-7951/2020/1450-79512002073Q.pdf

Djukic, G., & Ilic, B. (2020). Sustainability in higher education - a comparison of the Asia-Pacific region and Serbia. *Business Trends, 8*(1), 9-21.

Djukic, G.P., & Ilic, B.S. (2020). Sustainable development, social protection and responsibility. *İzmir Sosyal Bilimler Dergisi, 2*(2), 83-91.

Djuric, K., Cvijanovic, D., Prodanovic, R., Cavlin, M., Kuzman, B., & Lukac Bulatovic, M. (2019). Serbian Agriculture Policy: Economic Analysis Using the PSE Approach. *Sustainability, 11*(2), 309. doi:10.3390u11020309

Compilation of References

Dollar, D., & Kraay, A. (2010). *Growth is Good for the Poor*. World Bank.

Donaldson, C. (2021). Culture in the entrepreneurial ecosystem: A conceptual framing. *The International Entrepreneurship and Management Journal*, *17*(1), 289–319. doi:10.100711365-020-00692-9

Donaldson, T., & Preston, L. E. (1995). The stakeholder theory of the corporation: Concepts, evidence, and implications. *Academy of Management Review*, *20*(1), 65–91. doi:10.2307/258887

Donnelly-Smith, L. (2009). Global learning through short-term study abroad. *Peer Review: Emerging Trends and Key Debates in Undergraduate Education*, *11*(4), 12–15.

Donthu, N., & Gustafsson, A. (2020). Effects of COVID-19 on business and research. *Journal of Business Research*, *117*(September), 284–289. doi:10.1016/j.jbusres.2020.06.008 PMID:32536736

Dornan, P., & Woodhead, M. (2015). *How inequalities develop through childhood: Life-course evidence from young lives cohort study*. Academic Press.

Draskovic, V., & Jovovic, R. (2008). Knowledge Processes Innovation – Dynamic Approach to Changes of Enterprise in the Knowledge Economy. *Montenegrin Journal of Economics*, *7*(4), 35–46.

Dreher, A., Gaston, N., & Martens, P. (2008). Measuring globalisation. In Gauging its Consequences. Springer.

Dreher, A., & Gaston, N. (2008). Has globalization increased inequality? *Review of International Economics*, *16*(3), 516–536. doi:10.1111/j.1467-9396.2008.00743.x

Dreher, A., & Lohmann, S. (2015). Aid and growth at the regional level. *Oxford Review of Economic Policy*, *31*(3-4), 420–446. doi:10.1093/oxrep/grv026

Duflo, E. (2001). Schooling and labor market consequences of school construction in Indonesia: Evidence from an unusual policy experiment. *The American Economic Review*, *91*(4), 795–813. doi:10.1257/aer.91.4.795

Dugger, C. W. (2008). *Aid group says Zimbabwe misused $7.3 million*. Retrieved March 27, 2022, from https://www.nytimes.com/2008/11/03/world/africa/03zimbabwe.html

Dumay, J., Bernardi, C., Guthrie, J., & Demartini, P. (2016, September). Integrated reporting: A structured literature review. *Accounting Forum*, *40*(3), 166–185. doi:10.1016/j.accfor.2016.06.001

Dutta, S., & Lanvin, B. (Eds.). (2020). The Network Readiness Index: Accelerating Digital Transformation in a post-COVID Global Economy. Portulans Institute.

Dyer, G., & Parker, G. (2015). US attacks UK's constant accommodation with China. *Financial Times*. Accessed Oct 20, 2021. https://www.ft.com/content/31c4880a-c8d2-11e4-bc64-00144feab7de

Dziminsk, M., Fijałkowska, J., & Sułkowski, L. (2020). A Conceptual Model Proposal: Universities as Culture Change Agents for Sustainable Development. *Sustainability*, *12*(11), 4635. doi:10.3390u12114635

Dzingirai, M. (2021). The role of entrepreneurship in reducing poverty in agricultural communities. *Journal of Enterprising Communities: People and Places in the Global Economy*. doi:10.1108/JEC-01-2021-0016

Dzingirai, M. (2020). Demographic determinants of youth entrepreneurial success. *International Journal of Sustainable Entrepreneurship and Corporate Social Responsibility*, *5*(2), 1–16. doi:10.4018/IJSECSR.2020070101

EC (European Commission). (2020). *Digital Economy and Society Index (DESI) 2020: Thematic chapters*. https://digital-strategy.ec.europa.eu/

Eizaguirre, A., García-Feijoo, M., & Laka, J. P. (2019). Defining sustainability core competencies in business and management studies based on multinational stakeholders' perceptions. *Sustainability*, *11*(8), 2303. doi:10.3390u11082303

El Said, G. R. (2021). How did the covid-19 pandemic affect higher education learning experience? an empirical investigation of learners' academic performance at a university in a developing country. *Hindawi -. Advances in Human-Computer Interaction*, *2021*, 1–10. doi:10.1155/2021/6649524

Elboj-Saso, C., Cortés-Pascual, A., Íñiguez-Berrozpe, T., Lozano-Blasco, R., & Quílez-Robres, A. (2021). Emotional and Educational Accompaniment through Dialogic Literary Gatherings: A Volunteer Project for Families Who Suffer Digital Exclusion in the Context of COVID-19. *Sustainability*, *13*(1206), 1–16. doi:10.3390/su13031206

Elkington, J. (1997). *Cannibals with forks: The triple bottom line of 21st century business*. Capstone Publishers.

Ellington, J. K., Surface, E. A., Blume, B. D., & Wilson, M. A. (2015). Foreign language training transfer: Individual and contextual predictors of skill maintenance and generalization. *Military Psychology*, *27*(1), 36–51. doi:10.1037/mil0000064

Elsayid, E. (2016). *The Hidden Role of WB and IMF in Developing Countries. Egypt, Malaysia and Turkey*. AV Akademikerverlag.

Emerson, R. M., Fretz, R. I., & Shaw, L. L. (2011). *Writing ethnographic fieldnotes* (2nd ed.). The University of Chicago Press. doi:10.7208/chicago/9780226206868.001.0001

EU. (2018). *Operating budgetary balance*. https://ec.europa.eu/info/publications/operating-budgetary-balance-gni_hr

European Agency for Development in Special Needs Education. (2011). *Key principles for promoting quality in inclusive education: Recommendations for Practice European Agency for Development in Special Needs Education*. https://www.european-agency.org/sites/default/files/Key-Principles-2011-EN.pdf

European Commission. (2012). *Proposal for a Council Recommendation on the Validation of Non-Formal and Informal Learning*. European Commission.

Fair Trade International Annual Report. (2016-2017). https://annualreport16-17.fairtrade.net/en/

Farina, M. C., Opertti, M. R., Ji, M. L., & Sasu, M. N. (2007*). Regional Preparatory Workshop on Inclusive Education Eastern and Southeastern. Europe*. http://www.ibe.unesco.org/sites/default/files/Sinaia_Final_Report.pdf

Farkas, A. (2014). Conceptualizing Inclusive Education and Contextualizing it within the UNICEF Mission. UNICEF.

Farvaque, E., Refait-Alexandre, C., & Saïdane, D. (2011). Corporate disclosure: A review of its (direct and indirect) benefits and costs. *International Economics, 128*, 5–31. doi: (13)60001-3 doi:10.1016/S2110-7017

Fedderke, J., & Klitgaard, R. (2013). How much do rights matter? *World Development*, *51*, 187–206. doi:10.1016/j.worlddev.2013.05.009

Fielding, M., Bragg, S., Craig, J., Cunningham, I., Eraut, M., Gillinson, S., Horne, M., Robinson, C., & Thorp, J. (2005). *Factors Influencing the Transfer of Good Practice*. University of Sussex, Department for Education and Skills.

Fincham, R., Georg, S., & Neilsen, E. (Eds.). (2004). *Sustainable developmentand the university: New strategies for research teaching and practice*. Howick, Brevitas.

Finnan, C. (2000). Implementing School Reform Models: Why Is It So Hard for Some Schools and Easy for Others? In *Annual Meeting of the American Educational Research Association*. American Educational Research Association. Retrieved June 25, 2021, from the World Wide Web. https://files.eric.ed.gov/fulltext/ED446356.pdf

Compilation of References

Fiscal Council. (2019). Fiscal and Economic Trends in 2019 and Strategic Recommendations for Budget and Fiscal Policy in 2020. Author.

Fischer, C., Xu, D., Rodriguez, F., Denaro, K., & Warschauer, M. (2020). Effects of course modality in summer session: enrollment patterns and student performance in face-to-face and online classes. *The Internet and Higher Education, 45*(April). doi:10.1016/j.iheduc.2019.100710

Fischer, M., & Marcus, G. (1999), Introduction to the Second Edition. In Anthropology as Cultural Critique: An Experimental Moment in the Human Sciences (2nd ed.). University of Chicago Press.

Fiszbein, A., & Schady, N. R. (2009). *Conditional cash transfers: reducing present and future poverty.* World Bank Publications. doi:10.1596/978-0-8213-7352-1

Fitzgibbons, R. P. (2016). Transsexual attractions and sexual reassignment surgery: Risks and potential risks. *The Linacre Quarterly, 83*(2), 337–350. doi:10.1080/00243639.2015.1125574a PMID:26997675

Fleiss, P. (2021). Multilateral development banks in Latin America: recent trends, the response to the pandemic, and the forthcoming role. Economic Commission for Latin America and the Caribbean (ECLAC).

Fontdevila, C., & Verger, A. (2015). *The World Bank's Doublespeak on Teachers: Analysis of Ten Years of Lending and Advice.* Education International. Available at http://download.eiie.org/Docs/WebDepot/World_Banks_Double-speak_on_Teachers_Fontdevila_ Verger_EI.pdf

Frantzen, D. (2014). Is technology a one-size-fits-all solution to improving student performance? A comparison of online, hybrid and face-to-face courses. *Journal of Public Affairs Education, 20*(4), 565–578. doi:10.1080/15236803.2014.12001808

Freeman, R. E. (2004). The stakeholder approach revisited. *Zeitschrift für wirtschafts-und unternehmensethik, 5*(3), 228-254.

Freeman, C. P. (2019). Constructive Engagement? The US and the AIIB. *Global Policy, 10*(4), 667–676. doi:10.1111/1758-5899.12764

Freeman, R. E., Martin, K., & Parmar, B. (2007). Stakeholder capitalism. *Journal of Business Ethics, 74*(4), 303–314. doi:10.100710551-007-9517-y

Freiberg, D., Rogers, J., & Serafeim, G. (2019). How ESG issues become financially material to corporations and their investors. Harvard Business School. doi:10.2139srn.3482546

Friede, G., Busch, T., & Bassen, A. (2015). ESG and financial performance: Aggregated evidence from more than 2000 empirical studies. *Journal of Sustainable Finance and Investment, 5*(4), 210–233. doi:10.1080/20430795.2015.1118917

Fukuda-Parr, S. (2004). *Human development report 2004: Cultural liberty in today's diverse world.* Human Development Report.

Fullan, M. (2014). *Leading in a culture of change personal action guide and workbook.* John Wiley & Sons.

Gaddy, C. G., & Barry, W. I. (2015). Putin's rent management system and the future of addiction in Russia. In S. Oxenstierna (Ed.), *The Challenges for Russia's Politicized Economic System* (pp. 11–32). Routledge.

Gagne-Acoulon, S. (2020). *Zimbabwe's health minister charged for COVID-19 corruption.* Retrieved March 27, 2022, from https://www.occrp.org/en/daily/12594-zimbabwe-s-health-minister-charged-for-covid-19-corruption

Galiani, S., Gertler, P., Ajzenman, N., & Orsola-Vidal, A. (2016). Promoting handwashing behavior: The effects of large-scale community and school-level interventions. *Health Economics, 25*(12), 1545–1559. doi:10.1002/hec.3273 PMID:26461811

353

Gamage, K. A. A., de Silva, E. K., & Gunawardhana, N. (2020). Online delivery and assessment during COVID-19: Safeguarding academic integrity. *Education Sciences, 10*(11), 1–24. doi:10.3390/educsci10110301

Gatti, M., Chiucchi, M. S., & Montemari, M. (2018). Management control systems and integrated reporting: Which relationships? The case of the Azienda Ospedaliero Universitaria Ospedali Riuniti Ancona. *International Journal of Business and Management, 13*(9), 169–181. doi:10.5539/ijbm.v13n9p169

Gaudin, J.-P. (2002). *Pourquoi la gouvernance?* Presses de Sciences Po. doi:10.3917cpo.gaudi.2002.01

GDP, current prices. (2022, February 9). *International Monetary Fund.* Retrieved February 9, 2022, from https://www.imf.org/external/datamapper/NGDPD@WEO/RUS?year=2022

Georgescu, R. (2016) Analysis of socio-intercultural communication in organizations. *Scientific Bulletin – Economic Sciences, 15*(2).

Gereffi, G. (1994). The organization of buyer-driven global commodity chains. In G. Gereffi & M. Korzeniewicz (Eds.), *Commodity chains and global capitalism.* Praeger.

Gertz, G., & Kharas, H. (2019). *Beyond Neoliberalism: Insights from Emerging Markets.* The Brookings Institution.

Gervasius, N. (2020). *Namibia digital rights and inclusion: a paradigm initiative publication.* https://paradigmhq.org/wp-content/uploads/2021/05/lr-Namibia-Digital-Rights-Inclusion-2020-Report.pdf

Ghafar, A. (2020). Convergence between 21st century skills and entrepreneurship education in higher education institutes. *International Journal of Higher Education, 9*(1), 218–229. doi:10.5430/ijhe.v9n1p218

Gherheş, V., Stoian, C. E., Fărcaşiu, M. A., & Stanici, M. (2021). E-learning vs. Face-to-face learning: Analyzing students' preferences and behaviors. *Sustainability (Switzerland), 13*(8), 4381. Advance online publication. doi:10.3390u13084381

Ghiasy, R., & Zhou, J. (2017). The Silk Road Economic Belt: Considering security implications and EU–China cooperation prospects. SIPRI (Stockholm International Peace Research Institute) and Friedrich Ebert Stiftung (Germany).

Gidens, E. (2003). A world that eludes us. In Globalization myth or reality. Institute for Textbooks and Teaching Aids.

Gilbert, C. L., Vines, D., & Powell, A. (Eds.). (2000). *The World Bank: Structure and policies.* Cambridge University Press. doi:10.1017/CBO9780511560002

Giles, S. (2016). The Most Important Leadership Competencies, According to Leaders Around the World. Harvard Business Review. Retrieved fromhttps://hbr.org/2016/03/the-most-important-leadership-competencies-according-to-leaders-around-the-world

Glaser, B., & Strauss, A. (1967). *The discovery of grounded theory.* Aldine Publishing.

Glass, L. M., & Newig, J. (2019). Governance for achieving the Sustainable Development Goals: How important are participation, policy coherence, reflexivity, adaptation and democratic institutions? *Earth System Governance, 2,* 100031. doi:10.1016/j.esg.2019.100031

Glen, J., & Singh, A. (2005). Corporate governance, competition and finance: Rethinking lessons from the Asian crisis. *Eastern Economic Journal, 31*(2), 219–243.

Glewwe, P., & Kremer, M. (2006). Schools, teachers, and education outcomes in developing countries. Handbook of the Economics of Education, 2, 945-1017.

Glewwe, P. (2002). Schools and skills in developing countries: Education policies and socioeconomic outcomes. *Journal of Economic Literature, 40*(2), 436–482. doi:10.1257/jel.40.2.436

Compilation of References

Glewwe, P., Maiga, E., & Zheng, H. (2014). The contribution of education to economic growth: A review of the evidence, with special attention and an application to Sub-Saharan Africa. *World Development*, *59*, 379–393. doi:10.1016/j. worlddev.2014.01.021

Global Policy. (n.d.). https://www.globalpolicy.org

Gluckman, M. (1968). The utility of the equilibrium model in the study of social change. *American Anthropologist*, *70*(2), 219–237. doi:10.1525/aa.1968.70.2.02a00010

Goldberg, A. E. (2018). *Transgender students in higher education*. Accessed on 7 August 2021, through https://williamsinstitute.law.ucla.edu/publications/trans-students-higher-education/

Goldberg, A. E., Beemyn, G., & Smith, J. Z. (2019). What is needed, what is valued: Trans students' perspectives on trans-inclusive policies and practices in higher education. *Journal of Educational & Psychological Consultation*, *29*(1), 27–67. doi:10.1080/10474412.2018.1480376

Göler, D. (2016). Elusive Migration Systems. Lessons from Europe's New Migratory Map. *Bulletin of the Serbian Geographical Society*, *96*(2), 42–49. doi:10.2298/GSGD1602038G

Golubovic, N. (2009). Social capital and economic-theoretical 'imperialism' [Društveni kapital i ekonomsko-teorijski 'imperijalizam']. *Proceedings of the "Matica Srpska" for Social Sciences*, *128*, 63-73.

Gómez-Mejía, A. (2017). The Concept of Technology in the History of Economic Thought. From the Classics to Schumpeter, Evolutionism and today. *Revista Libre Empresa*, *14*(2), 199–214. doi:10.18041/libemp.2017.v14n2.28210

Government of the Republic of Serbia (2021). *Social Inclusion Team- Social inclusion, Poverty statistics, Who are the poor in Serbia?* [Socijalno uključivanje, Statistika siromaštva, Ko su siromašni u Srbiji?]. Author.

Graen, G. B., Hui, C., & Gu, Q. L. (2004). A new approach to socio-intercultural cooperation. *LMX Leadership*, 225–246. https://www.researchgate.net/profile/George_Graen2/publication/292729391_A_NEW_APPROACH_TO_SOCIOIN-TERCULTURAL_COOPERATION/links/56b0dde408ae9c1968b97809.pdf

Graham, J., Amos, B., & Plumptre, T. (2003). *Governance principles for protected areas in the 21st century*. Institute on Governance, Parks Canada, and the Canadian International Development Agency.

Granberg, L., & Sätre, A.-M. (2017), *The Other Russia. Local experience and societal change*, Routledge.

Gransow, B., & Price, S. (2019). Social Risk Management at AIIB – Chinese or International Characteristics? *Journal of Chinese Political Science*, *24*(2), 289–311. doi:10.100711366-018-9553-8

Grant, J., Mottet, L., Tanis, J., Harrison, J., Herman, J., & Keisling, M. (2011). *Injustice at every turn: A Report of the National Transgender Discrimination Survey*. National Center for Transgender Equality and National Gay and Lesbian Task Force.

Greenaway, D., Gullstrand, J., & Kneller, R. (2005). Exporting may not always boost firm productivity. *Review of World Economics*, *141*(4), 561–582. doi:10.100710290-005-0045-5

Greif, A. (2000). The fundamental problem of exchange: A research agenda in historical institutional analysis. *European Review of Economic History*, *4*(3), 251–284. doi:10.1017/S1361491600000071

Grenot-Scheyer, M., Jubala, K. A., Bishop, K. D., & Coots, J. J. (1996). The inclusive classroom. Westminster: Teacher Created Materials. Centre for Economic & Social inclusion.

Griffin, P. (2006). The World Bank. *New Political Economy*, *11*(4), 571–581. doi:10.1080/13563460600991028

Grove, H., Clouse, M., & Xu, T. (2020). Stakeholder capitalism strategies and opportunities for corporate governance. *Journal of Governance & Regulation*, *9*(4), 59–68. doi:10.22495/jgrv9i4art5

Guay. (2016). *An example of a global institution: The International Organization for Migration.* https://www.futurelearn.com/info/

Guralnick, M. J. (2001). A Framework for change in early childhood inclusion. In M. J. Guralnich (Ed.), *Early Childhood inclusion: Focus on change* (pp. 3–35). Brookes.

Gyas, R. M. (2018). Unmasking the Practices of Nurses and Socio-intercultural Health in Sub-Saharan Africa: A Useful Way to Improve Health Care? *Journal of Evidence-based Integrative Medicine*, *23*, 1–5.

Gyimah-Brempong, K., & Aziedu, E. (2008, November). *Aid and human capital formation: some evidence.* African Development Bank/UNECA Conference on Globalization, Institutions and Economic Development in Africa.

Habermas, J. (1981). *The theory of communicative action: Reason and the rationalization of society.* Beacon Press.

Hacken, G. (1985). *Synergetics: Hierarchy of instabilities in self-organizing systems and devices.* Moscow: Mir.

Haenggi, M., Andrews, J. G., Baccelli, F., Dousse, O., & Franceschetti, M. (2009). Stochastic geometry and random graphs for the analysis and design of wireless networks. *IEEE Journal on Selected Areas in Communications*, *27*(7), 1029–1046. doi:10.1109/JSAC.2009.090902

Hair, J. F. J., Black, W. C., Babin, B. J., & Anderson, R. E. (2010). *Multivariate Data Analysis* (7th ed.). Prentice Hall.

Halinen, I., & Jarvinen, R. (2008). Towards Inclusive Education: The Case of Finland. *Prospects*, *38*(1), 77–97. doi:10.100711125-008-9061-2

Hall, R., & Jones, C. I., (1999). Why Do Some Countries Produce So Much More Output per Worker than Others? *Quarterly Journal of Economics, 114*(1), 83-116.

Hall, E. T. (1997). *Beyond Culture.* Random House Inc.

Hall, N., & Woods, N. (2018). Theorizing the role of executive heads in international organizations. *European Journal of International Relations*, *24*(4), 865–886. doi:10.1177/1354066117741676

Hall, P., & Gingerich, D. (2009). Varieties of capitalism and institutional complementarities in the political economy: An empirical analysis. *British Journal of Political Science*, *39*(3), 449–482. doi:10.1017/S0007123409000672

Hall, P., & Soskice, D. (2001). *Varieties of capitalism: The institutional foundations of comparative advantage.* Oxford University Press. doi:10.1093/0199247757.001.0001

Hambrick, D. C., Davison, S. C., Snell, S. A., & Snow, C. C. (1998). When groups consist of multiple nationalities: Towards a new understanding of the implications. *Organization Studies*, *19*(2), 181–205. doi:10.1177/017084069801900202

Hameiri, S., & Jones, L. (2018). China challenges global governance? Chinese international development finance and the AIIB. *International Affairs*, *94*(3), 573–593. doi:10.1093/ia/iiy026

Handley, S. M., & Angst, C. M. (2015). The impact of culture on the relationship between governance and opportunism in outsourcing relationships. *Strategic Management Journal*, *2015*(36), 1412–1434. doi:10.1002mj.2300

Hansen, H., & Tarp, F. (2000). Aid effectiveness disputed. *Journal of International Development*, *12*(3), 375–398. doi:10.1002/(SICI)1099-1328(200004)12:3<375::AID-JID657>3.0.CO;2-M

Hanushek, E. A. (1981). Throwing money at schools. *Journal of Policy Analysis and Management*, *1*(1), 19–41. doi:10.2307/3324107

Compilation of References

Haradhan, M. (2018). Qualitative Research Methodology in Social Sciences and Related Subjects. *Journal of Economic Development. Environment and People, 7*(1), 23–48.

Harford, T., & Klein, M. (2005). *Aid and the Resource Curse: How Can Aid Be Designed to Preserve Institutions.* Academic Press.

Harrison, R., Newholm, T., & Shaw, D. (2005). Introduction. In RThe ethical consumer. London: Sage Publications.

Hart, S. L. (2005). *Capitalism at the crossroads: The unlimited business opportunities in solving the world's most difficult problems.* Wharton School.

Harvey, D. (2007). *A brief history of neoliberalism.* Oxford University Press.

Hasenclever, A., Mayer, P., & Rittberger, V. (1997). *Theories of International Regimes.* Cambridge University Press. doi:10.1017/CBO9780511521720

Hattingh, J. (2002). On the imperative of sustainable development: A philosophical and ethical appraisal. In Environmental education, ethics andaction in Southern Africa (pp. 5–16). Human Sciences Research Council.

Hawawini, G. (2011). *The Internationalization of Higher Education Institutions: A Critical Review and a Radical Proposal.* Faculty & INSEAD Research Working Paper. The Business School for the World. https://sites.insead.edu/facultyresearch/research/doc.cfm?did=48726

Hayter, T. (1971). *Aid as imperialism.* Academic Press.

Hebib, E. (2013). How to develop a school - development and reform processes in the field of school education. Institute of Pedagogy and Andragogy, Faculty of Philosophy, University of Belgrade.

He, K., & Feng, H. (2019). Leadership Transition and Global Governance: Role Conception, Institutional Balancing, and the AIIB. *The Chinese Journal of International Politics, 12*(2), 153–178. doi:10.1093/cjip/poz003

Held, D., & Young, K. (2009). The world crisis: global financial governance: principles of reform (No. 43602). London School of Economics and Political Science, LSE Library.

Held, D. (2005). At the global crossroads: The end of the Washington Consensus andthe rise of global social democracy? *Globalizations, 2*(1), 95–113. doi:10.1080/14747730500085122

Held, D., & McGrew, A. (2008). *Globalization / anti-globalization: Beyond the greatdivide* (2nd ed.). Polity Press.

Helsper, E. (2014). Digital Inclusion in Europe: Evaluating Policy and Practice. In *Harnessing ICT for social action, a digital volunteering program. Discussion Paper.* European Commission, Directorate-General for Employment, Social Affairs, and Inclusion. http://eprints.lse.ac.uk/59998/

Henderson, J., Dicken, P., Hess, M., Coe, N., & Wai-Chung Yeung, H. (2002). Globalproduction networks and the analysis of economic development. *Review of International Political Economy, 9*(3), 436–464. doi:10.1080/09692290210150842

Heneghan, M., & Orenstein, M. A. (2019). Organizing for impact: International organizations and global pension policy. *Global Social Policy, 19*(1–2), 65–86. doi:10.1177/1468018119834730

Henry Jackson Initiative. (2012). *Towards a more inclusive capitalism.* The Henry Jackson Foundation Initiative.

Herold, M. H. (2018). Demystifying the link between institutional theory and stakeholder theory in sustainability reporting. *Economics. Management and Sustainability, 3*(2), 6–19. doi:10.14254/jems.2018.3-2.1

Heyneman, S. P. (2001). The growing international commercial market for educational goods and services. *International Journal of Educational Development, 21*(4), 345–359. doi:10.1016/S0738-0593(00)00056-0

Heyneman, S. P. (2004). Education and corruption. *International Journal of Educational Development, 24*(6), 637–648. doi:10.1016/j.ijedudev.2004.02.005

Heyneman, S. P. (2009). The failure of education for all as political strategy. *Prospects, 39*(1), 5–10. doi:10.100711125-009-9107-0

Heyneman, S. P. (2010). A comment on the changes in higher education in the former Soviet Union. *European Education, 42*(1), 76–87. doi:10.2753/EUE1056-4934420104

Heyneman, S. P. (2012). When models become monopolies: The making of education policy at the World Bank. In *Education strategy in the developing world: Revising the World Bank's education policy.* Emerald Group Publishing Limited. doi:10.1108/S1479-3679(2012)0000016007

Heyneman, S. P., & De Young, A. J. (Eds.). (2006). *The challenges of education in Central Asia.* IAP.

Hinds, P., Liu, L., & Lyon, J. (2011). Putting the global in global work: A socio-intercultural lens on the practice of cross-national collaboration. *The Academy of Management Annals, 5*(1), 135–188. doi:10.5465/19416520.2011.586108

Hisrich, R. D., Peters, M. P., & Shepherd, D. A. (2017). *Entrepreneurship.* McGraw-Hill Education.

History of BRICS. (2021). *BRICS.* https://infobrics.org/

Ho, M. (2016). *Investment in learning increases for fourth straight year.* Talent and Development. https://www.td.org/Publications/Magazines/TD/TD-Archive/2016/11/Investment-in-Learning-

Hoepner, M. (2001). *Corporate governance in transition: ten empirical findings on shareholder value and industrial relations.* Discussion Paper 01/5. Max-Planck-Institut für Gesellschaftsforschung.

Hoepner, M., & Jackson, G. (2001). *An emergent market for corporate control? The Mannesmann takeover and German corporate governance.* MPIfG Discussion Paper 01/4. Cologne: MPIf.G.

Hofstede, G. (2001). *Culture's Consequences: Comparing Values, Behaviors, Institutions, and Organizations across Nations* (2nd ed.). SAGE Publications.

Hofstede, G., Hofstede, G. J., & Minkov, M. (2010). *Cultures and organizations: Software of the mind. Socio-intercultural cooperation and its importance for survival* (3rd ed.). McGraw-Hill.

Holotik, S. I., Eliseeva, N. V., & Karpenko, S. V. (2002). Russia in 1992 - 2000: Economy, Power and society. *New Historical Bulletin, 8,* 164–203.

Hooghe, L., & Marks, G. (2014). Delegation and pooling in international organizations. *The Review of International Organizations, 10*(3), 305–328. doi:10.100711558-014-9194-4

Horpynych, O., & Ibrahimova, Z. (2020). Socio-intercultural model of the development of modern cities: A conceptual analysis. *Scientific and Theoretical Almanac Grani, 23*(4), 13–19. doi:10.15421/172036_

House, R. J., Hanges, P. J., Dorfmanand, P. W., & Gupta, V. (Eds.). (2004). *Culture, Leadership, and Organizations. The GLOBE Study of 62 Societies.* SAGE Publications, Inc.

Howitt, R. (2001). *Rethinking resource management: Justice, sustainability, and indigenous peoples.* Routledge.

Howlett, M., & Rayner, J. (2006). Convergence and divergence in 'new governance' arrangements: Evidence from European integrated natural resource strategies. *Journal of Public Policy, 26*(2), 167–189. doi:10.1017/S0143814X06000511

Hrnjica, S. (1997). A Child with Developmental Disabilities in Elementary School. The School of Pedagogy.

Compilation of References

Hrnjica, S., Rajovic, V., Colin, T., Krstic, K., & Kopunovic, D. (2009). *Tailor-made school: Handbook for ad with regular school students who have developmental difficulties.* Save the Children UK, Program for Serbia.

Hrvatić, N. (2007). Interkulturalna pedagogija –nove paradigme. *Pedagogijska istraživanja, 4*(2), 241-252.

https://doi.org/10.9774/GLEAF.4700.2005.su.00004

Hughes, B. M. (2019). *The Psychology of Brexit. From Psychodrama to Behavioural Science.* Springer. doi:10.1007/978-3-030-29364-2

Hulme, M. (2010). Moving beyond climate change. *Environment, 52*(3), 15–19.

Hu, M. K., & Kee, D. M. H. (2021). Strategic measures and tactical interventions for COVID-19 impact relief on SMEs. In N. Baporikar (Ed.), *Handbook of research on strategies and interventions to mitigate COVID-19 impact on SMEs* (1st ed., pp. 522–541). IGI Global. doi:10.4018/978-1-7998-7436-2.ch026

Humphrey, C. (2020). *All Hands on Deck: How to Scale Up Multilateral Financing to Face the COVID-19 Crisis.* ODI Emerging Analysis and Ideas.

Humphreys, M., & Bates, R. (2005). Political institutions and economic policies: Lessons from Africa. *British Journal of Political Science, 35*(3), 403–428. doi:10.1017/S0007123405000232

Hunt, J., & Smith, D. (2006). *Building Indigenous community governance in Australia: preliminary research findings.* CAEPR Working Paper No. 31, CAEPR, ANU.

Hunt, J., & Smith, D. E. (2007). *Indigenous Community Governance Project: Year two research findings.* CAEPR Working Paper No. 36, CAEPR, CASS, ANU.

Hurt, K. J. (2016). A theoretical model of training and its transference: The pivotal role of top management team composition and characteristics. *Human Resource Development International, 19*(1), 44–66. doi:10.1080/13678868.2015.1102007

Hussain, N., Rigoni, U., & Orij, R. P. (2018). Corporate governance and sustainability performance: Analysis of triple bottom line performance. *Journal of Business Ethics, 149*(2), 411–432. doi:10.100710551-016-3099-5

IDA & IMF. (2020). *Joint World Bank-IMF Debt Sustainability Analysis.* Retrieved September 15, 2021, from https://www.imf.org/en/About/Factsheets/Sheets/2016/08/01/16/39/Debt-Sustainability-Framework-for-Low-Income-Countries

Idowu, S. O., & Baldo, M. D. (2019). *Integrated Reporting.* Springer. doi:10.1007/978-3-030-01719-4

IFC Project Information & Data Portal. (2021a*). IFC | International Finance Corporation | World Bank Group.* https://disclosures.ifc.org/enterprise-search-results-home?f_region_description=ECAREG

IFC Project Information & Data Portal. (2021b, November 27). *International Finance Corporation.* https://disclosures.ifc.org/enterprise-search-results-home?f_region_description=ECAREG

IIRC & Kirchhoff. (2020). Closing the gap: the role of integrated reporting in communicating a company's value creation to investors. Investor Research Report.

IIRC. (2013). *The International IR Framework.* International Integrated Reporting Council. http:// www.theiirc.org/wp-content/uploads/2013/12/13-12-08-THE-INTERNATIONAL-IR-FRAMEWORK-2-1.pdf

Ilic, B., & Pavicevic, N. (2018). Selection of economic and ecological development rights of tourism using the method of multi-criteria decision-making-case study Gamzigradska Banja. Society of Economists, Economics (NIS, Medivest KT).

359

Ilic, B. S. (2019). Renewable Energy Sources Management and Role of Ecological Parks: Improving Quality of Life for Sustainable Development. In U. Akkucuk (Ed.), *Handbook Ethical and Sustainable Supply Chain Management in a Global Context* (pp. 220–228). IGI Global. doi:10.4018/978-1-5225-8970-9.ch014

Ilic, B. S. (2020). Social Component of Sustainable Development and Quality of Life: Region of the Balkans, Eastern Serbia. In U. Akkucuk (Ed.), *Handbook of Research on Creating Sustainable Value in the Global Economy* (pp. 452–462). IGI Global. doi:10.4018/978-1-7998-1196-1.ch026

Ilic, B., & Djukic, G. (2021). Introduction of crisis management for the purpose of positive changes in the age of COVID -19. In *Proceedings of 7th International ConferenceInnovation as the initiator of development* (Vol. 3, pp. 398–408). Faculty of Applied Management, Economics and Finance.

Ilic, B., Djukic, G., & Todosijevic, J. (2021). Cultural dimensions - the impact of differences and similarities on business in the COVID-19 era. *Proceedings of the 11th International Symposium on Natural Resources Management, 11*, 169-176.

Ilic, B., & Jovanovic, L. (2017). Quality of Serbian life as one of the components of sustainable development. *Proceeding of the 7th International Symposium on Natural Resources Management, 7*, 272-279.

Ilic, B., & Mihajlovic, D. (2017). Motivational theories and factors of sustainable and socially responsible business. *Proceedings of 9th International Scientific Conference Social actors before information technologies challenges in search for new vision of social peace, 9*, 312-325.

Ilic, B., Mihajlovic, D., & Karabasevic, D. (2016). Social component of sustainable development and quality of life in Serbia. *Srpska Nauka Danas, 1*(1), 413–423.

Ilic, B., Sovtic, K., & Mihajlovic, D. (2019). Economic and ecological sustainability of Serbia - a condition for raising quality and environmental protection. *Ecologica, 94*(26), 193–198.

ILO. (2015). *Policy Frame work*. http://www.ilo.org

Imenda, S. (2014). Is there a conceptual difference between theoretical and conceptual frameworks? *Journal of social sciences, 38*(2), 185–195. doi:10.1080/09718923.2014.11893249

IMF Launches New SDR Basket Including Chinese Renminbi, Determines New Currency Amounts. (2016, September 30). *International Monetary Fund*. https://www.imf.org/ru/News/Articles/2016/09/30/AM16-PR16440-IMF-Launches-New-SDR-Basket-Including-Chinese-Renminbi

IMF. (2020). *New Policy Frame Work for a Lower for Longer World*. https://www.imf.org/en/News/

Ingerson, M. C., Donaldson, T., Harris, J. D., Keevil, A., Phillips, R. A., Agle, B. R., ... Mitchell, R. K. (2015). Normative Stakeholder Capitalism: Getting from Here to There. *Business & Professional Ethics Journal, 34*(3), 377–406.

Institute of Directors in Southern Africa. (2012). Practice Notes: King III Chapter 9. = Institute of Directors in Southern Africa.

International Integrated Reporting Council (IIRC). (2016a). *Creating Value. The Cyclical Power of Integrated Thinking and Reporting*. International Integrated Reporting Council.

International Labour Organization (ILO). (2014). *An enabling environment for sustainable enterprises*. https://www.ilo.org/wcmsp5/groups/public/---ed_emp/---emp_ent/---ifp_seed/documents/publication/wcms_175476.pdf

International Monetary Fund. (2015a). *Financing for Development: Revisiting the Monterrey Consensus*. Retrieved September 10, 2021, from https://www.imf.org/en/Publications/Policy-Papers/Issues/2016/12/31/Financing-For-Development-Revisiting-the-Monterrey-Consensus-PP4966

Compilation of References

International Monetary Fund. (2015b). *Financing for Development: Enhancing the Financial Safety Net for Developing Countries*. Retrieved September 10, 2021, from https://www.imf.org/en/Publications/Policy-Papers/Issues/2016/12/31/Financing-for-Development-Enhancing-the-Financial-Safety-Net-for-Developing-Countries-PP4965

IPA – Interreg – CBS (2021). *Territorial and socio-economic analysis of the programme area*. Interreg IPA Programme 2021-2021.

ITU (International Telecommunication Union). (2020). Global ICT Regulatory Outlook 2020: pointing the way forward to collaborative regulation. ITU Publications.

ITU. (2021). Towards building inclusive digital communities: ITU toolkit and self-assessment for ICT. *Accessibility Implementation, 3*. https://www.itu.int/pub/D-PHCB-TOOLKIT.01-2021

Ivancic, D. & Stancic, Z. (2013). Creating an inclusive school culture. *Croatian Journal of Rehabilitation Research, 49*(2), 139-157.

Ivan, O. R. (2018). Integrated Reporting in the Context of Corporate Governance. Case study on the Adoption of Integrated Reporting of Romanian Companies listed on BSE. *Valahian Journal of Economic Studies, 9*(2), 127–138. doi:10.2478/vjes-2018-0024

Ivwighreghweta, O., & Igere, M. A. (2014). Impact of the internet on academic performance of students in tertiary institutions in Nigeria. *Journal of Information and Knowledge Management, 5*(6), 47–56.

Jaeger, P. T., Thompson, K. M., Katz, S., M., & Decoster, E. J. (2012). The Intersection of Public Policy and Public Access: Digital Divides, Digital Literacy, Digital Inclusion, and Public Libraries. *Public Library Quarterly, 31*(1), 1-20. . doi:10.1080/01616846.2012.654728

Jahnukainen, M. (2011). Different Strategies, Different Outcomes? The History and Trends of the Inclusive and Special Education in Alberta (Canada) and in Finland. *Scandinavian Journal of Educational Research, 55*(5), 489–502. doi:10.1080/00313831.2010.537689

James, S., Herman, J., Rankin, S., Keisling, M., Mottet, L., & Anaf, M. (2016). *The report of the 2015 US Transgender Survey*. National Center for Transgender Equality.

Jandric, M., & Molnar, D. (2017). *Quality of employment and labor market in Serbia*. Friedrich-Ebert Foundation, Belgrade Office.

Jeavons, M., & Thandi, J. (2021). *AA view: The benefits of ESG*. https://insights-north-america.aon.com/responsible-investing/aon-the-benefits-of-esg-integration-report

Jimaa, S. (2011). The impact of assessment on students learning. *Procedia: Social and Behavioral Sciences, 28*, 718–721. doi:10.1016/j.sbspro.2011.11.133

Johnson, S. D., Aragon, S. R., Shaik, N., & Palma-Rivas, N. (2000). Comparative analysis of learner satisfaction and learning outcomes in online and face-to-face learning environments. *Journal of Interactive Learning Research, 11*(1), 29–49.

Johnstone, I. (2021). The G20, climate change and COVID-19: Critical juncture or critical wound? *Fulbright Review of Economics and Policy, 1*(2), 227–245. doi:10.1108/FREP-05-2021-0031

Jones, L., & Hameiri, S. (2021). COVID-19 and the failure of the neoliberal regulatory state. *Review of International Political Economy*, 1–25. doi:10.1080/09692290.2021.1892798

Jones, P. W. (2007). *World Bank financing of education: Lending, Learning and Development*. Routledge. doi:10.4324/9780203965931

Jovanovic, B. M., & Langovic, A. (2009). Intercultural Challenges of Globalization. Megatrend University.

Jovanovic, M. (2004). *Intercultural Management*. Megatrend University of Belgrade.

Joyce, P. (2018). The effectiveness of online and paper-based formative assessment in the learning of English as a second language. *PASAA, 55*. https://files.eric.ed.gov/fulltext/EJ1191739.pdf

Kabir, M. N. (2019). *Knowledge-Based Social Entrepreneurship: Understanding Knowledge Economy, Innovation, and the Future of Social Entrepreneurship*. Springer. doi:10.1057/978-1-137-34809-8

Kahn, M. (1995). Concepts, definitions, and key issues in sustainable development: the outlook for the future. *Proceedings of the 1995 International Sustainable Development Research Conference*, 2-13.

Kaisara, G., & Bwalya, K. J. (2020). Investigating the e-learning challenges faced by students during Covid-19 in Namibia. *International Journal of Higher Education, 10*(1), 308. doi:10.5430/ijhe.v10n1p308

Kalinowska, A., & Batorczak, A. (2017). Uczelnie wy˙zsze wobec wyzwa´n celów zrównowa˙zonego rozwoju. Zeszyty Naukowe Politechniki Sl˛askiej. *Organizacja i Zarz˛adzaniez, 104*, 281–290.

Karamatic-Brcic, M. (2011). Purpose and goal of inclusive education. University of Zadar, Croatia [Svrha i cilj inkluzivnog obrazovanja. Sveučilište u Zadru, Hrvatska]. *Acta Iadertina, 8*(1). https://hrcak.srce.hr/19009

Karnani, A. (2011). *Fighting Poverty Together*. Palgrave MacMillan. doi:10.1057/9780230120235

Katada, S. N. (2016). At the Crossroads: The TPP, AIIB, and Japan's Foreign Economic Strategy. *AsiaPacific Issues, 125*, 1–8.

Katzenstein, P. J. (1996). Introduction: Alternative Perspectives on National Security. In P. J. Katzenstein (Ed.), *The Culture of National Security* (pp. 1–32). Columbia University Press.

Kavkler, M., Babuder, M. K., & Magajna, L. (2015). Inclusive Education for Children with Specific Learning Difficulties: Analysis of Opportunities and Barriers in Inclusive Education in Slovenia. *CEPS Journal, 5*(1), 31–52. doi:10.26529/cepsj.152

Kaya, A., & Woo, B. (2021). China and the Asian Infrastructure Investment Bank (AIIB): Chinese Influence Over Membership Shares? *The Review of International Organizations*. Advance online publication. doi:10.100711558-021-09441-1

Kayser, O., & Budinich, V. (2015). *Scaling up business solutions to social problems: A practical guide for social and corporate entrepreneurs*. Springer. doi:10.1057/9781137466549

Keefer, P., & Stasavage, D. (2002). Checks and balances, private information, and the credibility of monetary commitments. *International Organization, 56*(4), 751–774. doi:10.1162/002081802760403766

Keohane, R.O., & Victor, D. (2011). The regime complex for climate change. *Perspectives on Politics, 9*(1), 7–23.

Kesteven, S., & Smith, D. E. (1984). Contemporary Land-Tenure in Western Arnhem Land: An Investigation of Traditional Ownership, Resource Development and Royalties. Report to the Australian Institute of Aboriginal Studies and the Northern Land Council.

Keyton, J. D., Ford, J., & Smith, F. L. (2012). Communication, collaboration and identification as facilitators and constraints of multiteams systems. *Multiteam Systems: An Organization Form for Dynamic and Complex Environments, 21*, 173–190.

Compilation of References

Khalil, R., Mansour, A. E., Fadda, W. A., Almisnid, K., Aldamegh, M., Al-Nafeesah, A., Alkhalifah, A., & Al-Wutayd, O. (2020). The sudden transition to synchronized online learning during the COVID-19 pandemic in Saudi Arabia: A qualitative study exploring medical students' perspectives. *BMC Medical Education, 20*(1), 1–10. doi:10.118612909-020-02208-z PMID:32859188

Khan, S. (2012). *Topic Guide on Social Exclusion.* International Development Department, University of Birmingham. www.gsdrc.org

Khan, Z. R., Rodrigues, G., & Balasubramanian, S. (2016, January). *Ethical consumerism and apparel industry-towards a New Factor Model* [Paper presentation]. 33rd International Business Research Conference, Dubai, UAE.

Kilbourne, W., McDonagh, P. P., & Prothero, A. (1997). Sustainable consumption and the quality of life: A micromarketing challenge to the dominant social paradigm. *Journal of Macromarketing, 17*(1), 4–21. doi:10.1177/027614679701700103

King, K. (2002). Banking on knowledge: The new knowledge projects of the World Bank. *Compare: A Journal of Comparative Education, 32*(3), 311–326. doi:10.1080/0305792022000007472

King, P. M., & Baxter Magolda, M. B. (2005). A Developmental Model of Intercultural Maturity. *Journal of College Student Development, 2005*(46), 571–592. doi:10.1353/csd.2005.0060

Kingston, K. J. (2013). *The impact of high-speed internet connectivity at home on eighth-grade student achievement* [Doctoral dissertation, University of Nebraska]. https://digitalcommons.unomaha.edu/cgi/viewcontent.cgi?article=1050&context=studentwork

Kivirauma, J., & Ruoho, K. (2007). Excellence through Special Education? Lessons from the Finnish School Reform. *International Review of Education, 53*(3), 283–302. doi:10.100711159-007-9044-1

Klees, S. J., Stromquist, N. P., Samoff, J., & Vally, S. (2019). The 2018 world development report on education: A critical analysis. *Development and Change, 50*(2), 603–620. doi:10.1111/dech.12483

Knowledge management practices in Turkish global institutions. (n.d.). *Journal of Enterprise Information Management, 20*(2), 209–221. doi:10.1108/17410390710725788

Koehn, P. H. (2007). Peaceful and sustainable development? Middle-management entrepreneurship and transnational competence in China. *East Asia (Piscataway, N.J.), 24*(3), 251–263. https://doi.org/10.1007/s12140-007-9017-9

Kokovic, D. (2009). Culture and ecological values. *Annual Review of the Faculty of Philosophy, 1/2*(34), 207–215.

Komarkova, I., Conrads, J., & Collado, A. (2015). *Entrepreneurship Competence: An Overview of Existing Concepts. Policies and Initiatives.* JRC Science Hub.

Kooiman, J. (2003). *Governing as Governance.* Sage Publications.

Koskinen, Y. (Ed.). (2013). *Corporate social responsibility and organization risk. Theory and empirical evidence.* Retrieved from http://www.ecgi.global/sites/default/files/working_papers/documents/SSRN-id1977053.pdf

Köster, K. (2010). *International Project Management.* SAGE Publications Ltd.

Kothari, C. R. (2004). *Research methodology: Methods and technics* (2nd revised edition). New Age International Publishers.

Krais, B. (1999). On Pierre Bourdieu's Masculine Domination. *Travail, Genre et Sociétés, 1*(1), 214–221. doi:10.3917/tgs.001.0214

Kramarz, T., & Momani, B. (2013). The World Bank as Knowledge Bank: Analyzing the Limits of a Legitimate Global Knowledge Actor. *The Review of Policy Research, 30*(4), 409–431. doi:10.1111/ropr.12028

Kremer, M., & Holla, A. (2009). Improving education in the developing world: What have we learned from randomized evaluations? *Annual Review of Economics*, *1*(1), 513–542. doi:10.1146/annurev.economics.050708.143323 PMID:23946865

Krishnaratne, S., & White, H. (2013). *Quality education for all children? What works in education in developing countries*. International Initiative for Impact Evaluation (3ie).

Krivokapic, Dj., & Mesanovic, E. (2016). *Leasing Workers - A Guide to the Rights of Workers Temporarily Engaged through Employment Agencies*. Share Olof Palme Foundation and International Center.

Krstic, G., & Soskic, D. (2016). Economic statistics. Center for Publishing Activities of the Faculty of Economics.

Krüger, D., & David, A. (2020, February). Entrepreneurial education for persons with disabilities—a social innovation approach for inclusive ecosystems. Frontiers in Education, 5, 3.

Kucherov, D., & Manokhina, D. (2017). Evaluation of training programs in Russian manufacturing companies. *European Journal of Training and Development*, *41*(2), 119–143. doi:10.1108/EJTD-10-2015-0084

Kukovec, D., Mulej, M., & Šarotar Žižek, S. (2018). Professional Languages Alone Do Not Suffice for Successful and Socially Responsible Internal Communication between Different Cultures. *Naše gospodarstvo/Our Economy*, *64*(3), 47-55. DOI: doi:10.2478/ngoe-2018-0017

Kumar, N., & Arora, O. (2019). Financing Sustainable Infrastructure Development in South Asia: The Case of AIIB. *Global Policy*, *10*(4), 619–624. doi:10.1111/1758-5899.12732

Kuratko, D. F., & Morris, M. H. (2018). Examining the future trajectory of entrepreneurship. *Journal of Small Business Management*, *56*(1), 11–23. doi:10.1111/jsbm.12364

Kuruc, K. (2018). *The IMF and Fragile States: Assessing Macroeconomic Outcomes. Background Papers*. Independent Evaluation Office of the IMF.

Labour Force survey in Serbia. (2014). *SORS*. https://www.stat.gov.rs/sr-Latn / areas / labor-market /labor-force-survey

Labour Market dynamics in the third quarter. (2021). *SORS*. https://www.stat.gov.rs/sr-latn/vesti/20211130-anketa-o-radnoj-snazi-iii-kv-2021/?s=2400

Lackéus, M. (2015). Entrepreneurship in Education: What, Why, When, How. *Long Range Planning*, *48*, 215–227.

Lackéus, M. (2020). Comparing the impact of three different experiential approaches to entrepreneurship in education. *International Journal of Entrepreneurial Behaviour & Research*, *26*(5), 937–971. doi:10.1108/IJEBR-04-2018-0236

Lane, C. (2004). *Institutional transformation and system change: changes in corporate governance of Germancorporations* (Reihe Soziologie / Institut für Höhere Studien, Abt. Soziologie, 65). Wien: Institut für Höhere Studien (IHS). https://nbn-resolving.org/urn:nbn:de:0168-ssoar-220637

Langford, M., Sumner, A., & Yamin, A. E. (Eds.). (2013). *The Millennium Development Goals and Human Rights: Past, Present and Future*. Cambridge University Press. doi:10.1017/CBO9781139410892

Lans, T., Blok, V., & Wesselink, R. (2014). Learning apart and together: Towards an integrated competence framework for sustainable entrepreneurship in higher education. *Journal of Cleaner Production*, *62*, 37–47. doi:10.1016/j.jclepro.2013.03.036

Law on the Fundamentals of the Education System. (2009). *Official Gazette of RS, 72*.

Lee, J. (2021, September 25). ESG boost for small businesses. *The Star Malaysia*, 1–8. https://www.thestar.com.my/business/business-news/2021/09/25/esg-boost-for-small-businesses

Compilation of References

Lee, C., Lee, H., Lee, J., & Park, J. (2014). A multiple group analysis of the training transfer model: Exploring the differences between high and low performers in a Korean insurance company. *International Journal of Human Resource Management, 25*(20), 2837–2857. doi:10.1080/09585192.2014.934887

Lee, J., & Negrelli, K. (2018). Cultural Identification, Acculturation, and Academic Experience Abroad: A Case of a Joint Faculty-Led Short-Term Study Abroad Program. *Journal of International Students, 8*(2), 1152–1072. https://doi.org/10.32674/jis.v8i2.138

LeRoy, G. (2005). *The Great American Jobs Scam: Corporate Tax Dodgingand the Myth of Job Creation.* Berrett-Koehler Publishers.

Lettinga, D., & van Troost, L. (Eds.). (2015). *Can Human Rights Bring Social Justice?: Twelve Essays.* Amnesty International Netherlands.

Lima Magalhães, M. (2011). *Cleber Cristiano Prodanov Jesuítas, culturas nativas y colonos: relaciones socio-interculturales en América Latina Diálogos.* Academic Press.

Lim, D. H., & Nowell, B. (2014). Integration for training transfer: Learning, knowledge, organizational culture, and technology. In *Transfer of Learning in Organizations* (pp. 81–98). Springer. doi:10.1007/978-3-319-02093-8_6

Lim, W. M. (2017). Inside the sustainable consumption theoretical toolbox: Critical concepts for sustainability, consumption, and marketing. *Journal of Business Research, 78*, 69–80. doi:10.1016/j.jbusres.2017.05.001

Lindqvist, E., Sigurjonsson, H., Möllermark, C., Rinder, J., Farnebo, F., & Lundgren, T. (2017, June). Quality of life improves early after gender reassignment surgery in transgender women. *European Journal of Plastic Surgery, 40*(3), 223–226. doi:10.100700238-016-1252-0 PMID:28603386

List of All Projects. (2021, June 24). *New Development Bank.* https://www.ndb.int/projects/list-of-all-projects/?country_name=4&status_name=1

Lord, J. E., Raja, D. S., & Blanck, P. (2013). Beyond the orthodoxy of rule of law and justice sector reform: A framework for legal empowerment and innovation through the convention on the rights of persons with disabilities. *World Bank Legal Review, 4*, 45.

Lozano, R., Carpenter, A., & Huisingh, D. (2015). A review of 'theories of the firm and their contributions to Corporate Sustainability. *Journal of Cleaner Production, 106*, 430–442. doi:10.1016/j.jclepro.2014.05.007

Lückmann, P., & Feldmann, C. (2017). Success factors for business process improvement projects in small and medium sized enterprises - Empirical evidence. *Procedia Computer Science, 121*, 439–445. doi:10.1016/j.procs.2017.11.059

Lukač-Zoranić, A. Ivanović R. A. (2014), *Interkulturalno obrazovanje: Nužnost današnjice Interkulturalno obrazovanje: Nužnost današnjice /Intercultura educationa: necessity o nowadays, Zbornik radova II Međunarodne konferencije* "Bosna i hercegovina i euroatlantske integracije - Trenutni izazovi i perspektive", god. 2, br. 2, tom II, UDK 37-01, Pravni fakultet Biha ći Centar za društvena istraživanja Internacionalnog Burč Univerziteta, Bihać, 2014, str. 1081-1999.

Ly, B. (2020). The rationale of European countries' engagement in AIIB. *Cogent Business & Management, 7*(1), 1772619. Advance online publication. doi:10.1080/23311975.2020.1772619

Lytovchenko, I. (2016). Corporate university as a form of employee training and development in American companies. *Advanced Education, 0*(5), 35–41. doi:10.20535/2410-8286.62280

Madzar, Lj. (2015). Economic effects of the interactions of globalization and culture. In *Globalization and Culture* (pp. 20–32). Institute of Social Sciences, Center for Economic Research. https://www.idn.org.rs/biblioteka/Ekonomisti2015.pdf

Maimbo, S. M., & Zadek, S. (2017). *Roadmap for a sustainable financial system*. Retrieved from http:// unepinquiry. org/publication/roadmap-for-a-sustainable-financial-system/

Malay Mail. (2021, October 15). Finance minister: Wage subsidy programme applications hit RM12.94b as at Oct 1. *Malay Mail Malaysia*, p. 5. https://www.malaymail.com/news/malaysia/2021/10/15/finance-minister-wage-subsidy-programme-applications-hit-rm12.94b-as-at-oct/2013687

Manetovic, E. (2016). Serbian National Identity: A Look Beyond the Modernization Paradigm. *Serbian Science Today, 1*(1), 18–29.

Mannila, S. (2015). Informal Employment and Vulnerability in Less Developed Markets. In J. Vuori, R. Blonk, & R. H. Price (Eds.), *Sustainable Working Lives*. Springer. doi:10.1007/978-94-017-9798-6_2

Maqableh, M., Jaradat, M., & Azzam, A. (2021). Exploring the determinants of students' academic performance at university level: The mediating role of internet usage continuance intention. *Education and Information Technologies, 26*(4), 4003–4025. doi:10.100710639-021-10453-y PMID:33584119

Marcus, G., & Fischer, M. M. J. (1999). *Anthropology and Cultural Critique: An Experimental Moment in the Human Sciences* (2nd ed.). University of Chicago Press.

Marika, R., Ngurruwutthun, D., & White, L. (1992). Always together, yaka gäna: Participatory research at Yirrkala as part of the development of a Yolngu education. *Convergence (Toronto), 25*, 23–39.

Marini, A., & Genereux, R. (1995). The challenge of teaching for transfer. In A. McKeough, J. Lupart, & A. Marini (Eds.), *Teaching for Transfer: Fostering Generalization in Learning* (pp. 1–19). Lawrence Erlbaum Associates, Inc.

Marković, Lj., & Prnjat, Z. (2011). Incorporating Socio-intercultural Communicative Competence in ESP Courses: Design of Materials and Activities for the Students of Economics, Finance and Trade. In B. Đorić-Francuski (Ed.), *Image_Identiy_Reality* (pp. 83–96). Cambridge Scholars Publishing.

Marks, S.P. (2005). The human rights framework for development: Seven approaches. *Reflections on the Right to Development*, 23-60.

Martin, A. (2005). DigEuLit – A European Framework for Digital Literacy: A Progress Report. *Journal of e-Literacy, 2*, 130-136.

Martin, A., & Grudziecki, J. (2006). DigEuLit: Concepts and Tools for Digital Literacy Development. *Innovation in Teaching and Learning in Information and Computer Sciences, 5*(4), 249–267. doi:10.11120/ital.2006.05040249

Martin, H. J. (2010). Improving training impact through effective follow-up: Techniques and their application. *Journal of Management Development, 29*(6), 520–534. doi:10.1108/02621711011046495

Masino, S., & Niño-Zarazúa, M. (2016). What works to improve the quality of student learning in developing countries? *International Journal of Educational Development, 48*, 53–65. doi:10.1016/j.ijedudev.2015.11.012

Mason, E. S., & Asher, R. E. (1973). The World Bank since Bretton Woods; the origins, policies, operations, and impact of the International Bank for Reconstruction and Development and the other members of the World Bank group: the International Finance Corporation, the International Development Association [and] the International Centre for Settlement of Investment Disputes. Brookings Institution Press.

Mason, J. (2002). *Qualitative researching*. Sage.

Compilation of References

Mässing, C. (2017). *Success factors and challenges for E-learning Technologies in the Namibian Higher Education System: A case study of the University of Namibia* [Bachelor's thesis, University of Skövde]. https://www.diva-portal.org/smash/get/diva2:1111480/FULLTEXT01.pdf

Mather, M., & Sarkans, A. (2018). Student perceptions of online and face-to-face learning. *International Journal of Curriculum and Instruction, 10*(2), 61–76.

Matkovic, G. (2014). *Poverty Measurement-Theoretical Concept, Situation and Recommendations for the Republic of Serbia*. Team for Social Inclusion and Poverty Reduction of the Government of the Republic of Serbia.

Mattingly, C. (2006). Pocahontas goes to the clinic: Popular culture as lingua franca in a cultural borderland. *American Anthropologist, 108*(3), 494–501. doi:10.1525/aa.2006.108.3.494 PMID:20706562

Mayer, C.-H., & Louw, L. (2012). Managing cross-cultural conflicts in organizations. *International Journals of Cross-Cultural Management, 12*(1), 3–8. doi:10.1177/1470595811413104

Mayer, C.-H. (2011). *The meaning of sense of coherence in transcultural management*. Waxmann.

Mayer, C.-H., & Boness, C. M. (2011). Culture and conflict in urban Tanzania: Professionals' voices in educational organizations. *African Journal on Conflict Resolution, 11*(2), 59–83. https://doi.org/10.4314/ajcr.v11i2.69833

McArthur, J. W., & Werker, E. (2016). Developing countries and international organizations: Introduction to the special issue. *The Review of International Organizations, 11*(2), 155–169. doi:10.100711558-016-9251-2

McCann, D., & Berry, C. (2017). *Shareholder Capitalism, System Crisis*. New Economics Foundation.

McKie, A. (2020). *Lack of study space and poor connections hinder online learning*. Retrieved October 11, 2021, from https://www.timeshighereducation.com/news/lack-study-space-and-poor-connections-hinder-online-learning

McKinnon, R. I. (1989). Financial liberalization and economic development: A reassessment of interest-rate policies in Asia and Latin America. *Oxford Review of Economic Policy, 5*(4), 29–54. doi:10.1093/oxrep/5.4.29

Mendez, A. (2019). Latin America and the AIIB: Interests and Viewpoints. *Global Policy, 10*(4), 639–644. doi:10.1111/1758-5899.12733

Mendez, A., & Turzi, M. (2020). *The Political Economy of China–Latin America Relations. The AIIB Membership*. Springer. doi:10.1007/978-3-030-33451-2

Mensah, J., & Casadevall, S. R. (2019). Sustainable development: Meaning, history, principles, pillars, and implications for human action: Literature review. *Cogent Social Sciences, 5*(1), 1653531. doi:10.1080/23311886.2019.1653531

Merhi, T. E. T. C. (2021). Transexualidade na atenção primária de saúde: Um relato de experiência em uma unidade de uma cidade em Goiás. *Brazilian Journal of Development, 7*(1), 7074–7082. doi:10.34117/bjdv7n1-479

Methé, B. A., Nelson, K. E., Pop, M., Creasy, H. H., Giglio, M. G., Huttenhower, C., ... Mannon, P. J. (2012). A framework for human microbiome research. *Nature, 486*(7402), 215.

Meuleman, L., & Niestroy, I. (2015). Common but differentiated governance: A meta governance approach to make the SDGs work. *Sustainability, 7*, 12295-12321.

Meyer, S. D., & Hathaway, W. (1993). Competition and cooperation in social movement coalitions. Lobbying for peace in the 1980s. *Berkeley Journal of Sociology, 38*, 157–183.

Michaelowa, K., & Weber, A. (2008). *Aid effectiveness in primary, secondary and tertiary education*. Background paper prepared for the Education for All Monitoring Report.

Michaelowa, K., & Weber, A. (2006). Aid effectiveness in the education sector: A dynamic panel analysis. In *Theory and practice of foreign aid*. Emerald Group Publishing Limited.

Miletic, D., & Sovtic, K. (2018). Poverty as a national and regional problem of the Republic of Serbia [Siromaštvo kao nacionalni i regionalni problem Republike Srbije]. *Proceeding Regional Development and Border Cooperation, II International Scientific Conference*, 339-350.

Milner, H. V. (2005). Globalization, Development, and International Institutions: Normative and Positive Perspectives. *Perspectives on Politics, 3*(4), 833–854. doi:10.1017/S1537592705050474

Milutinović, J., & Zuković, S. (2007). Obrazovanje i kulturni pluralizam. *Pedagogija, 62*(1), 23–33.

Ministry of Economy Sector for Regional Development and Strategic Economic Analysis Republic of Serbia. (2013). *Serbia Regional Development Report.* Author.

Ministry of Finance Belgrade of Serbia. (2019). *Macroeconomic and Fiscal Data.* Author.

Ministry of Foreign Affairs and International Trade. (2019). *Impact on Zimbabwe and the region of the unilateral sanctions imposed by the United States of America and the European Union*. Retrieved September 20, 2021 from http://www.zimfa.gov.zw/index.php/component/k2/item/49-impact-on-zimbabwe-and-the-region-of-the-unilateral-sanctions-imposed-by-the-united-states-of-america-and-the-european-union

Ministry of Public Service, Labour and Social Service. (2020). *Zimbabwe Progress Review Report of Sustainable Development Goals (SDGs)*. Retrieved September 10, 2021, from https://www.mpslsw.gov.zw/download/zimbabwe-sdgs-progress-report-december-2020-pdf/

Mittler, P. (2004). *Working towards Inclusive Education*. David Fulton Publishers Ltd.

Mladenovic, B. (2017). *Poverty in the Republic of Serbia 2006-2016.* Team for Social Inclusion and Poverty Reduction of the Government of Serbia.

Mochizuki, Y., & Fadeeva, Z. (2010). Competences for sustainable development and sustainability: Significance and challenges for ESD. *International Journal of Sustainability in Higher Education, 11*(4), 391–403. doi:10.1108/14676371011077603

Mohammad, W. M. W., & Wasiuzzaman, S. (2021, June). Environmental, social and governance (ESG) disclosure, competitive advantage and performance of firms in Malaysia. *Cleaner Environmental Systems, 2*, 1–11. doi:10.1016/j.cesys.2021.100015

Mohanakumari, D., & Magesh, R. (2017). Competency Development through Training and Development: An Empirical Study. *Indian Journal of Scientific Research, 14*(1), 69–70.

Monbiot, G. (2016). *How did we get into this mess? Politics, equality, nature.* Verso Books.

Morgan, G., Rocha, G., & Poynting, S. (2005). Grafting Cultures: Longing and Belonging in Immigrants' Ottaviano G.I.P., G. Peri (2005), Cities and cultures. *Journal of Urban Economics, 58*, 304–337.

Morphy, H. (2007). *Becoming Art: Exploring Cross-Cultural Categories*. Berg.

Morten. (2003). *Global Institutions and development: Framing the world?* https://www.researchgate.net

Movius, L. (2010). Cultural Globalisation and Challenges to traditional communication Theories. *Journal of Media and Communication, 2*(1). https://www.researchgate.net/publication/267254633_Cultural_Globalisation_and_ChallenGes_to_traditional_CommuniCation_theories

Moyo, D. (2009). Why foreign aid is hurting Africa. *The Wall Street Journal, 21*, 1-2.

Compilation of References

Muddiman, D. (2000). Theories of Social Exclusion and The Public Library: the chapter. In *Open to All?* (pp. 1–15). The Public Library and Social Exclusion. https://core.ac.uk/download/pdf/11879329.pdf

Muduli, A., Vinita, K., & Ali, Q. (2018). Pedagogy or andragogy? – Views of Indian graduate business. *IIMB Management Review*, *21*(3), 161–178.

Muha, A. V. (2003). Sodobni položaj nacionalnih jezikov v luči jezikovne politike [Modern position of national languages regarding to the language policy]. Ljubljana: Filozofska fakulteta

Muhumed, M. M., & Sayid, A. G. (2016). The World Bank and IMF in Developing Countries: Helping or Hindering? *International Journal of African and Asian Studies*, *28*, 39–49.

Muller, S. (2008). Accountability constructions, contestations, and implications: Insights from working in a yolngu cross-cultural institution, Australia. *Geography Compass*, *2*(2), 1–19. doi:10.1111/j.1749-8198.2007.00087.x

Murray & Raynolds. (2007). Globalization and its antimonies: Negotiating a FairTrade Movement. In Fair Trade: The challenges in transforming globalization. Routledge.

Murray, M. C., & Perez, J. (2014). Unraveling the digital literacy paradox: How higher education fails at the fourth literacy. *Issues in Informing Science and Information Technology*, *11*, 85–100. doi:10.28945/1982

Mustaffa, A. H., Ahmad, N., & Bahrudin, N. Z. (2021). A systematic literature review on barriers to green financing participation worldwide. *Global Business and Management Research*, *13*(4), 66–79.

Mwasalwiba, E. S. (2010). Entrepreneurship education: A review of its objectives, teaching methods, and impact indicators. *Education + Training*, *52*(1), 20–47. doi:10.1108/00400911011017663

Mwasalwiba, E., Dahles, H., & Wakkee, I. (2012). Graduate Entrepreneurship in Tanzania: Contextual Enablers and Hindrances. *European Journal of Scientific Research*, *76*, 386–402.

Myers, M. D., & Tan, F. B. (2003). *Beyond Models of National Culture in Information Systems Research*. IGI Global.

Myrdal, G. (1992). The Equality Issue in World Development. In Nobel Lectures, Economics, 1969-1980. Singapore: World Scientific Publishing.

Nakib, M., & Dey, P. K. (2018). The journey towards integrated reporting in Bangladesh. *Asian Economic and Financial Review*, *8*(7), 894–913. doi:10.18488/journal.aefr.2018.87.894.913

Namibia Statistics Agency (NSA). (2012). *Namibia 2011 population and housing census main report*. https://cms.my.na/assets/documents/p19dmn58guram30ttun89rdrp1.pdf

Na-nan, K. (2010). A causal model of factors affecting transfer of training. *Journal of Education*, *9*(1), 93–109.

Narlikar & Odell. (2006). *The Strict Distributive Strategy for a Bargaining Coalition: The Like Minded Group in the World Trade Organization*. Academic Press.

National Development Strategy 1. (2020). *National Development Strategy 1- January 2021 – December 2025: Towards a prosperous & empowered upper middle income society by 2030*. Retrieved September 1, 2021, from https://www.veritaszim.net/sites/veritas_d/files/NDS.pdf

National Strategy for Sustainable Development of Serbia. (2008). Available at: http: / /indicator.sepa.gov.rs/slike/pdf/o-indikatorima/nacionalna-strategija-odrzivog-razvoja-srbije

Nazli, N. N. N. N., & Khairudin, S. M. H. S. (2018). The factors that influence transfer of training and its effect on organizational citizenship behaviour. *Journal of Workplace Learning*, *30*(2), 121–146. doi:10.1108/JWL-09-2017-0080

NDIA (National Digital Inclusion Alliance). (2021). *Digital Inclusion: Definition*. https://www.digitalinclusion.org/definitions/

Neagu, G., Berigel, M., & Lendzhova, V. (2021). How Digital Inclusion Increase Opportunities for Young People: Case of NEETs from Bulgaria, Romania, and Turkey. *Sustainability*, *13*(7894), 7894. Advance online publication. doi:10.3390u13147894

Neck, H. M., & Greene, P. G. (2011). Entrepreneurship education: Known worlds and new Frontiers. *Journal of Small Business Management*, *49*(1), 55–70. doi:10.1111/j.1540-627X.2010.00314.x

Newig, J., Vob, J.P., & Monstadt, J. (2007). Governance for sustainable development in the face of ambivalence, uncertainty and distributed power: An introduction. *Journal of Environment Policy Plan, 9*, 185-192.

Newman, J., Barnes, M., Sullivan, H., & Knops, A. (2004). Public participation and collaborative governance. *Journal of Social Policy*, *33*(2), 203–223. doi:10.1017/S0047279403007499

Ng, E. (2021). What is ESG and why does it matter for business and investors? *South China Morning Post*. https://www.scmp.com/business/companies/article/3132470/what-esg-and-why-does-it-matter-businesses-and-investors

Ng, K. H., & Ahmad, R. (2018). Personality traits, social support, and training transfer: The mediating mechanism of motivation to improve work through learning. *Personnel Review*, *47*(1), 39–59. doi:10.1108/PR-08-2016-0210

Ng, T. H., Lye, C. T., Chan, K. H., Lim, Y. Z., & Lim, Y. S. (2020). Sustainability in Asia: The roles of financial development in environmental, social and governance (ESG) performance. *Social Indicators Research*, *150*(1), 17–44. doi:10.100711205-020-02288-w

Niinimäki, K. (2007). *Eettisenkuluttamisentulevaisuuskuvia. Futura, 4*, 58–75.

Noll, G., Older-Aguilar, D., Gregory Rosston, G., & Ross, R. R. (2001). The Digital Divide: Definitions, Measurement, and Policy Issues. Bridging the Digital Divide, 1-28.

Nonaka, I., & Takeuchi, H. (1995). *The knowledge-creating company*. Oxford University Press.

Noorizan, M. M., Afzan, N. F., & Akma, A. S. (2016). The moderating effects of motivation on work environment and training transfer: A preliminary analysis. *Procedia Economics and Finance*, *37*, 158–163. doi:10.1016/S2212-5671(16)30107-1

North, D. C. (1990). *Institutions, Institutional Change and Economic Performance*. Cambridge University Press. doi:10.1017/CBO9780511808678

NSA. (2021). *NSDI metadata browser*. http://geofind.nsa.org.na/

Nsouli, S. M. (2003). *The Changing Institutional Needs of the Transition Economies and the Role of the IMF*. Paper presented to the East-West Conference, Vienna, Austria.

Nunes, L. R. (2016). *Metamorfoses: identidades e papéis de género. Um estudo com Transhomens* [Master's thesis]. Universidade de Évora, Portugal.

Nursen, İ., Tomruk, M., Sevi, S., Karadibak, D., & Savc, S. (2018). The relationship between learning styles and academic performance in TURKISH physiotherapy students. *BMC Medical Education*, *18*(291), 1–8. doi:10.118612909-018-1400-2 PMID:30514280

Nur, Y. F. A., Ruhizan, M. Y., & Bekri, R. M. (2015). Learning transfer in national occupational skill standard (NOSS) system and workplace learning: How training design affect it? *Procedia: Social and Behavioral Sciences*, *174*, 156–163. doi:10.1016/j.sbspro.2015.01.641

Compilation of References

Nwanji, T. I., & Howell, K. E. (2007). A review of the two main competing models of corporate governance: The shareholdership model versus the stakeholdership model. *Corporate Ownership and Control, 5*(1), 9–23. doi:10.22495/cocv5i1p1

Nyambegera, S. M., Kamoche, K., & Siebers, L. Q. (2016). Integrating Chinese and African culture into human resource management practice to enhance employee job satisfaction. *Journal of Language. Technology and Entrepreneurship in Africa, 7*(2), 118–139.

O'Connell, M., & Ward, A. M. (2020). Shareholder Theory/Shareholder Value. Encyclopedia of Sustainable Management, 1-7.

O'Donnell, G. (1999). Horizontal accountability in new democracies. In A. Schedler, L. Diamond, & M. F. Plattner (Eds.), *The Self-Restraining State: Power and Accountability in the New Democracies*. Lynne Rienner Publishers.

O'Malley, P. (1998). Indigenous governances. In M. Dean & B. Hindess (Eds.), *Governing Australia: Studies in contemporary rationalities of government* (pp. 156–172). Cambridge University Press.

O'Sullivan, M. A. (2000). *Contests for Corporate Control. Corporate governance and economic performance in the United States and Germany*. Oxford University Press.

Obschonka, M., Stuetzer, M., Audretsch, D. B., Rentfrow, P. J., Potter, J., & Gosling, S. D. (2016). Macropsychological Factors Predict Regional Economic Resilience during a Major Economic Crisis. *Social Psychological & Personality Science, 7*(2), 95–104. doi:10.1177/1948550615608402

Odom, S. L. (2002). Learning about the barriers to facilitators of inclusion for young children with disabilities. In S. L. Odom (Ed.), *Widening the circle: Including children with disabilities in preschool programs* (pp. 1–9). Teachers' college Press.

OECD. (2001). *Understanding the Digital Divide*. https://www.oecd.org/digital/ieconomy/1888451.pdf

OECD. (2016). *Innovating Education and Educating for Innovation: The Power of Digital Technologies and Skills*. OECD Publishing. doi:10.1787/9789264265097-

OECD. (2020). *Strengthening online learning when schools are closed - The role of families and teachers in supporting students during the COVID-19 crisis*. OECD. https://read.oecd-ilibrary.org/view/?ref=136_136615-o13x4bkowa&title=Strengthening-online-learning-when-schools-are-closed

Official Gazette of the Republic of Serbia, No. 149/20.

Official Gazette of the Republic of Serbia, No. 74/10, 4/12, 44/18 - State Law 69/19.

Oliver. (2019). *BMC Public Health*. https://bmcpublichealth.biomedcentral.com

Oliver, C. (1997). Sustainable competitive advantage: Combining institutional and resource-based views. *Strategic Management Journal, 18*(9), 697–713. doi:10.1002/(SICI)1097-0266(199710)18:9<697::AID-SMJ909>3.0.CO;2-C

Oliver, J., Vesty, G., & Brooks, A. (2016). Conceptualising integrated thinking in practice. *Managerial Auditing Journal, 31*(2), 228–248. doi:10.1108/MAJ-10-2015-1253

Oljača, M. (2006). Stereotipi i predrasude u vaspitno-obrazovnom procesu. In *Modeli stručnog usavršavanja nastavnika za interkulturalno vaspitanje i obrazovanje*. Filozofski fakultet.

Olufemi, O. T., Adediran, A. A., & Oyediran, W. O. (2018). Factors affecting students' academic performance in colleges of education in southwest, Nigeria. *Brock Journal of Education, 6*(10), 43–56.

371

Organisation for Economic Co-operation and Development (OECD). (2020). *The impact of COVID-19 on student equity and inclusion: supporting vulnerable students during school closures and school re-openings.* https://www.oecd.org/coronavirus/policy-responses/the-impact-of-covid-19-on-student-equity-and-inclusion-supporting-vulnerable-students-during-school-closures-and-school-re-openings-d593b5c8/

Oshewolo, S. (2011). Poverty Reduction and the Attainment of the MDGS in Nigeria: Problems and Prospects. *Africana, 5*(2), 211–238.

Oviawe, J. I. (2018). Revamping Technical Vocational Education and Training through Public-Private Partnerships for Skill Development. *Makerere Journal of Higher Education, 10*(1), 73–91. doi:10.4314/majohe.v10i1.5

Oxenstierna, S. (Ed.). (2015). *The Challenges for Russia's Politicized Economic System.* Routledge. doi:10.4324/9781315757780

Paechter, M., & Maier, B. (2010). Internet and higher education online or face-to-face? students' experiences and preferences in e-learning. *The Internet and Higher Education, 13*(4), 292–297. doi:10.1016/j.iheduc.2010.09.004

Page, D. (2008). Systematic literature searching and the bibliographic database haystack. *Electronic Journal of Business Research Methods, 6*(2), 171–180.

Parahoo, K. (2006). *Nursing research: Principles, process and issues.* Palgrave Macmillan.

Parasuram, K. (2006). Variables that affect teachers' attitudes towards disability and inclusive education in Mumbai, India. *Disability & Society, 21*(3), 231–242. doi:10.1080/09687590600617352

Parizek, M., & Stephen, M. D. (2020). The long march through the institutions: Emerging powers and the staffing of international organizations. *Cooperation and Conflict, 56*(2), 204–223. doi:10.1177/0010836720966017

Parmar, B. L., Freeman, R. E., Harrison, J. S., Wicks, A. C., Purnell, L., & De Colle, S. (2010). Stakeholder theory: The state of the art. *The Academy of Management Annals, 4*(1), 403–445. doi:10.5465/19416520.2010.495581

Pasalic-Kreso, A. (2003). The Genesis of the maturation of the idea of inclusion or inclusion in the function of reducing inequality in education. In A. Pasalic-Kreso (Ed.), *Inclusion in Education of Bosnia and Herzegovina* (pp. 2–24). Department of Pedagogy, Faculty of Philosophy in Sarajevo.

Pattberg, P., & Stripple, J. (2008). Beyond the public and private divide: Remapping transnational climate governance in the 21st century. *International Environmental Agreements: Politics, Law and Economics, 84*(4), 367–88.

Paul, J., & Jefferson, F. (2019). A comparative analysis of student performance in an online vs. face-to-face environmental science course from 2009 to 2016. *Frontiers of Computer Science, 1*(November), 7. Advance online publication. doi:10.3389/fcomp.2019.00007

Paulo, S., Shewbridge, C., Nusche, D., & Herzog, H. D. (2009). Evaluation and assessment frameworks for improving school outcomes: common policy challenges. *Education and Training Policy, 21*, 1–10. https://www.oecd.org/education/school/46927511.pdf

Pedota, L. (2011). *Indigenous intercultural universities in Latin America: Interpreting interculturalism in Mexico and Bolivia* [Thesis]. Loyola University. http://ecommons.luc.edu/luc_theses/516

Pejovich, S. (2008). *Law, Informal Rules and Economic Efficiency – The Case for Common Law.* Edward Elgar. http://www.fintp.hr/upload/files/ftp/2009/1/badjun2.pdf

Penco, L., Ivaldi, E., Bruzzi, C., & Musso, E. (2020). Knowledge-based urban environments and entrepreneurship: Inside EU cities. *Cities (London, England), 96*, 102443. doi:10.1016/j.cities.2019.102443

Compilation of References

Perakis, R., & Savedoff, W. (2015). Does results-based aid change anything? Pecuniary interests, attention, accountability and discretion in four case studies. *CGD Policy Paper, 52.*

Perez, C. (2002). *Technological Revolutions and Financial Capital: The Dynamics of Bubbles and Golden Ages.* Edward Elgar Editorial. doi:10.4337/9781781005323

Perotti, A. (1995). *Interkulturalni odgoj i obrazovanje.* Educa.

Peters, B.G. (2018). *The Logic of Policy Design.* https://www.elgaronline.com/view

Petrović i sar. (2010). Kako budući učitelji vide položaj Roma u sistemu obrazovanja? In *Socijalna pedagogija u nastajanju –traženje odgovora na probleme društveno –isključenih grupa.* Jagodina: Pedagoški fakultet.

Petrov, P., Dijkstra, H., Đokić, K., Zartsdahl, P. H., & Mahr, E. (2019). All hands on deck: Levels of dependence between the EU and other international organizations in peacebuilding. *journal of European Integration, 41*(8), 1027–1043. doi:10.1080/07036337.2019.1622542

Phillips, V., & Barker, E. (2021). Systematic reviews: Structure, form and content. *Journal of Perioperative Practice, 31*(9), 349–353. doi:10.1177/1750458921994693 PMID:34228554

Piechota, G. (2014). The Role of social media in Creating Socio-intercultural Dialogue and Overcoming Prejudice –a Comparative Analysis of Pilot Survey Results. *KOME – An International Journal of Pure Communication Inquiry, 2*(2), 37-63.

Pineda, E., Valencia, O., & Andrian, L. (2020). *Possible macro-fiscal consequences of COVID-19 in Latin America.* Inter-American Development Bank.

Piron, L. H., & O'Neil, T. (2016). Integrating human rights into development: donor approaches, experiences and challenges (No. 111914). The World Bank.

Plummer, D., Kearney, S., Monagle, A., Collins, H., Perry, V., Moulds, A., & Lewis, C. (2021). *Skills and Competency Framework-Supporting the development and adoption of the Information Management Framework (IMF) and the National Digital Twin.* Academic Press.

Plumptre, T., & Graham, J. (1999). *Governance and Good Governance: International and Aboriginal Perspectives.* Institute on Governance.

Pookulangara, S., Shephard, A., & Mestres, J. (2011). University community's perception of sweatshops: A mixed method data collection. *International Journal of Consumer Studies, 35*(4), 476–483. doi:10.1111/j.1470-6431.2010.00950.x

Popesku, C. (Ed.). (2021). *The Impact of COVID-19 on Inclusive Education at the European Level.* European Agency for Special Needs and Inclusive Education. https://www.european-agency.org/sites/default/files/COVID-19-Impact-Literature-Review.pdf

Porter, T. (2009). Global governance as configurations of state/non-state activity. In J. Whitman (Ed.), *Palgrave advances in global governance.* Palgrave Macmillan. doi:10.1057/9780230245310_5

Pradhan, R. P., Arvin, M. B., Nair, M., & Bennett, S. E. (2020). Sustainable economic growth in the European Union: The role of ICT, venture capital, and innovation. *Review of Financial Economics, 38*(1), 34–62. doi:10.1002/rfe.1064

Prahalad, C. K., & Hart, S. L. (2002). Strategy and business. *The Fortune at the Bottom of the Pyramid, 26,* 2–14.

Pricewaterhousecooper, L. (2003). *Shareholders' Questions: Questions That May Be Asked At 2003 Shareholders' Meetings.* Pricewaterhouse Cooper.

Prinsloo, C. (2019). AIIB Membership for African Countries: Drawcards and Drawbacks. *Global Policy, 10*(4), 625–630. doi:10.1111/1758-5899.12734

PRME. (2018). *Search Participants*. Principles for Responsible Management Education. Available online: http://www.unprme.org/participation/index.php

Prnjat, Z. (2015). Welcome to Serbia: Using Blogs in an English for Tourism Course. *Proceedings of the 2nd International Conference on Teaching English for Specific Purposes and New Language Learning Technologies*, 478-484.

Projects | Multilateral Investment Guarantee Agency | World Bank Group. (2021). *MIGA*. https://www.miga.org/projects?host_country%5B%5D=495&project_status=All&env_category=All&project_type=All&board_date%5Bmin%5D=&board_date%5Bmax%5D=&title=&project_id=

Projects. (2021). *World Bank*. https://projects.vsemirnyjbank.org/ru/projects-operations/projects-list?countrycode_exact=RU&os=0

Psacharopoulos, G., & Arriagada, A. M. (1986). The educational composition of the labour force: An international comparison. *Int'l Lab. Rev., 125*, 561.

Putnam, R. (1993). *Making Democracy Work: Civic Traditions in Modern Italy*. Princeton University Press.

PwC Malaysia. (2021). *Family business survey 2021: The Malaysian chapter*. https://www.pwc.de/de/mittelstand/family-business-survey/pwc-intes-family-business-survey-2021.pdf

Radakovic, M. (2012). Problems in the construction of collective national identity. *Political Magazine, 11*(3), 153-169.

Raja, E., & Nagasubramani, P. C. (2018). Impact of modern technology in education. *Journal of Applied and Advanced Research, 3*(1). Advance online publication. doi:10.21839/jaar.2018.v3S1.165

Rajovic, V., & Jovanovic, O. (2010). Professional and private experience with people with special needs and attitudes of regular school teachers towards inclusion. *Psychological Research, 13*(1), 91-106.

Rakonic Leskovar, I. (2018). School librarian in inclusive education. *Librarianship* [in Croatian. *Knjižničarstvo, 22*(1-2), 29–44.

Ramos, T. B., Caeiro, S., Pires, S. M., & Videira, N. (2018). How are new sustainable development approaches responding to societal challenges? *Sustainable Development, 26*(2), 117–121. doi:10.1002d.1730

Randa, I. O. (2021). Corporate Social Responsibility Interventions for Namibia's Post-COVID-19 Sustainable Banking Sector. In Handbook of Research on Strategies and Interventions to Mitigate COVID-19 Impact on SMEs (pp. 48-73). IGI Global. doi:10.4018/978-1-7998-7436-2.ch003

Randa, I. O., & Atiku, S. O. (2021). SME Financial Inclusivity for Sustainable Entrepreneurship in Namibia During COVID-19. In Handbook of Research on Sustaining SMEs and Entrepreneurial Innovation in the Post-COVID-19 Era (pp. 373-396). IGI Global. doi:10.4018/978-1-7998-6632-9.ch018

Rangan, K., Chase, L., & Karim, S. (2012). *Why every company needs a CSR strategy and how to build it*. Harvard Business School Working Paper No. 12–088.

RATEL (Regulatory Agency for Electronic Communications and Postal Services). (2020). *An Overview of the Telecom and Postal Services Markets in the Republic of Serbia in 2019*. Author.

Ratkovic, M. S., Hebib, E. D., & Saljic, Z. S. (2017). Inclusion in education as a goal and content of reforms of modern school systems, *Teaching and Education, 66*(3), 437–450.

Compilation of References

Ravallion, M. (2013). *The Idea of Antipoverty Policy.* NBER Working Paper Series.

Ravallion, M. (2016). The World Bank: Why it is still needed and why it still disappoints. *The Journal of Economic Perspectives*, *30*(1), 77–94. doi:10.1257/jep.30.1.77

Raynolds, D. L., & Long, M. A. (2007). Fair/Alternative Trade: Historical and empirical dimensions. In L. T. Raynolds, D. L. Murray, & J. Wilkinson (Eds.), *Fair Trade: Thechallenges in transforming globalization.* Routledge. doi:10.4324/9780203933534

Raynolds, L. T. (2012). Fair Trade: Social regulation in global food markets. *Journal of Rural Studies*, *28*(3), 276–287. doi:10.1016/j.jrurstud.2012.03.004

Raynolds, L. T., & Greenfield, N. (2015). Fair Trade: Movements and markets. In L. T. Raynolds & E. A. Bennett (Eds.), *Handbook of Research on Fair Trade.* Edward Elgar Publishing. doi:10.4337/9781783474622.00010

Raynolds, L., Douglas, M., & Heller, A. (2007). Regulating sustainability in the coffeesector: A comparative analysis of third-party environmental and social certification initiatives. *Agriculture and Human Values*, *24*(2), 147–163. doi:10.100710460-006-9047-8

Reimers, F. M. (2009). Global competency. *Harvard International Review*, *30*(4), 24–27.

Ren, S., Wei, W., Sun, H., Xu, Q., Hu, Y., & Chen, X. (2020). Can mandatory environmental information disclosure achieve a win-win for a firm's environmental and economic performance? *Journal of Cleaner Production*, *250*, 119530. doi:10.1016/j.jclepro.2019.119530

Reynolds, A. D., Kadiu, I., Garg, S. K., Glanzer, J. G., Nordgren, T., Ciborowski, P., Banerjee, R., & Gendelman, H. E. (2008). Nitrated alpha-synuclein and microglial neuroregulatory activities. *Journal of Neuroimmune Pharmacology*, *3*(2), 59–74. doi:10.100711481-008-9100-z PMID:18202920

Rhodes, R. (2005). The unholy trinity of governance. The Blake Dawson Waldron Lecture, National Museum of Australia.

Ribeiro, L., Rosário, P., Núñez, J. C., Gaeta, M., & Fuentes, S. (2019). First-year students background and academic achievement: The mediating role of student engagement. *Frontiers in Psychology*, *10*, 2669. Advance online publication. doi:10.3389/fpsyg.2019.02669 PMID:31920775

Ribot, J. C. (2002). *Democratic decentralization of natural resources: Institutionalizing popular participation.* World Resources Institute.

Richardson, I. E. (2004). *H. 264 and MPEG-4 video compression: video coding for next-generation multimedia.* John Wiley & Sons.

Riddell, R. (2008). *Does foreign aid really work?* Oxford University Press.

Robins, H. S., Campregher, P. V., Srivastava, S. K., Wacher, A., Turtle, C. J., Kahsai, O., ... Carlson, C. S. (2009). Comprehensive assessment of T-cell receptor β-chain diversity in αβ T cells. *Blood. The Journal of the American Society of Hematology*, *114*(19), 4099–4107. PMID:19706884

Robinson, O. (2014). Sampling in interview-based qualitative research: A theoretical and practical guide. *Qualitative Research in Psychology*, *11*(1), 25–41. doi:10.1080/14780887.2013.801543

Rodrik, D. (2000). *Institutions for High-Quality Growth: What they are and how to acquire them.* Working Paper 7540.

Rodrik, D., Subramanian, A., & Trebbi, F. (2004). Institutions Rule: The Primacy of Institutions over Geography and Integration in Economic Development. *Journal of Economic Growth*, *9*(2), 131–165. doi:10.1023/B:JOEG.0000031425.72248.85

Rolle, L., Ceruti, C., Timpano, M., Falcone, M., & Frea, B. (2015). Quality of life after sexual reassignment surgery. In *Management of Gender Dysphoria* (pp. 193–203). Springer. doi:10.1007/978-88-470-5696-1_23

Rosenau, J. N. (2000). Change, complexity, and governance in globalizing space. In J. Pierre (Ed.), *Debating governance* (pp. 167–200). Oxford University Press.

Rosenzweig, M. R., & Schultz, T. P. (1982). Market opportunities, genetic endowments, and intrafamily resource distribution: Child survival in rural India. *The American Economic Review, 72*(4), 803–815.

Rosinski, P. (2011). Global coaching for organizational development. *The International Journal of Coaching in Organizations, 8*(2), 49–66.

Rossi, A. (2013). Does Economic Upgrading Lead to Social Upgrading in Global Production Networks? Evidence from Morocco. *World Development, 46*, 223–233. doi:10.1016/j.worlddev.2013.02.002

Rostow, W. W., & Rostow, W. W. (1990). *The stages of economic growth: A non-communist manifesto.* Cambridge University Press.

Rowbottom, N., & Locke, J. (2016). The emergence of Integrated Reporting. *Accounting and Business Research, 46*(1), 83–115. doi:10.1080/00014788.2015.1029867

Roxana-Ioana, B., & Petru, S. (2017). Integrated Reporting for a Good Corporate Governance. *Ovidius University Annals. Economic Sciences Series, 17*(1), 424–428.

Rozman, R. (2007). Pomeni in zahtevnost analiziranja za boljše odločanje [Meaning and complexity of analysis for better decision making]. In Zbornik referatov 13. Strokovnega posvetovanja o sodobnih vidikih analize poslovanja in organizacije [Collection of 13th edition of professional papers on professional consultations on modern aspects of business analysis and organization] (pp. 9-23). Portorož: Zveza ekonomistov Slovenije.

Rozman, R. (2008). Spreminjanje ulture v združbah [Changing culture in organizations]. In 9. znanstveno posvetovanje o organizaciji [9th Scientific consultation on the organization] (pp. 57-59). Ljubljana: Fakulteta za organizacijske vede.

Rozman, R. (2010). Razmerja med organizacijskimi procesi upravljanja in ravnateljevanja, koordinacije in odločanja [Relationships between organizational processes of management and governance, coordination, and decision-making]. In 11. znanstveno posvetovanje o organizaciji: Koordinacijski in komunikacijski vidiki organizacije združb [11th Scientific organizational consultation: Coordination and communication aspects of the organization entities] (pp. 15-21). Ljubljana: Fakulteta za organizacijske vede UM.

RSWEBSOLS. (2021). *Internet connectivity and its impact on students in Australia.* Retrieved October 12, 2021 from https://www.rswebsols.com/tutorials/internet/internet-connectivity-impact-students-australia

Russia and the Organization for Economic Cooperation and Development (OECD). (2016, November 2). *The Ministry of Foreign Affairs of the Russian Federation.* https://www.mid.ru/organizacia-ekonomiceskogo-sotrudnicestva-i-razvitia-oesr-/-/asset_publisher/km9HkaXMTium/content/id/2511808

Russia's cooperation with the World Bank. (2016, November 1). *The Ministry of Foreign Affairs of the Russian Federation.* https://www.mid.ru/vsemirnyj-bank-vb-/-/asset_publisher/km9HkaXMTium/content/id/2511066

Sadokhin, A. P. (2014). *The Introduction in intercultural communication theory: study guide.* KNORUS.

Saiz Álvarez, J. M. (2009). La Organización de Cooperación de Shanghai. Claves para la creación de un futuro líder mundial. *Revista de Economía Mundial, 23*, 307–326.

Saldana, J. (2016). *The coding manual for qualitative researchers* (3rd ed.). Sage Publications.

Compilation of References

Samans, R., & Nelson, J. (2020*). Integrated Corporate Governance: A Practical Guide to Stakeholder Capitalism for Boards of Directors*. Geneva: World Economic Forum.

Samsha. (2017). *Smart Goals fact sheet*. https://www.samhsa.gov

Sanders, W. (2003). *Participation and representation in the 2002 ATSIC elections*. CAEPR Discussion Paper No. 252, CAEPR, ANU.

Sanders, W. (2004). *Thinking about Indigenous community governance*. CAEPR Discussion Paper No. 262, CAEPR, ANU.

Santos, W. S. (2014). Uma reflexão pós-crítica sobre corpo, gênero, sexualidade no ambiente educacional. *Revista Sem Aspas*, *3*(1), 7.

Santti, J., & Salminen, J. (2015). Development of Teacher Education in Finland 1945-2015. *Hungarian Educational Research Journal*, *5*(3), 1–18.

Sapic, J. (2021). *Digital Inclusion 101: A Two-Fac Story*. https://socijalnoukljucivanje.gov.rs/sr

Save the children. (2003). *Annual report*. Retrieved, July 2021. https://www.savethechildren.org/content/dam/usa/reports/annual-report/annual-report/sc-2003-annualreport.pdf

Saviano, J. P. S. B. M., & Carrubbo, F. P. L. (2014). The contribution of VSA and SDL perspectives to strategic thinking in emerging economies. *Managing Service Quality*, *24*(6), 565–591. doi:10.1108/MSQ-09-2013-0199

Savic, N., & Radojicic, Z. (2011). Digital Divide in the Population of Serbia. *Issues in Informing Science and Information Technology, 8*. http://iisit.org/Vol8/IISITv8p245-258Savic293.pdf

Savin-Baden, M., Cousin, G., & Major, C. H. (2010). *New approaches to qualitative research: wisdom and uncertainty*. Routledge. doi:10.4324/9780203849873

Savoia, A., Easaw, J., & McKay, A. (2010). Inequality, Democracy, and Institutions: A Critical Review of Recent Research. *World Development*, *38*(2), 142–154. doi:10.1016/j.worlddev.2009.10.009

Schacter, M. (2000). *When accountability fails: A framework for diagnosis and action. Policy Brief No. 9*. Institute on Governance.

Schedler, A. (1999). Restraining the state: conflicts and agents of accountability. In A. Schedler, L. Diamond, & M. F. Plattner (Eds.), *The Self-Restraining State: Power and Accountability in the New Democracies*. Lynne Rienner Publishers.

Schein, E. H. (1990). Organizational culture. *American Psychologist*.

Schein, E. H. (2010). *Organizational culture and leadership*. John Wiley & Sons.

Schinasi, G. J., & Truman, E. M. (2010). *Reform of the global financial architecture*. Bruegel Working Paper, No. 2010/05, Bruegel.

Schramade, W., & Schoenmaker, D. (2018). *Royal Philips: A sustainable finance case*. Rotterdam School of Management Erasmus University.

Schroder, B. (2006). Native science, intercultural education, and place-conscious education: An Ecuadorian example. *Educational Studies*, *32*(3), 307–317. https://dx.doi.org/10.1080/03055690600845438

Schuelka, M. J. (2018). Implementing inclusive education. In *Helpdesk Report: Knowledge, evidence and learning for development*. University of Birmingham. https://assets.publishing.service.gov.uk/media/5c6eb77340f0b647b214c599/374_Implementing_Inclusive_Education.pdf

Schumpeter, J.A. (2000). Entrepreneurship as innovation. *Entrepreneurship: The social science view*, 51-75.

Scott, J. C. (1998). *Seeing Like a State: How Certain Schemes to Improve the Human Condition Have Failed*. Yale University Press.

Sekerin, V. D., Gaisina, L. M., Shutov, N. V., Abdrakhmanov, N. K., & Valitova, N. E. (2018). Improving the quality of competence-oriented training of personnel at industrial enterprises. *Calitatea*, *19*(165), 68–72.

Sekulovic, M. (2004). *Essays on transition*. Faculty of Economics in Nis.

Selman, P. (2001). Social capital, sustainability, and environmental planning. *Planning Theory & Practice*, *2*(1), 13–30. doi:10.1080/14649350122850

Selvaggi, G., & Bellringer, J. (2011). Gender reassignment surgery: An overview. *Nature Reviews. Urology*, *8*(5), 274–282. doi:10.1038/nrurol.2011.46 PMID:21487386

Sen, A. (2014). Development as freedom (1999). *The globalization and development reader: Perspectives on development and global change*, 525.

Setia, N., Abhayawansa, S., Joshi, M., & Huynh, A. V. (2015). Integrated reporting in South Africa: Some initial evidence. *Sustainability Accounting, Management and Policy Journal*, *6*(3), 397–424. doi:10.1108/SAMPJ-03-2014-0018

Shahibi, M. S., & Ku Rusli, N. K. K. (2017). The influence of internet usage on student's academic performance. *International Journal of Academic Research in Business & Social Sciences*, *7*(8), 873–887. doi:10.6007/IJARBSS/v7-i8/3301

Shakhray, S. M. (Ed.). (2016). *The Collapse of the USSR: Documents and Facts (1986–1992)*. Kuchkovo Field. http://www.fa.ru/org/div/museum/SiteAssets/Pages/1917-2017/%D0%A8%D0%B0%D1%85%D1%80%D0%B0%D0%B9%20%D0%A1.%D0%9C.%20%D0%A0%D0%B0%D1%81%D0%BF%D0%B0%D0%B4%20%D0%A1%D0%A1%D0%A1%D0%A0.%20%D0%94%D0%BE%D0%BA%D1%83%D0%BC%D0%B5%D0%BD%D1%82%D1%8B%20%D0%B8%20%D1%84%D0%B0%D0%BA%D1%82%D1%8B.pdf

Shantz, A., & Latham, G. P. (2012). Transfer of training: Written self-guidance to increase self-efficacy and interviewing performance of job seekers. *Human Resource Management*, *51*(5), 733–746. doi:10.1002/hrm.21497

Shaw, D., & Clarke, I. (1999). Belief formation in ethical consumer groups: An exploratory study. *Marketing Intelligence & Planning*, *17*(2), 109–119. doi:10.1108/02634509910260968

Shaw, D., Shiu, E., & Clarke, I. (2000). The contribution of Ethical Obligation and Self identity to the theory of planned behaviour: An exploration of ethical consumers. *Journal of Marketing Management*, *16*(8), 879–894. doi:10.1362/026725700784683672

Shea, T. M., & Bauer, A. M. (1997). *An Introduction to special education: A social systems perspective*. Brown & Benchmark.

Sheinis, E. Y. (2022, February 8). *Council of Mutual Economic Assistance*. The Great Russian Encyclopedia. https://bigenc.ru/domestic_history/text/3589191

Shen, Q., Chung, J. K. H., Challis, D., & Cheung, R. C. T. (2007). A comparative study of student performance in traditional mode and online mode of learning. *Computer Applications in Engineering Education*, *15*(1), 30–40. doi:10.1002/cae.20092

Sheth, J. N. (2011). Impact of emerging markets on marketing: Rethinking existing perspectives and practices. *Journal of Marketing*, *75*(4), 166–182. doi:10.1509/jmkg.75.4.166

Compilation of References

Shirley, M. M. (2005). Institutions and Development. In C. Ménard & M. M. Shirley (Eds.), *Handbook of New Institutional Economics*. Springer. doi:10.1007/0-387-25092-1_25

Shuja, A., Qureshi, A. I., Schaeffer, D. M., & Zareen, M. (2019). Effect of m- learning on students' academic performance mediated by facilitation discourse and flexibility. *Knowledge Management & E-Learning, 11*(2), 158–200.

Sibanda, D. M. (2016). *Zimbabwe position paper on Sustainable Development Goals (SDGs)*. Retrieved September 10, 2021, from https://www.scribd.com/document/510783065/Sibanda-SDG-Position-Paper-Presentation-11-May-2016-1

Siewart, R. (2007). *Ministerial powers to seize assets of service providers in prescribed areas within the Northern Territory*. Background Briefing, Parliament House. Available at <http://www.rachelsiewert.org.au/files/campaigns/extras/Briefing_on_NT_seizure_powers.pdf>

Silva, E. (2009). Measuring skills for 21st century learning. *Phi Delta Kappan, 90*(9), 630–634. doi:10.1177/003172170909000905

Simoulin, V. (2003). La gouvernance et l'action publique: Le succès d'une forme simmélienne. *Droit Social*, (54), 307–328. doi:10.3917/drs.054.0307

Sinkovec, B., & Cizelj, B. (2013). *Entrepreneurial Education & Innovation: Developing Entrepreneurial Mindset for knowledge Economy*. University of Wolverhampton, Knowledge Economy Network (KEN). Retrieved from https://www.knowledge-economy.net/uploads/documents/2013/workshops/wolverhampton/Wolverhampton%20Workshop%20-%20Analytical%20Compendium.pdf

Sirili, N., Frumence, G., Kiwara, A., Mwangu, M., Goicolea, I., & Hurtig, A. K. (2019). Public private partnership in the training of doctors after the 1990s¢ health sector reforms: The case of Tanzania. *Human Resources for Health, 17*(1), 1–11. doi:10.118612960-019-0372-6 PMID:31118038

Smith, D. E. (1995). Representative politics and the new wave of native title organisations. In J. Finlayson & D. E. Smith (Eds.), Native Title: Emerging Issues for Research, Policy and Practice. CAEPR Research Monograph No. 10. CAEPR, ANU.

Smith, D. E. (1996). From cultural diversity to regionalism: The political culture of difference in ATSIC. In P. Sullivan (Ed.), Shooting the Banker: Essays on ATSIC and Self-determination. North Australia Research Unit, ANU.

Smith, D. E. (2004). *From Gove to governance: Reshaping Indigenous governance in the Northern Territory*. CAEPR Discussion Paper No. 265, CAEPR, ANU.

Smith, D. E. (2007). Networked governance: Issues of process, policy, and power in a West Arnhem Land regional initiative. *Ngiya: Talk the Law. Governance in Indigenous Communities, 1*, 24–52.

Smith, J. A., Flowers, P., & Larkin, M. (2009). *Interpretative phenomenological analysis: Theory, method and research*. Sage.

Social Inclusion and Poverty Reduction Team. (2019). *Report on digital inclusion in the Republic of Serbia for the period from 2014 to 2018*. https://socijalnoukljucivanje.gov.rs/wp-content/uploads/2019/07/Izvestaj_o_digitalnoj_ukljucenosti_RS_2014-2018_lat.pdf

Social inclusion and poverty reduction unit. (2021). *Absolute poverty*. https://socijalnoukljucivanje.gov.rs/sr/социјално-укључивање-у-рс/статистикасиромаштва/апсолутно-сиромаштво/

Sommer, C. (2017). *Drivers and constraints for adopting sustainability standards in small and medium-sized enterprises (SMEs)*. Discussion paper. Deutsches Institut fur Entwicklungspolitik (DIE). https://www.econstor.eu/bitstream/10419/199511/1/die-dp-2017-21.pdf

SORS. (2018). *Publication.* https://www.stat.gov.rs/sr-latn/publikacije/

Soskice, D. (1999). Divergent production regimes: coordinated and uncoordinated market economies in the 1980s and 1990s. *Continuity and Change in Contemporary Capitalism, 38*, 101-134.

Soter, M. (2016). Theoretical Modelling of Socio-intercultural Communication Process. *Journal of Advocacy, Research and Education, 6*(2).

Spaulding, M. (2009). Perceptions of academic honesty in online vs. face-to-face classrooms. *Journal of Interactive Online Learning, 8*(3), 183–198.

Speziale, M. T. (2019). Theoretical perspectives on purposes and users of integrated reporting: a literature review. *Integrated Reporting*, 13-60.

Sretenov, D. (2008). *Creating an inclusive kindergarten.* Center for Applied Psychology.

St Clair, A. L. (2006). The World Bank as a transnational expertised institution. *Global Governance, 12*(1), 77–95. doi:10.1163/19426720-01201007

Stanimirovic, D. (1986). Attitudes of visually impaired people towards the blind. *Psychology, 19*, 104–119.

Stankovic, B. (2008). *Living Standards Study: Serbia 2002-2007: Poverty Profile in Serbia 2002-2007.* Statistical Office of the Republic of Serbia.

Statistical Yearbook of the Republic of Serbia. (2016). SORS.

Stead, R. H., Dixon, M. F., Bramwell, N. H., Riddell, R. H., & Bienenstock, J. (1989). Mast cells are closely apposed to nerves in the human gastrointestinal mucosa. *Gastroenterology, 97*(3), 575–585. doi:10.1016/0016-5085(89)90627-6 PMID:2666250

Steensma, T. D., Biemond, R., de Boer, F., & Cohen-Kettenis, P. T. (2011). Desisting and persisting gender dysphoria after childhood: A qualitative follow-up study. *Clinical Child Psychology and Psychiatry, 16*(4), 499–516. doi:10.1177/1359104510378303 PMID:21216800

Steger, M. (2013). Globalization: A very short introduction. Oxford. doi:10.1093/actrade/9780199662661.001.0001

Stephen, M. D., & Skidmore, D. (2019). AIIB in the Liberal International Order. *The Chinese Journal of International Politics, 12*(1), 61–91. doi:10.1093/cjip/poy021

Steyn, M. (2014). Organisational benefits and implementation challenges of mandatory integrated reporting: Perspectives of senior executives at South African listed companies. *Sustainability Accounting, Management and Policy Journal, 5*(4), 476–503. doi:10.1108/SAMPJ-11-2013-0052

Stiglitz, J., Sen, A., & Fitoussi, J.P. (2009). *Report by the Commission on the Measurement of Economic Performance and Social Progress.* Academic Press.

St-Jacques, B., Hammerschmidt, M., & McMahon, A. P. (1999). Indian hedgehog signaling regulates proliferation and differentiation of chondrocytes and is essential for bone formation. *Genes & Development, 13*(16), 2072–2086. doi:10.1101/gad.13.16.2072 PMID:10465785

Stojanovic, B. (2005). *Game theory - elements and application.* PE Official Gazette and Institute for European Studies.

Stojanovic, D., Ilic, B., & Mihajlovic, D. (2017). Sustainable development in Serbia in correlations with foreign direct investment. *21st International Scientific Conference on Economic and Social Development, 21*, 101-108.

Compilation of References

Stoker, G. (1998). Governance as theory: Five propositions. *International Social Science Journal, 155*(155), 17–28. doi:10.1111/1468-2451.00106

Stracke, C. M. (2011). Competence Modelling, Competence Models and Competence Development-An Overview. In *Competence Modelling for Vocational Education and Training*. Innovations for Learning and Development.

Stratford, E., & Davidson, J. (2002). Capital assets and intercultural borderlands: Socio-cultural challenges for natural resource management. *Journal of Environmental Management, 66*(4), 429–440. doi:10.1006/jema.2002.0597 PMID:12503497

Streeck, W. (2001). *The transformation of corporate organization in Europe: an overview.* MPIfG Working Paper 01/8, December 2001. MPIfG/Cologne/Germany.

Strohmer, D. C., Grand, S. A., & Purcell, M. J. (1984). Attitudes toward persons with disability: An examination of demographic factors, social context and specific disability. *Rehabilitation Psychology, 29*, 131–145.

Structure of Earnings Survey. (2016). *Eurostat Press Office.* https://ec.europa.eu/eurostat/documents/2995521/7762327/3-08122016-AP-EN.pdf/3f02c5ed-81de-49cb-a77e74396bac2467

Stubbs, S. (1998). *What is Inclusive Education? Concept Sheet.* Enabling Education Network (EENET). Retrieved 16 October 2003. www.eenet.org.uk/theory_practice/whatisit.shtml

Study on Coordination Mechanisms. (n.d.). www.unescap.org/sites/default/files/

Suazo, M. M., Martínez, P. G., & Sandoval, R. (2009). Creating psychological and legal contracts through human resource practices: A signaling theory perspective. *Human Resource Management Review, 19*(2), 154–166. doi:10.1016/j.hrmr.2008.11.002

Sullivan, P. (2005). Searching for the socio-intercultural, searching for the culture, in The Independent Commission for Good Governance in Public Services (TICGG). *The good governance standard for public services.* http://www.opm.co.uk/icggps/download_upload/Standard.pdf

Sundaram, J. K. (2015). *Pathways Through Financial Crisis: Argentina Pathways through Financial Crisis.* Retrieved September 15, 2021 from https://law-journals-books.vlex.com/vid/pathways-through-financial-crisis-argentina-56822020

Surface, E. A. (2012). Training need assessment: Aligning learning and capability with performance requirements and organizational objectives. In M. A. Wilson, W. Bennett, S. G. Gibson, & G. M. Alliger (Eds.), *The handbook of work analysis: The methods, systems, applications and science of work measurement in organizations.* Routledge.

Sweeney, P. D., & McFarlin, D. B. (2002). *Organizational behavior, solutions for management.* McGraw-Hill.

Swinkels. (2019). *How ideas matter in public policy: A review of concepts, mechanisms, and methods.* Academic Press.

Szmigin, I., Carrigan, M., & McEachern, M. G. (2009). The conscious consumer: Taking the flexible approach to ethical behavior. *International Journal of Consumer Studies, 33*(2), 224–231. doi:10.1111/j.1470-6431.2009.00750.x

Tajudeen, E., Olusola, A. T., & Ademola, B. A. G. (2017). Interest rate liberalization, financial development and economic growth in Sub-Saharan African economies. *African Journal of Economic Review, 5*(2), 109–129.

Takala, M., Pirttimaa, R., & Tormanen, M. (2009). Inclusive Special Education: The Role of Special Education Teachers in Finland. *British Journal of Special Education, 36*(3), 162–172. doi:10.1111/j.1467-8578.2009.00432.x

Tallberg, J., & Zürn, M. (2019). The legitimacy and legitimation of international organizations: Introduction and framework. *The Review of International Organizations, 14*(4), 581–606. doi:10.100711558-018-9330-7

Tarp, F., & Director, U. N. U. (2009). *Aid effectiveness.* A Note Prepared Based Both on Joint Work with Channing Arndt and Sam Jones Including an Unpublished Report for NORAD and 2009 UNU-WIDER Research Paper Entitled "Aid and Growth: Have We Come Full Circle?" Dated September 2009, 1-22.

Tatar, H. E. (2020). IMF, World Bank, and the European Union With the Perspective of New Institutional Economics. In I. Akansel (Ed.), *Comparative Approaches to Old and New Institutional Economics* (pp. 217–238). IGI Global. doi:10.4018/978-1-7998-0333-1.ch013

Teegen, H. (2003). International NGOs as global institutions: Using social capital to impact multinational enterprises and governments. *Journal of International Management, 9*(3), 271–285. doi:10.1016/S1075-4253(03)00037-1

Thalheimer, W. (2018). *The learning-transfer evaluation model.* Available at: https://www.worklearning.com/wp-content/uploads/2018/02/Thalheimer-The-Learning-Transfer-Evaluation-Model-Report-for-LTEM-v11a-002.pdf

The Role of the WTO in Global Development Policy. (2004). In B. von Hoffmann (Ed.), Global Governance (pp. 101–129). Academic Press.

The Star. (2021, July 29). Mustapa: Lack of integrity detrimental. *The Star*, 1–7.

The World Bank in Russia. (2021). *World Bank.* https://www.vsemirnyjbank.org/ru/country/russia

Thelen, K. (2000). Timing and temporality in the analysis of institutional evolution and change. *Studies in American Political Development, 14*(1), 101–108. doi:10.1017/S0898588X00213035

Thill, J. V., & Bovee, C. L. (2002). *Essentials of business communication.* South End Press.

Thomson, I. (2015). 'But does sustainability need capitalism or an integrated report' a commentary on 'The International Integrated Reporting Council: A story of failure. *J. Critical Perspectives on Accounting, 27*, 18–22. doi:10.1016/j.cpa.2014.07.003

Todaro, M. P., & Smith, S. C. (2003). Economic Development (8th ed.). Pearson Education Pvt. Ltd.

Torres-Díaz, J., Duart, J.M., Gómez-Alvarado, H.F., Marín-Gutiérrez, I., & Segarra-Faggioni, V. (2016). Internet use and academic success in university students. *Media Education Research Journal*, 61-70. doi:10.3916/C48-2016-06

Trompenaars, F., & Hampden-Turner, C. (2012). Riding the Waves of Culture: Understanding Cultural Diversity in Business (3rd ed.). Nicholas Brealey Publishing.

Trompenaars, F., & Asser, M. N. (2010). *The global M and A Tango: Cross-cultural dimensions of mergers and acquisitions.* McGraw-Hill.

Trompenaars, F., & Woolliams, P. (2003). *Business Across Cultures.* Capstone Publishing Ltd.

Trost, J. A. (1986). Statistically non-representative stratified sampling: A sampling technique for qualitative studies. *Qualitative Sociology, 9*(1), 54–57. doi:10.1007/BF00988249

Tubulingane, S. B. (2018). *Analysis of the impact of demographic and economic factors on internet services satisfaction levels in Windhoek, Namibia* [Masters Dissertation, University of Namibia]. https://repository.unam.edu.na/bitstream/handle/11070/2304/tubulingane_2018.pdf?sequence=1&isAllowed=y

Turnbull, W. (2005). *Evaluation of current governance arrangements to support regional investment under the NHT and NAP.* Canberra, Australia: Departments of Environment and Heritage and Agriculture, Fisheries and Forestry.

UK Committee for UNICEF. (2021). *Closing the Digital Divide for Good: an end to the digital exclusion of children and young people in the UK.* https://apo.org.au/sites/default/files/resource-files/2021-06/apo-nid312856.pdf

382

Compilation of References

Umrani, A. I., Johl, S. K., & Ibrahim, M. Y. (2015). Corporate governance practices and problems faced by SMEs in Malaysia. *Global Business and Management Research, 7*(2), 71–77.

UN (United Nations). (1994). Salamanca Statement and Framework for Action on Special Needs. *Education World Conference on Special Needs Education: Access and Quality.* https://www.european-agency.org/sites/default/files/salamanca-statement-and-framework.pdf

UN (United Nations). (2012). *Bridging the digital divide by reaching out to vulnerable populations 5 Chapter Five. United Nations E-Government Survey.* Author.

UN (United Nations). (2020b). *E-Government Survey 2020.* UN.

UN. (1995). *UN Documents: Overview of Secretary-General's Reports.* https://www.securitycouncilreport.org/un-documents/document/unro-s1995-1.php

UN. (2015). *Handbook on Measuring Quality of Employment – a Statistical Framework.* United Nations Economic Commission for Europe.

UN. (2020a). *World Summit on Information Society (WSIS).* https://publicadministration.un.org/en/Themes/ICT-for-Development/World-Summit-on-Information-Society

UNDP. (2017). *Inclusive Development.* Accessed on 15th July 2021, through http://www.undp.org/content/undp/en/home/ourwork/povertyreduction/focus_areas/focus_inclusive_development.html

UNESCO. (1997). *Education for a sustainable future: A transdisciplinary vision for concerted action.* UNESCO. https://en.unesco.org/themes/education/

UNESCO. (2005). *Guidelines for Inclusion: Ensuring Access to Education for All.* http://www.ibe.unesco.org/sites/default/files/Guidelines_for_Inclusion_UNESCO_2006.pdf

UNESCO. (2012). *Youth and skills: Putting education to work.* Retrieved from https://unesdoc.unesco.org/ark:/48223/pf0000218003

UNESCO. (2020). *Participation in Education: Children out-of-school in education (Finland and Serbia).* http://uis.unesco.org/en/country/fi?theme=education-and-literacy

UNESCO. (2021). *Participation in Education.* http://uis.unesco.org/en/country/fi?theme=education-and-literacy

UNESCO. (2022). *UNESCO – Inclusive education.* http://www.unesco.org/education/sne/

UNICEF. (2015). *For every child, a fair chance: The promise of equity.* UNICEF.

UNICEF. (2020). *Bridging the Digital Divide in Serbia For the Most Vulnerable Children, Education is important.* UNICEF. https://www.unicef.org

United Nations Educational, Scientific and Cultural Organization (UNESCO). (2008a). Background Note. A Review of Education for Sustainable Development (ESD) Policies from a Cultural Diversity and socio-intercultural Dialogue Perspective. Unpublished document. UNESCO/CLT/CPD/CPO20/11/2008. Paris: UNESCO.

United Nations Educational, Scientific and Cultural Organization (UNESCO). (2008b). UNESCO Concept Note. Towards a New Cultural Policy Profile. UNESCO/CLT/CPD 01/08/2008. Paris: UNESCO.

United Nations Educational, Scientific and Cultural Organization (UNESCO). (2008c). ESD Lens, version 2, draft 1: Comments from a cultural diversity perspective. Unpublished document. Paris: UNESCO.

United Nations. (2015). *Millennium Development Goals Report, Lessons Learned in Implementing the MDGs: Assessing Progress in Africa toward the Millennium Development Goals. Economic Commission for Africa, Addis Ababa, Ethiopia.* Retrieved September 20, 2021, from https://www.afdb.org/fileadmin/uploads/afdb/Documents/Publications/MDG_Report_2015.pdf

United Nations. (2016a). *The Sustainable Development Goals Report 2016.* Author.

United Nations. (2016b). *The changing political economy of globalization: Multilateral Institutions and the 2030 Agenda.* Retrieved July 20, 2021, from https://www.un.org/ecosoc/sites/www.un.org.ecosoc/files/files/en/2016doc/2016-globalization-mtg-bcknote.pdf

United Nations. (2016c). *The Sustainable Development Goals Report 2016.* United Nations Publications Department of Economic and Social Affairs (DESA). Retrieved September 10, 2021, from https://www.un.org/development/desa/publications/sustainable-development-goals-report-2016.html

United Nations. (2019). *Global sustainable development report: The future is now - Science for achieving sustainable development.* https://sustainabledevelopment.un.org/globalsdreport/2019

United Nations. (2020). *Policy brief: education during Covid-19 and beyond.* https://www.un.org/development/desa/dspd/wp-content/uploads/sites/22/2020/08/sg_policy_brief_covid-19_and_education_august_2020.pdf

University of Huddersfield. (2017). *Policy Frame work. Inspiring Global Professionals.* Author.

UNO. (2001). *Indicators of Sustainable Development.* https://www.un.org/

van der Nest, D. (2004). *The impact of black economic empowerment on the management of small companies in South Africa.* Retrieved August 16, 2017, from https://ujdigispace.uj.ac.za/bitstream/handle/10210/319/ImpactofBEEontheMngofSMEinSouthAfrica.pdf?sequence=1

van Dijk, J. (2010). *Social Aspects of the New Media* [Społeczne aspekty nowych mediów]. Wydawnictwo Naukowe PWN.

Van Dijk, J. G. M. (2017). Digital Divide: Impact of Access. In P. Rossler, C. A. Hoffner, & V. Z. L. V. Liesbet (Eds.), *The International Encyclopedia of Media Effects* (pp. 1–11). John Wiley & Sons. doi:10.1002/9781118783764.wbieme0043

Van Reusen, A. K., Shoho, A. R., & Barker, K. S. (2001). High School Teacher Attitudes toward Inclusion. *High School Journal, 84*, 7–20.

Vasilic, N., & Brkovic, P. (2017). *National Culture as a Determinant of Attitudes About Leadership Styles.* School of Business. http://www.vps.ns.ac.rs/SB/2017/2.3.pdf

Vassilakopoulou, P., & Hustad, E. (2020). Bridging Digital Divides: A Literature Review and Research Agenda for Information Systems Research. *Information Systems Frontiers.* Advance online publication. doi:10.100710796-020-10096-3 PMID:33424421

Velte, P., & Stawinoga, M. (2017). Integrated reporting: The current state of empirical research, limitations and future research implications. *Journal of Management Control, 28*(3), 275–320. doi:10.100700187-016-0235-4

Veltri, S., & Silvestri, A. (2020). The value relevance of corporate financial and non-financial information provided by the integrated report: A systematic review. *Business Strategy and the Environment, 29*(8), 3038–3054. doi:10.1002/bse.2556

Venables, A. (1999). *Regional integration agreements: a force for convergence and divergence?* Annual World Bank Conference on Development Economics. Working paper 2260.

Venkataraman, S. (2019). *Stakeholder approach to corporate sustainability: A review.* Indian Institute of Management Kozhikode Working Papers, (319).

Compilation of References

Verboven, H., & Vanherck, L. (2016). Sustainability management of SMEs and the UN sustainable development goals. *Uwf UmweltWirtschaftsForum*, *24*(2–3), 165–178. doi:10.100700550-016-0407-6

Vercic, A. T., Verčič, D., & Sriramesh, S. (2012). Internal communication: Definition, parameters, and the future. *Public Relations Review*, *38*(2), 223–230. doi:10.1016/j.pubrev.2011.12.019

Vervaart, B. (2018). *Varieties of Capitalism Revisited: Empirical Testing of Country Cluster Classifications and the Implications for Other Empirical Work* [Doctoral dissertation]. Hertie School of Governance.

Veselinovic, P. (2013). National Economy. Faculty of Economics.

Veselinovic, P., Micic, V., & Miletic, D. (2012). Serbia – zone of poverty and social exclusion. *Economics Of Agriculture*, *59*(2), 305–318.

Vetráková, M., Ďurian, J., Seková, M., & Kaščáková, A. (2016). Employee Retention and Development in Pulp and Paper Companies. *BioResources*, *11*(4), 9231–9243.

Vetterlein, A. (2012). Seeing like the World Bank on poverty. *New Political Economy*, *17*(1), 35–58. doi:10.1080/135 63467.2011.569023

Vianna, C. (2018). *Políticas de educação, gênero e diversidade sexual: Breve história de lutas, danos e resistências*. Autêntica.

Viener, J. (1950). *The Customs Union Issue*. Carnegie Endowment for International Peace.

Visser, W. (2005). Corporate citizenship in South Africa: A review of progress since democracy. *Journal of Corporate Citizenship*, *18*, 18–20.

Vives, A. (2004). The role of multilateral development institutions in fostering corporate social responsibility. *Development*, *47*(3), 45–52. doi:10.1057/palgrave.development.1100065

Vladimirova, I. G. (2001). Globalization of World Economy: Challenges and Implications. *Corporate Management*, *3*(1). https://www.cfin.ru/press/management/2001-3/10.shtml

von Borzyskowski, I., & Vabulas, F. (2019). Hello, goodbye: When do states withdraw from international organizations? *The Review of International Organizations*, *14*(2), 335–366. doi:10.100711558-019-09352-2

Voting Powers. (2021, November 27). *The World Bank*. https://www.worldbank.org/en/about/leadership/votingpowers

Vrcelj, S. (2005). *U potrazi za identitetom –iz perspektive komparativne pedagogije*. Rijeka: Graftrade/Hrvatsko futurološko društvo.

Vreeland, J. R. (2019). Corrupting International Organizations. *Annual Review of Political Science*, *22*(1), 205–222. doi:10.1146/annurev-polisci-050317-071031

Vujacic, M., & Djevic, R. (2013). Inclusive education: conceptual definition, principles and characteristics. *Topics*, *2*(37), 753-768.

Vuletic, V. (2003). *Globalization - Myth or Dread*. http://velikimali.org/wp-content/uploads/2017/03/biltenvelikimali_3.pdf

Wagner, L., & D'Aiglepierre, R. D. J. (2010). *Aid and Universal Primary Education* (No. 201022). Academic Press.

Wagner, A. (2011). *The origins of evolutionary innovations: a theory of transformative change in living systems*. OUP Oxford. doi:10.1093/acprof:oso/9780199692590.001.0001

Walker, A. (1997). Introduction: the strategy of inequality. In A. Walker & C. Walker (Eds.), *Britain divided: the growth of social exclusion in the 1980s and 1990s*. Child Poverty Action Group.

Walker, J., Pearce, C., Boe, K., & Lawson, M. (2019). *The Power of Education to fight Inequality: How increasing educational equality and quality is crucial to fighting economic and gender inequality. Oxfam Briefing Paper*. Oxfam International.

Wals, A. E. (2010). Mirroring, Gestaltswitching and transformative social learning: Stepping stones for developing sustainability competence. *International Journal of Sustainability in Higher Education, 11*(4), 380–390. doi:10.1108/14676371011077595

Wang, J. S. (2018). Practice and exploration of establishing blood purification training center with ppp (Public Private Partnership) model. Academic Journal of Second Military Medical University, 19-23.

Wang, Y. (2018). The Political Economy of Joining the AIIB. *The Chinese Journal of International Politics, 11*(2), 105–130. doi:10.1093/cjip/poy006

Ward, T., & MacKenzie, J. (2020). ESG in small and mid-sized quoted companies : Perceptions, myths and realities. Quoted Companies Alliance.

Watts, L., & Hodgson, D. (2019). *Social Justice Theory and Practice for Social Work: Critical and Philosophical Perspectives*. Springer. doi:10.1007/978-981-13-3621-8

WBI. (2008). *World Bank Institute Annual Report 2008*. World Bank Institute.

WBI. (2015) *Leadership: The World Bank Institute's Leadership for Development Program*. World Bank Institute. https://wbi.worldbank.org/wbi/content/leadership-world-bankinstitute%E2%80%99s-leadership-development-program

Weaver, C. (2010). Reforming the World Bank. In J. Clapp & R. Wilkinson (Eds.), *Global Governance, Poverty, and Inequality* (pp. 112–131). Routledge.

Weber, M. (2008). The business case for corporate social responsibility: A company-level measurement approach for CSR. *European Management Journal, 26*(4), 247–261. doi:10.1016/j.emj.2008.01.006

Weber, M., Hellmann, I., Stadler, M. B., Ramos, L., Pääbo, S., Rebhan, M., & Schübeler, D. (2007). Distribution, silencing potential and evolutionary impact of promoter DNA methylation in the human genome. *Nature Genetics, 39*(4), 457–466. doi:10.1038/ng1990 PMID:17334365

Weeks, J. (2000). O Corpo e a sexualidade. In G. L. Louro (Ed.), *O corpo educado* (pp. 35–82). Autêntica.

WEF (Global Economic Forum). (2021). *Global Gender Gap Report 2021*. https://www3.weforum.org/docs/WEF_GGGR_2021.pdf

Weiss, M. A. (2018). Asian Infrastructure Investment Bank (AIIB). *Current Politics and Economics of South, Southeastern, and Central Asia, 27*(1/2), 1–29.

Weiss, R. S. (1994). *Learning from strangers: The art and method of qualitative interview studies*. The Free Press.

Welfens, J. J. P. (2015). Innovation, Inequality and a Golden Rule for Growth in an Economy with Cobb-Douglas Function and an R&D Sector. *IZA DP, 8996*. https://ftp.iza.org/dp8996.pdf

Williams, D., & Young, T. (1994). Governance, the World Bank and Liberal Theory. *Political Studies, 42*(1), 84–100. doi:10.1111/j.1467-9248.1994.tb01675.x

Compilation of References

Williams, N. M. (1982). A boundary is to cross observations on Yolngu boundaries and permission. In N. M. Williams & E. S. Hunn (Eds.), *Resource Managers: North American and Australian Hunter-Gatherers.* Australian Institute of Aboriginal Studies Press.

Williamson, O. E. (1991). Comparative economic organization: The analysis of discrete structural alternatives. *Administrative Science Quarterly, 1991*(2), 269–296. doi:10.2307/2393356

Williamson, O. E. (1996). *The Mechanisms of Governance.* Oxford University Press.

Williamson, O. E. (2008). Outsourcing: Transaction cost economics and supply chain management. *The Journal of Supply Chain Management, 2008*(44), 5–16. doi:10.1111/j.1745-493X.2008.00051.x

Williamson, T., & Dom, C. (2010). *Sector budget support in practice. Synthesis report, Overseas Development Institute and Mokoro.* ODI.

Wilson, I., & Madsen, S. R. (2008). The influence of Maslow's humanistic views on an employee's motivation to learn. *The Journal of Applied Management and Entrepreneurship, 13*(2), 46–62.

Wong, W. C., Batten, J. A., Ahmad, A. H., Mohamed-Arshad, S. B., Nordin, S., & Adzis, A. A. (2021). Does ESG certification add firm value? *Finance Research Letters, 39*(April), 101593. doi:10.1016/j.frl.2020.101593

Woods, N. (2006). *The globalizers: The IMF, the World Bank and their borrowers.* Cornell University.

World Bank Group | Bank of Russia. (2021). *Bank of Russia.* http://www.cbr.ru/today/ms/smo/wb/#highlight=%D0%B2%D1%81%D0%B5%D0%BC%D0%B8%D1%80%D0%BD%D0%BE%D0%B3%D0%BE%7C%D0%B1%D0%B0%D0%BD%D0%BA%D0%B0

World Bank Group. (2018, October 2). *Russia and the World Bank: International Development Assistance.* World Bank. https://www.worldbank.org/en/country/russia/brief/international-development

World Bank. (2009). *Annual report.* Retrieved from http://siteresources.worldbank.org/EXTAR2009/Resources/62239771252950831873/AR09_Complete.pdf

World Bank. (2010). *About Us.* Retrieved from http://go.worldbank.org/3QT2P1GNH0

World Bank. (2013). *Inclusion matters: The foundation for shared prosperity.* World Bank.

World Bank. (2013). *Projects-Operations/Environmental-and-Social-Policies.* https://www.worldbank.org/

World Bank. (2015). *Reimbursable Advisory Services in Europe and Central Asia (ECA): Expanding Options for Our Clients: Global Knowledge, Strategy, and Local Solutions.* World Bank.

World Bank. (2016). *Open Learning Campus.* World Bank. https://olc.worldbank.org/

World Bank. (2016d). *World Bank Annual Report 2016.* World Bank.

World Bank. (2018). *AFCC2/RI-ACBF Regional Capacity Building Project (P122478).* Retrieved September 20, 2021, from https://projects.worldbank.org/en/projects-operations/project-detail/P122478

World Bank. (2021). *Zimbabwe Economic Update: COVID-19 Further complicates Zimbabwe's economic and social conditions.* Retrieved September 1, 2021, from https://www.worldbank.org/en/country/zimbabwe/publication/zimbabwe-economic-update-covid-19-further-complicates-zimbabwe-s-economic-and-social-conditions

World Bank: projects in Russia. (2021, November 27). *The World Bank.* https://projects.worldbank.org/en/projects-operations/projects-list?countrycode_exact=RU&os=0

World Business Council for Sustainable Development. (2020). *Building long-term business resilience*. https://docs.wbcsd. org/2020/09/WBCSD_Vision_2050_Building_longterm_business_resilience

Wren, B., Launer, J., Reiss, M. J., Swanepoel, A., & Music, G. (2019). Can evolutionary thinking shed light on gender diversity? *BJPsych Advances*, *25*(6), 351–362. doi:10.1192/bja.2019.35

Wright, M. (1999). Influences on learner attitudes towards foreign language and culture. *Educational Research*, *41*(2), 197–208. https://doi.org/10.1080/0013188990410207

Xiao, R. (2016). China as an institution-builder: The case of the AIIB. *The Pacific Review*, *29*(3), 435–442. doi:10.10 80/09512748.2016.1154678

XINHUANET. (2020). *Namibia to provide laptops, internet access to help college students learn amid COVID-19*. Retrieved October 10, 2021, from http://www.xinhuanet.com/english/2020-06/08/c_139123647.htm

Yani-de-Soriano, M., & Slater, S. (2009). Revisiting Drucker's theory: Has consumerism led to the overuse of marketing? *Journal of Management History*, *15*(4), 452–466. doi:10.1108/17511340910987347

Yaw, D. C. (2008). Tools for transfer. *Industrial and Commercial Training*, *40*(3), 152–155. doi:10.1108/00197850810868658

Yesufu, L. O. (2018). Motives and Measures of Higher Education Internationalisation: A Case Study of a Canadian University. *International Journal of Higher Education*, *7*(2), 155–168. doi:10.5430/ijhe.v7n2p155

Yildizhan, B. Ö., Yüksel, Ş., Avayu, M., Noyan, H., & Yildizhan, E. (2018). Effects of Gender Reassignment on Quality of Life and Mental Health in People with Gender Dysphoria. *Türk Psikiyatri Dergisi*, *29*(1). PMID:29730870

Zajda, J. (2010). Globalization and the Politics of Education Reform. In The Politics of Education Reforms. Springer.

Zaromatidis, K., Papadaki, A., & Glide, A. (1999). Cross-cultural comparison of attitudes toward persons with disabilities: Greeks and Greek-Americans. *Psychological Reports*, *84*(3_suppl), 1189–1196. doi:10.2466/pr0.1999.84.3c.1189 PMID:10477938

Zhao, J., Gou, Y., & Li, W. (2019). A New Model of Multilateral Development Bank: A Comparative Study of Road Projects by the AIIB and ADB. *Journal of Chinese Political Science*, *24*(2), 267–288. doi:10.100711366-018-9580-5

Zhu, J. (2020). Is the AIIB a China-controlled Bank? China's Evolving Multilateralism in Three Dimensions (3D). *Global Policy*, *10*(4), 653–659. doi:10.1111/1758-5899.12763

Zhu, Q., Sarkis, J., & Lai, K.-H. (2012). Examining the effects of green supply chain management practices and their mediations on performance improvements. *International Journal of Production Research*, *2012*(50), 1377–1394. doi:1 0.1080/00207543.2011.571937

Zolochevskaya, E. Y., Zubanova, S. G., Fedorova, N. V, & Yana, E. (2021). *Education policy: the impact of e-learning on academic performance*. E3S Web of Conferences. doi:10.1051/e3sconf/202124411024

Zucker, K. J., Lawrence, A. A., & Kreukels, B. P. (2016). Gender dysphoria in adults. *Annual Review of Clinical Psychology*, *12*(1), 217–247. doi:10.1146/annurev-clinpsy-021815-093034 PMID:26788901

Zumente, I., & Bistrova, J. (2021). Do Baltic investors care about environmental, social and governance (ESG)? *Entrepreneurship and Sustainability Issues*, *8*(4), 349–362. doi:10.9770/jesi.2021.8.4(20)

Костовић, С., & Ђерманов, J. (2006). *Изазови интеркултурализма и школа, У: Љ. Суботић (ур.), Сусрет култура, Зборник радова са 4.* Међународнох.

About the Contributors

Neeta Baporikar is currently Professor/Director (Business Management) at Harold Pupkewitz Graduate School of Business (HP-GSB), Namibia University of Science and Technology, Namibia. Prior to this, she was Head-Scientific Research, with the Ministry of Higher Education CAS-Salalah, Sultanate of Oman, Professor (Strategic Management and Entrepreneurship) at IIIT Pune and BITS India. With more than a decade of experience in the industry, consultancy, and training, she made a lateral switch to research and academics in 1995. Prof Baporikar holds D.Sc. (Management Studies) USA, Ph.D. in Management, the SP Pune University, INDIA with MBA (Distinction) and Law (Hons.) degrees. Apart from this, she is an external reviewer, Oman Academic Accreditation Authority, Accredited Management Teacher, Qualified Trainer, FDP from EDII, Doctoral Guide, and Board Member of Academic and Advisory Committee in accredited B-Schools. She has to her credit many conferred doctorates, is a member of the international and editorial advisory board, reviewer for Emerald, IGI, Inderscience, etc, and authored more than 300 scientific refereed papers and 30 plus books in the area of entrepreneurship, strategy, management, and higher education.

* * *

María Teresa Alcívar-Avilés is a Ph.D. in Business Sciences from Nebrija University (Spain). She is the Director of the Master in Finances and Business Economics, The Catholic University of Santiago de Guayaquil (Ecuador). Specialized in International Commerce, she has been the president and founder of ASOFLEX (Association of Producers and Exporters of Tropical Flowers) and COPEI (Ecuadorian Organization of Exports and Investment). She has worked for the Chilean/Ecuadorian Chamber of Commerce and has been awarded by the Top-ten Women Economists in the Region of Guayas (Ecuador).

Dileep Baburao Baragde is presently working as Assistant Professor at G.S. Moze College, Pune. He has completed MSc. (Computer Science) and M.B.A. (Computer Management) from Pune University. He has been awarded his PhD (Organizational Management) from SP Pune University. He is having total 12 years of teaching experience. He has published 13 Research paper national and international level. He has published 5 chapters in International Reference Book of Management. He has published 5 books having ISSN/ISBN. His area of interest are Business Innovation, Knowledge Management, and Information Technology. He is very popular among the students as hard-working teacher.

Elena Burdenko is the author of more than 200 scientific publications. She directs the scientific work of students and postgraduates as the supervisor of their dissertations. She has been teaching at higher educational institutions for more than 30 years as a professor of the Department of Political Economy and History of Economics at Plekhanov Russian University.

Uriel Hitamar Castillo-Nazareno is a Ph.D. in Business Sciences from Nebrija University (Spain) with post-graduate studies in Argentina, Israel, and Spain. He has been provost at the University of Esmeraldas (Ecuador) and has worked for the Ecuadorian government as a counselor for SENPLADES (National Planning and Development System for Ecuador).

Tatjana Cvetkovski was born in Belgrade. She graduated from the Faculty of Organizational Sciences, University of Belgrade, took her Master's degree at the same institution and acquired her PhD at the Faculty of Business Studies, Megatrend University in Belgrade. From 1998 to 2000 she was engaged at the Faculty of Organizational Sciences as an associate. From 2000 she has been employed at the Megatrend University. Since 2011 she is a full time professor at the Faculty of Business Studies. In two terms she was a Vice-Dean and from March 2016 until April 2018 she was the Dean of the Faculty of Business Studies of the Megatrend University. In the Ministry of Education, Science and Technological Development, she has been engaged since 2018 until 2020 as Minister adviser for Higher Education. She has participated in several projects including: Managing the transformation of enterprises, Serbian Ministry of Science and Technology, Faculty of Organizational Sciences (Center for Project Management), 1998-2000. Strategic networking options of the Serbian economy in the world economic trends – the impact of electronic commerce on the restructuring of the domestic market, the Ministry of Science, Technology and Environment, Graduated school of Business Studies, 2006-2010. Development of a five-year strategic business plan and annual business plan of the Republic Geodetic Authority, 2009. National Strategy for the inflow of foreign capital in order to reintegrate Serbia into international economic developments, 2011-2015, Ministry of Science and Technological Development of Serbia, Graduated school of Business Studies, Megatrend University. She participated as a lecturer at several seminars held for pharmaceutical companies, tourism organizations and NGOs. She is a member of the Association of Belgrade Economists, since 1999 and from 2010 the member of the Editorial Board of the International Journal of Applied Economics "Megatrend Review". From 2018 she is a member of Commission for Accreditation and Quality Assurance - Field of humanities and social sciences, National Entity for Accreditation and Quality Assurance in Higher Education. She is author of several books and monographs, and more than 100 papers published in journals and conferences of national and international importance, as well as themed collections.

Teresa Dieguez is a Doctor on Economics, MBA on Prospective and Organizational Strategy, Master on Innovation and Technological Transfer, Specialist on Strategy and Entrepreneurship, PhD Student on Social Development and Sustainability.

Ramnath Dixit is a Behavioral Training Facilitator and Proprietor at Squirrel Interventions, a training and development entity. He has been conducting behavioral training workshops for global organizations on areas of leadership, communication, customer service, team building and various other topics of business relevance. In a career spanning over 15 years he has delivered trainings at over 125 organizations spanning 25 industry verticals and covering more than 7000 participants. Ramnath has to his credit a research paper related to Training & Development, published in a Scopus Indexed Journal. Some of his noteworthy credentials include the following: Life-member and Diploma in Training &

About the Contributors

Development (Dip. T & D from ISTD, New Delhi, India), Certified Behavioral Trainer (Dale Carnegie Training, India), Neuro-linguistic Practitioner (School of Excellence, India) and Belbin Team Role Assessor (CERT, India). He is currently pursuing his research from Symbiosis International (Deemed University) (SIU), Pune, India.

Gordana Djukic graduated from the University of Belgrade, Faculty of Economics, Serbia, 2006. She defended her master's thesis in 2010 at the same faculty. She defended her doctoral dissertation in 2016 and received her PhD in economics from John Naisbitt University, Faculty of Management in Zajecar. She has acquired the scientific research title of Research Associate in 2017 at the Institute of Economic Sciences in Belgrade. She is author and coauthor on many national and international papers and chapters writing with eminent worlds famous professors.

Mufaro Dzingirai is a PhD candidate in Business Management at Midlands State University and a lecturer in the Department of Business Management, Midlands State University. He is also a Senior Fellow at Zarawi Trust. He received his Master of Commerce in Strategic Management and Corporate Governance degree from Midlands State University in 2016. He was hired as a teacher by the Ministry of Education from 2014 to 2016. In 2013, he received the MSU Book Prize. His research interests include Higher Education, Strategy, Management, Finance, Entrepreneurship, and Development.

Meng Kui Hu, Chartered Banker, MBA, is a former senior banker with 26 years of banking experience in commercial and corporate banking. He is actively involved in various governmental agencies, providing his expertise in banking, financial technology and best practices for Small and Medium Enterprises (SMEs). He is presently a member of the United Nations ESCAP Sustainable Business Network (ESBN) and its Vice Chair for Digital Economy Task Force. He also serves as a member of the Examination Committee with the Asian Institute of Chartered Bankers (AICB). He earned his Master of Business Administration degree from the University of Strathclyde, UK, and has authored two books entitled "SME Challenges and Solutions" and "Transforming Family Businesses". He also writes regularly on financing and business for various publications. He is currently pursuing his PhD candidacy with Universiti Sains Malaysia, Malaysia. He speaks English, Malay, Mandarin, and Cantonese.

Biljana Ilic, PhD, was born on 10/01/1970, in Zajecar, Serbia. She graduated on Business Higher School of Belgrade University, in 1996. She continued further education on the Faculty of Management Zajecar, Megatrend University of Belgrade, in 2007. She Graduated on the Faculty of Management in Zajecar, in 2009. She received the degree of Master of Academic Studies in Management on the same faculty, defended master thesis with mark 10.00, and acquired the title of master manager. She defended her doctoral thesis titled "Strategic directions of regional economic and environmental development of the tourist potential of Gamzigrad Spa", in April, 2016, mark 10.00. She was elected as associated professor at the Faculty of Management in Zajecar on July, 2021. Biljana is the author and coauthor of many papers and books chapters with eminent professors, published in Domestic and International Conferences and Journals.

Amit Uttam Jadhav is presently working as Assistant Professor at G.S.Moze College, Pune. He has completed MA (Economics) from Pune University. He has been awarded his PhD (Economics) from SP Pune University. He is having total 13 years of teaching experience. He has published 08 Research paper national and international level. He has published 2 chapters in International Reference Book of Management. He has published 1 book having ISSN/ISBN. He is very popular among the students as hard-working teacher.

Jagbir Singh Kadyan is an Academician, Researcher, Trainer & Consultant. PhD in CSR Corporate Social Responsibility, Post graduate in Commerce, Economics & Management. Accredited Management Teacher by AIMA-All India Management Association, New Delhi, India, Certified CSR- Corporate Social Responsibility Professional by ICSI- Institute of Company Secretary of India. Research interest include CSR-Corporate Social Responsibility; Corporate Governance; Business Management (Marketing; OB&HRM and Accounting, Finance & Taxation). Successfully conducted FDP- faculty development programs; Presented & published over 40 research papers in national & international seminars & conferences; authored books; evaluated PhD thesis; edited research journal; reviewed research papers and completed two innovation research projects awarded by University of Delhi, India. Presently, he is working as Assistant Professor, Dept. of Commerce, Swami Shraddhanand College, University of Delhi and is also Honorary Director, IndoGlobal Institute of Management, Training & Research, New Delhi, India.

Sneha Kadyan is a social science researcher with demonstrated experience and performance at all organisations and institutes in academic and professional development across diverse social issues. Knowledge innovator with methodological proficiency in qualitative and quantitative skills and analysis with 4 award winning research projects PhD level in 4 years. Unique perspective as a professor, scholar and researcher in global institutional environments. Excellent relationship builder -team worker with collaborative research across the globe. Presently she is working as Lecturer, Jindal Global Business School, O.P. Jindal Global University, Haryana, India.

Daisy Mui Hung Kee, PhD, MBA, is an associate professor at the School of Management, Universiti Sains Malaysia in Penang, Malaysia. Her areas of interest are in human resource management, organisational behaviour, work values, leadership, psychosocial safety climate, entrepreneurship, and small and medium enterprises. She earned her Master of Business Administration degree from the School of Management, Universiti Sains Malaysia, and her doctoral degree in business and management from the International Graduate School of Business of the University of South Australia. In 2006 she received the Merdeka Award from the Australia Malaysia Business Council of South Australia.

Vaishali Mahajan has 19 years of teaching Management subjects to the Masters(MBA) students. currently serves as Associate Professor and Head of the Department of Marketing Department at Symbiosis Centre for Management and Human Resource Development, Symbiosis International (Deemed), Pune. Her research interests' area includes service marketing, on line marketing, and consumer buying behavior. She has presented several papers in the reputed international conferences.

Rodgers Ndava holds a Master of Commerce in Strategic Management and Corporate Governance degree from Midlands State University (MSU) and a Bachelor of Commerce in Business Management (Honours) majoring in Finance from the same institution. He is a former Zimbabwe Revenue Authority (ZIMRA) employee hired on a seasonal basis. He is a keen scholar on Tax Compliance, Small Business Management, Entrepreneurship, Finance, and Strategic Management.

About the Contributors

Kannan Rajagopal worked in the Health Care and Automobile Sectors as Assistant Director and Director respectively for 22 years in the Strategy, HR and Marketing domains. Worked with both Domestic and International Automobile OEM and After-Market customers and Channels before taking up full-time Academic Profession. Possessing two decades of experience in Business Strategy, HR, Marketing and Selling of Products and Services both in India and International Market. Successful track record of developing comprehensive strategies on Brand, Distribution, Marketing and Sales strategy that enhanced the market share, profitability and customer loyalty of the organization exponentially. Presently working as Associate Professor of Marketing, Strategy and Innovation at SCMHRD, Symbiosis International University, Pune. Presented several papers in international conferences. Holding two doctoral PhD degrees, one in Applied Marketing and the other in Human Resource Development. Published papers in Scopus and ABDC Journals. Authored and Published Book Chapters in IGI Global and Springer.

Isaac O. Randa is serving as a senior faculty in the area of Accounting and Finance at HP-GSB, Namibia University of Science and Technology, Namibia, and has university teaching experience of more than a decade and a half at the graduate and postgraduate levels. His research interest is in the areas of Finance and Governance. Dr. Randa is also a qualified Insurance Professional.

Jose Manuel Saiz-Alvarez is Ph.D. in Economic and Business Sciences, Universidad Autónoma de Madrid, Spain. Ph.D. in Sociology, Universidad Pontificia de Salamanca, Spain. Visiting professor, Universidad Católica de Santiago de Guayaquil, Ecuador. International researcher, CEIEF-Universidad de Santiago de Chile. Officially accredited in Spain by ANECA. Regular member, Mexican Academy of Sciences and Accademia Tiberina già Pontificia, Italy. He was a research professor, Tecnológico de Monterrey, Mexico, and member of the National System of Researchers of Mexico. Director for BA Doctoral Studies, Universidad Nebrija, Spain. Professor, Universidad Pontificia de Salamanca, Spain, and Universidad Alfonso X El Sabio, Spain. Academic leader, Tecnológico de Monterrey, Mexico. Diploma of Recognition, The House of Representatives from the Capitol of Puerto Rico. Honor Diploma, Universitatea Valahia din Targoviste, Romania. Honorary Professor, Universidad Autónoma de Madrid, Spain. Who's Who in the World since 2011.

Vinita Sinha is a Professor (OB & HR) at Symbiosis Center of Management & Human Resource Development, a constituent of Symbiosis International University, Pune, India. She is doctorate in Psychology and Masters in Psychology with specialization in Organizational Behavior. She also holds Post Graduate Diploma in Human Resource Management, Post Graduate Diploma in Health Psychology & Behavior Modification and Masters Diploma in Higher Education and Andragogy. She has 14 years of work experience in core teaching and research. She is also a recognized research supervisor at Symbiosis International University. Her areas of interest in teaching and research stretch out from Psychology to OB & HR viz. evolving trends in management and education, social media, accreditation, psychological issues at work, quality aspects of work, psychological well-being, work stress, role stress, attrition trends, etc. She has presented many papers in international conferences and published more than 30 research papers in refereed international and national journals of repute.

José G. Vargas-Hernández, M.B.A., Ph.D., Member of the National System of Researchers of Mexico and a research professor at University Center for Economic and Managerial Sciences, University of Guadalajara. Professor Vargas-Hernández has a Ph. D. in Public Administration and a Ph.D. in

Organizational Economics. He has undertaken studies in Organisational Behaviour and has a Master of Business Administration, published four books and more than 200 papers in international journals and reviews (some translated to English, French, German, Portuguese, Farsi, Chinese, etc.) and more than 300 essays in national journals and reviews. He has obtained several international Awards and recognition.

Index

21st Century Maritime Silk Road 2, 18

A

academic performance 39-43, 45-59, 73
Accredited Regional Development Agencies 277, 284
ADB 12-13, 17, 107, 148-149, 303-305, 311-312
AIIB 1-17, 237
Alternative Consumerism 82, 98

B

best practices 68, 73-74, 139, 141, 149, 153, 156, 233-234, 329
business sustainability 139-141, 143, 145, 148, 152-153, 156

C

collaboration 6, 13-14, 27, 42, 64, 67-69, 72, 99, 107, 112, 139, 164-165, 234, 296, 303, 315, 318, 322-323, 329-330, 333, 336
competency development 285-291, 293-296, 299, 302
Concessional Lending 219
contact learning 39, 45, 48, 59
cooperation programs 198-199
COVID-19 pandemic 25, 29-32, 35, 40, 42-43, 52, 54-56, 58, 64, 99-100, 102, 106, 108, 112, 116, 123, 129, 140, 142-143, 147, 149, 152, 259
culture 4, 6, 23, 33, 62, 71-72, 74-75, 79, 82-83, 88-92, 95, 98, 111, 119, 121-122, 125, 130-131, 133-135, 137-138, 153, 157-162, 164-168, 171-174, 187, 189-190, 214, 249, 263, 266, 270, 281, 299, 305, 320, 322-328, 330, 332-336

D

development 1-7, 9-18, 20-23, 25-29, 32-34, 36, 38-39, 41-42, 57-58, 60-62, 64-68, 70-79, 83, 85, 90, 96-97, 99-123, 125-126, 129-134, 136-137, 139-140, 142-144, 148-156, 168, 170-172, 174, 176-179, 182, 187-192, 194, 196, 198-201, 204-206, 208-212, 214-218, 220-227, 229-232, 234-235, 237-251, 253-254, 257-266, 269, 274, 276-321, 323, 325-330, 333, 335-336
Digital Divide 20-21, 25, 29, 31, 33-38
Digital Economy and Society Index (DESI) 19, 28-30, 35, 38
digital effectiveness 19, 23
digital inclusion 19-23, 25, 28-30, 32-38
digital transformation 19, 22, 26-28, 30, 32-33, 35, 38, 65
disability 23, 61, 73, 123, 131, 135-136, 138

E

Economic Development Institute (EDI) 292-294, 302
educational aid 220-221, 223-225, 228, 230, 235-236
Educational Aid Effectiveness 220
Educational Growth and Development 220
e-government 19, 24-25, 28-30, 34, 37-38
e-learning 35, 39, 42-43, 45-48, 50, 54, 56-59, 149, 290, 292
emerging economies 165, 175-177, 181-182, 195-196, 306
entrepreneurship 18, 60-62, 64-67, 71-72, 74-79, 113, 153, 155, 177, 192, 195, 207, 215, 254, 257, 277, 296, 301, 331, 333-334
Environmental, Social, and Governance (ESG) Principles 113, 139-156, 197
epistemic community 302
equality 23, 32, 37, 39, 53, 59, 73-75, 78-79, 93, 103, 105, 119-122, 126, 131, 161, 194, 317, 320
equity 26, 57, 60, 67, 72, 78-80, 98, 126, 133, 143-144, 182, 230, 237, 293, 302, 328
ERP 13, 18
ESG integration 139-142, 144-153, 156
ESG principles 140-141, 144-146, 148-149, 151,

153, 156

ethical consumption 80-83, 90, 92-93, 98

Europe 2-3, 7, 18-21, 27-28, 35, 38, 118-119, 122-123, 125, 133, 137, 169, 174, 206, 215, 247, 264, 266, 268, 283, 301, 332

Extended Fund Facility (EFF) 219

F

Faculty 19, 39-40, 42, 45, 47-48, 50, 59, 66, 118, 134-136, 280-283

Fair Trade 80, 83, 87, 93, 95-98

Financialisation 197

Flexible Credit Line (FCL) 219

foreign aids 220

framework 14, 23, 29, 34, 36, 38, 65, 73, 76, 94, 101-102, 108-109, 116, 126, 134, 136, 152, 159, 163-164, 168-169, 173, 177, 179-187, 190, 192, 194, 199, 217, 241, 244-245, 250-251, 257-259, 264-266, 283, 285, 289, 293-294, 296, 300, 304, 308, 313, 321-322, 324, 327-330

G

GAAT 303

GDP 2, 4, 8, 15, 30, 111, 200, 202-203, 208, 210-211, 215-216, 264-265, 267, 279, 303, 306

gender 20, 25, 37, 40, 60-64, 66-67, 71-74, 76-79, 90, 98, 102-105, 120, 128-130, 137, 229, 237, 247, 273, 321

gender equality 73, 78-79, 103, 105

gender equity 72, 79, 237

global education 40, 122, 129, 133, 138, 296

global institutions 99-113, 116, 118, 138-141, 148-150, 153, 156, 176, 181, 244-248, 251, 254, 256-257, 260, 285-286, 289, 291-294, 296, 301-303

Globalization 17, 21, 27, 64, 77, 81, 95-97, 101, 113-116, 118-119, 121-122, 133-135, 137-138, 175, 240-241, 286, 295, 302, 306, 315, 322, 328

governance 1-2, 4, 9, 15-16, 19, 95, 99, 104-106, 110, 112-114, 139, 141, 144-145, 148, 152, 154-155, 157-184, 187-197, 200, 204, 218, 234-235, 244-246, 254, 258, 260, 295, 297, 300-301, 315-316, 335

governance and neoliberalism 175

growth 1-2, 4-6, 9, 11, 15, 21, 23, 26, 29, 37-38, 45-46, 65, 74, 77, 79-80, 103, 118, 138, 141, 147-149, 177, 179, 181-182, 187, 189, 196-197, 200, 202, 206, 214-215, 219-221, 223-225, 231-233, 237-240, 242, 245, 251-252, 255-256, 261-262, 267, 276-280, 284, 287, 304, 314, 316-317, 319,

321, 328-330

H

heping hueqi 1, 15

Heping Juequi 18

higher education 36, 39-40, 43-45, 47, 52-57, 59-61, 64-65, 67-68, 71-76, 78, 132-134, 221, 223, 226, 232, 241, 275, 300, 302, 332

human rights 60-61, 72-73, 76-77, 79, 121-122, 124-125, 131, 168, 246-247, 320-321

Hyperinflation 262, 284

I

IBRD 199-200, 204-205, 208-209, 258, 287, 293, 303, 305, 307, 309-311

ICT 19-23, 25, 27, 31-33, 35-36, 38, 44-48, 52, 59, 77, 331

ICT Development 38

IDA 100, 102-103, 105, 107, 111, 114, 204, 208-209, 258, 303, 309-311

ILO 100-102, 110, 148, 150, 154, 245, 247, 259-260, 291, 302-303, 305

IMF 100-105, 107, 109-111, 113-114, 148, 177-179, 199-204, 212, 214-219, 239, 244-245, 247, 259-260, 286, 291, 294-295, 299-300, 302-305, 307-309, 312, 315

inclusive capitalism 175-176, 179-182, 187, 189-190, 192-193, 197

inclusive development 29, 39, 60-61, 66-67, 72, 78-79, 99-100, 102, 108-109, 112, 117, 220, 285

inclusive education 31, 118-123, 125-127, 130-138

Inclusive Growth 23, 79

inclusiveness 31, 80, 160

Industry 4.0 3, 13, 18

institution 4-5, 40, 68, 103, 121, 128, 142, 157, 172, 193, 215, 217, 221, 228, 243-244, 249, 251-254, 256-257, 260, 286-287, 292, 300, 302, 315

Integrated Corporate Governance 195, 197

integrated reporting 152, 175, 179-184, 186-197

Interculturality 336

International aid 220-223, 225-238

International Bank for Reconstruction and Development 198-199, 201, 204-205, 217, 287, 293, 304-305, 307, 309

International Commerce 1

International Labour Organization (ILO) 100-102, 110, 148, 150, 154, 245, 247, 259-260, 291, 302-303, 305

International Monetary Fund (IMF) 100-105, 107,

Index

109-111, 113-114, 148, 177-179, 199-204, 212, 214-219, 239, 244-245, 247, 259-260, 286, 291, 294-295, 299-300, 302-305, 307-309, 312, 315

internet 18-21, 24-25, 27-31, 33-34, 38-59, 131

IoT 13, 18, 33, 38

K

Kaizen 13, 18

Knowledge management 56-57, 170, 245, 256, 260, 284, 286, 297, 324, 336

L

Learning and Development 131, 229, 285, 298, 300

learning transfer 285-286, 289, 291-292, 294, 296, 300

LFS 267-269, 284

Local Economic Development 277, 284

M

MDG 115, 243

N

National Development Strategy 1 99, 108, 114, 117

National Rejuvenation 3, 14-15, 18

Neoliberalism 175-178, 193, 197

New Development Bank 15, 199, 212, 215-216

NGO 31, 88, 243

NRI 19, 26

O

organization 4, 9, 11, 68, 81, 95-96, 98, 100, 122, 132, 138, 150, 154, 157-158, 164-166, 169, 174, 178, 180, 182-183, 185, 198-200, 205, 210-212, 214-215, 217-218, 223, 226-227, 230, 236, 238, 243, 245-248, 250, 254-255, 257, 259-260, 264, 287, 290-292, 296-297, 302, 305, 307, 312, 315, 317, 319-321, 325-327, 329-330, 332-333, 335-336

Organization for Economic Cooperation and Development 199, 210-211, 217-218, 287

organizational 8, 64, 82, 85, 153, 158-163, 165, 167, 169, 171, 197, 285-287, 289, 299-300, 318-330, 335-336

organizational development 318-320, 325-330, 335-336

P

peace 1, 16, 73, 122, 131, 137, 210, 243, 245-247, 281,

284, 321, 328, 330, 334

planning 18, 76, 97, 140, 146, 148-149, 173, 188-189, 191, 229, 233-235, 239, 244, 250-253, 256-259, 265, 276, 308

policy 2, 5, 9, 15-18, 21, 23, 25, 27, 32-36, 38, 43, 57-58, 60, 99, 103, 105, 109-114, 116, 119, 125-126, 131, 133, 140, 153, 156, 158-159, 161-163, 166-168, 171-177, 179, 181, 189-192, 194, 196-197, 200-202, 204, 209, 215-216, 224, 228, 232-235, 238, 240-242, 244-260, 262, 265, 270, 276-278, 280-282, 287-288, 293-294, 299, 303, 314, 316, 329, 334

poverty 2, 5, 7, 23-24, 30-32, 37-38, 40, 73, 100-101, 103-104, 113, 123, 176-177, 194, 202, 204, 215, 219, 221-222, 224, 230-231, 240, 242-243, 245, 261-263, 265-266, 268-284, 287, 295, 301, 303, 314-316, 328, 330

poverty indicators 261, 274

power 1-7, 10, 12-15, 18, 37, 47, 70, 77, 79, 81, 83, 114, 119, 157-158, 161-162, 167, 172-174, 194, 216, 244-245, 263-265, 297, 306, 309, 323, 326

Precautionary and Liquidity Line (PLL) 219

purchasing practices 80

Q

qualitative research 80, 84, 94, 97-98, 114, 181, 195

R

Regional Development 18, 261-265, 276-278, 282, 284

relative poverty 269-270, 284

Reputational Capital 82, 98

Return on Training Investment (ROTI) 294, 302

Russia 7, 9-10, 13-14, 16-17, 198-218, 277, 306, 315

S

SDG 100, 104-105, 221, 243, 264

Serbia 19-20, 26, 28-37, 118, 120, 125-134, 136, 261-284, 335

SFRY 264, 274-275, 284

Shareholders Capitalism 197

Silk Belt 1, 6

Silk Road Economic Belt 2, 16, 18

Small and Medium Enterprises (SMEs) 139-140, 142-143, 149, 152, 155-156, 195

SMEs 10, 74, 139-156, 179, 187, 189, 195, 298

social exclusion 19, 21, 23-26, 30-31, 36-38, 61, 67, 125, 278-279, 283, 329

social status 39, 43, 59, 116, 293

social sustainability 82, 98, 206
socio-intercultural 157-161, 163-170, 174, 318-336
Sociology 95, 97-98, 137, 334
SORS 265, 269, 276, 280, 282-284
stakeholder capitalism 179-180, 183, 193-195, 197
Stand-By (SBA) 219
student 27, 39-43, 45-59, 61, 66-67, 70-71, 89, 131-132, 220, 223, 227, 229, 241, 331-333
Student Social Status 59
sustainability 21, 35-36, 56, 58, 64-66, 72, 74-76, 78-79, 82, 96-98, 100-101, 107, 109, 111, 113-114, 116, 122-123, 133, 139-145, 147-149, 152-156, 171, 173, 175-176, 179-180, 182-184, 186-187, 191-194, 196-197, 206, 232, 235, 245, 252-255, 259, 261, 264-265, 276, 280-281, 295, 329
sustainable development 18, 21, 23, 25, 28, 34, 60-62, 65, 72, 74-76, 79, 99-105, 108-110, 112-118, 122-123, 134, 139-140, 143-144, 148-149, 155-156, 174, 182, 190, 192, 194, 204, 212, 221, 223, 227, 243, 245, 247, 259-264, 266, 279-284, 330, 333
Sustainable Development Directions 261
Sustainable Development Goals 60-61, 99-100, 103, 113-116, 139-140, 149, 155-156, 221, 227, 243, 245, 264, 279, 284
Sustainable Development Goals (SDGs) 61, 100, 114-116, 139-140, 149, 156, 221, 227, 243, 245
Sustainable Entrepreneurship 76, 79, 113, 195

T

third world countries 262, 284, 288
trade 1, 3-5, 7, 10, 13-14, 18, 21, 80, 82-83, 87, 93, 95-98, 100, 105-107, 114, 122, 153, 177-178, 197, 201, 207, 209, 222, 225, 231, 248-249, 253, 262, 303-304, 306-309, 312, 315-317, 334
training intervention 289-290, 292, 302
training investments 289
training transfer 285-286, 288-290, 292, 294, 296-300, 302
transformation 3-4, 6-7, 12, 19-20, 22, 26-28, 30, 32-33, 35, 38, 65, 102, 138, 157-160, 162-166, 168, 172, 174, 188-189, 199, 210, 220-221, 321, 324, 327, 330
Transgender 62-63, 67, 71-72, 74-76, 79

U

UNESCO 65, 78, 122, 128-130, 132-133, 136-138, 167, 174, 225-226, 230, 232, 234, 236, 239, 283, 287

W

welfare 1-2, 5, 102-104, 106-109, 122, 144-145, 176, 231, 236, 251, 276, 293
World Bank 12-15, 26, 76-77, 100-107, 109-111, 114-115, 137, 148, 155, 177-179, 198-201, 204-210, 212, 215-218, 224, 226, 229-232, 235, 237, 239-241, 244-247, 258, 260, 280, 283, 286-287, 290-305, 307-312, 314-316
WTO 100-102, 178, 200, 245, 260, 303-304, 312-313, 315

Z

Zimbabwe 99-100, 102-115, 314

Recommended Reference Books

IGI Global's reference books are available in three unique pricing formats:
Print Only, E-Book Only, or Print + E-Book.

Shipping fees may apply.

www.igi-global.com

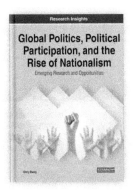

ISBN: 9781799873433
EISBN: 9781799873457
© 2021; 213 pp.
List Price: US$ **175**

ISBN: 9781799841562
EISBN: 9781799841579
© 2021; 374 pp.
List Price: US$ **195**

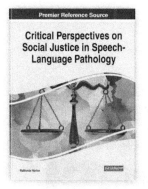

ISBN: 9781799871347
EISBN: 9781799871361
© 2021; 355 pp.
List Price: US$ **195**

ISBN: 9781799837299
EISBN: 9781799837312
© 2021; 301 pp.
List Price: US$ **185**

ISBN: 9781799870043
EISBN: 9781799870067
© 2021; 290 pp.
List Price: US$ **195**

ISBN: 9781799836650
EISBN: 9781799836674
© 2021; 301 pp.
List Price: US$ **195**

Do you want to stay current on the latest research trends, product announcements, news, and special offers?
Join IGI Global's mailing list to receive customized recommendations, exclusive discounts, and more.
Sign up at: **www.igi-global.com/newsletters**.

Publisher of Timely, Peer-Reviewed Inclusive Research Since 1988

www.igi-global.com   Sign up at www.igi-global.com/newsletters   facebook.com/igiglobal   twitter.com/igiglobal   linkedin.com/igiglobal

Ensure Quality Research is Introduced to the Academic Community

Become an Evaluator for IGI Global Authored Book Projects

 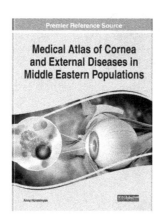 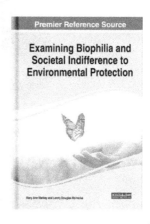 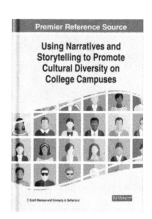

The overall success of an authored book project is dependent on quality and timely manuscript evaluations.

Applications and Inquiries may be sent to:
development@igi-global.com

Applicants must have a doctorate (or equivalent degree) as well as publishing, research, and reviewing experience. Authored Book Evaluators are appointed for one-year terms and are expected to complete at least three evaluations per term. Upon successful completion of this term, evaluators can be considered for an additional term.

If you have a colleague that may be interested in this opportunity, we encourage you to share this information with them.

Increase Your Manuscript's Chance of Acceptance
IGI Global Author Services

Copy Editing & Proofreading

Professional, native English language copy editors improve your manuscript's grammar, spelling, punctuation, terminology, semantics, consistency, flow, formatting, and more.

Scientific & Scholarly Editing

A Ph.D. level review for qualities such as originality and significance, interest to researchers, level of methodology and analysis, coverage of literature, organization, quality of writing, and strengths and weaknesses.

Figure, Table, Chart & Equation Conversions

Work with IGI Global's graphic designers before submission to enhance and design all figures and charts to IGI Global's specific standards for clarity.

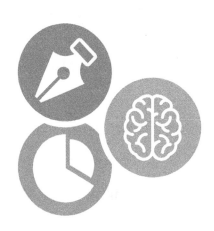

- Professional Service
- Quality Guarantee & Certificate
- Timeliness
- Affordable Pricing

What Makes IGI Global Author Services Stand Apart?

Services/Offerings	IGI Global Author Services	Editage	Enago
Turnaround Time of Projects	3-5 Business Days	6-7 Busines Days	6-7 Busines Days
Pricing	Fraction of our Competitors' Cost	Up to **2x** Higher	Up to **3x** Higher

Learn More or Get Started Here:

For Questions, Contact IGI Global's Customer Service Team at cust@igi-global.com or 717-533-8845

6,600+ E-BOOKS.
ADVANCED RESEARCH.
INCLUSIVE & ACCESSIBLE.

IGI Global e-Book Collection

- **Flexible Purchasing Options** (Perpetual, Subscription, EBA, etc.)
- Multi-Year Agreements with **No Price Increases** Guaranteed
- **No Additional Charge** for Multi-User Licensing
- No Maintenance, Hosting, or Archiving Fees
- Transformative **Open Access Options** Available

Request More Information, or Recommend the IGI Global e-Book Collection to Your Institution's Librarian

Among Titles Included in the IGI Global e-Book Collection

Research Anthology on Racial Equity, Identity, and Privilege (3 Vols.)
EISBN: 9781668445082
Price: US$ 895

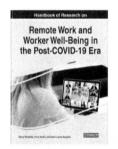

Handbook of Research on Remote Work and Worker Well-Being in the Post-COVID-19 Era
EISBN: 9781799867562
Price: US$ 265

Research Anthology on Big Data Analytics, Architectures, and Applications (4 Vols.)
EISBN: 9781668436639
Price: US$ 1,950

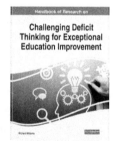

Handbook of Research on Challenging Deficit Thinking for Exceptional Education Improvement
EISBN: 9781799888628
Price: US$ 265

Acquire & Open

When your library acquires an IGI Global e-Book and/or e-Journal Collection, your faculty's published work will be considered for immediate conversion to Open Access *(CC BY License)*, at no additional cost to the library or its faculty *(cost only applies to the e-Collection content being acquired)*, through our popular **Transformative Open Access (Read & Publish) Initiative**.

For More Information or to Request a Free Trial, Contact IGI Global's e-Collections Team: eresources@igi-global.com | 1-866-342-6657 ext. 100 | 717-533-8845 ext. 100

Have Your Work Published and Freely Accessible
Open Access Publishing

With the industry shifting from the more traditional publication models to an open access (OA) publication model, publishers are finding that OA publishing has many benefits that are awarded to authors and editors of published work.

Freely Share Your Research

Higher Discoverability & Citation Impact

Rigorous & Expedited Publishing Process

Increased Advancement & Collaboration

Acquire & Open

When your library acquires an IGI Global e-Book and/or e-Journal Collection, your faculty's published work will be considered for immediate conversion to Open Access *(CC BY License)*, at no additional cost to the library or its faculty *(cost only applies to the e-Collection content being acquired)*, through our popular **Transformative Open Access (Read & Publish) Initiative**.

- Provide Up To **100%** OA APC or CPC Funding
- Funding to Convert or Start a Journal to **Platinum OA**
- Support for Funding an **OA Reference Book**

IGI Global publications are found in a number of prestigious indices, including Web of Science™, Scopus®, Compendex, and PsycINFO®. The selection criteria is very strict and to ensure that journals and books are accepted into the major indexes, IGI Global closely monitors publications against the criteria that the indexes provide to publishers.

PsycINFO®   **IET Inspec**

Learn More Here: For Questions, Contact IGI Global's Open Access Team at openaccessadmin@igi-global.com

www.igi-global.com

CPSIA information can be obtained
at www.ICGtesting.com
Printed in the USA
BVHW011746110622
639438BV00004B/39